D0772854

SPECIAL EDUCATION IN A DIVERSE SOCIETY

Herbert Grossman
San Jose State University

Allyn and Bacon
Boston • London • Toronto • Sydney • Tokyo • Singapore

Series Editor: Ray Short
Editorial Assistant: Christine M. Shaw
Marketing Manager: Ellen Mann
Editorial-Production Administrator: Annette Joseph
Editorial-Production Coordinator: Susan Freese
Editorial-Production Service: TKM Productions
Composition Buyer: Linda Cox
Manufacturing Buyer: Louise Richardson
Cover Administrator: Linda Knowles
Cover Designer: Suzanne Harbison

Library of Congress Cataloging-in-Publication Data

Grossman, Herbert
    Special education in a diverse society / Herbert Grossman.
       p. cm.
    Includes bibliographical references and index.
    ISBN 0-205-15516-2
    1. Special education—Social aspects—United States.
2. Minorities—Education—United States.   3. Discrimination in
education—United States.   4. Education equalization—United
States.   I. Title.
    LC3981.G76   1994
    371.9'0973—dc20   94-980
                                              CIP

Printed in the United States of America

10 9 8 7 6 5 4 3 2 1   99 98 97 96 95 94

Photo Credits: Pages xviii, 22, and 240: Brian Smith; pages 62, 216, and 254: Jim Pickerell; pages 104 and 140: Will Faller; pages 184, 310, and 356: Stephen Marks.

*For the many students and citizens of Tuskegee
who treated me like just another congo drum–playing professor,
the Black Forest, the Elks Club,
and Groovy*

CONTENTS

PREFACE

In a democracy, schools are expected to provide citizens with much of the knowledge and skills they need to meet the challenges of life and to profit from the opportunities life presents them. To be truly democratic, a society should assure all students the same opportunity to succeed in school, regardless of their ethnic and socioeconomic-class background, the geographic area in which they live and study, their gender, or their disability. Unfortunately, many students are poorly served by and fail to succeed in both the regular and special education systems. Among these are students from non-European ethnic backgrounds—especially African American, Native American, and Hispanic American students—students from employed and unemployed poor families, rural students, and students whose school experiences are adversely affected by gender biases.

Although a great deal has been written about ethnic, socioeconomic-class, and gender issues in regular education, few authors have tackled the relationship between these factors and students' experiences in special education. This book is designed to fill this void by examining the influence of ethnic, socioeconomic-class, and gender factors on the special education careers of students with disabilities and students who are gifted and talented. The text explores the role these factors play in both the misidentification of students who do not have disabilities and the denial of special education services to students who should be enrolled in special education. It describes the influence of these factors on students' dissimilar rates of success in the special education programs in which they participate, explores the causes of these differences, and suggests specific ways special educators can eliminate these differences by providing students with the services that most fit their individual needs.

Special Education in a Diverse Society has been written for students who are preparing to become special educators. However, because very few special educators are exposed to the kind of information included in this text, practicing special educators who have completed their training will also find it useful.

The activities and exercises in the book were also written with the special education student in mind. In some states, special educators can receive their credentials without first having to obtain a regular education teaching credential. Most of these special education students will have little, if any, classroom experience when they read this book. In other states, special education is a second credential. In these states, many students will have taught for a number of years before returning to school for their special education training; all of them will have completed student teaching. Therefore, some of the exercises and activities in the text were designed for students who have had classroom experience and others were prepared with the inexperienced student in mind.

Although the focus of the text is special education, it examines special education in the context of its interrelationship with regular education. This is important for many reasons. Many students with disabilities are referred for special education services from regular education. Most students with disabilities and gifted and talented students are mainstreamed for part of the day in regular education programs. Many of them are eventually returned to regular education programs. In addition, regular and special educators take many of the same preservice courses, operate in the same school buildings, share similar philosophies of education, and probably have fairly similar attitudes toward ethnic, socioeconomic-class, and gender issues and deal with these issues in similar ways.

The text begins by examining the inequities that exist in the educational careers of diverse groups of students with disabilities. Chapter 1 details such inequities as the overrepresentation and underrepresentation of certain groups of students in special education programs, the different success rates among students with disabilities from diverse backgrounds, and the culturally, contextually, and linguistically inappropriate special education services many students receive.

Chapters 2 and 3 discuss the causes of the current disparities in the outcomes of students who belong to different ethnic and socioeconomic-class groups. Chapter 4 describes how special educators can eliminate these disparities. It also includes techniques for increasing respect for diversity, reducing prejudice, and improving intergroup relationships among students with disabilities. Chapter 5 examines the many ways the context of students' lives can impede their progress in special education programs. It then highlights what teachers can do to adapt their special educational approaches to the contextual needs of students with disabilities who are immigrants or refugees, migrants, rural, homeless, and so on. Chapter 6 describes communicatively appropriate special educational approaches. It focuses on how special educators can succeed with students who are limited English proficient, speak and write in nonstandard English dialects, or use different communication styles.

Chapters 7 and 8 deal with gender and sexual orientation issues in special education. Chapter 7 focuses on the possible causes of gender inequalities in special education. Chapter 8 examines legal requirements and describes what special educators can do to eliminate gender bias, provide students with gender-appropriate special education services, and assist students with sexual orientation problems.

Chapters 9, 10, and 11 detail how special educators can employ the principles developed in earlier chapters to adapt their assessment, instructional, and classroom management techniques to the diverse needs of students with disabilities. Chapter 9 presents the legal requirements of nonbiased assessment and describes how special educators can improve the assessment process by emphasizing prereferral procedures, adapting their assessment techniques to their students' characteristics, and selecting less biased assessment approaches and materials. Chapter 10 explains how special educators can select instructional techniques that suit students' relationship styles, cognitive styles, motivational styles, self-concepts, interests, and types of acculturation. Chapter 11 examines the many discriminatory classroom management techniques that teachers unwittingly use with diverse students with special needs and describes how special educators can improve their classroom management approaches by adapting their techniques to their students' characteristics and by empowering them.

The text includes an unusually large number of references. Two reasons for this are especially significant: to avoid ethnic, socioeconomic-class, and gender stereotypes and to present all sides of controversial issues.

Different ethnic groups have different values. Students from varied ethnic backgrounds do not behave in the same ways nor do they share the same beliefs and values. Subgroups within these larger ethnic groups also differ. Although not all students fit the following generalizations, Mexican American students tend to be exposed to much more traditional values and role models than the Nicaraguan American students who were exposed to values that were encouraged by the Sandinistas after their assumption of power. Filipino females tend to grow up in a society in which the roles that the genders fulfill are much more alike than in Vietnam. Chinese American, Japanese American, Samoan American, Vietnamese American, and Hmong American students have very different experiences and cultural backgrounds. Native Americans who maintain their traditional life-styles live differently than those who have acculturated to the mainstream European American culture.

There is diversity among students brought up in families with similar ethnic backgrounds. Parents who want their children to maintain their own ethnic identities may encourage and even pressure them to maintain traditional values, attitudes, and behavior patterns to a much greater degree than parents who want to assimilate and acculturate into the American mainstream. For example, Mexican migrant workers and their children who plan to return to Mexico may be less motivated to adopt European American values and behavior patterns than those who intend to settle in the United States permanently.

Students from different socioeconomic-class backgrounds are also influenced by dissimilar cultural experiences. Students from the same socioeconomic class may not be equally motivated to maintain their cultural heritages. Students in upwardly mobile low-income families and those who identify with and wish to join or emulate the middle class may be less likely to accept traditional values or roles than students who are content with their economic situation.

Regional differences create diversity among ethnic and socioeconomic groups. For example, Mexican American students who live in border towns in Texas, New Mexico, and Arizona and Cuban Americans who live in areas with large Hispanic American populations, such as Miami, are much more likely to be exposed to the traditional Latino cultural life-styles and attitudes than Mexican American and Cuban American students who live in other parts of the country. Likewise, students from low-income families growing up in Appalachia have somewhat different experiences and exposure to middle-class values and behavior patterns than students from cities such as New York, Detroit, or Atlanta, and they may be more likely to behave in traditional ways than urban students.

It is extremely important to avoid stereotypic overgeneralizations about all non-European American, all poor, all immigrant, or all refugee students. Therefore, research is included about the various subgroups of these large groups.

Many of the issues that are examined in this book are so controversial that it seemed necessary to present the evidence in support of and against each of the various positions that appear in the literature. Hopefully, this has been done in a way that allows students to examine all sides of an issue and arrive at informed decisions.

Every attempt was made to include the most current research. Nevertheless, some of the references may appear dated. This typically occurs when the bulk of the research about a topic or work in a field was completed in the 1970s and early 1980s. Examples of these are the considerable amount of research conducted in the 1970s regarding the efficacy of assessing nonstandard English dialect-speaking students in standard English and the validity of the pluralistic norms included in such assessment procedures as the System of Multicultural Pluralistic Assessment and the culture-specific tests developed for African Americans during this period.

Individual readers may find some of the terminology used in the book not completely to their liking. This is unavoidable. People use the same term in different ways and different terms for the same concept. The terms *mildly retarded, mildly developmentally disabled, educable mentally retarded, students with mild developmental disabilities, students with significant challenges,* and *differently abled students* all refer to the same group of students or special education category. The terms *poor, low income, lower class, employed and unemployed poor,* and *working class; gender* and *sex;* and *gender bias* and *sexism* are also used interchangeably at times.

To some individuals, one term is definitely preferable to the others because of the term's connotation. What may appear to some to be minor changes in terminology often signify major differences in point of view. *Culturally different* does not mean the same thing as *culturally deprived* or *culturally disadvantaged.* And what may seem to be an inconsequential difference in terms when referring to groups of people (e.g., *Chicano* versus *Mexican American* and *Latino; Black* versus *AfroAmerican, African-American,* and *African American; American Indian* versus *Native American,* and *native American;* and *Pilipino* versus *Filipino*) may mean a great deal to the people who are being labeled. In such cases, no terminology will satisfy everyone. Even if it did, it is entirely possible that many terms will change and become dated in the not too distant future.

In most cases, I have attempted to handle the problem of terminology by using the most current terms. When a number of terms are in use and if there is no overwhelming reason to prefer one to the other, I have used several current terms for the same concept. In a few cases, I have used the term I prefer even though it may not be the one "in fashion." I hope that the reader will look beyond the controversy over terminology to the more substantial issues dealt with in the text. Socioeconomic-class, ethnic, and gender issues are controversial enough in their own right.

ACKNOWLEDGMENTS

I wish to gratefully acknowledge the following individuals who reviewed the manuscript: Isaura Barrera, The University of New Mexico; Catherine Collier, Cross-Cultural Developmental Education Services; and Ramon M. Rocha, State University of New York at Geneseo.

1

THE PROBLEM

A mind is a terrible thing to waste.
(United Negro College Fund advertisement
slogan, 1972)

EDUCATIONAL INEQUITIES

This introductory chapter describes the mind-wasting problems of non-European American students, students from employed and unemployed poor families, and students who are exposed to gender-biased teaching experience in the regular and special education systems.

Ethnic and Socioeconomic-Class Inequities

The population of the United States is rapidly becoming less European American (1–5). By the year 2000, non-European Americans are expected to comprise one-third of the U.S. population. The three fastest growing groups are Hispanic Americans, African Americans, and Southeast Asian Americans. The two largest minority groups, 30 million African Americans and 20 million Hispanic Americans, will comprise almost a third of the total school enrollment. Currently, non-European American students are the majority in the 25 largest school districts in the country.

The number of children and youth living in poverty is also continuing to rise. Between 1979 and 1989, the numbers of Hispanic American, European American, and African American children living in poverty increased by 29, 25, and 6 percent, respectively, leading to an overall increase of 19 percent. This section examines the disparities between the school experiences and educational outcomes of non-European American students as well as students from employed and unemployed poor families and their European American middle- and upper-class peers.

Regular Education
Many non-European American students and students from employed and unemployed poor families do very well in school. However, as the following statistics indicate, the lack of educational success that characterizes these students as a whole is a national disaster.

The average achievement of African American, Native American, Hispanic American, and poor students is consistently lower than that of middle- and upper-class European American students at every grade level (6–17). By the

1

eleventh and twelfth grades, only 25.7 percent of European American students have repeated at least one grade level. The corresponding figures for African American and Hispanic American students are 39.0 and 40.8, respectively; for Hispanic American males, the percentage is 54.2 (16).

A smaller percentage of African American, Hispanic American, and Native American students graduate from high school (7, 18–28). Although the dropout rate of African American students has improved dramatically in recent years, in large cities where the vast majority of African American students are poor, more than half of them drop out (7). On a nationwide basis, Native Americans have the highest dropout rate. In Alaska and California, their dropout rates have been estimated at 90 and 70 percent, respectively (25, 28). The Hispanic dropout rate is almost as high. In some areas, such as New York City, the rate has been as high as 80 percent. As a group, Asian Pacific Americans have a low dropout rate. However, combining the statistics for all Asian Pacific Americans is misleading. Those students who come from developing countries where they and their families had little access to formal education have very high dropout rates.

Many non-European American high school graduates perform very well during their high school years, but, on average, their achievement leaves much to be desired. In comparison to European American students, African American, Hispanic American, and Native American students who graduate from high school are less likely to have studied computers or to have enrolled in high-level academic courses such as algebra, geometry, trigonometry, chemistry, physics, biology, and foreign languages. These students are also more likely to have taken remedial math and science classes (9, 16).

The results for students who are poor and have either an African American or Hispanic American background are especially discouraging. In comparison to middle-class African American and Hispanic American students, they are even more likely to drop out of school, to achieve less while in school, and to earn lower grades. They are also more likely to be enrolled in general and vocational programs than academic programs and in remedial rather than advanced or honors classes.

Special Education

Poor and non-European American students experience three major problems in relation to special education:

1. They are misrepresented—overenrolled as well as underenrolled—in special education programs. Those who are misplaced in special education are denied the kind of education they would profit from in regular education programs, whereas those who are inappropriately kept in the regular education system are deprived of the special education services their disabilities require.
2. Those who are correctly placed in special education often receive services that are culturally inappropriate and ill suited to the socioeconomic and geographic factors, as well as other factors that shape the context of their lives.

3. Students who are limited English proficient or who speak a nonstandard English dialect often experience a third problem—linguistically inappropriate services.

Misrepresentation.   Although some studies have found the contrary (31, 33, 34, 64), poor, African American, Hispanic American, and Native American students have been and are still grossly misrepresented in those special education programs in which placement decisions are subject to assessment bias (e.g., programs for students with learning disabilities, behavior disorders, mild developmental disabilities, gifts and talents, and so on versus those for students with physical or sensory disabilities) (29, 30, 32, 33, 35–63, 65–74). Prior to the passage of Public Law (PL) 94-142, these groups were typically overrepresented in programs for students with behavior disorders, serious emotional problems, communication disorders, and developmental disabilities (especially for those who were considered educable mentally retarded); they were underrepresented in programs for students with learning disabilities and in programs for gifted and talented students.

In many school districts, even when students' assessment results were similar, it was not uncommon to place poor, African American, Hispanic American, and Native American students in programs for students with emotional problems, behavior disorders, and developmental disabilities. European American students, especially those from the middle class, on the other hand, were usually placed in programs for students with learning disabilities. For example, in 1981, 46 percent of the African American students placed in special education were in programs for the retarded, in comparison to 22 percent of European American students; whereas only 26 percent of African American students in special education programs were enrolled in programs for students with learning disabilities, in comparison to 40 percent of European American students (71). (See Chapter 9 for a more detailed discussion of ethnic and socioeconomic bias in the distribution of students among various special education categories.)

The situation has changed considerably in the last decade. Some positive results have been achieved. The underrepresentation of non-European American and poor students in programs for the gifted and talented has lessened somewhat. In some areas, their enrollment in special education is proportional to their share of the local population (33, 34). And in many areas, programs for students with learning disabilities have ceased to be reserved primarily for European Americans.

Nevertheless, poor, African American, Hispanic American, and Native American students, especially those who are limited English proficient, are still grossly misrepresented in special education programs. The type of misrepresentation they experience differs from state to state and from school district to school district. In many states and school districts, these students are still underrepresented in programs for the gifted and talented and overrepresented in special education classes for students with behavior disorders, learning disabilities, serious emotional problems, communication disorders, and mild developmental disabilities.

Overall, Hispanic Americans and Native Americans tend to be overrepresented in programs for students with learning disabilities and underrepresented in programs for the gifted and talented, but again this varies from school district to school district. Asian American students tend to be underrepresented in programs for students with learning disabilities, serious emotional problems, and behavior disorders and overrepresented in programs for students with speech disorders. In fact, in some school districts, as many as 50 percent of the Asian American students receiving special education services are in such programs. African Americans experience the greatest overrepresentation in programs for students with disabilities. Although they account for only 12 percent of the elementary and secondary school population, they constitute 28 percent of the total enrollment in special education. They are especially overrepresented in programs for students with mild developmental disabilities.

Special educators disagree about the implications of these statistics. (See Chapters 2 and 3 for a detailed discussion of this controversy.) Some are not troubled because they believe that, for a variety of reasons, poor and non-European American students are less likely to be gifted and more likely to have behavior disorders, emotional problems, communication disorders, learning disabilities, and developmental delays. Many others, however, view this misrepresentation as a problem that needs to be corrected. These special educators concede that there is no reason to assume that all groups of students should be represented in each special education category in exactly the proportion that they represent the population of a school district, state, or country. However, they claim that in many school districts and regions these students are not being placed in the educational programs that would be most beneficial to them. They believe this results in depriving some students of the kind of education they can profit from in regular education programs and programs for gifted and talented and in denying other students the special education services that their disabilities require.

Some special educators feel that either of the previous positions can be correct, depending on the situation. One panel on the cause of disproportionality in programs for students with mild developmental disabilities posed the issue this way:

> The key issue is not disproportionality per se but rather the validity of referral and assessment procedures and the quality of instruction received, whether in the regular classroom or in special education settings. If needed and effective educational services are provided in the least restrictive environment to students validly targeted, then any resulting inequality in minority representation in those programs would not constitute an inequity. . . . Disproportion is a problem if children are invalidly placed in programs for mentally retarded students. . . . Disproportion is a problem if children are unduly exposed to the likelihood of EMR placement by being in schools or classes with poor-quality regular instruction. . . . Disproportion is a problem if the quality and academic relevance of instruction in special classes block students' educational progress, including decreasing the likelihood of their return to the regular classroom. (46, pp. 5, 18–20)

Non-European American students who are limited English proficient are even more likely to be misrepresented in special education programs. Although a

number of new bilingual special education programs for limited-English-proficient gifted and talented students have been initiated in recent years, on a nationwide basis, these students continue to be underrepresented in such programs. In
some school districts, these students continue to be overrepresented in programs
for students with learning disabilities, behavior disorders, and mild developmental disabilities. Beginning in the early 1980s, however, limited-English-proficient
students in many other districts were underrepresented in these same programs
(51, 61, 71, 72).

A PERSONAL ACCOUNT BY HARIM ZAYAS

At the age of nine, I was referred to a speech therapist for a speech impediment. What
really occurred was that my Spanish speaking mother assisted me with my spelling
homework, and I would learn to pronounce words according to her instructions. For
example, she taught me to say the letters *ch* as they are pronounced in the word *cheat*.
So when it came to a word like *machine*, I would mispronounce it, and, even after
being encouraged to say it correctly, I would only do as I was instructed by my
mother. The constant therapy received for this "speech impediment" eventually created in me a low self-worth for not overcoming this matter. It wasn't until many years
later that an English speaking, culturally sensitive teacher informed me that I did not
have a speech problem. (75, p. 12)

To some educators, underrepresentation of limited-English-proficient students in programs for students with behavior disorders, emotional problems,
learning disabilities, and mild developmental disabilities is an improvement because it signifies that fewer of them are being misplaced in programs for students
with disabilities. Others are dissatisfied with the change. They claim that many
poor immigrant and refugee students need these kinds of special education services even more than the English-proficient non-European American students
who are born in the United States because of the extreme physical and psychological deprivation they experienced before they emigrated to the United States.
These educators note that limited-English-proficient students with disabilities
who remain in mainstream bilingual education programs are instructed by teachers who are not prepared to provide them with the special education services they
require (56).

Culturally, Contextually, and Linguistically Inappropriate Services.　The vast
majority of special educators who teach in ethnically diverse schools are not
knowledgeable about their students' religious beliefs, values, customs, life-styles,
learning styles, and so on. They do not know about the ways in which the economic problems of students living in poverty affect their learning. They are unaware of the trauma many refugee students experienced prior to arriving in the
United States. And they do not appreciate the difficulty limited-English-proficient
students experience while trying to learn in a language they do not understand

and adjust to a strange and often frightening school environment. As a result, many poor and non-European American students (especially those who are immigrants, refugees, or limited English proficient) are often exposed to assessment, instruction, classroom management, and counseling techniques that are appropriate only for European American middle-class students with disabilities (56, 76–80).

Inappropriate services can create many problems. For example, having been assessed in culturally unsuitable ways, these students may have individual education plans with goals that do not fit their needs. Taught in teaching styles that do not match their culturally influenced learning styles, they may progress less rapidly than their European American peers. When they are exposed to culturally and contextually inappropriate classroom management techniques, they are less likely to change their behavior and be accepted in mainstream classes. Counseled in inappropriate ways, they can have difficulty understanding, appreciating, and accepting the knowledge and advice their teachers give them. And when their parents are exposed to similarly culturally inappropriate counseling, the parents are less likely to become involved in their children's education. (See Chapter 3.)

Very few special educators are bilingual, and many of those who are have not been trained to provide bilingual special education services. (See Chapter 3.) As a result, non-European American, limited-English-proficient students with disabilities are usually instructed by monolingual teachers who are unable to provide them with the services they are entitled to in the language they can understand. The Office of Special Education of the U.S. Department of Education has concluded, "Studies have documented apparent discrepancies in the levels of referral and placement of limited English proficient children in special education. The Department of Education has found that services provided to limited English proficient students often do not respond primarily to the pupil's academic needs. These trends pose special challenges for special education in the referral, assessment, and services for our Nation's students from non-English language backgrounds" (7).

Program Effectiveness.   Many researchers have studied the effectiveness of the special education services provided to students with disabilities and gifted and talented students. However, very few of their studies have yielded information about whether these services are equally effective with poor and middle- and upper-class, European American and non-European American, and English-proficient and limited-English-proficient students. The limited evidence available suggests that most, but not all, programs specifically designed to deliver culturally and linguistically appropriate services to non-European American or limited-English-proficient students with disabilities or gifted and talented are effective, at least to some degree (82–85, 88, 90–93).

Special programs that are not designed with the needs of poor, non-European American, and limited-English-proficient students in mind tend to be about as ineffective as regular education programs. Studies about the effectiveness of special education programs for limited-English-proficient, non-European, and poor students are very limited and include only African American, Hispanic American, Native American, and poor students. With very few exceptions, research suggests that these students earn lower grades and score lower on standardized tests than their European American middle-class peers. They are also less likely to be returned to mainstream classes, to graduate from high school, to continue their studies after high school, to achieve vocational success, to be employed, or to earn a good living (76, 80, 81, 86, 87, 89, 94-96). One researcher noted, "Ethnic minority children generally, and Black economically disadvantaged children in particular, are not reaping comparable instructional benefits from these special programs, as are their white counterparts. As a matter of fact, the data reveal a striking parallel between Black students who drop out of "special programs" and those who are disadvantaged by their socioeconomic backgrounds, and who tend to drop out of "regular education" (80, p. 14).

Poor students are especially likely to do poorly in special education, regardless of their ethnic background. For example, a national study found that when students with disabilities were divided into four groups based on their socioeconomic status, their dropout rates were lowest quartile—26.7 percent, second quartile—25.0 percent, third quartile—17.2 percent, and highest quartile—6.7 percent. Thus, the dropout rate for students in the two lowest socioeconomic-class groups was almost four times as great as that of students in the highest group (93).

Because most of the data currently available are based on studies that included a limited number of students who are unrepresentative of both the many different kinds of disabilities students can have and the variety of ethnic backgrounds in the schools, they should be considered suggestive rather than conclusive. Nevertheless, they do raise concerns about the effectiveness of the special education services currently being provided to non-European American and poor students.

Informal discussions with educators indicate that the implications of these statistics are controversial. Some feel that ethnic and socioeconomic-class differences in the outcomes of special education programs are intolerable. Others do not expect the special education system to eliminate the disparities that pervade the regular education system and society in which it operates.

Gender Inequities

Although students' performance and participation in school cannot be predicted on the basis of their gender alone, on the average, males and females have somewhat different experiences in both the regular and special education systems. These differences are discussed next.

Regular Education

When students are given the opportunity to select their courses and activities, males and females make somewhat different choices (97–107). Females tend to enroll in fewer advanced math courses (especially intermediate algebra and calculus), computer courses, and science courses—the courses that are so important for admission to college and success in many technological and scientific fields. This generalization characterizes females from many Asian Pacific American backgrounds, Native Americans, and European American and Hispanic American females from poor backgrounds. It is not true of African American females, in general, or females from European American, Filipino American, and Vietnamese American middle-class backgrounds.

There is considerable evidence that males and females choose very different vocational education courses and aspire to different careers (108–122). Females comprise over 90 percent of the students in cosmetology, clerical, home economics, and health courses, and less than 10 percent of the students in courses that deal with agriculture, electrical technology, electronics, appliance repair, auto mechanics, carpentry, welding, and small engine repair. In general, Hispanic American , Southeast Asian American, and poor European American males are more likely than females to plan to work outside the home and to aspire to professional careers that require at least a bachelor's degree or higher. These gender differences do not apply to the same extent to middle-class European American, Vietnamese American, Filipino American, and African American students.

Although the gender gap on standardized achievement tests and school grades has narrowed in recent years (123–128), male and female students still have different success rates in many academic subjects and skills (129–163). However, many of those rates do not apply to all ethnic groups and socioeconomic classes. African American, Hispanic American, European American, and Native American females receive higher grades than males on tests of verbal skills in elementary and secondary school. In elementary school, females, with the exception of Native Americans, tend to score higher than males on mathematics skills tests. Beginning in high school, females, again with the exception of Native Americans, do better than males on tests of basic computational skills. However, with the exception of African American and some Asian Pacific American groups, females score less adequately than males on mathematics tests involving complex mathematical skills, word problems, and visual-spatial tasks.

In elementary school, there are few, if any, gender differences in students' science achievement. In secondary school, males tend to score higher then females on tests of physical and earth science information but not on tests of health science information. Poor and African American males are exception to this generalization.

Females are less likely to get into trouble for behavioral problems. They are also less likely to be disciplined by their teachers or suspended from school (164–168).

Special Education

Misrepresentation.   Males are much more likely to be enrolled in special education programs for students with developmental disabilities, behavior disorders, emotional disturbances, and learning disabilities (37, 38, 53). Data that need updating to determine if they still apply to students currently suggest that this disparity may be the result of misplacing males—especially African American, Hispanic, and poor males—in these programs and denying some female students with cognitive or emotional problems the special education services they require.

Although fewer females than males are enrolled in programs for students with emotional problems, there is some evidence that they have more emotional problems than males (169–178). Females are more likely to regard themselves as sad or depressed. In general, they are more fearful, anxious, and timid. Until recently, this was especially noticeable among European American and Hispanic American females in courses such as science and math, traditionally thought to be in the so-called male domain (175, 178). African American females are typically no more and perhaps even less anxious than African American males in these courses (174). Recently, however, females have reportedly been less anxious in these courses, perhaps because they are less likely to be perceived to be in the male domain (172).

With the exception of African American students, females tend to be less self-confident about school than males, especially in courses such as mathematics and science, in competitive situations, and when they lack objective information about how well they have done or can do (179–187). Females are apt to react less positively than males to difficult and challenging situations and are less likely to take risks in school (188–189). In general, they are less persistent and perform less adequately than males following failure or the threat of failure (190–191). Finally, female students tend to seek the assistance and approval of adults more than males do (192–195).

These characterizations do not apply to all females, of course. They are more likely to apply to a greater degree to poor females and to Hispanic American and Asian Pacific American females who are brought up in families that adhere to traditional ideas about sex roles than to European American middle-class females, and are least likely to apply to African American females (112, 196–197). However, these characteristics do apply to other ethnic groups and to many females regardless of their ethnic or socioeconomic backgrounds. Some of the students who behave in these ways may be conforming to gender stereotypes. Others may have emotional problems and not be receiving the help they require.

Program Effectiveness.   Very few studies of the effectiveness of special education programs have yielded information about whether they are equally effective with males and females. The data about gender differences in academic achievement are inconsistent (198–200). One study found no differences; another reported that males outscored females on achievement tests; and a third found that female students tend to earn higher grades and score better on verbal but not mathematics tests. In one study, male students' self-descriptions indicated that they had more self-confidence than females. Males appear to gain more vocational skills in school, experience less unemployment, and earn more as young adults (81, 200). However, the data on which these tentative descriptions are based are much too sketchy to yield any firm conclusions about possible gender differences.

PROGRAM EFFECTIVENESS

- By what standards should special educators judge the achievements of their programs?
- Should special education programs be expected to avoid the ethnic, socioeconomic-class, and gender disparities in student achievement, graduation, postschool employment, and other areas that are characteristic of regular education and society in general?

ORGANIZATION OF THE TEXT

The eleven chapters in this book are designed to help special educators recognize and reduce ethnic, socioeconomic-class, and gender educational disparities and inequities. This chapter has described the problems that need to be addressed. Chapters 2 through 4 examine the causes of and solutions to ethnic and socioeconomic-class inequities in special education. Chapters 5 through 8 discuss the knowledge needed by special educators to provide students with contextually, linguistically, and gender-appropriate special education services. Chapters 9 through 11 assist special educators in selecting nonbiased/nonsexist assessment, instructional, and classroom management approaches for their students.

RESEARCH-BASED APPROACH

Throughout the text, there is a heavy emphasis on research findings. Enough is known about the role of ethnic, socioeconomic, and gender factors in special education for teachers to take these factors into account when they assess, instruct, manage, and counsel their students without basing their decisions on inaccurate or prejudicial stereotypes. The following are two examples of how knowledge of ethnic, socioeconomic-class, and gender factors can help special educators.

Most regular educators tend to employ competitive instructional techniques because they believe such methods bring out the best in students. Other educators, especially those who teach in special education program, stress cooperative approaches because they think such approaches improve relationships among students, prepare them to function in a democratic society, and lead to higher levels of achievement. However, as you will see in later in this book, research indicates that, males, in general, and certain European Americans and Asian Pacific Americans perform better in competitive learning situations, whereas females, in general, and ethnic groups such as African Americans, Hispanic Americans, and Hawaiian Americans perform better in cooperative learning situations.

Educators who act on their preference for competitive or cooperative learning without considering their students' gender and ethnically influenced learning styles will not meet the needs of all students. Educators who are aware of ethnic and gender differences in learning styles can make reasoned choices. If they want to maximize students' academic achievement, they can use cooperative techniques with some students and competitive ones with others. However, if their goal is to help students be able to act competitively when competition is required and cooperatively when cooperation is required, they might employ techniques designed to expand students' behavioral repertoires. In either case, a knowledge of gender and ethnic differences in preferences for competitive and cooperative learning environments would certainly help.

Some primary-grade special education teachers use material reinforcers such as food, toys, or time to use especially desirable classroom equipment. Symbolic rewards such as gold stars, checks, or points that can be converted into material rewards at a later time may also be used to motivate students. Others prefer to use interpersonal motivational techniques such as praising students, telling students they are proud of them, patting them on the back, sending home a note about them, and so on. Research indicates that most females, Hispanic Americans, African Americans, and certain other ethnic groups are more receptive to personal rewards, but most males and European Americans are more responsive to impersonal ones, especially in the lower grades. A knowledge of students' ethnic and gender-influenced preferences can help a special educator select effective reinforcers.

Some words of caution about research-based teaching are in order. Although researchers know a considerable amount about some topics, many important issues remain to be studied. Sometimes what is known is obsolete. What was true of group a few years ago may not be true today and even less so tomorrow. For example, generalizations that characterized the Southeast Asian students who were brought to the United States by their well-educated, middle- and upper-class, urban parents in the early 1970s do not describe the children of the uneducated, poor, rural boat people who came to the United States in the 1980s and 1990s. The first group of children may have had considerable difficulty adjusting to U.S. schools. However, the second group of children—most of whom never attended school and who had to survive the trauma of running blockades, avoiding pirates, and being confined in detention camps for many years until they finally resettled in the United States—typically have much more serious academic and emotional problems. As a result, they are also more likely to require special education services.

Many researchers fail to control for socioeconomic differences when they study the cognitive skills, learning styles, and so on of different ethnic groups of students with disabilities. Since a smaller percentage of European American children currently live in families below the poverty level than Hispanic American and African American children, differences that are observed among uncontrolled samples of these groups cannot be attributed solely to ethnicity. Conclusions about educationally relevant differences between African American and European American students with disabilities based on comparisons between African American poor students and European American middle-class students should have no influence on educational policy and practices. Unfortunately, this is not the case.

Much of the information about socioeconomic-class, ethnic, and gender differences among students has been gained by looking at questions derived from the researchers' gender, ethnic, or class perspective that is different from that of the students studied. Much information is based on studying these students in laboratories, presenting them with hypothetical situations and asking what they would do. This kind of information may be scientific, exact, objective, and reproducible, but it may also be less valid and therefore less useful than knowledge gained by actively participating in and understanding the students' in-school and out-of-school lives.

Finally, and perhaps most importantly, there is an ever-present danger that special educators will overgeneralize research findings to students to whom they do not apply. All students do not conform to the stereotypic behavior patterns of the gender, ethnic, and socioeconomic-class groups to which they belong. Even when people behave in stereotypic ways, they all do not behave the same. There are important differences among students brought up in families with similar ethnic backgrounds. Parents who want their children to maintain their own ethnic identities may pressure them to maintain their traditional values, attitudes, and behavior patterns to a much greater degree than parents who wish to assimilate and acculturate into the U.S. mainstream. Migrant workers and their children who plan to return to Mexico may be less motivated to adopt European American values and behavior patterns than those who plan to settle here permanently. Native American students who plan to continue to live on their reservations may be less motivated to adapt to European American ways than those who plan to leave the reservations. Similar differences occur between African Americans who want to integrate fully into European American society and those who want to maintain their African American identities.

Although students from poor backgrounds are more likely to be brought up to fulfill traditional roles than middle-class students, this may be less true for students in upwardly mobile families and students who identify with and wish to join or emulate the middle class than for those who are content with their lifestyle. This may also be less important for poor students growing up in Appalachia than for poor students from New York City who have somewhat different life experiences and much more exposure to middle-class values and behavior patterns.

For these and other reasons, generalizations about gender, ethnic, and socioeconomic-class differences among students can be very misleading. Despite these cautions, however, it is important to recognize that some descriptions of socioeconomic-class or ethnic groups tend to apply to the majority of their members and some gender differences cut across socioeconomic-class, ethnic, and geographic boundaries.

Such generalizations can be helpful. They can sensitize special educators to the *possibility* that their students may have certain stereotypic attitudes, preferences, values, learning styles, and behavior patterns. However, special educators should never assume that their students will *necessarily* think and behave in these ways. It is as important to avoid relating to students on the basis of incorrect stereotypes as it is to avoid being insensitive to the role that ethnic, socioeconomic-class, or gender-influenced attitudes and behavior may play in some students' lives. As long as special educators keep these limitations in mind and strive to be informed consumers of research-based knowledge, they will be more effective with exceptional students, especially with those groups who traditionally have not performed well in today's diverse society.

SUMMARY

There are great ethnic, socioeconomic-class, and gender disparities in the extent to which students are effectively served by regular and special education. Some students are misplaced in special education, some are denied the special education services they require, and many are provided culturally, linguistically, or gender-inappropriate services. Educators can avoid these problems by taking ethnic, socioeconomic-class, and gender factors in consideration when they assess, instruct, manage, and counsel their students.

ACTIVITIES

1. Compare the ethnic composition of the school or school district in which you are working to the ethnic composition of the special education program it offers. If there are disparities, determine whether they fit the patterns described in this chapter.

2. Examine the gender composition of the various special education programs being offered. Does it fit the nationwide pattern?

REFERENCES

References 1–5 discuss population trends.

1. Bureau of the Census. (1988a). *Hispanic Population in the United States: Current Population Reports, Series P-20, No. 438.* U.S. Department of Commerce, Washington, DC: U.S. Government Printing Office.

2. Bureau of the Census. (1988b). *Money, Income and Poverty Status in the United States (Advance Data from the March 1989 Current Population Survey): Current Population Reports, Series P-60, No.* 166 U.S. Department of Commerce, Washington, DC: U.S. Government Printing Office.

3. Bureau of the Census. (1988c). *The Black Population in the United States: Current Population Reports, Series P-20, No. 442.* U.S. Department of Commerce, Washington, DC: U.S. Government Printing Office.

4. National Information Center for Children and Youth with Handicaps. (1988). *Minority Issues in Special Education: A Portrait of the Future.* Washington, DC: Author.

5. Puente, T. (1991). Latino child poverty ranks swell. *Hispanic Link Weekly Report, 9* (35), 1, 2, 8.

References 6–17 deal with the low success rates of non-European American and poor students.

6. Educational Testing Service. (1989). *Who Reads Best?* Princeton, NJ: Author.

7. Individuals with Disabilities Education Act (20 U.S.C., Sections 1400–1485; Education of the Handicapped Act Amendments of 1990).

8. Johnson, M. L. (1984). Blacks in mathematics: A status report. *Journal for Research in Mathematics Education, 15* (2), 145–153.

9. National Assessment of Education Progress. (1988a). *Computer Competence: The First National Assessment.* Princeton, NJ: Educational Testing Service.

10. National Assessment of Education Progress. (1988b). *The Mathematics Report Card: Are We Measuring Up?* Princeton, NJ: Educational Testing Service.

11. National Assessment of Education Progress. (1988c). *The Science Report Card: Elements of Risk and Recovery.* Princeton, NJ: Educational Testing Service.

12. National Assessment of Education Progress. (1990a). *The Reading Report Card, 1971–1978: Trends from the Nation's Report Card.* Princeton, NJ: Educational Testing Service.

13. National Assessment of Education Progress. (1990b). *The Writing Report Card, 1984–1988: Findings from the Nation's Report Card.* Princeton, NJ: Educational Testing Service.

14. National Black Child Development Institute. (1990). *The Status of African American Children: Twentieth Anniversary Report.* Washington, DC: Author.

15. National Center for Educational Statistics. (1989). 1987 high school transcript study. In *National Center for Educational Statistics. Digest of Educational Statistics 1989.* Washington, DC: U.S. Department of Education.

16. National Council of La Raza. (1990). *Hispanic Education: A Statistical Report.* Washington, DC: Author.

17. Office of Educational Research and Improvement, National Center for Educational Research. (1990). *National Education Longitudinal Study. A Profile of the American Eighth Grader: NELS: 88 Student Descriptive Summary.* Washington, DC: U.S. Department of Education.

References 18–28 focus on the high dropout rates of non-European American and poor students.

18. American Council on Education, Office of Minority Concerns. (1989). *Minorities in Higher Education: Eighth Annual Status Report, 1989.* Washington, DC: Author.

19. Arciniega, T. A., & Moray, A. I. (1985). *Hispanics and Higher Education: A CSU Imperative. Final Report of the Commission on Hispanic Under-representation.* Long Beach: California State University, Office of the Chancellor.

20. Aspira. (1983). *Racial and Ethnic High School Dropout Rates in New York City.* ERIC ED 254 600.

21. Astin, A. (1982). *Minorities in American Higher Education.* San Francisco: Jossey-Bass.

22. Bureau of Indian Affairs. (1988, March). *Report on B. I. A. Education: Final Review Draft.* Washington, DC: Department of the Interior.

23. Hirano-Nakanishi, M. J., & Diaz, R. L. (1982). *Differential Educational Attainment Among "At-Risk" Youth: A Case Study of Language Minority Youth of Mexican Descent and Low Socioeconomic Status.* Los Alamitos, CA: National Center for Bilingual Research.

24. Illinois State General Assembly. (1985). *A Generation Too Precious to Waste.* ERIC ED 268 198.

25. National Public Radio Broadcast. (1990, September). *On the Alaskan Native American.* Washington, DC: All Things Considered.

26. New York Alliance for Public Schools. (1985). *A Study of the Identification, Monitoring, and Tracking of Potential High School Student Dropouts for the New York City Board of Education: Executive Summary. Final Report.* ERIC ED 273 720.

27. Rumberger, R. W. (1983). Dropping out of high school: The influence of race, sex, and family background. *American Education Research Journal, 20,* 199–220.

28. Steinberg, L., Blinde, P. L., & Chan, K. S. (1984). Dropping out among language minority youth. *Review of Educational Research, 54,* 113–132.

References 29–75 include evidence regarding ethnic and socioeconomic-class differences in student enrollment in special education.

29. Achey, V. H., & Woods, S. B. (1988). *Increasing Minority Participation in the Greensboro Academically Gifted Program without Changing Entrance Criteria.* ERIC ED 302 999.

30. Benavides, A. (1988). *High Risk Predictors and Prereferral Screening for Language Minority Students. Revised.* ERIC ED 298 702.

31. Bernard, R., & Clarizio, H. (1981). Socioeconomic bias in special education placement decisions. *Psychology in the Schools, 18,* 178–183.

32. Bowman, J. E. (1988). *A Study of Special Education Referral and Placement Practices in Montgomery County Public Schools (Maryland).* ERIC ED 301 004.

33. Brosnan, F. L. (1983). Overrepresentation of low socioeconomic minority students in special education programs in California. *Learning Disabilities Quarterly, 6* (4), 517–525.

34. Cegelka, P. T., Lewis, P., & Rodriguez. A. M. (1987). Status of educational services to handicapped students with limited English proficiency: Report of a state-wide study in California. *Exceptional Children, 54* (3), 220–227.

35. Chinn, P. C., & Hughes, S. (1987). Representation of minority students in special education classes. *Remedial and Special Education, 8* (4), 41–46.

36. Collins, R., & Camblin, L. D. (1983). The politics and science of learning disability classification: Implications for Black children. *Contemporary Education, 54* (2), 113–118.

37. DBS Corp. (1986). *Elementary and Secondary School Civil Rights Survey, 1984. National Summaries.* ERIC ED 271 543.

38. DBS Corp. (1987). *Elementary and Secondary School Civil Rights Survey, 1986. National Summaries.* ERIC ED 304 485.

39. Dew, N. (1984). The exceptional bilingual child: Demographics. In P. C. Chinn (Ed.), *Education of Culturally and Linguistically Different Children.* Reston, VA: Council for Exceptional Children.

40. Figueroa, R. A., Sandoval, J., & Merino, B. (1984). School psychologists and limited English proficient (LEP) children: New competencies. *Journal of School Psychology, 22* (2), 131–143.

41. Florey, J., & Tafoya, N. (1988). *Identifying Gifted and Talented American Indian Students: An Overview.* ERIC ED 296 810.

42. Garcia, S. B. (1985). Characteristics of limited English proficient Hispanic students served in programs for the learning disabled: Implications for policy, practice, and research (Part I). *Bilingual Special Education Newsletter.* Austin: University of Texas.

43. Gelb, S. A., & Mizokawa, D. D. (1986). Special education and social structure: The commonality of "exceptionality." *American Education Research Journal, 23* (4), 543–557.

44. Goodale, R., & Williams, I. J. (1984). *Minority Students in Special Education: A School System, Parent Advocacy and State Department Perspective.* ERIC ED 250 847.

45. Gregory, J. F. (1986). *A Secondary Analysis of HSB Data Related to Special Education.* ERIC ED 276 219.

46. Heller, K. A., Holtzman, W. H., Jr., & Messick, S. (1982). *Placing Children in Special Education: A Strategy for Equity.* Washington, DC: National Academy Press.

47. Holtzman, W. H., Jr., Ortiz, A., & Wilkinson, C. Y. (1986). *Characteristics of Limited English Proficient Hispanic Students in Programs for the Mentally Retarded: Implications for Policy, Practice, and Research.* ERIC ED 290 309.

48. Horner, C. M., Maddux, C. D., & Green, C. (1986). Minority students and special education: Is overrepresentation possible? *NASSP Bulletin, 70* (492), 89–93.

49. Jones, D. H., Sacks, J., & Bennet, R. E. (1985). A screening method for indentifying racial overrepresentation in special education placement. *Education Evaluation and Policy Analysis, 7* (1), 19–34.

50. MacMillan, D. L. (1988). *"New" EMR's. Chapter One.* ERIC ED 304 829.

51. Martinez, H. (Ed.). (1981). *Special Education and the Hispanic Child, Proceedings from the Second Annual Colloquium on Hispanic Issues.* New York: ERIC Clearinghouse on Urban Education, Institute for Urban and Minority Education, Teachers College, Columbia University.

52. Melsky, J. T. (1985). Indentifying and providing for the Hispanic gifted child. *NABE Journal, 9* (3), 43–56.

53. Messick, S. (1984). Assessment in context: Appraising student performance in relation to instructional quality. *Educational Researcher, 13* (3), 3–8.

54. Murphy, J., & Simon, R. (1987). *Minorities Issues in Special Education: A Portrait of the Future. News Digest#9.* Washington, DC: National Information Center for Handicapped Children and Youth.

55. National Information Center for Children and Youth with Handicaps. (1988). *Minority Issues in Special Education: A Portrait of the Future.* Washington, DC: Author.

56. Nuttall, E. V., Landurand, P. M., & Goldman, P. (1983). *A Study of Mainstreamed Limited English Proficient Handicapped Students in Bilingual Education.* ERIC ED 246 583.

57. Nuttall, E. V., Landurand, P. M., & Goldman, P. (1984). A critical look at testing and

evaluation from a cross-cultural perspective. In P. C. Chinn (Ed.), *Education of Culturally and Linguistically Different Exceptional Children*. Reston, VA: Council for Exceptional Children.

58. Ochoa, A. M., Pacheco, R., & Omark, D. R. (1988). Addressing the learning disability needs of limited-English proficient students: Beyond the language and race issues. *Learning Disabilities Quarterly, 11*, 257–264.

59. Office of Civil Rights. (1987). *Elementary and Secondary School Civil Rights Survey, 1986. National Summaries*. ERIC ED 304 485.

60. Plata, M., & Chinn, P. C. (1989). Students with handicaps who have cultural and language differences. In R. Gaylord-Ross (Ed.), *Integration Strategies for Students with Handicaps*. Baltimore: Brookes.

61. Pyecha, J. A. (1981). A study of the implementation of Public Law 94-142 for handicapped migrant children. In *Disparities Still Exist in Who Gets Special Education* (GAO Report). Gaithersburg, MD: General Accounting Office, U.S. Government.

62. Ramirez, B. (1990). Federal policy and the education of American Indian exceptional children and youth: Current status and future directions. In M. J. Johnson & B. Ramirez (Eds.), *American Indian Exceptional Children and Youth. Report of a Symposium*. ERIC ED 322 706.

63. Ramirez, B. A., & Johnson, M. J. (1988). *American Indian Exceptional Children: Improved Practices and Policy*. ERIC ED 298 713.

64. Reschly, D. J. (1985). *Myths and Realities in Minority Special Education Overrepresentation*. ERIC ED 271 911.

65. Reschly, D. J. (1988). Minority MMNR overrepresentation and special education reform. *Exceptional Children, 54* (4), 316–323.

66. Ryan, M. B. (1988). *Assessing Limited English Proficient Students for Special Education*. ERIC ED 316 045.

67. Schwenn, J. O., Hamon, G. T., & Jones, J. R. (1989). *Research on Service Patterns for Exceptional Children in the Rural Southeast*. ERIC ED 316 989.

68. Serwatka, T., Dove, T., & Hodge, W. (1986). Black students in special education: Issues and implications for community involvement. *Negro Educational Review, 37* (1), 17–26.

69. Serwatka, T. S., Deering, S., & Stoddard, A. (1989). Correlates of the underrepresentation of Black students in classes for gifted students. *Journal of Negro Education, 58* (4), 520–530.

70. Sleeter, C. E. (1986). Learning disabilities: The social construct of a special education category. *Exceptional Children, 53* (1), 46–54.

71. U.S. Comptroller General. (1981). *Disparities Still Exist in Who Gets Special Education*. Washington, DC: General Accounting Office.

72. Willig, A. C. (1986). Special education and the culturally and linguistically different child: An overview of issues and challenges. *Reading, Writing, and Learning Disabilities, 2*, 161–173.

73 Yancey, E. (1990). *Increasing Minority Participation in Gifted Programs*. ERIC ED 324 393.

74. Yourofsky, K. G. (1984). *Bilingual-Special Education Needs Assessment*. ERIC ED 250 868.

75. Zayas, H. (1981). *Bilingual Special Education Personnel Preparation National Task Oriented Seminar*. Washington, DC: Association for Cross-Cultural Education and Social Studies, Inc.

References 76–80 focus on culturally, contextually, and linguistically inappropriate special education services.

76. Cardoza, D., & Rueda, R. S. (1986). Educational and occupational outcomes of Hispanic learning-disabled high school students. *Journal of Special Education, 20* (1), 111–126.

77. Cegelka, P. T., Lewis, R., & Rodriguez, A. M. (1987). Status of educational services to handicapped students with limited English proficiency: Report of a statewide study in California. *Exceptional Children, 54* (3), 220–227.

78. Rodriguez, R., Prieto, A. G., & Rueda, R. S. (1984). Issues in bilingual/multicultural special education. *NABE Journal, 8* (3), 55–65.

79. Salend, S. J., & Fradd, S. (1986). Nationwide availability of services for limited-English proficient handicapped students. *Journal of Special Education, 20* (1), 127–135.

80. Wyche, L. G., Sr. (1989). The Tenth Annual Report to Congress: Taking a significant step in the right direction. *Exceptional Children, 56* (1), 14–16.

References 81–96 discuss the effectiveness of the special education services with different groups of students.

81. Asch, A. (1984). The experience of disability: A challenge for psychology. *American Psychologist, 39* (5), 529–536.

82. Berney, T. D., & Cantalupo, D. (1990). *Bilingual Education Talented Academy: Gifted and Talented, Project BETA, 1988–1989. Evaluation Section Report and Executive Summary. OREA Report.* ERIC ED 322 679.

83. Berney, T. D., & Hriskos, C. (1990). *Great Opportunities for Optional Resources to Improve the Talents of Gifted Bilingual High School Students: Project GO-FOR-IT, 1988–1989. OREA Report.* ERIC ED 321 539.

84. Berney, T. D., & Keyes, J. (1998). *Computer Writing Skills for Limited English Proficient Students Project (COMPUGRAPHIA. LEP), 1987–1988.* ERIC ED 311 719.

85. Berney, T. D., & Velasquez, C. (1990). *Project COMPUOCC. LEP Evaluation Section Report and Executive Summary. OREA Report.* ERIC ED 322 678.

86. Blackorby, J., & Kortering, L. J. (1991). A third of our youth? A look at the problem of high school dropout among students with mild handicaps. *Journal of Special Education, 25* (1), 102–113.

87. Bruck, M. (1985). The adult functioning of children with specific learning disabilities: A follow-up study. In I. Siegel (Ed.), *Advances in Applied Developmental Psychology.* Norwood, NJ: Ablex.

88. Foster, C. G. (1986). Special education program for Native American exceptional students and regular program staff. *Rural Special Education Quarterly, 8* (3), 40–43.

89. Harnisch, D. L., Lichtenstein, S. J., & Langford, J. B. (1989). *Digest on Youth in Transition: Volume 1.* ERIC ED 279 118.

90. Lichtenstein, S. J. (1987). *A Study of Selected Post-School Employment Patterns of Handicapped and Nonhandicapped Graduates and Dropouts.* Unpublished doctoral dissertation, Urbana-Champaign.

91. Miller, R. C., Berney, T. D., Mulkey, L., & Saggese, R. (1988). *Chapter 1/P.S.E.N. Remedial Reading and Mathematics Program, 1986–1987. Final Evaluation Report and Evaluation Summary. OREA Evaluation Report.* ERIC ED 302 049.

92. O'Connor, S. C., & Spreen, O. (1988). The relationship between parents' socioeconomic status and education level, and adult occupational and educational achievement of children with learning disabilities. *Journal of Learning Disabilities, 21* (3), 148–153.

93. Owings, J., & Stocking, C. (1986). *High School and Beyond, a National Longitudinal Study for the 1980's. Characteristics of High School Students Who Identify Themselves as Handicapped.* ERIC ED 260 546.

94. Palmateer, R. (1988). *Educare: Evaluation of a Transition Program for Culturally Disadvantaged and Educationally Handicapped Youth. Executive Summary.* ERIC ED 305 791.

95. Weissman, C. S., Archer, P., Liebert, D. E., Shaw, E., & Schilley, D. (1984). *The Impact of Early Intervention and Other Factors on Mainstreaming. Final Report, 3/1/83–4/30/84.* ERIC ED 245 033.

96. Welsh, W., & Schroedel, J. (1982). *Predictors of Success for Deaf Graduates of the Rochester Institute of Technology* (Paper Series #46). Rochester, NY: Department of Planning and Evaluation Systems, National Technical Institute for the Deaf.

References 97–107 deal with gender differences in academic interests and activities.

97. Alspach, P. A. (1988). *Inequities in the Computer Classroom: An Analysis of Two Computer Courses.* ERIC ED 301 180.

98. Chen, M. (1986). Gender and computers: The beneficial effects of experience on attitudes. *Journal of Educational Computing Research, 2* (3), 265–282.

99. Goertz, M. (1989). *Course Taking Patterns in the 1980's.* Princeton, NJ: Educational Testing Service.

100. Klinzing, D. G. (1985). *A Study of the Behavior of Children in a Preschool Equipped with Computers.* ERIC ED 255 320.

101. Lee, V. E., & Ware, N. C. (1986). *When and Why Girls "Leak" Out of High School Mathematics: A Closer Look.* Paper presented at the annual meeting of the American Educational Research Association, San Francisco.

102. Linn, M. C. (1983). *Fostering Equitable Consequences from Computer Learning Environments.* ERIC ED 242 626.

103. Lockheed, M., & Frakt, S. (1984). Sex equity: Increasing girls use of computers. *The Computing Teacher, 11* (8), 16–18.

104. Parsons, J. E. (1984). Sex differences in mathematics participation. In M. W. Steinkamp & M. L. Meehr (Eds.), *Women in Science: Advances in Motivation and Achievement* (Vol. 2). Greenwich, CT: JAI Press.

105. Rampy, L. (1984). *We Teach Children: Computer Literacy as a Feminist Issue.* ERIC ED 240 028.

106. Silvern, S. B., Countermine, T. M., & Williamson, P. A. C. (1982). *Young Children Interacting with a Computer.* Paper presented at the annual meeting of the American Educational Research Association, New York.

107. Stage, E. K., & Kreinberg, N. (1982). *Equal Access to Computers*. Paper presented at the semiannual meeting of the American Educational Research Association Special Interest Group: Research on Women in Education, Philadelphia.

References 108–122 are concerned with gender differences in vocational training and career aspirations.

108. American College Testing Program. (1989). *State and National Trend Data for Students Who Take the ACT Assessment*. Iowa City: Author.

109. Dao, M. (1987). *From Vietnamese to Vietnamese American*. Unpublished manuscript. San Jose State University, Department of Special Education, San Jose, CA.

110. Falkowski, C. K., & Falk, W. W. (1983). Homemaking as an occupational plan: Evidence from a national longitudinal study. *Journal of Vocational Behavior, 22* (2), 227–242.

111. Farmer, H. S., & Sidney J. S. (1985). Sex equity in career and vocational education. In S. Klein (Ed.), *Handbook for Achieving Sex Equity Through Education*. Baltimore: John Hopkins University Press.

112. Grossman, H. (1984). *Educating Hispanic Students: Cultural Implications for Instruction, Classroom Management, Counseling and Assessment*. Springfield, IL: Thomas.

113. Gupta, N. (1982). *The Influence of Sex Roles on the Life Plans of Low-SES Adolescents*. ERIC ED 235 434.

114. Hannah, J. S., & Kahn, S. E. (1989). The relationship of socioeconomic status and gender to occupational choices of grade 12 students. *Journal of Vocational Behavior, 34* (2), 161–178.

115. Holmes, B. L., & Esses, L. M. (1988). Factors influencing Canadian high school girls' career motivation. *Psychology of Women Quarterly, 12* (3), 313–328.

116. Jensen, E. L., & Hovey, S. Y. (1982). Bridging the gap from high school to college for talented females. *Peabody Journal of Education, 59* (3), 153–159.

117. Kelly, K. R., & Cobb, S. J. (1991). A profile of the career development characteristics of young gifted adolescents: Examining gender and multicultural differences. *Roeper Review, 13* (4), 202–206.

118. Odell, K. S. (1989). Gender differences in the educational and occupational expectations of rural Ohio youth. *Research in Rural Education, 5* (3), 37–41.

119. Pido, A. J. A. (1978). *A Cross-Cultural Change of Gender Roles: The Case of Pilipino Women Immigrants in Midwest City, U.S. A*. ERIC ED 159 244.

120. Smith, E. J. (1982). The Black female adolescent: A review of the educational, career, and psychological literature. *Psychology of Women Quarterly, 6*, 261–288.

121. Vasquez, M. J. T. (1982). Confronting barriers to the participation of Mexican American women in higher education. *Hispanic Journal of Behavioral Sciences, 4* (2), 147–165.

122. Wells, J. (1983). *Statement of the National Coalition for Women and Girls in Education*. Washington, DC: National Coalition for Women and Girls in Education.

References 123–128 deal with the narrowing of the gender gap in academic ability and achievement.

123. Becker, C., & Forsyth, R. (1990). *Gender Differences in Grades 3 through 12: A Longitudinal Analysis*. Paper presented at the annual meeting of the American Educational Research Association, Boston.

124. Coladarci, T., & Lancaster, L. N. (1989). *Gender and Mathematics Achievement: Data from High School and Beyond*. ERIC ED 308 207.

125. Feingold, A. (1988). Cognitive gender differences are disappearing. *American Psychologist, 43*, 95–103.

126. Halpern, D. F. (1989). The disappearance of cognitive gender differences: What you see depends on where you look. *American Psychologist, 44*, 455–464.

127. Hyde, J. S., & Linn, M. C. (1988). Gender differences in verbal abilities: A meta-analysis. *Psychological Bulletin, 104* (1), 53–69.

128. Mullin, I., & Jenkins, L. (1988). *The Science Report Card: Elements of Risk and Recovery*. Princeton, NJ: Educational Testing Service.

References 129–146 discuss gender differences in verbal and mathematics achievement.

129. Allred, R. A. (1990). Gender differences in spelling achievement in grades 1 through 6. *Journal of Educational Research, 83* (4), 187–193.

130. Armstrong, J. M. (1981). Achievement and participation of women in mathematics. *Journal for Research in Mathematics Education, 12*, 356–372.

131. Benbow, C. P., & Stanley, J. C. (1982). Consequences in high school and college of sex differences in mathematical reasoning ability: A longitudinal perspective. *American Educational Research Journal, 19* (4), 598–622.

132. Benbow, C. P., & Stanley, J. C. (1983). Sex differences in mathematical reasoning ability: More facts. *Science, 222,* 1029–1031.

133. Brandon P. R., Newton, B. J., & Hammond, O. W. (1987). Children's mathematics achievement in Hawaii: Sex differences favor girls. *American Educational Research Journal, 24* (3), 437–461.

134. Conner, J. M., & Serbin, L. A. (1980). *Mathematics, Visual-Spatial Ability, and Sex Roles (Final Report).* Washington, DC: National Institute of Education.

135. Eastman, S. T., & Kendrl, K. (1987). Computer and gender: Differential effects of electronic search on students' achievement and attitudes. *Journal of Research and Development in Education, 20* (3), 41–48.

136. Fennema, E., & Carpenter, T. (1981). Sex-related differences in mathematics: Results from the national assessment. *Mathematics Teacher, 74* (7), 554–559.

137. Fox, L., Brody, L. A., & Tobin, D. (Eds.). (1980). *Women and the Mathematical Mystique.* Baltimore: Johns Hopkins University Press.

138. Fox, L., & Cohn, S. (1980). Sex differences in the development of precocious mathematical talent. In L. Fox, L. A. Brody, & D. Tobin (Eds.), *Women and the Mathematical Mystique.* Baltimore: Johns Hopkins University Press.

139. Harris, C. S. (1986). *A Summary of the Language Arts Achievement of Students in a Phase-Elective Mini-Course System as Compared to the Language Arts Achievement of Students in a Traditional Program (1986).* ERIC ED 280 064.

140. Hyde, J. S. (1981) How large are cognitive gender differences? A meta-analysis using w and d. *American Psychologist, 36,* 892– 901.

141. Marshall, S. P. (1984). Sex differences in students' mathematics achievement: Solving computations and story problems. *Journal of Educational Psychology, 76* (2), 194–204.

142. Midgley, C. (1983). Expectations, values, and academic behaviors. In J. T. Spence (Ed.), *Achievement and Achievement Motivation.* San Francisco: W. H. Freeman.

143. Scott-Jones, D., & Clark, M. L. (1986). The school experience of Black girls: The interaction of gender, race, and socioeconomic status. *Phi Delta Kappan, 67* (7), 520–526.

144. Sharp, L. M. (1989). *The SAT-M Gap: Looking at Micro Level Data.* ERIC ED 307 292.

145. Sherman, J. (1981). Girls' and boys' enrollment in theoretical math courses: A longitudinal study. *Psychology of Women Quarterly, 5,* 681–689.

146. Simmons,W. (1990). *Black Male Achievement: Strategies for Ensuring Success in School.* Paper presented at the Annual meeting of the National Black Child Development Institute. Washington, DC.

References 147–155 relate to gender differences on visual spatial tasks.

147. Burnett, S. A., & Lane, D. M. (1980). Effects of academic instruction on spatial visualization. *Intelligence, 4,* 233–242.

148. Fennema, E. H., & Carpenter, T. P. (1981). Sex-related differences in mathematics: Results from national assessment. *Mathematics Teacher, 74,* 554–559.

149. Harris, L. J. (1981). Sex-related variations in spatial skill. In L. S. Liben, A. H. Patterson, & N. Newcombe (Eds.), *Spatial Representation and Behavior Across the Life Span.* New York: Academic Press.

150. Linn, M. C., & Petersen, A. C. (1985). Emergence and characterization of sex differences in spatial ability: A meta-analysis. *Child Development, 56,* 1479–1498.

151. Linn, M. C., & Petersen, A. C. (1986). Gender differences in spatial ability. In J. S. Hyde & M. C. Linn (Eds.), *The Psychology of Gender: Advances through Meta-Analysis.* Baltimore: John Hopkins University Press.

152. McGee, M. G. (1979). Human spatial abilities: Psychometric studies and environmental, genetic, hormonal, and neurological influences. *Psychological Bulletin, 86,* 889–918.

153. Nash, S. C. (1979). Sex-role as a mediator of intellectual functioning. In M. A. Witting & A. C. Petersen (Eds.), *Sex-Related Differences in Cognitive Functioning: Developmental Issues.* New York: Academic Press.

154. Petersen, A. G. (1979). Hormones and cognitive functioning in normal development. In M. A. Witting & A. C. Petersen (Eds.), *Sex-Related Differences in Cognitive Functioning: Developmental Issues.* New York: Academic Press.

155. Richmond, P. G. (1980). A limited sex difference in spatial test scores with a preadolescent sample. *Child Development, 51,* 601–602.

References 156–163 focus on gender differences in science achievement.

156. Becker, B. J. (1989). Gender and science achievement: A reanalysis of studies from two meta-analyses. *Journal of Research in Science Teaching, 26* (2), 141–169.

157. Hueftle, S. J., Rakow,S. J., & Welch, W. W. (1983). *Images of Science*. Minneapolis: University of Minnesota Press.

158. Hyde, J. S., & Linn, M. C. (1986). *The Psychology of Gender: Advances through Meta-Analysis*. Baltimore: John Hopkins University Press.

159. Maehr, M. L., & Steinkamp, M. (1983). *A Synthesis of Findings on Sex Differences in Science Education Research*. ERIC ED 229 226.

160. Malone, M. R., & Fleming, M. L. (1983). The relationship of student characteristics and student performance in science as viewed by meta-analysis research. *Journal of Research in Science Teaching, 20,* 481–495.

161. Shaw, E. L., Jr., & Doan, R. L. (1990). An investigation of the differences in attitude and achievement between male and female second and fifth grade science students. *Journal of Elementary Science Education, 2* (1), 10–15.

162. Steinkamp, M. W., & Maehr, M. L. (1983). Affect, ability, and science achievement: A quantitative synthesis of correlational research. *Review of Educational Research, 53,* 369–396.

163. Steinkamp, M. W., & Maehr, M. L. (1984). Gender differences in motivational orientations toward achievement in school science: A quantitative synthesis. *American Educational Research Journal, 21* (1), 39–59.

References 164–168 indicate that females are less likely to get into trouble for behavioral problems, be disciplined by their teachers, or be suspended from school.

164. Center, D. B., & Wascom, A. M. (1987). Teacher perceptions of social behavior in behaviorally disordered and socially normal children and youth. *Behavior Disorders,12* (3), 200–206.

165. Duke, D. L. (1978). Why don't girls misbehave more than boys in school? *Journal of Youth and Adolescence, 7* (2), 141–157.

166. Epstein, M. H., Cullinan, D., & Bursuck, W. D. (1985). Prevalence of behavior problems among learning disabled and nonhandicapped students. *Mental Retardation and Learning Disability Bulletin, 213,* 30–39.

167. Ludwig, G., & Cullinan, D. (1984). Behavior problems of gifted and nongifted elementary school girls and boys. *Gifted Child Quarterly, 28* (1), 37–39.

168. National Black Child Development Institute. (1990). *The Status of African American Children: Twentieth Anniversary Report*. Washington, DC: Author.

References 169–178 describe gender differences in emotional reactions and problems.

169. Baron, P., & Perron, L. M. (1986). Sex differences in the Beck Depression Inventory scores of adolescents. *Journal of Youth and Adolescents, 15* (2), 165–171.

170. Brody, L. R. (1984). Sex and age variation in the quality and intensity of children's emotional attributions to hypothetical situations. *Sex Roles, 11* (1), 51–59.

171. Grossman, H., & Grossman, S. (1994). *Gender Issues in Education*. Boston: Allyn and Bacon.

172. Hadfield, O. D., & Maddux, C. D. (1988). Cognitive style and mathematics anxiety among high school students. *Psychology in the Schools, 25,* 75–83.

173. Harlow, L. L., Newcomb, M. D., & Bentler, P. M. (1986). Depression, self-derogation, substance use and suicide ideation: Lack of purpose in life as mediational factor. *Journal of Clinical Psychology, 42,* 353–358.

174. Haynes, N. M., Comer, J. P., & Hamilton-Lee, M. (1988). Gender and achievement status differences on learning factors among black high school students. *Journal of Educational Research, 81* (4), 233–237.

175. Marsh, H. W. (1987). *The Content Specificity of Math and English Anxieties: The High School and Beyond Study*. ERIC ED 300 402.

176. Reynolds, W. (1984). Depression in children and adolescents. *School Psychology Review, 13,* 171–182.

177. Worchel, F., Nolan, B., & Wilson, V. (1987). New perspectives on child and adolescent depression. *Journal of School Psychology, 25* (4), 411–414.

178. Wynstra, S., & Cummings, C. (1990). *Science Anxiety: Relation with Gender, Year in Chemistry Class, Achievement, and Test Anxiety*. ERIC ED 331 837.

References 179–187 discuss gender differences in self-confidence.

179. Armstrong, J. M., & Kahl, S. (1980). *A National Assessment of Performance and Participation of Women in Mathematics (Final Report).* Washington, DC: National Institute of Education.

180. Brush, L. (1980). *Encouraging Girls in Mathematics: The Problem and the Solution.* Boston: Abt.

181. Eccles (Parsons), J., Adler, T. F., Futterman, R., Goff, S. B., Kaczala. C. M., Meece, J., & Midgley, C. (1983). Expectations, values, and academic behaviors. In J. T. Spence (Ed.), *Perspective on Achievement and Achievement Motivation.* San Francisco: W. H. Freeman.

182. Fox, L. H., Brody, L., & Tobin, D. (Eds.). (1980). *Women and the Mathematical Mystique.* Baltimore: Johns Hopkins University Press.

183. Hyde, J., & Fennema, E. (1990). *Gender Differences in Mathematics Performance and Affect: Results of Two Meta-Analyses.* Paper presented at the annual meeting of the American Educational Research Association, Boston.

184. Levine, B. (1990). *Arithmetic Development: Where Are the Gender Differences?* Paper presented at the annual meeting of the American Educational Research Association, Boston.

185. Reyes, L. H. (1984). Affective variables and mathematics education. *Elementary School Journal, 84* (5), 558–581.

186. Sherman, J. (1980). Mathematics, spatial visualization, and related factors: Changes in girls and boys, grades 8–11. *Journal of Educational Psychology, 72,* 476–482.

187. Stevenson, H. W., & Newman, R. S. (1986). Long-term prediction of achievement and attitudes in mathematics and reading. *Child Development, 57,* 646–659.

References 188–191 focus on gender differences in risk taking and reaction to failure.

188. Ginsburg, H. J., & Miller, S. M. (1982). Sex differences in children's risk-taking behavior. *Child Development, 53* (2), 426–428.

189. Licht, B. G., Linden, T. A., Brown, D. A., & Sexton, M. (1984). *Sex Differences in Achievement Orientation: An "A" Student Phenomenon.* ERIC ED 252 783.

190. Miller, A. (1986). Performance impairment after failure: Mechanisms and sex differences. *Journal of Educational Psychology, 78* (6), 486–491.

191. Reyes, L. H. (1984). Affective variables and mathematics education. *Elementary School Journal, 84* (5), 558–581.

References 192–195 discuss gender differences in seeking teacher feedback, support, and help.

192. Brutsaert, H. (1990). Changing sources of self-esteem among girls and boys in secondary school. *Urban Education, 24* (40), 432–439.

193. Nelson-LeGall, S., & Glor-Scheib, S. (1983). *Help-Seeking in Elementary Classrooms: An Observational Study.* ERIC ED 230 286.

194. Stewart, M. J., & Corbin, C. B. (1988). Feedback dependence among low confidence preadolescent boys and girls. *Research Quarterly for Exercise and Sport, 59* (2), 160–164.

195. Sullivan, H. J. (1986). Factors that influence continuing motivation. *Journal of Educational Research,* 80(2), 86–92.

References 196–197 deal with ethnic differences in female roles.

196. Dao, M. (1987). *From Vietnamese to Vietnamese American.* Unpublished manuscript. San Jose State University, San Jose, CA.

197. Simpson, G. (1984). The daughters of Charlotte Ray: The career development process during the exploratory and establishment stages of Black women attorneys. *Sex Roles, 11* (1/2), 113–139.

References 198–200 focus on gender differences in the results of special education services.

198. Dannenbring, G., & Lanning-Ventura, S. (1985). *Academic Growth Made By Learning Disabled Students.* ERIC ED 280 202.

199. Harnisch, D. L., & Fisher, A. T. (1989). *Digest on Youth in Transition.* ERIC ED 318 163.

200. Porter, M. E. (1988). *How Vocational Teachers Rate Classroom Performance of Students with Mild Handicaps Using Curriculum-Based Vocational Assessment Procedures.* ERIC ED 308 639.

2

ETHNIC AND
SOCIOECONOMIC-CLASS DISPARITIES:
INTRINSIC CAUSES

Claiming that students who suffer the inequities of the U.S. educational system are responsible for their problems permits the status quo to continue.

A number of educators claim that many poor and non-European American students arrive at their school building's doorstep already predisposed to do poorly in the regular education system and to require special education services. They believe that these students are more likely to suffer biomedical problems, to inherit less intellectual potential than their peers, and to come from culturally deprived or disadvantaged backgrounds. They attribute the high percentage of failure among these students, their overrepresentation in special education programs for students with disabilities, and their underrepresentation in programs for gifted and talented students to these factors. Many other educators disagree with these explanations and consider them to be examples of blaming the victims for problems inflicted on them by others. This chapter examines whether certain non-European American and poor students come to school predisposed to fail and to require special education services.

BIOMEDICAL PROBLEMS

The living conditions of many poor African American, European American, Hispanic American, and Native American students place them at greater risk for biomedical problems. Poor health care and nutrition can cause neurological problems, which in turn can cause students to do poorly in school and require special education. Most poor parents do not abuse drugs during pregnancy. However, some people believe that in comparison to middle-class European American children, children of these poor parents are more likely to suffer the results of exposure to harmful substances because their mothers abuse drugs and alcohol while they are pregnant. (Whether this is actually true or not is discussed below.) If current trends continue, poor African American, European American, Hispanic American, and Native American students may also suffer the unfortunate effects of being born HIV positive in greater relative numbers than their European American middle-class peers.

Health Care and Nutrition

As a group, poor families, especially the millions of families whose incomes fall below the poverty line, do not have adequate access to prenatal and postnatal health care (7, 10). In fact, the percentage of poor mothers who receive prenatal care has actually decreased in recent years (1). As a result, poor children are more likely to suffer the consequences of complications of pregnancy and delivery, prematurity, low birth weight, and the learning, emotional, and behavior problems these conditions can cause (2, 3, 6, 7, 13, 14–16). From 6 to 8 percent of children who are born with a moderately low birth weight will have developmental problems. Among those born with severe low birth weight, the percentage is twice as large (5, 8). As the mortality rate from these complications has declined and more infants who are born with these risky conditions survive, the number of poor children who suffer from the kinds of disabilities that require special education has increased.

Poor parents are also less able to provide their children with the same nutrition and medical care that their more advantaged peers receive. This can also cause their children to develop learning and behavior problems (11, 12). Thus, because of inadequate medical care and nutrition, poor children may experience a higher incidence of problems such as developmental and learning disabilities, attention deficit disorders, and behavior disorders (4, 9). Also, because African American and Hispanic American children are more likely than European Americans to be born poor, they are at greater risk to experience these problems.

Fortunately, the deleterious effects of low birth weight and other perinatal problems can be counteracted in many cases by providing youngsters with proper care. In addition, the harmful effects of malnutrition appear to occur primarily when severe malnutrition is present, which is typically not the case with most U.S. students from poor or poverty backgrounds. Also, these effects may be reversible.

Thus, for the present, we do not know the exact effects of limited access to medical care and poor nutrition on the incidence of disabilities that require special education. Nor can we estimate the portion of the misrepresentation in special education programs such situations cause. When considered as a whole, it seems reasonable to expect that the disproportionately small share of the medical and nutritional benefits received by poor families contributes to both the educational problems these students experience in regular education and their misrepresentation in some special education categories. However, whether these problems are a very significant factor is a moot point that can only be answered by more research.

Substance Abuse

Some individuals believe that parental substance abuse contributes to the lack of academic success of African American, Native American, and poor students in school and their overenrollment in special education. They claim that African

American, Native American, and poor parents abuse substances such as alcohol, marijuana, cocaine, and so on during pregnancy more frequently than middle-class European American parents. And as a result, their children are born with more birth defects, perform less adequately in school, and are more likely to require special education.

Substance abuse does cause both severe and subtle birth defects and a variety of learning and behavioral problems (17–19, 22, 26–28, 30, 32–35, 38, 39, 41, 43–46, 52, 53). Even supposedly less severe forms of substance abuse such as smoking cigarettes during pregnancy can cause children to develop learning, social adjustment, and behavior problems (24, 30). Fortunately, only some substance-exposed children actually develop the difficulties these dangerous substances may cause (49, 53). The reasons for this are largely unknown. However, one has been identified: Good prenatal care reduces the likelihood that substance-exposed children will actually suffer the potential problems for which they are at risk (32, 41).

Substance-exposed children do not suffer all of the possible problems that exposure can cause (27, 32, 41, 49). The problems experienced by children of substance-abusing parents can vary. Approximately 2 to 17 percent will suffer from severe congenital defects, developmental disabilities, cerebral palsy, seizure disorders, and so on (23, 49). Many others will develop normally at first, then demonstrate learning and behavioral problems as they approach school age.

POTENTIAL PROBLEMS OF SUBSTANCE-EXPOSED CHILDREN

Congenital Defects
- Central nervous system damage
- Retarded physical growth
- Abnormal facial and cranial features
- Severe and mild developmental disabilities
- Seizure disorders

Learning and Language Disabilities
- Expressive language difficulties
- Communicative difficulties and language delays
- Impaired hand-eye coordination and other forms of motor performance
- Perceptual, auditory-processing, and word-retrieval difficulties
- Impaired conceptualizing abilities
- Difficulty organizing information
- Perseveration and low tolerance for change
- Difficulty adjusting to simultaneous stimulations
- Distractibility, hyperactivity, poor impulse control, low frustration tolerance
- Short attention span and decreased ability to focus attention and concentrate

Emotional and Behavioral Problems
- Irritability and hypersensitivity
- Avoidance of eye contact
- Difficulty in forming attachments with adults and establishing and maintaining relationships with peers
- Behavioral extremes and emotional instability
- Constantly testing limits set by adults
- Difficulty understanding social cues

Substance-exposed students often function adequately under adult guidance and in structured learning and play situations. They have great difficulty, however, adjusting to situations that require them to provide their own structure, initiative, or organization. They do much better in one-to-one situations or when they have to cope with only one individual, task, or toy. When these students have to deal with group situations or multiple activities, materials, tasks, or people, they quickly become overstimulated, overwhelmed, and disorganized.

Many, but not all, substance-exposed children suffer additional insults and injuries (21, 23, 29, 31, 32, 34, 42, 43). Their parents tend to have a host of additional medical and social problems. A mother who is unable to stop abusing drugs for her children's sake during her pregnancy is often unable to care for them after they have been born. (The fact that a mother abuses drugs during pregnancy is often an indication that her children will receive inadequate care.) Those who are poor tend to abandon their children in the hospital, which often leads to eventual foster care placement. "Growing numbers of crack babies simply are being abandoned in hospitals by their crack-smoking mothers. As for those babies who are discharged, the vast majority go from the hospital nursery to chaotic home environments characterized by deep poverty and little physical or emotional nurturing. With one strike already against them, these babies are at high risk for the second strike—neglect and abuse by crack-using adults" (43, p. 19).

Presently, we are unable to determine when and to what extent substance-exposed children's problems are caused by physiological factors or the environmental disadvantages often associated with substance-abusing parents. For now, the prudent position is that these students' learning and behavioral problems can best be understood as resulting from the interaction of both biological and environmental factors.

The number of mothers who abuse drugs while they are pregnant and the number of drug-exposed infants is unknown. Surveys of the percentage of parents who expose their unborn infants to harmful substances have yielded results that range from from 0.4 to 27 percent of the parents tested or questioned, depending on the hospital and the neighborhood surveyed (21, 25, 37, 48, 51). Their number is growing at an alarming rate (36). Estimates of the number of infants that may be affected yearly by crack alone range from 48,000 to 375,000 (20, 21, 43, 47, 51).

There appears to be evidence that poor, African American, Native American, and inner-city mothers in general abuse these substances while they are pregnant more frequently than other mothers (40, 43, 49, 50). However, some researchers believe that the difference between their rates of drug abuse and those of European American middle-class mothers is overstated because European American middle-class mothers are better able to hide their substance abusing-behavior from the authorities (24, 43). "A minority woman who uses drugs or alcohol during pregnancy is almost ten times more likely to be reported to child-abuse authorities than is a white woman. White middle-class mothers—along with other white middle-class cocaine users—find it easier to hide their substance abuse than do poor, minority women" (43, p. 21).

Even if the difference is overstated, there is evidence that substance-abusing poor parents in general, and non-European poor parents in particular, are less able to obtain the good prenatal care that reduces the likelihood that substance-exposed children will actually suffer the potential problems for which they are at risk. Thus, it may be that the children of these groups of people are at even greater risk than European American middle-class children.

Although African American, Native American, and poor students are currently more likely to suffer from such problems than European American middle-class students, it is unclear what proportion of their school problems and overenrollment in special education is caused by their parents' substance abuse during pregnancy. It may well turn out to be too small to account for much of the disparity between the educational experiences of different ethnic groups and socioeconomic classes.

SUBSTANCE-EXPOSED CHILDREN

> The media have painted a dire picture of infants who were exposed to alcohol and other drugs in utero. . . . Children who were prenatally exposed to substances are unique, but as a whole they are more like than different from other children. . . . There is a danger in this label in that it can engender a self-fulfilling prophecy: Children will become what their parents and teachers expect them to become. Given the current view of drug exposure this would be an unfair prophecy. (49, pp. 1, 24)

Acquired Immune Deficiency Syndrome (AIDS)

The dramatic increase in the number of AIDS-exposed infants who are born HIV positive is adding to the number of children who demonstrate problems similar to those who are exposed to drugs (54–56). As better methods of prolonging their lives are developed, more and more HIV-positive students will require special education services.

Non-European American poor children are disproportionately affected by AIDS (57–58). In one national study, African Americans and Hispanic Americans represented 53 percent and 23 percent, respectively, of the reported cases (58). Although the number of students affected by AIDS is still small, if their numbers continue to grow and if non-European American poor children continue to be disproportionately affected, there may be a rise in their disproportionate representation in special education programs.

GENETIC DIFFERENCES/INFERIORITY

In the not too distant past, it was both acceptable and commonplace to justify colonialism, slavery, gross economic inequality, the inferior status of women, racial segregation, immigration restriction, sterilization of the poor, unequal educational opportunities, and a host of other inequities on the basis of imagined genetic differences (59, 61, 69, 72). Abraham Lincoln was not immune to the point of view prevalent during his time. Despite his Emancipation Proclamation, he maintained, "There is a physical difference between the white and black races which I believe will forever forbid the two races living together on terms of social and political equality. And inasmuch as they cannot so live, while they do remain together there must be the position of superior and inferior, and I as much as any other man am in favor of having the superior position assigned to the white race" (63, p. 35).

Most of these conditions are no longer acceptable in our society. However, some individuals still believe that certain groups of students—most notably African American, Hispanic American, and poor students—are less successful in school, overrepresented in special education programs for the mildly developmentally disabled, and underrepresented in classes for the gifted and talented because they inherit different amounts or kinds of intelligence (62, 64–76, 70–71). The following quotes by Shockley and Jensen are representative of this position:

> Nature has color-coded groups of individuals so that statistically reliable predictions of their adaptability to intellectually rewarding and effective lives can easily be made and profitably be used by the pragmatic man-in-the-street. (70, p. 375)

> The most parsimonious hypothesis—one that would comprehend virtually all the established facts about the white-black IQ difference without the need to postulate any environmental factors besides those that are known to affect IQ and on which blacks in general are less advantaged—is that something between one-half and three-fourths of the average IQ difference is attributable to genetic factors, and the remainder to environmental factors and their interaction with genetic differences. (67, p. 227)

Currently, there are two major theories of how genetic differences operate to create presumed ethnic and socioeconomic-class intellectual differences. These theories and the evidence regarding them are presented next.

Meritocracy Theory

The meritocracy theory offers an explanation for why poor students, especially those who come from poverty backgrounds, tend to have lower IQ scores than middle- and upper-class students. According to the theory, U.S. society is a meritocracy in which all people have an equal opportunity to succeed. Those who do not succeed lack either the ability or the motivation to do so. Thus, it is to be expected that those who remain in the working class, especially those who are below the poverty level and those who do poorly in school, lack either the motivation or the intelligence to do better. In other words, proponents of this theory offer a simple explanation for poor students' lack of achievement in school, their overrepresentation in programs for the mildly developmentally disabled, and their underrepresentation in programs for the gifted and talented. If their parents were smarter, they would learn more and earn more. Herrenstein has stated, "1. If differences in mental abilities are inherited, and 2. if success requires these abilities, and 3. if earnings and prestige depend on success, 4. then social standing (which reflects earnings and prestige) will be based to some extent on inherited differences among people" (64, p. 58–59).

Various authors (60, 65, 68) have suggested that there are many millions of people in the working class, especially those below the poverty level, with what they call *cultural familial retardation.* They believe that these individuals suffer from two related problems. They inherit limited intellectual potential from their parents, and they are brought up by their parents in

> families which are unable—due to their own lack of intellectual ability—to provide their children with the support that they need to acquire and maintain a reasonable standard of living. . . . Having low mental ability, exacerbated by a lack of parental encouragement, support, and proper modeling, the cultural familial retarded settle permanently into the lowest of the lower socioeconomic strata of society, become life-long clients of welfare programs, drift from job to job, are easily exploited, and reproduce an inordinately large posterity that will perpetuate this grim circumstance. (68, pp. 3–4, 8)

Levels of Cognitive Ability

For many years, educators and others who believed that different ethnic groups and socioeconomic classes inherited dissimilar intellectual potentials claimed the groups inherited varying *amounts* of intelligence. Since 1969, however, many of them have accepted a theory of intelligence first proposed by Jensen, which states that poor and African American students tend to inherit different *types or levels* of intelligence rather than different amounts of intellectual ability. According to Jensen, there are two types of intelligence, which he calls Level I and Level II. "Level I ability consists of rote learning and primary memory; it is the capacity to register and retrieve information with fidelity and is characterized essentially by a relative lack of transformation, conceptual coding, or other mental manipulation intervening between information input and output. Level II ability, in contrast, is characterized by mental manipulation of inputs, conceptualization, reasoning, and problem solving: it is essentially the general intelligence (g) factor common to most complex tests of intelligence" (66, p. 99).

Although all individuals and groups supposedly inherit the ability to use Level I (rote learning and associative learning) to solve problems more or less to the same degree, they supposedly inherit different capacities to use Level II (conceptual ability). Jensen and others have claimed that African Americans and poor students do not score as high as European American and middle- and upper-socioeconomic-class students on intelligence tests because they tend to be endowed with a diminished capacity for Level II intellectual functioning. "The hypothesis in its most simple and extreme form states that low- and middle socioeconomic-status groups differ in Level II but not Level I ability" (66, p. 104).

Implications

Individuals who believe that genetics play a role in causing socioeconomic-class and ethnic differences in school outcomes do not agree about how educators should handle these differences. Educators who believe the influence of genetic differences can be mitigated typically recommend that schools provide students with experiences and training that will counteract the effects of genetic differences.

Those who think the effects of genetics are unmodifiable suggest that teachers should accommodate their goals for students, their instructional approaches, and their classroom management techniques to the intellectual differences among their students. These individuals have also provided suggestions for adapting instructional approaches to the different kinds of intellectual operations characteristic of Level I and Level II intellectual functioning. They believe that ethnic groups and socioeconomic classes require different educational approaches, and so are not troubled by the fact that European American middle- and upper-class students are more likely to be assigned to courses of study (tracks) for high-potential students in which teachers stress independent study and higher level cognitive skills, while Hispanic American, African American, and poor students are overrepresented in tracks for low-potential students in which teachers stress instructional techniques that involve concrete repetitive drill and practice. These individuals also find it understandable that Hispanic American, African American, and poor students are overrepresented in special education programs for students of limited intellectual potential and underrepresented in programs for gifted and talented students.

Criticisms

The claim that different ethnic groups and socioeconomic classes inherit different kinds or amounts of intelligence is based on four assumptions: (1) U.S. society is a meritocracy. (2) Individuals from different ethnic and socioeconomic class backgrounds inherit different amounts of intelligence or learning potential. (3) Ethnic group and socioeconomic classes differ in their abilities to use Level I or Level II types of intellectual operations when solving problems. (4) Level I and Level II differences are genetically determined. These assumptions and the arguments against them offered by their critics are discussed next.

1. *U.S. society is a meritocracy.* Many people have argued that the United States is not a meritocracy (73–76). They claim that schools do not provide a level playing field that enables all students to achieve their potential. Instead of being designed to provide all students with the knowledge and skills they need to succeed in life regardless of their ethnic and socioeconomic-class backgrounds, schools are biased against the groups that perform poorly. In fact, some individuals propose that myths about the democratizing influences of schools are propaganda used to legitimize the privileged positions of the middle- and upper-socioeconomic classes by convincing poor and non-European American students and parents that they are not capable of profiting from the education offered them. In this way, poor and non-European American students and their parents will blame their lack of success in school on themselves. They will believe that they merit their eventual inferior positions in society because they did not take advantage of the opportunities afforded them in school. (See Structured Reproduction in Chapter 3.)

The evidence presented throughout this book confirms that schools are not a level playing field. Schools that serve primarily middle- and upper-class European American students have many more resources than schools who serve primarily non-European and poor students. (See Chapter 3.) The United States is far from a perfect meritocracy. For example, even when certain groups of students do well in school, the amount of money they earn is not always commensurate with their educational attainment. It is true that European American males who have earned a high school diploma obtain higher-paying jobs than those who have not graduated high school. However, research indicates that non-European American students, especially African Americans and Hispanic Americans, who graduate from high school do not earn significantly more than those of their peers who do not complete high school. Given the same level of education, students' earnings depend more on how high up the socioeconomic ladder their parents are (75–76).

Moreover, despite the corrective effects that affirmative action has had, middle- and upper-class European American job seekers still receive preference over their non-European and poor competitors in certain sectors. (See Structured Reproduction in Chapter 3.) Thus, there is no justification for believing that poor students who do not do well in school and families that remain poor or below the poverty level are responsible for the state of affairs in which they find themselves.

2. *Individuals from different ethnic and socioeconomic class backgrounds inherit different amounts of intelligence or learning potential.* There are a number of reasons for questioning this assumption. Supporters of the genetic explanation base their conclusion that intelligence is inherited primarily on the results of research on twins. They claim these studies indicate the following:

- Intelligence test scores of identical twins are more similar than those of fraternal twins.
- Identical twins reared apart have very similar intelligence test scores despite being brought up in different environments.
- The IQ scores of adopted children resemble those of their natural parents to a greater degree than expected.

However, these studies have been criticized on a number of grounds (77–87). Researchers who are critical of the theory claim that the studies were flawed methodologically. They suggest that because identical twins are treated more similarly by their parents than fraternal twins, the greater similarity in their test scores could be caused by the similar treatment they receive. They point out that the twins in the adoption studies tended to be placed in homes of families with the same socioeconomic backgrounds as their natural parents, thereby introducing the possibility that environmental factors accounted for the similarity between their scores and those of their natural parents. They also note that African American children adopted by European American families score much higher on intelligence tests than one would expect if they had inherited a fixed amount of intelligence from their biological parents.

Another reason for doubting that some non-European American groups such as African Americans inherit less intelligence than European Americans is that environmental factors are the more likely explanation of the difference in scores between African American and European American students. For example, within each socioeconomic class, African American students who grow up in racially mixed neighborhoods score higher on intelligence tests because they are exposed to the contents of tests that reflect the experiences of European Americans (83). In addition, almost without exception, studies of African American children's performance on tests purported to measure their intellectual functioning indicate that poor students do not perform as well as their middle-class peers and that socioeconomic class is a more powerful predictor of how children will perform than ethnic background (78, 88–92).

3. *Ethnic group and socioeconomic classes differ in their abilities to use Level I or Level II types of intellectual operations when solving problems.* Research on Jensen's two-level theory has indicated that poor, African American, and Hispanic American students do score lower than middle-class and European American students on tests that are purported to measure Level II abilities (78, 87, 93, 99–103, 105, 107). However, a number of researchers have criticized the results of these studies for the following reasons (94–98, 104, 106, 108, 109):

- The differences obtained in these studies are not as strong or as consistent as those originally reported by Jensen. Some studies have found relationships between Level II scores and ethnicity but not for socioeconomic status, for one ethnic group but not another, or for socioeconomic status but not for ethnicity. Contrary to Jensen's theory, most studies have found differences between ethnic groups and socioeconomic classes on tests that are purported to measure Level I abilities.

- The differences observed between the scores of European American middle-class students and African American, Hispanic American, and poor students on so-called intelligence tests are more likely to be due to test bias than to real differences in intellectual ability. (See Chapter 9.)

- There is evidence that the reason why there is greater difference between the scores of European American and middle-class students and the scores of African American, Hispanic American, and poor students on tests of Level II abilities than on Level I abilities is that the tests of Level II abilities are more biased against African American students. Finally, because training students on the use of specific strategies for solving Level II type problems has been shown to raise the low scores of poor, African American, and Native American students, it appears that the difference in scores on these tests are due to exposure rather than heredity (95, 106, 108).

- Tests of intelligence, including those used to study students' Level I and Level II abilities, are poor predictors of scholastic achievement and therefore are invalid measures of intelligence. There is no reason to look for explanations for why groups of students have different Level I and Level II intellectual abilities because the tests used to measure these intellectual abilities do not measure intelligence nor predict how students will perform in school. (See Chapter 9.)

As will be seen in Chapter 9, the results of studies that appear to support the two-level theory are based on invalid assessment instruments that cannot be used to measure or evaluate students' intelligence. The content, language, and format of standardized tests that purport to measure intelligence are neither culture free nor culture fair. Assessors employ them in a biased manner. They are also poor predictors of non-European and poor students' academic achievement and learning potentials. Comparisons of the assumed intelligence of different groups based on the results of biased instruments and assessors are invalid, misleading, and harmful. They do not explain or justify ethnic or socioeconomic-class differences in students' achievement or their enrollment in special education programs.

4. *Level I and Level II differences are genetically determined.* Some educators grant the possibility that ethnic groups and socioeconomic class differences on intelligence tests reflect real differences in intellectual ability but disagree that their cause is genetic. They argue that there have been no studies to investigate the reasons why some students do less well on problems that involve conceptual learning (Level II) than on tasks requiring associate and rote learning (Level I). They also claim that since there is no evidence that these differences are inherited, there is no reason to attribute these differences to genetic factors rather than to such environmental factors as different exposure at home to the kinds of mental operations measured by the tests, inadequate preparation for the tasks on the tests in biased and prejudicial school systems, and so on.

Conclusions

There is no evidence that genetically determined differences in intellectual ability contribute significantly to ethnic and socioeconomic-class educational disparities or that ethnic groups and socioeconomic classes inherit different intellectual potentials. Differences that have been observed occur because current methods of evaluating intelligence are biased against the groups who perform least adequately on them and because our imperfect society has not yet achieved the assumptions underlying the meritocracy theory.

CULTURAL DEPRIVATION/ EDUCATIONAL DISADVANTAGE

In the 1960s, at the same time that the genetic explanation of the low rates of success among non-European American and poor students and their disproportionate enrollment in special education programs was rejected by increasing numbers of educators, the theory of cultural deprivation gained a great deal of acceptance (110–123). According to this theory, certain non-European American students—especially African Americans, Hispanic Americans, and the children of poor parents—are brought up in inferior cultural environments that deprive them of the skills, attitudes, and acceptable behaviors that are transmitted to students who grow up in the superior European American middle-class culture. As a result, they are ill prepared to succeed in school either academically or behaviorally. As Bloom described them, culturally deprived students have "experiences in homes which do not transmit the cultural patterns necessary for the type of learning characteristics of the schools and the larger society" (112, p. 4).

The term used to label such students has undergone a number of modifications since the 1960s. First, it was changed from *culturally deprived* to *culturally disadvantaged* to signify that these students were not cultureless (deprived of a culture) but brought up in a culture that placed them at a disadvantage. Then *culturally disadvantaged* was replaced by *educationally disadvantaged* to indicate that the whole of students' cultures were not being indicted, but merely the way they prepared students to function in school. Today, few educators would publicly proclaim that certain non-European American and poor students are brought up in inferior cultures, but numerous educators are on record as believing that some students are ill prepared to succeed in school because their culture places them at an educational disadvantage. In fact, the U.S. Department of Educations spends millions of dollars on educational programs for "educationally disadvantaged students."

Characteristics

According to the theory of cultural deprivation, disadvantaged and advantaged students differ in terms of their cognitive skills, linguistic ability, self-concepts, levels of educational aspiration, locus of control, and social behavior.

Cognitive Skills

Educationally disadvantaged students are assumed to have "special difficulty in developing concepts of an abstract nature and generalizing" (112, p. 71). They are also considered to be deficient in the "semi-autonomous essential processes demanded for adequate skill in the use of linguistic and mathematical symbols and for the analysis of causal relationships" (117, p. 236). In other words, their thinking processes are concrete and convergent/conforming rather than abstract and creative.

According to the theory, these cognitive deficits occur because educationally disadvantaged students' parents do not interact sufficiently with them; stimulate them intellectually through conversation, field trips, books, magazines, encyclopedias; correct their misperceptions; nor encourage their curiosity. As McCloskey stated,

> Intellectual stimulation between adult and child is relatively slight. Adults seldom talk with children. Parents who work at physical tasks for long hours, often during evening hours, are too tired or inaccessible for conversation with children. . . .
>
> Disadvantaged children have not developed sufficient cognitive and reasoning skills essential for typical rates and dimensions of school progress. These deficiencies accumulate partly from prolonged restriction to the limited experiences of culturally and intellectually impoverished homes and neighborhoods. . . . Disadvantaged children's communication capabilities are elementary. Analytic conversations with adults at home are limited. There, children learn, think, and speak largely about concrete matters of immediate import. Generalities and long-range goals are seldom discussed or recognized. (121, pp. 6, 16)

Katz stated it this way:

> In crowded lower-class homes, where mothers often are away at work during the day and both parents lack intellectual sophistication, the child's early efforts at verbal and cognitive mastery are less likely to be favorably reinforced than in middle-class homes, resulting in lower expectations of reward for intellectual effort. (138, p. 19)

Linguistic Ability

The language of educationally disadvantaged students is supposedly deficient for two reasons. First, it is perceived to be structurally deficient. It is full of grammatical errors, lacks prepositions and other forms that are necessary to perceive and express logical relationships, uses tenses incorrectly, and is repetitive, dull, and colorless.

> Language in the lower class is not as flexible a means of communication as in the middle class. It is not as readily adapted to the subtleties of the particular situation, but consists more of a relatively small repertoire of stereotyped phrases and expressions which are used rather loosely without much effort to achieve a subtle correspondence between perception and verbal expression. Much of lower class language consists of a kind of incidental "emotional" accompaniment to action here and now. In contrast, middle-class language, rather than being a mere accompaniment to ongoing activity serves more to represent things and events not immediately present. Thus middle-class language is more abstract and necessarily somewhat more flexible, detailed and subtle in its descriptive aspects. (118, pp. 118, 119)

Second, educationally disadvantaged students' use of language is supposedly inadequate because the environments in which they grow up offers "inadequate opportunities to use language in cognitively complex ways" (158, p. 303). These deficits are attributed to parents who provide children with poor language models and spend insufficient time communicating with children (112, 114, 116, 167). "In the deprived home, language usage is more limited. Much communication is through gestures and other non-verbal means. When language is used, it is likely to be terse and not necessarily grammatically correct" (112, pp. 70–71).

> Compared with other children whose families provide them with adequate or extensive spoken language stimulation, children from lower socioeconomic families may be less fortunate. . . . For example, often missing is an atmosphere of family conversation where a child's questions are answered—extending his vocabulary and giving him a right to stand up for and explain his point of view. Also missing in some homes of this type is a family environment which sets an example for acceptable speech and reading patterns. And, children from meager family situations are too often not exposed to a variety of toys and play materials of different colors, shapes, and sizes which challenge the child's ingenuity with his hands and mind, and learn only "restricted" types of language. (167, pp. 332–333)

Self-Concepts and Self-Esteem

Non-European American students—especially those from African American, Native American, Hispanic American, and poor backgrounds—are thought to have poor self-concepts and low self-esteem. This is attributed to a variety of causes. Supposedly, they lack successful role models in their families and communities with whom to identify. Repeated failure in school and other competitive situations is assumed to lower their self-images. They are also believed to suffer a loss of self-esteem when they compare their lives and living conditions with those of their middle-class and European American peers. "Disadvantaged children have relatively impoverished self-concepts. From quite realistic appraisals of their experiences, these children have acquired the attitude that they cannot achieve as much as their middle- or upper-class counterparts" (127, p. 5).

Levels of Educational Aspirations

Disadvantaged students are assumed to have low educational and career aspirations. "Their expectations and aspirations are correspondingly low. Many have learned to '*not hope for too much.*' As a result, they are less motivated by goals that fuel the efforts of pupils who have acquired larger aspirations from richer experiences" (121, p. 5).

Disadvantaged students' supposed low level of aspirations are attributed to the following four factors.

- Their parents do not expect them to do well in school.
- They perceive that their culture and environment do not prepare them to compete successfully with their more advantaged peers.
- Their life experiences, and those of their parents, quickly teach them that it is unrealistic to expect that they will accomplish very much.

- Many of them, especially African American males, lack role models because of the absence of fathers in the house. Because the male parent represents the external world and serves as a role model for dealing with life outside the family, and the female parent represents the internal/family world, students without fathers are not motivated to succeed because do not see that model at home (115, 120, 123).

Locus of Control

Theoretically, disadvantaged students have little faith that they are in control of their own lives. Their fatalistic, pessimistic, and dependent attitude amounts to an external locus of control. Their poor performance in school is assumed to be caused in part by the fact that they attribute their poor performance to fate, chance, and various circumstances beyond their control and do not believe they can determine whether they will succeed.

Disadvantaged students' presumed external locus of control is attributed to the following three factors:

- Parents of disadvantaged students do not train their children to function independently nor praise them for doing so.
- Parents of disadvantaged students are too harsh and authoritarian and as a result fail to encourage autonomy or positive self-expectations.
- The very conditions of being poor and powerless convince students that they and their parents cannot exercise control over their lives.

"Deprivation impels a child to adopt fatalistic attitudes about the probability that he can meet even his most basic physical needs, let alone his emotional and social needs" (121, p. 24).

Social Behavior

Disadvantaged students are described as misbehaving more often and presenting more discipline problems in school than other students. The theory of cultural deprivation also offers a number of explanations for why this is so (110, 113, 115, 120–122). Consider the following:

- The environment in which disadvantaged students grow up does not encourage acceptable behavior because much of the behavior they observe in their neighborhoods would be unacceptable in school.
- Because their parents stop supervising them at an early age, they are socialized by peer groups that model socially unacceptable values and behavior.
- The lack of fathers at home leaves many of them, especially African American students, without models of appropriate behavior to emulate.
- Raising males in a matriarchal setting causes them to overcompensate in exaggeratedly aggressive, masculine ways and leads to "desperate efforts of males in lower class culture to rebel against their early overprotective, feminizing environments and to find a masculine identity" (113, p. 9).

Implications

Some educators who subscribe to the theory of cultural/educational disadvantage are pessimistic about the possibilities that schools can overcome its presumed effects. This was especially true in the 1960s and 1970s.

> Class-cultural factors largely account for the conspicuous differences between the slum and the suburban school. Each school has a class character imposed upon it by the social setting in which it exists; this, and not staff inefficiency, racial discrimination, or inequitable provisions of resources, is the main reason for the virtues of one and the defects of the other. The implication is one that reformers find hard to accept—to wit, that no matter how able, dedicated, and hard-working the teachers, no matter how ample the facilities of the school or how well designed its curriculum, no matter how free the atmosphere of the school from racial or other prejudice, the performance of pupils at the lower end of the class-cultural scale will always fall short not only of pupils at the upper end of the scale, but also of what is necessary to make them educated workers. (124, p. 142)

Educators who do not believe that the effects of cultural disadvantage can be reversed tend to favor lowering expectations for educationally disadvantaged students, modifying their curriculum, using alternative instructional strategies that involve concrete teaching techniques, and segregating them from the mainstream by placing them in separate tracks. They find it reasonable that such students are overrepresented in special education programs such as those for individuals with mild developmental disabilities, learning disabilities, and behavior disorders.

Many other supporters of the theory of cultural/educational disadvantage believe that it is possible to combat the characteristics they attribute to the educationally disadvantaged. They tend to support additional funding to schools that serve educationally disadvantaged students; programs such as Head Start and Upward Bound to compensate for students' educational disadvantage; school integration to expose non-European American students to the influence of the more positive, advantaged culture of majority students; affirmative action to provide students with the added resources they are thought to require in order to compete successfully with their more advantaged peers; and parent education programs to help parents prepare children to succeed in school.

> The litany of past and present innovation, strategies, and acronyms is endless—Parent Child Centers, Upward Bound, Chapter 1, Head Start, Job Corps, Follow Through, Home Start. These programs, including their predecessors and progenitors, are primarily the Great Society's compensatory efforts based on beliefs and assumptions that if only the appropriate method, environment, parenting style, money, program, materials, and personnel were implemented, underachieving minority students would catch up with white children. This deficit view assumes that black children, because of cultural, biological, environmental, and social differences, lack the adaptations and knowledge necessary for school achievement. (136, pp. 1–2)

Criticisms

These beliefs concerning the supposed impact of cultural disadvantages have been criticized on a number of grounds since the 1960s (125–152). In general, critics claim the descriptions of so-called disadvantaged students and the cultural/familial factors these characteristics are attributed to are incorrect, unscientific, and prejudiced. "These terms carry the weight of authority and scholarship instead of the label of ignorant prejudice" (133, p. 63).

Some of their specific criticisms include the following:

• Many of the characteristics that are attributed to cultural disadvantage are actually the result of poor peoples' inability to afford and obtain the resources available to the middle and upper classes, and the disadvantages many poor immigrants experience because of their limited English proficiency (126, 145–150). Since many more non-European American students than European American students come from lower socioeconomic-class backgrounds, many of the apparent cultural differences between them are actually the result of financial factors. Although poor parents want their children to do well in school, many of them are unemployed, underemployed, underpaid, and undereducated. Thus, they are unable to provide their children with the childhood experiences needed to prepare them for school or the educational and financial support they require to assist their youngsters during their educational careers. The following comments by educators about the poor parents of the Hispanic students with whom they worked illustrate this point of view:

> Spanish-speaking parents believe in the educational system but do not know how to help their youngsters. . . . How can a man with a second grade level of education help his son figure out an algebra equation? (134, p. 169)

> Among poor families, the necessities of the day-to-day existence such as trips to the grocery store or laundromat, emergency health needs, car trouble, etc. are of primary importance. . . . It is not uncommon for a 7- or 8-year-old girl to stay home from school to baby sit for younger siblings so that Mother can go to work, for a bilingual child to be taken along as "translator" when monolingual parents have medical or legal appointments, or for ten-year-olds to take major responsibility for preparing meals at home for "working family members." (134, p. 72)

Critics complain that society spends less on the economically disadvantaged. They believe that local and state governments should spend more, not less, on schools that serve predominantly poor students. They favor programs designed to assist and supplement poor parents' efforts. Examples are day care and preschool programs; programs that train parents to participate in their children's education; and equal opportunity, open admissions, and affirmative action programs that provide students with access to educational programs and the added resources they require to compete successfully with their more economically advantaged peers. They believe such programs are necessary for poor European

American and non-European American students to achieve their potential in school.

Critics maintain that educators should have a realistic picture of both the kinds of educational support and assistance that parents can provide their children, and the way their financial situation impacts on their children's functioning in school. They advise educators to adapt their educational approaches to these realities. Until this happens, the critics believe, many children of poor parents will continue to fail in regular education. These children will be misplaced into special education programs because educators mistakenly believe that the learning and behavior problems their economic disadvantages create are caused by learning or developmental disabilities.

• Because students with similar socioeconomic-class and ethnic backgrounds (e.g., African American poor students) are actually exposed to very different living conditions, the theory of cultural/educational disadvantage offers misleading overgeneralizations. Within the same socioeconomic class or ethnic group, there are great differences in terms of such factors as parents' educational aspirations for their children; family size; housing conditions; frequency of parent-child cultural activities like trips to the zoo, library, museums, and movies; frequency and type of adult-child conversation; preschool and kindergarten attendance; and so on. Therefore, students with similar socioeconomic-class and ethnic backgrounds grow up to be very dissimilar. Also, many of them do not conform to cultural stereotypes (146, 151, 152).

> There are substantial variations in children's outcomes across families that are identical in parents' education and work history, family income, family size, and other standard measures of social and economic well-being. . . . Differences in family behavior and attitudes have large and important long-term effects on children's academic performance. (131, pp. 528, 543)

> A broad rubric such as "educationally deprived" does little if anything toward defining characteristics and educational needs of children. . . . Defining children by social economic level and then designing educational programs for this group will not suffice. . . . The terms "educationally deprived" or "disadvantaged" therefore are of little or no use for educators seriously concerned with providing meaningful educational experiences for Afro-American children, in particular, and for all children in general. (143, pp. 127, 133)

• The theory has a harmful effect on students because the curriculum offered to educationally disadvantaged students is based on lowering standards, modifying the content, utilizing less effective instructional strategies, and placing them in separate tracks (125, 128, 132, 139, 140). (See Structured Reproduction in Chapter 3.)

> The development of compensatory education programs has traditionally been informed by the belief that disadvantaged students can benefit most from a less challenging curriculum, and limited achievement goals. Thus, Chapter I services, provided through the Federal Education Consolidation and Improvement Act, comprise

currricula stressing basic skills in reading and mathematics, vocational rather than academic programs, and a slower instructional pace. . . . Students receive more instruction in factual and lower-level skills—drill and practice—and less in higher-order skills. [This] hampers the ability of low achieving students to develop thinking skills, lowers their learning expectations and stigmatizes them as inferior. (140, p. 1)

The cultural deprivation explanation has provided the substance for the educational self-fulling prophecy which shackles the lives of these low-status children. Because they are "culturally deprived," low-status children are not expected to perform academically up to the norms of other children—the curriculum is watered down and they are placed, for the most part, in slow-learning classes or slow tracks. And because they are treated that way and, at times, told that they are intellectually slow and culturally deprived, they are not motivated to learn and they do not learn. (129, p. 7)

- The theory blames the victim and diverts people's attention away from the school's contribution to students' problems (127, 130).

Since both the academic opportunity structure and the occupational opportunity structure of the larger society are assumed to be open and accessible, failure becomes the fault of the individual, his family, his environment, or his culture. Since the *cream rises to the top,* it is implied that the people who remain at the bottom are either low in ability or psycho-motivationally defective. Further, if whole groups remain at the bottom, it follows that something must be wrong with their particular form of social organization or culture. . . . The cultural deprivation theory, because its focus is on the family and individual personality traits, subtly calls attention away from the schools themselves as precipitators of school success and failure. (130, pp. 340, 341)

Research

Cognitive Ability

- *Poor parents' and some non-European American parents' communication, teaching, and parenting styles impede their children's cognitive development and academic achievement.*

The evidence does not support this claim. First, as discussed previously, there is no evidence that students from different socioeconomic-class and ethnic backgrounds differ in cognitive (intellectual) ability. (See also Chapter 9.) Second, there is little reason to accept the claim that poor parents impede their children's cognitive development by providing them with an impoverished language environment (154, 155). Early researchers believed that poor parents restrict the development of thought in their children because they "use a restricted language code, in which messages are short, are not made explicit, and are bound to the context in which the message occurs. Middle-class speakers, in contrast, use an elaborated code in which messages are made explicit and context-free." Middle-class mothers also differ from working class parents on the "quality of speech, sentence length, syntactic complexity, use of abstract nouns and verbs, and adjective-verb-ratio" (174, p. 280).

However, the studies this claim was based on were typically not conducted in natural settings, such as children's homes, but in laboratory settings, which have been shown to make poor parents anxious and less fluent (144, 168, 178). Research in naturalistic settings indicates that poor parents do not use a restricted language code with their children (162, 163). In addition, there is no evidence that complex linguistic forms are superior to simplistic forms or that complex linguistic forms are necessary for adequate development of children's cognitive skills, reading ability, or academic achievement (161, 174, 175). In the absence of such evidence, there is little reason to assume the type of language employed by students' parents affects student's cognitive development.

Third, as just noted in the previous section, parenting/teaching styles do not affect students' cognitive development.

Fourth, although parenting and teaching styles do contribute to students' school success (165, 169, 177, 181), there is no evidence that the styles used by different ethnic groups and socioeconomic class affect children's academic achievement. The early studies that appeared to demonstrate that African American and poor people's parenting styles impeded their children's success in school were poorly controlled. Like the studies on communication styles, the studies did not take into account the fact that poor parents behave differently in experimental settings (such as laboratories) and in more natural settings (such as their own homes and apartments). Also, researchers did not control for the fact that parents use different teaching techniques for the real-life tasks and those involved in laboratory experiments.

Later studies that better controlled for these factors found fewer and often no socioeconomic-class differences in parenting/teaching styles (153, 156, 159, 164, 172). As a result, researchers concluded that earlier researchers who asserted that the teaching style of poor parents is less efficient than the style employed by middle-class parents were merely expressing their biases and preferences for middle-class norms (174).

Linguistic Proficiency

- *Non-European and poor students do not have the linguistic skills necessary to succeed in school.*

Many studies of students' linguistic proficiency have affirmed the existence of socioeconomic-class and ethnic group differences in oral language (167), vocabulary (166, 180), and syntactic usage (170). To some educators, these differences indicate that middle-class and European American students have acquired a higher level of linguistic skills than poor and African American students. Other educators, however, interpret these results in terms of linguistic differences rather than linguistic deficiencies. They feel that certain groups of linguistically able students *appear* to have poorly developed linguistic skills because of a mismatch between the way they and their teachers use language. For example, Slaughter and Epps (1987) stated, "Lower income Black children are quite 'verbal,' but . . . the norms governing when and how they should speak are different from middle-class norms. To be effective educators, teachers need to know some of these norms, to adapt them to their own classroom behaviors, and, conversely, to point out the differences between in-school and out-of-school speech to the students" (176, p. 9).

A number of studies have documented the poor match between the way teachers engage African American students in conversations and the way these students use language in their homes and communities. For example, African American adults seldom ask questions that require children to state something that the children realize adults already know. Rather, they are asked to talk about things about which adults are unaware. Teachers, on the other hand, often ask questions about things that they obviously know more about than their students. Thus, in the early grades, African American students are often puzzled about why teachers are asking them for information that they already know. African American adults tend to ask about things related to children's experiences, whereas teachers often ask questions about things outside their students' life experiences. As a result, students are unprepared to discuss things about which they have no direct experience or understanding. Some African American parents issue direct orders to students such as, "Do such and such," whereas European American teachers are often more indirect and say things such as, "Why don't you do such and such?" or "You might want to do such and such." Therefore, African American students are not always aware that their teachers have required them to do something and have not merely made a suggestion that they can choose to accept or reject (157, 163).

The use of nonstandard speech by African American and Hispanic students does have an effect on students' academic achievement. However, this effect is the result of the way teachers react to their speech patterns, not the speech patterns themselves. Teachers of nonstandard English speakers, especially those who believe standard English to be a more preferable/correct version of English, tend to spend too much time correcting students' "grammatical and dialectic pronunciation errors" instead of teaching them the skills they need to acquire (158, 171). In addition, many teachers think that students who do not speak standard English are less intelligent. These teachers have lower academic expectations for the students, and they evaluate the oral and written work of the students to be lower than comparable work of standard English-speaking students (160, 179). They are also more likely to disapprove of such students (169). (See Prejudice and Discrimination in the Educational System in Chapter 3.)

Auditory Discrimination

- *Disadvantaged students have poor auditory discrimination skills.*

Although there is a modest relationship between auditory discrimination and reading achievement, there is little evidence that African American, Hispanic American, or poor students have poor auditory discrimination skills. During the 1960s, a number of researchers reported that these students scored lower on tests of auditory discrimination (182, 185, 190, 191). However, these differences were actually the result of biased assessment procedures.

Many African American, Hispanic American, and poor students speak non-standard forms of English that utilize somewhat different sounds. As a result, when they are required to discriminate between unfamiliar sounds that are included in standard English but not in their dialects and languages, they are unable to do so. On the other hand, when these students are given auditory discrimination tests in their own languages or dialects, African American, Hispanic American, and poor students do not demonstrate any auditory discrimination problems (183, 184, 186–189, 192).

Self-Concept

- *Educationally disadvantaged students' poor self-concepts interfere with their achievement in school.*

Research reveals that students' self-concepts have a significant effect on the way they behave both in and out of school. Positive self-concepts have been shown to enhance learning and encourage acceptable behavior; poor self-concepts impede achievement and lead to emotional and behavioral problems. However, there is little evidence that poor, African American, and Hispanic American students have poorer self-concepts than their European American middle-class peers.

Some studies, primarily those done in the 1960s, found weak but statistically significant relationships between students' self-concepts and their ethnic and socioeconomic-class backgrounds. In general, poor, African American, Native American, and Hispanic American students had lower self-concepts than European American middle-class students (198, 199, 201, 203, 204, 208, 213, 216).

More recent studies of Native American students completed since the 1960s confirmed these earlier findings. Many Native American students, especially those with the greatest exposure to the European American culture and school system, have lower self-esteem than European Americans (207). Most studies of Hispanic American students' self-concepts done since the 1960s indicate that these students do not have lower self-concepts (202, 206, 209, 217). The vast majority of studies, especially those done after the 1960s, have revealed that poor and African American students' self-concepts are at least as high, if not higher, than those of middle-class European Americans (193–195, 200, 202, 205, 208, 210–212, 214, 215, 218).

The following are four of the common explanations for why African American and Hispanic American students, including those from poor backgrounds, do not have low self-concepts despite their poor neighborhoods, the discrimination they experience, and their low academic success rates.

1. The prevailing view that African Americans and other non-European American groups suffer from poor self-concepts is a product of a European American perspective. European American researchers and commentators do not realize that most non-European American children and their parents do not accept the dominant society's view that they are inferior and incapable. They are not aware that African American, Native American, Hispanic American, and other non-European American families have always attempted to coun-

teract the messages students receive about their "inferiority" and have done so with increasing success since the black, brown, and red power movement of the late 1960s and 1970s (197, 210, 212).

To act as if the only influence upon the formation of self-concepts is that of the dominant culture negates the idea of the child having any other culture or a socialization process that might counteract such a negative view. Such conclusions assume that all a Black or Indian child will get from his family socialization is a carbon copy of the negative stereotyping and evaluation of the white racist culture. . . . Either from ethnocentric distortion or from the negation of the culture of the minority group, researchers leave only psychopathological explanations for observed behavior (i.e., academic failure due to "poor self-concept." (210, p. 17)

Blacks have not really believed that white equals goodness and purity. Their self-concept has never entirely been controlled by whites. . . . Blacks have struggled to show their children that the white view of blacks as inferior is incorrect as well as immoral. (212, p. 139)

The supposed negative self-image of the Mexican-American is, in reality, our own stereotype projected onto him. "Anglos" tend to think of Mexican-Americans in negative ways, and conclude they see themselves in the same light. (197, p. 218)

2. Many non-European American poor students grow up and attend schools in their neighborhood primarily with students like themselves, and are not actually exposed to the more advantaged groups nor to the prejudice many have against them.
3. Many poor non-European American students do not have poor self-concepts because they experience less stress and tension than middle-class European American students. Unlike middle-class students, they are not trying to live up to high expectations since family's, teachers', and self-expectations for them are not as high.
4. Non-European American and poor students who believe that discrimination, not lack of effort or ability, is the cause of many of their problems do not accept blame for not doing well and do not lose self-respect. Middle-class students tend to blame themselves for their lack of success and thus experience a loss of self-esteem.

Academic and Vocational Aspirations and Expectations

- *Disadvantaged students, especially males, do not aspire or expect to do well in school because their parents do not have high aspirations for them, do not expect them to do well, and do not provide them with acceptable male role models.*

Research offers little support for this supposition. The most telling argument against it are studies of students' academic and vocational aspirations done in the 1960s through 1980s that have consistently indicated that African Americans' aspirations are as high, if not higher than, their European American peers (219–222). The difference between the groups is not their aspirations, but the extent to which they believe they will achieve their aspirations.

African American students start off placing even greater value on education than European American students. However, after attending school for a few years, they often end up expecting that they will not achieve the level of education to which they aspire.

Parents' aspirations and expectations for their children in school and their evaluations of their children's academic ability do affect students' confidence about their academic abilities, their academic and occupational aspirations, and the courses they select. However, research about ethnic and socioeconomic-class differences in these parental characteristics is inconsistent. Some studies have found that poor, African American, and Hispanic American parents expect their children to do less well in school and do not encourage them as much as European American middle-class parents (126, 223–225). Other studies indicate that African American and poor parents have as high, if not higher, *aspirations* for their children than European American middle-class parents. Again, the difference lies in the fact that African American and poor parents do not expect their children's academic or vocational achievement to fulfill their aspirations for them, so they are willing to accept lower levels of achievement than European American middle-class parents (135, 141, 142, 226–228).

Research that appears to indicate that African American students do not have high educational aspirations and are not encouraged to set high goals for themselves is often culturally insensitive, biased, and invalid (135, 137, 142). European American researchers do not consider the role of the African American community. Through individuals outside the family—such as teachers, trusted adults, neighbors, community groups and agencies, and so on—the community encourages African American students to set high achievement goals for themselves. Therefore, research that includes only the influence of students' families does not present a true picture of the encouragement African American students receive within their culture. Researchers also focus too exclusively on individual achievement. Because African American students are more cooperative and interested in group goals, researchers who do not include students' desire to contribute to the advancement of African Americans as a group underestimate their achievement orientation.

Locus of Control

- *Many disadvantaged students have an external locus of control that has a negative effect on their academic and vocational achievement.*

The research evidence used to support this claim is questionable for the following two reasons:

1. Research about the locus of control of poor, African American, and Hispanic American students has produced mixed results. Some studies have found that these groups have an external locus of control (177, 229); others have found they do not (126, 231, 233, 234).
2. It is unclear if the research that shows that students with an internal locus of control tend to achieve more in school than those whose locus of control is ex-

ternal applies equally to middle-class European American students and to poor and non-European American students (181, 231). Studying locus of control from a European American point of view, researchers failed to recognize the special circumstances of many poor and non-European American students. These researchers mistakenly thought that all students with an internal locus of control attributed their successes and failures to their skill, ability, and effort, whereas all students with an external locus of control attributed their successes and failures to fate and chance. In so doing, researchers did not realize that many non-European American students with an external locus of control believe, often correctly, that the environment they encounter both in and out of school is so hostile and prejudiced that despite their best efforts, skills, and abilities they will not be able to accomplish their goals (138, 230, 232).

In a society that is fair, as it tends to be for most middle-class European Americans, students with an internal locus of control should do better in school. This is because they will try harder to succeed and to improve when they do poorly. However, in the case of poor students, African Americans, Native Americans, and Hispanic Americans who exist in a racist and prejudiced environment, an internal locus of control may be self-destructive. This is because it may lead students to blame themselves or hold themselves responsible for failure caused by unfairness, prejudice, and economic injustice. Students with an internal locus of control who are not doing well because of discrimination may blame themselves and give up, but students who correctly understand that external factors are to blame may strive to change them, especially if they are supported by others who hold similar beliefs and have similar characteristics.

> "Feelings of fate control" may in fact be valid perceptions of institutional barriers (for example, tracking and negative teacher attitudes) which prevent black students from actually exercising any significant and meaningful control over their own lives. . . . The way to solve the learning difficulties encountered by black students is to remove the institutional barriers which prevent them from exercising any significant and meaningful control over their intellectual and personal destinies rather than *blaming* the black family for something over which it has no control. (232, p. 75)

Father Absence

- *Many of the educational and behavioral problems of poor students, especially African American males, are caused at least in part by the absence of a father in the family.*

During the 1960s and 1970s, a number of studies found that students—especially African American males—growing up in one-parent families headed by females performed less adequately on tests purported to measure intelligence and moral development, had lower academic and vocational aspirations, achieved less, were more aggressive in school, and were less well adjusted (115, 165, 235, 237, 239, 240, 242, 243, 246, 249). However, these early studies have been justly criticized.

Most of the researchers failed to control for socioeconomic-class differences. This is a very important omission because families that are deprived of the income of fathers were and are more likely to fall into the poor or poverty groups. Currently, 46 percent of European American, 66 percent of Hispanic American, and 67 percent of African American children living in single-parent female-headed families live in poverty (256). In the 1960s and early 1970s, fewer women were in the work force, the discrepancy between what working women and men earned was even greater than today, and there were fewer resources (such as day-care centers) and other supports available to single-parent families. Thus, the differences observed in these studies could well have been due to socioeconomic-class factors.

Most subsequent studies that were better controlled and a number of studies done in the 1960s and 1970s reported results that contradict the findings of the early studies (173, 181, 219, 236, 241, 242, 247, 250, 253). Researchers typically found either no relationship between the presence of students' fathers at home and their adjustment in or out of school, or a relationship that was so small that it accounted for very little of the differences observed between successful and unsuccessful students. In addition, the relationship tended to be confined to only poor students. These facts suggest that the small relationship between children's adjustment and the presence or absence of their fathers is primarily the result of the loss of income poor families experience rather than the absence of a male role model.

The early studies misunderstand and misrepresent the nature of poor and African American families (238, 244, 245, 251, 252, 254). Culturally insensitive European American researchers underestimated the strength of African American families. They designed studies and interpreted the results of these studies while they were unaware of the role that families, teachers, trusted adults, neighbors, community groups and agencies, and churches play in encouraging, guiding, and supporting African American students. It is also incorrect to assume that fathers who are legally not a part of the family are actually absent. Many males who are separated or divorced from the children's mothers or pretend to be absent and uninvolved so their families can qualify for welfare and other forms of assistance, often play significant roles in their lives.

Researchers may have also projected their sexist points of view on the African American family (137, 238, 248, 255). African American families are much more egalitarian and nonsexist than many European American families. Gender roles are much less stereotyped; mothers can be role models for activities and functions that are usually reserved for males in the European American culture. So, even when males are absent, females can often provide the necessary role models.

Conclusions

The validity of the cultural deprivation/educational disadvantage theory can be evaluated in terms of the following three questions:

1. *Do the characteristics attributed to educationally disadvantaged students negatively affect educational outcomes?* Research indicates that students' auditory discrimination skills, locus of control, level of aspiration, and self-concept do affect their achievement in school. The assumed negative influence of students' use of nonstandard English, parental teaching styles, and father absence are not supported by research.
2. *Do African American, Hispanic American, and poor students have these characteristics to a greater degree than European American and middle-class students?* There is no evidence that poor, African American, and Hispanic American students have poor auditory skills. Research on their locus of control is mixed. However, it is likely that even when these students appear to have an external locus of control, they may be accurately perceiving the obstacles they face in a society rife with prejudice rather then attributing their successes and failure to fate, luck, or chance. Contrary to what the theory predicts, these students have as high, if not higher, aspirations and self-concepts as middle-class European American students.
3. *If African American, Hispanic American, and poor students have these characteristics to a greater degree than European American and middle-class students, are the differences caused by cultural/familial factors rather than racism, economic disadvantage, and so on?* The few differences observed in African American, Hispanic American, and poor students versus European American and middle-class students and their families that have been confirmed by research are more likely to be caused by the prejudiced and hostile environment they face and the limited opportunities their lack of financial resources impose of them than by cultural differences.

SELF-QUIZ

INTRINSIC CAUSES

- Some educators believe that many poor, African American, Hispanic American, and Native American students come to school already predisposed to fail in regular education and to require special education services. Do you agree?
- What is your opinion about the extrinsic factors that some educators feel contribute to these students' learning and behavior problems?
- Do you agree or disagree that poor, African American, Hispanic American, and Native American students are exposed to an inordinate amount of biomedical problems that cause disabilities?
- Do you think that poor, African American, Hispanic American, and Native American students tend to inherit less intellectual potential than European American students?
- Do you think that poor, African American, Hispanic American, and Native American students are brought up in disadvantaged cultures?

SUMMARY

Some educators believe that many poor, African American, Native American, and Hispanic American students are more likely to suffer biomedical problems, to inherit less intellectual potential than their peers, and to come from culturally deprived or disadvantaged backgrounds. They attribute the high percentage of failure among these students and their overrepresentation in special education programs for students with disabilities and their underrepresentation in programs for gifted and talented students to the educational problems these conditions can create.

Although poor, African American, Native American, and Hispanic American students are more likely to suffer biomedical problems, it is unlikely that these problems are a major cause of their lack of achievement in the regular education system or their misrepresentation in special education programs. Research does not support the contention that they inherit less intellectual potential than others. The early research on cultural deprivation/disadvantage was done from a European American point of view. Better controlled and more culturally sensitive studies refute the idea that poor, African American, and Hispanic American students are brought up in deprived or disadvantaged cultures.

ACTIVITIES

1. The following are the major contentions of those who believe that cultural disadvantage is an important cause of the educational problems of many students. Ask some of your European American middle-class colleagues or peers to tell you their opinion about which, if any, of these assumptions are characteristic of African American, Hispanic American, or poor students. Ask some of your African American or Hispanic American colleagues or peers, or colleagues or peers from poor backgrounds, if they were ever told or believed any of these assumptions.
   a. Their parents' communication, teaching, and parenting styles impede their cognitive development and academic achievement.
   b. They do not have the linguistic skills necessary to succeed in school.
   c. They have poor auditory discrimination skills.
   d. Their poor self-concepts interfere with their achievement in school.
   e. They do not aspire or expect to do well in school because their parents do not have high aspirations for them, do not expect them to do well, and do not provide them with acceptable male role models.
   f. They have an external locus of control that has a negative effect on their academic and vocational achievement.
   g. Many of their educational and behavioral problems are caused at least in part by the absence of a father in the family.
2. Improve your understanding of the problems of children born addicted to substances such as alcohol and drugs by visiting a program that serves them.

REFERENCES

References 1–16 deal with the effects of poor nutrition and health care on students' behavior and school success.

1. Baumeister, A. A., Kupstas, F., & Klindworth, L. M. (1990). New morbidity: Implications for prevention of children's disabilities. *Exceptionality, 1*, 1–16.
2. Escalona, S. K. (1982). Babies at double hazard: Early development of infants at biological and social risk. *Pediatrics, 70*, 670–675.
3. Food Research and Action Center. (1984). *The Widening Gap: The Incidence and Distribution of Infant Mortality and Low Birthweight in the United States-1978–1982.* Washington, DC: Author.
4. Galler, J. R. (Ed.). (1984). *Human Nutrition: A Comprehensive Treatise: Vol. 5. Nutrition and Behavior.* New York: Plenum.
5. Hoy, E. A., Bill, J. M., & Sykes, D. H. (1988). Very low birthweight: A long-term developmental impairment? *International Journal of Behavioral Development, 11*, 37–67.
6. Hughes, D., Johnson, K., Rosenbaum, S., Butler, W., & Simons, J. (1988). *The Health of America's Children: Maternal and Child Health Data Book.* Washington, DC: Children's Defense Fund.
7. Institute of Medicine. (1985). *Preventing Low Birthweight.* Washington, DC: National Academy Press.
8. Kopp, C. B., & Kaler, S. R. (1989). Risk in infancy: Origins and implications. *American Psychologist, 44* (2), 224–230.
9. Lane, J. M., & Johnson, C. L. (1981). Prevalence of iron deficiency. In *Report of the Eighty-Second Ross Conference on Pediatric Research.* Columbus, OH: Ross Laboratories.
10. Lieberman, E., Ryan, K., Monson, R., & Schoenbaum, S. (1987). Risk factors accounting for racial differences in the rate of premature birth. *New England Journal of Medicine, 317*, 743–748.
11. Lozoff, B. (1988) Behavioral alterations in iron deficiency. *Advances in Pediatrics, 35*, 331–360.
12. Lozoff, B. (1989). Nutrition and behavior. *American Psychologist, 44* (2), 231–236.
13. National Center for Clinical Infant Programs. (1986). *Infants Can't Wait: The Numbers.* Washington, DC: Author.
14. National Center for Health Statistics. (1987). *Advance Report of Final Natality Statistics,*
1985. (Monthly vital statistics report, vol. 36). Washington, DC: Author.
15. R. W. Johnson Foundation. (1983). *A National Collaborative Study.* Princeton, NJ: Author.
16. Shapiro, S., McCormick, M. C., Starfield, B. H., & Crawley, B. (1983). Changes in infant morbidity associated with decreases in neonatal mortality. *Pediatrics, 72*, 408–415.

References 17–53 discuss the prevalence and effects of parental substance abuse.

17. Adler, T. (1989). Cocaine babies face behavior deficits. *American Psychological Association Monitor, 20* (7), 14.
18. Archer, L. D. (1987). *Program Strategies for Preventing Fetal Alcohol Syndrome and Alcohol Related Birth Defects.* DHHS Publication No. (ADM) 87–1482.
19. Aronson, M., Kyllerman, M., Sobel, J. G., Sandin, B., & Olegard, R. (1985). Children of alcoholic mothers: Developmental, perceptual, and behavioral characteristics as compared to matched controls. *Acta Paediatricia Scandinavica, 74*, 27–35.
20. Besharov, D. J. (1989). The children of crack, will we protect them? *Public Welfare, 47* (4), 6–11.
21. Besharov, D. J. (1990). Crack children in foster care. *Children Today, 19*, 21–35.
22. Brooks-Gunn, J., & McCarton, C. (1991). *Effects of Drugs In-Utero on Infant Development.* Washington, DC: National Institute of Child Health and Human Development, Report to Congress.
23. Burkett, B., Yasin, S., & Palow, D. (1990). Perinatal implications of cocaine exposure. *Journal of Reproductive Medicine, 35* (1), 35–42.
24. Chasnoff, I., Landress, H., & Barrett, M. (1990). The prevalence of illicit drug and or alcohol use during pregnancy and discrepancies in mandatory reporting in Pinellas County, Florida. *New England Journal of Medicine, 322*, 1202–1206.
25. Chavin, W., & Kandall, S. R. (1990). Between a rock and a hard place: Perinatal drug abuse. *Pediatrics, 85*, 223–225.
26. Cohen, S. (1985). *The Substance Abuse Problems, Vol II. New Issues for the 1980's.* Redding, CA: Hawthorn Press.

27. Cole, C., Ferara, V., Johnson, D., Jones, M., Schoenbaum, M., Tyler, R., Wallace, V., & Poulsen, M. (1989). *Today's Challenge: Teaching Strategies for Working with Young Children Pre-natally Exposed to Drugs/Alcohol.* Los Angeles: Los Angeles Unified School District.

28. Dow-Edwards, D. L. (1988). Developmental effects of cocaine. *National Institute of Drug Abuse Research Monographs, 88,* 290–303.

29. Finnegan, L. (1989). *Drug Dependency in Pregnancy: Clinical Management of Mother and Child.* Washington, DC: National Institute of Drug Abuse Service Research Monograph Service, U. S. Government Printing Office.

30. Fried, P. A., & O'Connell, C. M. (1987). A comparison of the effects of prenatal exposure to tobacco, alcohol, cannabis, and caffeine on birthsize and subsequent growth. *Neurotoxicology and Teratology, 9,* 79–85.

31. Gittler, J., & McPherson, M. (1990). Prenatal substance abuse. *Children Today, 19,* 3–7.

32. Griffith, D. (1991, May). *Intervention Needs of Children Prenatally Exposed to Drugs.* Congressional testimony before the House Select Committee on Special Education.

33. Haflon, N. (1989). *Hearing: Born Hooked, Confronting the Impact of Perinatal Substance Abuse.* Select Committee on Children, Youth and Families, U.S. House of Representatives, April 27.

34. Howard, J., Beckwith, L., Rodning, C., & Kropenske, V. (1989). Development of young children of substance-abusing parents: Insights from seven years of intervention and research. *Zero to Three, 9,* 8–12.

35. Kronstadt, D. (1989). *Pregnancy and Cocaine Addiction: An Overview of Impact and Treatment.* San Francisco: Far West Laboratory for Educational Research and Development.

36. Miller, G. (1989). *Hearing: Born Hooked, Confronting the Impact of Perinatal Substance Abuse.* Select Committee on Children, Youth and Families, U.S. House of Representatives, April 27.

37. New York City HRA Office of Management Analysis. (1990). Report issued on January 31. New York: Author.

38. *New York Times.* (1989). *Crack's Toll Among Babies: A Joyless View of Even Toys.* September 17.

39. Petitti, D. B., & Coleman, C. (1990). Cocaine and the risk of low birth weight. *American Journal of Public Health, 80* (1), 25–28.

40. Phillipson, R. (1988). The fetal alcohol syndrome: Recent international statistics. *Australia and New Zealand Journal of Developmental Psychology, 14* (3 & 4), 211–221.

41. Poulsen, M. (1991). *Schools Meet the Challenge: Educational Needs of Children at Risk Due to Substance Exposure.* Sacramento: Resources in Special Education.

42. Reed, B. (1987). Developing women sensitive drug dependent treatment services: Why so difficult? *Journal of Psychoactive Drugs, 19* (2), 151–164.

43. Rist, M. C. (1990). The shadow children. *American School Board Journal, 177* (1),19–24.

44. Straus, A. (1981). Neonatal manifestations of maternal phencyclidine (PCP) abuse. *Pediatrics, 66,* 4.

45. Streisstguth, A. P. (1989). *Prenatal Alcohol Exposure and Child IQ, Achievement and Classroom Behavior at Age 7.* Paper presented at the annual meeting of the Society for Research in Child Development, Kansas City, MO.

46. Streisstguth, A. P., Clarren, S. K., & Jones, K. L. (1985). Natural history of the fetal alcohol syndrome: A 10-year follow-up of eleven patients. *Lancet, 2* (8446), 85–91.

47. U.S. Department of Health and Human Services, Office of Inspector General. (1990). *Crack Babies.* Washington, DC: Author.

48. U. S. National Center for Health Statistics. (1989). *Advance Report of Final Natality Statistics, 1987.* Vol 38, No. 3, Supplement, June 29. Washington, DC: U.S. Department of Health and Human Services.

49. Vincent, L. J., Poulsen, M. K., Cole, C. K., Woodruff, G., & Griffith, D. R. (1991). *Born Substance Exposed, Educationally Vulnerable.* Reston, VA: Council for Exceptional Children.

50. Wescott, S. M. (1990). Time to address a preventable tragedy. *Winds of Change, 5* (3), 30–34.

51. Weston, R. R., Ivins, B., Zuckerman, B., Jones, C., & Lopez, R. (1989). Drug-exposed babies: Research and clinical issues. *Zero to Three, 9,* 1–7.

52. Wilson, G. S. (1989). Clinical studies of infants and children exposed prenatally to heroin. *Annals of The New York Academy of Sciences, 562,* 183–194.

53. Zuckerman, B. (1991). Drug-exposed infants: Understanding the medical risk. *The Future of Children, 1* (1), 26–35.

The prevalence and effects of pediatric acquired immune deficiency syndrome (AIDS) is the focus of references 54–58.

54. Belman, A. L., Diamond, G., Dickson, D., Horoupian, D., Llena, J., Lantos, G., & Rubinstein, A. (1988). Calcification of the basal ganglia in infants and children with acquired immunodeficiency syndrome. *American Journal of Diseases of Children, 36*, 1192–1199.
55. Belman, A. L., Ultmann, M. H., Horouopian, D., Novick, B. D., Spiro, A. J., Rubinstein, A., Kurtzberg, D., & Cone-Wesson, B. (1985). Neurological implications in infants with acquired immunodeficiency syndrome. *Annals of Neurology, 18*, 560–566.
56. Epstein, L. G., Sharer, L. R., Oleske, J. M., Cannon, E. M., Gouldsmit, J., Bagdon L., Robert-Guroff, M., & Koenigsberger, M. R. (1986). Neurological manifestations of HIV infection in children. *Pediatrics, 78*, 678–688.
57. Mays, V. M. (1987). *Epidemiology of AIDS among Ethnic Minorities.* Paper presented at the annual meeting of the American Psychological Association, New York.
58. Task Force on Pediatric AIDs. (1989). Pediatric AIDS and human immunodeficiency virus infection. *American Psychologist, 44* (2), 258–264.

Genetic explanations of ethnic and socioeconomic differences in school outcomes are presented in references 59–72.

59. Agassiz, L. (1850). The diversity of origin of the human races. *Christian Examiner, 49*, 110–145.
60. Blatt, B. (1981). *In and Out of Mental Retardation.* Baltimore: University Park Press.
61. Davenport, C. B. (1911). *Heredity in Relation to Eugenics.* New York: Holt.
62. Eysenck, H. J. (1973). *The Inequality of Man.* London: Temple Smith.
63. Gould, S. J. (1981). *The Mismeasure of Man.* New York: W. W. Norton.
64. Herrnstein, R. J. (1973). *IQ in the Meritocracy.* Boston: Little, Brown.
65. Jensen, A. R. (1971). *A Two-Factor Theory of Familial Mental Retardation.* ERIC ED 060 577.
66. Jensen, A. R. (1974). Interaction of Level I and Level II abilities with race and socioeconomic status. *Journal of Educational Psychology, 66* (1), 99–111.
67. Jensen, A. R. (1981). *Straight Talk about Mental Tests.* New York: Free Press.
68. Latham, G. L. (1987). *Breeding Poverty? Great Issues Lecture.* ERIC ED 293 232.
69. Popenoe P., & Johnson, R. H. (1918). *Applied Eugenics.* New York: Macmillan.
70. Shockley, W. (1971). Models, mathematics, and the moral obligation to diagnose the origins of Negro IQ deficits. *Review of Educational Research, 41* (4), 369–377.
71. Spuhler, J. N., & Lindzey, G. (1967). Racial differences in behavior. In J. Hirsch (Ed.), *Behavior-Genetic Analysis.* New York: McGraw-Hill.
72. Thorndike, E. L. (1931). *Human Learning.* New York: Century.

References 73–76 discuss the fallacy of the meritocracy theory.

73. Goldberg, A. S. (1974). *Mystery of the Meritocracy.* Madison, WI: Institute for Research on Poverty, University of Wisconsin.
74. Goldberg, A. S. (1974). *Professor Jensen, Meet Miss Burks.* Madison, WI: Institute for Research on Poverty, University of Wisconsin.
75. Jencks, C., Smith, M., Acland, H., Bane, M. J., Cohen, D., Gintis, H., Heyns, G., & Michelson, S. (1972). *Inequality: A Reassessment of the Effect of Family and Schooling in America.* New York: Harper & Row.
76. Rumberger, R. W. (1983). The influence of family background on education, learnings, and wealth. *Social Forces, 3*, 755–773.

Arguments and evidence against the genetic explanation of educational disparities are included in references 77–87.

77. Bronfenbrenner, U. (1972). Is 80% of intelligence genetically determined? In U. Bronfenbrenner (Ed.), *Influence on Human Development.* Hinsdale IL: Dryden.
78. Green, R. B., & Rohwer, W. D., Jr. (1971). SES differences on learning and ability tests in black children. *American Journal of Educational Research, 8* (4), 601–609.
79. Kamin, L. J. (1973). Text of Dr. Kamin's presentation denying that proof exists that IQ test scores are hereditary. *South Today, 4* (8), 1–5.
80. Kamin, L. J. (1974). *The Science and Politics of I.Q.* Hillsdale, NJ: Erlbaum.

81. Mensh, E., & Mensh, H. (1991). *The IQ Mythology: Class, Race, Gender, and Inequality*. Carbondale, IL: Southern Illinois University Press.

82. Moore, E. G. J. (1986). Family socialization and the IQ test performance of traditionally and transracially adopted black children. *Developmental Psychology, 22,* 317–326.

83. Moore, E. G. J. (1987). Ethnic social milieu and black children's intelligence achievement. *Journal of Negro Education, 56* (1), 44–52.

84. Persell, C. H. (1981). Genetic and cultural deficit theories: Two sides of the same racist coin. *Journal of Black Studies, 12* (1), 19–37.

85. Scarr, S. (1968). Environment bias in twin studies. *Eugenics Quarterly, 15,* 34–40.

86. Scarr, S. (1971). Race, social class and IQ. *Science, 174,* 1285–1295.

87. Vernon, P. E., & Mitchell, M. C. (1974). Social-class differences in associative learning. *Journal of Special Education, 8* (4), 297–311.

The role of socioeconomic class factors in predicting differences in scores on tests of intellectual functioning within ethnic groups is discussed in references 88–92.

88. Bardouille-Crema, A., Black, K. N., & Feldhusen, J. (1986). Performance on Piagetian tasks of black children of differing socioeconomic levels. *Developmental Psychology, 22* (6), 841–844.

89. Blau, Z. S. (1981). *Black Children/White Children*. New York: Free Press.

90. Hall, V. C., & Kaye, D. B. (1980). Early patterns of cognitive development. With commentary by Sandra W. Scarr. *Monographs of the Society for Research in Child Development, 45* (2), Serial No. 184.

91. Scarr, S. (1981). *Race, Social Class, and Individual Differences in I.Q.* Hillsdale, NJ: Erlbaum.

92. Yando, R., Seitz, V., & Zigler, W. (1979). *Intellectual and Personality Characteristics of Children*. Hillsdale, NJ: Erlbaum.

References 93–109 present research and discussion regarding the theory of genetically determined ethnic group and socioeconomic-class differences in Level I and Level II abilities.

93. Bee, H., Barnard, K., Eyres, S., Gray, C., Hammond, M., Speitz, A., Snyder, C., & Clark, B. (1982). Prediction of IQ and language skills from perinatal status, child performance, family characteristics, and mother-infant interaction. *Child Development, 53,* 44–75.

94. Borkowski, J. G., & Krause, A. (1983). Racial differences in intelligence: The importance of the executive system. *Intelligence, 7,* 379–395.

95. Bridgeman, B., & Buttram, J. (1975). Race differences on nonverbal analogy test performance as a function of verbal strategy training. *Journal of Educational Psychology, 67* (4), 586–590.

96. Butcher, H. J. (1972). Comments on Arthur Jensen's "Do schools cheat minority children?". *Educational Research, 14* (2), 87–100.

97. Humphreys, L. G., & Dachler, P. (1969). Jensen's theory of intelligence. *Journal of Educational Psychology, 60,* 419–426.

98. Humphreys, L. G., & Dachler, P. (1969). Jensen's theory of intelligence: A rebuttal. *Journal of Educational Psychology, 60,* 432–433.

99. Jensen, A. R. (1969). How much can we boost IQ and scholastic achievement? *Harvard Educational Review, 39,* 1–123.

100. Jensen, A. R. (1971). The role of verbal mediation in development. *Journal of Genetic Psychology, 118,* 39–70.

101. Jensen, A. R. (1973). *Genetics and Education*. New York: Harper & Row.

102. Jensen, A. R. (1973). *Level I and Level II Abilities in Three Ethnic Groups*. ERIC ED 080 646.

103. Jensen, A. R., & Inouye, A. R. (1980). Level I and level II abilities in Asian, white, and black children. *Intelligence, 4,* 41–49.

104. Nisbet, J. (1972). Comments on Arthur Jensen's "Do schools cheat minority children?" *Experimental Research, 14* (2), 87–100.

105. Orn, D. E., & Das, J. P. (1972). IQ, socioeconomic status, and short-term memory. *Journal of Educational Psychology, 63,* 327–333.

106. Schubert, J., & Cropley, A. (1972). Verbal regulation of behavior and IQ in Canadian Indian and white children. *Developmental Psychology, 7,* 295–301.

107. Sigel, I. (1982). The relationship between parental distancing strategies and the child's cognitive behavior. In L. Laosa & I. Sigel (Eds.), *Families as Learning Environments for Children*. New York: Plenum.

108. Skanes, G. R., Sullivan, A. M., Rowe, E. J., & Shannon, E. (1974). Intelligence and transfer: Aptitude by treatment interactions. *Journal of Educational Psychology, 66,* 563–568.

109. Vernon, P. (1972) Comments on Arthur Jensen's 'Do schools cheat minority children. *Experimental Education*, 14 (2), 87–100.

Cultural deprivation theory is discussed in references 110–123.

110. Bacon, M. K., Child, I. L., & Barry, H. (1963). A cross cultural study of correlates of crime. *Journal of Abnormal and Social Psychology*, 66, 291–300.

111. Bandura, A., & Walters, R. H. (1959). *Adolescent Aggression*. New York: Ronald.

112. Bloom, B. S., Davis, A., & Hess, R. (1965). *Compensatory Education for Cultural Deprivation*. New York: Holt, Rinehart & Winston.

113. Bronfenbrenner, U. (1967). *The Psychological Costs to Quality and Equality in Education*. ERIC ED 113 405.

114. Deutsch, C. P. (1964). Auditory discrimination and learning: Social factors. *Merrill-Palmer Quarterly*, 10, 277–296.

115. Deutsch , M. (1960). Minority group and class status as related to social and personality factors in scholastic achievement. *Society for Applied Anthropology*, Monograph No. 2.

116. Hess, R. (1970). Social class and ethnic influences on socialization. In P. Hussen (Ed.), *Manual of Child Psychology* (Vol. 2). New York: Wiley.

117. Hunt, J. (1964). The psychological basis for using pre-school environment as an antidote for cultural deprivation. *Merrill-Palmer Quarterly*, 10, 209–248.

118. Jensen, A. R. (1968). Social class and verbal learning. In M. Deutsch, I. Katz, & A. R. Jensen. (Eds.), *Social Class, Race and Psychological Development*. New York: Holt, Rinehart & Winston.

119. Lewis, O. (1966). The culture of poverty. *Scientific American*, 215, 19–25.

120. McClelland, D. C. (1961). *The Achieving Society*. New York: Van Nostrand.

121. McCloskey, E. F. (1967). *Urban Disadvantaged Pupils: Characteristics, Environments, Potentials*. Portland, OR: Northwest Regional Educational Laboratory.

122. Miller, W. B. (1958). Lower class culture as a generating milieu of gang delinquency. *Journal of Social Issues*, 14 (30), 5–19.

123. Pettigrew, T. F. (1964). *A Profile of the Negro American*. Princeton, NJ: Van Nostrand.

Reference 124 focuses on the implications of the cultural deprivation theory.

124. Banfield, E. (1970). *The Unheavenly City*. Boston: Little, Brown.

References 125–144 contain criticism of the concepts culturally deprived, culturally disadvantaged, and educationally disadvantaged and the procedures used with students with these labels.

125. Adams, M. J. (1986). Teaching thinking to Chapter 1 students. In B. I. Williams, P. A. Richmond, & B. J. Mason (Eds.), *Designs for Compensatory Education: Conference Proceedings and Papers*. ERIC ED 293 913.

126. Bender, P. S., & Ruiz, R. A. (1974). Race and class as differential determiners of underachievement and underaspiration among Mexican-Americans and Anglos. *Journal of Educational Research*, 68 (2), 51–55.

127. Bowles, S., & Gintis, H. (1976). *Schooling in Capitalist America: Educational Reform and the Contradictions of Economic Life*. New York: Basic Books.

128. Calfee, R. (1986). Curriculum and instruction: Reading. In B. I. Williams, P. A. Richmond, & B. J. Mason (Eds.), *Designs for Compensatory Education: Conference Proceedings and Papers*. ERIC ED 293 912.

129. Clark, K. B., Deutsch, M., Gartner, A., Keppel, G., Lewis, H., Pettigrew, T., Plotkin, L., & Reissman, F. (1972). *The Educationally Deprived: The Potential for Change*. New York: Metropolitan Applied Research Center.

130. Cummings, S. (1977). Explaining poor academic performance among black children. *Educational Forum*, 41 (3), 335–346.

131. Datcher-Loury, L. (1989). Family background and school achievement among low income blacks. *Journal of Human Resources*, 24 (3), 528–544.

132. Dolye, W. (1986). Vision and reality: A reaction to issues in curriculum and instruction for compensatory education. In B. I. Williams, P. A. Richmond, & B. J. Mason (Eds.), *Designs for Compensatory Education: Conference Proceedings and Papers*. ERIC ED 293 918.

133. Goodman, Y. T. (1969). The culturally deprived child: A study in stereotyping. *Integrated Education*, 7 (4), 58–63.

134. Grossman, H. (1984). *Educating Hispanic Students: Cultural Implications for Instruction, Classroom Management, Counseling and Assessment.* Springfield, IL: Thomas.

135. Gurin, P., & Epps, E. (1975). *Black Consciousness, Identity and Achievement.* New York: Wiley & Sons.

136. Irvine, J. J. (1991). *Black Students and School Failure: Policies, Practices, and Prescriptions.* New York: Praeger.

137. Irvine, R. W. (1978). The black family and community: Some problems in the development of achievement values. *Negro Educational Review, 29* (3–4), 249–254.

138. Katz, I. (1969). A critique of personality approaches to negro performance, with research suggestions. *Journal of Social Issues, 25* (3), 13–27.

139. Levin, H. M. (1987). *New Schools for the Disadvantaged.* Unpublished manuscript, Stanford University, Stanford, CA.

140. Passow, A. H. (1990). *Enriching Compensatory Education Curriculum for Disadvantaged Students.* New York: ERIC Clearinghouse on Urban Education, Teachers College, Columbia University.

141. Sowell, T. (1976). Patterns of black excellence. *The Public Interest, 43,* 26–58.

142. Staples, R. (1976). *Introduction to Black Sociology.* New York: McGraw-Hill.

143. Sullivan, A. R. (1972). The influence of social processes on the learning abilities of Afro-American School Children: Some educational implications. *Journal of Negro Education, 41* (2) 127–136.

144. Tulkin, S. (1972). An analysis of the concept of cultural deprivation. *Developmental Psychology, 6,* 326–339.

The relative influences of cultural, linguistic, and socioeconomic-class factors on school achievement are discussed in references 145–150.

145. Laosa, L. M. (1982). School, occupation, culture, and family: The impact of parental schooling on the parent-child relationship *Journal of Educational Psychology, 74* (6), 791–827.

146. Laosa, L. M. (1984). Ethnic, socioeconomic, and home language influences upon early performance on measures of abilities. *Journal of Educational Psychology, 76* (6), 1178–1198.

147. Macias, R. F. (1979). *Mexicano/Chicano Sociolinguistic Behavior and Language Policy in the United States.* Unpublished doctoral dissertation, Georgetown University.

148. Rosenthal, A. S., Milne, A., Ginsburg, A., & Baker, K. A. (1981). *A Comparison of the Effects of Language Background and Socioeconomic Status on Achievement Status among Elementary School Students.* Draft final report, subcontract #b43601 from System Development Corporation under contract # 300-75-0332. Washington, DC: U.S. Department of Education.

149. So, A. Y., & Chan, K. S. (1982). *What Matters? The Relative Impact of Language Background and Socioeconomic Status on Reading Achievement.* Los Alamitos, CA: National Center for Bilingual Research.

150. Valencia, R. R., Henderson, R. W., & Rankin, R. J. (1981). Relationship of family constellation and schooling to intellectual performance of Mexican American children. *Journal of Educational Psychology, 73* (4), 524–532.

References 151–152 deal with the low validity of ethnic and socioeconomic-class profiles in identifying students who do not fit their ethnic and socioeconomic-class stereotypes.

151. Stodolosky, S. S., & Lesser, G. (1967). Learning patterns in the disadvantaged. *Harvard Educational Review, 37,* 546–593.

152. Trotman, F. K. (1977). Race, IQ, and the middle class. *Journal of Educational Psychology, 69* (3), 266–273.

References 153–181 deal with ethnic and socioeconomic differences in cognitive verbal skills.

153. Adams, J. L., & Ramey, C. T. (1980). Structural aspects of maternal speech to infants reared in poverty. *Child Development, 51,* 1280–1284.

154. Bee, H., Van Egeren, L., Striessguth, P. A., Nyman, B. A., & Leckie, M. S. (1969). Social class differences in maternal teaching strategies and speech patterns. *Developmental Psychology, 1* (6), 726–734.

155. Bernstein, B. (1961). Social class and linguistic development. In A. Halsey, J. Floud, & C. Anderson (Eds.), *Education, Economy and Society.* Glencoe, IL: Free Press.

156. Borduin, C. M., Henggeler, S. W., Sanders-Walls, M. , & Harbin, F. (1986). An evaluation of social class differences in verbal and nonverbal maternal controls, maternal sensitivity and child compliance. *Child Study Journal, 16* (2), 95–112.

157. Brice-Heath, S. (1982). Questioning at home and at school: A comparative study. In G. Spindler (Ed.), *Doing Ethnography: Educational Anthropology in Action.* New York: Holt, Rinehart & Winston.

158. Collins, J. (1988). Language and class in minority education. *Anthropology and Education Quarterly, 19* (4), 299–326

159. Farron, D. C., & Ramey, C. T. (1980). Social class differences in dyadic involvement during infancy. *Child Development, 51,* 254–257.

160. Ford, C. E. (1984). The influence of speech variety on teachers' evaluation of students with comparable academic ability. *TESOL Quarterly, 18* (1), 25–40.

161. Gibson, E., & Levin, H. (1975). *The Psychology of Reading.* Cambridge, MA: MIT Press.

162. Hall, W., & Dore, J. (1980). *Lexical Sharing in Mother-Child Interaction.* Technical Report No. 161. Urbana: University of Illinois, Center for the Study of Reading.

163. Hall, W., & Tire, W. (1979). *The Communicative Environment of Young Children: Social Class, Ethnic, and Situational Differences.* Technical Report No. 125. Champaign, IL: University of Illinois at Urbana-Champaign, Center for the Study of Reading.

164. Henggeler, S. W., & Tavormina, J. B. (1980). Social class and race differences in family interaction: Pathological, normative, of confounding methodological factors? *Journal of Genetic Psychology, 137,* 211–222.

165. Hess, R. D., & Shipman, V. (1968). Maternal influences upon early learning: The cognitive environment of urban preschool children. In R. D. Hess & R. M. Bear (Eds.), *Early Education.* Chicago: Aldine.

166. Hill, E. H., & Giammatto, M. C. (1963). Social economic status and its relationship to school achievement in elementary school. *Elementary English, 40,* 465–470.

167. Howard, M. J., Jr., Hoops, H. R., & McKinnon, A. J. (1970). Language abilities of children with different socioeconomic backgrounds. *Journal of Learning Disabilities, 3* (6), 328–335.

168. Labov, W. (1972). Academic ignorance and black intelligence. *Atlantic Monthly, 229,* 59–67.

169. Laosa, L. M. (1979). Inequality in the classroom: Observational research on teacher-student interactions. *Aztlan, 8,* 51–66.

170. Loban, W. D. (1963). *The Language of Elementary School Children.* Research Report No. 1. Champaign, IL: National Council of Teachers of English.

171. Piestrup, A. (1973). *Black Dialect Interference and the Accommodation of Reading Instruction in First Grade.* Monograph No. 4. Berkeley, CA: University of California-Berkeley, Language-Behavior Research Laboratory.

172. Rogoff, B., & Gardner, W. (1984). Adult guidance of everyday cognition. In B. Rogoff & J. Lave (Eds.), *Everyday Cognition: Its Development in Social Context.* Cambridge, MA: Harvard University Press.

173. Scheinfeld, D. R. (1983). Family relationships and school achievement among boys of lower-income urban black families. *American Journal of Orthopsychiatry, 53* (1), 127–143.

174. Scott-Jones, D. (1984). Family influences on cognitive development and school achievement. *Review of Research in Education, 11,* 259–304.

175. Simon, H. (n.d.). *Black Dialect Interference and Classroom Interaction.* Unpublished manuscript, University of California-Berkeley, School of Education.

176. Slaughter, D. T., & Epps, W. G. (1987). The home environment and academic achievement of black American children and youth: An overview. *Journal of Negro Education, 56* (1), 3–20.

177. Solomon, D., Hirsch, J. G., Scheinfeld, D. R., & Jackson, J. C. (1972). Family characteristics and elementary school achievement in an urban ghetto. *Journal of Consulting and Clinical Psychology, 39* (3), 462–466.

178. Sroufe, L. A. (1970). A methodological and philosophical critique of intervention-oriented research. *Developmental Psychology, 2,* 140–145.

179. Taylor, J. B. (1983). Influence of speech variety on teachers' evaluation of reading comprehension. *Journal of Educational Psychology, 75* (5), 662–667.

180. Templin, M. C. (1957). *Certain Language Skills in Children: Their Development and Interrelationships*. Minneapolis: University of Minnesota Press.

181. Wilson, K. R., & Allen, W. R. (1987). Explaining the educational attainment of young black adults: Critical familial and extra-familial influences. *Journal of Negro Education, 56* (1), 64–76.

Research on ethnic and socioeconomic-class differences in auditory discrimination is found in references 182–192.

182. Baratz, J. A. (1969). A bidialectic task for determining language proficiency in economically disadvantaged Negro Children. *Child Development, 40,* 889–901.

183. Bartel, N. R., Grill, J. J., & Bryen, D. N. (1973). Language characteristics of black children: Implications for assessment. *Journal of School Psychology, 11* (4), 351–364.

184. Bryen, D. N. (1976). Speech-sound discrimination ability on linguistically unbiased tests. *Exceptional Children, 42* (4), 95–201.

185. Clark, A. D., & Richards, C. J. (1964). Auditory discrimination among economically disadvantaged and nondisadvantaged preschool children. *Exceptional Children, 33,* 259–262.

186. Evans, J. S. (1974). Word-pair discrimination and imitation abilities of preschool Spanish-speaking children. *Journal of Learning Disabilities, 7* (9), 49–56.

187. Fowles, B. R., & Kimple, J. A. (1972). Language tests and the "disadvantaged" reader. *Reading World, 11* (3), 183–195.

188. Karger, G. (1970). *The Effect of Black English on the Performance of Lower Class Black Children on the Wepman Auditory Discrimination Test*. Unpublished manuscript, School of Education, Harvard University, Cambridge, MA.

189. Mathewson, G. C., & Pereyra-Suarez. D. M. (1975). Spanish language interference with acoustic-phonetic skills and reading. *Journal of Reading Behavior, 7* (2), 187–196.

190. Oakland, T. D. (1969). Auditory discrimination and socioeconomic status as correlates of reading ability. *Journal of Learning Disabilities, 2,* 32–39.

191. Ralph, J. B. (1965). Language development in socially disadvantaged children. *Review of Educational Research, 35,* 389–400.

192. Ross, H. W. (1979). Wepman Test of Auditory Discrimination: What does it discriminate? *Journal of School Psychology, 17* (1), 47–54.

The relationship between ethnic and socioeconomic-class background and self-concept is the focus of references 193–218.

193. Arnez, N. (1972). Enhancing the black self-concept through literature. In J. Banks (Ed.), *Black Self-Concept: Implications for Education and Social Science*. New York: McGraw-Hill.

194. Banks, J. A. , & Grambs, D. (Eds.). (1972). *Black Self-Concept: Implications for Education and Social Sciences*. New York: McGraw-Hill.

195. Baughman, E. E. (1971). *Black Americans: A Psychological Analysis*. New York: Academic Press.

196. Braroe, N. W. (1975). *Indian and White: Self Image and Interaction in a Canadian Plains Community*. Stanford, CA: Stanford University Press.

197. Carter, T. P. (1968). Negative self-concept of Mexican-American students. *School and Society, 96,* 217–219.

198. Coopersmith, S. (1967). *The Antecedents of Self-Esteem*. San Francisco: Freeman.

199. Deutsch, M. (1960). *Minority Group and Class Status as Related to Social and Personality Factors in Scholastic Achievement*. Society for Applied Anthropology, Monograph 2. Ithaca, NY: Cornell University Press.

200. Douglas, L. A. (1970). Comparative analysis of the relationships between self-esteem and certain selected variables among youth from diverse racial groups. *Dissertation Abstracts, 31* (2A), 641–641.

201. Evans, F. B., & Anderson, J. G. (1973). The psychocultural origins of achievement and achievement motivation: The Mexican-American family. *Sociology of Education, 46,* 396–416.

202. Healy, G. W., & DeBlassie, R. R. (1974). A comparison of Negro, Anglo, and Spanish American adolescents' self concepts. *Adolescence, 33,* 15–24.

203. Heaps, R. A., & Morrill, S. G. (1979). Comparing the self-concepts of Navajo and white high school students. *Journal of American Indian Education, 18* (3), 12–14.

204. Hishiki, P. (1969). The self-concepts of sixth grade girls of Mexican-American descent. *California Journal of Educational Research, 20,* 56–62.

205. Ladner, J. (1973). The urban poor. In R. P. Rothman & W. Wilson (Eds.), *Through Different Eyes: Black and White Perspectives on American Race Relations*. New York: Oxford University Press.

206. Larned, D. T., & Muller, D. (1979). Development of self-concept in Mexican American and Anglo students. *Hispanic Journal of Behavioral Sciences, 1* (2), 179–185.

207. Luftig, R. L. (1982), *The Effects of Schooling on the Self-Concept of Native American Students.* ERIC ED 220 227.

208. McDaniel, E. L. (1967). *Relationship between Self-Concept and Specific Variables in a Low-Income Culturally Different Population.* ERIC ED 019 124.

209. Muller, D., & Leonetti, R. (1974). Self-concepts of primary level Chicano and Anglo students. *California Journal of Educational Research, 25,* 57–60.

210. Parry, R. (1982). Poor self-concept and differential academic achievement: An inadequate explanation of school performance of black and Native American children. *Canadian Journal of Native Education, 10* (1), 11–24.

211. Patton, S. M., Walberg, H. J., & Yeh, E. G. (1973). Ethnicity, environmental control, and academic self-concept in Chicago. *American Educational Research Journal, 10,* 85–91.

212. Poussaint, A. R. (1974 August). Building a strong self-image in the black child. *Ebony,* pp. 136–143.

213. Schwartz, A. J. (1969). *Comparative Values and Achievement of Mexican-American and Anglo Pupils.* Los Angeles: Center for the Study of Evaluation, University of California, Los Angeles. Occasional Report No. 37.

214. Trowbridge, N. T. (1973). Self-concept and socioeconomic status in elementary-school children. *American Educational Research Journal, 9,* 525–537.

215. Wells, E. E. (1978). *The Mythical Negative Black Self Concept.* San Francisco: R & E Research Associates.

216. Ziller, R. C., Hagey, J., Smith, M. D. C., & Long, B. H. (1969). Self-esteem: A self-social construct. *Journal of Consulting and Clinical Psychology, 33* (1), 84–95.

217. Zirkel, P. A. (1973). Self-concept and the "disadvantage" of ethnic group membership and mixture. *Review of Educational Research, 41,* 211–225.

218. Zirkel, P. A., & Moses, E. G. (1971). Self-concept and ethnic group membership among public school students. *American Educational Research Journal, 8,* 253–265.

Research that deals with students' level of aspiration is discussed in references 219–222.

219. Bales, K. B. (1979). The single parent family aspirations and academic achievement. *Southern Journal of Educational Research, 13* (4), 145-160.

220. Castenell, L. A. (1983). Achievement motivation: An investigation of adolescents' achievement patterns. *American Educational Research Journal, 20* (4), 503–510.

221. DeBord, L. W., Griffin, L. J., Clark, M. (1977). Race and sex influences in the schooling processes of rural and small town youth. *Sociology of Education, 42,* 85–102.

222. George, V. D. (1981). Occupational aspirations of talented black and white adolescent females. *Journal of Non-White Concerns in Personnel and Guidance, 9* (4), 137–145.

References 223–225 found that middle-class parents have higher aspirations for their children and expect and encourage them to attain more education.

223. Baker, D. P., & Entwisle, D. R. (1987). The influence of mothers on the academic expectations of young children: A longitudinal study of how gender differences arise. *Social Forces, 65* (3), 670–694.

224. Brooks, J. S., Whiteman, M., Lukoff, I. F., & Gordon, A. S. (1979). Maternal and adolescent expectations and aspirations as related to sex, ethnicity, and socioeconomic status. *Journal of Genetic Psychology, 135,* 209–216.

225. Lareau, A. (1987). Social class differences in family school relationships: The importance of cultural capital. *Sociology of Education, 60,* 73–85.

References 226–228 found that poor and African American parents have as high, if not higher, aspirations for their children.

226. Goodwin, L. (1976). A critical comment on success-value research. *American Journal of Sociology, 81,* 1151–1155.

227. Kandel, D. B. (1971). Race, maternal authority, and adolescent aspiration. *American Journal of Sociology, 76* (6) 999–1020.

228. Rodman, H., & Voydanoff, P. (1978). Social class and parents' range of aspirations for their children. *Social Problems, 25,* 333–344.

Students' locus of control is the focus of references 229–234.

229. Brown, D., Fulkerson, K. F., Furr, S., & Ware, W. B. (1984). Locus of control, sex role orientation, and self-concept in black and white third-and sixth-grade male and female leaders in a rural community. *Developmental Psychology, 20* (4), 717–721.

230. Cummings, S. (1977). Family socialization and fatalism among black adolescents. *Journal of Negro Education, 46* (1), 62–75.

231. Epps, E. G. (1969) Negro academic motivation and performance: An overview. *Journal of Social Issues, 25* (3), 5–11.

232. Gurin, P., Gurin, G., Lao, R. C., & Beattie, M. (1969). Internal-external control in the motivational dynamics of negro youth. *Journal of Social Issues, 25* (3), 29–53.

233. Knight, G. P., Kagan, S., Nelson, W., & Gumbiner, J. (1978). Acculturation of second-and third-generation Mexican American children: Field independence, locus of control, self esteem, and school achievement. *Journal of Cross-Cultural Psychology, 9* (1), 87–97.

234. Willig, A. C., Harnisch, D. L., Hill, K. T., & Maehr, M. L. (1983). Sociocultural and educational correlates of success-failure attributions and evaluation anxiety in the school setting for black, Hispanic and anglo children. *American Educational Research Journal, 20* (3), 385–410.

References 235–255 discuss the effects of father absence on students' cognitive development and school achievement.

235. Collins, M. A. (1970). Achievement, intelligence, personality, and selected school-related variables in Negro children from intact and broken families attending parochial schools in central Harlem. *Dissertation Abstracts International, 30,* 5280A–5281A.

236. Fowler, P. C., & Richards, H. C. (1978). Father absence, educational preparedness, and academic achievement: A test of the confluence model. *Journal of Educational Psychology, 70* (4), 595–601.

237. Havinghurst, R. J., & Neugarten, B. L. (1967). *Society and Education.* Boston: Allyn and Bacon.

238. Hill, R. (1972). *Strengths of Black Families.* New York: National Urban League.

239. Hoffman, M. L. 1971). Father absence and conscience development. *Developmental Psychology, 4* (3), 400–406.

240. Jaffe, B. D. (1966). The relationship between two aspects of socioeconomic disadvantage and the school success of 8th grade Negro students in a Detroit junior high school. *Dissertation Abstracts, 27,* 1546A.

241. Kukuk, C. R., Levine, D. U., & Meyer, J. K. (1978). Neighborhood predictors of reading achievement in six big city school districts: A path analysis. *Multiple Linear Regression Viewpoints, 8* (3), 27–43.

242. LeCorgne, L. L., & Laosa, L. M. (1976). Father absence in low-income Mexican-American families: Children's social adjustment and conceptual differentiation of sex role attributes. *Developmental Psychology, 12* (5), 470–471.

243. Lessing, E. E., Zagorin, S. W., & Nelson, D. (1973). WISC subtest and IQ score correlates of father absence. *Journal of Genetic Psychology, 117,* 181–195.

244. Liebow, E. (1967). *Tally's Corner.* Boston: Little, Brown.

245. McAdoo, H. (1977). Family therapy in the black community. *American Journal of Orthopsychiatry, 47* (1), 75–79.

246. Peterson, R. A., DeBord, L., Peterson, C. L., & Livingston, S. K. (1966). *Educational Supportiveness of the Home and Academic Performance of Disadvantaged Boys.* Nashville: Institute on Mental Retardation and Academic Development, George Peabody College for Teachers.

247. Prom-Jackson, S., Johnson, S. T., & Wallace, M. G. (1987). Home environment, talented minority youth and school achievement. *Journal of Negro Education, 56* (1), 111–121.

248. Scanzoni, J. (1971). *The Black Family in Modern Society: Patterns of Stability and Security.* Chicago: University of Chicago Press.

249. Sciara, F. J. (1975). Effects of father absence on the educational achievement of urban black children. *Child Study Journal, 5,* 45–55.

250. Scott-Jones, D. (1984). Family influences on cognitive development and school achievement. *Review of Research in Education, 11,* 254–304.

251. Solomon, B. (1976). *Black Empowerment.* New York: Columbia University Press.

252. Stack, C. (1975). *All Our Kin: Strategies for Survival in a Black Community.* New York: Harper & Row.

253. Svanum, S., Bringle, R., & McLaughlin, J. E. (1982). Father absence and cognitive performance in a large sample of six-to-eleven-year-old children. *Child Development, 83,* 136–143.

254. Williams, M. (1974). *Community in a Black Pentecostal Church.* Pittsburgh: University of Pittsburg Press.

255. Willie, C. (Ed.). (1976). *The Family of Black People.* Columbus, OH: Merrill.

Reference 256 discusses ethnic differences in poverty rates.

256. Baumeister, A. A., Kupstas, F., & Klindworth, L. M. (1990) New morbidity: Implications for prevention of children's disabilities. *Exceptionality, 1,* 1–16.

3

ETHNIC AND
SOCIOECONOMIC-CLASS DISPARITIES:
EXTRINSIC CAUSES

*When I began my "educational career" I spoke almost no English. By
the time I was able to understand my teachers I must have been two
years behind grade level. Although my parents were uneducated they
preached the value of education. They expected me to complete high
school and hoped that I would go on to college. My teachers did not.
Looking back at those years in retrospect I now can see that they treated
me as if I were incapable of learning. It did not make a difference that
well over half of us were Mexican-American—you would not have
thought so to look at the curriculum. They never mentioned our foods,
our holidays, our culture, or our contributions. It was always the
Anglo culture. It was always hurry up and become Americanized
which was idiotic since we were Americans. At the time I realized none
of this. I had introjected their image of me as a loser. By the time I was
12, I was a psychological dropout. When I turned seventeen I made it
official. It was not until the second year of my tour of duty in the Army
that I became aware that I had the potential to learn. I returned to
school, graduated and went on to college and graduate school determined to prevent as many Mexican-American students as possible from
suffering the same fate that I almost suffered. (50, pp. 5–6)*

The previous chapter dealt with the ideas of those who attribute some non-European American and poor students' lack of success in school and misrepresentation in special education programs to the students themselves. Actually, the research described in this and subsequent chapters indicates that many of the
causes of their problems in school and overrepresentation in some school districts' programs for students with emotional problems, behavior disorders, and
developmental disabilities lie outside of the students. This chapter describes how,
with the exception of some excellent bilingual and multicultural education programs, the U.S. educational system provides these students with contextually and
culturally inappropriate instruction, classroom management, counseling, and assessment services that do not suit their educational and psychological needs.

Many teachers, psychologists, and administrators are prejudiced against non-
European American and poor students. School officials often have attempted to
maintain segregated educational settings by assigning non-European American
and poor students to low-ability tracks and groups, and misplacing them in special education programs. When these students realize that schools as well as society in general are structured in ways that reproduce ethnic and socioeconomic-

class inequality, many of them become alienated and angry. They resist the prejudice and hostility they experience by refusing to do their homework, not attending classes, and dropping out of school. Some well-meaning teachers and administrators misplace ineligible students in special education to help them obtain the individual instruction and increased teacher attention they think these students need.

In some school districts, African American, Hispanic American, and limited English proficient students are overrepresented in programs for students with emotional problems, behavior disorders, and developmental disabilities. Research included in this chapter indicates that some school districts that lack the bilingual special education teachers and psychologists necessary to assess and instruct limited English proficient students with disabilities too often discourage their staff from referring and accepting such students in special education, even when they require placement. Other districts establish similar policies and procedures out of fear that they will be sued for misplacing non-European American students in special education. In some cases, bilingual and monolingual teachers who do not have confidence that the special education programs in their districts will provide limited English proficient and non-European American students the culturally and linguistically appropriate services they require are reluctant to refer these students.

CONTEXTUALLY INAPPROPRIATE EDUCATIONAL APPROACHES

The educational approaches that predominate in most schools are ill suited to the context or conditions of many poor and non-European American students' lives. (See Chapter 5.) For example, immigrant and refugee students are especially unlikely to receive the education services they require, are apt to do poorly in school, and are likely to be misplaced in special education programs (1–7). (See Chapter 5.) Too often, they do not receive the assistance they require to overcome the culture shock they experience upon entering a new and strange environment. As a result, they may react angrily and aggressively toward teachers and systems they do not understand and to which they cannot easily adjust, or they may become sullen, depressed, and withdrawn. These behaviors can lead educators to refer such students to be assessed for the kinds of emotional problems that require special educational services. This is especially true of students who have never attended school because they come from rural areas or internment camps and/or grew up in cultures that have no written languages.

Even when their culture shock passes, these students need more help than they typically receive in learning how to learn in classes taught in foreign languages and unfamiliar teaching styles. This, too, can interfere with their learning and lead them to be inappropriately placed in special education programs for students with learning disabilities or developmental disabilities.

Refugee students who suffer the psychological effects of the war, famine, and persecution they experienced at home or in internment camps are most likely to lack the assistance they need to overcome their problems. Educators who work with refugee and immigrant students need skills in instructing students with special needs and managing the special problems they bring to school. They also need to maintain a high degree of tolerance for behavior that students cannot control while adjusting to their new educational environments.

Like foreign-born students, Native American students who live on reservations live in a region separate from mainstream America where they speak a language other than English. They, too, are ill prepared to adjust to and profit from a curriculum typically offered in mainstream schools that encourage beliefs and values that conflict with their culture and that is often taught in a language they do not understand, by teachers who are unprepared to succeed with them in schools (8, 9). Like immigrant students, they are susceptible to experiencing culture shock, identity conflicts, and feelings of alienation, confusion, and frustration.

Contextual problems make it difficult for poor non-European American migrant students to actualize their potential for learning (10–16). Attending school irregularly, losing considerable time traveling with their families from job to job, and enrolling in numerous schools during the academic year—all contribute to their poor achievement. Lack of a stable home base, inadequate medical care, poverty, and prejudice are examples of other contextual problems that complicate their lives. In addition, while migrant students can be helped by educational programs geared to their needs, school systems that have been designed for students who are permanent members of the community often add to their problems rather than help solve them.

Rural students with disabilities face many contextual problems (17–27). Those from rural families that rely on seasonal activities such as fishing, agriculture, timber, and so on may not be able to attend school during certain times of the year. In addition, it is difficult for school systems to provide services to small numbers of students scattered over vast land areas with major transportation problems.

The contextual problems that confront poor homeless students with disabilities are horrendous (28–45). Many do not have their basic food, clothing, and shelter needs met. They have four times as many health problems and twice as many chronic diseases, but they have less access to medical care and are less able to follow the health regimes prescribed by physicians. They move from place to place and shelter to shelter and attend school erratically. They are more likely to need special education services than students who lead more stable lives. However, the transient nature of their existence makes it difficult, if not impossible, for poor homeless students to comply with school systems' insistence on receiving certain documents or to be available for long periods of time while schools implement their inflexibly slow-moving special education assessment and placement processes.

When one considers the numbers of poor urban, rural, homeless, and migrant students and the large numbers of immigrant and refugee students whose contextual needs are not met by the U.S. educational system, it becomes clear that many students are not receiving an appropriate education. Thus, contextually inappropriate educational approaches contribute significantly to the problems of poor and non-European American students.

CULTURALLY INAPPROPRIATE EDUCATIONAL APPROACHES

An increasing number of individuals have come to believe that schools have not adapted their educational approaches to the cultural needs of their non-European and poor students (46–49). (See Chapter 4.) They tend to claim that schools in the United States, like many other aspects of life, have historically served the needs of the European American middle-class majority. They argue that once the European Americans succeeded in wresting control of the territory that presently comprises the United States from the Native Americans and Mexicans who shared it with them, they installed their approach to life from the Atlantic to the Pacific.

This is not to say that other cultures did not continue to survive. However, they survived in a powerless state. Most Native Americans were confined to their reservations; African Americans were subjected to stringent restrictions—first slavery and then segregation; and the Hispanic Americans who inhabited the lands taken from Mexico were considered to be inferior and treated as second-class citizens. Thus, for many years, the European American way of life, including the educational system that developed to serve the needs of the upper-class and middle-class European Americans who had the power and influence to shape it, reigned supreme with no effective challenges.

Over the years, many events contributed to a change in the status quo. Immigration from Mexico, Puerto Rico, and other Latin American countries, as well as China, Japan, the Philippines, and Eastern Europe increased the numbers of persons who were not prepared for or able to adapt easily to the established educational system. Segregation was ended in most areas of U.S. life, including education. The working class unionized and gained political power. Large numbers of African Americans and Hispanics Americans gained the right to vote. With all of these developments, the demand for educational reform grew louder and louder.

One of these demands was for the modification and elimination of biased programs. Some reformers believed that programs such as Head Start attempted to compensate for unreal deprivations or to change students' socioeconomic class, culturally determined behavior, and learning styles.

> Child rearing practices not in accord with mainstream values have generally been seen . . . as unfortunate personal practices that indicate a lack of information or training. Black families in particular have been labelled "pathological," black mothers deficient, and black children deprived.

Since the problem is seen to rest with individuals, it is assumed that it is individuals who need to change. Millions of dollars have been expended both to provide poor, frequently non-European American, children with educational experiences that their own homes "lack" or to provide poor and minority parents with training that would enable them to raise children "properly." (49, pp. 46–47)

The entire intervention model of Head Start rests on an assumption of linguistic and cognitive deficits which must be remedied if the child is to succeed in school. . . . The theoretical base of the deficit model employed by Head Start programs denies obvious strengths within the Negro community and may inadvertently advocate the annihilation of a cultural system which is barely considered or understood by most social scientists. . . . Education for culturally different children should not attempt to destroy functionally viable processes of the sub-culture. . . . Head Start has failed because its goal is to correct a deficit that simply does not exist. (46, pp. 112, 116, 124, 125)

A second demand was to make education more culturally relevant. Many reformers insisted that school personnel should be sensitized to the importance of educationally relevant ethnic and socioeconomic-class cultural differences and the special challenges and problems poor students have to deal with because of their economic situations. They wanted educators to be trained to take such differences into consideration when planning school programs and selecting instructional, classroom management, counseling, and assessment techniques for non-European American and poor students. They believed such training would help students in the mainstream and correct their misrepresentation in special education.

This belief is still current. It is clearly reflected in the following quotation, which summarizes the results of a national survey of the opinions of special education experts and parents of exceptional students about the state of the educational services for non-European American students with disabilities:

The current educational system has a mainstream cultural bias which adversely affects the education of students from minority backgrounds. This bias is manifested in preconceived expectations about children from diverse cultures that are limiting and inaccurate. In addition, lack of awareness, sensitivity and understanding of diverse cultures by school personnel interfere with the education of students and the development of productive relationships with parents. . . . In general, the current instruction curricula, materials/methods and service delivery models are inadequate for meeting the educational needs of children from minority backgrounds. . . . Existing methods are not adequate to correctly assess/identify students from diverse backgrounds and determine appropriate educational services. Therefore, there is an overrepresentation or underrepresentation of students from minority backgrounds in various educational programs. (47, pp. 5–7)

The opinions of these experts is supported by a great deal of research evidence. This research is discussed in detail in Chapters 4 and 9 through 11. The following two examples illustrate these research findings.

Students from different cultural backgrounds have different *learning* styles. (See Chapter 10.) When educators do not adapt their educational approaches to these differences, mismatches between teachers' culturally influenced teaching styles and students' culturally influenced learning styles occur. This can cause students to do poorly in school and to be referred to and accepted into programs for students with learning disabilities and/or cognitive disabilities.

Students from different cultures also have different *behavioral* styles. (See Chapter 11.) Students who come from different ethnic or socioeconomic backgrounds than their teachers may be viewed as troublesome if they behave in ways that are acceptable in their homes and communities but not in school (50). For example, African American students who are brought up to be more active, emotionally responsive, and assertive than many middle-class European American students are often inappropriately referred to and accepted into special education programs for students with behavior disorders and serious emotional problems. (See Chapter 11.)

PREJUDICE AND DISCRIMINATION IN THE EDUCATIONAL SYSTEM

It has been clear for many years that teachers', psychologists', and school administrators' behavior toward poor and certain non-European students reflects the biases that exist in the larger society. As a result, these students often fall behind in school, misbehave, and are misplaced in special education programs. From the 1960s to the 1980s, research repeatedly documented the prejudice and discrimination that non-European American students experienced in U.S. schools. To a considerable degree, the groups that bore the brunt of this biased approach were those that populated the particular school or school system. For example, Stein reported that in an area with substantial numbers of African American and Puerto Rican American students "at every grade level the curriculum is 'modified' to the teacher's image of what the child can be expected to do—even in kindergarten where Black and Puerto Rican children are taught to hang up their clothes and 'take turns,' while white children are taught 'numbers and letters'" (55, pp. 168–169).

Bennett and Harris cited the following results of their survey of the attitudes of a group of European American teachers to support their conclusion that the European American faculty of the school they studied was rife with prejudice against Black students. "Many of the teachers would not live in a desegregated neighborhood, did not favor mandatory school desegregation, felt the civil rights movement had done more harm than good, and felt that the problems of prejudice were exaggerated. One-third believed that Blacks and whites should not be allowed to intermarry. Furthermore, the majority of the teachers perceived their white students to be superior intellectually, socially, and in other characteristics related to school achievement" (52, pp. 420–421).

Becker described the attitude of teachers toward the Portuguese American students in a Rhode Island community as follows: "Teachers' attitudes and behavior reflected stereotypes of the Portuguese student as intellectually inferior, noneducationally oriented, socially backward. . . . The teachers expressed feelings of alienation from their students. . . . When the teachers' feelings about the Portuguese were examined closely, many revealed patterns of racism, ethnocentrism and cultural superiority. . . . There was definite resistance to cultural diversity" (51, p. 4).

Working-class non-European students often are treated in an even more discriminatory manner than their middle-class peers. For example, in his classical study comparing the way teachers treated African American students from different socioeconomic-class backgrounds, Rist documented how teachers acted out their prejudices against poor students.

> When a teacher bases her expectations of performance on the social status of the student and assumes that the higher the social status, the higher the potential of the child, those children of low social status suffer a stigmatization outside of their own choice or will. Yet there is a greater tragedy than being labeled as a slow learner, and that is being treated as one. The differential amounts of control-oriented behavior, the lack of interaction with the teacher, the ridicule from one's peers, and the caste aspects of being placed in lower reading groups all have implications for the future life style and value of education for the child. . . . Given the treatment of poor children from the beginning of their kindergarten experience, for what class strata are they being prepared other than that of the lower class? It appears that the public school system not only mirrors the configurations of the larger society, but also significantly contributes to maintaining them. Thus the system of public education in reality perpetuates what it is ideologically committed to eradicate—class barriers which result in inequality in the social and economic life of the citizenry. (54, pp. 107–108)

Reviews of the educational system done in the 1990s indicate that prejudice and discrimination are very much alive and well. For example, The National Black Child Development Institute described the educational conditions for African Americans in Selma, Alabama, 20 years after the school system was supposedly desegregated: "Selma schools are desegregated, although African American children largely remain in separate classes due to a racially discriminatory tracking system. Children are tracked into three levels, with level I designated as the college preparatory track. . . . *Ninety-seven percent of African American children were placed in levels II and III, and African American faculty were not assigned to teach at the higher levels.*" One student reported, "In sixth grade I was next to the top of my class. Yet my sixth grade teacher referred me to level III classes" (53, p. 12).

Anecdotal evidence suggests that most educators believe that they are not biased against non-European American and poor students. Many researchers have found little or no prejudice or discrimination among the educators they studied (56–63). However, as the following research indicates, many teachers were and continue to be biased.

Biased Expectations

Although a few studies failed to find significant ethnic and class differences in educators' expectations for their students, most studies have found such bias. Beginning in preschool and continuing through their college careers, educators and education students tend to expect the European American middle-class students in their classes to do better academically than non-European American and poor students. In addition, they expect European American middle-class students to be more intelligent, even when students' achievement test scores, grades, and school histories would predict otherwise. In experiments in which educators were given the exact same information about students except for their ethnic or socioeconomic backgrounds, the educators attributed higher academic and intellectual potential to European American students than to African American students (64, 65, 68, 69, 71, 76, 79) and Hispanic American students (66, 70, 72, 79). The teachers had the same prejudicial expectations for middle-class students in comparison to poor students (65, 73, 75, 76).

All too often, teachers have overly optimistic expectations for Asian Pacific Island American students (67, 74, 77, 78). Dao offered the following observation:

> There is an assumption that Asian Americans, in general, are a model minority. This notion is related to the stereotypic perception that Asian-American families place high priority on education and push their children to succeed in school. . . . Although there have been impressive occupational and educational achievements by Asian-Americans in the past, these achievements should not obscure the changes now occurring in the Asian American population. . . . The growing and changing Asian-American student population includes many children from families with life and educational experiences vastly different from children from established Asian-American families. Among the Mein and Hmong refugees, for example, the unemployment rate is 90%. Recent immigrant or refugee children from these families face the triple burden of simultaneously learning English and the new school curriculum, adjusting to a new culture, and surviving an impoverished environment. (67, p. 594)

Educators also maintain prejudicial behavioral expectations for non-European American students, especially African Americans, whom they expect to be more disruptive and deviant than European Americans. (See Chapter 11.)

Biased Evaluation

Although a few studies have not found teacher bias (57, 61), most studies done in the 1970s and 1980s indicate that teachers tend to evaluate African American, Hispanic American, and poor students' academic performance and behavior in a biased manner (80–85, 88–91). For example, although neither ethnicity nor social class is ever the sole criterion educators use when assigning students to ability groups, teachers often assign non-European American and poor students to lower ability groups than objective data such as test scores would warrant.

Some teachers also evaluate African American students' behavior in a biased manner. When these teachers evaluate the severity or deviancy of students' behavior problems, they judge the exact same transgressions as more severe or deviant when they are committed by African American male students. They evaluate European American females higher than they evaluate African American females in the areas of responsibility, compliance, persistence, performance, ability, and relationships with others. African American students who are seen as fun loving, happy, cooperative, energetic, and ambitious by African American teachers are viewed as talkative, lazy, fun loving, high strung, and frivolous by their European American teachers.

Teachers also tend to allow their judgments about students' work to be influenced by whether students express themselves in Black English (the English dialect many African Americans speak, especially, but not exclusively, those from poor backgrounds), a working-class dialect (a variety of nonstandard dialects spoken by individuals from poor backgrounds), a Spanish accent, or Standard English (the English used in grammar books, textbooks, newspapers, television news programs, and typically by most middle- and upper-class European Americans). In general, teachers incorrectly rate the quality and accuracy of the English of speakers of Standard English higher than non-Standard English. More importantly, even when students' work is identical or of equal quality, these teachers judge the oral and written work of students who speak in a Black English, Spanish, or a working-class accent to be poorer than students who speak Standard English. Also, African American students who speak Black English are rated lower than those who speak more standard English (58, 60, 61, 63, 64, 66, 68, 69).

As noted in Chapters 2 and 9, at one time many educators may not have perceived this as a biased approach to evaluation. In the 1960s and early 1970s, researchers typically used European American middle-class students' scores on tests prepared in Standard English as the norm to which they compared the scores of students who spoke non-Standard English. As a result, they concluded that Black English and working-class English were inferior to Standard English. By the mid-1970s, the results of research studies that did not make that methodological error led most authors to conclude that these varieties of English are actually equally effective and valid forms of communication. Many scholars, especially those from African American backgrounds, encourage schools to incorporate Black English into the curriculum, rather than attempt to eradicate it. "Black children must be educated to learn and believe that deviation from the normative pattern of standard English is not an indication that they are abnormal. . . . Whites should not become reference points for how Black children are to speak and behave. One's family and community and how one measures up to one's peers should provide some of these reference points. Black children's encounters with the white world should be filtered through a Black frame of reference, which includes the use of Black English" (59, p. 215).

Apparently, many teachers still believe that Standard English is superior to other forms of English. That is, instead of correctly viewing Black English and Spanish and working-class dialects and accents as different, they view them as deficient. Also, these teachers continue to allow their beliefs to prejudice their evaluations of students.

There is no reason to assume that the biases found in the preceding studies have disappeared. However, since they were done in the 1970s and mid-1980s, additional research is needed to determine whether the situation has improved significantly in recent years.

Although a few studies have not found any bias (43, 45, 49, 71, 79, 85), most studies indicate that when teachers and school psychologists refer students to special education programs, evaluate them for possible placement in special education programs, or select the most appropriate placement for them, their evaluations of non-European American and poor students are biased (70, 72, 73, 75, 82, 84, 86, 88, 94–108). Teachers are more likely to refer poor and non-European American students for evaluation for possible placement in special education programs for students with disabilities and less likely to refer them to programs for gifted and talented students. When evaluating poor and non-European American students for special education placement, educators judge their work, performance, intellectual potential, and social skills to be lower than objective data would suggest.

When deciding on the most appropriate placement for students with the exact same behavioral and academic problems, regular educators, special educators, and school psychologists are more likely to choose a special education placement program for poor and non-European American students—especially if they are both poor and non-European—and a regular education placement for European American middle-class students. When they choose a special education placement for students, they are likely to recommend a program for students with mild developmental disablities for poor and non-European American students and a program for students with learning disabilities for European American middle-class students. They also are likely to recommend more restrictive, custodial, environments for non-European American students than for European American students (94, 100, 104, 105).

Being poor and African American places students at even greater risk to be on the receiving end of teacher bias. For example, teachers are 3.5 times more likely to identify poor African American students as developmentally disabled than their European American peers (72). Teachers are also more likely to refer poor African American students to programs for students with disabilities and less likely to refer them to programs for the gifted and talented. (See Chapter 9.) "Professionals in education may view cultural differences among Black students as indicators of deficiencies. This perception can lead to a student being identified as being below normal or abnormal on measures of adaptive behavior and social development. Scoring low or scoring as abnormal on these measures can in turn lead to placement in classrooms for emotionally disturbed and educable mentally retarded pupils" 107, p. 21).

There is some evidence that teachers are more likely to perceive students from a different ethnic background than their own as needing special education (91). If this is true, it is just as necessary to modify non-European American teachers' evaluations of European American students as it is to correct European American teachers' evaluations of non-European American students.

There is also evidence that teachers evaluate Asian Pacific American students in a biased manner (86, 92, 93). (See Table 3–1.) There appear to be three reasons for this. First, believing that all of them are good students, some teachers fail to notice these students' academic problems and neglect to refer those with learning disabilities for special education evaluation (93). As Yao stated, "Many school teachers share a myth: that all Asian American youngsters are diligent, respectful,

**TABLE 3–1   Teachers' Perceptions of Asian American
and European American Students**

European Americans	Asian Americans
More extroverted	Less extroverted
Less cheerful	More cheerful
Less emotionally stable	More emotionally stable
Less kind	More kind
Less obedient	More obedient
Less disciplined	More disciplined
Less cooperative	More cooperative
Less patient	More patient
More prone to anger	Less prone to anger
Less academically competent	More academically competent
Less able to concentrate	More able to concentrate
Less organized	More organized
Less persevering	More persevering
Less adequate memory	More adequate memory

Source: 92.

intelligent, good students. But teachers should not be dismayed if they find the opposite is true in their classrooms" (93, p. 82).

Second, Asian American students tend to internalize their emotional problems rather than act them out. Even though they may be experiencing serious emotional problems, their suffering is less obvious and less disruptive than that of students who act out their problems. As a result, they are less likely to be noticed by teachers or to be referred for special education services (86). For example, Kim reported that many troubled Asian Pacific American students "resort to passivity and conformity. . . . Their quietness, inconspicuousness, withdrawal, and non-threatening stance in the classroom tend to make them less noticeable. A teacher might not recognize a certain behavioral manifestation of passivity as a sign of poor adjustment. [In addition] teachers tend to perceive passive Asian American children as being better adjusted to the classroom as compared to passive Caucasian children" (87, pp. 83–84).

Third, because teachers welcome the quiet unobtrusive behavior of many Asian Pacific Americans, they often fail to recognize when this type of behavior may be a sign of problems. Takeuchi pointed out that "the quiet passive behavior of Asian American students should not be unquestionly encouraged. Rather, it often signifies problems in verbalization needing attention" (78, p. 2).

Biased Treatment

In addition to having biased expectations for non-European American and poor students and evaluating them in a discriminatory manner, most, but not all, studies indicate that many teachers treat them unfairly. Some of the discriminatory ways many educators treat African American, Native American, and Hispanic students are discussed next (52, 53, 71, 110–112, 114–117, 119–127).

In comparison to European American students, teachers praise African Americans less and criticize them more. The praise they give them is more likely to be routine, rather than feedback for a particular achievement or behavior. When teachers do praise them for a specific behavior, it is more likely to be qualified ("Your work is almost good enough to be put on the board") or, in the case of females, more likely to be for good behavior than for academic work.

Teachers interact more with European American students than with African Americans, especially males, and give European Americans more attention. In comparison to European American students, educators are less likely to respond to African American male students' questions or to direct questions to them. Unlike the preferential treatment many teachers give their brightest European American students, they give bright African American students, especially females, the least attention and criticize them the most. Although European American teachers typically demonstrate considerable concern and interest in European American females' academic work, they pay less attention to African American female students' academic work than to their social behavior. Teachers encourage European American female students in intellectual and academic areas, whereas they encourage and praise African American females in areas involving social skills. In addition, European American females are more likely to receive trusted duties and special high-prestige assignments; African American female students' duties typically involve social responsibilities.

Educators tend to use different classroom management techniques with African American and European American students. In general, teachers of classes with high percentages of African American students are more likely to be authoritarian and less likely to use an open classroom approach. Teachers spend more time on the lookout for possible misbehavior by African American students, especially males. When male students misbehave, educators are especially prone to criticize the behavior of African American males and to use more severe punishments, including corporal punishment and suspension. When females misbehave, teachers treat African Americans more harshly than they treat European Americans.

Grant described the effect this can have on African American females' perception of the role that is most suitable for them in the following way: "The emphasis on black girls' social rather than academic skills, which occurs particularly in white-teacher classrooms, might point to a hidden cost of desegregation for black girls. . . . While such skills assuredly are helpful in high-status adult roles, the lesser attention to black girls' work might diminish motivation for gaining credentials to enter such positions. Black girls' everyday schooling experiences seem more likely to nudge them toward stereotypical roles of black women than toward alternatives" (71, p. 109).

Teachers relate to Hispanic American students in much the same way that they treat African American students. Although Hispanic American students tend to prefer more positive reinforcement and feedback from their teachers than most European American students (see Chapters 10 and 11), teachers praise them less often and give them less positive feedback when they answer correctly or perform well. Teachers are also less likely to encourage them, to accept their ideas, and to direct questions to them.

Research about the ways in which teachers treat Native Americans is sparse. There is some evidence that teachers and their aides tend to speak to and attend to Native Americans less often than they do to European American students (117). However, this may be partly the result of teachers' failure to recognize the nonverbal ways Native American students ask for help and attention.

Poor students also receive unfair treatment in school (109, 113, 118, 121). Beginning in primary school, teachers give them less attention and fewer rewards. Educators provide poor students, especially males, with fewer social and instructional contacts and with more disciplinary and control contacts. When disciplining students, teachers in schools that serve predominantly poor students are more likely to endorse or use corporal punishments, verbal punishments, or suspension than teachers in middle-class schools.

Apparent and Real Lack of Bias

Bias against non-European American students and poor students is not quite as pervasive as the preceding text suggests. African American teachers tend to be less prejudiced than European American teachers toward African American students (71, 123). Only some European Americans are biased against non-European American students and poor students. There is some evidence that the ratio of non-European American to European American teachers on the staff of a school district has an effect on the discriminatory treatment students receive. For example, in one study, a high percentage of African American teachers in a school district was associated with (1) a decrease in the overrepresentation of African American students in special education programs for students with mild and severe developmental disabilities; (2) a decrease in their overrepresentation among students who were disciplined by corporal punishment, suspension, or expulsion; (3) a decrease in their dropout rates; (4) a decrease in their underrepresentation in programs for gifted and talented students; and (5) an increase in their high school graduation rates (129).

At least in some cases, however, the apparent lack of bias against students who belong to a different ethnic group may not be real (123, 125, 128). Many European American and African American teachers are not aware of their biases against students from ethnic backgrounds different from their own. In order to hide their true feelings and attitudes from themselves, some European American and African American teachers may give students a double message without realizing it. They consciously praise students who belong to a different ethnic group more than they do students who share their ethnic background, but they unknowingly treat them negatively by giving them less nonverbal positive attention, maintaining a greater distance from them, and touching them less often.

European American teachers exhibit more unconscious discrimination than African American teachers do. In addition to negative, nonverbal communication, they also give African American students less positive feedback when they answer questions correctly and fewer helpful hints when they call on them to answer questions. Simpson and Erickson stated, "Naturalistic observational studies in the classroom may show overcompensatory behavior on the part of black and white teachers. However, the nonverbal behaviors may indicate a natural preference or comfortableness with students of one's own race" (123, p. 185).

Implications

Many educators believe that much of the disruptive behavior, inadequate motivation, lack of participation in school, and poor achievement demonstrated by many poor and non-European American students is partially caused by the biased evaluations, expectations, and treatment they receive in school. Thus, these problems will not be solved until teachers correct their biased attitudes, beliefs, and treatment of non-European American and poor students.

These educators also believe that teacher bias contributes to the unnecessary suspension of many African American, Hispanic American, and poor students, as well as their overrepresentation in special education programs for the behavior disordered and emotionally disturbed (53, 130–132). They feel that non-European American and poor students will not receive the kind of regular education or special education services they deserve until educators behave more democratically and serve the needs of the population as a whole. The elimination of teacher prejudice and discrimination is the first and most important step educators can take to ensure that only students who require special education services are referred to and accepted into special education programs and that once accepted, they receive culturally appropriate special education services.

Conclusions

Prejudice and discrimination against non-European American and poor students is still rampant. Not all teachers are biased, however. A few studies have found that ethnic and class differences do not influence the way educators perceive, judge, and relate to students. Those that have uncovered bias did not find that all teachers behaved in a biased manner. In fact, a few studies found that some teachers evaluate and treat opposite-race students better than same-race students. However, when the evidence is considered as a whole, it is clear that teachers' conscious and unconscious prejudice against certain non-European American and poor students influences teachers' relationships with them, expectations for them, evaluation of their work, choices of which instructional and classroom management techniques to use with them, and decisions about whether they would be better served in regular education or special education programs. In turn, these teacher biases affect the students' performance in and attitudes toward school and contribute to their misrepresentation in special education programs.

| SELF-QUIZ | STUDENT RESISTANCE TO PREJUDICE |

- What is your opinion about the following statement? "In a prejudiced society, students' militant behavior in school that is aimed at correcting injustices may be positive and acceptable, even though teachers and others may find it disruptive, be uncomfortable with it, and feel threatened by it."

STRUCTURED REPRODUCTION

As noted at the beginning of this chapter, schools reproduce the inequalities found in society at large. One of the many missions of schools is to perpetuate the values, ideals, and attitudes of the societies they serve. Since U.S. society does not completely live up to the high ideals it espouses, much of what is transmitted from generation to generation is what actually *is* rather than what *should be*. This applies to ethnic and socioeconomic-class issues as well as to many other aspects of life in the United States. Because many of the prevailing societal views and values about ethnicity and socioeconomic class are biased, students are exposed to an educational structure that reproduces the ethnic and socioeconomic-class disparities in outcomes.

Some educators with a neo-Marxist perspective see purpose behind the bias in the schools' structure. They believe it is only one of many biased structures that the European American middle- and upper-class (especially males) have set up throughout society to maintain their economic and social power and position. That is, they believe that those who exercise control and power in U.S. society—middle- and upper-class European American males—structure its institutions, including schools, to maintain their special positions by reproducing the inequality that serves their interests (133–146). Thus, they use schools to maintain an ethnic, class, and gender division of labor.

According to these theorists, schools provide non-European Americans, poor, and female students with the kinds of educational experiences that maintain them as a source of cheap, though well-prepared, labor for their enterprises. On the other hand, more affluent European males are trained to be the leaders of society. At the same time, schools teach poor, non-European American,and female students to accept the status quo—their economic and social inferiority. Giroux described three ways in which schools could be said to reproduce inequality:

> First, schools provided different classes and social groups with knowledge and skills they needed to occupy their respective places in a labor force stratified by class, race, and gender. Second, schools were seen as reproductive in the cultural sense, functioning in part to distribute and legitimate forms of knowledge, value, language, and modes of style that constitute the dominant culture and its interests. Third, schools were viewed as part of a state apparatus that produced and legitimated the economic and ideological imperatives that underlie the state's political power. (138, p. 258)

Grant and Sleeter stated,

School plays a major role in the culture students develop. Like the family and neighborhood, school affects how students understand and pursue their life chances. It provides an institutional ideology, socializing agents, and an experiential context within
which students define and shape the way they think about their personal dreams. The
school context, containing social relations defined by race, social class, and gender, can
produce a student culture in which young people accept and live out their parents'
place in a stratified society, in spite of the school's espoused mission as equalizer and
escalator to a better life. (140, p. 19)

Reproduction theorists criticize the schools for the disparity between the
lower level of funding for schools that serve students from poor and non-European American neighborhoods, the use of tracking and ability grouping to separate European American middle-class students from other students, and the use
of the community college system to prevent working-class and minority students
from enrolling in four-year colleges. They claim that females, especially non-European American and poor females, are exposed to two separate but related
forces in the schools—those designed to maintain middle- and upper-class hegemony over the poor and those designed to maintain male hegemony over females. The following quotation is an example of reproduction theorists' point of
view. Although it focuses on Native American females' educational experiences
in government-run schools, it exemplifies what they think about the education
many non-European women receive. "The government's master plan for Indian
women has been to generate an endless stream of domestics, and to a lesser extent, secretaries. The vocational choices for native children in boarding schools
have always been sexist: boys do woodworking, car repair, house painting or
farmwork; while girls do domestic or secretarial work. . . . When we look at the
occupations of native women in this country today, it should come as no surprise
to find us locked into the nations' female work ghetto employees; it was designed
that way" (145, pp. 47–48).

Resistance, Production, and Transformation

Neo-Marxist reproduction theorists suggest that while students are being exposed to ethnic, socioeconomic-class, and gender biases in school and in society at
large, they are also being exposed to ideas and experiences that contradict these
biases. They note that egalitarian ideas are available in the media and in the materials students read in school. In addition, many teachers do not believe in the current class, ethnic, and gender biases. Thus, bombarded by conflicting messages,
students do not passively accept the biases presented to them. Instead, they are
constantly involved in a process of accommodating to some messages and resisting others (147–169).

According to reproduction theorists, especially those with a neo-Marxist perspective, students are alienated, distrustful, angry, and disillusioned about the
problems inherent in attending schools that are structured to maintain gender in-

equality, but many of them also realize that schools are merely one aspect of a society structured against them. These theorists believe that many students also know that even if they do well in school, a society stratified along ethnic, socio-economic-class, and gender lines will not afford them the same benefits that European American upper-class males receive from succeeding in school. Therefore, instead of acquiescing to the educational system for payoffs they do not believe will be forthcoming, they battle against the system to maintain their own sense of identity.

There are significant ethnic, socioeconomic-class, and gender differences in the way students resolve these contradictions (147, 155, 169). This makes sense when one considers the fact that students from different ethnic, socioeconomic-class, and gender backgrounds have somewhat different options available to them for resolving the contradictory pressures they experience.

Some students accommodate more than they resist; others actively resist the biased education they receive and the inferior position it threatens to place them in. Some defy schools' ethnic, socioeconomic-class, and gender biases in nonconstructive ways. They purposefully misbehave in aggressive or sexual ways, tune out their teachers, refuse to do their homework, come to school late, drop out before graduating, decide not to participate in higher education, and so on (148, 149, 161–163, 165, 169). Other students battle the same forces in constructive ways. They reject the biased ideas to which they are exposed. Instead, they assert their own experiences, heighten their own sense of self-identity, and graduate from school with new understandings of their gender, ethnicity, and class and with the knowledge, skills, values, and self-awareness they require to contribute to transforming society (144, 155, 156, 158). Thus, for some students, schools reproduce the stereotypes prevalent in society, whereas in other cases, schools actually help students to reject these stereotypes.

Some theorists believe that society and schools are not equally biased against all non-European students. They believe that the European American dominant class differentiates between voluntary immigrants and involuntary, subordinated castelike groups such as African Americans, Native Americans, Puerto Rican Americans, and Mexican Americans. According to these theorists' way of thinking, voluntarily immigrants are those who chose to come to the United States; involuntary immigrants are those who were brought here as slaves (e.g., African Americans) or those who were incorporated into the United States against their will by conquest (e.g., Native Americans and Mexican Americans). Voluntary immigrants are likely to be accepted into society as equals once they have assimilated. They also tend to be the preferred non-European Americans because they most resemble the original northern European American settlers of the continent. Involuntary groups, however, are unlikely to be accepted as equals, regardless of what they do, for three reasons: the history of their relationship with the dominant European Americans; the myths European Americans have created about their innate inferiority in order to justify the conquest of their land, the eradication of their culture, and the enslavement of their ancestors; and the fact that they do not resemble European Americans in either looks or behavior.

European Americans are willing to accept voluntary immigrants into their country clubs and into some high-status positions. School personnel are willing to tolerate their cultural differences, at least to some degree. Involuntary castelike groups are not treated as well, socially or vocationally. In school, the cultural differences between them and European Americans are devalued, disliked, and squashed because these groups have been deemed inferior for hundreds of years.

According to these theorists, students from the subordinated groups are less willing to play the educational game according to the rules established by their oppressors. They reject and resist school because of the prejudicial treatment they receive, regardless of how much they accomplish academically. Their point of view has been aptly expressed by Ogbu.

All minority children encounter social adjustment and academic learning problems, at least initially. For some minority groups these tend to diminish over time, so that they eventually learn more or less successfully. For some other minority groups the problems tend to persist and may even increase in magnitude and seriousness. . . . The main factor differentiating the more successful from the less successful minorities appears to be the nature of the history, subordination, and exploitation of the minorities, and the nature of the minorities' own instrumental and expressive responses to their treatment which enter in the process of their schooling.

[These subordinate minorities] develop a new sense of social identity in opposition to the social identity of the dominant group after they have become subordinated and they do so in reaction to the way that dominant-group members treat them in social, political, economic, and psychological domains. [They] do not really believe that they have an equal chance with white Americans to get ahead through education. They tend to reject or attack the criteria by which academic achievement is measured and also the use of educational qualifications or measures as a criterion for employment in some situations.

The relationship between involuntary minorities and white Americans, who control the public schools, characterized by conflict and distrust, contributes to the minorities' social adjustment and academic performance problems. . . . Involuntary minorities do not necessarily accept or interpret school rules of behavior and standard practices in the same way that white people and immigrants do. The latter seem to endorse the rules and standard practices as necessary. . . . Involuntary minorities appear, on the other hand, to interpret the same rules and standard practices as an imposition of the white frame of reference, which does not necessarily meet their educational needs.

[As a result, those involuntary minorities students who are rebelling against the schools] do not work hard, and spend limited time on academic tasks; they avoid taking "hard"/"difficult"/"white" courses; they tend to be satisfied with average grades; although the children may do their homework, they do not routinely study; they do not usually separate academic tasks from their activities; they seem to prefer peer solidarity to schoolwork and easily submit to peer pressures that take them away from their schoolwork; they distrust school authorities with whom they are frequently in conflict; and they have a tendency to resist following school rules and standard practices.* (163, pp. 317, 323, 324, 333, 334)

---

*Reproduced by permission of the American Anthropological Association from *Anthropology & Education Quarterly* 18:4, December 1987. Not for further reproduction.

Like those who believe in the cultural difference explanation, those who share Ogbu's point of view want schools to offer culturally relevant and culturally appropriate educational experiences to minorities. However, they also believe that society as a whole must be reformed in ways that give non-European American students confidence that if they succeed in school, they will reap the benefits of their success.

Implications

Although neo-Marxist reproduction theorists believe that it is important to eliminate class, ethnic, and gender inequities in the schools, their ultimate goal is to transform the very nature of the public schools. Neo-Marxists want teachers to prepare students to resist the reproductive forces of society in more constructive ways and, above all, to change both the schools and the social and economic structure of the society they serve instead of preparing students to fit into the capitalist status quo (144, 170, 171). "The ultimate purpose of radical pedagogy is not simply one of changing people's consciousness or restructuring schools along more democratic principles; the latter aims are important but are reformist in nature and incomplete when viewed within a radical problematic. At the core of any radical pedagogy must be the aim of empowering people to recognize and work for a change in the social, political, and economic structure that constitutes the ultimate source of class-based power and domination" (137, p. 427).

Criticisms

Many educators are critical of the major assumptions underlying the theory of structured reproduction. Some critics question whether schools are actually structured in ways that reproduce the inequalities found in society at large. Many more believe that even if schools do help to reproduce inequality, there is no evidence that this is part of a purposeful plan by those in power to maintain the status quo. Also, many educators do not agree with the distinction between voluntary immigrants and castelike groups. For example, Treuba challenged the claim that Mexican Americans are a castelike group:

> Ogbu has described castelike groups, and Mexican Americans in particular, as being composed of individuals who live involuntarily in this country, occupy menial positions, and remain at the bottom of the educational and economic ladder, failing to incorporate into mainstream American society. . . . In the case of Mexicans, classified by Ogbu as an exemplary castelike group, we have obtained recent empirical evidence from studies showing that there is educational progress, an increase in English language proficiency, and upward mobility taking place among the Mexican families in California and Arizona, and that the improvement is incremental across generations over a period of time. (172, pp. 276–277).

Treuba went on to explain that the apparent lack of progress of many Mexican Americans in states such as California is not due to their castelike condition but to the large numbers of recent immigrants who have not had time to be incorporated into the U.S. educational, economic, and social systems.

> The overwhelming majority of people who recognize themselves as Mexicans (85%) are either foreign born or first generation U.S. born. . . . High dropout rates are much more characteristic of the Mexican born, who constitute a large proportion of the current Latino population in the state. Dropout rates among the U.S. born Latinos are not much higher than those of all Californians. Comparing the occupational profiles of Mexican born with those of U.S. born, and both with that of all Californians, we find the following distribution: Highly skilled jobs, professional, teacher, manager, technician, sales clerk, account for 5% of Mexican born, 12% of U.S. born Mexican origin, and 27% of all Californians. Service jobs account for 14%, 33%, and 34% respectively. Semiskilled jobs represent respectively 21%, 20%, and 19%. Farm jobs, 15%, 6%, and 3%. Unskilled, 45%, 29%, and 17%. (172, p. 277)

Research

There is a great deal of evidence to support the contention that the structure of U.S. schools contributes to the reproduction of ethnic and socioeconomic-class inequality. Examples of the relevant research are presented here.

Financing

Local and state governments spend less money on educating poor and non-European American students and provide them with less adequate instructional materials and equipment, especially in the areas of computer technology and science (173–185). Per-pupil expenditures for schools serving students in poor and non-European communities are considerably below those for European American middle-class students. For example, in Kentucky, the per-pupil costs ranged from a low of $1,800 to a high of $4,200. In Texas, the per capita expenditure on education in the 100 poorest school districts was less than $3,000, compared to the more than $7,000 spent on pupils attending the 100 richest school districts. In New Jersey, the gap between the amount of money spent per pupil by the richest and poorest districts was over $10,000 (180). The per-pupil expenditure for students in New York City (with a predominantly European American poor student population) was $4,351, compared to $6,605, $6,539, and $5,852 in the three surrounding suburban counties (183).

The results of these disparities are reflected in the availability of equipment and materials, especially computers and science laboratory equipment; the availability of academic and nonacademic course offerings; the quality of the educational staff; and so on. Karp described the effects of the disparities in spending for education in the following way:

> These numbers translate into daily injustices for school kids. Princeton's high school science students study in seven modern, well-equipped labs and student athletes can play golf, field hockey and lacrosse in addition to baseball, basketball and football. In Jersey City, middle-school science students have no labs at all while in East Orange, NJ, the track team practices in a second floor corridor. In rural Kentucky, elementary schools have done without music and art teachers. In one poor Texas district students

study computer science by pretending to type on an artificial paper replica of a computer keyboard. (180, pp. 1, 14)

Even programs specifically designed to serve poor students are underfinanced. At the height of their financial support in 1980, compensatory educational programs served only 57 percent of the 9,000,000 eligible students. Since then, the program has experienced repeated cutbacks. Even Head Start reaches only 18 percent of eligible students (174).

Tracking and Ability Grouping

As stated earlier, research confirms that poor and non-European American students are much more likely to be placed in low-track and low-ability groups than European American middle-class students. Tracking and ability grouping has been justified on a number of grounds; for example, "that students learn better when they are grouped with other students who are similar to them academically; that the placement process used to sort students into groups is accurate and fair and, in addition, reflects past achievements and innate abilities; that slower students develop more positive attitudes in relation to themselves and their schools if they are not sorted into groups with students who are more capable; that it is easier for teachers to accommodate individual differences in homogeneous groups; that similar students are easier to manage" (187, p. 94). However, research on these approaches indicates that they typically do more harm than good (184, 186–197).

Students placed in low-ability groups do not learn better. After reviewing the research, Lake concluded, "Once in a low track, students rarely switch tracks after grade three. Schools do not help them to move into a higher track. By the end of the primary grades students are set into rigid ability tracks correlating to their race and socioeconomic status. The effects last even longer than the school years" (191, p. abstract).

In a similar vein, Oakes reported the following:

> The typical ways elementary schools respond to students' performance may help to "fix" students' perceptions of their ability to learn and, over time, may actually exaggerate initial differences among them. . . . At the high school level, whether a student is enrolled in an academic (college-preparatory) or non-academic program has an independent effect on achievement. Students who are initially similar in background and aptitude exhibit increased achievement differences resulting from their placements in higher and lower tracks. . . . Students placed in low-ability groups in elementary school are likely to continue in these tracks in middle schools and junior highs; in senior high they typically are found in non-college-preparatory tracks.
>
> In the data about curriculum paths, course offerings, and track-related classroom differences, we find that the differentiated structure of schools often throws up barriers to achievement and participation of poor and minority students. Measures of ability work against them, which leads to minimal course offerings at their schools and these students' disproportionate placement in groups identified as "slow." Once in these classes, their success seems to be further inhibited by the type of knowledge they are taught and by the quality of the learning experiences that are afforded. (194, pp. 115–116, 118–119)

Students in low tracks and ability groups do not improve their self-esteem. On the contrary, they experience a loss of self-esteem and a worsening of their attitudes toward school.

Many poor and non-European American students do not receive the instructional approaches and attention they require. In fact, research clearly demonstrates the opposite. Schools spend less money on students in low-ability groups. They are counseled less often. Students are exposed to a watered-down curriculum and treated poorly by their teachers. They are called on less often, criticized more often, praised less frequently, given less help and feedback, counseled less often, and so on.

Management problems are typically increased rather than diminished by grouping students into low-ability groups and tracks because students tend to be more disruptive and teachers tend to interrupt the academic work more often to deal with discipline problems. After studying the effects of ability grouping, Eder concluded, "Students in low groups were instructed in an environment characterized by disruptions from the teacher as well as from other members. In other words, those students who were likely to have more difficulty learning were inadvertently assigned to groups whose social contexts were much less conducive for learning" (188, p. 159).

Finally, students are not placed in ability groups in an accurate and fair manner. As noted earlier, non-European American and poor students are often assigned to low-ability groups in a biased manner when objective evaluation of their academic functioning would not justify their placement. Also, in some cases, ability grouping is used to resegregate students not to enhance their learning.

Community colleges serve to track students rather than to provide them with the the opportunity to achieve their potential (198–202). Research reveals that non-European and poor students are grossly overrepresented in the two-year college system. Many of the programs in which they enroll do not lead to viable occupations. The majority of students drop out before completing their programs. Of those who graduate, few go on to earn degrees at four-year colleges. As a result, the community/two-year college system serves to segregate non-European American students in an educational system that does not typically lead to the completion of a four-year college degree or the attainment of sufficient vocational skills to obtain a high-paying or prestigious job. The following quotations are representative of the conclusions of many of the critics of the community college system:

> The rise of two year systems in some cities raises the unmistakable impression that such systems were established in order to preserve the status quo and to enable senior institutions to remain inaccessible to minority students. (201, pp. xiii–xiv)

> The two year college system in the United States is a system of whites, it is controlled and operated by whites, and reserves its major rewards for whites. (199, p. 42)

> Hispanics have made few appreciable gains in either their participation or achievement in community colleges. The fact remains that few Hispanics earn college credentials, graduate, or transfer to senior institutions. (200, p. 139)

TABLE 3–2   Socioeconomic-Class Differences in School Structure

	Poor Neighborhood	Middle-Class Neighborhood
Campus	fenced in; security guards	open; no security guards
Selection of courses	no choice of courses	students select courses
Dress code	dress code	no dress code
Teacher resources invested in	vocational and general tracks	academic track
Courses emphasized	physical education, home economics, industrial arts, business education, special education	science, math, language arts, fine arts, foreign languages
Program for mentally gifted minors	none available	available
Academic courses	restricted to basic level	many advanced courses offered
Industrial arts courses and apprenticeship programs geared to	blue-collar jobs	white-collar jobs
Graduates advised to attend	two-year colleges	four-year colleges

Source: 181

Table 3–2 shows results of a study that compares two comprehensive high schools that serve students in a poor and in an affluent neighborhood in the same city.

Resistance, Production, and Transformation

Although there has not been a great deal of research on the topic, the available evidence suggests that many non-European and poor students are alienated, distrustful, angry, and disillusioned about the schools they attend and believe that even if they do well in school, they will not obtain the same benefits that European American upper-class males receive from succeeding in school (203–207). Studies indicate that many African American middle school and high school students feel alienated and distrustful about their teachers, the schools they attend, and the American political system (202, 206, 207). Research also suggests that although African American students think that getting a good education is important, many of them do not believe that education necessarily leads to a good job (204, 205). In one study, over 50 percent of the 10- to 15-year-old African American students in their study did not believe that a high school diploma led to a good job (204). Although they did not report specific percentages, the authors of another study observed that many African American male high school students had similar doubts. Those authors speculated, "If African American male youth feel that racism hampers the 'cashing in of their educational check,' it is probably valid to assume that they will not take full advantage of the educational opportunities that their schools have to offer" (205, p. 12).

There is also evidence that Native American and African American high school graduates often do not reap the benefits a high school diploma affords most European American students. For example, a recent study indicated that, with rare exceptions, Native American students who graduated from high school obtained the same "menial or service-industry positions" as dropouts (208).

Conclusions

One may believe that schools *simply reflect* the biases that permeate society—"Education does not create the sexual division of labour, nor the kinds of work available in the labour market, nor the class relationships of society, but it rarely does anything to undermine them" (136, p. 20). Or one may believe that European American middle- and upper-class males *purposely* structure schools in ways that reproduce their power in society—"Schools provided different classes and social groups with knowledge and skills they needed to occupy their respective places in a labor force stratified by class, race, and gender" (137, p. 258). Whether the current situation is purposeful or not, it is clear that despite the progress that has occurred in providing equal educational opportunities to all students, the regular and special education systems both perpetuate inequality in school and in the larger society and cause many students to misbehave, tune out, and drop out.

We currently lack the knowledge to predict which students will accept the prevailing biases more than they resist them and which will resist more than succumb. In addition, we certainly cannot predict the manner in which those students will resist.

SCHOOL RESEGREGATION

Some individuals claim that ability grouping and tracking, strict disciplinary measures, and special educational programs are often employed to resegregate desegregated school systems and to reinstitute the unequal educational opportunity that accompanies segregation rather than to improve instruction and classroom management. "Many school systems remain segregated 'even after a court ordered desegregation plan has been fully implemented.' Through such practices as unequal application of disciplinary measures, ability grouping and educational placement, minority students continue to receive uneven and unfair treatment. They have been, in effect, resegregated" (209, p. 184).

Considerable evidence supports this contention (202–225). The use of more severe forms of discipline and ability grouping and tracking was increased significantly in desegregated school systems, especially in the South during the late 1960s and 1970s (129, 210, 212, 221, 223, 225). Desegregation has also been accompanied by a tendency toward the inflexible administration of strict disciplinary codes and an increased use of corporal punishment and suspensions with African American students (217, 218). For example, during the first year of the desegregation of the Milwaukee school system, of the 22 schools that increased their African

American student enrollment,16 had increases in their suspension rates. Of the 11 schools that experienced a decline in African American student enrollment, 8 also experienced a decrease in their suspension rates (218).

For well over 100 years, desegregation has often led to the expansion of special education programs (220). For instance, the first ungraded classes for students who were mentally, physically, or morally defective or truant in New York were initiated in reaction to compulsory education laws (214). These programs served primarily poor and immigrant students. In California, the establishment of special education programs for the mentally retarded occurred during the same year that separate schools for different ethnic groups were abolished (214, 220).

Analyzing the origins of the special education programs in such areas as New York and California, Gelb concluded,

> The ungraded classes were not created with reference to a theory, but to meet the needs of a school system whose normal procedures could not accommodate previously excluded children and those with different linguistic backgrounds. The categorical labeling of these children may be understood as an attempt to confer medical validity to classifications derived out of social necessity. . . . Medical labels used to classify and separate students in California evolved from exemptions initially based on race. Regulations establishing separate schools for black, Chinese American, Japanese American, and Indian children were all written separately prior to the creation of public special education for mentally retarded children. The introduction of special services for mentally retarded children in 1947 coincided with the repeal of laws separating children by ethnic background. The medical label of mental retardation permitted segregation of minority students within schools that were no longer legally permitted to exclude them. (214, p. 10)

In the 1970s and 1980s, school desegregation typically resulted in the expansion of special education programs for students with mild developmental, emotional, and behavioral problems and the disproportionate placement of African American and Hispanic Americans in these programs (129, 211, 213, 214, 220, 224). The following quotes are representative of the opinions of educators who believe special education has been serving to segregate those non-European American students who create problems for the system because they are ill served by it.

In 1969, an African American special educator wrote,

> The current plight of the Black is, in fact, a direct result of the regular school's failure to cope with individual and collective differences in learning and conduct of an increasing number of pupils. Regular schools have been the major force for accommodation of the "regular" Blacks and special education receives the "hard to break" Blacks. It is an unwritten pact between the two. . . . Special education is part of the arrangement for cooling out students. It has helped to erect a parallel system which permits relief of institutional guilt and humiliation stemming from the failure to achieve competence and effectiveness in the task given to it by society. Special education is helping the regular school maintain its spoiled identity when it creates special programs (whether psycho-dynamic or behavior modification) for the "disruptive child" and the "slow learner," many of whom, for some strange reason, happen to be Black and poor and live in the inner city. (216, p. 245)

In the 1980s, Goodale and Soden said of special education services for inner-city students,

> There is little incentive to maintain students who are experiencing education, social, or emotional difficulty in the regular education setting. It is easier to make a referral than to modify a program. Urban education is a challenging and demanding field. Special education is an easy available option which can reduce the demands on regular education. . . . Money spent for many mildly/moderately handicapped students to be placed in special education might better be spent to provide incentives to regular education. (215, p. 8)

In the 1990s, an African American educator offered the following advice to African American parents:

> Wake up! Please don't let your children become special education students. . . . "What might appear to be good to you, may not (in this case) be good for you." (224, p. 31)

GOOD INTENTIONS

Despite federal and state guidelines that govern eligibility for special education, some non-European American students who do not have disabilities are referred to and accepted into special education because educators believe they will receive more individual and remedial attention.

> Some individuals who support present practices suggest that if there are Black students who are misdiagnosed and misplaced in these classes, the net effect may not be detrimental to these students. These individuals propose, rather, that Black students who are misdiagnosed in this manner are probably having problems in the regular classrooms for some reason or another and placement in a special education classroom may serve to ameliorate these problems. The more individualized attention they receive, the slower pace of this type of classroom and so forth may serve to accomplish this. (107, p. 22)

Some educators refer limited-English-proficient students who appear to be having difficulty adjusting to and profiting from instruction in English to special education even though they are known not to be eligible for such programs, in the belief that they too will profit from the extra help they will receive. This practice has been justly criticized for number of reasons (107, 226–228), some of which are the following:

- It is against the law to place ineligible students in special education programs.
- It deprives students of an appropriate education because teacher expectations, instructional techniques, curriculum content and so on are inappropriate.
- It can lead to a self-fulfilling prophesy as students come to believe they have a disability and act accordingly.
- It relieves the pressure on regular education to become more responsive to needs of non-European American and limited-English-proficient students by placing the responsibility for the problem within the student.

GOOD INTENTIONS

- What is your opinion about the preceding justifications for placing limited-English-proficient and other non-European American students without disabilities in special education programs?
- Do you think the possible disadvantages outweigh the advantages or vice versa?

UNDERREPRESENTATION

As noted in Chapter 1, in recent years in some school districts, non-European American students—especially those who are limited English proficient—are underrepresented in programs for students with disabilities. The following three factors have contributed to the change (229–232):

- Some school officials want to avoid the fate of school districts that have been sued for misplacing students in special education programs.
- Some teachers want to protect students from the abuses many non-European students have experienced in special education programs.
- Some school districts have neither the bilingual personnel required to provide such students with nonbiased assessments nor the bilingual special educators necessary to provide them with bilingual special education services.

Litigation

There is evidence that the spate of court cases that were decided in favor of those who complained that school districts had misplaced non-European American students—especially those with limited English proficiency—in special education programs led to some unexpected side effects. Some school districts responded to the courts' actions by attempting to improve their placement procedures. However, fear of litigation led others to hesitate to place and to even stop placing eligible African American, Hispanic American, and limited-English-proficient students in special education programs, regardless of their need for such services (3, 229, 232). "Fear of litigation by school districts can lead to the under-identification of minority pupils in special education. Data collected by the California State Department of Education pupil count verifies the trend of shifting from over-identification of minorities in special education to under-representation" (232, p. 2).

Protection of Students

Evidence suggests that some educators who believe that special education programs are more likely to harm than help students refuse to refer African Americans and Hispanic Americans who may require special education services for evaluation. Thus, concern with the possible misplacement of students who do not require special education leads to the denial of special education to those who do require them. This tendency appears to be especially prevalent among bilingual education teachers who believe that special education classes staffed by nonbilingual teachers will not meet the linguistic needs of limited-English-proficient students.

Believing that they have to choose between linguistically appropriate regular education services that may not meet the special needs of their students and special education services that do not meet the linguistic needs of students, these teachers choose linguistically appropriate educational services. Their rational often is that special educational services offered in English cannot help students who do not understand their teachers. This is especially likely to be true of immigrant students. As one school official stated, "The tendency of teachers to quickly refer these children for special education consideration, the lack of linguistically and culturally appropriate assessment instruments for the students . . . who speak languages other than English and Spanish, and our very limited understanding of their cultures make us very reluctant to place a newly-arrived immigrant student who does not present a physical handicap into special education" (230, p. 53).

Personnel Shortages

There is a nationwide shortage of personnel who are culturally and linguistically competent to assess and instruct limited-English-proficient students in their native languages. This is especially true of students from countries that do not offer special education services to children with disabilities, since few if any of the immigrants that come from these countries arrive with competencies in special education.

SHORTAGES OF BILINGUAL SPECIAL EDUCATION PERSONNEL

The National Coalition of Advocates for Children studied the services currently provided to limited-English-proficient (LEP) students with disabilities. (3) One of the handful of Southeast Asian school psychologists currently employed in various schools in the United States reported, "Right now as a [Southeast Asian] school psychologist I have . . . at least 93 referrals from the school system" (3, p. 54) (Bilingual School Psychologist, Lowell Public Schools, MA).

A Burmese mother who wanted her daughter placed in a special education described her frustrating experiences with the school system:

> There was a gap of three months, March to May, when the COH [Committee on the Handicapped] did not get in touch with me. . . . When I called them this time, I was informed that I should try and locate an individual or agency to do the evaluation in Burmese. . . . I contacted a number of these agencies, but without any success.

Around this time, I also suggested that I might be allowed to interpret for my daughter. This suggestion they absolutely refused to entertain. It was also then that they informed me that it was incumbent upon me to find a Burmese-speaking psychologist. (3, p. 55) (Burmese Parent, NY)

A child advocate stated, "If in addition to being limited in his English proficiency, that child is also handicapped, that child is really doubly handicapped because he is very unlikely to get any sort of instruction or assistance in his own language" (3, p. 54).

Another advocate reported, "The Division of Special Education [and] the Board of Education have been well aware of the acute shortage of bilingual clinicians to evaluate children, and bilingual teachers to service children who have been recommended for placement in the bilingual special education program. To date, their efforts at recruitment have been almost totally unsuccessful" (3, p. 57) (Intergroup Relations Representative, Dade County Public Schools, FL).

Because school districts are reluctant to identify students who may have disabilities when the schools are unable to provide the bilingual assessment and educational services such students would require, many limited-English-proficient students with disabilities are not evaluated, placed, or even referred to special education (97, 230). "LEP handicapped children tend to be formally screened for handicaps, referred to the Special Education Department, assessed, and placed via an Individualized Educational Plan (IEP) when there are bilingual special education services available for them. When bilingual special education services are not available for them, LEP handicapped students tend to remain in bilingual education classrooms, without a formal IEP, without being formally identified as handicapped, and the Bilingual Education Department remains responsible for their education" (230, p. ii).

As Bergin pointed in 1980, this problem will continue as long as school district personnel have only two options for limited-English-proficient students— English-only special education classes and regular bilingual education classes— and as long as district personnel believe that they are more likely to be sued for misplacing such students in special education programs than for failing to provide them the linguistically appropriate services they require (229).

SUMMARY

A number of factors contribute to the poor academic achievement of many non-European American students and their overrepresentation in special education programs for students with disabilities. Their education is often contextually, culturally, and linguistically inappropriate. Too often, teachers, psychologists, and administrators are prejudiced against them. In some cases, these students are assigned to low-ability tracks and groups and misplaced in special education programs in order to maintain segregation. When they realize that both schools and society in general are structured in ways that reproduce ethnic and socioeconomic-class inequality, many of them resist the prejudice and hostility they experience in nonconstructive ways. Some well-meaning teachers and administrators misplace ineligible students in special education to help them obtain the individual instruction and increased teacher attention they think these students need.

In some school districts, African American and limited-English-proficient students are underrepresented in programs for students with emotional problems, behavior disorders, and developmental disabilities. Some school districts discourage their staff from referring and accepting such students in special education—even when the students require placement—out of a concern that they may be sued for misplacing non-European American students in special education. School districts that lack the bilingual special educators and psychologists necessary to assess and instruct limited-English-proficient students with disabilities sometimes establish similar policies and procedures. In some cases, teachers who do not have confidence that the special education programs in their districts will provide limited-English-proficient and non-European American students the culturally and linguistically appropriate services they require are reluctant to refer them.

ACTIVITIES

1. If you are an in-service teacher, ask a colleague to observe your teaching and to compare the way you relate to different groups of students by studying your behavior. Almost any aspect of your teaching could be examined. For example, your colleague might count the number of times you call on students who do and do not volunteer, assign students to particular chores, praise students' work, and so on. Then she or he can compare the results for different groups of students, such as European Americans and non-European Americans, poor and middle-class students, and so on. If you are a preservice teacher, make the same comparisons in someone else's class, or study the way your master teacher or your professors relate to students from different ethnic backgrounds.

2. Ask yourself whether your expectations for non-European American and poor students are accurate or prejudicial. Do you expect these students to achieve less and/or misbehave more than their test scores, grades, and previous performance would indicate? Do you evaluate their work objectively, or does their ethnic or socioeconomic background influence your conclusions?

3. If you are an in-service teacher, ask a colleague to evaluate some of your students' work that is difficult to judge objectively (e.g., essay questions or a writing sample rather than a math problem or a multiple-choice answer).

Compare your colleague's evaluations with your own to see if your evaluations of particular groups of students are biased.

4. Interview students in the courses you are taking who are from different ethnic and socioeconomic backgrounds about some of the issues discussed in this chapter. Do their opinions vary with their ethnic or socioeconomic-class backgrounds?

5. Review the textbooks and other materials your professors assign in the courses you are taking. Do these materials deal with the diversity issues inherent in the topics they cover? Do they focus exclusively or primarily on European Americans to the exclusion of other ethnic groups?

6. Compare your professors in terms the time they devote to the diversity issues inherent in the courses they teach. Do you find that some professors are more sensitive to and interested in diversity issues than others?

REFERENCES

References 1–7 discuss the special problems of immigrant and refugee students that are not met by the educational system.

1. Cervantes, R. C., Salgado de Snyder, V. N., & Padilla, A. M. (1988). *Post Traumatic Stress Disorder among Immigrants from Central America and Mexico*. Los Angeles: University of California, Spanish Speaking Mental Health Resource Center.
2. Juffer, K. A. (1983). Culture shock: A theoretical framework for understanding adaptation. In J. Bransford (Ed.), *Monograph Series: BUENO Center for Multicultural Education, 4,* 136–149.
3. First, J. M., & Carrera, J. W. (1988). *New Voices: Immigrant Students in the Public Schools.* Boston: National Coalition of Advocates for Students.
4. Nguyen, T. P. (1987). Positive self-concept in the Vietnamese bilingual child. In M. Dao (Ed.), *From Vietnamese to Vietnamese American: Selected Articles.* San Jose, CA: Division of Special Education and Rehabilitative Services, San Jose State University.
5. Olsen, L. (1988). *Crossing the Schoolhouse Border: Immigrant Students and the California Public Schools.* San Francisco: California Tomorrow.
6. Padilla, A. M., Lindholm, K. J., Alvarez, M., & Wagatsuma, Y. (1985). *Acculturative Stress*

in Immigrant Students: Three Papers. Los Angeles: University of California, Spanish Speaking Mental Health Resource Center.
7. Wei, T. T. D. (1980). *Vietnamese Refugee Students: A Handbook for School Personnel* (2nd ed.). ERIC ED 208 109.

References 8–9 discuss the unmet educational needs of Native American students.

8. Bureau of Indian Affairs. (1988, March). *Report on B. I. A. Education: Final Review Draft.* Washington, DC: Department of the Interior.
9. Chavez, R. C., Belkin, L. D., Hornback, J. G., & Adams, K. (1991). Dropping out of school: Issues affecting culturally, ethnically, and linguistically distinct student groups. *Journal of Educational Issues of Language Minority Students, 8,* 1–21.

The contextual problems of migrant students are discussed in references 10–16.

10. Center for Educational Planning. (1989). *Migrant Education Dropout Prevention Project Final Report.* ERIC ED 321 951.

11. Interstate Migrant Education Council. (1987). *Migrant Education: A Consolidated View.* ERIC ED 285 701.

12. Interstate Migrant Secondary Services Program. (1985). *Survey Analysis: Responses of 1070 Students in High School Equivalency Programs, 1984–1985.* ERIC ED 264 070.

13. Johnson, F., Levy, R., Morales, J., Morse, S., & Prokop, M. (1986). *Migrant Students at the Secondary Level: Issues and Opportunities for Change.* ERIC ED 270 242.

14. Lawless, Ken. (1986). *Neediest of the Needy: Special Education for Migrants. Harvesting the Harvesters. Book 8.* ERIC ED 279 473.

15. Migrant Attrition Project. (1987). *Migrant Attrition Project: Abstract of Findings.* Oneonta: State University of New York at Oneonta.

16. Rasmussen, L. (1988). *Migrant Students at the Secondary Level: Issues and Opportunities for Change.* Las Cruces: New Mexico State University, ERIC CRESS.

The special problems of rural students are described in references 17–27.

17. Berkeley, T. R., & Ludlow, B. L. (1991). Meeting the needs of special student populations in rural areas. In A. J. DeYoung (Ed.), *Rural Education: Issues and Practices.* New York: Garland.

18. Brown, D. L. (1989). Demographic trends relevant to education in nonmetropolitan America. In *Rural Education—A Changing Landscape.* Washington, DC: U.S. Department of Education.

19. Helge, D. (1984). The state of the art of rural special education. *Exceptional Children, 50,* 294–305.

20. Helge, D. (1989). *Rural Family-Community Partnerships: Resources.* ERIC ED 320 736.

21. Helge, D. (1991). *Rural, Exceptional, At Risk.* Reston, VA: Council for Exceptional Children.

22. Leadership for Special Education. (1989). A conversation with Robert R. Davila. *Education of the Handicapped,* September 13, 28.

23. National Council on Disabilities. (1989). *The Education of Students with Disabilities: Where Do We Stand?* Washington, DC: Author.

24. Students at Risk. (1990, October). *Education Week,* pp. 19, 26.

25. O'Connor, C., Murr, A., & Wingert, P. (1986). Affluent America's forgotten children, *Newsweek, 107* (22), 20–21.

26. Pollard, K. M., & O'Hare, W. P. (1990). *Beyond High School: The Experience of Rural and Urban Youth in the 1980's.* ERIC ED 326 363.

27. Phelps, M. S., & Prock, G. A. (1991). Equality of educational opportunity in rural America. In A. DeYoung (Ed.), *Rural Education Issues and Practice.* New York: Garland.

References 28–45 concern the contextual problems of homeless children and adolescents.

28. Bass, J. L., Brennan, P., Mehta, K. A., & Kodzis, S. (1990). Pediatric problems in a suburban shelter for homeless families. *Pediatrics, 85* (1), 33–38.

29. Bassuk, E. L., & Gallagher, E. M. (1990). The impact of homelessness on children. In N. A. Boxill (Ed.), *Homeless Children: The Watchers and the Waiters.* Binghamton, NY: Haworth.

30. Bassuk, F., & Rubin, L. (1987). Homeless children: A neglected population. *American Journal of Orthopsychiatry, 57* (2), 279–286.

31. Bowen, J. M., Purrington, G. S., Layton, D. H., & O'Brien, K. (1989). *Educating Homeless Children and Youth: A Policy Analysis.* Paper presented at the annual conference of the American Educational Research Association, San Francisco.

32. Eddowes, A., & Hranitz. J. R. (1989). Education children of the homeless. *Childhood Education: Infancy through Early Adolescence, 65* (4), 197–200.

33. Friedman, L., & Christiansen, G. (1990). *Shut Out: Denial of Education to Homeless Children.* ERIC ED 320 987.

34. Heflin, L. J., & Rudy, K. (1991). *Homeless and in Need of Special Education.* Reston, VA: Council for Exceptional Children.

35. Miller, D. S., & Linn, E. H. B. (1988). Children in sheltered homeless families: Reported health status and use of health services. *Pediatrics, 81,* 668–673.

36. Rafferty, Y., & Rollins, N. (1989). *Learning in Limbo: The Educational Deprivation of Homeless Children.* Long Island City, NY: Advocates for Children of New York.

37. Rafferty, Y., & Rollins, N. (1989). *Homeless Children: Educational Challenges for the 1990's.* ERIC ED 325 589.

38. Rescoria, L., Parker, R., & Stolley, P. (1991). Ability, achievement and adjustment in homeless children. *American Journal of Orthopsychiatry, 61* (2), 210–220.

39. Rivlin, L. G. (199). Home and homelessness in the lives of children. In N. A. Boxill (Ed.), *Homeless Children: The Watchers and the Waiters.* Binghamton, NY: Haworth.

40. Rosenman, M., & Stein, M. L. (1990). Homeless children: A new vulnerability. In N. A. Boxill (Ed.), *Homeless Children: The Watchers and the Waiters.* Binghamton, NY: Haworth.

41. Russell, S. C., & Williams, E. U. (1988). Homeless handicapped children: A special education perspective. *Children's Environments Quarterly, 5* (1), 3–7.

42. Schumack, S. (Ed.). (1987). *The Educational Rights of Homeless Children.* ERIC ED 288 915.

43. Stronge, J. H., & Helm, V. M. (1990). *Residency and Guardianship Requirements as Barriers to the Education of Homeless Children and Youth.* ERIC ED 319 845.

44. Stronge, J. H., & Tenhouse, C. (1990). *Educating Homeless Children: Issues and Answers.* Bloomington, IN: Phi Delta Kappa Educational Foundation.

45. Wright, J. D. (1990). Homelessness is not healthy for children and other living things. In N. A. Boxill (Ed.), *Homeless Children: The Watchers and the Waiters.* Binghamton, NY: Haworth.

The effects of cultural differences is dealt with in references 46–49.

46. Baratz, S. S., & Baratz, J. C. (1975). Early childhood intervention: The social science basis of institutional racism. *Harvard Educational Review, Reprint Series No. 5. Challenging the Myth: The Schools, the Blacks, and the Poor. pp.* 111–132.

47. Federal Regional Resource Center. (1991). *Exploring the Education Issues of Cultural Diversity.* Lexington: Interdisciplinary Human Development Institute, University of Kentucky.

48. Hurn, C. J. (1985). *The Limits and Possibilities of Schooling: An Introduction to the Sociology of Education* (2nd ed.). Boston: Allyn and Bacon.

49. Lubeck, S. (1988). Nested contexts. In L. Weis (Ed.), *Class, Race, and Gender in American Education* (pp. 46–47). Albany: State University of New York Press.

Reference 50 discusses reasons why students may get into trouble in school for behaving in ways that are acceptable in their communities.

50. Grossman, H. (1984). *Educating Hispanic Students: Cultural Implications for Instruction, Classroom Management, Counseling and Assessment.* Springfield, IL: Thomas.

Examples of the opinions of writers in the 1970s, 1980s, and 1990s about prejudice in schools are found in references 51–55.

51. Becker, A. (1980). *The Role of the School in the Maintenance and Change of Ethnic Group Affiliation.* ERIC ED 259 052.

52. Bennett, C., & Harris, J. J. (1982). Suspension and expulsion of male and black students: A case study of the causes of disproportionality. *Urban Education, 16* (4), 399–423.

53. National Black Child Development Institute. (1990). *The Status of African American Children: Twentieth Anniversary Report.* Washington, DC: Author.

54. Rist, R. C. (1971). Student social class and teacher expectations: The self fulfilling prophecy in ghetto education. *Harvard Educational Review Reprint Series No. 5. Challenging the Myths: The Schools The Blacks and the Poor.*

55. Stein, A. (1971). Strategies for failure. *Harvard Educational Review. Reprint Series No. 5. Challenging the Myths: The Schools The Blacks and the Poor.*

References 56–63 describe studies that did not find teacher bias.

56. Flynn, T. M. (1983). IQ tests and placement. *Integrated Education, 21,* 124–126.

57. Heller, E. J. (1985). Pupil race and elementary school ability grouping: Are teachers biased against black children? *American Educational Research Journal, 22* (4), 465–483.

58. Huebner, E. S., & Cummings, J. A. (1986). Influence of race and test data ambiguity upon school psychologists' decisions. *School Psychology Review, 15* (3), 410–417.

59. Jaeger, R., & Freijo, T. (1975). Race and sex as concomitants of composite halo in teachers' evaluative ratings of pupils. *Journal of Educational Psychology, 67* (2), 226–237.

60. Matuszek, P., & Oakland, T. (1979). Factors influencing teachers' and psychologists' recommendations regarding special class placement. *Journal of School Psychology, 17* (2), 116–125.

61. Moacdieh, C. (1981). *Grouping for Reading in the Primary Grades: Evidence on the Revisionist Theory.* ERIC ED 200 938.

62. Tobias, S., Zibrin, M., & Menell, D. (1983. *Special Education Referrals: Failure to Replicate Student-Teacher Ethnicity Interaction.* ERIC ED 224 221.

63. Wiley, M., & Eskilson, A. (1978). Why did you learn in school today? Teachers' perceptions of causality. *Sociology of Education, 51,* 261–269.

References 64–79 describe teachers' biased expectations for students.

64. Beady, C. H., & Hansell, S. (1980). *Teacher Race and Expectations for Student Achievement.* ERIC ED 200 695.

65. Bennet, C. I. (1979). The effects of student characteristics and task performance on teacher expectations and attributions. *Dissertation Abstracts International, 40,* 979–980–B.

66. Campos, F. (1983). *The Attitudes and Expectations of Student Teachers and Cooperating Teachers Toward Students in Predominantly Mexican American Schools: A Qualitative Data Perspective.* ERIC ED 234 026.

67. Dao, M. (1991). Designing assessment procedures for educationally at-risk Southeast Asian-American students. *Journal of Learning Disabilities, 24* (10), 594–601, 629.

68. Derlega, V., Wang, P., & Colson, W. (1981). *Racial Bias in Expectancies and Performance Attributions.* Unpublished manuscript, Old Dominion University, Norfolk, VA.

69. Dusek, J. B., & Joseph, G. (1983). The bases of teacher expectancies: A meta-analysis. *Journal of Educational Psychology, 75* (3), 327–346.

70. Figueroa, R. A., & Gallegos, E. A. (1978). Ethnic differences in school behavior. *Sociology of Education, 51,* 289–298.

71. Grant, L. (1984). Black females' "place" in desegregated classrooms. *Sociology of Education, 57,* 98–110.

72. Matute-Bianchi, M. E. (1986). Ethnic identities and patterns of school success and failure among Mexican-descent and Japanese-American students in a California high school: An ethnographic analysis. *American Journal of Education, 95* (1), 233–255.

73. Metheny, W. (1979). *The Influences of Grade and Pupil Ability Levels on Teachers' Conceptions of Reading.* ERIC ED 182 713.

74. Mizokawa, D. T., & Morishima, J. K. (1979). *Education for, by, and of Asian/Pacific Americans. I.* ERIC ED 199 355.

75. Ogbu, J. U. (1978). *Minority Education and Caste: The American in Cross-Cultural Perspective.* New York: Academic Press.

76. Smith, J. A. (1979). Ascribed and achieved student characteristics in teacher expectancy: Relationship of socioeconomic status to academic achievement, academic self-concept, and vocational aspirations. *Dissertation Abstracts International, 40,* 959–960-B.

77. Sue, S., & Kitano, H. H. L. (1973). Stereotypes as a measure of success. *Journal of Social Issues, 29* (3), 83–98.

78. Takeuchi, S. M. (1972). *Verbal Skills and the Asian American Student.* ERIC ED 097 395.

79. Wilkerson, M. A. (1980). The effects of sex and ethnicity upon teachers' expectations of students. *Dissertation Abstracts International, 41,* 637-A.

References 80–93 discuss bias in teachers' evaluations of students.

80. Davis, S. A. (1974). *Students' SES as Related to Teachers' Perceptions and Ability Grouping Decisions.* ERIC ED 090 487.

81. DeMeis, D., & Turner, R. (1978). Effects of students' race, physical attractiveness, and dialect on teachers' evaluations. *Contemporary Educational Psychology, 3,* 77–86.

82. Eaves, R. (1975). Teacher race, student race, and the behavior problem checklist. *Journal of Abnormal Child Psychology, 3* (1), 1–9.

83. Elliot, S. N., & Argulewicz, E. N. (1983). The influence of student ethnicity on teachers' behavior ratings of normal and learning disabled children. *Hispanic Journal of Behavioral Sciences, 5* (3), 337–345.

84. Granger, R. E., Mathews, M., Quay, L. C., & Verner, R. (1977). Teacher judgements of communication effectiveness of children using

different speech patterns. *Journal of Educational Psychology, 69* (6), 793–796.

85. Haller, E. J., & Davis, S. A. (1980). Does socioeconomic status bias the assignment of elementary school students to reading groups? *American Educational Research Journal, 17* (40), 409–418.

86. Ishi-Jordan, S. (1992). *Effects of Students' Racial or Ethnic Background on Teacher Expectations and Intervention Selection for Problem Behaviors.* Paper presented at the Topical Conference on Cultural and Linguistically Diverse Exceptional Children, Minneapolis, MN.

87. Kim, Y. J. (1983). Problems in the delivery of the school-based psycho-educational services to the Asian immigrant children. *Journal of Children in Contemporary Society, 15* (3), 81–89.

88. Marwit, K., Marwit, S., & Walker, E. (1978). Effects of student race and physical attractiveness on teachers' judgements of transgressions. *Journal of Educational Psychology, 70,* 911–915.

89. Scheinfeld, D. R. (1983). Family relationships and school achievement among boys of lower-income urban black families. *American Journal of Orthopsychiatry, 53* (1), 127–143.

90. Taylor, J. B. (1983). Influence of speech variety on teachers' evaluation of reading comprehension. *Journal of Educational Psychology, 75* (5), 662–667.

91. Tobias, S., Cole, C., Zibrin, M., & Bodlakova, V. (1981). *Bias in the Referral of Children to Special Services.* ERIC ED 208 637.

92. Wong, M. G. (1980). Model students? Teachers' perceptions and expectations of their Asian and white students. *Sociology of Education, 53,* 236–246.

93. Yao, E. L. (1987). Asian-immigrants students—Unique problems that hamper learning. *NASSP Bulletin, 71* (503), 82–88.

References 94–108 deal with teachers' and psychologists' biased evaluations of students in or referred to special education.

94. Amira, S., Abramowitz, S. I., & Gomes-Schwartz, B. (1977). Socially-charge pupil and psychologist effects on psychoeducational decisions. *Journal of Special Education, 11* (4), 433–440.

95. Argulewicz, E. N. (1983). Effects of ethnic membership, socioeconomic status, and home language on LD, EMR, and EH placements. *Learning Disability Quarterly, 6* (2), 195–200.

96. Argulewicz, E. N., & Sanchez, D. T. (1983). The special education evaluation process as a moderator of false positives. *Exceptional Children, 49* (5), 452–454.

97. Bickel, W. E. (1982). Classifying mentally retarded students: A review of placement practices in special education. In K. A. Heller, W. H. Holtzman, & S. Messick (Eds.), *Placing Children in Special Education: A Strategy for Equity.* Washington, DC: National Academy Press.

98. Collier, C. (1986). *The Referral of Hispanic Children to Special Education: A Comparison of Acculturation and Education Characteristics of Referred and Nonreferred Culturally and Linguistically Different Children.* ERIC ED 271 954.

99. Fetterman, D. M. (1986). Gifted and talented education: A national test case in Peoria. *Educational Evaluation and Policy Analysis, 8* (20), 155–166.

100. Frame, R. E., Clarizio, J. G., Porter, A. C., & Vinsonhaler, J. R. (1982). Interclinician agreement and bias in school psychologists' diagnostic and treatment recommendations for a learning disabled child. *Psychology in the Schools, 19,* 319–327.

101. Individuals with Disabilities Education Act (20 U.S.C., Sections 1400–1485; Education of the Handicapped Act Amendments of 1990).

102. Leinhardt, G., Seewald, A. M., & Zigmond, N. (1982). Sex and race differences in learning disabilities classrooms. *Journal of Educational Psychology, 74* (6), 835–843.

103. Low, B. P., & Clement, P. W. (1982). Relationships of race, and socioeconomic status to classroom behavior, academic achievement, and referral for special education. *Journal of School Psychology, 20* (2), 103–112.

104. Mercer, M. M. (1982). Reassessing the large number of black children in special education classes: A challenge for the 80's. *Negro Educational Review, 33* (1), 28–33.

105. Pickholtz, H. J. (1977). *The Effects of a Child's Racial-Ethnic Label and Achievement Differences on School Psychologists' Decisions.* Unpublished doctoral dissertation, Pennsylvania State University.

106. Prieto, A., & Zucker, S. (1980). *The Effects of Race on Teachers' Perceptions of Education Placement of Behaviorally Disordered Children.* ERIC ED188 427.

107. Serwatka, T., Dove, T., & Hodge, W. (1986). Black students in special education: Issues and Implications for community involvement. *Negro Educational Review, 37* (1), 17–27.

108. Tobias, S., Cole, C., Zibrin, M., & Menell, C. (1982). *Special Education Referrals: Failure to Replicate Student-Teacher Ethnicity Interaction.* ERIC ED 224 221.

Bias in teacher-student interactions is the focus of references 109–127.

109. Appleford, B., Fralick, P., & Ryan, T. J. (1976). *Teacher-Child Interactions as Related to Sex, Socio-Economic Status and Physical Attractiveness.* ERIC ED 138 869.

110. Barba, L. (1979). *A Survey of the Literature on the Attitudes Toward the Administration of Corporal Punishment in Schools.* ERIC ED 186 538.

111. Bickel, F., & Qualls, R. (1981). *The Impact of School Climate on Suspension Rates in the Jefferson County Public Schools.* Paper presented at the annual meeting of the American Educational Research Association, Boston.

112. Buriel, R. (1983). Teacher-student interactions and their relationship to student achievement: A comparison of Mexican-American children. *Journal of Educational Psychology, 75* (60), 889–897.

113. Friedman, P. (1976). Comparison of teacher reinforcement schedules for students with different social class backgrounds. *Journal of Educational Psychology, 68,* 286–293.

114. Glackman, T., Martin, R., Hyman, I., McDowell, E., Berv, V., & Spino, P. (1980). *Corporal Punishment in the Schools As It Relates to Race, Sex, Grade Level and Suspensions.* Philadelphia: Temple University, National Center for the Study of Corporal Punishment in the Schools.

115. Grant, L. (1985). Race-gender status, classroom interaction, and children's socialization in elementary school. In L. C. Wilkinson & C. B. Marrett (Eds.), *Gender Influences in Classroom Interaction.* New York: Academic Press.

116. Grossman, H., & Grossman, S. (1994). *Gender Issues in Education.* Boston: Allyn and Bacon.

117. Guilmet, G. M. (1979). Instructor reaction to verbal and nonverbal styles: An example of Navajo and Caucasian children. *Anthropology and Education Quarterly, 10,* 254–266.

118. Hamilton, S. (1983). The social side of schooling. *Elementary School Journal, 83,* 313–334

119. McGhan, B. R. (1978). *Teachers' Use of Authority and Its Relationship to Socioeconomic Status, Race, Teacher Characteristics, and Educational Outcomes.* ERIC ED 151 329.

120. Moody, C. D., Williams, J., & Vergon, C. B. (1978). *Student Rights and Discipline: Policies, Programs and Procedures.* ERIC ED 160 926.

121. Moore, W. L., & Cooper, H. (1984). Correlations between teacher and student background and teacher perception of discipline problems and disciplinary techniques. *Psychology in the Schools, 21,* 386–392.

122. Richardson, R. C., & Evans, E. T. (1991). *Empowering Teachers to Eliminate Corporal Punishment in the Schools.* Paper presented at the annual conference of the National Black Child Developmental Institute, Washington, DC.

123. Simpson, A. W., & Erickson, M. T. (1983). Teachers' verbal and nonverbal communication patterns as a function of teacher race, student gender and student race. *American Educational Research Journal, 20* (2), 183–198.

124. Stevens, L. B. (1983). *Suspension and Corporal Punishment of Students in the Cleveland Public Schools, 1981–1982.* Cleveland, OH: Office of School Monitoring and Community Relations.

125. Taylor, M. (1979). Race, sex and the expression of self-fulfilling prophecies in a laboratory teaching situation. *Journal of Personality and Social Psychology, 37* (6), 897–912.

126. Washington, V. (1982). Racial differences in teacher perception of first and fourth grade pupils on selected characteristics. *Journal of Negro Education, 51,* 60–72.

127. Woolridge, P., & Richman, C. (1985). Teachers' choice of punishment as a function of a student's gender, age, race and I.Q. level. *Journal of School Psychology, 23,* 19–29.

Apparent and real lack of bias and their effects are the the focus of references 128–132.

128. Feldman, R., & Donohoe, L. (1978). Nonverbal communication of affect in interracial dyads. *Journal of Educational Psychology, 70* (6), 979–986.

129. Meier, K. J., Stewart, J. Jr., & England, R. E. (1989). *Race, Class, and Education: The Politics of Second-Generation Discrimination.* Madison: University of Wisconsin Press.

130. Office for Civil Rights. (1982). *1980 Elementary and Secondary School Civil Rights Surveys*. Washington, DC: U.S. Department of Education.

131. Office of Civil Rights. (1987). *Elementary and Secondary School Civil Rights Survey, 1986. National Summaries*. ERIC ED 304 485.

132. Plata, M., & Chinn, P. C. (1989). Students with handicaps who have cultural and language differences. In R. Gaylord-Ross (Ed.), *Integration Strategies for Students with Handicaps*. Baltimore: Brookes.

References 133–146 discuss the role of schools in the reproduction of inequities in society.

133. Apple, M., & Weis, L. (Eds.). (1983). *Ideology and Practice in Schools*. Philadelphia: Temple University Press.

134. Bowles, S., & Gintes, H. (1977). *Schooling in Capitalist America*. New York: Basic Books.

135. Connell, R. W. (1989). Curriculum politics, hegemony, and strategies of social change. In H. A. Giroux & R. I. Simon (Eds.), *Popular Culture, Schooling and Everyday Life*. Granby, MA: Bergin & Garvey.

136. Deem, R. (1978). *Women and Schooling*. Boston: Routledge Kegan Paul.

137. Giroux, H. A. (1981). Hegemony, resistance, and the paradox of educational reform. In H. A. Giroux, A. N. Penna, & W. F. Pinar (Eds.), *Curriculum and Instruction: Alternatives in Education*. Berkeley, CA: McCutchan.

138. Giroux, H. A. (1983). Theories of reproduction and resistance in the new sociology of education: A critical analysis. *Harvard Educational Review, 53* (3), 257–293.

139. Giroux, H. A., & Penna, A. N. (1988). Social education in the classroom: The dynamics of the hidden curriculum. In H. A. Giroux (Ed.), *Teachers as Intellectuals: Toward a Critical Pedagogy of Learning*. Granby, MA: Bergin & Garvey.

140. Grant, C. A., & Sleeter, C. E. (1988). Race, class, and gender and abandoned dreams. *Teachers College Record, 90* (1), 19–40.

141. Irvine, J. J. (1989). *Black Students and School Achievement: A Process Model of Relationships among Significant Variables*. ERIC ED 310 220.

142. Kelly, G., & Nihlen, A. (1982). Schooling and the reproduction of patriarchy: Unequal workloads, unequal rewards. In M. Apple (Ed.), *Culture and Economic Reproduction in Education*. Boston: Routledge Kegan Paul.

143. Valli, L. (1986). *Becoming Clerical Workers*. Boston: Routledge Kegan Paul.

144. Weiler, K. (1988). *Women Teaching for Change: Gender, Class and Power*. Granby, MA: Bergin & Garvey.

145. Witt, S. H. (1979). Native women in the world of work. In T. Constantino (Ed.), *Women of Color Forum: A Collection of Readings*. ERIC ED 191 975.

146. Wolpe, A. (1981). The official ideology of education for girls. In M. McDonald, R. Dale, G. Esland, & R. Fergusson (Eds.), *Politics, Patriarchy and Practice*. New York: Falmer Press.

References 147–169 deal with student resistance to school.

147. Anyon, J. (1984). Intersections of gender and class: Accommodation and resistance by working class and affluent females to contradictory sex-role ideologies. *Journal of Education, 166* (1), 25–48.

148. Arnot, M. (1982). Male hegemony, social class and women's education. *Journal of Education, 164* (1), 64–89.

149. Bouie, A. (1981). *Student Perceptions of Behavior and Misbehavior in the School Setting: An Exploratory Study and Discussion*. San Francisco: Far West Laboratory for Educational Research and Development.

150. Comer, J. P. (1990, October). What makes the new generation tick? *Ebony, 45*, pp. 34–38.

151. Ford, D. Y. (1991). *Self-perceptions of Social, Psychological, and Cultural Determinants of Achievement among Gifted Black Students: A Paradox of Underachievement*. Unpublished doctoral dissertation, Cleveland State University, Cleveland, OH.

152. Ford, D. Y. (1992). The American achievement ideology and achievement differentials among preadolescent gifted and nongifted African American males and females. *Journal of Negro Education, 61* (1), 45–64.

153. Fordham, S. (1988). Racelessness as a strategy in Black students' school success: Coping with the burden of 'acting White.' *Urban Review, 18*, 176–207.

154. Fordham, S., & Ogbu, J. U. (1986). Black students' school success: Coping with the 'burden of acting white.' *Urban Review, 18* (3), 176–203.

155. Fuller, M. (1980). Black girls in a London comprehensive school. In R. Deem (Ed.), *Schooling for Women's Work*. Boston: Routledge and Kegan Paul.

156. Gaskell, J. (1985). Course enrollment in high school: The perspective of working class females. *Sociology of Education, 58* (1), 48–59.

157. Gibson, M. A. (1987). The school performance of immigrant minorities: A comparative view. *Anthropology and Education Quarterly, 18* (4), 262–275.

158. Kessler, S., Ashenden, R., Connell, R., & Dowsett, G. (1985). Gender relations in secondary schooling. *Sociology of Education, 58* (1), 34–48.

159. Matute-Bianchi, M. E. (1986). Ethnic identities and patterns of school success and failure among Mexican-descent and Japanese-American students in a California high school: An ethnographic analysis. *American Journal of Education, 95* (1), 233–255.

160. MacLeod, J. (1987). *Ain't No Makin' It: Leveled Aspirations in a Low-Income Neighborhood*. Boulder, CO: Westview.

161. Nieto, S. (1992). *Affirming Diversity: The Sociopolitical Context of Multicultural Education*. New York: Longman.

162. Ogbu, J. U. (1986). The consequences of the American caste system. In U. Meisser (Ed.), *The School Achievement of Minority Children: New Perspectives*. Hillsdale, NJ: Erlbaum.

163. Ogbu, J. U. (1987). Variability in minority school performance: A problem in search of an explanation. *Anthropology & Education Quarterly, 18* (4), 312–334.

164. Ogbu, J. U. (1990). Minority education in comparative perspective. *Journal of Negro Education, 59*, 45–57.

165. Simon, R. (1983). But who will let you do it? Counter-hegemonic possibilities for work education. *Journal of Education, 165* (3), 235–256.

166. Suarez-Orozco, M. M. (1987). Becoming somebody: Central American immigrants in the United States. *Anthropology and Education Quarterly, 18* (4), 287–299.

167. Weis, L. (1985). *Between Two Worlds: Black Students in an Urban Community College*. Boston: Routledge and Kegan Paul.

168. Weis, L. (1985). Excellence and student class, race and gender cultures. In P. Altbach, G. Kelly, & L. Weis (Eds.), *Excellence in Education: Perspective on Policy and Practice*. Buffalo: Prometheus Press.

169. Willis, P. (1981). Cultural production is different from cultural reproduction is different from social reproduction is different from production. *Interchange, 12* (2–3), 48–68.

References 170–171 include suggestions for preparing students to change both schools and society.

170. Hartsock, N. (1979). Feminist theory and the development of revolutionary strategy. In Z. Eisenstein (Ed.), *Capitalist Patriarchy and the Case for Socialist Feminism*. New York: Monthly Review Press.

171. Lather, P. (1984). Critical theory, curricular transformation and feminist mainstreaming. *Journal of Education, 166* (1), 49–62.

Reference 172 criticizes the theory that there are voluntary and castelike groups in the United States.

172. Treuba, H. T. (1988). Culturally based explanations of minority students' academic achievement. *Anthropology and Education Quarterly, 19* (3), 270–287.

References 173–185 deal with the inadequate educational services provided to non-European middle-class students.

173. Ascher, C. (1989). *Urban School Finance: The Quest for Equal Educational Opportunity*. New York: ERIC Clearinghouse on Urban Education.

174. Bastian, A., Fruchter, N., Gittell, M., Greer, C., & Haskins, K. (1986). *Choosing Equality*. Philadelphia: Temple University Press.

175. Becker, H. J. (1986). *Computer Survey Newsletter*. Baltimore, MD: Johns Hopkins University, Center for the Social Organization of Schools.

176. Center for Social Organization of School. (1983). *School Uses of Microcomputers: Reports from a National Survey, No. 3*.

177. Darling-Hammond, L. (1985). *Equality and Excellence: The Status of Black American Education*. New York: College Entrance Examination Board.

178. Furr. J. D., & Davis, T. M. (1984). Equity Issues and microcomputers: Are educators meeting the challenges? *Journal of Educational Equity and Leadership, 4*, 93–97.

179. Hood, J. F. (1984). *Update on the School Market for Microcomputers.* Westport, CT: Market Data Retrieval.

180. Karp, S. (1991). Rich schools, poor schools & the courts. *Rethinking Schools, 5* (2), 1–15.

181. Mickelson, R. A. (1980). Social stratification processes in secondary schools: A comparison of Beverly Hills High School and Morningside High School. *Journal of Education, 162* (4), 83–112.

182. National Assessment of Education Progress. (1988). *Computer Competence: The First National Assessment.* Princeton, NJ: Educational Testing Service.

183. New York City Board of Education. (1989). *A New Direction: 1989–1990 Budget Request.* New York: Author.

184. Oakes, J. (1983, May). Limiting opportunity: Student race and curricular differences in secondary vocational education. *American Journal of Education,* pp. 328–355.

185. O'Brien, E. M. (1989). Texas legislators impatient to solve unfairness of school financing system. *Black Issues in Higher Education, 6* (16), 23.

References 186–197 are concerned with the effects of tracking and ability grouping.

186. Brophy, J. (1983). Research on the self-fulfilling prophecy and teacher expectation. *Journal of Educational Psychology, 75* (5), 631–661.

187. Chun, E. W. (1988). Sorting black students for success and failure: The inequity of ability grouping and tracking. *Urban League Review, 11* (1–2), 93–106.

188. Eder, D. (1981). Ability grouping as a self-fulfilling prophecy: A micro-analysis of teacher-student interaction. *Sociology of Education, 54,* 151–162.

189. Gamoran, A. (1986). *The Stratification of High School Learning Opportunities.* Paper presented at the annual meeting of the American Educational Research Association, San Francisco.

190. Goodlad, J. (1984). *A Place Called School.* New York: McGraw-Hill.

191. Lake, S. (1985). *Update on Tracking and Ability Grouping.* ERIC ED 274 708.

192. Lee, V. (1986). *The Effect of Tracking on the Social Distribution of Achievement in Catholic and Public Secondary Schools.* Paper presented at the annual meeting of the American Educational Research Association, San Francisco.

193. Oakes, J. (1985). *Keeping Track: How Schools Structure Inequality.* New Haven: Yale University Press.

194. Oakes, J. (1988). Tracking in mathematics and science education: A structural contribution to unequal schooling. In L. Weis (Ed.), *Class, Race, and Gender in American Education.* Albany: State University of New York Press.

195. Rosenbaum, J. E. (1980). Track misperceptions and frustrated college plans: An analysis of the effects of tracks and track perceptions in the National Longitudinal Survey. *Sociology of Education, 53* (2), 74–88.

196. Simpson, W. (1990). *Black Male Achievement: Strategies for Ensuring Success in School.* Paper presented at the annual meeting of the National Black Child Development Institute, Washington, DC.

197. Slavin, R. (1986). *Ability Grouping in Elementary Schools: A Best Evidence Synthesis.* Baltimore: Johns Hopkins University Press.

The results of community colleges are discussed in references 198–202.

198. Astin, A. W. (1982). *Minorities in American Higher Education.* San Francisco: Jossey-Bass.

199. Moore, W. (1976). Black knight/white college. *Community and Junior College Journal, 6* (7), 18–20, 40–43.

200. Nora, A., & Rendon, L. (1988). Hispanic student retention in community colleges: Reconciling access with outcomes. In L. Weis (Ed.), *Class, Race, and Gender in American Education.* Albany: State University of New York Press.

201. Olivas, M. A. (1979). *The Dilemma of Access: Minorities in Two Year Colleges.* Washington, DC: Howard University Press.

202. Weis, L. (1983). Schooling and cultural production: A comparison of black and white lived cultures. In M. A. Apple & L. Weis (Eds.), *Ideology and Practice in Schooling.* Philadelphia: Temple University Press.

Alienation among African American students is the focus of references 203–208.

203. Fisher, S. (1981). Race, class, anomie, and academic achievement: A study at the high school level. *Urban Education, 16* (2), 149–173.

204. Ginsberg, E., Berliner, H. S., & Ostow, O. (1988). *Young People at Risk: Is Prevention Possible?* Boulder, CO: Westview Press.

205. Harris, W. G., & Blanchard, R. (1990). *A Select Group of African American Males' Perceptions of Barriers to Successfully Achieving the Typical Male Familial Role—Implications for Educators.* Paper presented at the annual meeting of the National Association for Multicultural Education, New Orleans.

206. Hirsch, B. J., & Rapkin, B. D. (1987). The transition to junior high school: A longitudinal study of self-esteem, psychological symptomatology, school life, and social support. *Child Development, 58*, 1235–1243.

207. Long, S. (1980). Personality and political revenge: Psychopolitical adaptation among black and white youth. *Journal of Black Studies, 11* (1), 77–104.

208. Utah researcher blames discrimination for Native American high school dropout rate. (1992). *Black Issues in Higher Education, 9* (9), 3.

Techniques for resegregating schools are discussed in references 209–225.

209. Carter, D. G. (1982). Second-generation school integration problems for blacks. *Journal of Black Studies, 13* (2), 175–188.

210. Children's Defense Fund. (1974). *Children Out of School.* Washington, DC: Children's Defense Fund of the Washington Research Project.

211. Cross, D. E., Long, M. A., & Ziajka, A. (1978). Minority cultures and education in the United States. *Education and Urban Society, 10* (3), 263–276.

212. Eyler, J., Cook. B. J., & Ward, L. E. (1983). Resegregation: Segregation within desegregated schools. In C. H. Rossell & W. D. Hawley (Eds.), *The Consequences of School Desegregation.* Philadelphia: Temple University Press.

213. Finn, J. D. (1982). Patterns in special education placement as revealed by the ORC surveys. In K. A. Heller, W. H. Holtzman, & S. Messick (Eds.), *Placing Children in Special Education.* Washington, DC: National Academy Press.

214. Gelb, S. A. (1983). *Special Education and Linguistic Minority Students: The Historical Bases of Discriminatory Practices.* ERIC ED 232 401.

215. Goodale, R., & Soden, M. (1981). *Disproportionate Placement of Black and Hispanic Students in Special Education Programs.* ERIC ED 204 873.

216. Johnson, J. L. (1969). Special education and the inner city: A challenge for the future or another means for cooling the mark out? *Journal of Special Education, 3* (3), 241–251.

217. Kritek, W. J. (1979) Teacher's concerns in a desegregated school in Milwaukee. *Integrated Education, 17* (1), 19–24.

218. Larkin, J. (1979). School desegregation and student suspension: A look at one school system. *Education and Urban Society, 11* (4), 485–495.

219. *Resegregation of Public Schools: The Third Generation.* (1989). Network of Regional Desegregation Assistance Centers.

220. Richardson, J. G. (1979). The case of special education and minority misclassification in California. *Educational Research Quarterly, 4* (1), 25–40.

221. Rogers, H. R., & Bullock, C. S. III. (1972). *Law and Social Change.* New York: McGraw-Hill.

222. Smith, G. R. (1983). Desegregation and assignment for children to classes for the mildly retarded and learning disabled. *Integrated Education, 21* (1–6), 208–211.

223. Smith, M., & Dziuban, C. D. (1977). The gap between desegregation research and remedy. *Integrated Education, 15,* 51–55.

224. Tillman, J. (1991). Wake up! Please don't let your children become special education students. *Black Issues in Higher Education, 8* (16), 31.

225. Trent, W. T. (1981). Expert opinion on school desegregation issues. In W. D. Hawley (Ed.), *Assessment of Current Knowledge about the Effectiveness of School Desegregation Strategies.* Nashville, TN: Institute for Public Policy Studies, Vanderbilt University.

References 226–228 discuss the practice of referring ineligible students to special education in order to provide them with additional educational services.

226. Cummins, J. (1984). *Bilingualism and Special Education.* Clevedon, England: Multilingual Matters.

227. Reschly, D. J. (1980). *Nonbiased Assessment.* Des Moines: Iowa Department of Instruction.

228. Willig, A. C. (1986). Special education and the culturally and linguistically different child: An overview of issues and challenges. *Reading, Writing, and Learning Disabilities, 2,* 161–173.

References 229–232 are concerned with the underrepresentation of non-European American students in special education programs for students with certain disabilities.

229. Bergin, V. (1980). *Special Education Needs in Bilingual Programs.* Rosslyn, VA: National Clearinghouse for Bilingual Education.

230. Nuttall, E. V., Landurand, P. M., & Goldman, P. (1983). *A Study of Mainstreamed Limited English Proficient Handicapped Students in Bilingual Education.* ERIC ED 246 583.

231. Ortiz, A. A., & Yates, J. R. (1981). *Exceptional Hispanics: Implications for Special Education Services and Manpower Planning.* A report of the Texas Education Agency, Council for Personnel Preparation of the Handicapped, Task Force on Exceptional Hispanics. Austin: University of Texas

232. Vasquez-Chairez, M. (1988). *Bilingual and Special Education: Procedural Manual for Program Administrators.* Crosscultural Special Education Series, Vol. 1. Sacramento: California State Department of Education.

4

EDUCATIONAL APPROACHES FOR STUDENTS FROM DIVERSE ETHNIC AND SOCIOECONOMIC-CLASS BACKGROUNDS

My childhood experience came from participation in a special education program where I was one of a handful of Spanish monolingual children. . . . I was faced with conflicting expectations. The English speaking dominant culture of the school often contrasted vividly with my home culture. As a handicapped individual, I was caught between two value systems and fought desperately for acceptance in both. I struggled to retain my Spanish identity while I was also trying to meet the success standards of a school set up by a culture totally foreign to me. This precarious position placed heavy demands on me as a child. A handicapped youngster must have extraordinary coping abilities in such a situation. (1)

Culturally appropriate special education is a well-accepted goal. Policy statements issued by the federal government and many professional organizations that serve students with disabilities emphasize the importance of multiculturalism. Federal laws such as Public Law (PL) 94-142 and the 1990 amendments to the act require that students with disabilities receive culturally appropriate special education services (2). Congress, however, has not defined the term *culturally appropriate*. As a result, there are many different approaches to providing culturally appropriate educational services that are aimed at solving problems such as increasing respect for diversity, reducing prejudice, improving interethnic group relations, and resolving cultural incompatibilities between students' learning and behavioral styles and special educators' instructional styles.

The lack of a legal definition of culturally appropriate education has left room for differences of opinion about the desirability and efficacy of these approaches with students in general. In addition, they are not equally suitable for students with disabilities. Approaches that can be effective with students with learning and sensory disabilities and average or better learning potential may not suit the needs of students with cognitive disabilities and immature students. Techniques that are appropriate for secondary school students may be inappropriate for elementary school students.

This chapter describes various approaches to these problems. It discusses the advantages and disadvantages of each approach, examines the suitability of techniques for students in special education, and summarizes the research evidence for their effectiveness. Most important, it assists readers in examining the controversies surrounding them and in developing their own points of view about these various approaches.

INCREASING RESPECT FOR DIVERSITY, REDUCING PREJUDICE, AND IMPROVING INTERETHNIC GROUP RELATIONS

Currently, schools in the United States are plagued by ethnic strife. Many groups of students are alienated from schools that reflect a European American cultural bias. Some educators argue that in times like these, special education cannot be culturally appropriate if it does not increase respect for diversity, reduce prejudice and discrimination, and help eliminate alienation. Many approaches for solving these problems have been suggested. These approaches include discussing the similarities and differences among different ethnic groups, including aspects of students' cultures in the curriculum, taking proactive steps to counter and correct bias and prejudice, and preparing students to emancipate themselves and transform society.

Discussions of Differences and Similarities

One approach to increasing respect for diversity and reducing prejudice that has received considerable support among educators is to teach students that all people have similar needs, desires, and problems, but have differences ways of satisfying and solving them. This approach is based on the assumption that when students realize that people who behave differently are actually the same, they will have more respect for the diversity they observe among human beings. "Children must be provided the concepts and experiences which are necessary to assist them in realizing the extent of the similarities, and the nature of the differences in their various human associations. In this manner, children are encouraged to develop an understanding and appreciation of human diversity" (3, p. 4).

Younger students and those with cognitive disabilities can study how all people need to eat well but eat different foods and prepare them differently; all humans need to keep warm and protect themselves against the elements but they use many different and equally effective ways of accomplishing these goals. Older students and those without cognitive disabilities can study the different ways people discipline their children, organize themselves into groups, handle interpersonal conflicts, schedule activities, express themselves verbally, nonverbally, and artistically, and so on. In classes that include students from diverse backgrounds, younger children can tell each other what they like to do to have a good time, what their favorite foods are, and so forth. Older students can describe how things are done at home, how respect is shown in their families, what is embarrassing and distasteful, how family members relate to each other, how late is late, what happens when children do not do what they are supposed to do, how parents discipline children, who does the disciplining, and so on. They can learn how different students like to have things done at school—whether they prefer a lot or very little teacher supervision and feedback, cooperative or competitive learning environments, lectures or discussions, individual or group work, and the like.

Criticisms

Some educators are not comfortable with this approach because they believe that it is better to focus exclusively on the similarities among people. They want educators to avoid discussing differences among people because they are concerned about the divisive effect it can have on relationships between different groups. The following quotations express this point of view: "When people focus on the differences among themselves they engender conflict and hostility" (4, p. 17). "We are all Americans and as Americans we would do well to be blind to the differences that divide us" (4, p. 17).

Certainly this is a valid concern, but proponents of the approach believe that because students also study the similarities among people, they will become decentered and avoid becoming ethnocentric. "My experience in teaching multicultural education courses leads me to believe that an effective way of decentering a person is to use his or her ethnic background as a cross-cultural bridge by showing the parallels between his or her group's experience and that of other ethnic groups. . . . Increasing awareness of such parallels in experiences can, I think, help develop mutual understanding and empathy between different ethnic groups and contribute to the process of depolarization" (5, p. 309).

As will be seen later in this chapter, the available evidence indicates that discussions of similarities and differences increase appreciation and respect for diversity. There is no evidence that discussions of this type cause the kinds of problems that concern its critics.

Inclusion of Students' Cultures in the Classroom

Numerous educators who believe that U.S. schools are too monocultural have recommended, if not demanded, that schools become more representative of today's pluralistic society. They have documented the lack of inclusion of non-European American cultures in the curriculum and have made a variety of suggestions for how educators can include students' cultures in the classroom (6–8, 10, 11, 13–16). The following quotes typify their reasoning:

> Through the omission of information, America's schools have become monocultural environments. They dispense a curriculum centered on western civilization that encapsulates only narrowly the truth, reality, and breadth of human experience. This curriculum reinforces institutional racism by excluding from discourse and from the ethos of the school and the classroom the intellectual thought, scholarship, history,

culture, contributions, and experience of minority groups. Schools have become sites for producing and making acceptable myths and ideologies that systematically disorganize and neutralize the cultural identities of minorities. Consequently, schools—where the hearts and minds of children are shaped and controlled—have been dominated for far too long by the attitudes, the beliefs, and the value system of one race and class of people. This is not a politically, socially, morally, or economically justifiable situation in a democratic, multicultural society. (14, p. 90)

All U.S. citizens need to master a common core of shared knowledge. However, the important question is: *Who will participate in the formulation of that knowledge and whose interests will it serve?* We need a broad level of participation in the identification, construction, and formulation of the knowledge that we expect all of our citizens to master. Such knowledge should reflect cultural democracy and serve the interests of all of the people within our pluralistic nation and world. (8, p. 126)

A multicultural approach that has been used by many regular and special educators to achieve these goals is to include aspects of students' cultures in the curriculum. They teach units on the foods, clothing, stories, legends, dances, and arts of the major ethnic groups in the United States. They select textbooks and other educational materials that include pictures of and stories about different ethnic groups. They listen to the music of different ethnic groups, discuss and celebrate their holidays, and note their historical and current contributions. On these occasions, some special educators also encourage students to bring to class things such as pictures, foods, games, photos, jewelry, pets, money, and musical instruments from home. Unfortunately, almost all of the available commercially prepared material is designed for students in regular education. Multicultural materials designed for students with developmental disabilities, learning and sensory disabilities, and so on are almost nonexistent. As a result, some students with disabilities, especially those with sensory impairments, are denied many potential multicultural school experiences.

Some experts note that multicultural education is usually included in special units or only on special occasions. They maintain that although this is a positive first step, multicultural education approaches are more effective when they are included in the ongoing, daily curriculum.

When educators add ethnic heroes and fragmented ethnic content to the curriculum, ethnic heroes and content are assumed to be nonintegral parts of the mainstream U.S. experience. Consequently, it is assumed sufficient to add special units and festivals to teach about ethnic groups and their cultures. Particularly in elementary social studies, ethnic content is taught primarily with special lessons and pageants on holidays and birthdays. Blacks usually dominate lessons during Black History Week or on Martin Luther King's birthday, but they are largely invisible in the curriculum during the rest of the year. (7, p. 533)

Some experts believe that teachers often teach students superficial inaccurate stereotypes. Thus, Pepper has advised, "Bias about Indians is often the result of inaccurate information. The realities of American Indian and Alaskan Native life are often oversimplified and distorted. Stylized accounts of Indian life reinforce the 'buckskin and feather' and the 'Eskimo and igloo' stereotypes. With such instruction, students are certain to develop misguided impressions of Indians" (13, p. 1).

Researchers note that merely celebrating special days, learning about selected heroes, eating ethnic foods, and building tepees and igloos does not help students understand the experiences, attitudes, problems, life-styles, and so on of different groups. They recommend that teachers focus more on these real-life current problems.

> Focusing on the strange and exotic traits and characteristics of ethnic groups is likely to reinforce stereotypes and misconceptions. The making of tepees does not reveal anything significant about contemporary American Indian values, cultures, or experiences. It merely adds to the classical Indian stereotype, which is so pervasive on television and in the wider society. Rather than focus on the exotic characteristics of ethnic groups the teacher should emphasize the common needs which all human groups share, such as the need to explain the unknown and the need for artistic expression, and the diverse ways in which American ethnic groups have solved the problems of survival. (11, p. 86)

> The infusion of fragmented ethnic content into the curriculum . . . results in the trivialization of ethnic cultures. The study of Mexican-American food or of native American tepees will not help students develop a sophisticated understanding of Mexican-American culture and of the tremendous cultural diversity among native Americans. (7, p. 533)

There is considerable validity to these authors' suggestions, especially for secondary school students in the mainstream and for gifted and talented students. However, it is unclear how applicable these recommendations are to students with disabilities. For example, immature students and those with cognitive disabilities may not be able to relate to some within-group differences or the more abstract aspects of culture. Therefore, special educators' decisions about which aspects of students' cultures to include in the curriculum should be based on an appreciation of their students' cognitive development and level of maturity.

Criticisms

Although few educators oppose demonstrating respect for cultural diversity in the ways just discussed, some believe many teachers go too far. They think that educators overemphasize the importance of the contributions of non-European American groups. They worry that educators do not teach students that American society was founded by European Americans and do not give sufficient attention to their belief that the United States owes its greatness to the Anglo-Saxon democratic principles the European settlers brought with them. They also believe that the inclusion of all cultures in the curriculum waters it down. For example, in a monograph entitled *Pluralism Gone Mad,* Thomas stated,

> Those who founded this nation wrote some important ideas into our national documents. It is those ideas that must be taught in our schools. . . . It is an ethos that supports diversity with limits . . . and a set of political principles that distinguishes us

from all other nations. . . . The American ethos has sustained us for over 200 years . . . and it will eventually lead us through the quicksand of pluralism gone mad . . . as we enter a third century as a free nation, the American ethos of freedom, opportunity, self-reliance, hard work, adherence to law, respect for individuals, and commitment to rigorous standards will become the norm of our schools. (16, pp. 27–29)

If the schools are expected to teach the cultures of all groups and the preferences of all political persuasions in our nation, then the curriculum will become so overloaded that little of substance will be accomplished. (16, pp. 16–17)

Other critics of multicultural education have stated,

"Multicultural education" should not take place at the expense of studies that transcend cultural differences; the truths of mathematics, the sciences, history, and so on, are not different for people of different races, sexes, or cultures, and for that reason alone their study is liberating. Nor should we further attenuate the study of the traditions of the West. Not only is knowledge of those traditions essential for any evaluation of our own institutions, it is increasingly relevant to our understanding of other nations, which in striking testament to the universality of the values they embody, are rapidly adapting Western practices to their own situations. (12, p. A23)

[Multicultural education] promotes cultural relativism instead of teaching students to respect and appreciate the best that has been produced in Western and in other cultures. (9, pp. A13, A22)

Proponents of multicultural education do not accept these criticisms. They believe that many groups besides Western Europeans contributed to the development of the United States. They do not agree that including the contributions of other groups diminishes the importance of the contributions of Western Europeans. In addition, they do not agree that including information about various ethnic groups will lead to a watering down of the curriculum because they do not expect schools to teach the cultures of all groups. Suzuki has explained,

Of course it would be impossible for any teacher to incorporate the experiences and perspectives of all the ethnic groups—there are more than 300—into the curriculum. I would suggest including at least those groups that are present in significant numbers in the local community, along with a few that may not be present. However, there would still be a massive amount of factual information even on these groups. Since there is little merit in having students memorize a lot of low-level facts about these groups, a conceptual approach that provides a framework for understanding the experiences and perspectives of all the groups would appear to be the most effective strategy. (5, p. 311)

There is little evidence that multicultural approaches have gone too far; in fact, the opposite appears to be true. However, very little multicultural information is included in regular or special education elementary and secondary school programs. What is included tends to be taught during special occasions, not infused into the ongoing curriculum.

Proactive Antibias
Curricular Approaches

Acknowledging a variety of cultures in the classroom and discussing why various ethnic and socioeconomic characteristics are equally acceptable demonstrate respect for students' cultural backgrounds. However, these instructional techniques do very little to reduce prejudice, discrimination, and intergroup hostility in the classroom. Some authors maintain that in order to accomplish these goals, special educators must take positive steps specifically designed to eliminate the prejudicial and discriminatory treatment students receive in school and to help resolve hostility, animosity, and suspicion between students from different cultural backgrounds (17–23). Research supports their position. Taking specific steps to improve students' relationships and perceptions of each other is more effective than merely talking at students or teaching them a unit about prejudice. Teaching students about the realities of prejudice in the United States accomplishes more than only including students' cultures in the curriculum. Also, a schoolwide approach that is designed to influence all students and to change the climate of the school is better than an approach that involves only a single class or group of students.

Eliminating Teacher Bias

Many experts on teacher bias have suggested that teachers should begin by monitoring their own behavior to be sure that they do not model prejudicial attitudes and behavior. Becoming aware of your own own prejudices and stereotypic perceptions and behavior is a necessary first step in changing them. Some of the exercises and activities in Chapter 3 are designed to enhance your awareness of your attitudes about cultural differences and the ways, if any, you encourage prejudice in your classroom. Reading the material and completing the self-quizzes and activities in this chapter should provide you with additional insight.

However, self-insight alone is insufficient, especially since the very structure of society supports certain biases. Real behavioral change requires determined effort over time. The following are some steps you might consider to improve your perceptions and behavior:

- Work with another teacher on changing a few of your behaviors or attitudes each month.
- Form a support group with other colleagues or ask your school to provide in-service training.
- Examine your instructional and classroom management techniques for the kinds of bias described in Chapter 3.

The following self-quiz is an example of the biased beliefs people harbor about one ethnic group.

SELF-
QUIZ   **BELIEFS ABOUT NATIVE AMERICANS**

Pepper has maintained that the following myths about Native Americans are commonplace in most textbooks and elementary school curricula. Which, if any, did or do you believe to be true?

1. American Indians and Alaskan Natives are a similar group of people who share a common language and culture and live together in similar places.
2. All American Indians and Alaskan Natives live on reservations.
3. American Indians and Alaskan Natives receive checks from the government because they are Indian.
4. The existing status of American Indians, their people, and their governments is the product of accepted principles of international law and equity.
5. American Indians are a defeated people.
6. The allotment Act (Dawes Act of 1887) was passed to civilize American Indians by making them private property owners.
7. Thanksgiving is a day of rejoicing that marks the advent of a mutually beneficial relationship between European settlers and Native people. (13, pp. 1–2)

SELF-
QUIZ   **PREJUDICE**

None of us is perfect; we all have acted in a prejudicial or discriminatory manner at one time or another. We all have difficulty changing our attitudes and behavior. The following questions are designed to help you acquire the self-insight you may need to improve. Ask yourself why you have used discriminatory approaches.

- Is it difficult for you to admit to yourself that you are prejudiced?
- Does change make you uncomfortable?
- Do you find that you resist a multicultural approach because sensitive topics upset people or create hostility or conflict?
- Are you concerned for your job or that your relationships with the administration, your colleagues, or the community will suffer if you do things differently, make waves, deal with ethnic hostility openly, or discuss ugly aspects of American history and culture?
- Do you think that you cannot make a significant contribution by yourself so it is not worth the effort or the risk?
- Do you feel that adapting a multicultural approach would require too much work?
- Do you lack information about some ethnic groups?

Eliminating Curricular Bias

Eliminating the bias found in classroom materials and in the content of courses can help prevent student bias. There are many published guidelines one can refer to for assistance (24–30). The following list of sources of bias is a good place to begin:

- Representing certain groups in an unflattering or demeaning manner (Jews are money-mad and stingy; Native Americans are savages; Mexican Americans are lazy; African Americans are on welfare; all gang members are African Americans or Hispanic Americans)
- Making overgeneralizations (African American families are always headed by females; Hispanic Americans always have many children)
- Omitting non-Europeans altogether or underrepresenting them
- Making revisions of the pictures and illustrations in a book to include significant numbers of non-European Americans without changing its contents
- Darkening illustrations of people with obvious European facial features to make them appear ambiguous
- Stereotyping in instructional material (presenting non-Europeans in stereotypic roles at work and play; attributing stereotypic personality characteristics such as studious Asian Americans and athletic African Americans)
- Assigning certain ethnic groups traditional and stereotypic roles that imply that they have limited abilities and potential or are less valuable to society (European Americans perform leadership roles, take the initiative, play the key roles in solving problems, give aid and assistance; non-European Americans are European Americans' helpers and the recipients of their assistance)
- Omitting the roles of non-Europeans in history, their contributions to science, and so on
- Describing other cultural heritages from a European American view (presenting only a European American perspective on such issues as wars and other conflicts between groups; calling Native American victories massacres and their defeats battles)
- Presenting problems such as drug abuse, poverty, homelessness, and crime as if they were restricted to non-European communities
- Including only a few non-Europeans' work in basal readers, literary anthologies, language arts kits, and so on
- Glossing over or ignoring such controversial or troublesome issues as slavery, oppression, poverty, prejudice, and injustice
- Setting non-Europeans off in boxes away from the main body of a text, which remains biased and one sided
- Describing families as two-parent families living in suburban middle-class neighborhoods in which the father goes to work in a suit and the mother stays home
- Employing only middle-class standards of success, such as a college degree, and working as a professional, executive, or entrepreneur
- Illustrating the final rung on the evolutionary ladder as a European American male

Teaching about Prejudice

Some experts think teachers need to inform students about the facts of racism in the United States if they want students to become less biased. Their point of view is expressed in the following quotations:

> The overt goals of multicultural education can be realized only when policy-makers, educators, and communities acknowledge the subtle (and sometimes not so subtle) forms of institutionalized racism that permeate the structures of schools and mediate the interactions between educators and students. In other words, unless it becomes "anti-racist education," "multicultural education" may serve only to provide a veneer of change that in reality perpetuates discriminatory educational structures. (31, pp. 127–128)

> Although the beautiful and heroic aspects of our history should be taught, so must the ugly and exclusionary. Rather than viewing the world through rose-colored glasses, antiracist multicultural education forces both teachers and students to take a long, hard look at everything as it was and is. (22, pp. 208–209)

> To truly address racism, instruction must enable teachers and students to analyze the inequities in power and economic status that determine race relations. (20, p. 1)

Some special educators teach students with disabilities about societal prejudices against them since they too are themselves victims of prejudice and discrimination. "Helping deaf children become aware of the ethnic and cultural differences between themselves and deaf persons of other ethnic groups or between themselves and hearing members of their own ethnic group is an important factor in their education, development and survival" (19, p. 71).

Very little has been published about the techniques special educators have used to teach students with disabilities about societal prejudice against them, and there are few antibias materials designed specifically for students with disabilities. A great deal has been written about how to teach students about prejudice in general. Proponents of antibias curricular approaches have offered teachers the following suggestions (20, 22, 31, 32):

- Make discussions of racism and discrimination an explicit aspect of the curriculum. Do not allow the truth about these problems to be swept under the carpet as something too ugly or un-American for discussion.
- Replace teaching about tepees, igloos, and other out-of-date stereotypes with discussions of actual current problems and issues in the lives of different ethnic groups. In the case of Native Americans, these issues could include fishing and hunting rights, land claims, self-rule, education and health issues, and the like.
- Introduce pertinent incidents of prejudice and discrimination in the news or in a particular field of study into the curriculum on a regular and timely basis.
- Have students examine television programs, movies, magazine articles, and textbooks for prejudice, bias, and stereotyping.
- Invite guest speakers who perform roles that counteract stereotypes. Talks by African American and Hispanic American lawyers and physicians can reduce students' stereotypes of such groups.

- Eliminate stereotypes by demonstrating to students that whatever the stereotype, there are many exceptions to the rule. "Although it is always important to understand how culture, language, gender and economic class influence such things as learning and communication style, it is equally crucial to understand that these factors are not *deterministic*. That is, not all Jewish students have an ethos for scholarship, not all African American students have a relational learning style, and not all Asian students are quiet and independent learners" (22, p. 254).

Some of these suggestions may be ineffective or even undesirable with some students with disabilities. Immature students and students with cognitive disabilities may not be able to relate to some of the concepts and issues included in these suggestions. Students with emotional problems or cognitive disabilities may be too sensitive and too easily upset by conflicts and hostility to cope with the ugliness of ethnic conflict, prejudice, and racism.

Improving Interethnic Group Relations and Resolving Intergroup Conflicts

There are many approaches to improving interethnic group relations. Many published materials designed to assist educators in improving interethnic group relations have proven to be effective with students in the mainstream (33–43). Unfortunately, their effectiveness with students with disabilities, young students, and immature students has not been evaluated.

Teacher-initiated activities and techniques have also been shown to work. These include organizing discussions in which students describe the prejudice that they have suffered, using role-playing activities to help students experience rejection and prejudice, and having students divide into groups on the basis of some arbitrary characteristic such as hair color, height, or alphabetical order and assign superior and subordinate roles to each group.

Exposing students to the life experiences of the refugee and immigrant students who they often ridicule and reject helps students to understand these groups and reduces prejudice against them. Themes such as Coming to America, Forced Out, Homeland Histories, and Our Lives have been used to encourage immigrant and refugee students to describe their experiences through art projects, murals, plays, and oral reports. Published materials specifically designed to teach students about the immigrant and refugee experience are also available (38).

It is also possible to request guest speakers from such groups as Children of War. Guest speakers provided by Children of War are children who have been victims of war. They participate in workshops throughout the United States that are designed to help other students understand the experiences of refugee children and their problems. Many cities have local chapters that can provide services to local schools (34). As noted earlier, teachers can do the same thing by having refugee students in the school describe their experiences in class or as part of an assembly program. The following quote describes the reaction of a student who was exposed to such information: "When I first heard other kids stand up and talk about what it is like to grow up in a country at war—like when I first heard

Guatemalans coming from their country and having been tortured at such a young age, I thought 'Oh, my God, wait a minute! My biggest worry is waking up at 7:00 so I can get to my classes on time! I don't have to think about my family disappearing.' It is a tremendous eye-opener to see what life is like for refugees here. It shocked me and my friends into realizing there is more to the world than our own experiences" (34, p. 52).

Many teachers prefer to avoid dealing with discriminatory incidents or intergroup friction in the form of fights, name calling, and threats. However, many experts suggest that teachers should handle them head-on. They advise teachers not merely to tell students, "We don't call others names in this room" or something to that effect. Rather, they should discuss such incidents not as isolated incidents but as a reflection of the society in which students are growing up. "Teachers generally avoid discussing such issues as racial name-calling, or peer relationships and how they develop among students. Yet, such issues are often the more potent aspects of the immediate social reality of students and can be used by teachers to give students a deeper, more personal understanding of broader social issues. By personalizing learning in this way, I believe that students will gain not only cognitive knowledge, but equally important, they will also develop greater empathy and sensitivity" (5, p. 313).

Interethnic group conflicts can be handled within the classroom or by means of various schoolwide entities. Student mediation panels composed of student volunteers who have been trained to mediate intercultural problems among their fellow students have proven successful at resolving the problems of students who are referred to the panel by teachers, counselors, and others. Interethnic advisory boards/forums made up of students, parents, staff, and community members are another effective way to respond to conflicts (34).

It is also possible to use a case-study method to examine how prejudice, discrimination, ethnic conflict, and the like occur and to discover how they can be avoided and resolved. Special educators can prepare cases on their own or use some that are available in the literature as models (44). To develop a case study for use in your classroom, consider the following:

- What issues do you want the students to consider?
- How does the situation look from the points of view of the students involved?
- What went wrong?
- What could have been done to avoid the problem?
- What should be done now?

Since students who require special education services have different disabilities, levels of maturity, and cognitive abilities, it is important for special educators to select only those approaches to improving interethnic group relations and resolving intergroup conflicts that are suitable for their particular students.

Schoolwide Approaches
Research indicates that the goals of multicultural education cannot be fully achieved in a one-time or one-classroom approach (14, 22, 45). Nieto has pointed out that "the entire 'culture' of the school must be changed if the impact of multi-

cultural education is to be felt, including curriculum and materials, institutional norms, attitudes and behaviors of teachers and other staff, counseling services, [and] the extent to which parents are welcome in the school" (22, p. 253).

The following are some of the many schoolwide programs that are designed to reduce prejudice and discrimination and to improve intergroup relations (34):

• Project REACH is a year-long, four-phase program that has been used successfully with middle school students (34). In the Human Relationship skills phase, students complete activities designed to enhance their self-esteem, self-awareness, interpersonal communication skills, and understanding of group dynamics. This is followed by the Cultural Self-Awareness phase, in which students examine their own culture, ethnicity, family history, or community. The third phase—Multicultural Awareness—is based on a set of booklets, the *Ethnic Perspectives Series,* that are designed to present American history from diverse ethnic points of view. In the final phase, Cross-Cultural Experience, students engage in dialogue and exchange ideas with students and adults from different ethnic backgrounds.

Research indicates that in comparison to students who have not participated in Project REACH, students who have completed the program have a greater sense of pride and know more about other cultures. They are more accepting of ethnic differences and more interested in learning about students from other backgrounds. They also engage in fewer incidents of putting down other students, name calling, and ethnic slurs (37, 39).

• A World of Difference provides a number of services, including community action and school-based programs, one of which is a 40-lesson program for secondary-level students on U.S. beliefs and values; prejudice, stereotyping, and discrimination; scapegoating; and racism (34).

• The Green Circle Program provides schools with workshops for students that are run by trained facilitators who guide students through understanding how they can include rather than exclude certain groups of individuals who appear to be different because of their religion, ethnic background, or disability (34).

Special education programs that are not integrated into the regular education program may not be able to participate in such schoolwide approaches. This is one more reason why programs for students with disabilities should be as integrated as possible into the mainstream.

Emancipatory and Transformational Approaches

Some educators believe that merely helping students to become informed about racism is not sufficient. They believe students, especially those who are the victims of prejudice, must also be taught how to resist and combat racism. This approach has been labeled *emancipatory multicultural education* and *education for empowerment* by its proponents (5, 8, 46–49). (See Chapter 3.) "Education for empowerment demands taking seriously the strengths, experiences, strategies, and goals members of oppressed groups have. It also demands helping them to analyze and understand the social structure that oppresses them and to act in ways that will enable them to reach their own goals successfully. . . . Education for empowerment also means teaching students how to advocate effectively for themselves as individuals as well as collectively" (48, p. 6).

Some educators suggest that resistance is insufficient. To their way of thinking, teachers should prepare students to change the biased discriminatory aspects of society. This approach has been called *transformational education* and *social reconstructionist education*. (See Chapter 3.)

> A transformative curriculum cannot be constructed merely by adding content about ethnic groups and women to the existing Eurocentric curriculum or by integrating or infusing ethnic content or content about women into the mainstream curriculum. When the curriculum is revised using either an additive or an infusion approach, the basic assumptions, perspectives, paradigms, and values of the dominant curriculum remain unchallenged and substantially unchanged, despite the addition of ethnic content or content about women. . . . A curriculum designed to empower students must be transformative in nature and help students to develop the knowledge, skills, and values needed to become social critics who can make reflective decisions and implement their decisions in effective personal, social, political, and economic action. (8, pp. 130–131)

According to some special educators, students with disabilities should also be prepared to advocate for themselves and change society's attitude and behavior toward them since they too are often the victims of prejudice and discrimination. Adult citizens with disabilities, including those with developmental disabilities, have actively participated in public demonstrations and other forms of self-advocacy. However, there is no research about the level of maturity required of students with disabilities in order to profit from activities designed to prepare them to advocate for themselves and help change society.

Criticisms

Suggestions for reducing prejudice meet with a mixed reception. Not many educators have gone on record as supporting the prejudicial treatment non-European American and poor students receive that is described in Chapter 3. Few educators would disagree that teachers' expectations for students, evaluation procedures, placement decisions, instructional techniques, curriculum materials, and classroom management techniques should be as free from bias as possible. However, there is considerable disagreement about whether schools should expose students to the negative aspects of the history of and the present circumstances in the United States—"the ugly realities of systematic discrimination [and the] ugly and exclusionary" (22, p. 208). There is also much debate about what role, if any, the schools should play in preparing students to be self-advocates and change agents. (See Chapter 3.)

**TECHNIQUES FOR INCREASING
RESPECT FOR DIVERSITY, REDUCING PREJUDICE,
AND IMPROVING INTERETHNIC GROUP RELATIONS**

State which of the following techniques you would be comfortable using with students with disabilities who had the cognitive ability and maturity to profit from them:

- Discussing similarities and differences
- Including students' cultures in the classroom
- Eliminating teacher bias
- Teaching about bias against people who are non-European American, poor, or disabled
- Exposing students to the life experiences of immigrant and refugee students
- Pairing students in ESL and bilingual education programs with students in special education programs
- Meeting discrimination and intergroup conflicts head-on
- Preparing students to advocate for themselves
- Preparing students to change society's attitudes and behavior toward them

LEARNING AND TEACHING STYLE INCOMPATIBILITIES

Non-European American and poor students with disabilities often are unprepared for the instructional techniques they are exposed to in school because their learning and behavioral styles do not match their teachers' instructional styles. There are at least four different ways in which special educators can handle the incompatibilities and discontinuities between students' cultural characteristics and the norms, expectations, and methods that prevail in most schools. They can *accommodate* their methods to students' cultural characteristics, help students to adjust to the approaches that are typically found in U.S. schools (*assimilation*), assist students to become *bicultural,* or *empower* students to resolve their cultural conflicts in their own ways. This chapter examines the arguments for and against each of these approaches. Chapters 9 through 11 describe how special educators can implement these techniques when they assess, instruct, and manage students, as well as work cooperatively with their parents.

Accommodation

Many special educators believe that when there are mismatches between their teaching and classroom management styles and students' learning and behavioral styles, they should adapt or accommodate their educational approaches to their students. This is also the position of many professional organizations. For example, the Council for Exceptional Children stated, "Professional personnel should be required to receive training in adapting instruction to accommodate children with different learning styles who are members of ethnic and multicultural groups. College and university preservice training programs should include clinical, practicum, or other field experiences with specific focus on learning about exceptional children from ethnic and multicultural groups" (55, pp. ix, 4).

Criticisms

A number of special educators have reservations about accommodating to cultural differences. Some of them believe that it is impractical; others believe that even if accommodation were feasible, it is undesirable. Their reasons are discussed here.

- *There are no monolithic cultures in the United States.*

Some individuals argue that even within such groups as Asian Pacific Island Americans, Hispanic Americans, and African Americans, people are so different that it is not possible to accommodate educational techniques to the cultural needs of any ethnic group. This point of view is presented in the following quotation about Hispanic Americans, but it applies to other ethnic groups as well:

> Latin America is composed of developed industrialized countries such as Argentina and Chile and basically under-developed countries such as Bolivia, Honduras, Belize and Panama. Some countries have a strong European cosmopolitan influence, others have an American influence and others are still predominantly Indian. Some have high rates of illiteracy while others have well-developed educational systems which are as fine or better than those found in some states in the U.S. How then can we talk about a Hispanic culture in the U.S. when Hispanics come here from such diverse countries? (4, pp. 9–10)

Other educators grant that there is great variability among members of a particular ethnic group. However, they claim that as important as these differences are, there are also many important similarities among the members. As an Hispanic American special educator stated, "When I am with a group of fellow Latinos I'm conscious of our differences. Cubanos, Mexicanos, Puerto Riquenos, Colombianos, we are all different. Yet when I find myself among non-Latinos I realize how much alike we Latinos are" (4, p. 10).

As will be seen throughout this text, research studies consistently reveal the existence of educationally relevant cultural differences among different ethnic, socioeconomic-class, and regional groups. Although these characteristics may not apply to all individuals in a particular group, they are common enough so that special educators should be alert to the *possibility* that they may be applicable to an individual student or parent.

- *It is impossible to accommodate educational approaches to the cultural needs of the many culturally different students found in any particular school system or often within a particular classroom.*

Many people do not believe that educators can accommodate their methods and techniques to the different cultural groups with whom they work. Some of their reasons are found in the following quotation from a special educator:

My school district, the Los Angeles County School District, has over one hundred different language/culture groups. How can anyone be expected to know about all these different cultures, and how can anyone be expected to apply what they do know? From what I have been told during in-service training, what are appropriate teaching technique for one group are inappropriate for another. How can I teach my Anglo students one way, my Latino students a second way, my Vietnamese students a third, my Korean students a fourth way, my Hmong, my Portuguese, etc., at the same time? Impossible! (4, pp. 15–16)

Other educators believe it is possible. They do not agree that each culture requires a unique educational approach. They point out that alternative methods of instructing students, organizing classrooms, and counseling parents are limited. For example, educators can encourage or require their students to work individually or in groups; they can motivate them through the use of competitive games or cooperative settings; they can allow them to work at their own pace or encourage them to work as quickly as possible; they can attempt to develop close personal relationships with them or maintain a "professional distance"; they can correct and criticize them in front of their peers or privately; they can encourage them to discuss controversial issues and express differences of opinion or emphasize similarities of experience and opinion; and they can teach abstract concepts or utilize methods that stress the concrete and learning by doing. Believing that educators are always choosing between alternatives as limited as these, proponents of accommodation think educators can easily adapt their methodology to the cultural needs of their students. There is little research to support either position. We do not know how effective educators can be when they have to accommodate their techniques simultaneously to many different groups in the same classroom (77).

- *It would not be a good idea for professionals involved in educating non-European American students to use misleading and even prejudicial description of their cultures.*

Some people are concerned that when educators attempt to be culturally relevant, they will believe misleading and outdated stereotypes about their students' cultures and adapt their educational practices to these incorrect beliefs. Some teachers do accept outdated or fictionalized versions of their students' cultures and focus on the quaint or unusual aspects of their life-styles. For example, some teachers of Native American students may believe that they still have life-styles like those depicted in Hollywood westerns (63). This suggests that educators should take great care to avoid these problems; it does not mean that they should not attempt to learn as much as they can about their students' cultural background.

Many educators are also concerned that teachers will fall victim to prejudicial stereotypes of non-European American students. The following statement reflects their view: "I believe enough good research has been done to dismiss bigoted stereotypes. . . . I, personally, get very tired of having to defend my culture against the mythical themes of the 'hot blooded, lazy, Latin'" (4, p. 11).

As the following quotations indicate, many other educators maintain that one of the most effective ways to combat such prejudice is to provide educators with accurate descriptions of the cultural characteristics of ethnic groups: "Regardless of the benefits that may accrue from public institutions refusing to acknowledge, *in public*, general descriptions of ethnic traits, it is my conviction that this very refusal has fostered the continued use of incorrect and often unjust stereotypes about ethnic groups" (65, p. 10). Another author has stated, "To identify differences related to Afro-Americans is, of course, a controversial issue; regardless of the disclaimers, values of good or bad, inferior or superior, are so ingrained in our society that the issue will still lead to reinforcement of stereotypes. . . . However, if we are to engage in an educational revolution aimed at promoting the success of a larger percentage of the Afro-American population, it is an area that must be explored" (74, p. 238).

- *Cultural descriptions can lead to misleading overgeneralizations.*

Some special educators are concerned that teachers may think that their knowledge of the cultural characteristics of different ethnic groups and socioeconomic classes is sufficient for them to understand an individual student or parent. This concern is expressed in the following statement:

> There are many common stereotypes of the Hispanic person such as never being on time, being deeply religious, etc. Those who work with Hispanics should be aware of this and guard against a generalized, stereotyped view of those they work with. This is not to say that a specific stereotype (like being deeply religious) may not apply to an individual. Rather, the individual should always be dealt with as a unique human being who may or may not exhibit certain attitudes, habits, and beliefs.
>
> A list of over-general attributes which describe certain socio-economic subgroups of Hispanics such as the poor who may be more apt to have certain problems in school or the Indian who may be more apt to believe in La Llorona will not make educators more sensitive. Educators must recognize that children come to us from an infinitely varied array of backgrounds and not assume that all Hispanic students come from poor or Indian backgrounds. (4, p. 12)

The possibility of overgeneralization is an ever-present danger. However, as the following statement indicates, many people believe that despite this possibility, educators should be aware of the cultural traits that may characterize their students: "It is important for educators to be aware of our culture just so long as they refrain from thinking that we are all exactly alike. Just as knowing one Anglo would not enable a Hispanic to know all Anglos, so too knowing a few Hispanic students does not enable an Anglo educator to 'know' all Hispanic students either as a group or individually" (4, p. 13).

- *To treat some students differently than others is discriminatory.*

Some critics of the accommodation position argue that since all people are basically the same, they should be treated the same. Not to do so, in their opinion, is unfair and discriminatory. Proponents of the accommodation position disagree. They grant that human beings are basically the same; they prefer success to failure, praise and recognition to criticism or condemnation, and acceptance and attention to rejection and inattention. However, those who believe in accommodation maintain that peoples' behavior in these situations is influenced by different cultural veneers. They have different criteria for success. They find different forms of praise and recognition rewarding. They differ in terms of when, where, why, and how they are willing to accept criticism or condemnation. They also express acceptance and rejection in their own culturally determined ways. Therefore, if teachers expect all individuals to behave the same way or interpret everyone's behavior from a single culturally determined point of view, they may fail to respond to the unique needs of many of their ethnic minority students.

In addition, the result of treating all students the same may be that those who do not fit the model used by their teachers are treated in a discriminatory manner. "When teachers ignore students' race and claim that they treat all children the same, they usually mean that their model of the ideal student is white and middle-class" (61, p. 54).

For example, Hilliard (59) advised that special educators who believe that providing students with the same instructional techniques, classroom management approaches, and so on have the mistaken notion that they are treating them equally and being fair to them. However, they are not treating all students the same but are dealing with some students in a culturally appropriate manner and others in a biased manner. Hilliard suggested that there is a more valid way of treating students the same, and that is to provide all students with culturally appropriate educational approaches. According to him, this may make it appear that students are being treated differently but they are actually being treated the same and in a nondiscriminatory manner.

- *Treating groups of students differently can result in lower expectations and standards for some non-European American groups. It can also lead European Americans to retaliate against those whom they believe are given preferential treatment.*

Anecdotal evidence, which needs updating, suggests that these are valid concerns (63, 77). In an attempt to be culturally relevant, some well-meaning educators do lower their standards for some students. For example, Thomas reported, "A young man whom I taught in senior high school is now attending a predominantly black college. He has an English teacher who happens to be white and who constantly tells blacks of the hard work whites at a nearby university receive. She further informs them (blacks) that she is not going to give work that is 'too difficult'—that they need not worry. . . . Such conduct is demeaning and, indeed, criminal on the part of the teacher, for blacks do not need missionaries to pity them; they need teachers to instruct them" (77, p. 320).

Kleinfeld reported the following conversation between a teacher whom she labels a cultural relativist and a Native American student: "After class, an Indian girl came up to the teacher and told her that she had been sick and had missed the last test. 'What should I study for it?' she asked. 'Don't worry,' the teacher replied. 'I'll make up a special test for you and you'll do well on it.' 'But I don't know what to study.' 'Don't worry,' repeated the teacher. 'I'll make it special for you. You'll do well'" (63, p. 271). Kleinfeld also found that many European American students resent the special treatment Native Americans receive from some teachers. "White students resent the easier assignments, tests, and grading system used exclusively for the Indians. They often take if upon themselves to redress the inequity" (63, p. 271).

There probably are many teachers like these, who reduce their standards for non-European American students and cause other students to express their resentment in nonconstructive ways. However, these teachers are not following the advice of educators who caution them to maintain realistic standards for non-European American students and not expect them to behave in an anti-social manner or to achieve less than others while they educate them in a culturally appropriate manner (59).

ACCOMMODATION: AN EXAMPLE OF A CULTURALLY COMPATIBLE EDUCATIONAL APPROACH

Hawaiian American students are often perceived as lazy and uninvolved by teachers who are unaware of the cultural incompatibilities that these individuals experience in school. In school, teachers constantly supervise students, set rules, make assignments, and regulate the classroom's resources. On the other hand, at home, when a Hawaiian American parent wants something done, he or she tells the children to do it and lets them organize themselves and take care of it. When teachers act more like Hawaiian American parents by withdrawing from supervising students and assuming that they will act responsibly, Hawaiian American students involve themselves in the classroom activities. An approach that has been used successfully to make the classroom routines more culturally compatible and involve Hawaiian students in classroom activities includes the following:

- The teacher models a routine or task and explains the procedure.
- The teacher instructs the students to perform the desired task, then withdraws as quickly as possible from supervising the group.
- The teacher lets the group determine how the task will be done, who the leader will be, who will perform which aspects of the task, and so on.
- The teacher does not interfere in order to impose her or his own cultural values about such things as fair play, sharing the workload equally, and so on (62).

Assimilation

A great many special educators believe that the best way to deal with cultural incompatibilities in students' learning styles, behavior styles, and communication styles is for students to adopt the school's European American culture. The reasons they typically cite for believing that assimilation should be the ultimate goal are discussed here.

- *Students will learn more effectively if they accommodate to the learning and behavior styles that prevail in schools.*
  Many educators believe that for non-European students to actualize their potential in school, "they must aspire to enter the middle class, adopt the middle-

class lifestyle, and use the middle-class value standard as a reference to judge their own behavior" (75, p. 20). There is little evidence to support this hypothesis. In fact, there is evidence that among some non-European groups, those who are most likely to be well adjusted and to succeed both academically and vocationally are not those who reject their ethnic identity; rather, they are those who identify with their own ethnic group (52–54, 62, 64, 67, 68, 73, 75, 76, 79, 80, 82). The reasons for this have not been well studied, but the following are some possible explanations:

- Students who have not assimilated bring the positive aspects of their cultures to the educational situation.
- Students who assimilate may substitute the poor attitudes toward school that characterize many European American students for the positive attitudes that prevail in their original culture.
- Students who maintain their cultural identity have more self-esteem and self-confidence than those who reject their cultural background.
- In comparison to monocultural students, bicultural students have a larger repertoire of learning strategies and coping techniques to apply to the tasks and challenges of school.
- Assimilated students may experience conflicts with their parents as well as identity conflicts, resentment, anger, and rebelliousness, all of which can interfere with students' learning.

- *Schools should not accommodate their expectations and approaches to those of disadvantaged/inferior non-European American cultures.*

Some special educators believe that schools should not accommodate to the cultural needs of non-European American students because the European American culture is superior to other cultures. Instead, they should encourage non-European American students and their parents to give up those cultural characteristics that have held back the progress of their native countries or ethnic groups. The following quotation exemplifies this point of view: "People come to this country to better themselves. If their native cultures are so great, why did they have to immigrate? If they aren't willing to accept the values that have helped the United States have the largest economy and the highest standard of living then they should return to the countries from which they came and settle for the limited opportunities they provide" (anonymous).

The idea that some cultures—especially the African American, Hispanic American, and Native American cultures—are inferior, deprived, or disadvantaged was discussed at length in Chapter 2 and rejected.

- *Non-European American students and their families should adapt to the mainstream culture in the schools because people living in the same country should all speak the same language, follow the same laws, and share the same morality.*

This idea is embodied in the following statements: "We cannot survive as a culture with different laws for different people. Everyone must pay taxes, serve in the army, respect private property and the rights of others regardless of where they were born or what religion they profess" (4, p. 13). Another author has stated, "Pluralism in our society has produced a moral climate that tells everyone to establish a sense of what is right and wrong *for you*. This trend has a way of blurring the limits of a moral code. In the educational arena this trend has produced a no-fault morality and relativistic values. . . . Schools, if they are to survive, must protect and articulate moral standards, ethical behavior, and historical principles of social cohesion. It is their function to teach the common beliefs that unite us as a free nation" (16, pp. 15–16).

These concerns are based on the incorrect assumption that persons who favor pluralistic approaches believe in complete cultural relativism. Pluralists typically recommend that diversity should be balanced against higher and universal values (5, 22, 58, 70). Two examples of this position follow:

> Because each cultural group proceeds from a different context, we can never reach total agreement on the "best" or most appropriate ways in which to lead our lives. . . .
>
> Nevertheless, it should also be stressed that above and beyond all cultures there are human and civil rights that need to be valued and maintained by all people. These rights guarantee that all human beings are treated with dignity, respect, and equality. Sometimes the values and behaviors of a group so seriously challenge these values that we are faced with a dilemma to reject it or to affirm the diversity it represents. If the values we as human beings hold most dear are ultimately based on extending rights rather than negating them, we must decide on the side of those more universal values. (22, pp. 278–279)

> I believe in a form of cultural pluralism in which universal and particularistic values would be dialectically balanced against each other. In particular, I believe that the universal values of equality, freedom, and democracy, which are among the most important values that have been promulgated under the concept of common school, should be balanced against the particularistic values associated with the maintenance of cultural diversity. But the freedom of an individual must be restrained to the extent that it imposes detrimentally on the freedom of others. Unfortunately, this two-sided nature of cultural pluralism is rarely underlined and, as a consequence, it is sometimes misunderstood as licence for runaway ethnicity, rather than as a way of avoiding such ethnocentric behavior. (5, pp. 300–301)

The contention that accommodating to cultural differences in the classroom necessarily leads to having two or more national languages and different laws for different cultural groups is also incorrect. Instructing students in their native languages while they learn English, permitting them to work at their own pace, developing the kinds of interpersonal relationships with them that make them feel comfortable, allowing them to choose whether to behave competitively or cooperatively, and so on does not necessarily lead to adopting two or more national languages, moral codes, or sets of laws.

- *Adapting educational approaches to students' cultural characteristics does not prepare them to function effectively in the mainstream European American dominated society.*

Educators who support this position argue that the real world is not nearly as tolerant or as flexible as some educators would like it to be. They maintain that because employers and others require individuals to conform to mainstream expectations and norms, accommodating to students' culturally influenced behavior patterns, learning styles, communication styles, concepts of punctuality, and so on dooms them to be uncompetitive and disadvantaged in the real world.

There is some truth to this concern. Americans do live in an imperfect society. Despite federal and state laws against discrimination, too many people with supervisory and administrative power over others continue to expect and insist that those over whom they have influence conform to their culturally determined standards. However, does that mean that educators should prepare their students to acquiesce to the prejudicial attitudes of these individuals? Who has the right to decide whether students should be encouraged and helped to submit to such abuse or to fight it—the students' teachers or the students themselves? (See Empowerment later in this chapter.)

Criticisms

Critics of the assimilation position offer the following reasons for preferring alternative solutions to cultural incompatibilities (50, 51, 56, 57, 65, 69, 81):

• Many students do not want to replace their values, attitudes, learning and behavior styles, and so on with those of the European American middle class. Requiring them to do so can cause them to become angry, resentful, suspicious, and rebellious, and to tune out their teachers or drop out of school.

• If students believe that their culture is inferior or if they agree that they should change their culturally determined ways of functioning, they may suffer a loss of self-esteem and self-confidence.

• Even if students want to change, it may be too difficult to accomplish since it is no easy task to change one's life-style and values. Thus, Longstreet has maintained that "there is a limited capability within each of us to modify the ethnic traits we absorb as children. We may change our accent or the way we smile but we cannot, intellectually or emotionally, change the multitude of traits that would have to be altered to change our basic ethnicity" (65, p. 20).

• Even if students succeed in changing, their efforts can create serious problems and unwanted side effects. When non-European American students act in ways that are less natural to them than to European American middle-class students who were brought up from their earliest years to behave in these ways, non-European Americans can become tense and nervous. They may also experience the guilt, shame, and anxiety that often result from rejecting one's culture.

• Students may experience identity conflicts if they are exposed to conflicting pressure from home, the community, and the schools.

• Students who assimilate may suffer the loss of friendship and experience outright hostility from peers who accuse them of trying to be "coconuts, oreos, or bananas" (brown, black, or yellow on the outside and white on the inside). This is especially likely to happen if there is movement within the students' culture toward increasing the groups' cultural pride or if there is a history of conflict and oppression between the students' ethnic group and the European American power structure.

An African American high school student who lived in a poor neighborhood and attended a predominantly white middle-class preparatory school described the experience this way: "When trying to live in two different worlds, one is in peril of not belonging to either of them. . . . Being put in a position of changing one's character every morning and afternoon to adapt to two different worlds endangers one's identity" (69, p. 337).

• There is little reason to assume that assimilation can work. It has been tried for years with very little success. This concern was expressed quite some time ago by one of the pioneers in the field of multicultural special education:

> Schools' past efforts to acculturate culturally different children have failed miserably. These children as a whole are still not being educated, and the school system cannot continue to ignore its ethical, legal, moral, and professional responsibilities to accommodate children as they are. It is highly presumptuous for any school system to assume the responsibilities of acculturating children when the potential emotional consequences of forced acculturation are so pernicious. If most educators realized the way in which they risk the mental health of culturally different children by insisting on acculturating them, they would look more favorably on their potential role in developing a culturally pluralistic society. (51, p. 555)

ASSIMILATION: AN EXAMPLE OF A LESS STRESSFUL APPROACH TO CHANGING STUDENTS

Papago parents teach their children through nonverbal means such as modeling and gesturing as well as economical speech. In school, children are expected to be verbal. At home and in their community, Papago children enjoy considerable autonomy. They are not rebuked by adults for interfering with their work or conversations nor forced to bow to the wishes of their elders. Because children are raised with few limitations on their freedom, they are not accustomed to being controlled, reprimanded, or punished by adults. In school, Papago children are expected to conform to many rules and procedures and they are exposed to punitive consequences if they do not.

Papago preschool teachers whose goal was to prepare Native American students to transit to European American schools did so without creating undue stress for them. For example, the teachers respected and accepted the students' desire not to participate and recite in class. They allowed children to learn by doing and by observing how their teachers did things. However, they also explained how things should be done. They combined physical activities with verbal activities, such as dancing and singing simultaneously. They also exposed them to the behavior that would eventually be required by presenting them with activities designed to entice them into improving their verbal skills and self-assertive classroom participatory behavior.

Teachers taught students to conform to school rules and procedures. However, because students were unaccustomed to so many limitations on their freedom, teachers did not use consequences to enforce rules. Instead, they repeatedly reminded students what was expected of them and patiently waited for them to conform. In these ways, teachers helped students to gradually adjust to the school's culture without unduly confronting the culturally determined learning and behavior styles that they brought with them to school. Macias described the teachers' approach: "Teachers continuously present their students with experiences which are typical of mainstream education and which necessitate the child's adjustment to culturally different ways of behaving and learning. Yet, of most importance, these same teachers act to mitigate the discontinuity of the necessary preschool experiences and ensure that the child's appreciation of his own culture is not eroded" (66, p. 378).

Biculturalism

Many educators do not believe that students should be expected to assimilate totally to the schools' way or that schools should accomodate completely to students' preferences (71, 72). They disagree that the schools' way is best and they do not think that schools can accommodate to an unlimited number of cultural differences. Additionally, they do not think that non-European American students should be required to choose between the ways of their family and the way school officials expect them to function. These educators propose a third alternative—biculturalism. Instead of having to choose between maintaining the values, beliefs, and practices of the home and rejecting the mainstream culture of the schools, or rejecting the culture of their home and adopting the school culture, students can identify with and accept both cultural systems and use each in appropriate situations.

There are two different bicultural approaches. Some educators who favor biculturalism believe that although neither the school's culture or the students' culture is superior, the school's culture is more appropriate in school and the students' culture is more appropriate at home and in their neighborhoods. Thus, they recommend that teachers prepare students to function one way at home and another way at school. Other educators view biculturalism as a process of mutual accommodation. They maintain that teachers should expect students to adjust to only some of the teaching procedures while teachers also accommodate to some aspects of their students' culture. Proponents of this form of biculturalism do not believe that students must leave all of their cultural characteristics at the doorstep of the school building—only those that conflict with the effective operation of the educational process (22, 72).

Nieto's conception of biculturalism is an example of this approach. "Mutual accommodation means accepting and building on students' language and culture as legitimate expressions of intelligence and as the basis for their academic success. On the part of students and families, it means accepting the culture of the school in such areas as expectations about attendance and homework and learning the necessary skills for work in school" (22, p. 259).

Proponents of mutual accommodation believe that both school and students are enriched by it. Teachers expand their repertoires of instruction and classroom management techniques, and bicultural students acquire a second way to react to challenges and tasks. Thus, both are able to adapt their approaches to the requirements of the situation (e.g., being cooperate or competitive, and assertive or nonassertive as needed).

In actual practice, this second approach to biculturalism is different from the first only in the degree to which teachers accommodate to students' cultural characteristics or require students to adjust to the school's culture. It does allow for some accommodation on the part of the school. However, it still requires students and their parents to acknowledge that the school's way is necessary if not superior in some areas.

Criticisms

Some educators see problems associated with both bicultural approaches. They do not believe either one is as fair as it is appears at first glance. They ask why only one cultural perspective has to predominate at all in schools that serve a pluralistic society and why the European American way should be the accepted way in school. These educators assert that although teachers may think they are communicating to students that neither the school's way or the home's way is more desirable, by stating that the European American way is best for even some school situations, they are communicating that it is also the better way. Critics also maintain that both bicultural approaches can place students in conflict situations if students' parents and friends do not believe that there should be only one cultural perspective in school or that the European American way is the best approach in any areas of the educational settings.

Empowerment

Some educators believe that the accommodation, assimilation, and bicultural models create problems for students because they are too teacher directed. These individuals prefer to empower students to choose how to resolve their cultural conflicts (48). This approach involves exposing students to the fact that there are various ways they may function, educating them about the possible advantages and disadvantages of each one and helping them to select the solution that they themselves favor.

Criticisms

Many educators who appreciate the good intentions of those who wish to empower students to make important decisions for themselves question whether the approach can work. They doubt that teachers can be neutral and impartial regarding students' choices, especially when the values involved are important to them. They wonder whether teachers can avoid communicating their preferences to students and if teachers can accept students' choices that interfere with the smooth progress of their class or rights of others.

Critics of the empowerment approach are also skeptical about students' abilities to make reasonable choices. They point out that until students reach adolescence, they are not mature enough to evaluate the alternatives among which they must choose. Critics also worry about the results of allowing even the best-prepared students to choose for themselves. They find it difficult to believe that students who are relative strangers to the United States can appreciate the ramifications of different alternatives. These educators ask whether adolescents can project themselves into the future and imagine how a employer might react if, as a result of choosing to remain true to their cultural backgrounds, they were unable or unwilling to engage in competitive behavior, to work at the same pace as others, to acknowledge their mistakes and errors, to discuss difficult interpersonal issues without a mediator, to accept public criticism, and so on.

Critics also point out that the empowerment approach may have only a limited positive effect on students' identity problems. It may encourage teachers to avoid placing students in conflict situations by not pressuring them to choose one cultural over another; however, it will not help students avoid identity conflicts if the choices they would like to make conflict with those that their parents or peers prefer.

Research

Special educators cannot accommodate completely to students learning styles (83, 88). The subject matter and skills to be learned by students impose a certain amount of structure on the teaching situation. Also, special educators' personalities influence the instructional styles that they can comfortably and effectively use with students. As a result, it is necessary for students to adjust to at least some of the unfamiliar approaches to which they are exposed in school. Thus, a bicultural approach is the most likely outcome of special educators' attempts to facilitate students adjustments to new and unfamiliar instructional styles. Fortunately, a bicultural approach is often the most effective. Research also suggests that educators can enhance students' learning and success in school by accommodating their instructional techniques to students' communication, learning, and motivational styles (77, 84–88). As noted in Chapter 5, expecting students to adjust to European American middle-class values and methods too rapidly places additional stress on them and creates identity conflicts. There is little evidence regarding the effectiveness of the empowerment approach.

Individual Differences

In practice, special educators do not use the same approach with each and every case of cultural incompatibility that occurs in their classes. Their responses to each situation depend on such factors as the importance they place on the particular cultural incompatibility or issue involved, the effect their students' behavior has on the classroom environment, and the attitude of the students or their parents toward the particular cultural trait. For example, with many exceptions, special educators are probably more likely to accommodate their approaches to students who feel uncomfortable in competitive situations or who prefer to work independently rather than in groups. These culturally influenced learning styles do not seriously impede the progress of the group as a whole.

Special educators may be a little less likely to accommodate to students who express their needs only in extremely subtle indirect ways or who resist admitting they don't know or understand something. These culturally influenced learning styles do not impede the progress of the group, but they do require extra work and sensitivity on the teacher's part. Special educators are probably least likely to accommodate to students who prefer to settle differences with their peers by fighting or who think it is better to be assertive and aggressive than compliant and conforming. These behaviors seriously interfere with the rights of others and tend to impede teachers' ability to manage the class.

Some special educators may be less willing to accommodate to cultural differences that go against their deeply held beliefs. There are those who prefer students to function in androgynous rather than gender-stereotypical ways. These educators may be less willing than those who are comfortable with gender-stereotypic roles to empower students to choose their own solutions to cultural conflicts when students' cultures encourage males to act like men and females to be ladies.

Special educators may refrain from encouraging the children of migrant workers to function biculturally if they and their parents do not plan to stay in the United States. They may also avoid attempting the assimilation and bicultural approaches with African American and Native American students who do not believe that European American values and life-styles are desirable. "Historically, American Indians have resisted acculturation and assimilation more than any other ethnic group. What this means is that by retaining traditional values and beliefs that are important to them, a natural conflict is set up in the classroom that must be handled by children of a very sensitive age" (60, pp. 45–46).

SELF-QUIZ

CRITICAL INCIDENTS

This self-quiz is designed to provide you with some insight into the approaches you may use to resolve diversity issues. First, describe how you think the teacher involved should handle each of the following critical incidents. Disregard the description of the teacher's point of view; instead, put yourself in the teacher's place—imagine what your viewpoint would be and state how you would deal with the problem. Next, decide which of the following alternatives best describes each of your solutions: assimilation, accommodation, biculturalism, or empowerment. If you prefer a number of different approaches to the incidents, try to determine the factors that led you to select the particular approaches you would use in each critical incident.

1. A second-grade Filipino child in a class for students with learning disabilities has been brought up to respect and depend on adult authority figures. He appears to be unable or unwilling to make choices such as selecting a book to bring home from the school library, choosing a partner, and deciding on which learning center work to do during free time without his teacher's guidance. The teacher feels that one role of an educator is to help young children learn to function more independently.

2. A parent who is representing the parents of all four of the Chinese American students in a third-grade class asks the teacher not to require their children to express their opinions in class because they are in school to learn what the teacher knows. He tells the teacher that Chinese Americans believe that children should be taught to respect the knowledge and opinions of adults. He adds that it is not a good idea for children to discuss their personal views of things about which they have little knowledge. The teacher believes students should be participants in the learning process, not merely banks into which teachers deposit information. The teacher also thinks that presenting problems and having students share their opinions about them is an effective technique for developing students' critical thinking skills.

3. After hearing a seventh-grade student tell his classmate that he would "get him" after school for what he said about his mother, the teacher tells the two students they should settle their arguments without fighting. The teacher reminds them that fighting is against the rules and warns them that if they fight after school they will get into trouble. The student who did the threatening replies that his parents expect him to stand up for himself, especially when someone says something derogatory about his family.

4. An eleventh-grade student in a predominantly poor neighborhood school complains that his teacher is too tough on him. He accuses the teacher of being insensitive to the students in the class because the teacher gives them too much homework. He also insists that as long as he does okay on tests, he should not be marked down every time he does not complete an assignment, because he has to work after school to earn money for the family expenses. Although the teacher realizes that the student is telling the truth, the teacher also feels that teachers in urban schools should expect as much from their students as teachers in more affluent suburban schools do. In the teacher's opinion, to expect less of students is to condemn them to life as second-class citizens.

SUMMARY

Public Law 94-142 and the 1990 amendments to the act require that students with disabilities receive culturally appropriate special education services. However, there are many different opinions about how to achieve this goal. Many educators believe that increased student respect for diversity, improved interethnic group relations, and a reduction in prejudice should be included among the outcomes of culturally appropriate special education. However, there is much disagreement about how best to accomplish these goals.

Special educators may employ at least four approaches to resolve cultural incompatibilities between students' learning and behavioral styles and special educators' instructional and classroom management styles. They can accommodate to students' cultural characteristics, require students to assimilate and adjust to their educational techniques, assist students to become bicultural, or empower them to resolve their cultural conflicts in their own ways. Since each approach has its advantages and disadvantages, special educators should examine and evaluate their ways of handling cultural incompatibilities.

ACTIVITIES

1. Ask a few of your fellow students or colleagues to answer the self-quizzes on prejudice and techniques for increasing respect for diversity, reducing prejudice, and improving interethnic group relations. If possible, include persons from different backgrounds. How do your responses compare to theirs? Are all of your responses similar? Do you notice any differences in the responses of individuals from different backgrounds?

2. Administer a quiz similar to the one on Native Americans about other ethnic groups to some of your peers or colleagues. What kinds of misconceptions do they have about these other groups?

3. Administer a quiz about students with disabilities to regular education teachers. What are their misperceptions about students with disabilities?

4. Compare the responses of students in regular education and special education programs to a quiz about one or more ethnic groups. Is one group of students less knowledgeable than the other?

5. Ask regular education students to describe their beliefs about students with disabilities. What are their misperceptions? Compare their misperceptions of students from other ethnic backgrounds to their misperceptions of students with disabilities.

6. Ask some of your colleagues or fellow students whether they believe that studying the characteristics of different ethnic groups is helpful or should be

avoided. Ask them if they think it is possible to adapt special educational approaches to cultural differences.

7. If you are currently teaching, ask your students which of the four approaches for dealing with cultural incompatibilities they would prefer you to use in class. Do your students' preferences match yours? Do students from different backgrounds have similar preferences?

8. Ask a few of your fellow students or colleagues to answer the four critical incidents on page 133. Include persons from different backgrounds. How do your responses compare to theirs? Are all of your responses similar? Do you notice any differences in the responses of individuals from different backgrounds?

REFERENCES

Reference 1 is for the quotation at the beginning of the chapter.

1. Zayas, H. (1981). *Bilingual Special Education Personnel Preparation National Task Oriented Seminar.* Association for Cross-Cultural Education and Social Studies, Inc. Washington, DC: Author.

Federal requirements regarding culturally appropriate special education are spelled out in reference 2.

2. Individuals with Disabilities Education Act (20 U.S.C., Sections 1400–1485; Education of the Handicapped Act Amendments of 1990).

References 3–5 are concerned with discussions about differences and similarities among people.

3. Glimps, B., & Hicks, J. (1983). *Planning for a Culturally Sensitive Program in the Preschool Setting.* ERIC ED 230 009.
4. Grossman, H. (1984). *Educating Hispanic Students: Cultural Implications for Instruction, Classroom management, Counseling, and Assessment.* Springfield, IL: Thomas.
5. Suzuki, B. H. (1984). Curriculum transformation for multicultural education. *Education and Urban Society, 16,* 294–322.

Reference 6 documents the omission of non-European Americans' holidays, contributions, values, and so on in texts and other reading materials.

6. Knafle, J. D., Rodriguez-Brown, F. V., & Budinsky, M. (1991) Values in American and Hispanic children's readers. *Journal of Educational Issues of Language Minority Students, 8,* 53–70.

References 7–16 discuss the advantages and disadvantages of including students' cultures in the classroom.

7. Banks, J. A. (1987). Social studies, ethnic diversity, and social change. *Elementary School Journal, 87* (5), 531–543
8. Banks, J. A. (1991). A curriculum for empowerment, action, and change. In C. Sleeter (Ed.), *Empowerment through Multicultural Education.* Albany: State University of New York Press.
9. Heller, S. (1989). Press for campus diversity leading to more closed minds, say critics. *Chronicle of Higher Education, 36,* November 8, A13, A22.
10. Loridas, L. (1988). *Culture in the Classroom: A Cultural Enlightenment Manual for Educators.* ERIC ED 303 941.
11. Mendenhall, P. T. (1982). Bicultural school organization and curriculum. In R. Barnhardt (Ed.), *Cross-Cultural Issues in Alaskan Education Vol. II.* Fairbanks: University of Alaska, Center for Cross-Cultural Studies.

12. National Association of Scholars. (1989). Is the curriculum biased? A statement by the National Association of Scholars. *Chronicle of Higher Education, 36,* November 8, A23.

13. Pepper, F. C. (1990). *Unbiased Teaching about American Indians and Alaska Natives in elementary Schools.* Charleston, WV: ERIC/CRESS.

14. Pine, G. J., & Hilliard, A. G. III. (1990). Rx for racism: Imperatives for America's schools. *Phi Delta Kappan, 71* (8), 593–600.

15. Sleeter, C. E., & Grant, C. A. (1988). *Making Choices for Multicultural Education.* Columbus, OH: Merrill.

16. Thomas, M. D. (1981). *Pluralism Gone Mad.* Bloomington, IN: Phi Delta Kappa Educational Foundation.

The importance of proactive antibias and antiracism approaches is stressed in references 17–23.

17. Banks, J. A. (1988). *Multiethnic Education: Theory and Practice* (2nd ed.). Boston: Allyn and Bacon.

18. Brandt, G. L. (1986). *The Realization of Anti-Racist Teaching.* London: Falmer Press.

19. Cohen, O. P., Fischgrund, J. E., & Redding, M. A. (1990). Deaf children form ethnic, linguistic and racial minority backgrounds: An overview. *American Annals of the Deaf, 135* (2), 67–73.

20. Mitchell, V. (1990). *Curriculum and Instruction to Reduce Racial Conflict.* New York: Teachers College, Columbia University, ERIC Clearinghouse on Urban Education.

21. Moultry, M. (1988). *Multicultural Education among Seniors in the College of Education at Ohio State University.* ERIC ED 296 634.

22. Nieto, S. (1992). *Affirming Diversity: The Sociopolitical Context of Multicultural Education.* New York: Longman.

23. Olneck, M. R. (1990). The recurring dream: Symbolism and ideology in intercultural and multicultural education. *American Journal of Education, 98* (2), 147–174.

References 24–30 offer guidelines, checklists, and suggestions for detecting prejudice and bias in curricular materials and instructional techniques.

24. Banks, J. A. (1984). *Teaching Strategies for Ethnic Studies.* Boston: Allyn and Bacon.

25. California State Department of Education. (1988). *Ten Quick Ways to Analyze Children's Books for Racism and Sexism.* Sacramento, CA: Author.

26. California State Department of Education. (n.d.). *Standards for Evaluation of Instructional Materials with Respect to Social Content.* Sacramento, CA: Author.

27. Cotera, M. P. (1982). *Checklists for Counteracting Race and Sex Bias in Educational Materials.* ERIC ED 221 612.

28. Ferguson, H. (1987). *Manual for Multicultural Education.* Yarmouth, ME: Intercultural Press.

29. National Education Association. (n.d.) *How Fair Are Your Children's Books?* Washington, DC: Author.

30. Office of Intergroup Relations. (1977). *Guide for Multicultural Education: Content and Context.* Sacramento, CA: California State Department of Education.

References 31–32 describe techniques for increasing respect for diversity and reducing prejudice, animosity, and alienation and their effectiveness.

31. Cummins, J. (1988). From multicultural to anti-racist education: An analysis of programmes and policies in Ontario. In T. Skutnabb-Kangas & J. Cummins (Eds.), *Minority Education: From Shame to Struggle.* Philadelphia: Multilingual Matters.

32. Kanpol, B. (1992). The politics of similarity within difference: A pedagogy for the other. *Urban Review, 24* (2), 105–131.

Programs and approaches to reduce prejudice and to improve interethnic and intercultural relationships are described in references 33–43.

33. Anti-Defamation League of B'nai B'rith. (1986). *The Wonderful World of Difference: A Human Relations Program for Grades K–8.* New York: Author.

34. Olsen, L., & Dowell, C. (1989). *Bridges: Promising Programs for the Education of Immigrant Children.* San Francisco: California Tomorrow.

35. Byrnes, D. A., & Kiger, G. (Eds.). (1992). *Common Bonds: Anti-Bias Teaching in a Diverse Society.* Wheaton, MD: Association for Childhood Education International Publications.

36. Cole, J. (1990). *Filtering People: Understanding and Confronting Our Prejudices.* Philadelphia: New Society Publishers.

37. Howard, G. (1989). Positive multicultural outcomes: A practitioner's report. *Multicultural Leader, 2* (1), 12–16.

38. Jorgensen-Esmaili, K. (1988). *New Faces of Liberty: A Curriculum for Teaching about Today's Refugees and Immigrants.* Berkeley, CA: Graduate School of Education, University of California, Berkeley.

39. Lynch, J. (1987). *Prejudice Reduction and the Schools.* New York: Nichols.

40. Panel of Americans. (1991). *No Dissin' Allowed.* New York: Author.

41. San Francisco Study Center. (n.d.). *Voices of Liberty.* San Francisco: Author.

42. Southern Poverty Law Center. (1991). *Teaching Tolerance.* Montgomery, AL: Author.

43. Teidt, I., & Teidt, P. (1986). *Multicultural Teaching: A Handbook of Activities, Information, and Resources.* Boston: Allyn and Bacon.

Descriptions of materials that can be employed in a case-study approach for dealing with ethnic conflict are included in reference 44.

44. Kleinfeld, J. (1990). *The Case Method in Teacher Education: Alaska Models.* Charleston, WV: ERIC/CRESS.

Reference 45 includes evidence that schoolwide approaches reduce prejudice and improve interethnic group relations in school.

45. Pate, G. S. (1989). Reducing prejudice in the schools. *Multicultural Leader, 2* (20), 1–3.

The works of authors who favor a transformational education or social reconstructionist education approach are listed in references 46–49 and in Chapter 3.

46. Mullard, C. (1985). Racism in society and school: History, policy, and practice. In F. Rizvi (Ed.), *Multiculturalism As an Educational Policy.* Victoria, Australia: Deakin University Press.

47. Quality Education for Minorities Project. (1990). *Education that Works: An Action Plan for the Education of Minorities.* Cambridge, MA: MIT Press.

48. Sleeter, C. (Ed.). (1991). *Empowerment through Multicultural Education.* Albany: State University of New York Press.

49. Wood, G. H. (1984). Schooling in a democracy: Transformation or reproduction. *Educational Theory, 34* (3), 219–239.

References 50–82 discuss the different ways students and educators can respond to cultural incompatibilities in school and examine their advantages and disadvantages.

50. Alley, J. (1980). Better understanding of the Indochinese students. *Education, 101,* 111–114.

51. Bernal, E. (1974). A dialogue on cultural implications for learning. *Exceptional Children, 40,* 552–563.

52. Buriel, R. (1984). Integration with traditional Mexican-American culture and sociocultural adjustment. In J. L. Martinez Jr. & R. H. Mendoza (Eds.), *Chicano Psychology* (2nd ed.). Orlando, FL: Academic Press.

53. Buriel, R., & Saenz, E. (1980). Psychocultural characteristics of college bound and non-college bound Chicanos. *Journal of Social Psychology, 110,* 245–251.

54. Cloud, N. (1991). Acculturation of ethnic minorities. In A. M. Ambert (Ed.), *Bilingual Education and English as a Second Language: A Research Handbook 1988–1990.* New York: Garland.

55. Council for Exceptional Children. (n.d.). *Council for Exceptional Children's Policies Manual.* Reston, VA: Author.

56. Ellis, A. A. (1980). *The Assimilation and Acculturation of Indochinese Children into American Culture.* ERIC ED 213 484.

57. ERIC/CUE. (1985). The social and psychological adjustment of Southeast Asian Refugees. *Urban Review, 17* (2), 147–152.

58. Higham, J. (1984). *Send These to Me: Immigrants in Urban America.* Baltimore, MD: Johns Hopkins University Press.

59. Hilliard, A. G. III. (1992). *Language, Culture, and Valid Teaching.* Paper presented at the Topical Conference on Cultural and Linguistically Diverse Exceptional Children, Minneapolis, MN.

60. Hornett, D. M. (1990). Elementary-age tasks, cultural identity, and the academic performance of young American Indian children. *Action in Teacher Education, 12* (3), 49.

61. Irvine, J. J. (1991). *Black Students and School Failure: Policies, Practices, and Prescriptions.* New York: Praeger.

62. Jordan, K., Tharp, R. G., & Baird-Vogt, L. (1991). Cross-culturally compatible schooling. In M. Saravia-Shore & S. F. Arvizu (Eds.), *Cross-Cultural Literacy: Ethnographies of Communication in Multiethnic Classrooms.* New York: Garland.

63. Kleinfeld, J. (1975). Positive stereotyping: The cultural relativist in the classroom. *Human Organization, 34* (3), 269–274.

64. Landsman, M., Padilla, A., Clark, C., Liederman, H., Ritter, P., & Dornbusch, S. (1990). *Biculturality and Academic Achievement among Asian and Hispanic Adolescents.* Paper presented at the annual meeting of the National Association for Bilingual Education, Tuscon, AZ.

65. Longstreet, W. S. (1978). *Aspects of Ethnicity.* New York: Teachers College Press.

66. Macias, J. (1987). The hidden curriculum of Papago teachers: American Indian strategies for mitigating cultural discontinuity in early schooling. In G. Spindler & L. Spindler (Eds.), *Interpretive Ethnography of Education: At Home and Abroad.* Hillsdale, NJ: Erlbaum.

67. Melville, M. B. (1980). Selective acculturation of female Mexican migrants. In M. B. Melville (Ed.), *Twice a Minority: Mexican American Women.* St Louis: Mosby.

68. Morales, R. F. (Ed.). (1983). *Bridging Cultures.* Los Angeles: Asian American Health Training Center.

69. Niera, C. (1988). Building 860. *Harvard Educational Review, 58* (2), 337–342.

70. Patrick, J. L. (1986). Immigration in the curriculum. *Social Education, 50* (3), 172–176.

71. Ramirez, M., & Castenada, A. (1974). *Cultural Democracy, Bicognitive Development and Education.* New York: Academic Press.

72. Saville-Troike, M. (1978). *A Guide to Culture in the Classroom.* Rosslyn, VA: National Clearinghouse for Bilingual Education.

73. Santiseban, D., & Szapocznik, J. (1982). Substance abuse disorders among Hispanics: A focus on prevention. In R. M. Becerra, M. Karno, & J. I. Escobar (Eds.), *Mental Health and Hispanic Americans: Clinical Perspectives.* New York: Grune & Stratton.

74. Shade, B. J. (1982). Afro-American cognitive style: A variable in school success. *Review of Educational Research, 52,* 219–244.

75. So, A. Y. (1987). High-achieving disadvantaged students: A study of low SES Hispanic language minority students. *Urban Education, 22* (1), 19–35.

76. Szapocznik, J., Kurtines, W. M., & Fernandez, T. (1979). *Bicultural Involvement and Adjustment in Hispanic American Youths.* ERIC ED 193 374.

77. Thomas, E. W. (1978). English as a second language—For whom? *The Crisis, 85* (9), 318–320.

78. Tharp, R. (1989). Psychocultural variables and constants: Effects on teaching and learning in schools. *American Psychologist, 44* (2), 349–359.

79. Torres-Matrullo, C. M. (1980). Acculturation, sex-role values and mental health among mainland Puerto Ricans. In A. M. Padilla (Ed.), *Acculturation: Theory, Models, and Some New Findings.* Boulder, CO: Westview Press.

80. Vigil, J. D. (1982). Chicano high schoolers: Educational performance and acculturation. *Educational Forum, 47* (1), 58–73.

81. Wei, T. T. D. (1980). *Vietnamese Refugee Students: A Handbook for School Personnel.* ERIC ED 208 109.

82. Wong-Rieger, D., & Quintana, D. (1987). Comparative acculturation of Southeast Asian and Hispanic immigrants and sojourners. *Journal of Cross-cultural Psychology, 18* (3), 345–362.

Limitations on educators' abilities to adapt to students' learning styles are discussed in reference 83.

83. Hyman, R., & Rosoff, B. (1984). Matching learning and teaching styles: The jug and what's in it. *Theory into Practice, 23* (1), 35–43.

References 84–88 provide evidence that matching instructional techniques to students' personal characteristics enhances learning.

84. Carbo, M. (1984). Research in learning style and reading: Implications for instruction. *Theory into Practice, 23* (1), 72–76.

85. Dunn, R. (1984). Learning style: State of the art. *Theory into Practice, 23* (1), 10–25.

86. Hare, B. R., & Levine, D. U. (1985). Effective schooling in desegregated settings: What do we know about learning style and linguistic differences? *Equity and Choice, 1* (2), 13–18.

87. Mickler, M. L., & Zippert, C. J. (1987). Teaching strategies based on learning styles of adult learners. *Community/Junior College Quarterly, 11,* 33–37.

88. Smith, L. H., & Renzulli, J. S. (1984). Learning style preferences: A practical approach for classroom teachers. *Theory into Practice, 23* (1), 44–50.

5

CONTEXTUALLY APPROPRIATE SPECIAL EDUCATION

In addition to the issues of cultural diversity and a changing school population, we must also acknowledge and address the social context in which children live if we are to provide a free appropriate education for all children. More than ever before in our country's history, children are living in poverty and unsafe neighborhoods, being raised in single-parent families and by teenage mothers, exposed to drugs, and lacking appropriate prenatal and basic health care. (173, p. 23)

The techniques special educators use to assess, instruct, and manage students with disabilities are often designed for middle-class students from stable homes with two native-born, well-educated parents who understand the way schools work and have the time and resources to help their children gain the most that they can from their school experiences. Many students do not grow up in these kinds of families, however. Because the contexts of their lives are different, they do not profit as much from traditional educational approaches.

This chapter discusses the effects of various contextual factors on students' school experiences. It describes the additional problems students with disabilities may face because of the circumstances of their lives and it suggests specific ways in which special educators can reduce or even eliminate these potential problems. Some of the topics included in this chapter are immigrant and refugee students, children of illegal immigrants, migrant students, students from cultures that have a history of unequal cross-cultural relationships with European Americans, students in rural and isolated areas, abused and neglected students, and students whose parents are unable to provide them with adequate child care.

IMMIGRANT AND REFUGEE STUDENTS

Immigrant and refugee students experience many contextual problems in U.S. schools that interfere with their learning (1–23). When these students do not learn English or subject matter as rapidly as expected, teachers should investigate and attend to the possible contextual causes of their slower-than-expected progress. Too often, however, teachers react to the academic difficulties of these students by placing them in low-ability tracks and groups or referring them for special education placement. To avoid these mistakes, teachers should be sensitive to a variety of potential contextual problems.

VIEWPOINTS FROM THE NATIONAL COALITION OF ADVOCATES FOR STUDENTS

> Immigrant students are clustered along with minority American students in classes which teach the answers to questions on minimum competency exams. So there is very little enrichment, there's very little encouragement for critical thinking or some of the other skills that are so very important for success in later life. (John Ratliff, Attorney, Legal Services of Greater Miami) (13, p. 48)

> Immigrant students tend to become tracked for failure and geared toward low-level jobs. They are steered away from college prep courses. (Diana Rivera, La Llave Case Advocate, La Puente, New York) (13, p. 48)

Culture Shock

When people have to adjust to a culture that is significantly different from their own, they often become confused, anxious, and frustrated because they do not know what is expected of them in different situations. They often cannot solve interpersonal problems and do not know what is and is not acceptable behavior in the new culture. They may become angry at people whose behavior they cannot understand and they may feel anxious and fearful about not being able to function adequately in the new culture or sad and depressed over the loss of their familiar way of life. All of this disorientation and confusion is called *culture shock* (1, 9).

Students who immigrate to the United States from other countries can suffer culture shock in school. They may become angry, anxious, sad, or depressed; some may withdraw from their teachers whereas others may act aggressively toward them. These behaviors can lead educators to refer such students to be assessed for the kinds of emotional problems that require special educational services. A description of the plight of an Hispanic American student who suffers culture shock follows:

> The very first day in the first grade the Mexican American child starts with a handicap no humane society should place on the shoulders of a mere child. English is the language of the classroom. He speaks no English or he speaks inadequate English. The whole program is designed to make him an Anglo. . . . He doesn't want to become an Anglo or he doesn't know how. . . . The Anglo concepts and values that prevail are unintelligible to him. . . . There is nothing in the atmosphere from which he can draw any comfort. Nothing he can relate to. . . . He is one scared kid. (21, p. 3)

The following is an excerpt from the responses of a Japanese teacher studying in the United States about what a European American teacher should know about the background of a recently arrived Japanese student. It provides examples of specific differences that can cause immigrant students to experience culture shock in U.S. schools.

A: There is a lot of memorization. . . . Most students would expect a teacher to teach them rather than ask them questions or raise discussions. When I first came here, I expected all the professors to be lecturing us rather than asking us questions. At first, I was very embarrassed; it was hard for me to follow.

Q: Sometimes a problem is created when a teacher picks out a student and corrects him.

A: I think it might cause the student to react in a negative way. He might try to keep to himself. If the teacher corrects mistakes in class, the student might be very embarrassed.

Q: What kinds of other adjustment problems would a Japanese student face?

A: The small daughter of a friend of mine from Japan was having difficulties when she entered school here. When she started to go to school, she used to come back every day, crying. It appears that in her math class, she was doing the math according to the Japanese way. An American student corrected her by saying, "This is not the way." And every time she wrote something, the American boy erased it. Since she could not speak any word of English, she had no way of indicating that she was doing it the Japanese way, she had no way but to cry. The teacher thought that the child was kind of nervous and somewhat strange. The child apparently had a hard time for the first two months; now she is doing fine. (7, pp. 24–27)

Identity Conflicts

Many immigrant students may experience identity conflicts during the acculturation process if they are pressured at home and in their community to maintain the traditional values of their culture while at the same time they are pressured at school to accept new cultural values (24–26). Some students adopt the culture of the school and try to abandon the traditions of their families. If they do this, they may be punished by their parents and suffer from feelings of guilt and shame. Other students may reject the pressures of school and satisfy their parents, but by doing so, they risk getting into trouble with their teachers and school administrators (26).

Rudolf Vecoli, Director of the Immigration History Research Center at the University of Minnesota in St. Paul, stated, "The immigrant child lives between two cultures—that of the family, and that of the mainstream society. He is thus exposed to the conflicting values of home, peer group, school, to clashing definitions of the good life, and to the tug and pull of competing loyalties" (13, p. 21). Reine Leroy, Intergroup Relations Representative from Dade County Public Schools in Florida, has added, "He is living in two worlds. During the day, he is American. He is trying to 'Americanize himself.' He is trying to fit in. He has a lot of peer pressure to deal with. And when he comes home at night, he is Haitian. And that is very hard. He has two different sets of rules to follow" (13, p. 21).

A Chinese American high school student who immigrated to the United States when she was 10 years old expressed her identity conflict in this way: "I don't know who I am. Am I the good Chinese daughter? Am I an American teenager? I always feel I am letting my parents down when I am with my friends because I act so American, but I also feel that I will never really be an American. I never feel really comfortable with myself anymore" (25, p. 30).

Some non-European American students born in the United States are brought up by parents who want them to assimilate and to adjust to the culture of the school. Many others are torn between conflicting messages and pressures regarding the right and wrong ways to live their lives. The school's role in exacerbating Hispanic American and Indian American students' identity conflicts is described in the following statements:

> Cultural conflicts between home and school cause youth to either choose one or the other. This causes conflicts in personality, adjustment, etc. He needs to act one way at school and when he gets home, uses a different language and a different set of cultural values. If the school allowed him to be himself, he wouldn't have the problem. (24, p. 122)

> The more schools pressure Punjabi children to conform to prevailing norms for behavior, the more tightly their parents supervised their behavior and advised against too much social contact with nonPunjabi peers. Punjabi parents defined "becoming Americanized" as forgetting one's roots and adopting the most disparaged traits of the majority group, such as young people making decisions on their own without parental counsel, leaving their families at age 18 to live independently, dating, dancing, and friendship between the sexes.
>
> Parents constantly admonish their young that they will dishonor themselves, their families, and their community if they adopt the values and behaviors of majority peers. (8, p. 269)

Language and Teaching Style Differences

Having to adjust to a new language and a strange teaching style can be traumatic for some students. The difficulty some immigrant students experience trying to learn in classrooms taught in foreign languages and unfamiliar teaching styles can cause them to be inappropriately placed in special education programs for the learning disabled or the retarded. This is especially true of students who have never attended school because they came from rural areas or internment camps and/or grew up in cultures that have no written language. If these students feel anxious, angry, resentful, or ashamed of their difficulties and act out their emotions, they may be referred to special education programs for students with behavior disorders or emotional problems.

Wei has described some of the following difficulties Vietnamese American students often experience in U.S. schools where they are taught in a language foreign to them and in an unfamiliar teaching style:

> There are three categories of educational difficulties that the Vietnamese child must face: (1) different learning styles and classroom activities; (2) a change in the student-teacher relationship; and most of all (3) the language barrier.
>
> *Differences in learning style and classroom activities.* The Vietnamese educational system promotes a passive type of learning where the students learn by listening, watching, and imitating their teachers. The open type of classroom common in many

American schools is perceived by the Vietnamese as confusing and disorganized. Since Vietnamese students are used to a lecture method, team teaching and active class participation are uncommon and strange to many of them. They are not used to group activities and do not know how to react. Independent projects or library research are foreign to them, and they need to be guided with patience.

The student-teacher relationship. The American teachers' friendliness and informality are shocking to the Vietnamese students and hard for them to accept. The absence of honorific terms in the English language compounds the problem and makes the Vietnamese students feel uneasy and uncomfortable when talking with their teachers. They are reluctant to ask questions in class because such behavior seems aggressive and disrespectful to them. Their confusion is increased when, to their surprise, their teachers reward such behavior in class.

Since they are not accustomed to talking in front of the class, they are shy and uncomfortable when asked to do so in the American classroom. They do not volunteer answers because they have been taught to be modest. If they need help, they probably will not ask for it.

The language barrier. The language problem can be very acute when there is only one or very few Vietnamese students in the school. The lack of communication or understanding between the child and the school authority can cause a small misunderstanding to grow into a large emotional or discipline problem. I remember a woman principal who asked me if a little boy in a kindergarten class knew Kung Fu because of his uncontrolled strength. Being the only Vietnamese in the school, he was totally confused and bewildered with no one to turn to for help. His tension had built to an explosive limit. Once explanations were given to him in Vietnamese, he was a changed child.

The language barrier also limits the child's social contacts with American peers. A high school teacher was concerned when a Vietnamese boy changed from being friendly and cooperative to being antisocial. A talk with the boy revealed that he did not know enough English to communicate with his peers, and as a result, he was slowly withdrawing from them. He was frustrated because he could not say "maybe later" or "not at this time" when he was asked to join in an activity. His abrupt responses seemed rude to his classmates, further frustrating him, and in effect, discouraging other social interaction.

Many of the directions and explanations in the American classroom are verbal. . . . You can imagine the tremendous amount of self-control and self-discipline that a non-English-speaking child must maintain in order to keep quiet and not disturb others. He can rely only on visual clues. These are not always dependable and mean that the child will always be one step behind the others. This causes his/her reactions and behavior to be out of place. (22, pp. 13–14)

STATEMENT OF A CHINESE AMERICAN IMMIGRANT STUDENT

I started to hate myself when I failed to answer the teacher's questions . . . because I couldn't express my answers in English. Then I began to hate everything in the world, including my parents because they took me to this country. (13, p. 25)

Previous Educational Experiences

There are vast differences in the educational experiences of immigrant students. Some have attended school before they arrive in the United States. Many others are too young to have participated in the educational programs of their countries of origin. Immigrant students from industrialized countries such as Taiwan, Korea, and so on typically have very different school experiences than those who come from Haiti, El Salvador, Laos, and Cambodia. Their experiences in a nonindustrialized environment may not provide them with the knowledge they require in the United States.

Preschool immigrant students are exposed to their own rich culture instead of the cultural experiences that most mainstream educators and school administrators expect and value. As a result, they may begin school already behind because they do not know what their teachers expect them to know about the alphabet, numbers, colors, and places, even though they know a great deal about other areas not included in the traditional curriculum. If their teachers fail to capitalize on what these children do know, these students may soon fall even further behind. Then, frustrated by trying to produce at the level of the other students, they may act out their anger by behaving in ways that are disruptive to other students or they may give up trying, withdraw, and tune out their teachers.

The different school experiences of immigrant children is described in the following quotation:

> Some have been exposed to one hour a day of political indoctrination as their sole education, while others have put in eight-hour school days, six days a week covering all major academic areas. . . . There are dramatic contrasts between rural and urban education. For example, in Mexico. . . . 75% of those in urban areas finish the 6th grade, compared to only 15% of those in rural areas. In El Salvador most rural area schools don't go beyond second grade and operate with few materials or trained teachers. . . .
>
> Most students from Southeast Asia in the past decade have had disrupted school histories because of war, and have lived for a period in refugee camps. Depending on the camp's location and who ran it, a student may have had a few hours a day or less of instruction. Most camps had minimal if any books or instructional materials and few educated teachers. (25, p. 21)

Immigrant students who are accustomed to philosophies of life and education far different from those that prevail in the United States may have adjustment problems in school. This may be especially true of students from communist or former communist countries such as Cuba and Russia, who have been taught such very different ideas about economics, history, international relationships, interpersonal relationships, and so on from those included in the courses taught in U.S. schools (14, 19). Students whose educational experience has focused on the following may have considerable difficulty dealing with the ideas and ideals presented to them in the United States: "Three important objectives of present Cuban education are to determine the types of crimes that 'American imperialism' has committed in different parts of the world, to explore the many advantages of socialism over capitalism and to recognize other people's struggles against imperialism around the world" (19, p. 37).

Conflicting Demands

Immigrant students often are faced with demands that conflict with those of the schools they attend. If they are the only person in the family who can speak some English, they may have to interpret for their parents during school hours at meetings with community agencies. If they are the oldest child, they may have to care for their siblings instead of attending school. Also, if they came to the United States on their own as unaccompanied minors, they may have family back home who are dependent on them.

Rudolf Vecoli, Director of the Immigration History Research Center at the University of Minnesota in St. Paul, stated, "At quite an early age . . . children serve as interpreters for their parents and help their families confront many adult tasks. For example, if their tenement has no heat in the winter, the school child who knows English might be the one to place a telephone call. . . . These immigrant children face much more responsibility and pressure than the average American school child" (13, p. 21). Oscar Chacon, Coordinator on the National Advisory Panel for Comite El Salvador in Cambridge, Massachusetts, added, "A lot of people, 13–14–year-olds boys for example, that have come into the United States alone, by themselves, or just with a friend, are supposed to come and stay at a parent's or relative's house. But they know that they have sisters, they have brothers, they sometimes have parents that are waiting for them to support them . . . and they cannot do it by attending school" (13, p. 27).

Impoverished Living Conditions

Many immigrants and most refugees arrive in the United States with few economic resources to support them. As a result, many of them move into relatively impoverished environments, which can seriously impede students' ability to succeed in school. Many do not find employment; those who do earn very low wages. As a result, immigrants are much more likely to live below the poverty level (4). Too often, parents do not have the financial resources to provide children with an adequate diet, health care, sleeping arrangements, materials necessary to progress in school, and so on. The home environment is often too crowded and noisy for students to prepare their lessons. To stated,

> Immigrants tend to settle in relatively deteriorating areas of inner cities where educational facilities are already poor and heavily used. In the absence of sufficient additional assistance, the influx of immigration adds an almost unbearable burden on the resources of the school. The home living condition of immigrant children is equally a serious drawback in terms of learning environment. Many of these immigrants live in crowded houses and apartments occupied by more than one family. The children may have no quiet place at home to do their homework or to study. (20, p. 7)

Native American and Rural Students

Native American students who grow up on reservations and attend schools run by and designed for European American students are in a position that is somewhat analogous to that of immigrant students (27–29). Like foreign-born students, they too live in a region separate from mainstream America where they speak a language other than English. They too are ill prepared to adjust to and profit from the education typically offered in mainstream schools. This is especially true if the curriculum is culturally irrelevant, encourages beliefs and values that conflict with those of their communities, and is taught by teachers who are unfamiliar with the students' culture and native language.

Rural children who migrate to urban areas often have similar experiences (30–34). For example, the following problems have tended to characterize many Appalachian students and their families who have moved to urban northern cities:

> Appalachian youth are less likely to seek, or readily accept, school personnel support such as sponsorship or encouragement by a particular teacher or counselor. . . . They are less likely to participate in school activities.
>
> Youth do not identify with their schools especially in junior and senior high school, since most youth are placed in an unfamiliar neighborhood. . . . Familism requires that family situations take priority over education. . . . High absenteeism is at least in part a result of youth being needed at home to help care for siblings and household matters. The traditional migration process, in the three to five years after initial settlement in urban areas. . . . can mean moving several times to find satisfactory neighborhoods, jobs, schools, doctors, and shopping areas. . . . Parents may encourage students into career/practical skills and vocational classes rather than college preparatory or advanced placement classes. . . . Class differences cause Appalachian youth to feel "looked down on" and the lack of attention given to Appalachian culture only adds to a defeated self-image. Differences in language, dress, and values are seen by other classes as deficiencies or inferiority. (32, pp. 99–101)

Students who move between middle America to the coasts, or between the South and North, or who are bused from one ethnic neighborhood to another can suffer similar problems, albeit to a lesser degree.

RURAL STUDENTS IN URBAN SCHOOLS

> To say that Appalachians are poorly served by urban public schools is an understatement. Ethnographic studies of teaching and learning in urban primary and secondary schools have documented the biases of social class and ethnicity faced by urban Appalachian students. These biases are manifest in such routine practices as grouping children for instruction in reading and mathematics, segregating them by perceived ability, retaining students in grade, and administering Ritalin to young children labeled as hyperactive. (30, p. 125)

Illegal/Undocumented Immigrants

Although the children of illegal immigrants are entitled to a free education, they are not always afforded their rights (35–38). Undocumented immigrant students who have disabilities are entitled to the same special education services as students who are in the United States legally. However, they are less likely to receive them because their parents are reluctant to take an active or assertive role with governmental agencies such as schools. Padilla described the plight of the undocumented immigrant family vis-à-vis employers and community authorities in the following manner: "They are considered to be a menace to the country since they are here illegally; cannot find employment that is more than subsistence level and which is long and back breaking and for which they are frequently cheated out of wages; find it next to impossible to obtain needed health or social services because of fear of deportation if they have to admit to being here illegally . . . and are essentially powerless to counter discriminatory behaviors directed against them" (37, p. 3).

Attorney Peter Roos (Multicultural Training and Advocacy, San Francisco), who advocates for children reported, "One way or another, vigilante principals and people who are misinformed are asking kids for their papers and denying them access to schooling on the basis that they do not have them, or refuse to produce them" (13, p. 41).

Enforcement of immigration laws can also interfere with students' education. Audrey Yamagata-Noji, Commissioner of Orange County (California) Human Relations, stated, "There appears to be a pattern developing with INS (Immigration and Naturalization Service) focusing their attention around school sites. Last spring . . . the school was a site for an immigration raid. Approximately 10 parents were arrested. . . . They were taking their children there. . . . Of course, after that . . . many went down and pulled their children out of school for several weeks" (13, p. 64). Gilberto Cardenas of Thomas Rivera Center in San Diego reported, "INS harassment also affects the drop-out rate. . . . You may have a child who is born in the United States, whose father is undocumented [but] the mother is here legally, born in the U.S. The INS apprehends the father, and the family moves. They're pulled out of school for six months and re-enter again" (13, p. 64).

Refugee Experiences

Refugee students who have experienced war, famine, persecution, and other forms of suffering in their native lands or internment camps prior to coming to the United States bring to school additional problems that can interfere with their functioning. The following are some descriptions of the problems such experiences can create for students (39, 40):

> Vietnamese students came to the United States not only as immigrants to this new land, but also as refugees. Immigrants leave their homeland on their own volition, with many possibilities of motivation for the move, whereas refugees have no choice but to leave or to suffer. Refugees are in fact driven away from their homeland—they are pushed out.
>
> Studies have shown that this type of forced migration and the experience of being uprooted involuntarily causes more psychological problems to refugees than to immigrants. With this in mind, an educator must be concerned about the mental well-being of students who have lived in conditions of violence and sociopolitical turmoil before coming to this country. Such students have been exposed to loss, extended violence,

prolonged threat, and terrorization. They may have witnessed violence inflicted to members of their family or to close friends. Their exodus to this country has been paved with dangers and life threatening situations such as poverty, starvation, drowning at sea, rape, murder, piracy, life in a refugee camp, and the possibility of the separation of the family. (15, p. 1)

Describing school life in Central America, Oscar Chacon, Coordinator on the National Advisory Panel for Comite El Salvador in Cambridge, Massachusetts, stated, "There are countless situations where children . . . were in the classroom where their teachers . . . were killed by armed people in different countries in Central America. And that is something that definitely affects a kid's performance and the overall ability for them to adapt into the school system" (13, p. 22).

Life in Cambodia for schoolchildren has been described this way by researcher David Gilbert: "Many teachers were executed. . . . Schools were destroyed and children sent to live on 'work farms' often separated from their families. . . . Almost half the population died, either by starvation, disease, execution, or the war" (13, p. 22). Another author stated, "I remember teaching a spelling lesson to mostly Cambodian youngsters, and I was using a hangman game. One youngster said to me, 'You know, that is how my parents died'" (25, p. 66).

Teachers, psychologists, and other professionals need to be aware of the contextual causes of refugee students' problems. When they are not, they may not give students the help they need and they may inappropriately refer students to special education.

Prejudice

Brought up in fairly homogeneous societies, many immigrant students get their first taste of ethnic prejudice when they begin to attend the U.S. school system. Native American students who leave their reservations to attend schools run by and attended by European Americans, and rural students who migrate to urban areas, often have similar experiences. Students who experience prejudicial treatment from other students may form self-protective gangs and their antagonisms may affect the way they function in school. If they also receive prejudicial treatment from teachers and/or other school personnel, they may react in a number of ways. (See Chapter 3.)

PREJUDICE IN THE SCHOOLS

American students always picked on us, frightened us, made fun of us and laughed at our English. They broke our lockers, threw food on us in cafeteria, said dirty words to us, pushed us on the campus. Many times they shouted at me "Get out of here, you Chink, go back to your country." Many times they pushed me and yell on me. I've been pushed, I had gum thrown on my hair. I've been hit by stones, I've been shot by air gun. I've been insulted by all the dirty words in English. All this really made me frustrated and sad. [Reported by a Chinese American limited-English-proficient student.]

The Americans tell us to go back to our own country. I say we don't have a country to go back to. I wish I was born here and nobody would fight me and beat me up. They don't understand. I want to tell them if they had tried to cross the river and were afraid of being caught and killed and lost their sisters, they might feel like me. [Reported by a Cambodian American student.] (25, pp. 34–35)

In school, Punjabi teenagers are told they stink, directly by white students and indirectly by their teachers. They are told to go back to India. They are accused of being illegals. They are physically abused by the majority students, who spit at them, refuse to sit by them in class or on buses, crowd in front of them in line, stick them with pins, throw food at them and worse. They are labelled troublemakers if they defend themselves. . . . They are criticized for their hairstyle, their diet, and their dress. They are faulted because they place family ahead of individual interests, defer to the authority of elders, accept arranged marriages, and believe in group decision making. [Reported by a researcher] (8, p. 268)

Strengths

Although it is true that most immigrant and refugee students experience many contextual problems that can interfere with their functioning in school, they also have unique strengths that teachers can use in the classroom (8, 41). Those who leave their native lands to emigrate to the United States tend to be the active strivers and survivors—those who are best prepared to make sacrifices for their family's future. The strengths needed to make the decision to leave and to survive the leaving stand them in good stead in the United States.

In addition, compared to many native-born Americans, most immigrant and refugee students and their parents are more likely to view education as the major and often only way for them to improve their vocational and economic status. As a rule, these students see education as a way to repay their parents for the sacrifices they made to bring them to this country and to help those family members left behind. They appreciate the opportunity that was often denied their parents in their native countries to obtain an education (8, 41). For example, Suarez-Orozco described the attitudes of Central American immigrants and refugees in the following manner:

Universally, informants reported that schooling was the single most significant avenue for status mobility. It is important to note that the majority of my parent-informants had been pushed out of school in their native lands. Some could not afford the luxury of schooling in remote rural areas of Central America. Others had to face hard physical labor at an early age to contribute to the family's income. The parents were mostly laborers and semiskilled laborers. The current opportunities open to their children in the new land were seen by many parents in contrast to their own experiences in Central America. . . .

Most of the Central American students I came to know well were keenly aware of the degree of parental sacrifice involved in getting out of the country of origin. . . . Students saw their parents become janitors, maids, busboys, and in some cases, take two jobs so they could go to school to receive the education the parents themselves never had.

The majority of my informants had one or more members of their nuclear family still residing in a war-torn Central American nation. Most of my informants worked about four hours a day, commonly after school, to help their relatives and those left behind with remittances. . . . Schooling efforts in the new land were framed in reference to a wish to "rescue" those relatives still in Central America. (41, pp. 291–292)

Helping Immigrant and Refugee Students

Special educators who work with refugee and immigrant students, Native American students who have grown up on reservations, and rural students in urban areas should adapt their educational approaches to the context of their students' lives. They also need to accept a certain amount of problematic behavior, which students cannot control while they are adjusting to their new educational environments.

Although almost all of the students discussed in this section experience at least some of the problems described here, none of them experience all of these problems. In addition, some of these students no longer experience many of these problems, especially if they have had time to assimilate. Therefore, it is important to understand the particular circumstances and contextual problems of each student and to treat each as an individual. The following information may be helpful in individualizing approaches to the particular needs of individual students.

Immigrant students with disabilities who have spent the first four, five, or more years of their lives somewhere else require a number of years to adjust to the way things are done in the United States, even if they and their parents want to learn the new ways as quickly as possible. Thus, if a student from another country has not been here at least for a few years, the teacher can assume that the student's classroom functioning will be affected by at least some of the problems described here. If a student has recently arrived and is just beginning to attend school, the teacher should anticipate that the student will experience some degree of culture shock. The same would apply to many other students who have to adjust to unfamiliar school environments, including Native American students, rural students, and students who attend schools that serve children and youth from a different socioeconomic class.

Students' cumulative folders should include information concerning where they were born and how long they have been in the United States. Their folders may also contain information about whether they previously attended school and, if so, the kind of school experiences they had. This is extremely important for refugee students who may have spent two or more years in refugee camps where there were no schools and for students from rural areas in developing countries where schooling may not have been compulsory or available. If students' cumulative folders do not contain this information, the teacher should be able to obtain it from the students themselves, if they are old enough, or their parents or guardians.

Some information about Native American or rural students can be obtained from their cumulative folder. However, the teacher may have to rely on the students themselves, their parents, and sometimes agencies that are working with the students for most of the information that is needed.

Culture Shock

Imposing the school's culture on students with disabilities without regard to the culture they bring with them can cause them to experience even greater degrees of culture shock than they already do. However, building bridges between their home culture and the culture of the classroom can help manage the severity of the culture shock they will encounter.

Culture brokers have been used successfully to assist non-European American students (recent immigrants, second-generation Americans, and native Americans, African Americans, and others who are not knowledgeable about the ways of European American schools) to adjust to unfamiliar school environments (45, 46, 49). *Culture brokers* are bicultural individuals—usually other students, assistant teachers, paraprofessionals, or parent volunteers—who are equally knowledgeable about and comfortable in both the non-European American students' culture and the culture of the school. Although it is not essential, it is helpful for them to have experienced and solved the kinds of problems that face the students they are going to help. Typically, they belong to the same ethnic groups as the non-European American students; however, some people believe that European Americans who are very familiar with a particular non-European American culture can also serve as culture brokers.

Culture brokers help bridge the gap between the school's and non-European American students' culture by performing three roles: translators of the academic subculture to the student's ethnic subculture, translators of the student's ethnic subculture to the academic subculture, and role models (45, pp. 122–126). As translators to students' subcultures, they teach students which behaviors are appropriate in various situations, explain the possible motivations behind European Americans' actions or their reactions to the students' behavior, and so on. As translators to the academic subculture, they help teachers and peers understand and appreciate the students' feelings, attitudes, motives, and behavior. As models, they demonstrate the appropriate behavior necessary to be successful in the new culture. The following statement by a Peruvian American student with an African American, European American, and Native American background illustrates the usefulness of a cultural broker:

> My first day in school I didn't understand anything at all. I didn't speak English, I didn't understand the black students. I didn't understand the white students and there were hardly any Latinos. I was real scared. Then they assigned me a buddy. She was black and Latino like me and she was in the eighth grade too. I went to all of her classes with her and never went anywhere during recess, lunch, or any time without her.
>
> She told me that the other students were trying to figure out what I was, black, Latino, or what. I looked like I could be black but didn't speak or act black. She helped

me understand things. She taught me what to do when people started up with me. She taught me how to do things right in school. And she explained why the black kids acted that way.

Little by little I learned how to act in school. I even learned how to be black. Now I can act Latino, black, or white. (42)

Cultural assimilators have also helped students who are unfamiliar with U.S. school practices to understand and adjust to them. Cultural assimilators typically consist of a series of problematic situations with a number of alternate ways of behaving in the situation or perceiving the situation. Students choose which alternative is one they would follow or how they would perceive the situation. Then they discuss each alternative's advantages and disadvantages, appropriateness or inappropriateness, and accuracy or inaccuracy in the United States (43, 44, 47, 48).

CULTURAL ASSIMILATOR

What Should You Do?
- You are sitting in the classroom talking with classmates when the teacher enters the room. The teacher gave out papers to the class and you didn't get one.
- The teacher is talking to the class, and you didn't understand part of his lecture.
- You are talking to a friend and you want to end the conversation because you are in a hurry.
- Your teacher gave you a homework assignment that you aren't able to do. It's due the next day.

How Should You Feel?
- You see an American classmate walking toward you. You stop and say hello. Your classmate smiles, says "Hello, how are you," and continues walking.

Why Do People Behave That Way?
- A man gets on the bus and goes all the way to the back to get a seat by himself even though there is a seat next to you.
- One of your women teachers sometimes sits on her desk when teaching, wears slacks to class, and often talks with students informally after class. (44)

Including aspects of the students' home culture in the classroom by putting up pictures of their native country, arranging for classroom demonstrations of the cooking, music, or dancing of the students' place of birth, and discussing the students' country of origin can make the classroom environment a little less strange and help smooth the students' transition. Tolerating symptoms of culture shock in the classroom when they occur, so long as they are not too disruptive, will avoid putting extra pressure on students to adjust faster than they are able. Providing alternatives when the activity of the moment is not appropriate can sometimes prevent the students from having unpleasant experiences. For example, some students may not be ready for male-female recreational activities, competitive games, or showering nude in front of others. Perhaps other options can be made available. Providing alternative foods and snacks to replace what the students' religions prohibit them from eating or are unaccustomed to eating can show concern and respect for them and their customs. Such sensitivity also avoids placing students in a conflict situation.

Identity Conflicts

Teachers can avoid having students develop identity conflicts by not pressuring them to do things the way the teachers are used to having them done. Examples of such pressure could include calling on students who do not volunteer or feel comfortable speaking up in class, asking students to state publicly whether they agree with the previous speaker, or requiring students to admit their mistakes and apologize for them verbally when their culturally determined ways are just as effective.

The previously mentioned techniques for reducing culture shock—such as including students' language, heritage, and cultural values in the curriculum and using teaching styles that are familiar to students—reduce pressure on students either to assimilate completely at the expense of the their original cultures or to reject the school's culture in order to maintain their own. Special educators can use many different activities to demonstrate their respect for students' cultural heritages. For example, students can prepare multicultural calendars that include the important dates in the history of students' countries of origin and the holidays celebrated in their native countries. They can present written, oral, or videotaped reports to their classmates and write and perform in skits on themes such as Coming to America, What I Miss, Forced Out, Homeland History, and so on. Teachers can also include literature and films about immigrants in their curricula.

There is a large amount of published materials available to special educators. They include descriptions of educational programs that have proven to be effective approaches for immigrant and refugee students, curriculum guides for teaching about immigrant and refugee students, lists of books suitable for students about immigrants and refugees, and lists of films, videos, and so on. (50–55)

As one person, a teacher's influence on students' identity conflicts is limited; a schoolwide approach initiated and encouraged by school administrators can accomplish much more. As Sleeter and Grant, stated, "If one wants children to learn to value America's cultural diversity . . . it is not enough simply to tell children that these should be valued. The whole environment of the school must be teaching this" (56, p. 150). Still, it would certainly be beneficial for a teacher to do everything possible that would help students avoid identity conflicts.

Language and Teaching Styles

Research indicates that instructing students for part of the day in their native languages while they are learning English as a second language helps them adjust better to attending schools where almost every transaction is in English (8). (See Chapter 6.) The Bilingual Education Act of 1988 provides that limited-English-proficient students may be instructed bilingually for three years, and up to five years if needed, in order to bridge the transition from their native language to English. When bilingual education is not a viable option, students can be placed in programs that combine sheltered English instruction in which basic English is used to teach students their academic subjects and English as a second language instruction is used to improve their advanced English skills. Although not as desirable as bilingual education, these programs are preferable to merely submerging non-English-proficient-students in regular classes that are taught in English in which they either swim or sink. (See Chapter 6.)

Adapting instructional and classroom management techniques to the learning styles of these students while they acquire the skills necessary to learn in U.S. classrooms can enhance their learning. (See Chapter 11.) It may also reduce the likelihood that students will be frustrated, angry, anxious, or resentful in class.

Readiness Skills/Previous Educational Experience

Immigrant students' academic readiness skills and knowledge will be different from those of most students in their classes. If they have not attended school prior to coming to the United States, they will lack a great deal of knowledge and skill that children acquire in school. If they attended school irregularly, there will be huge gaps in what they know and can do. Even if they attended school regularly, they will not have learned many of the things that are included in the curriculum of the typical U.S. school. Therefore, it is essential to provide these students with a curriculum that is as individualized to their needs as possible. This can be done by starting at a student's current level of functioning, including the concepts and skills the student has acquired, being watchful for and filling in gaps, and using teaching techniques that complement the student's learning styles.

Illegal Status

Special educators can help ensure that children with disabilities of undocumented immigrants enroll in school and receive the special education services they require. Since many immigrant parents and children are unfamiliar with the U.S. school system, special educators can make sure students and parents are aware that the Supreme Court has upheld their rights to a free and appropriate education and can inform them of the rights guaranteed them under Public Law (PL) 94-142. Since they live in fear of being discovered and deported, special educators can avoid requesting information about students' immigration status or documents related to immigration questions. Teachers may also assure students and their families that their immigration status is confidential.

Refugee Experiences

Special educators can make the class a safe haven for students who have suffered the traumatic experiences that cause families to leave their homelands precipitously. Students who do not yet feel secure in their new surroundings and who are frightened by physical aggression or threats of aggression or even verbal conflicts among students may need to feel that their teachers will protect them from the possibility that they will be caught up in these events. If they are unable to handle discussions of themes such as war, starvation, crime, and so on, students may need to be allowed to engage in another activity or leave the class until the discussions have terminated. Students who have survived the ordeals or refugee camps by becoming hardened and tough and engaging in activities that are considered delinquent in the United States require understanding when they continue to behave in these ways in school. Although special educators should not accept the behavioral patterns refugee students acquired to survive terrible situations, they should not view the students as bad or punish them. A more appropriate and fairer approach would be to explain that although their behavior may have been necessary while they were refugees, their situation in the United States is now different and they no longer need to behave that way. (See Chapter 11.)

Unequal Cross-Cultural Relationships

The history of the relationship between the students' groups and the group the teacher represents (usually the dominant culture) can affect the students' classroom behavior and success in school (12). Students who have personally experienced prejudice, oppression, rejection, or abuse by European Americans or who have been brought up to anticipate and be wary of such treatment may be suspicious of the teacher's motives. They may reject the teacher's friendship, act provocatively and disrespectfully, or rebel against the teacher's authority. This certainly could apply to African American and Hispanic American students who have experienced the discriminatory treatment described in Chapter 3.

Other groups of students may also be suspicious of and hostile toward their teachers. The history of the relationships between Native Americans and the oppressive European American immigrants to this country, the current relationships between the two groups, and the discriminatory treatment Native American students experience in school give them good reason to be critical of and suspicious of European Americans in general and European American teachers in particular. Some Vietnamese American students have been told by their parents to be wary of Americans who betrayed them by withdrawing from the war and leaving behind many Vietnamese people who fought alongside them and supported them. As a result of the damage Korean American businesses suffered in Los Angeles in 1992, some Korean American students may harbor resentments against African Americans. "Growing up Indian in White America entails learning legends about historical atrocities committed by whites against Indians as well as personally experiencing white prejudice and discrimination in daily encounters" (29, p. 18).

An individual teacher may not merit such feelings on the part of his or her students, but their existence in the students' attitudes can adversely affect how these students function in class and in school. Students who are alienated, hostile, and suspicious of another group, such as the dominant society, and its institutions and organizations can bring this hostility to school. They may disbelieve and reject much of what they are taught in class. For example, even at a young age, some students may already disbelieve the concept "your friend, the police officer." As these students progress through the grades, they may reject both their teachers' and the textbooks' interpretations of American and world history (e.g., the role of Christopher Columbus, the causes of the Civil War, desirability of U.S. intervention in Central America, labeling the events in Los Angeles a riot rather than a rebellion, etc.), as well as the standard explanations of how the U.S. economic and political systems function. Their opinions about the best way to solve the current issues facing the United States and the world may be at odds with those of their teachers. They may believe, sometimes with justification, that their teachers are insensitive to their cultural needs and indifferent—or even prejudiced—toward them. As a result, they may be suspicious of their teachers' motives.

Although some students keep their feelings to themselves in class, many others—especially the older ones—act on their feelings. In doing so, they may repeatedly challenge their teachers' statements and demonstrate a lack of respect and disregard for their teachers' authority by not following rules, acting bored, making sarcastic and provocative comments, and purposely disrupting the class. Some students may withdraw from what they consider to be an irrelevant and prejudicial education by ignoring their teachers, arriving late, and cutting class. These students may function in this way, regardless of whether the teacher merits such reactions because of what teachers, in general, represent to them.

Parents who are suspicious of the European American school system and believe that non-European and poor students are often misplaced in special education programs may resist the suggestions they receive from special educators and relate to school personnel in an uncooperative manner. If they also communicate their concerns to their sons and daughters, it may cause additional problems between students and their teachers.

If you, as a teacher, have alienated students in your class or if you are the recipient of their anger, resentment, and distrust of the system, tell them that you understand how they feel and why they might feel that way, but explain how things are different in your classroom. If students act out their anger or resentment in class, tolerate behavior problems that do not seriously disrupt the class. However, make it clear that although you understand how they feel, they will not be allowed to interfere with other students' right to learn. When students withdraw from classroom participation, ignore you, arrive late, cut classes, and so on, explain that there are better ways of expressing their feelings and solving the problem than denying themselves an education. Earn their trust and confidence by utilizing a multicultural approach when you instruct, assess, and counsel students and manage their behavior (see Chapters 9–11), and advocate for their rights when they are mistreated or victimized by prejudice.

It is also important for a teacher to correct any misperceptions students' families may have about him or her and to develop positive relationships with families before it becomes necessary to solve problems and resolve issues. Communicating the positive accomplishments of their children, inviting them to visit the class and to participate in class events, and seeking their input and feedback about curriculum can help establish a relationship of mutual respect and confidence. (See Chapter 4 for a detailed discussion of techniques for dealing with suspicion and alienation.)

CONTEXTUAL PROBLEMS

List and compare the possible contextual problems that each of the following students may be experiencing. Although there is insufficient information to really understand these students, it is possible to be sensitive to potential problems they may be facing because of the context of their lives.

Martín is a 5-year-old Hispanic American student in a bilingual kindergarten program who has been referred for evaluation for possible placement in special education. He was born in a rural town in Mexico and came to the United States with his parents when he was 3 years old. Very little is known about Martín's parents because they resist providing information to school authorities. However, it is known that both parents speak only Spanish.

Jaime is a 12-year-old English-proficient Hispanic American student who came to this country when he was 7 months old. After spending 3 years in a bilingual program, he was transitioned to the regular English program. He was recently evaluated and placed in a special day class.

Jewel is a 5-year-old African American student in a regular kindergarten class who has been referred for evaluation for possible placement in special education. She lives in a predominantly poor African American neighborhood. Both her parents dropped out of high school when they were 16 and 17 years old.

Rashid is a 9-year-old African American student who was just accepted for placement in a special education program for students with behavior disorders. He lives in a predominantly middle-class African American neighborhood. Both his parents are college graduates.

Hoa is a 6-year-old Vietnamese American student who came to this country from a rural area when she was 4 years old. After escaping from Vietnam by boat, she was kept in a camp for refugees for 17 months before coming to the United States. After spending 1 year in a regular kindergarten program, she was evaluated, found to have developmental disabilities, and placed in a special day class.

Mai is an English-proficient 9-year-old Vietnamese American student. She was born in the United States. Both her parents were born in Vietnam and came to the United States when the U.S. forces left Vietnam in the 1970s. She is in a pull-out resource specialist program for students with learning disabilities because of her difficulty in mathematics.

MIGRANT STUDENTS

Migrant students' dropout rate, which has been estimated at between 45 and 57 percent, is the highest rate of any group in the United States (60, 62, 65). Even while migrant students are attending school, they often fail to actualize their potential for learning because of both the contextual aspects of their lives and the school system's inability or unwillingness to provide them with a contextually appropriate education (56–70). Dyson has described some of the unique contextual problems with which migrant students must deal: "Imagine the problems a migrant child must face as he shifts from one school to another—perhaps as many as three times a year. Very often the migrant child does not use English as the primary language; he is not accepted readily by his classmates because he is 'different'; educational approaches and textbooks tend to vary from school to school; and many times instructors are not willing to bother with a student who will be in the classroom only a few weeks" (59, p. 1).

The negative results of these problems are all too prevalent. "Inevitably this constant interruption of learning, lack of continuity, absence from school during travel time, and often blatant discrimination by local communities and school personnel all contribute to migrant students falling behind . . . and getting disinterested in an educational system which cannot provide the needed continuous education" (66, p. 4). These problems can be ameliorated to a considerable degree by educational programs geared to the needs of migrant students. Unfortunately, schools often add to students' problems rather than help solve them. As Dyson stated, "It is an unfortunate but undeniable reality that our educational system has been developed for, and geared toward, the permanent community resident" (59, p. 1).

The multiple health problems and poverty that afflict migrant students place them at greater risk for various kinds of disabilities (56). However, migrant children with disabilities are especially likely to be shortchanged by the schools.

> Migrant children with special needs are faced by a cruel double jeopardy. Special education students face serious academic difficulties even when they come from stable, affluent homes; when they are given the additional burdens of migrancy, they risk being crushed. . . . Real leadership and dedicated commitment are required if these students are to get the educations they deserve. . . . The perception that they are disadvantaged makes teachers less alert to giftedness than they might be. . . . Nature puts as many geniuses among migrants as among non-migrants. . . . The opposite is worse, being larger in scale: thousands upon thousands of migrant children are diagnosed as learning impaired or mentally disabled when, in fact, their abilities are well within the normal range. . . . We must stop branding migrant children as deficient when they are merely different. (65, p. 1)

Helping Migrant Students

The following suggestions for adapting educational approaches to the context of migrants students' lives appear repeatedly in the literature (57–63, 68–70). While many of these suggestions are directed to regular education teachers, they are especially important for special educators.

- Utilize a multicultural approach to make the classroom more relevant to students and to help students bridge the gap between their experiences and the culture of the school. (See Chapter 4.)
- Include English as a second language instruction, sheltered English approaches, and bilingual paraprofessionals to facilitate limited-English-proficient students' academic learning and their acquisition of English language skills. (See Chapter 6.)
- Because migrant students tend to be characterized by inconsistent enrollment and attendance in a number of difference schools, do not assume that students have been receiving the special education assistance they need or that they have even attended special education programs on a regular basis.
- Identify and help students with the academic problems they experience because of their disabilities and their irregular school attendance.
- Provide students with successful role models by inviting individuals who have escaped from the vicious cycle many migrant families are caught in to be guest speakers, tutors, and so on.
- Help students become acquainted with the community, the services the community offers, and how their lives can be improved by making use of those services. Fieldtrips can be especially useful.
- Provide students with opportunities to learn career and vocational skills other than farm work that will increase their employability.
- Encourage and assist parents to become involved in their children's education. Research indicates that even if parents are unable to help students with their schoolwork because they themselves have not attended or succeeded in school, their children will learn more and have better attitudes about school if parents are interested in and discuss their children's education with them (60).

RURAL STUDENTS

The rural communities that students with disabilities call home cannot and should not be stereotyped. These students may be living on remote islands, in rural farming areas, deserts, Arctic villages, Native American reservations, isolated mountainous regions, and so on. Economically, they may come from stable farming communities or economically depressed mining towns. Their communities may be connected to each other and to a large urban area by accessible roads that are open all year round, their connecting roads may be impassable during the winter, or their only means of transportation to other areas may be by plane. The special education program they attend may be located in such a remote and sparsely populated area that it consists of one class that serves only a handful of students with many different disabilities and provides little in the way of additional services. It may be located close enough to a group of small towns to provide different services for students with different disabilities and a range of ancillary services. Or it may be a residential facility located far from where the students' families live. Despite these significant variations, there are some important contextual factors about which special educators who work with students with disabilities from and in rural areas should be aware (71–89).

Although students in rural schools face economic and social strains at least as difficult as those confronting students who attend inner-city schools, their problems receive far less attention than those of urban students (76, 87). The dropout rate for rural students from regular education, between 40 and 50 percent, is more than twice the national average. The rate for students in special education, 36 percent, is 50 percent higher than the national average (78, 82, 86).

Research indicates that rural students with disabilities experience a greater number of problems and are exposed to many more adverse conditions than non-rural students (72, 76, 80, 84). However, special educators are often unaware of their contextual problems. In one study, rural students scored significantly poorer than nonrural students on 34 of 39 risk and problems factors (76). In comparison to nonrural students with disabilities, rural students are twice as likely to come from poor families. They are significantly more likely to have illiterate parents, to be children of substance abusers, to be abused, and to have lower self-esteems. They also have a greater tendency to be substance abusers, to experience depression, and to attempt suicide. As one researcher has stated, "It is apparent that the image of rural children leading wholesome, trouble-free lives compared with youth in more crowded settings is in need of revision" (76, p. 3).

Contextual Problems

Helge described the obstacles facing special educators in rural areas as follows: "Problems associated with implementing comprehensive special education services are compounded by vast land areas, scattered populations, and isolation. Remote and impoverished districts also suffer from a lack of social, psychological, and family counseling services" (76, p. 2). Transportation difficulties to get to remote locations, vast distances between population groups, impassable roads during inclement weather, and low population density make it difficult to provide special education services to some students. These factors also prevent many families from being involved in the the special education process, and make it extremely difficult to offer services at reasonable costs.

Loss of farming, mining, timber, coal, and gas jobs has led to an exacerbation of poverty. This has lowered an already small tax base for education and other services. It also limits what local governments can provide. As a result, although rural communities expend a greater percentage of their local resources on education, they are less able to afford more costly special education services, especially those that are required for students with low-incidence disabilities. Rural areas are also less able to afford technological tools such as computers, interactive television, and so on that could help in overcoming the logistics problems previously mentioned.

The following description indicates that on some impoverished Native American reservations, the situation for those with disabilities is especially dismal:

Public transportation is not available on most reservations and mobility continues to be a significant problem for the disabled as well as the general population. Other services such as personal care are also rarely available, and in order to receive such services, the disabled individual who wants independence must be willing either to remain or to re-settle in an off-reservation community or urban environment. Dirt floors, substandard housing, and other inconveniences such as lack of indoor toilets make it almost impossible for many disabled people to be independent in most Indian communities. Governmental and other support for such programs have not yet reached most Indian communities. . . . Tribally operated programs also have difficulty obtaining adequate funds for their programs. Allocation of funds is not calculated on what services the disabled require or are entitled to, but are calculated based on figures or budgets for care and education of Indian children who are not disabled. (77, pp. 258, 260)

Remoteness, poverty, and the unavailability of the many amenities found in urban areas makes it difficult to attract and keep adequate numbers of qualified, well-trained professionals such as medical personnel and nutritionists. The scarcity of prenatal care programs and nutrition programs that result from the lack of human resources leads to many biomedical problems that increase the number of children and youth with disabilities. The failure to recruit sufficient special educators, psychologists, and other personnel who serve students with disabilities leads to a decrease in the services available to meet their special needs. For example, there is often a lack of medical, social, and psychological services. Respite care and foster care are often unavailable.

Evidence that needs to be updated suggests that factors such as low tax bases, logistical problems, and lack of qualified personnel have combined to create a disturbing situation. Although rural students account for less than 30 percent of the total population, the majority of unserved or underserved students with disabilities live in rural areas (74). Too often, the special educational services that are offered are provided by uncertified and poorly prepared personnel.

Children with disabilities from rural families that rely on seasonal activities such as fishing, agriculture, timber, and so on may not be able to attend school during certain times of the year. Inconsistent attendance makes it especially difficult for special educators to do what is necessary to help students overcome their disabilities and to actualize their potential. (See Table 5–1.)

Motivational Factors

A number of factors have combined to keep the educational and vocational aspirations of rural students at a very low level: low self-esteem; high rates of poverty; low levels of parental education; parental encouragement to accept jobs that do not require a college education, to join the military, or to attend a trade school rather than a college; and a scarcity of jobs that require higher education (73, 81, 85, 87). In fact, rural youth who remain in rural areas as adults have the lowest educational aspirations of youth in the United States (73).

TABLE 5–1   Issues Differentiating Rural and Urban Communities as They Serve Children with Disabilities

Issue	Rural	Urban
Transportation	Long distances, high costs, climatic and geographic barriers	Problems associated with desegregation (e.g., busing)
Geography	Social and professional isolation, long distances from services, geographic barriers	Problems associated with access (e.g., wheelchairs)
Personnel turnover	30–50% among special education related personnel	Less teacher turnover
Difficulties in serving particular disabilities	Low-incidence disabilities hardest to to serve, favorable attitude toward mainstreaming	Adequate numbers of students with low-incidence disabilities to cluster services, attitude toward mainstreaming less favorable
Backlog of children for assessment	Lack of available services (e.g., personnel, agency programs, funds, etc.)	Bureaucratic and organizational barriers
Type of roles	Generalists who perform a variety of tasks and teach a variety of subjects to students with different disabilities	Specialists in one topic area, one age, or one disability group
Availability of technical resources	Advanced technologies less often available, particularly for students	Modern technologies more prevalent and more available for student use

Source: Adapted from *Rural, Exceptional, At Risk* by D. Helge, 1991, pages 11–13. Copyright 1991 by The Council for Exceptional Children. Reprinted with permission.

Cultural Factors

Some rural attitudes can also present obstacles to special educators (75, 76). For example, the tradition of taking care of one's own sometimes makes families too independent to welcome help in the form of special education, counseling, or social services—and even to identify students with disabilities—because they may view this as going on the "government dole." Many rural families are reluctant to participate in such school matters as IEP meetings because they see the schools as authority figures to be avoided. Many of them do not know about special education or their rights under PL 94-142. The tradition of making do with what they have sometimes leads agencies that serve students with disabilities to settle for less. As a rule, people in rural communities are less responsive than other people to statements about what they have to do for students with disabilities and they are more motivated to provide appropriate services when the initiative is theirs.

Some rural communities, such as Native American communities, have very different cultural heritages that require modifications in mainstream special education approaches to make them compatible with their heritage. Also, families living in isolated rural areas that do not offer special education services are sometimes unwilling to send children with disabilities to live in other areas with dissimilar cultures.

Contextual, Motivational, and Cultural Strengths

Special educators should also be aware of the contextual and cultural strengths that exist in rural communities (75, 76, 79). These include a tendency to trust their neighbors, close nuclear and extended family ties, a sense of community that leads rural citizens to aid their neighbors and volunteer to help those with disabilities, and a strong sense of personal accountability. Marrs stated, "Rural Americans take pride in helping each other solve problems; they know each other, are aware of needs and resources, and are willing to share what they have if their neighbors need it" (80, p. 361).

Appropriate Special Education Services

The following suggestions for providing appropriate special education services to students in rural areas have been made by experts in the field (75, 78, 89–103). Although many of these suggestions may apply to other situations, they are especially important in rural settings.

1. *Involve students' parents and their extended families as much as possible in the education process.* Especially when human resources are in short supply, parents can serve as volunteers in class and tutors at home. They can support and guide other parents who have just found out that their children have disabilities through the initial difficulties of accepting that children have disabilities, learning about the disabling condition, identifying where to obtain the needed services, and so on. Volunteer parents also may be able to share child-care responsibilities to provide respite.

Although urban parents may lend more credence to the pronouncements, suggestions, and advice of professionals than other parents, the opposite is often the case in rural families. Helge stated, "Discussion/support groups led by parents are much more successful than those led by professionals. Rural programs frequently find that a public service announcement made by a parent stating that he is not affiliated with the agency . . . is particularly successful" (75, p. 2).

Since rural parents often tend to avoid authority figures in the schools, it is especially important to establish a positive rapport with parents through social contacts, nonthreatening social events or meetings, and noncounseling activities. It is also helpful to assist them with their stated needs that are not related to their children's disability before attempting to visit their homes or to help them with special education issues. Providing free child care and starting off with a meal can increase parent willingness to cooperate with educators.

2. *Use creative means to solve communication/transportation problems in isolated areas.* Use the community's informal communication network and enlist the support of the important people in the community. These people may be the cooperative extension worker, the gas station attendant who speaks to everyone in the community, a well-respected church member, and so on. Work closely with other agencies and personnel—such as home health agents, county demonstration workers, public health workers, bookmobile librarians, and utility meter readers—who visit families or provide services to families of children with disabilities.

3. *Augment the qualified professional personnel available with trained paraprofessionals (if funds are available) and with trained community volunteers and students' parents.* In rural areas, individual concerned community members, social clubs, librarians, local small businesspersons, church groups, volunteer fire departments, 4–H clubs, chambers of commerce, veterans' groups, and other organizations are all good sources of human resources to augment the efforts of paid professionals and paraprofessionals. Although volunteerism has declined in urban areas, Kirmer and colleagues reported, "Recruiting volunteers is not a problem in rural America. The main problem is keeping them busy" (96, p. 366).

4. *Consider using itinerant teachers as consultants to the regular school personnel to avoid the problems inherent in removing students from their communities and placing them in residential programs that do not reflect students' cultures.*

5. *Adapt IEP and other legal requirements to the realities of the community.* Parents who live in cultures that do not have written languages or who do not read should not be sent written communications nor required to give their written consent to IEPs and other forms. Students should not be expected to attend school on religious holidays, and important work should not be scheduled in areas that rely on seasonal occupations (e.g., agriculture, fishing, etc.) during times when students are least likely to be able to comply with school attendance and homework policies.

6. *Employ technology to reach and teach rural students with disabilities.* Current special education practices that are based on communication among individuals working in comparatively close contact are less effective in rural settings. Technological tools such as videodiscs and videotapes, interactive television, instructional television, computers, and citizens band radios can improve instruction, enhance communication, and sometimes avoid the necessity of having to remove students from their communities in order to provide them with the special education they require. Helge pointed out, "The use of modern technology assists in overcoming serious service delivery problems associated with sparse populations, scarce resources, and difficult terrain" (94, p. 358).

7. *Adapt the curriculum content and instructional strategies to the students' cultural and socioeconomic-class characteristics.* (See Chapter 11.)

MIDDLE-CLASS AND AFFLUENT
SUBURBAN STUDENTS

Many special educators tend to overlook the contextual problems facing students who grow up in middle-class and affluent suburbs. Contrary to the view presented in many basal readers, television programs, magazine articles, and education textbooks, children and youth with disabilities who live in middle-class and affluent suburbs often lead lives that are far from idyllic. In some cases, their parents are too involved in their own careers to provide them with the supervision, support, attention, and affection they need. Parents who are concerned that if their children do not get into the right preschool they will be not be in the track that leads to acceptance by the right college and eventually to the right career may have great difficulty accepting their children's disabilities. As a result, they may pressure their children when they are older to study more than they can, learn faster than they are able, and earn higher grades than they are capable of obtaining.

Students who live in families that share child custody may find themselves living disjointed, unstable lives. Unless they have duplicates of all the education support materials they require at both of their homes, their likelihood of completing a particular assignment may depend in part on which home they are living in during a particular week. If they spend some nights of the week in one home and the remainder of the nights in another, they may forget to bring all of their school materials and books with them when they go from one to another.

Growing up in more affluent circumstances, some students may have more money at their disposal to abuse drugs, alcohol, cars, and so on. They may have the means to spend their time in amusement arcades instead of attending school and they may have more expensive electronic games at home to tempt them away from their schoolwork.

For these and other reasons, special educators should be as concerned about possible contextual problems among their more affluent students as they are about any other groups of students with disabilities.

INADEQUATE, NEGLECTFUL, AND ABUSIVE CHILD CARE

Some students with disabilities do not receive adequate child care. As noted in Chapter 2, through no fault of their own, parents of very poor students are often unable to provide their children with the same nutrition and medical care that more advantaged children receive. Many poor parents are also unable to give their children the financial support they need to succeed in school.

Students do not have to be poor to suffer inadequate child care. Many middle-class and upper-class parents do not adequately care for children with disabilities. Divorced parents may use students as pawns in their battles with each other. As noted in Chapter 2, regardless of their ethnic or socioeconomic-class background, parents who abuse drugs and alcohol are often unable to care for their children while they are under the influence of these substances. In addition, they may be unable to care for their children financially and psychologically even when not under the influence if their lives are consumed by drug problems. In some cases, the inadequate care students receive amounts to neglect or abuse.

Neglect and Abuse

The number of abused and neglected children and youth has risen precipitously in recent years. Although about 2 million cases of child abuse and neglect are officially reported annually, conservative estimates suggest that the number of children and adolescents that actually suffer abuse and neglect is two to three times the reported amount. Thus, between 10 and 15 percent of the U.S. population suffers from maltreatment (113). Whether this reflects a real increase in the prevalence of these problems or merely a greater willingness to report the abuse is somewhat unclear. However, it is clear that far too many students suffer the effects of neglect and psychological, physical, and sexual abuse.

Neglected children have many problems, but those who suffer actual abuse are much worse off. Fink and Janssen described the effects of abuse on adolescents as follows: "Systematic abuse causes significant dysfunction in intellectual, emotional, developmental, and motoric ability. Systematic abuse creates substantial 'at risk' conditions among adolescents for psychological, interpersonal, academic, medical, and legal problems. Self-image, motivation, personal satisfaction, and success in the workplace are negatively impacted. Systematic maltreatment is an experience that dominates and delimits personal competence and effectiveness" (114, p. 32).

Abused students tend to demonstrate serious behavior problems in school. However, the form their problems take depends on how they react to the abuse. Those who act out against others tend to be aggressive and abusive toward others. If they have been sexually abused, they may abuse others sexually or at least act out sexually. Those who turn away from others are likely to reject friendly overtures from others and withdraw from interpersonal relationships. In general, whatever the outward manifestations of their problems, abused children tend to mistrust others, especially adults. They also have low self-concepts. In comparison to nonabused students, they are more likely to develop conduct and emotional problems, to abuse drugs and alcohol, to lack the motivation and energy necessary to succeed in school, and to misunderstand and be suspicious of the behavior and intentions of others.

The tendency to misperceive others makes it especially necessary for teachers to be careful when selecting classroom management techniques for abused children. Because they have been maltreated in the past, they are less able to tolerate any kind of negative consequences, even mild ones. For example, students who have been locked up alone may have extreme difficulty coping with time out in an isolated area. Corporal punishment can have disastrous repercussions, especially with students who have been physically abused.

Abused students may view authoritative teachers who take charge of their classrooms as abusive. They may even experience praise as manipulative attempts to control them. Students who have been sexually abused may be threatened by friendly and warm teachers. They may recoil from any form of physical contact, no matter how innocent. Some of them may imagine that their teachers are on the verge of abusing them.

Research indicates that there is a strong interrelationship between disability and child abuse. On the one hand, in comparison to their peers who have no disabilities, children with disabilities suffer from a higher rate of child abuse (105, 111, 119, 121, 127, 130, 134, 135). Students with developmental, physical, sensory, and multiple disabilities are especially likely to be abused. Researchers have identified the following three factors that place students with disabilities at risk for abuse (116, 118, 120, 121, 131, 133):

1. Certain characteristics of students with disabilities—such as demanding behavior, high-pitched crying, unresponsiveness, helplessness, and dependency—can cause parents/caretakers to behave abusively toward them.
2. Parents may not be able to respond appropriately to children with disabilities or deal constructively with the added stress such children create in their lives if they also have to cope with other marital, financial, emotional, psychological, or social problems. This is even more likely to be true of parents who do not have sufficient information about atypical child development, special techniques for caring for children with disabilities, and so on.
3. Children with disabilities are more vulnerable to child abuse if their disabilities make them more dependent on adults, less able to defend themselves, less able to tell others when they are abused, and less able to know the difference between acceptable and unacceptable adult behavior.

On the other hand, child abuse may cause children to become disabled. Physical disabilities such as cerebral palsy, emotional problems, cognitive deficits, brain damage, and learning disabilities can all result from child abuse (104, 107–109, 111–112, 123).

To avoid these potential problems and to help students overcome them, special educators need to know which, if any, of their students have been abused or neglected. Although others may be the source of such information, teachers are often the first persons to suspect and report possible cases of child abuse and neglect to the appropriate authorities. Every state has passed laws that require educators to report observations that lead them to suspect the possibility of child abuse. Therefore, special educators need to be sensitive to the signs and symptoms of possible child abuse. Because most teachers need additional training to be able to identify the signs of possible child abuse (122), it is important that they seek such training from their school districts or teacher preparation programs. Special educators can also avail themselves of some of the material currently available to improve their level of competency (108, 125, 126, 128).

IDENTIFYING NEGLECTED AND ABUSED STUDENTS

The following physical and behavioral symptoms should alert educators to the possibility of child abuse and the need for additional investigation. However, keep in mind that these symptoms may also be caused by other problems.

Physical Abuse
- Unexplained cuts, bruises, burns, fractures, and welts
- Wary of adult contact
- Apprehensive when other students cry
- Aggressive or withdrawn
- Resists going home
- Fear of parents
- Reports abuse by parents

Physical Neglect
- Consistent hunger
- Poor hygiene
- Inappropriate dress
- Consistent lack of supervision
- Unattended physical or medical problems
- Abandonment
- Begging or stealing food
- Early arrival and late departure from school
- Constant fatigue, listlessness, or falling asleep in class
- Alcohol or drug abuse
- Delinquency
- Reports of parental neglect

Sexual Abuse
- Difficulty in walking or sitting
- Torn or stained clothing
- Pain or itching in genital area
- Venereal disease
- Pregnancy
- Unwilling to change for gym
- Withdrawal, fantasy, or infantile behavior
- Bizarre, sophisticated, or unusual sexual behavior, preoccupations, or knowledge
- Poor peer relationships
- Running away
- Reported sexual abuse

Emotional Maltreatment
- Speech disorders
- Lag in physical development
- Failure to thrive
- Sucking, biting, rocking
- Antisocial, destructive behavior
- Sleep disorders
- Compulsions, phobias, obsessions
- Behavior extremes—compliant, passive, demanding, aggressive
- Mental or emotional developmental lag
- Attempted suicide

Source: Adapted from *Abuse and Neglect of Exceptional Children* by C. L. Warger, S. Tewey, and M. Megivern, 1991. Copyright 1991 by The Council for Exceptional Children. Reprinted with permission.

There are a number of ways to help students who are known to have been abused (106, 114, 115, 117, 124, 129, 131, 132). Educators should maintain a classroom climate that makes abused students feel comfortable and secure. An assessment of whether students have actually suffered any of the potential negative results of child abuse that can interfere with their cognitive functioning, powers of attention and concentration, ability to relate positively to others, and so on is also helpful. The assessment may be followed up by utilizing special education techniques to deal with these negative results and by avoiding the use of classroom management techniques that can be inappropriate for abused students.

> As a teacher you are entrusted with a real treasure—a child's spirit. It can grow and flourish or it can be crushed. For the abused child, the school may be the only avenue of escape, a place where s/he can feel safe. Your classroom can support the child's needs if you:
>> Promote an accepting environment in your classroom.
>> Be warm and loving.
>> Create an individualized program for the maltreated child.
>> Give the maltreated child additional attention wherever possible. (132, p. 3)

When it is desirable or necessary to discuss students' abusive experiences with them, students should be reassured that it is not their fault, they are not in trouble, they have not done anything wrong, and they are not bad persons because of the actions of others. Asking prying questions and making judgmental statements about the adult abusers should be avoided. If students describe their abusive experiences, the teacher should not appear shocked, surprised, or horrified. The discussion should be reported in a timely manner to the person who has been legally designated by the school administration.

Runaway and Homeless Children and Youth

Between 1,000,000 and 1,500,000 children and youth run away from home each year (160). These children and youth suffer a great many problems (147, 160, 169, 171). Prior to running away, they may have suffered severe maltreatment, including physical and sexual abuse. (See previous section.) In comparison to children and youth who live at home, runaway and homeless children and youth are more likely to engage in self-destructive behavior, abuse drugs and alcohol, have medical and psychological problems, attempt suicide, be involved in illegal activities in order to obtain money, and have serious school problems. Because they attend school erratically, move from place to place, do not have the documents required by schools and lack parents or guardians to speak and sign for them, these children and youth are also much less likely to receive the special education services they require.

Estimates of the number of homeless children range from 272,773 to 1,600,000 (142, 143). The plight of homeless children and youth is especially horrendous (136–146,148–172). In comparison to those who live in homes, homeless students have more developmental delays, emotional problems, behavior disorders, and sleep disorders. They are more likely to be aggressive and noncompliant, shy and withdrawn, anxious, tired, and restless. They have greater difficulty forming relationships with others and they are also more likely to exhibit symptoms associated with stress and low self-esteem. Studies indicate that approximately 50 percent of homeless children are clinically depressed, over 50 percent have contemplated suicide, and between 31 to 50 percent need psychiatric evaluation. Although they have four times as many health problems and twice as many chronic diseases, they have less access to medical care and are less able to follow the health regimes prescribe by physicians.

The contextual problems that confront homeless children interfere with their schooling to the point that anywhere from 28 to 43 percent of them do not even attend school. Heflin and Rudy stated,

> The combination of physical, psychological, intellectual, and behavioral outcomes of homelessness for children and youth may make it difficult for them to achieve in school. Homelessness has been described as a "breeding ground" for disabling conditions. . . . Although they are clearly at risk for academic failure, the transient nature of most homeless students makes the time-consuming task of assessment and referral for special services almost impossible. Given the high percentages of homeless students experiencing school problems, child counts in special education should reflect service provision to a considerable number of learners with exceptionalities who are homeless. Analyses not only fail to document the existence of homelessness among students in special education, they also demonstrate that homeless students are often denied access to any educational opportunities. . . . A variety of legal, financial, bureaucratic, social, and familial barriers serve to effectively exclude homeless children and youth from accessing educational opportunities. (151, pp. 15–17)

The Individuals with Disabilities Education Act of 1991 (IDEA), the most recent version of PL 94-142, guarantees students with disabilities the right to a free and appropriate education. The McKinney Homeless Assistance Amendments Act of 1990 encourages schools to accommodate the process they use to identify, place, and serve homeless students with disabilities to the conditions in which homeless students find themselves. However, well-intentioned laws alone cannot solve the contextual problems runaway and homeless students with disabilities face. Therefore, to be effective, special educators have to adapt their approaches to the realities of these students' lives. The following suggestions have been offered by experts in the field:

- *Focus on making sure students' basic needs are met.* Students who are struggling with problems concerning transportation to school, food, clothing, sleep, and school supplies are unable to give their all to their studies. Assist students and their families to obtain the social, medical, financial, and other support services they require. Be discrete in order to avoid embarrassing them. Use techniques that empower parents to deal with these agencies in order to strengthen their child-care role and foster more positive parent-child relationships. However, if necessary, advocate for those families who meet with resistance from service agencies.
- *Provide students with a safe environment in which they can feel secure, relax their guard, act their age, and be themselves.* Runaway and homeless students often have learned to distrust adults who may have been unable or unwilling to care for them. They may be on their guard against anticipated disappointments, rejections, and abuse. They may also have had to assume adultlike responsibilities before they were ready to do so.
- *Assign students personal space.* Since homeless and runaway students are unlikely to have space of their own—their own room, closet, bed, place at a dinner table, and so on—providing them with a space in their classroom that they can call their own and mark with symbols of their identity can improve their sense of self-worth and stability.
- *Assess students' skills, knowledge, abilities, and strengths and weaknesses in great detail.* Although this is desirable for all students with disabilities, it is especially important for students who attend school irregularly, enroll in many different schools, and often do not complete assignments when they do attend.
- *Encourage students to become autonomous and independent so that they come to believe that they can be in control of their own lives.* Runaway and homeless students' living conditions tend to lead them to develop an external locus of control.
- *Maintain the kinds of flexibility necessary to incorporate students into your program for whatever amount of time they are able to attend.* Allowing students to progress at their own pace, individualizing their assignments, and using modules and computerized instruction are tools that can provide needed flexibility.
- *Encourage and assist students to attend your program even when it becomes difficult for them to do so.* Do not penalize students who are unable to attend, complete assignments, and so on because of contextual problems.

- *Work closely with other agencies that are assisting your students and their families.* Collaborative efforts are more effective than individualistic uncoordinated approaches.

PROBLEMS OF ADOLESCENCE

As any adolescent psychology textbook will certify, adolescence is an especially difficult developmental phase. The problems that many adolescents face can seriously impact the school functioning of students without disabilities. For students with disabilities, dealing with their emergent sexual drives, deciding who they are and who they want to be, and making decisions that will affect their entire lives can be more important and pressing than completing their schoolwork.

The available evidence suggests that teenage pregnancy may occur at a higher rate and at a younger age among females with disabilities than in the general population (173). Although some teenage parents are or become dropouts, many continue in school. Adolescent parents who are also students have to balance and juggle the responsibilities of bringing up children and the demands of school; however, those with disabilities are more vulnerable to these difficulties (175). Problems such as these can sap the energy of students without disabilities. Students with disabilities may find it almost impossible to deal with such problems and succeed in school. In addition, many teenagers with disabilities have to deal with the temptations and results of substance abuse (174). Students who bring such problems to school may have a difficult time learning.

To be effective with adolescents with disabilities, special educators need to be sensitive to the potential problems that adolescents bring with them to school. They should be able to adapt their expectations and teaching strategies to their students' problems, and to help them obtain the additional outside assistance they may require. Space does not permit a discussion of these topics. However, these issues are dealt with in considerable detail in the references at the end of the chapter (173–176).

CONTEXTUAL VERSUS CULTURAL FACTORS

Special educators sometimes incorrectly attribute some of their students' contextually influenced attitudes, behavior, and problems to cultural factors. For example, children of migrant workers have difficulty succeeding in school because they miss a great deal of school time while they are traveling from place to place and attend various schools in which they have to cope with different curricula, expectations, procedures, teaching and classroom management styles, and so on. As a result, despite their intense desire to succeed in school, they may become discouraged about and give up on education. Special educators who teach in schools in which most of their Hispanic American students' parents are migrant workers tend to misperceive their students' *loss* of interest in school as a *lack* of interest in school. Many of them thereby conclude that all Hispanic Americans devalue education. Some migrant workers and their children who move back and forth across the border between the United States and Mexico may not be motivated to learn English or assimilate to the way things are done in the United States. Thus, some special educators who have little exposure to other Hispanic Americans may mistakenly believe that for cultural reasons, Hispanic Americans in general are disinterested in assimilating or learning English.

Some parents avoid contact with the school because of their illegal status; some cannot afford the child care required to attend school meetings and functions; others cannot speak English well enough to participate in such functions or even understand the announcements that are sent home. Special educators who are unaware of the role played by these contextual factors may incorrectly attribute some parents' lack of attendance at IEP meetings, school functions, open houses, back-to-school days, and so on to a culturally influenced lack of interest in their children's education.

Many special educators are not aware that some non-European American and poor parents are suspicious about the motives of teachers and school administrators because of the misplacement of children from their ethnic group or socioeconomic class in special education. The history of unequal cross-cultural relationships between their ethnic or socioeconomic-class group and the group to which the special educators belong is also a reason for suspicion. As a result, some educators may mistakenly assume that these students and their parents are brought up to be suspicious and hostile in general.

A number of special educators are not aware of the extent to which racism and structured reproduction have helped to create a huge unemployment problem among African American teenage and adult males. These educators are too quick to assume that African Americans are lazy and shiftless because they hang out in the neighborhood during the day. Unaware of the inability of many African American males to support a family, some educators assume that African American males are brought up to avoid marriage and family responsibilities.

Some special educators do not take into account the effects of the trauma, abuse, neglect, and culture shock many Asian Pacific American refugee students experience. These educators may mistakenly attribute the students' reticence and lack of participation in class to culturally influenced learning and behavior styles.

As these examples demonstrate, it is essential that special educators understand the contextual aspects of their students' lives and avoid attributing the effects of contextual factors to cultural factors. This is one way that teachers can avoid harmful, prejudicial beliefs about students and their cultures.

SUMMARY

Many students are faced with contextual problems that can seriously impede their ability to succeed in school and lead them to be inappropriately referred to special education. Immigrant and refugee students, migrant students, students from cultures that have a history of unequal cross-cultural relationships with European Americans, students in rural and isolated areas, abused and neglected students, and students whose parents are unable to provide them with adequate care all need a contextually appropriate education. If they also have disabilities, special educators should adapt their approaches to these students' contextual problems and strengths.

ACTIVITIES

1. If you are currently teaching or student teaching and you have not already done so, find out your school district's procedures and policies on identifying and reporting cases of suspected child abuse.

2. Enhance your understanding and appreciation of homeless and runaway students by visiting a local shelter for homeless families or runaway youth.

REFERENCES

References 1–23 describe the problems of immigrant and refugee students and their families.

1. Adler, P. S. (1975). The transitional experience: An alternative view of culture shock. *Journal of Humanistic Psychology, 15,* 13–23.

2. Buell, L. H. (1984). *Understanding the Immigrant Mexican.* San Diego, CA: Los Amigos Research Associates.

3. Carlin, J. E. (1979). The catastrophically uprooted child: Southeast Asian refugee children. In J. D. Call, J. D. Noshpitz, R. L. Cohen, & I. N. Berlin (Eds.), *Basic Handbook of Child Psychiatry: Vol I.* New York: Basic Books.

4. Chan, K. S. (1980). *Limited English Speaking, Handicapped, and Poor: Triple Threat in Childhood.* ERIC ED 247 686.

5. Cloud, N. (1991). Acculturation of ethnic minorities. In A. M. Ambert (Ed.), *Bilingual Education and English as a Second Language: A Research Handbook 1988–1990.* New York: Garland.

6. Eisenbruch, M. (1988). The mental health of refugee children and their cultural development. *International Migration Review, 22* (2), 282–300.

7. Geschwind, N. (1974). *Cross-Cultural Contrastive Analysis: An Exploratory Study.* Unpublished master's thesis, University of Hawaii, Honolulu.

8. Gibson, M. A. (1987). The school performance of immigrant minorities: A comparative view. *Anthropology and Education Quarterly, 18* (4), 262–275.

9. Juffer, K. A. (1983). Culture shock: A theoretical framework for understanding adaptation. In J. Bransford (Ed.), *Monograph Series: BUENO Center for Multicultural Education, 4,* 136–149.

10. Lee, E. (1988). Cultural factors in working with Southeast Asian refugee adolescents. *Journal of Adolescence, 11,* 167–179.

11. Mortland, D. A., & Egan, M. G. (1987). Vietnamese youth in American foster care. *Social Work, 32* (3), 240–245.

12. Mostek, K. (1985). *Exploring the Definition of Culture Shock and Second Language Learning in Elementary School—Grades 4–8.* ERIC ED 270 975.

13. National Coalition of Advocates for Students. (1988). *New Voices: Immigrant Students in U. S. Public Schools.* Boston: Author.

14. North Carolina Department of Public Instruction. (1983). *Here They Are . . . What Do We Do?* Raleigh, NC: Author.

15. Nguyen, T. P. (1987). Positive self-concept in the Vietnamese bilingual child. In M. Dao (Ed.), *From Vietnamese to Vietnamese American: Selected Articles.* San Jose, CA: Division of Special

Education and Rehabilitative Services, San Jose State University.

16. Padilla, A. (1980). Acculturation: Theory, models, and some new findings. *American Association for the Advancement of Science Symposium Series* (No. 39). Boulder: Westview Press.

17. Padilla, A. M., Lindlholm, K. J., Alvarez, M., & Wagatsuma, Y. (1985). *Acculturative Stress in Immigrant Students: Three Papers.* Spanish Speaking Mental Health Research Center Occasional Paper No. 20. Los Angeles: Spanish Speaking Mental Health Research Center, University of California, Los Angeles.

18. Rumbalt, R., & Ima, K. (1988). *The Adaptation of Southeast Asian Refugee Youth: A Comparative Study.* ERIC ED 299 372.

19. Silva, H. (1985). *The Children of Mariel from Shock to Integration: Cuban Refugee Children in South Florida Schools.* ERIC ED 261 136.

20. To, C. (1979). *The Educational and Psychological Adjustment Problems of Asian Immigrant Youth and How Bilingual-Bicultural Education Can Help.* Paper presented at the annual conference of the National Association of Asian American and Pacific Island Education, San Francisco.

21. Ulibari, S. (1970). *Stereotypes and Caricatures.* Paper presented at the National Education Task Force de La Raza Staff Training Institute, Albuquerque, NM.

22. Wei, T. T. D. (1980). *Vietnamese Refugee Students: A Handbook for School Personnel* (2nd ed.). ERIC ED 208 109.

23. Westmeyer, J., Neider, J., & Callies, A. (1989). Psychosocial adjustment of Hmong refugees during their first decade in the United States: A longitudinal study. *Journal of Nervous and Mental Disease, 177* (3), 132–139.

Identity conflicts of immigrant students are discussed in references 24–26.

24. Grossman, H. (1984). *Educating Hispanic Students: Cultural Implications for Instruction, Classroom Management, Counseling, and Assessment.* Springfield, IL: Thomas.

25. Olsen, L. (1988). *Crossing the Schoolhouse Border: Immigrant Students and the California Public Schools.* San Francisco, CA: California Tomorrow.

26. Ramirez, M., & Castaneda, A. (1974). *Cultural Democracy, Bicognitive Development and Education.* New York: Academic Press.

References 27–29 describe the experiences of Native American students in non-Native American settings.

27. Bureau of Indian Affairs. (1988, March). *Report on B. I. A. Education: Final Review Draft.* Washington, DC: Department of the Interior.

28. Chavez, R. C., Belkin, L. D., Hornback, J. G., & Adams, K. (1991). Dropping out of school: Issues affecting culturally, ethnically, and linguistically distinct student groups. *Journal of Educational Issues of Language Minority Students, 8,* 1–21.

29. Lin, R. (1987). A profile of reservation high school girls. *Journal of American Indian Education, 26* (2), 18–28.

The adjustment problems of rural students in urban settings are the focus of references 30–34.

30. Obermiller, P. J., Borman, K. M., & Kroger, J. A. (1988). The Lower Price Community School: Strategies for social change from an Appalachian street academy. *Urban Education, 23* (2), 123–132.

31. Maloney, M. E., & Borman, K. M. (1987). Effects of schools & schooling upon Appalachian children in Cincinnati. In P. J. Obermiller & W. W. Philliber (Eds.), *Too Few Tomorrows: Urban Appalachians in the 1980's.* Boone, NC: Appalachian Consortium Press.

32. McCoy, C. B., & McCoy, H. V. (1987). Appalachian youth in cultural transition. In P. J. Obermiller & W. W. Philliber (Eds.), *Too Few Tomorrows: Urban Appalachians in the 1980's.* Boone, NC: Appalachian Consortium Press.

33. Swift, D. (1988). *Preparing Rural Students for an Urban Environment.* Las Cruces: New Mexico State University, ERIC CRESS.

34. Vaughn, D., & Vaughn, P. R. (1986). *Preparing Rural Students for an Urban Work Environment.* ERIC ED 270 243.

References 35–38 discuss and document the special difficulties facing illegal immigrants and refugees.

35. Carrera, J. W. (1989). *Education Undocumented Children: A Review of Practices and Policies.* Las Cruces: University of New Mexico, ERIC CRESS.

36. Gardner, C., & Quezada-Aragon, M. (1984). *Undocumented Children: An Ongoing Issue for the Public Education System.* Las Cruces: University of New Mexico, ERIC CRESS.

37. Padilla, A. (1987, Spring.) Human rights in the human service of Central Americans. *Spanish Speaking Mental Health Research Center*, pp. 1–4.

38. Stepick, A., & Portes, A. (1986). Flight into despair: A profile of recent Haitian refugees in South Florida. *International Migration Review*, 20 (2), 329–350.

The stress experienced by refugees from countries engaged in civil wars is the focus of references 39–40.

39. Cervantes, R. C., Salgado de Snyder, V. N., & Padilla, A. M. (1988). *Post-Traumatic Stress Disorder among Immigrants from Central America and Mexico*. Spanish Speaking Mental Health Research Center. Occasional Paper No. 24. Los Angeles: Spanish Speaking Mental Health Research Center, University of California, Los Angeles.

40. Padilla, A. M. (1987, Spring.). Post traumatic and psychosocial stress: The Central American experience. *Spanish Speaking Mental Health Research Center*, pp. 5–6.

Reference 41 describes the strengths of immigrant and refugee students.

41. Suarez-Orozco, M. M. (1987). Becoming somebody: Central American immigrants in the United States. *Anthropology and Education Quarterly*, 18 (4), 287–299.

Techniques and materials for reducing culture shock are included in references 42–49.

42. Aranguri-Oshiro, R. (1987). Personal communication.

43. Fiedler, F., Mitchell, T., & Triandis, H. C. (1971). The culture assimilator: An approach to cross-cultural training. *Journal of Applied Psychology*, 55, 95–102.

44. Ford, C. K., & Silverman, A. M. (1981). *American Cultural Encounters*. San Francisco: Alemany Press.

45. Gentemann, K. M., & Whitehead, T. L. (1983). The culture broker concept in bicultural education. *Journal of Negro Education*, 52 (2), 118–129.

46. Herzog, J. D. (1972). The anthropologist as broker in community education: A case study and some general propositions. *Council on Anthropology and Education Newsletter*, 3, 9–14.

47. Rosita, A., & Adamopoulos, J. (1976). An attributional approach to culture learning: The culture assimilator. *Topics in Cultural Learning IV*. Honolulu: East West Culture Learning Institute.

48. Triandis, H. C. (1975). Culture training, cognitive complexity and interpersonal attitudes. In R. W. Brislin, S. Bochner, & W. J. Lonner (Eds.), *Cross-Cultural Perspectives on Learning*. Beverly Hills, CA: Sage.

49. Wyatt, J. D. (1978–1979). Native involvement in curriculum development: The native teacher as cultural broker. *Interchange: A Journal of Educational Studies*, 9, 17–28.

Suggestions for helping immigrant and refugee students adjust to and succeed in school and lists of books, materials, films, and so on that are concerned with immigrants and refugees are listed in references 50–54.

50. California Tomorrow. (1989). *Bridges: Promising Programs for the Education of Immigrant Children*. San Francisco: Author.

51. Chang, H. N. (1990). *Newcomer Programs: Innovative Efforts to Meet the Educational Challenges of Immigrant Students*. San Francisco: California Tomorrow.

52. Friedlander, M. (1991). *The Newcomer Program: Helping Immigrant Students Succeed in School*. Washington, DC: National Clearinghouse for Bilingual Education.

53. Jorgensen-Esmaili, K. (1988). *New Faces of Liberty: A Curriculum for Teaching about Today's Refugees and Immigrants*. Berkeley, CA: Graduate School of Education, University of California, Berkeley.

54. National Council of La Raza. (1986). *Beyond Ellis Island: Hispanics—Immigrants and Americans*. Washington, DC: Author.

The importance of schoolwide approaches to multiculturalism is the focus of reference 55.

55. Sleeter C. E., & Grant, C. A. (1988). *Making Choices for Multicultural Education: Five Approaches to Race, Class, and Gender*. Columbus, OH: Merrill.

References 56–70 discuss migrant students and their families.

56. Baca, L., & Harris, K. (1988). Teaching migrant exceptional children. *Teaching Exceptional Children, 20,* 32–35.

57. Center for Educational Planning. (1989). *Migrant Education Dropout Prevention Project Final Report.* ERIC ED 321 951.

58. Chavkin, N. F. (1991). *Family Lives and Parental Involvement in Migrant Students' Education.* Las Cruces: New Mexico State University, ERIC CRESS.

59. Dyson, D. D. (1983). *Migrant Education: Utilizing Available Resources at the Local Level.* Las Cruces, NM: ERIC/CRESS.

60. Henderson, A. (1987). *The Evidence Continues to Grow: Parent Involvement Improves Student Achievement.* ERIC ED 315 199.

61. Herrington, S. (1987). How educators can help children of the road. *Instructor, 97,* 36–39.

62. Interstate Migrant Education Council. (1987). *Migrant Education: A Consolidated View.* ERIC ED 285 701.

63. Interstate Migrant Secondary Services Program. (1985). *Survey Analysis: Responses of 1070 Students in High School Equivalency Programs, 1984–1985.* ERIC ED 264 070.

64. Johnson, F., Levy, R., Morales, J., Morse, S., & Prokop, M. (1986). *Migrant Students at the Secondary Level: Issues and Opportunities for Change.* ERIC ED 270 242.

65. Lawless, Ken. (1986). *Neediest of the Needy: Special Education for Migrants. Harvesting the Harvesters. Book 8.* ERIC ED 279 473.

66. Mattera, G. (1987). *Models of Effective Migrant Education Programs.* Las Cruces: New Mexico State University, ERIC CRESS.

67. Migrant Attrition Project. (1987). *Migrant Attrition Project: Abstract of Findings.* Oneonta: State University of New York at Oneonta.

68. Rasmussen, L. (1988). *Migrant Students at the Secondary Level: Issues and Opportunities for Change.* Las Cruces: New Mexico State University, ERIC CRESS.

69. Salerno, A. (1991). *Migrant Students Who Leave School Early: Strategies for Retrieval.* Las Cruces: New Mexico State University, ERIC CRESS.

70. Simich-Dudgeon, C. (1986). *Parent Involvement and the Education of Limited-English Proficient Students.* ERIC ED 279 205.

The special problems inherent in providing special education services to rural students are described in references 71–88.

71. Berkeley, T. R., & Ludlow, B. L. (1991). Meeting the needs of special student populations in rural areas. In A. J. DeYoung (Ed.), *Rural Education: Issues and Practices.* New York: Garland.

72. Brown, D. L. (1989). Demographic trends relevant to education in nonmetropolitan America. In *Rural Education—A Changing Landscape.* Washington, DC: U.S. Department of Education.

73. Cobb, R. A., McIntire, W. G., & Pratt, P. A. (1989). Vocational and educational aspirations of high school students: A problem for rural America. In R. Quaglia (Ed.), *Research in Rural Education, 6* (20), 123.

74. Helge, D. (1984). The state of the art of rural special education. *Exceptional Children, 50,* 294–305.

75. Helge, D. (1989). *Rural Family-Community Partnerships: Resources.* ERIC ED 320 736.

76. Helge, D. (1991). *Rural, Exceptional, At Risk.* Reston, VA: Council for Exceptional Children.

77. Joe, J. R. (1988). Governmental policies and disabled people in American Indian communities. *Disability, Handicap, and Society, 3* (3), 253–262.

78. Leadership for Special Education. (1989, September 18). A conversation with Robert R. Davila. (1989). *Education of the Handicapped,* p, 28.

79. Marrs, L. W. (1984). A bandwagon without music: Preparing rural special educators. *Exceptional Children, 50* (4), 334–342.

80. Marrs, L. W. (1984). Should a special educator entertain volunteers? Independence in rural America. *Exceptional Children, 50* (4), 361–366.

81. McGranahan, D. A. (1988). Rural workers at a disadvantage in job opportunities. *Rural Development Perspectives, 4,* 7–12.

82. National Council on Disabilities. (1989). *The Education of Students with Disabilities: Where Do We Stand?* Washington, DC: Author.

83. National Rural Studies Committee. (1989). Percentage of rural poor exceeds urban rate: Program mix needed to ameliorate conditions. *Rural Postscript, 7.*

84. O'Connor, C., Murr, A., & Wingert, P. (1986). Affluent America's forgotten children, *Newsweek, 107* (22), 20–21.

85. O'Hare, W. P. (1988). *The Rise of Poverty in Rural America*. ERIC ED 302 350.

86. Phelps, M. S., & Prock, G. A. (1991). Equality of educational opportunity in rural America. In A. DeYoung (Ed.), *Rural Education Issues and Practice*. New York: Garland.

87. Pollard, K. M., & O'Hare, W. P. (1990). *Beyond High School: The Experience of Rural and Urban Youth in the 1980's*. ERIC ED 326 363.

88. Students at Risk. (1990, October). *Education Week*, pp. 19, 26.

Techniques for providing appropriate services in rural areas are the focus of references 89–103.

89. Baker, B. O. (1991). Technological delivery systems and applications for K–12 instruction in rural schools. In A. J. DeYoung (Ed.), *Rural Education: Issues and Practices*. New York: Garland.

90. ERIC/CRESS. (1987). *Interactive Distance Learning Technologies for Rural and Small Schools: A Resource Guide*. Charleston WV: Author.

91. Exceptional Children. (1984). Rural special education services, activities, and products. *Exceptional Children, 50* (4), 368–369.

92. Gear, G. H. (1984). Providing services for rural gifted children. *Exceptional Children, 50* (4), 326–331.

93. Helge, D. (1984). Models for serving rural students with low-incidence handicapping conditions. *Exceptional Children, 50* (4), 313–324.

94. Helge, D. (1984). Technologies as rural special education problem-solvers. *Exceptional Children, 50* (4), 351–359.

95. Hofmeister, A. M. (1984). Technological tools for rural special education. *Exceptional Children, 50*, 344–349.

96. Kirmer, K., Lockwood, L., Mickler, W., & Sweeney, P. (1984). Regional rural special education programs. *Exceptional Children, 50* (4), 306–311.

97. Luhman, A., & Fundis, R. (1989). *Building Academically Strong Gifted Programs in Rural Schools*. Charleston WV: ERIC/CRESS.

98. McIntosh, D. K., & Raymond, G. I. (1988). Training special education teachers in rural areas: A viable model. *Rural Special Education Quarterly, 9* (1), 2–5.

99. Miller, B. (1991). *Teaching and Learning in the Multigrade Classroom: Student Performance and Instructional Routines*. Charleston WV: ERIC/CRESS.

100. Oliver, J. P., & Howley, C. (1992). *Charting New Maps: Multicultural Education in Rural Schools*. Charleston WV: ERIC/CRESS.

101. Olmstead, K. (1989). *Touching the Past, Enroute to the Future: Cultural Journalism in the Curriculum of Rural Schools*. Charleston WV: ERIC/CRESS.

102. Sherwood, T. (1989). *Nontraditional Education in Rural Districts*. Charleston WV: ERIC/CRESS.

103. Theobald, P. (1992). *Rural Philosophy for Education: Wendell Berry's Tradition*. Charleston WV: ERIC/CRESS.

References 104–135 discuss the interrelationship between disability and child abuse and the educator's role in helping students who have been abused.

104. Allen, R., & Wasserman, G. A. (1985). Origins of language delay in abused infants. *Child Abuse and Neglect, 9* (3), 335–340.

105. Ammerman, R. T., VanHasselt, V. B., Hersen, J., McGonigle, J. J., & Lubetsky, M. J. (1989). Abuse and neglect in psychiatrically hospitalized multihandicapped children. *Child Abuse and Neglect, 13*, 335–343.

106. Broadhurst, D. (1986). *Educators, Schools and Child Abuse*. Chicago: National Committee for the Prevention of Child Abuse.

107. Caplan, P., & Dinardo, L. (1986). Is there a relationship between child abuse and learning disability? *Canadian Journal of Behavioral Science, 18* (4), 367–380.

108. Caplan, P., Watters, J., White, G., Parry, R., & Bates, R. (1984). Toronto multi-agency child abuse research project: The abused and the abuser. *Child Abuse and Neglect: The International Journal, 8*, 343–351.

109. Cohen, S., & Warren, R. D. (1987). Preliminary survey of family abuse of children served by United Cerebral Palsy Centers. *Developmental Medicine and Child Neurology, 29*, 12–18.

110. Council for Exceptional Children. (1979). *We Can Help: Specialized Curriculum for Educators in the Prevention and Treatment of Child Abuse and Neglect*. Reston, VA: Author.

111. Diamond, L. J., & Jaudes, P. K. (1983). Child abuse in a cerebral-palsied population. *Developmental Medicine and Child Neurology, 25*, 169–174.

112. Fatout, M. F. (1990). Consequences of abuse on the relationships of children. *Families in Society, 71* (2), 76–81.

113. Fink, A. H., & Janssen, K. N. (1990). *Abused/Neglected Adolescents: Programming for Their Educational Needs.* Paper presented at the National Conference on Adolescents with Behavior Disorders, Miami.

114. Fink, A. H., & Janssen, K. N. (1992). The management of maltreated adolescents in school settings. *Preventing School Failure, 36* (3), 32–36.

115. Garabino, J., & Authier, K. J. (1987). The role of educators. In J. Garabino, P. E. Brookhouser, & K. J. Authier (Eds.), *Special Children Special Risks: The Maltreatment of Children with Disabilities.* Hawthorne, NY: Aldinede Gruyter.

116. Glaser, D., & Bentovim, A. (1979). Abuse and risk to handicapped and chronically ill children. *Child Abuse and Neglect, 3,* 565–575.

117. Hurwitz, B. D. (1985). Suspicion: Child abuse. *Instructor, 94* (4), 76–78, 81, 125.

118. Jaudes, P. K., & Diamond, L. J. (1985). The handicapped child and child abuse. *Child Abuse and Neglect, 9,* 341–347.

119. Kirkham, M. A., Schinke, S. P., Schilling, R. F., Meltzer, N. J., & Norelius, K. L. (1986). Cognitive-behavioral skills, social supports, and child abuse potential among mothers of handicapped children. *Journal of Family Violence, 1* (3), 235–245.

120. Marion, M. (1982). Primary prevention of child abuse: The role of the family life educator. *Family Relations, 31* (4), 575–582.

121. Mayer, P., & Brenner, S. (1989). Abuse of children with disabilities. *Children's Legal Rights Journal, 10* (4), 16–20.

122. McIntyre, T. (1990). The teacher's role in cases of suspected child abuse. *Education and Urban Society, 22* (3), 300–306.

123. Mullins, J. B. (1986). The relationship between child abuse and handicapping conditions. *Journal of School Health,* 56(4), 134–136.

124. National Center on Child Abuse and Neglect. (1984). *The Educator's Role in the Prevention and Treatment of Child Abuse and Neglect.* Washington, DC: U.S. Department of Health and Human Services, Administration for Children, Youth, and Families, Children's Bureau.

125. National Clearinghouse on Child Abuse and Neglect. (1991). *Curricula.* Washington, DC: Author.

126. National Clearinghouse on Child Abuse and Neglect. (1991). *Prevention Programs: Training Materials.* Washington, DC: Author.

127. Nesbit, W. C., & Karagianis, L. D. (1982). Child abuse: Exceptionality as a risk factor. *The Alberta Journal of Educational Research, 28,* 69–76.

128. Ohman, L. (1988). The NEA: Professional organization and advocate for teachers. In A. Maney & S. Wells (Eds.), *Professional Responsibilities in Protecting Children: A Public Health Approach to Child Sexual Abuse.* New York: Praeger.

129. Shaman, E. J. (1986). Prevention programs for children with disabilities. In M. Nelson & K. Clark (Eds.), *The Educator's Guide to Preventing Child Sexual Abuse.* Santa Cruz, CA: Network Publications.

130. Tharinger, D., Horton, C. B., & Miller, S. (1990). Sexual abuse and exploitation of children and adults with mental retardation and other handicaps. *Child Abuse and Neglect, 14,* 301–312.

131. Warger, C. L., Tewey, S., & Megivern, M. (1991). *Abuse and Neglect of Exceptional Children.* Reston, VA: Council for Exceptional Children.

132. Wolverton, L. (1988). *Teaching the Abused Migrant Child: What's a Teacher to Do?* Las Cruces: New Mexico State University, ERIC CRESS

133. Zantal-Weiner, K. (1987). *Child Abuse and the Handicapped Child.* ERIC Digest No. E446. Reston VA: Council for Exceptional Children.

134. Zirpoli, T. J. (1990). Physical abuse: Are children with disabilities at greater risk? *Intervention in School and Clinic, 26* (1), 6–11.

135. Zirpoli, T. J., Snell, M. E., & Lloyd, B. H. (1987). Characteristics of persons with mental retardation who have been abused by care givers. *Journal of Special Education, 21* (2), 31–41.

References 136–172 concern the educational problems of homeless and runaway children and adolescents.

136. Bass, J. L., Brennan, P., Mehta, K. A., & Kodzis, S. (1990). Pediatric problems in a suburban shelter for homeless families. *Pediatrics, 85* (1), 33–38.

137. Bassuk, E. L., & Gallagher, E. M. (1990). The impact of homelessness on children. In N. A. Boxill (Ed.), *Homeless Children: The Watchers and the Waiters.* Binghamton, NY: Haworth.

138. Bassuk, F., & Rosenberg, L. (1988). Why does family homelessness occur? *American Journal of Public Health, 78,* 783–788.

139. Bassuk, F., & Rosenberg, L. (1990). Psychosocial characteristics of homeless children and children with homes. *Pediatrics, 85,* 257–261.

140. Bassuk, F., & Rubin, L. (1987). Homeless children: A neglected population. *American Journal of Orthopsychiatry, 57* (2), 279–286.

141. Bowen, J. M., Purrington, G. S., Layton, D. H., & O'Brien, K. (1989). *Educating Homeless Children and Youth: A Policy Analysis.* Paper presented at the annual conference of the American Educational Research Association, San Francisco.

142. Burns, S. (Ed.). (1991). Homelessness demographics, causes and trends. *Homewords, 3* (4), 1–3.

143. Cavazos, L. F. (1990). *U.S. Department of Education Report to Congress on the Education for Homeless Children and Youth Program for the Period October 1, 1988 through September 30, 1989.* Washington, DC: U.S. Department of Education.

144. Children's Defense Fund. (1988). *What Every American Should Be Asking Political Leaders in 1988: About Children and the Future, about Leadership and Vision, about National Values and Priorities.* Washington, DC: Author.

145. Eddowes, A., & Hranitz. J. R. (1989). Education children of the homeless. *Childhood Education: Infancy through Early Adolescence, 65* (4), 197–200.

146. Ely, L. (1987). *Broken Lives: Denial of Education to Homeless Children.* Washington, DC: National Coalition for the Homeless.

147. Faber, E., McCoard, D., Kinast, C., & Baum-Falkner, D. (1984). Violence in families of adolescent runaways. *Child Abuse and Neglect, 2* (3), 173–192.

148. Friedman, L., & Christiansen, G. (1990). *Shut Out: Denial of Education to Homeless Children.* ERIC ED 320 987.

149. Gewirtzman, R., & Fodor, I. (1987). The homeless child at school: From welfare hotel to classroom. *Child Welfare, 66* (3), 237–245.

150. Hall, J. A., & Maza, P. L. (1990). No fixed address: The effects of homelessness on families and children. In N. A. Boxill (Ed.), *Homeless Children: The Watchers and the Waiters.* Binghamton, NY: Haworth.

151. Heflin, L. J., & Rudy, K. (1991). *Homeless and in Need of Special Education.* Reston, VA: Council for Exceptional Children.

152. Jackson, S. (1989). *The Education Rights of Homeless Children.* Cambridge, MA: Center for Law and Education.

153. Kayne, A. (1989). *Annotated Bibliography of Social Science Literature Concerning the Education of Homeless Children.* Cambridge, MA: Center for Law and Education.

154. Layzer, J. I., Goodson, B. D., & deLange, C. (1986). Children in shelters. *Children Today, 15,* 6–11.

155. Linehan, M. F. (1989). Homeless children: Educational strategies for school personnel. *PRISE Reporter, 21* (2), 1–2, insert.

156. Mihaly, L. K. (1991). *Homeless Families: Failed Policies and Young Victims.* Washington, DC: Children's Defense Fund.

157. Miller, D. S., & Linn, E. H. B. (1988). Children in sheltered homeless families: Reported health status and use of health services. *Pediatrics, 81,* 668–673.

158. Neiman, L. (1988). A critical review of resiliency literature and its relevance to homeless children. *Children's Environments Quarterly, 5* (19), 17–25.

159. Palenski, J. E., & Launer, H. M. (1987). The "process" of running away: A redefinition. *Adolescence, 22* (86), 347–362.

160. Powers, J. L., Eckenrode, J., & Jaklitsch, G. (1988). *Running Away from Home: A Response to Adolescent Maltreatment.* ERIC ED 296 228.

161. Rafferty, Y., & Rollins, N. (1989). *Learning in Limbo: The Educational Deprivation of Homeless Children.* Long Island City, NY: Advocates for Children of New York.

162. Rafferty, Y., & Rollins, N. (1990). *Homeless Children: Educational Challenges for the 1990's.* ERIC ED 325 589.

163. Rescoria, L., Parker, R., & Stolley, P. (1991). Ability, achievement and adjustment in homeless children. *American Journal of Orthopsychiatry, 61* (2), 210–220.

164. Rivlin, L. G. (199). Home and homelessness in the lives of children. In N. A. Boxill (Ed.), *Homeless Children: The Watchers and the Waiters.* Binghamton, NY: Haworth.

165. Rosenman, M., & Stein, M. L. (1990). Homeless children: A new vulnerability. In N. A. Boxill (Ed.), *Homeless Children: The Watchers and the Waiters.* Binghamton, NY: Haworth.

166. Russell, S. C., & Williams, E. U. (1988). Homeless handicapped children: A special education perspective. *Children's Environments Quarterly, 5* (1), 3–7.

167. Schumack, S. (Ed.). (1987). *The Educational Rights of Homeless Children.* ERIC ED 288 915.

168. Stronge, J. H., & Helm, V. M. (1990). *Residency and Guardianship Requirements as Barriers to the Education of Homeless Children and Youth.* ERIC ED 319 845.

169. Stronge, J. H., & Tenhouse, C. (1990). *Educating Homeless Children: Issues and Answers.* Bloomington, IN: Phi Delta Kappa Educational Foundation.

170. Waxman, L. D., & Reyes, L. M. (1987). *A Status Report on Homeless Families in America's Cities: A 29–City Survey.* ERIC ED 296 018.

171. Witt, V. (Ed.). (1988). *Children's Defense Budget: FY 1989. An Analysis of Our Nation's Investment in Children.* Washington, DC: Children's Defense Fund.

172. Wright, J. D. (1990). Homelessness is not healthy for children and other living things. In N. A. Boxill (Ed.), *Homeless Children: The Watchers and the Waiters.* Binghamton, NY: Haworth.

The problems of adolescents with disabilities are discussed in references 173–176.

173. Kleinfeld, A., & Young, R. (1989). Risk of pregnancy and dropping out of school among special education adolescents. *Journal of Social Health, 59* (8), 359–361.

174. Leone, P. (1991). *Alcohol and Other Drugs: Use, Abuse, and Disabilities.* Reston, VA: Council for Exceptional Children.

175. Muccigrosso, L., Scavarda, M., Simpson-Brown, R., & Thalacker, B. E. (1991). *Double Jeopardy: Pregnant and Parenting Youth in Special Education.* Reston, VA: Council for Exceptional Children.

176. Schultz, J., & Adams, D. (1987). Family life education needs of mentally disabled adolescents. *Adolescence, 22* (85), 220–230.

Reference 177 includes the quotation at the begining of the chapter.

177. Federal Regional Resource Center. (1991). *Exploring Educational Issues of Cultural Diversity.* Lexington, KY: University of Kentucky, Federal Regional Resource Center.

6

COMMUNICATIVELY APPROPRIATE SPECIAL EDUCATION

There's no good way to teach kids in a language they
don't understand.

In a pluralistic society, students with disabilities come to school speaking different languages and dialects and using different verbal and nonverbal communication styles. This chapter discusses how special educators can take these differences into account when they instruct and assess students.

LIMITED ENGLISH PROFICIENCY

The limited-English-proficient (LEP) population is the fastest growing group in the United States. Although estimates vary of how many LEP children and adolescents are now in U.S. schools, it is probable that almost 8 million U.S. youngsters have a non-English background either because they were born elsewhere or they grew up in the United States in a home where another language was spoken. Over 3 million of these students scored in the lowest 20 percent on tests of English proficiency. Over 5 million scored in the lower 40 percent. Whichever of these two figures one uses, it is clear that millions of students are not proficient enough in English to function in English-only classes without considerable difficulty (2). Experts suggest that approximately 10 percent of the student population requires special education services. Using this guideline to estimate the number of LEP students who require special education yields an estimate of between 354,900 and 528,400. Currently, the vast majority of these students are not receiving linguistically appropriate special education services. Thus, the Education of the Handicapped Act Amendments of 1990 stated, "Services provided to limited English proficient students often do not respond primarily to the pupil's academic needs. These trends pose special challenges for special education in the referral, assessment, and instruction services for our Nation's students from non-English language backgrounds" (1).

The appropriate instructional services required by LEP students has been the subject of a number of court decisions and federal laws. In 1974, in *Lau* v. *Nichols,* the Supreme Court unanimously decided that schools must provide special assistance to LEP students in the form of linguistically appropriate educational services (8). In 1979, in *Dyrcia S. et al.* v. *Board of Education of the City of New York,* the court determined that LEP students with disabilities had the same right (5). The Bilingual Education Act of 1968, the Education for Handicapped Children Act of

1974 (Public Law 94-142) and the 1990 amendments to the act, the Equal Educational Opportunities Act of 1972, Section 504 of the Rehabilitation Act of 1973, and the Civil Rights Act of 1964 also require school districts to provide linguistically appropriate educational services to LEP students with disabilities (1, 3, 4, 6, 7, 9).

Schools may satisfy the requirement that LEP students receive linguistically appropriate services by providing students with instruction in their native language (bilingual education), English as a second language (ESL), sheltered English (also called structured English), or a combination of these approaches. These various ways of providing linguistically appropriate special education services are discussed in this section.

Bilingual Special Education

In the not too distant past, many people argued that the best way to work with LEP students was to immerse them in English as quickly and as completely as possible. Now we know from research that English immersion programs are less desirable than teaching students subject matter in their native languages (bilingual education) while they are also learning English as a second language. The three main reasons for this are the following:

1. It takes only a year or two for students to become proficient enough in a second language to carry on everyday conversations—basic interpersonal communication skills (BICS). However, it usually takes at least five years to reach the level of proficiency in a second language that is required to learn subject matter—cognitive academic learning proficiency (CALP) (11). Thus, if students are instructed in subject matter too soon in a second language, they will not be able to benefit optimally from such instruction.

A bilingual educator stated, "The fact is, it takes time to learn English. But we cannot forego learning other content areas while they're in the process of acquiring English. Put a child in a class for a year or two to learn English and meanwhile forget learning math, forget art, forget social studies. I don't think we can do that" (11, p. 57). A principal of a school designed to prepare immigrant students for the regular school in their area stated, "We know that the kind of English we are talking about is not just fluency, being able to converse, being able to make small talk. We are talking about academic English . . . the English you need to evaluate, criticize, voice your opinion. That kind of English requires a lot of study and requires a certain amount of cultural literacy in the American context. It takes time to acquire it. We know for a fact that what these kids most need is time—time in the school system" (11, p. 64).

2. There is considerable evidence that switching students from their native language to a new language before they have acquired CALP can stunt their language development in either language. On the other hand, once students have acquired CALP in one language, they are able to transfer their understanding of the logic and rules of language to the learning of a second language (11, 12). Thus, students taught in their native language until they have developed sufficient linguistic skills read better and learn more in school than those who are immediately taught in a second language.

3. Rejecting students' native languages can alienate students and lead them to develop poor self-concepts.

Knowledge about effective bilingual special education practices has grown considerably during recent years. Readers who wish to know more about bilingual special education methods are referred to the references at the end of the chapter (10, 12).

Although bilingual special education is the preferable approach, it is not a practical alternative in the vast majority of schools because most school districts lack bilingual special education personnel and/or are faced with providing services to LEP students in many different languages. Assuming that a bilingual special educator could serve 15 LEP students and that it was possible to assign students who all spoke the same language to each teacher (a very unlikely assumption), it would require between 23,000 and 35,000 bilingual special educators to serve all LEP students with disabilities.

Between 1979, when the federal government began to provide financial assistance to encourage universities to train bilingual special educators, and 1987, universities that prepared bilingual special educators produced only 257 graduates (13). Since 1987, there has been a decrease rather than an increase in the number of university programs in the field. Therefore, it is reasonable to assume that there are probably significantly fewer than 1,000 trained bilingual special educators to fill at least 23,000 positions. In addition, except for a few programs that train special educators to work with students who speak a Native American language and one program that trains teachers to work with students who speak a Chinese or a Filipino dialect or Vietnamese, these programs all focus on Spanish-speaking students. Thus, students who speak any of the almost 200 languages that are not included in these programs and students who live in areas that are not served by any of these programs cannot count on being taught by trained bilingual special educators.

Some school districts provide bilingual special education services by teaming a monolingual special educator with a bilingual aide who provides LEP students with disabilities with the additional bilingual instruction they need. However, their numbers are also limited by the lack of potential bilingual aides and the money to hire enough bilingual aides to serve LEP students who speak many different languages. This is an especially difficult problem for school districts that serve a linguistically diverse population—such as the Los Angeles School District, which serves students who speak over 100 different languages. As a result, a number of school districts have opted for English-as-a-second-language or sheltered English programs for their LEP students with disabilities.

English as a Second Language

In recent years, the art of teaching students a second language has become much more of a science. As a result, educators are now achieving a great deal of success in English as a second language (ESL) programs. In the 1980s, a few special educators began to experiment with using ESL instructional techniques and materials with LEP students with disabilities (10, 15–19). They found that the principles of effective ESL instruction also applied to students with disabilities. However, materials and techniques had to be adapted to the students' learning, cognitive, and sensory disabilities. Anecdotal evidence suggests that ESL approaches that are adapted to the special needs of students with disabilities help them to become proficient in English. However, there is no research to confirm this.

Unfortunately, very few special education personnel preparation programs train teachers to use ESL techniques. Therefore, this option is not readily available to students and school districts. As Cloud has pointed out, "Currently, a paucity of TESOL (Teachers of English to Speakers of Other Languages) programs provide cross-over training in special education, and few special education programs encourage specializations in TESOL. Professionals are left to find their own training opportunities at conferences and workshops" (15, p. 2).

Sheltered English/Structured Immersion

In a sheltered English/structured English approach, students are taught subject matter in a modified/controlled English vocabulary at their level of English comprehension. Teachers omit difficult words and forms, explain new vocabulary words (often in students' native languages), and employ as many nonverbal gestures, audiovisual aids, and other materials as possible. Gersten and Woodward described the approach in the following manner: "With structured immersion all instruction is done in the commonly used language of the school. . . . However, *all instruction is conducted at a level understood by students*. Superficially, structured immersion may seem similar to what the U.S. court outlawed in 1974; that is, a sink-or-swim approach for those not proficient in the language of the dominant culture. But there is a critical difference: teachers do not assume that the children understand English. Difficult new words are pretaught, sometimes using the child's native language" (26, p. 75).

Research indicates that students improve their second language proficiency and learn subject matter in well-planned sheltered English programs staffed by trained teachers (24–27). However, very few LEP students with disabilities are enrolled in sheltered English programs.

English Submergence

As already noted, most LEP students with disabilities are not in bilingual special education, ESL, or sheltered English programs (28–30). One study shows that the IEPs of only 2 percent of LEP students with disabilities included bilingual instruction in their native language and none included ESL instruction. The authors concluded, "The results of this study suggest that a student's bilingualism and level of English proficiency exert little influence on the IEP Committee's selection of instructional goals and objectives" (30, pp. 563, 567).

Thus, LEP students with disabilities without CALP and often BICS English fluency are submerged in the regular special education program and are taught in English without regard to their linguistic needs. Submerged in English without the skills necessary to profit from the instruction they receive, students are at risk for joining the ranks of students with disabilities who tune out their teachers, cut classes, and drop out of special education before graduating from high school.

ESL PROGRAMS VERSUS SUBMERGENCE PROGRAMS

Compare the experiences of the following three students. A student in an English submergence program reported:

> I just sat in my classes and didn't understand anything. Sometimes I would try to look like I knew what was going on, sometimes I would just try to think about a happy time when I didn't feel stupid. My teachers never called on me or talked to me. I think either they forgot I was there or else wished I wasn't. I waited and I waited, thinking someday I will know English. (11, p. 62)

Two other students made the following comparison between their experiences in ESL and a regular class taught in English.

> My ESL teacher helped me a lot in my first year here. I could relax there. I wasn't afraid. . . . In my other classes I was always confused and lost and I didn't want to ask anything because of my bad English. (11, p. 62)

> My first school I didn't want to go, just to stay home. When I went I just sat there and didn't understand anything. . . . No one talked to me and I couldn't say anything. I didn't know what was going on. My second school had an ESL teacher who taught me from the ABC's and helped me learn many more things. (11, p. 62)

DIALECTIC DIFFERENCES

In the past, many educators believed that the English dialect spoken by many poor African American students (Black English/Ebonics), the dialects spoken by Native Americans, Hispanic Americans, and Hawaiian Americans, as well as certain regional dialects spoken by poor European Americans such as the ones spoken in Appalachia (Mountain English) and in the greater New York City metropolitan area (New Yorkese) interfered with learning to read and write standard

English correctly. Critics of nonstandard dialects also believed that many dialects were inferior forms of English and should be eradicated. Today, as noted in Chapter 2, educators tend to consider dialect variations to be linguistic differences rather than linguistic deficiencies. Nevertheless, they still disagree about how to handle them in school.

Legal Aspects

Since the 1970s, schools have had to provide students with linguistically appropriate educational services that take into account their nonstandard English dialects. In 1972, the Equal Educational Opportunities Act stated that "no state shall deny equal educational opportunity to an individual by . . . the failure by an educational agency to take appropriate action to overcome language barriers that impede equal participation by its students in its instructional program" (6).

In 1979, a United States district court judge ruled in favor of 15 African American students who claimed that they were denied an equal education because their school did not take their nonstandard English dialect into account. Although this ruling affected only schools within the jurisdiction of the court, it set a national tone. Judge Joiner, the presiding judge, reflected the knowledge of the day in his ruling.

> The court does not believe that language differences between "Black English" and standard English to be a language barrier in and of itself.
>
> The unconscious but evident attitude of teachers toward the home language of the plaintiffs causes a psychological barrier to learning by the student. . . . The child who comes to school using the "Black English" system of communication and who is taught that this is wrong, loses a sense of values related to mother and close friends and siblings and may rebel at efforts by his teacher to teach reading in a different language.
>
> If a barrier exists because of the language used by the children in this case, it exists not because the teachers and students cannot understand each other, but because in the process of attempting to teach the students how to speak standard English the students are made somehow to feel inferior and are thereby turned off from the learning process. (31, pp. 18, 26, 36, 41–42)

The court required the school district to help the teachers of the plaintiff children at the King School to identify those children speaking Black English and the language spoken as a home or community language in order to use that knowledge in teaching such students how to read Standard English. However, the court did not provide guidelines for how teachers should use their knowledge of Black English to teach students. As a result, two very different educational approaches are being employed in schools to deal with mismatches between the English dialects spoken by many students and the oral and written English used by their teachers and found in almost all textbooks and curriculum materials: bidialectalism and appreciation.

Speaking

Bidialectalism

Many individuals believe that speakers of nonstandard dialects should be taught to express themselves in Standard English as well as their nonstandard dialects and to use each form when it is appropriate for a given situation. The objectives of bidialectal programs, although expressed in various ways, usually include the following:

1. To create an awareness of the need for "functional flexibility" in oral communication (i.e., the ability to use language for varying purposes),
2. To develop an understanding of the education, social and economic ramifications of unproductive communication skills, and
3. To provide opportunities to develop and practice the alternative style of communication (i.e., mainstream English), while not eradicating the importance and function of "home language." (41, p. 211)

The following three reasons are typically cited in support of bidialectalism.

1. *Although nonstandard English dialects are not substandard, they interfere with students' academic progress* (34, 41). The evidence regarding this contention is mixed. Most studies have found that speakers of nonstandard dialects do not have difficulty learning to read (37, 52, 54, 57–59, 62, 63). Some researchers have reported findings that indicate that Black English and Native American English dialect speakers have difficulty learning to read Standard English (53, 64). However, the cause of the relationship between reading difficulty and nonstandard dialect usage that has been observed in some studies is unclear. Although some educators believe that these results indicate that nonstandard dialects interfere with learning, three other explanations have been offered.

First, students of nonstandard English dialects tend to be from poor backgrounds. It is the many factors associated with having a poor background, not the students' nonstandard dialect, that account for students' lack of progress in reading. Support for this hypothesis lies in the fact that within the various groups that speak nonstandard dialects, such as African Americans, Hawaiian Americans, and so on, nonstandard dialects are much more prevalent among poor than middle-class students.

Second, educators' prejudicial attitudes against certain nonstandard English dialects interfere with students' learning. As noted in Chapters 2 and 3, teachers of nonstandard English speakers, especially those who believe Standard English to be a more desirable or correct version of English, tend to believe that students do not understand something if they cannot explain it in Standard English. They think that students who do not speak Standard English are less intelligent; they have lower academic expectations for them; they evaluate both their oral and written work to be lower than comparable work of standard English-speaking students; and they are more likely to disapprove of them.

Third, teachers spend too much time correcting students' dialectic vocabulary and grammatical and pronunciation "errors." There is considerable evidence that many teachers focus on dialectical differences that are not true errors rather than concentrate their efforts on improving students' higher-level skills and relate to them in unproductive ways (55, 56, 60, 61, 65). The following description illustrates how insistence on standard English speech can interfere with good teaching:

> A sixth-grade math teacher was quite disturbed because his students referred to the concept of lowest common denominator as "breaking it down more smaller." The students obviously understood the concept and had demonstrated, on the chalk board and in class and homework papers, that they could apply the concept to solve math problems. The teacher kept correcting the students because his perception was, "These kids obviously don't know how to arrive at lowest common denominators." When queried as to how, then, were the students able to solve problems involving the concept, his explanation was, "You can't do anything if you don't know the right word for it."
>
> The teacher's solution was to waste the next few days drilling his students on the spelling and textbook terminology of various mathematical operations that they already knew how to perform! (60, p. 89)

On balance, the evidence does not support the contention that students' nonstandard dialects interfere with their learning. As Padak has commented, "One need not speak a dialect in order to understand it" (46, p. 150).

2. *Competency in oral Standard English is necessary for students to learn to write Standard English.* Although it is true that nonstandard forms of English intrude in students' writing when they are first learning to write Standard English, most experts in the field agree that it is not necessary for students to be able to *speak* Standard English in order to *write* Standard English. They point out that many nonstandard English speakers can write Standard English. They also note that the longer students remain in school, the fewer nonstandard English forms intrude in their writing (40). In addition, critics remind others that writing is not speech written down: "Learning to write standard English does not mean first learning to speak it. . . . Forcing Chicanos to change their way of speaking English in order to learn to write makes no more sense than forcing an east Texas child, or a child from Boston or the Bronx to drop their speech peculiarities and replace them with midwestern English so that they can learn to write" (81, p. 25).

3. *Standard English is necessary for vocational success and in other areas in which nonstandard dialect speakers are branded as uneducated and ill prepared* (38, 42, 48). The following quotation typifies this line of thinking:

> There are many dialects in every language, but the standard form is that which is acceptable for purposes of state, business, or other everyday transactions. It is the official language of the country, and anyone who is successful in that country uses it. Those who use the nonstandard language are forever relegated to the most menial jobs and stations in life. . . . If blacks are prepared to accept the hypothesis of "black English," then they ought to be prepared to accept the relegation to "black jobs." If their preparation is second class, their lives will be second class. (49, pp. 318, 320)

It is true, as noted in previous chapters, that many members of U.S. society are prejudiced against certain nonstandard English dialects. However, many educators believe the solution to the problem is to combat discrimination, not accommodate and acquiesce to it. Dean and Fowler suggested the following quite some time ago:

> Previously, people who have applied for a job have been judged on clothing and hair styles. These discriminations have been lessened by change of public opinion. Then, people were judged on the color of their skin or their sex. These prejudices, while still present, are being lessened with the "help" of legislation. . . . Yet proponents of bidialectalism state that a person must speak standard English to be hired for a "good job." . . . White middle-class society has reexamined its values in the previously mentioned areas of hair style, clothing, race and sex. Surely that society can have its eyes opened once again. (36, pp. 305–306)

Moreover, many individuals believe that schools have an important role to play in correcting discrimination against nonstandard English dialects. On the other hand, many individuals have pointed out that community attitudes are difficult, if not impossible, to change quickly. They argue that schools should prepare students to succeed in the meantime.

Those who believe that students should be taught the ability to communicate in Standard English in appropriate situations have offered the following guidelines and principles (41, 61, 66, 67–70, 72, 75, 76, 78, 83):

- Motivate students to want to become bidialectic. Employ age-appropriate motivational techniques. The older the students are, the more they can appreciate the advantages, value, and importance of becoming bidialectic.
- Correct students' misperceptions that Standard English is the "white man's" language.
- Avoid creating resistance among students. For example, do not correct students; instead, discuss alternative acceptable ways of saying the same things in different situations.
- Concentrate on those dialect characteristics that are most stigmatized by the community and that most hamper success. For example, nonstandard grammar (double negatives, nonagreement of subject and verb, *them* for *those*) is viewed much more negatively than nonstandard pronunciation (70).

Many techniques have been employed to help students become bidialectic. Techniques vary, depending on the point of view of the educators. The most common approach is the method of *contrastive analysis*. In this method, students in regular and special education programs are taught to use both standard and nonstandard forms for expressing the same ideas in both dialects and to identify when to use each one (32, 33, 41, 50, 61, 66, 72, 76, 78, 83). In some cases, audio- and videotaping has been used to help students experience the difference in their language. Typically, this approach involves the following seven steps:

1. Identify nonstandard dialect speakers. This is usually done informally, but some instruments are available (78).
2. Explain that there are different dialects.
3. Contrast and teach the differences. Lists and descriptions of dialect differences for a number of dialects are available (88–93). Very young children may not be mature enough to recognize, label, and contrast dialect differences.
4. Teach students to distinguish between home English and school and work English and to use the most appropriate one for a given situation.
5. Drill students in substituting standard forms for nonstandard ones.
6. Provide students with opportunities to practice standard forms in class.
7. Evaluate the results. This last step can be done informally or by using a formal instrument (86).

Research indicates that contrastive analysis increases students' use of Standard English in the classroom; little data are available about its effects on students' language usage outside of school.

Some educators use ESL instructional techniques to assist limited-English-proficient students to teach nonstandard dialect speakers to speak Standard English (85). However, many educators object to the use of a method designed to teach non-English speakers with students who speak English, albeit in a nonstandard dialect. "English as a second language is a must for those who have just entered this country; however, I find it distressing when the term is applied to English for my Black brethren who have been in this English-speaking country for generations" (49, p. 318).

Many educators stress the importance of helping students to resolve their ambivalence and resistance and to increase their motivation to learn and use Standard English (73, 82, 87). Unlike limited-English-proficient students who need to learn English in order to survive in the United States, nonstandard English speakers already speak English. They often feel no need to learn a second English dialect that is different from the English spoken and accepted by their family, friends, and neighbors. In addition, they often resent teachers' attempts to make them do so.

Educators have employed discussions about the advantages of using Standard English on the job to increase students' understanding of the economic importance and value of speaking Standard English. Role-playing job interviews in which students speak Standard and nonstandard English and asking students to judge which applicant would be hired has also been tried. Exposing students to the speech of celebrities from their background who speak Standard English, and inviting successful non-European businesspersons who speak Standard English to deliver the message that Black English does not open many doors in U.S. society have all been used in this endeavor.

An African American female teacher has described how she used herself as a model for her Black English dialect speakers. Her rationale for doing so follows: "As the students' teacher, I assumed the students perceived me to be competent with status and having control over the learning resources. As a black person, I assumed these black students would view me as being similar and would identify with me. As a seemingly successful person, I assumed the students would view my success, in part, the result of my being able to speak standard English" (82, p. 106).

Changing the attitude of all of the students in a class so they are no longer resistant to and are supportive of a bidialectical approach and then having students engage in cooperative learning activities designed to improve their bidialectical skills can be effective (73). Another technique is to expose students to the example of people who changed their way of speaking and profited from the change. Reading *Pygmalion* or *My Fair Lady* or watching the movie and discussing the lessons the characters teach illustrate this approach.

Some individuals believe that exposing students to public criticism by correcting their dialects in front of others and teaching Standard English are too confrontational to students and create unnecessary resistance. They believe less confronting methods, such as reading literature in Standard English aloud to students and including works by non-European American writers, are more effective means for increasing students' understanding of and ability to use Standard English.

Despite the fact that many teachers are currently trying to make students bidialectic, research suggests that attempts to teach nonstandard English speakers to speak Standard English have backfired.

> The teaching of standard English to all learners is an implicitly and explicitly stated goal of the American school. Yet the national performance of the American school in teaching standard English to nonstandard speakers is dismal. On almost every reported measure at the national or state level, children from nonstandard English speaking communities achieve lower competency levels in the language of education than children who come from standard English speaking communities. The result has been an overplacement of nonstandard English speaking children in special education classes, speech-language pathology clinical services, and compensatory education classes, and an underplacement of these children in classes for talented and gifted students. . . . In addition this failure has contributed to diminished student self-esteem, lowered teacher expectations, and discipline problems. (48, p. 156)

In addition, the limited research available leaves a number of urgent questions unanswered, such as the following:

- Is there any value to teaching students to speak Standard English besides avoiding discrimination in the community?
- Does encouraging students to speak Standard English also encourage the community to continue to discriminate against nonstandard English speakers?
- Should school officials or the students themselves decide whether they should become bidialectical?

- Can all students learn a second dialect through the approaches offered in school?
- What student characteristics foster or impede second dialect learning?
- Which are the most effective approaches to second dialect teaching?
- Which techniques work best with which students?
- What negative side effects accompany schools' attempts to make students bidialectical?
- What are the best ways to avoid these unwanted effects?

Appreciation

Many educators reject the bidialectal approach. They believe that as long as students can understand spoken and written Standard English, they should be allowed or even encouraged to express themselves in their own dialects in any and all situations (36, 72). The appreciation approach has been described as follows:

> Teachers who employ this approach accept the fact of linguistic equality of the two dialects (standard and Black) and believe that the Black dialect is a competent form of communication. There are no drills to bring out contrasts or comparison between Black and standard English. Teachers, instead, look for additional techniques to bring out the verbal facility that is already present—not merely the potential of verbal ability. . . . This requires special consideration in the language arts—allowing students to use their own dialects or accents without correction in reading, by the teachers dictating oral spelling tests in both dialects if found helpful . . . by accepting Black dialect grammar in written composition, etc. (36, p. 305)

Proponents of the appreciation approach to dialect differences offer the following reasons for their position:

- *Efforts to teach students to speak Standard English do not work.* There is considerable evidence that highly motivated individuals can learn Standard English if they are given intensive instruction and interact on a frequent basis with Standard English speakers. However, the way students are taught to speak Standard English in school does not produce an increase in the frequency or correctness of students use of Standard English in the classroom, much less outside of school (35, 39, 44). Labov and Harris stated, "Underlying grammatical patterns of standard English are apparently learned through 'meaningful' and intensive interaction with those who already use standard English grammar, not simply by exposure in the mass medial or in schools" (44, p. 22).

- *Dialect speakers who are required to speak Standard English become less fluent and have difficulty expressing themselves.* This proposition has not been researched very well; however, there is some evidence to support it (48).

- *Teaching students Standard English before they are completely fluent in their original dialects stunts their language development.* In the words of Kochman, switching from one dialect to another "does not develop the child's ability to use language beyond what he is already capable of doing. . . . It is concerned with *how* the child says something rather than *how well* he says it" (43, p. 91). There is no research regarding this supposition.

- *It is not possible to encourage students to learn a second dialect without also communicating that their way of speaking is less desirable.* As an English teacher stated, "No matter how carefully I explained my purpose and assured them that I was not judging their parents, grandparents, race, or culture . . . my students still resented my correcting them although most of the time they accepted my corrections in good humor" (47, p. 49).

- *Acceptance and appreciation of nonstandard dialects by schools and teachers improves students' self-esteem* (72). Davis and Armstrong stated the following:

> Black children must be educated to learn and believe that deviation from the normative pattern of standard English is not an indication that they are abnormal. They must be helped to understand that these negative social and psychological views have resulted and can continue to result in low self-esteem, identity crisis, and self-hatred. An appreciation of Black habits, values, and goals is essential for Black children to develop a positive Black self-identity. The issue of Black English is a "good" place to start. Whites should not become reference points for how Black children are to speak and behave. (72, p. 215)

- *Teaching Standard English to nonstandard dialect speakers is a form of political and cultural subjugation.* Nonstandard English-speaking students and their teachers often have different perceptions of the implications of Standard English. Teachers tend to view it as a way to learn more effectively and get ahead in the real world; students often view it as "talking white," denying their heritage, and giving in to the European American power structure. (45, 60). Some individuals tend to believe that the solution to dialectal inequality can be achieved only by eliminating the power differential in society.

> If one culture possesses hegemony over the other, the less-powerful culture generally adopts the language of the more powerful but not without serious consequences for and potential danger to the harmonious relationship between the two groups. For even as the less-powerful speech community is expanding its linguistic repertoire to incorporate the language of the predominant group, simultaneously its loyalty to the mother tongue and native culture is intensified. . . . In the school setting, the linguistic norms and cultural context of white America prevail and the speech norms and cultural identity of the Black community are forced to give sway to those of the more powerful cultural group. (60, pp. 88–89)

Proponents of appreciation favor activities that instill pride in students about their language and that further their language development. High on the list of recommended activities include playing audio- and videotapes of well-known nonstandard dialect speakers reading plays and novels written in nonstandard dialects, and encouraging students to write nonstandard dialect fiction.

Writing

Teaching dialect speakers to write Standard English has been the focus of considerable research and discussion. Anecdotal evidence suggests that few people believe that it is unnecessary to teach nonstandard dialect speakers to write Standard English. In fact, many educators who favor the appreciation approach to oral language support a bidialectal approach to written language. They believe students should be encouraged to speak any way they prefer but they should be taught to write in Standard English. Anecdotal evidence suggests that most teachers currently follow this approach. However, research is needed to determine whether this is actually the case.

Some authors have advised teachers to use written English rather than oral English to teach Standard English skills because it does not subject students to public scrutiny and it is more effective (45, 70).

> Writing provides the means through which black students can experience language and develop alternative mechanisms for using it effectively. . . . Unlike speech, the writing process is slow paced and requires deliberate thinking and planning. Extensive revision and edition allows the student to focus on vocabulary, grammar, and syntactical problems as well as those in content and organization. Because there are no gestures or other nonverbal expressions to help communicate ideas, the written language must be shaped and fashioned so that it alone can convey the intended message. (45, p. 168)

The references at the end of the chapter provide additional information about techniques for teaching Standard English writing skills to nonstandard dialect speakers (37, 69, 71, 76, 77, 79, 80). Research, however, indicates that the instructional techniques currently being used to teach Standard English writing skills are no more effective than those used to teach oral skills (37, 73). This is probably because in most schools students do not write enough to learn the necessary skills; writing a few sentences or filling out blank spaces in workbooks is insufficient.

SELF-
QUIZ   **STANDARD ENGLISH**

What is your opinion about the following statement? Do you believe that students should be encouraged to speak and/or write in Standard English because of the prejudices of society, especially employers? Or do you feel that it is society's obligation to become less prejudiced?

> Language is personal and private; therefore, offering instruction to "improve" speech indicates criticism not only of the language but also of the person. However, since the "real world" is judgmental and critical, we do students a great disservice by continuing to ignore this serious issue. (84, pp. 22–23)

COMMUNICATION STYLE

Mismatches between students' and teachers' communication styles can impair students' learning in much the same way as mismatches between students' and teachers' language proficiency. Many times, it is difficult for special educators to understand what their students are telling them about how they feel or think, and sometimes misunderstandings occur. For example, teachers who are unaware of students' culturally influenced communication styles may mistakenly believe that they are shy, insecure, disrespectful, and so on. Likewise, students who are unfamiliar with their teachers' communication styles may not be able to distinguish when their teachers are serious and when they are joking. Therefore, to communicate effectively with students, special educators should be aware of the communication style differences between them and their students. The following are some examples of typical communication styles. The references at the end of the chapter provide more in-depth information.

Formal versus Informal Communication

All cultures have rules that people are expected to follow when they communicate with each other, but the expectations of some cultures are much more flexible than others. Some groups expect strict adherence to communication conventions in certain situations, such as when children are addressing parents and other adults or when subordinates are communicating with those who have more status and/or power than they have. Other cultures are much more relaxed and informal about communication codes. Strict codes of communication may be designed to show respect for others, to avoid open demonstrations of conflict and disagreement, or to avoid causing individuals to "lose face."

The communication styles of Hispanic Americans and some Asian Pacific American groups tend to be much more formal than either the African American or European American communication styles. "Because one of the ways in which Hispanics demonstrate their respect for each other is through the maintenance of certain formal conventions like the use of the formal *usted* rather than the informal *tu* in conversation, Hispanics may mistake an Anglo's less formal approach to interpersonal relationships as a sign of disrespect" (100, p. 130). Also, consider the following: "In Asian cultures the communication interaction is very structured and predictable. . . . The individual's status in the situation will define the role that he or she is expected to play in communication. These roles are usually defined by tradition and are often highly formalized. For communication to proceed smoothly, each participant must behave in the expected manner by using verbal and nonverbal behaviors appropriate to one's role" (107, p. 46).

Emotional versus Subdued Communication

When people communicate, are they expected to be considerate of other people's sensibilities—their reactions to what is communicated to them and how it is communicated? Or are the rights of individuals to express their feelings, regardless of how others might be affected, considered more paramount? Some cultures protect individuals' rights to express their feelings and require their members to learn to tolerate, accept, and deal with the the expression of intense feelings. Cultures that are more concerned with protecting people's sensibilities expect feelings to be communicated in a subdued way. African Americans and European Americans tend to be very different in this regard. "Whites want social interaction to operate at an emotionally subdued level. To realize this goal they first establish the rule that expressive behavior shall be subdued, which develops sensibilities capable of tolerating only relatively subdued outputs. . . . Black cultural norms desire levels of public interaction that are more emotionally intense. Consequently they allow individuals to express themselves at the level at which feelings are felt" (105, p. 117).

Although students are allowed to protest the decisions of their teachers, they are expected to do so in an acceptable manner. Because of communication style differences, when African American students express their positions passionately, European American teachers (many of whom tend to value cool-headed reasoning) may perceive these expressions as being beyond the bounds of acceptability (105).

Direct versus Indirect Communication

Do people express themselves directly, openly, and frankly, or do they speak indirectly and politely in order to maintain smooth interpersonal relationships? Should teachers be indirect or frank when they have to criticize students' work or behavior? As the following quotes about Southeast Asian Americans and Filipino Americans indicate, many Asian Pacific American groups shun European American frankness. Nguyen stated, "American straightforwardness is considered at best impolite if not brutal. In Indochina, one does not come directly to the point. To do so is, for an American, a mark of honesty and forthrightness while a person from Indochina sees it as a lack of intelligence or courtesy" (109, p. 6). Howells and Sarabia remarked, "The [Filipino] student will sometimes employ a mediator in communicating with the teacher. While this procedure may appear strange to the Anglo teacher, the child may have had numerous experiences at home with difficult-to-approach adults which have required the services of a mediator. This may be especially true if the teacher is held in high esteem" (101, p. 19).

If a special educator uses an indirect approach to tell students when he or she wants them to do something, will the students who are accustomed to a more direct approach understand that they are actually expected to comply? For example, African American students and students from poor backgrounds who are accustomed to being told directly what they should and should not do may not understand just how serious their teachers are when they are spoken to in an indirect manner (94).

Poetic and Analogous Communication

Some groups use a more poetic communication style or explain things by means of analogies rather than clear and concise terms and relationships. When teachers and students use different communication styles, there is the real possibility of miscommunication between them. Educators who prefer direct expression may also mistakenly think that some African American and Hispanic American students who use a more poetic and analogous speech pattern are sidestepping issues, that they cannot think straight, or that they have communication problems (100).

Honesty

Cultures have very different ideas about exactly what honest communication is and even if honest communication is desirable. No culture expects people to be completely honest. Other issues besides honesty—such as the relative importance placed by the culture on maintaining one's honor or "face," avoiding disagreement and conflict, avoiding personal responsibility, and so on—influence a group's opinion about how honest communication should be. In fact, in some cultures, when people communicate it is more important to maintain smooth interpersonal relationships than to tell the truth. For example, "falsehood carries no moral structure for a Cambodian, Laotian, or Vietnamese. The essential question is not whether a statement is true or false, but what the intention of the statement is. Does it facilitate interpersonal harmony? Does it indicate a wish to change the subject? Hence, one must learn the 'heart' of the speaker through his/her words" (109, pp. 6–7).

Even within cultures, subgroups have different attitudes about honest communication. In the European American culture, some individuals feel that people should take responsibility for, pay the price for, and stand up for one's actions, whereas many politicians believe that it is appropriate to use such techniques as damage control, spin control, and plausible deniability to color the truth and even hide it from the voters .

In some cultures, a promise to do something or to comply with an expectation may not be meant literally. If a refusal would lead to an awkward or uncomfortable interpersonal moment or insult a person, especially someone in a position of authority, a promise may be little more than a way of maintaining smooth interpersonal relationships. Thus, some students do not have the slightest intention of complying with a behavioral plan they have agreed to or a contingency contract they have signed.

Responses to Guilt and Accusations

When individuals are accused of doing the wrong thing, how do they express guilt and remorse or proclaim their innocence? European American students tend to express guilt by lowering their eyes and avoiding eye contact. When they are falsely accused, they may issue vigorous denials. Kochman described the European American reaction in the following way: "If they are innocent, they issue a vigorous and defensive denial—especially if the charge is serious. If they are guilty and are not trying to pretend otherwise, their response is subdued and embarrassed" (105, p. 93). African American students tend to lower their eyes as a sign of respect, not as an admission of guilt. They do not experience the same need to proclaim their innocence by emotional statements when they are not guilty. Because European Americans and African Americans respond differently when they admit or deny guilt, they may each assume the other has communicated their guilt when they have not.

Educators who do not know that African American students tend to avoid direct eye contact with authority figures or elders as a sign of respect and submission may judge their students' behavior by their own standards—which is exemplified by the expression, "Look me in the eye and tell me the truth." When African American students avert their eyes while being confronted about their behavior, teachers may misinterpret their lack of eye contact as indicating insincerity and guilt. "When whites . . . issue a vigorous and defensive denial—the kind that whites often use when they feel *falsely* accused—blacks consider this a confirmation of guilt since they believe only the truth would have been able to produce a protest of such intensity" (105, p. 92).

Themes Discussed

All cultures have unwritten rules about what should or should not be talked about and with whom. Because teachers and students may have culturally determined different expectations about what students should be willing to discuss with their teachers or their peers, it is important to know what students are and are not comfortable discussing. The following are some examples of themes that some students may be reluctant to discuss with teachers.

Needs
In some cultures, people are so sensitive to others' needs that it is unnecessary for individuals to be open and direct about their needs. Thus, it is important to ask whether individuals from a student's cultural background express their needs openly or expect others to be sensitive to their feelings and problems. This is especially true for Hispanic Americans. "Mexican American children seldom ask for help. Their socialization has accustomed them to the expectation that their needs will be noticed and help provided without its having to be asked for. This type of socialization results in children learning to be sensitive to the needs and feelings of others" (110, p. 15). Also, consider the following: "Educators should be tuned into these subtle expressions of need. They should not assume that because Hispanic students have not expressed a need for help or understanding in a direct and forthright manner, they do not need special attention or consideration" (100, p. 96).

Admission of Errors and Mistakes

Do people admit when they are wrong or have made a mistake? Students who have difficulty accepting responsibility for their errors and mistakes or apologizing to others for cultural reasons may be misperceived as defiant or stubborn. In Spanish-speaking countries, language forms make it easy for people to avoid accepting responsibility for their mistakes. An Hispanic American educator explained it this way:

> Let's pretend I missed the plane which brought me to this conference. Maybe it was my fault, and maybe not. Perhaps my husband turned off the alarm. Or perhaps my car would not start. But whatever rationalization I use, if I express myself in English it is my fault. The only way I can express what happened in English is to say "I missed the plane." So I think it would be better to express myself in Spanish. That way I don't have to feel guilty about what happened. I simply say, *"El avion me dejo."* That means the plane left me. . . . If I were to drop this glass, some of you would say to yourselves, "she dropped the glass," implying that I'm clumsy. Others of you would say, *"se cayo el vaso."* Somehow the glass managed to slide out of my hand and break itself. (103, pp. 6–7)

Should students be required to admit that they made a mistake or to apologize for something they did? Would that make students lose honor? Perhaps students should learn to accept verbally both responsibility for and the consequences of their behavior. But some students may be willing to accept the consequences of their behavior while resisting admitting their responsibility to others. In such cases, it may be more effective to permit them to avoid having to admit their errors and mistakes.

Disagreement, Unwillingness, and Inability

Are people expected to say when they are unwilling or unable to do something? Are they likely to express disagreement? When people say they too feel or believe as others do or that they will do something, do they mean it? Or is this just their way of avoiding an unpleasant moment? "In the midst of a great cultural emphasis on harmony and respect in Japan one speaker will rarely directly contradict another or even answer a question with a direct 'no.' Even in situations in which Americans can perceive 'nothing personal' to be conveyed by a 'no' answer, the Japanese will usually find one of at least 16 different ways of saying 'no' without using the literal equivalent" (98, p. 47). Grossman has added, "Hispanics often find themselves in difficulty if they disagree with an Anglo's point of view. To them, direct argument or contradiction appears rude and disrespectful. On the surface they seem agreeable, manners dictating that they do not reveal their genuine opinion openly unless they can take time to tactfully differ" (100, p. 131).

Can teachers count on students to do the things they commit themselves to do? Some students are brought up to believe that not following through on promises and saying something that is not so are acceptable behavior when doing so contributes to interpersonal harmony or helps someone save "face." When students do not fulfill a contract, do they think of it as lying or irresponsible behavior? Or do they believe that their behavior is appropriate?

An American who is not familiar with the Filipino culture might become annoyed when a Pilipino speaker says he or she will "try to come" and does not appear for the appointment. . . . The American probably does not know that when the Pilipino speaker says "I'll try" he or she usually means one of the following: 1. "I cannot do it, but I do not want to hurt feeling by saying no." 2. "I would like to, but I am not sure you really want me to come. Please insist that I do." 3. "I will probably come, but I will not say yes because something may prevent me from coming. I have no control over what may happen." (96, pp. 32–33)

Will students be able to ask questions or request help when they do not understand something? "A Japanese youth . . . will not insult the teacher's efforts by saying, 'I don't understand.' [He or she] will nod politely even while not understanding and attribute the difficulty to his or her own lack of diligence" (94, p. 19).

Facts versus Feelings
Many cultural groups frown on displays and discussions of feelings but expect their members to discuss matters of fact. For this reason, when students have problems it is important to know whether they are comfortable discussing feelings such as resentment, anger, shame, guilt and the like. "In the USA as well as in northern European cultures and many oriental groups, the expression of emotion is limited. Southern European cultures and some Latin American groups seem to permit the incredible in this matter of expressing emotions" (106, p. 4).

Sensitive and Controversial Topics
What are sensitive subjects from which people generally shy away? Depending on the group, topics such as politics, sex, religion, finances, and so on may be acceptable or unacceptable topics of conversation. "East Indian American students would not respond or give opinions about the existence of god because they are afraid of being rude and offensive to anyone (maybe even the teacher) with their opinions. They are taught not to be this way. . . . On the other hand European American students felt totally comfortable discussing this question. . . . As a matter of fact, they felt they were being totally honest and straightforward in letting everyone know how they felt about the issue" (112, p. 2).

How well do individuals have to know each other and what kind of relationship do they have to have in order to be able to discuss sensitive or intimate topics? When and under what circumstances will students be willing to discuss sensitive topics with their teachers? In some cultures, people will discuss sensitive issues only with family members and extremely close friends.

Affection

Do people demonstrate affection easily? Do they do so verbally or physically? Would students welcome or reject their teachers' display of affection? What are the acceptable ways teachers can express their affection for students? Is a pat on the back or an arm on the shoulder acceptable or are displays of affection limited to verbal statements? Although many students welcome physical touching, it is taboo behavior in some cultures. For example, the Hispanic American culture encourages more physical displays of affection than the European American culture. "Hispanics tend to show affection and acceptance through touching. Friends are likely to kiss when they meet. Males are likely to hug each other or pat each other on the back as well as shake hands. And it is not unusual for people to hold others by the arm or place their hands on their shoulders when conversing. Therefore, educators should utilize physical contact when expressing approval and acceptance of their Hispanic student, especially the young ones" (100, p. 97).

Group Processes

How do groups arrive at decisions and resolve disagreements? Do groups have leaders? Do leaders make decisions or lead the group to arrive at their own decisions? Are differences of opinion discussed openly or are they sidestepped? Would students be comfortable participating in the decision-making process or would they prefer to have decisions made by their teachers? Would they feel comfortable expressing opinions and feelings that differ from others in the group? Would they be able to participate in discussions of controversial issues or feel comfortable about deciding group issues by a public vote? Students who have been trained to avoid public conflicts and disagreements may be unable to participate in discussions of controversial issues, express opinions that are different from a previous speaker's viewpoints, or even vote on what the group should or should not do.

The following describes the ways in which group processes, as practiced in Asian Pacific American and Hispanic American groups, can often differ from the typical European American approach: "Because being a member of a group is so important, the ability to work harmoniously with a group is highly valued. . . . The goal of group problem solving is to reach consensus, not to compete for acceptance and approval of one's idea or position at the expense of others in the group. Directness and forthrightness are not valued, and people who display these traits are considered to be rude and impolite" (106, p. 47).

How many people speak at a time? European Americans expect that even in group situations only one person will speak and the others will wait their turn and listen. This is not true of all cultures. Leggio stated, "In Arab countries and in many Latin American ones, conversations are invitations for everybody to join" (106, p. 4). Irvine added, "In a heated discussion, blacks frequently make their points whenever they can enter the discussion. Deference is given to the person who considers his or her point most urgent. Turn-taking is the style of whites, who usually raise their hands to be recognized. Teachers find black students impolite, aggressive, and boisterous when they cut off another student or fail to restrain themselves so that every student can have a turn to talk" (102, p. 29). Many European Americans expect groups to function quietly. However, African Americans, Mediterranean Americans, and Hispanic Americans are comfortable with much higher levels of what may seem like noise to European Americans.

Conflict Resolution

Are conflicts faced and dealt with in a straightforward manner or swept under the table? Should teachers bring conflicts between students into the open to resolve them? At home, are youngsters who disagree allowed or encouraged to argue and/or fight it out or are they required to settle their differences peacefully and shake hands and make up? Is it better to intervene when students have conflicts or permit them to settle their conflicts themselves? Should students be required to shake hands and "make friends"? African American students are brought up to settle their conflicts in a much more open manner than many European American middle-class students and teachers. Teachers' intolerance of their behavior contributes to their being mislabeled behavior disordered.

Taking Turns

The time a person must wait to begin to respond or to introduce a new topic after another person has completed a statement varies with different cultures. Students from cultures that require longer pauses may feel left out or blocked out of classroom discussions because others who are used to shorter pauses take the floor before they do (94).

COMMUNICATION STYLE

People are not always comfortable with the way others communicate. For example, some individuals feel uncomfortable when people speak their mind in an emotional or frank manner; others find subdued or indirect expression difficult to understand and overly polite. State your preferences, if you have any, about the following aspects of people's communication styles. Do you feel more comfortable with one than the other? Do you think one is more preferable than the other? Would you attempt to change those aspects of students' communication styles that you feel are less desirable or acceptable?

- In general, are you more comfortable when students speak their minds in an emotional, passionate, excited, spontaneous manner or in a subdued, calm, controlled manner?
- Do you prefer direct, open, frank communication with students or indirect, polite communication?
- Would you rather students communicate their feelings, opinions, values, judgments, and so on directly, factually, and frankly or indirectly in order to protect people's honor or to maintain smooth interpersonal relationships?
- Do you prefer that students express their needs directly or openly or would you rather that they do so indirectly?
- Would you rather that students admit their mistakes, accept responsibility for their actions, and apologize when they have wronged someone or would you be satisfied if they are contrite and sorry without admitting so to others?

- When students disagree with others or are unwilling or unable to do something, would you rather that they say so directly or indirectly?
- Are you more comfortable with confronting and resolving conflicts directly or do you prefer to avoid them as much as possible?

NONVERBAL COMMUNICATION

Special educators are often unaware of the cultural differences in students' nonverbal communication styles. This is unfortunate because nonverbal communication can be an even more important clue to student's thoughts, feelings, and attitudes than their actual words. Some examples of these differences and their effects are described below. More detailed discussions of the topic are found in the references.

Emotion

Cultures differ in the way people are expected to express their emotions. In some Asian Pacific cultures, students laugh or giggle when they are embarrassed. Some cultures bring up males and females to express their feelings differently. For example, in some groups, only males can express anger; females never talk sharply or snap at others. When females are angry, they smile and their voices become softer. Because cultures differ regarding the ways in which they express emotions and feelings, special educators cannot always judge how students are feeling by referring to the ways in which they themselves behave when they are upset, embarrassed, angry, and so on. To understand their students' feelings, teachers need to be sensitive to the subtle and often not so subtle clues that are obvious to those who are able to recognize them.

Defiance

European Americans typically express anger and defiance by silent stares. African Americans roll their eyes and many Asian Pacific Americans force a smile when they are angry. As Johnson explained, among African Americans, especially females, "rolling the eyes is a non-verbal way of expressing impudence and disapproval of the person who is in the authority role and of communicating every negative label that can be applied to the dominant person. . . . Often white teachers (who are in an authority role and who have contact with Black children) will miss the message communicated by Black children when they roll their eyes" (104, pp. 18, 57).

African American and Hispanic American females will often stand with their hand or hands on their hips when they are angry or defiant. Johnson advised that "most Black people know to 'cool it' when Black women take this stance. The non-verbal message communicated when a Black female takes this stance is: 'I'm really mad, now. You better quit messing with me'" (104, p. 57).

Submissiveness

How do students express their respect for authority? In some cultures, looking an adult in the eye is a sign or respect and submission. In other cultures, avoiding eye contact communicates the same message. As a result, teachers may misinterpret the nonverbal messages communicated by students from other cultural backgrounds. The ways African American, Asian Pacific American, Hispanic American, and other non-European American students are taught to show respect and submission is typically different from the way European American students are expected to behave. As a result, European Americans often misinterpret the lack of eye contact among their non-European American students.

> Asians generally tend to use repeated head nodding, avoidance of direct eye contact, and minimal spontaneous verbalization, and to refrain from making critical comments, as a way of showing deference toward an authority figure. (107, p. 49)

> Occasional avoidance of eye contact by Oriental children may be classified as submissive behavior. . . . Such avoidance of eye contact provides others with a distorted image of an Oriental child—as being timid, shy, insecure, suspicious, undependable, and lacking self confidence. (112, p. 69)

> Avoidance of eye contact by a Black person communicates "I am in a subordinate role and I respect your authority over me," while the dominant culture member may interpret avoidance of eye contact as "Here is a shifty, unreliable person I'm dealing with." (104, p. 18)

The way some African Americans males walk away from a reprimand can also reveal whether or not they have accepted it. "If the young Black male walks away in a natural manner then the reprimand was received positively; if he walks away with a 'pimp strut' it means that the young Black male has rejected the reprimand and in fact is non-verbally telling the authority person to 'go to hell'" (104, p. 19). Also, in some cultures, a youngster may behave submissively while grumbling about the fact that he or she has to comply; in other cultures, grumbling would be a sign of severe disrespect (99).

Physical Contact

In comparison to European Americans, non-European American groups are more likely to touch each other in many different situations. Differences between European Americans and Haitian Americans and Hawaiian Americans and their implications are described in the following quotations:

Haitian children are very physical. . . . We use our hands. . . . If a child wants to speak, instead of saying: "Hi, Johnny," he will touch the other child automatically. (108, p. 62) (Olga Bzdyk, Director of Head Start Program, Homestead, FL)

Children will often simply lay a friendly hand on an adult they are trying to reach, rather than make a verbal approach. For Western teachers such touching on the part of Hawaiian youngsters can cause discomfort and is often not understood, leaving the teacher with a vague sensation of being pawed at or hung on, and the child with a feeling of having been ignored.

One part of the body not commonly touched by Hawaiians is the head, which is considered tabu throughout Polynesia. . . . By contrast, one of the few touching gestures which is natural and comfortable for Westerners is a friendly pat on the head or tousling a youngster's hair. . . . Although not on a conscious level Hawaiians react quite negatively to such behavior, with emotions ranging from a vague feeling of discomfort to resentment and anger and a feeling of physical violation. (95, p. 2)

Agreement and Disagreement

How do people communicate yes and no, agreement and disagreement, willingness and unwillingness, and so on? "There is a marked tendency on the part of Westerners to feel that the meaning of head-nods are universal, up-and-down to mean 'yes' and side-to-side to mean 'no.' . . . Hawaiians raise there eyebrows to say 'yes,' sometimes simultaneously jerking the head back slightly and lowering the corners of the mouth" (95, p. 4).

Beckoning

European Americans call others with their finger or upturned palms. In some cultures, this is a sign of disrespect or is used only for dogs. For example, among Hawaiian Americans, "in beckoning someone, the finger is never used nor the upright hand. Both these gestures to the Hawaiians are extremely abrupt and rude. People are called to come by placing the hand sideways, palm facing the center of the body, and beckoning with the hand in that position" (95, p. 4).

A similar problem can occur with Filipino American students. "The familiar 'come here' gesture made by curling the forefinger in an upward manner becomes a frightening 'you have done something wrong' signal to the Pilipino child. Pilipinos, as well as some other Asian groups, use a palm down sign to indicate 'come here' which is often confused with the Anglo gesture 'go back'" (101, p. 19).

SUMMARY

Students with disabilities speak many different languages and dialects and use various communication styles. Linguistically appropriate special education services for LEP students should include bilingual special education, ESL, and sheltered English approaches. Unfortunately, the vast majority of LEP students with disabilities are placed in English submersion programs. Although students who speak nonstandard dialects can learn to read and write Standard English without learning to speak Standard English, many educators insist on teaching standard speech to them. Special educators who understand their students' communication styles can communicate effectively with them.

ACTIVITIES

1. If you are currently teaching in a school with a significant number of non-European American students, listen to and observe their speech and communication styles. If you are not currently teaching, observe and listen to your peers in class. Do you notice any of the dialect and communication style differences described in this chapter? How sensitive are you to these differences?

2. Interview some nonstandard English dialect speakers about their experiences in school. Did/do their dialects interfere with their learning? How did/do their teachers and/or professors react to their dialects?

3. Ask some of your peers from different ethnic and socioeconomic backgrounds to describe their communication styles in terms of the characteristics included in this chapter. To what extent do their communication styles conform to the stereotypes discussed? Ask them to rate their acculturation to the European American middle-class mainstream culture. Is there a relationship between their type of acculturation and their communication style preferences?

REFERENCES

References 1–2 discuss the large number of limited-English-proficient students in the United States.

1. Education of the Handicapped Act Amendments of 1990 (Individuals with Disabilities Education Act) (20 U.S.C., Sections 1400–1485).

2. Woodrow, K. A. (1988). *Measuring Net Immigration to the United States: The Emigrant Population and Recent Emigration Flows.* Paper presented at the annual meeting of the Population Association of American, New Orleans.

The right of LEP students with disabilities to a linguistically appropriate education is the focus of references 3–9.

3. Bilingual Education Act of 1968.
4. Civil Rights Act of 1964.
5. *Dyrcia S. et al.* v. *Board of Education of the City of New York* (1979). 79 c. 2562 (E.D.N.Y.).
6. Equal Educational Opportunities Act of 1972.
7. Education of All Handicapped Children Act of 1974 (PL 94-142).

8. *Lau v. Nichols* (1974). 414 U.S. 563.

9. Rehabilitation Act of 1973.

Bilingual education and bilingual special education approaches are the focus of references 10–14.

10. Baca, L. M., & Cervantes, H. (1989). *The Bilingual Special Education Interface* (2nd ed.). Columbus, OH: Merrill.

11. Olsen, L. (1988). *Crossing the Schoolhouse Border: Immigrant Students and the California Public Schools*. San Francisco: California Tomorrow.

12. Cummins, J. (1984). *Bilingualism and Special Education: Issues in Assessment and Pedagogy*. San Diego: College Hill Press.

13. Garcia, R. L. (1982). *Teaching in a Pluralistic Society: Concepts, Models, Strategies*. New York: Harper & Row.

14. Medina, M. A. (1987) *Teacher Training Programs in Bilingual Special Education*. Unpublished masters thesis, San Diego State University, San Diego, CA.

References 15–19 focus on ESL techniques with students who have disabilities.

15. Cloud, N. (1988). *ESL in Special Education*. ERIC ED 303 044.

16. Cloud, N. (1990). Planning and implementing an English as a second language program. In A. L. Carrasquillo & R. E. Baecher (Eds.), *Teaching the Bilingual Special Education Student*. Norwood, NJ: Ablex.

17. Dew, N. (1985). Delivering ESL instruction to handicapped LEP children. *Elementary ESOL Education News, 7* (2), 10.

18. Duran, E. (1985). Teaching fundamental reading in context to severely retarded and severely autistic adolescents of limited English proficiency. *Adolescence, 20* (78), 433–440.

19. Spolsky, B. (1988). Bridging the gap: A general theory of second language learning. *TESOL Quarterly, 22,* 377–396.

Examples of model ESL lessons adapted for use with students with disabilities are included in references 20–23.

20. Fairfax County Schools. (1986). *Teaching Directions Using a Controlled Prepositional Vocabu-*lary. *Supplementary Lessons for Use with Limited English Proficient (LEP) Students Enrolled in ESL or Special Education Classes. Grades K-3*. ERIC ED 279 157.

21. New York City Board of Education. (1984). *Day By Day in English: An ESL-SEDAC Daily Living Skills Resource Activities Guide*. Brooklyn, NY: Division of Special Education, New York City Board of Education.

22. Ratleff, J. E. (1988). *Instructional Strategies for Crosscultural Students with Special Needs*. Sacramento, CA: Resources in Special Education.

23. Sorenson, S. (1991). *Working with Special Students in English/Language Arts. Teaching Resources in the ERIC Database (TRIED) Series*. ERIC ED 326 902.

References 24–27 discuss sheltered English approaches and their effectiveness.

24. Chamot, A. U., & O'Malley, J. M. (1986). *A Cognitive Academic Language Learning Approach: An ESL Content-Based Curriculum*. Rosslyn, VA: National Clearinghouse for Bilingual Education.

25. Crandall, J. (Ed.). (1987). *ESL Through Content Area Instruction: Mathematics, Science, Social Studies*. Englewood Cliffs, NJ: Prentice Hall.

26. Gersten, R., & Woodward, J. (1985). A case for structured immersion. *Educational Leadership, 43* (1), 75–79.

27. Northcutt, M., & Watson, D. (1986). *Sheltered English Teaching Handbook*. San Marcos, CA: AM Graphics & Printing.

References 28–30 document the linguistically inappropriate special education services provided to LEP students.

28. Cegelka, P. T., Lewis, R., & Rodriguez, A. M. (1987). Status of educational services to handicapped students with limited English proficiency: Report of a statewide study in California. *Exceptional Children, 54,* 220–227.

29. Harris, K. C., Rueda, R. S., & Supanchek, P. (1990). A descriptive study of literacy events in secondary special education programs in linguistically diverse schools. *Remedial and Special Education, 11* (4), 20–28.

30. Ortiz, A. A., & Wilkinson, C. Y. (1989). Adapting IEP's for limited English proficient students. *Academic Therapy, 24* (5), 555–568.

Legal requirements regarding nonstandard English dialects is the focus of reference 31.

31. *Martin Luther King Junior Elementary School Children* v. *Ann Arbor School District Board of Education,* 451 F. Supplement 1324 (Michigan 1978); 463 F. Supplement 1027 (Michigan 1978); No. 7–71861, Slip Op. (Michigan, July 12, 1979).

References 32–51 focus on the various approaches to dialect differences.

32. Adger, C. T., Wolfram, W., & Detwyler, J. (in press). New roles for special educators in language differences. *Teaching Exceptional Children.*

33. Adger, C. T., Wolfram, W., Detwyler, J., & Harry, B. (1993) Confronting dialect minority issues in special education: Reactive and proactive perspectives. *Proceedings of OBEMLA Research Conference.* Washington, DC: Government Printing Office.

34. Adler, S. (1987). Bidialectalism: Mandatory or elective? *Asha, 29* (1), 41–44.

35. Ash, S., & Myhill, J. (1983). *Linguistic Correlates of Interethnic Conflict.* Philadelphia: University of Pennsylvania, Linguistics Laboratory.

36. Dean, M. B., & Fowler, E. D. (1974). An argument for appreciation of dialect differences in the classroom. *Journal of Negro Education, 43* (3), 302–309.

37. Farr, M. (1986). Language, culture, and writing: Sociolinguistic foundations of research on writing. In E. Z. Rothkopf (Ed.), *Review of Research on Education, 13,* pp. 195–223.

38. Ferguson, A. M. (1982). A case for teaching standard English to Black students. *English Journal, 71* (3), 38–40.

39. Graff, D., Labov, W., & Harris, W. (1983). *Testing Listeners' Reactions to Phonological Markers of Ethnic Identity: A New Method for Sociolinguistic Research.* Paper presented at the annual meeting of the New Ways of Analyzing Variations in English, Montreal.

40. Groff, P. (1980). Black English and the teaching of spelling. In J. Schwartz (Ed.), *Teaching the Linguistically Diverse.* New York: New York State English Council.

41. Harris-Wright, K. (1987). The challenge of educational coalescence: Teaching nonmainstream English-speaking students. *Journal of Childhood Communication Disorders, 11* (1), 209–215.

42. Hochel, S. S. (1983). *A Position Paper on Teaching the Acquisition of the Mainstream Dialect in Kindergarten and Elementary School.* ERIC ED 238 060.

43. Kochman, T. (1969, Spring/Summer). Culture and communication: Implications for Black English in the classroom. *Florida Foreign Language Reporter,* pp. 89–92, 172–174.

44. Labov, W., & Harris, W. (1983). *De facto Segregation of Black and White Vernacular.* Paper presented at the annual meeting of the New Ways of Analyzing Variations in English, Montreal.

45. Lipscomb, D. (1978). Perspectives on dialects in Black students' writing. *Curriculum Review, 17* (3), 167–169.

46. Padak, N. D. (1981). The language and educational needs of children who speak Black English. *Reading Teacher, 35* (2), 144–151.

47. Simmons, E. A. (1991). Ain't we never gonna study no grammar? *English Journal, 80* (8), 48–51.

48. Taylor, O. L. (1986). A cultural and communicative approach to teaching standard English as a second dialect. In O. L. Taylor (Ed.), *Treatment of Communication Disorders in Culturally and Linguistically Diverse Populations.* San Diego: College-Hill Press.

49. Thomas, E. W. (1978). English as a second language—For whom? *The Crisis, 85* (9), 318–320.

50. Wolfram, W., Detwyler, J., & Adger, C. T. (1992) *All about Dialects: Instructors Manual.* Washington, DC: Center for Applied Linguistics.

51. Wood, B. S., & Curry, J. (1969). Everyday talk and school talk of the city Black child. *Speech Teacher, 18* (4), 282–296.

References 52–65 shed light on the relationship between nonstandard dialects and reading.

52. Anastasiow, N. J., Levine-Hanes, M., & Hanes, M. L. (1982). *Language and Reading Strategies for Poverty Children.* Baltimore: University Park Press.

53. Barth, J. L. (1979). Nonstandard English and native students: When is a difference a disability? *British Columbia Journal of Special Education, 3* (4), 357–363.

54. Bougere, M. B. (1981). Dialect and reading disabilities. *Journal of Research and Development in Education, 14* (4), 67–73.

55. Collins, J. (1988). Language and class in minority education. *Anthropology and Education Quarterly, 19* (4), 299–326.

56. Dandy, E. B. (1988). *Dialect Differences: Do They Interfere?* ERIC ED 294 240.

57. Gibson, E., & Levin, H. (1975). *The Psychology of Reading.* Cambridge, MA: MIT Press.

58. Lass, B. (1980). Improving reading skills: The relationship between the oral language of Black English speakers and their reading achievement. *Urban Education, 14* (4), 437–447.

59. Levine-Hanes, M., & Hanes, M. L. (1979). *Developmental Differences in Dialect, Function Word Acquisition and Reading.* Paper presented at the annual meeting of the International Reading Association, Atlanta.

60. McGinnis, J., & Smitherman, G. (1978). Sociolinguistic conflict in the schools. *Journal of Non-White Concerns in Personnel and Guidance, 6* (2), 87–95.

61. Pflaum, S. W. (1978). Minority student language and reading acquisition. In S. E. Pflaum-Connor (Ed.), *Aspects of Reading Education.* Berkeley, CA: McCutchan.

62. Simons, H. (n.d.). *Black Dialect Interference and Classroom Interaction.* Berkeley, CA: School of Education, University of California.

63. Sims, R. (1976). What we know about dialects and reading. In P. D. Allen & D. J. Watson (Eds.), *Findings of Research in Miscue Analysis: Classroom Implications.* Urbana IL: National Council of Teachers of English.

64. Strand, C. M. (1979). *Bidialectalism and Learning to Read.* Unpublished doctoral dissertation, University of Michigan, Ann Arbor, MI.

65. Washington, V. M., & Miller-Jones, D. (1989). Teacher interaction with nonstandard English speakers during reading instruction. *Contemporary Educational Psychology, 14* (3), 280–312.

Techniques for helping students acquire bidialectal skills are described in references 66–87.

66. Adler, S. (1979). *Poverty Children and Their Language.* New York: Grune & Stratton.

67. Anderson, E. (1989). *Students' Language Rights.* ERIC ED 311 959.

68. British Columbia Department of Education. (1981). *English as a Second Language/Dialect Resource Book for K–12.* Victoria, BC: Author.

69. Brooks, C. (Ed.). (1985). *Tapping Potential: English Language Arts for the Black Learner.* Urbana IL: National Council of Teachers of English.

70. Christian, D. (1987). *Vernacular Dialects in U.S. Schools.* ERIC ED 289 364.

71. Cronnell, B. (Ed.). (1981). *The Writing Needs of Linguistically Different Students. Proceedings of a Research Practice Conference Held at the Southwest Regional Laboratory for Educational Research and Development.* ERIC ED 210 932.

72. Davis, B. G., & Armstrong, H. (1981). The impact of teaching Black English on self-image and achievement. *Western Journal of Black Studies, 5* (3), 208–218.

73. Eubanks, I. M. (1991). Nonstandard dialect speakers and collaborative learning. *Writing Instructor, 10* (3), 143–148.

74. Farr, M., & Daniels, H. (1986). *Language Diversity and Writing Instruction.* New York: ERIC Clearinghouse on Urban Education, Institute for Urban and Minority Education.

75. Kizza, I. (1991). *Black or Standard English: An African American Student's False Dilemma.* ERIC ED 342 008.

76. Koenig, L. A., & Biel, C. D. (1989). A delivery system of comprehensive language services in a school district. *Language, Speech, and Hearing Services in Schools, 20* (4), 338–365.

77. Larson, D. A. (1989). "Snow White" and language awareness. *Journal of Teaching Writing, 6* (1), 171–179.

78. Love, T. A. (1991). *A Guide for Teaching Standard English to Black Dialect Speakers.* ERIC ED 340 248.

79. Morris, R. W., & Louis, C. N. (1983). *"A Writing of Our Own." Improving the Functional Writing of Urban Secondary Students.* Final Report. ERIC ED 241 668.

80. Nembhard, J. P. (1983). A Perspective on teaching Black dialect speaking students to write standard English. *Journal of Negro Education, 52* (1), 75–82.

81. Penfield, J. (1982). *Chicano English: Implications for Assessment and Literary Development.* ERIC ED 255 050.

82. Reed, D. F. (1983). Helping Black high school students speak standard English. *English Journal, 72* (2), 105–108.

83. Reynoso, W. D. (1984). *Standard English Acquisition*. ERIC ED 246 693.

84. Robbins, J. F. (1988). Employers' language expectations and nonstandard dialect speakers. *English Journal, 77* (6), 22–24.

85. Schierloh, J. M. (1991). Teaching standard English usage: A dialect-based approach. *Adult Learning, 2* (5), 20–22.

86. Shipley, K. G., Stone, T. A., & Sue, M. B. (1983). *Test for Examining Expressive Morphology*. Tuscon, AZ: Communication Skill Builders.

87. Taylor, H. (1991). Ambivalence toward Black English: Some tentative solutions. *Writing Instructor, 10* (3), 121–135.

References 88–93 provide descriptions of differences between Standard English and some nonstandard dialects.

88. Owens, R. E. (1988). *Language Development*. Columbus, OH: Merrill.

89. Hemingway, B. L., Montague J. C. Jr., & Bradley, R. H. (1981). Preliminary data on revision of a sentence repetition test for language screening with Black first grade children. *Language, Speech, and Hearing Services in Schools, 12,* 145–152.

90. Labov, W. (1972). *Language in the Inner City: Studies in Black English Vernacular*. Philadelphia: University of Pennsylvania Press.

91. Labov, W. (1974). *The Study of Nonstandard English*. Urbana, IL: National Council of Teachers of English.

92. Wolfram, W. A., & Christian, D. (1975). *Sociolinguistic Variables in Appalachian Dialects*. Arlington, VA: Center for Applied Linguistics.

93. Wolfram, W. A., & Fasold, R. W. (1974). *The Study of Social Dialects in American English*. Englewood Cliffs, NJ: Prentice Hall.

References 94–112 describe differences in verbal and nonverbal communication styles.

94. Wolfram, W., & Adger, C. T. (1993). *Language Differences Across Dialects*. Baltimore: Baltimore City Public Schools.

95. Anthony, A. P. (n.d.). *Hawaiian Nonverbal Communication: Two Classroom Applications*. Honolulu: University of Hawaii at Manoa, Department of Indo-Pacific Languages.

96. Boseker, B. J., & Gordon, S. L. (1983). What Native Americans have taught us as teacher educators. *Journal of American Indian Studies, 22* (3), 20–24.

97. California State Department of Education. (1986). *Handbook for Teaching Pilipino-Speaking Students*. Sacramento, CA: Author.

98. California State Department of Education. (1987). *Handbook for Teaching Japanese-Speaking Students*. Sacramento, CA: Author.

99. Goodwin, M. H. (1990). *He-Said-She Said: Talk as Social Organization Among Black Children*. Bloomington: Indiana University Press.

100. Grossman, H. (1984). *Educating Hispanic Students: Cultural Implications for Instruction, Classroom Management, Counseling, and Assessment*. Springfield, IL: Thomas.

101. Howells, G. N., & Sarabia, I. B. (1978). Education and the Pilipino child. *Integrated Education, 16* (2), 17–20.

102. Irvine, J. J. (1991). *Black Students and School Failure: Policies, Practices, and Prescriptions*. New York: Praeger.

103. Jaramillo, M. L. (1973). *Cautions When Working with the Culturally Different Child*. ERIC ED 115 622.

104. Johnson, K. R. (1971, Spring/Fall). Black kinetics: Some nonverbal communication patterns in the Black culture. *Florida Reporter*, pp. 17–20, 57.

105. Kochman, T. (1981). *Black and White Styles in Conflict*. Chicago: University of Chicago Press.

106. Leggio, P. (n.d.). *Contrastive Patterns in Nonverbal Communication among Different Cultures*. Trenton, NJ: Office of Equal Opportunity, New Jersey State Department of Education.

107. Matsuda, M. (1989). Working with Asian parents: Some communication strategies. *Topics in Language Disorders, 9* (3), 45–53.

108. National Coalition of Advocates for Students. (1988). *New Voices: Immigrant Students in U.S. Public Schools*. Boston: Author.

109. Nguyen, L. D. (1986). Indochinese cross-cultural adjustment and communication. In M. Dao & H. Grossman (Eds.), *Identifying, Instructing and Rehabilitating Southeast Asian Students with Special Needs and Counseling Their Parents*. ERIC ED 273 068.

110. Rodriguez, J. (n.d.). *An In-Service Rationale for Educators Working with Mexican American Students*. Stanford, CA: Chicano Fellow, Stanford University.

111. Sra, D. (1992) *A Comparison of East Indian American and European American Students*. Unpublished manuscript. San Jose, CA: San Jose State University, Division of Special Education.

112. Yao, E. L. (1979) Implications of biculturalism for the learning process of middle-class Asian children in the United States. *Journal of Education, 16* (4), 61–72.

7

CAUSES OF
GENDER DISPARITIES

*We are still in the early stages of learning what the
causes are of specific gender differences.*

As noted in Chapter 1, males and females have very different experiences in school. Depending on their ethnic and socioeconomic-class background, they choose different courses, participate in different extracurricular activities, aspire to different careers and occupations, and earn different scores on standardized achievement tests. Male students tend to score higher than females in the upper ranges of tests of advanced mathematics skills, but they do not perform as well as females in language arts and basic computational skills. Thus, their lower performance is in the areas that are most likely to lead students to be referred to programs for students with learning disabilities and mild developmental disabilities.

Depending on their ethnic background, girls tend to be less self-confident than boys in situations that are in the "male domain" such as mathematics and physics courses, in competitive situations, and when they lack objective information about how well they have done or can do. They tend to react less positively than boys to difficult and challenging situations and they are less likely to take risks and perform less adequately than boys following failure or the threat of failure. They are also more likely to attribute their poor performance to lack of ability rather than lack of effort or motivation. Additionally, they tend to seek the assistance and approval of adults more than boys do.

Males are more likely to get into trouble for behavioral problems, to be disciplined by their teachers, and to be suspended from school. They are also more likely to be referred to and accepted into programs for students with behavioral and emotional problems. Some educators believe that males require the special services provided by programs for students with developmental disabilities, behavior disorders, emotional disturbances, and learning disabilities more than females do. Other educators claim that the gender imbalance is caused by the over-referral of males—especially African Americans, Native Americans, and Hispanic Americans—who do not have disabilities and the underreferral and underenrollment of females with cognitive or emotional problems who are denied the special education they require.

This chapter examines the causes of gender imbalances in enrollment patterns in special education programs and gender differences in students' academic achievement, school participation, and behavior. The following chapter discusses techniques that educators can employ to solve these problems.

BIOLOGICAL PREDISPOSITIONS

Many people believe that biology is a major cause of the gender differences observed in school. Physiological factors that are thought to contribute to these differences include dissimilarities in females' and males' hormonal systems, the lateralization and specialization of their right and left brains, and their vulnerability to neurological damage.

Hormonal Differences

Some researchers have proposed that the higher levels of male hormones, such as testosterone, make males more active, assertive, and aggressive (1, 4–6, 11–13, 16, 21). They suggest that teachers are intolerant of the male behavior patterns these hormonal differences create, overreact to their students' behavior, and overrefer them to special education programs for students with emotional and behavioral problems.

It is true that males exhibit more behavior problems and get into more trouble in school than females (22–26). There also is evidence that teachers, especially females, tend to be less tolerant of male behavior patterns (27–29) and use more punitive management techniques with males (30, 31). However, these facts do not answer the question of whether teachers should be more tolerant of male behavior patterns or whether males' aggressive, assertive, and active behavior is caused by hormonal rather than cultural differences.

Research indicates that males and females do have different levels of testosterone and that this does affect their levels of activity and aggression and their emotional reactions (1, 4–6, 11–13, 16). It is not clear however, whether the higher levels of testosterone observed in males *cause* them to behave more assertively and aggressively than females or merely *predispose* them to do so when environmental conditions encourage them to behave in these ways.

Lateralization and Specialization

A number of researchers believe that male-female differences in verbal achievement are largely due to differences in the age at which and the extent to which their brains' right hemispheres and left hemispheres become specialized in mathematical and verbal functioning (3, 11). Although there are many different theories about exactly how cerebral specialization may cause gender differences, one that is more widely accepted than others is based on the fact that hemispherical specialization in certain functions (e.g., verbal, visual-spatial, and mathematical reasoning) occurs earlier in females than in males. This theory proposes that early development of females' brains and their greater hemispheric specialization provides them with a head start that improves their verbal functioning.

Research results regarding gender differences in hemispheric specialization are not entirely consistent. On balance, considerable evidence of differences in cerebral lateralization between males and females exists (3, 7–10, 14, 15, 17–20).

Researchers have found that hemispheric specialization in females begins earlier, perhaps as early as three months of age, and develops to a greater degree. However, research has not yet established a direct causal relationship between these physiological differences and the ages at which the genders acquire initial language skills or their scores on tests on verbal skills (3). Thus, more research is needed before the biological explanation for this gender disparity can be proven.

Predisposition versus Determinism

Educators disagree about the extent to which hormonal and lateralization/specialization differences make gender disparities inevitable. Some think that these differences cause definite gender disparities in behavior and learning. Many others view them not as complete determiners of how individuals behave, but as one of several interacting influences. In this view, aptly expressed by Maccoby and Jacklin in 1974, behavioral differences that have a biological base can still be modified by environmental events.

> We suggest that societies have the option of minimizing, rather than maximizing, sex differences through their socialization practices. A society could, for example, devote its energies more toward moderating male aggression than toward preparing women to submit to male aggression, or toward encouraging rather than discouraging male nurturance activities. In our view, social institutions and social practices are not merely reflections of the biologically inevitable. A variety of social institutions are viable within the framework set by biology. It is up to human beings to select those that foster the life styles they most value. (11, p. 374)

Although research since 1974 has provided considerable information about the possible biological bases of gender differences, the field is still relatively ignorant about which gender differences have a biological component. In addition, very little research has been conducted to determine the extent to which biological factors cause versus merely predispose males and females to function differently, whether some biological predispositions are more resistant to change than others, and the psychological costs, if any, people pay when they behave in ways that contradict their biological predispositions.

Vulnerability to Neurological Damage

Some educators and researchers attribute the overenrollment of males in classes for students with developmental and learning disabilities to a higher incidence of genetic defects and pre- and postnatal damage among males that impedes the development of their intellectual abilities. There is considerable evidence that males are more vulnerable to the kinds of mild and severe neurological damage that require special educational services. Males are more likely to suffer spontaneous abortions and stillbirths; complications of pregnancy and birth such as toxemia and placenta praevia; genetic disorders such as Down syndrome; neurological damage, including cerebral palsy, encephalitis, and seizure disorders; and other conditions such as attention deficit disorder and autism (32–43). Thus, it appears reasonable that males should comprise a greater percentage of the children and youth enrolled in programs for students with learning disabilities, developmental disorders, and speech disorders. However, other factors also contribute, perhaps to a greater degree, to the disproportionate enrollment of males and females in special education programs.

Conclusions

The possibility that male-female differences in hormonal levels and brain specialization/lateralization contribute significantly to differences in their academic success and their misrepresentation in special education programs for students with learning disabilities, mild developmental disabilities, behavior disorders, and emotional problems is basically unsubstantiated. It is also possible that as society and the education it provides students become less sexist, male-female differences in students' attitudes, behavior, academic achievement, and so on will decrease. As more is learned about non-European American and nonmiddle-class students, researchers will find that many of the male-female differences observed among European American middle-class students do not apply to other ethnic groups and socioeconomic classes. As a result, the need to question whether biological factors contribute to gender differences will diminish.

It is not known whether some physiological predispositions are more resistant to change than others. Nor are the psychological costs known, if any, that people pay when they behave in ways that contradict their physiological predispositions. Therefore, when educators react to students' gender-specific behaviors that may have a physiological component, they have little to guide them regarding either the extent to which such behavior can be changed or the possible costs involved in attempting to eliminate the behavior rather than to modify it.

On the other hand, it is probable that males' greater vulnerability to neurological damage during the prenatal, natal, and postnatal periods does contribute to an undetermined degree to their overrepresentation in special education programs for students with learning and developmental disabilities. It is unlikely, however, that this factor is a major cause of the gender differences in enrollment patterns observed in almost every school district in the United States.

DIFFERENTIAL REINFORCEMENT

Everyday life experiences confirm that males and females learn gender-stereotypic roles in part because they tend to be rewarded for behaving differently (e.g., playing with different toys, communicating in different styles, settling arguments differently, enrolling in different courses, participating in different sports, etc.) and negatively reinforced for behaving similarly (e.g., boys crying about bruises and scrapes, girls playing in an active and boisterous manner, etc.). Considerable research evidence supports this explanation. Although different ethnic and socioeconomic groups may not all share the same ideas about the sex roles children should learn, parents tend to reward their children for behaving in ways that they feel are gender appropriate and punish them for behaving in ways that they feel are gender inappropriate (11, 44–47). Teachers also use rewards and punishments to modify their students' behavior, although they differ about the kinds of behavior they want students to exhibit.

Children, even toddlers and preschoolers, also reinforce each other for behaving in gender-stereotypical fashions (48–51). Children in general and males in particular reward each other for playing with the right toys, in the right way, and with the right sex, and for relating to each of the sexes in acceptable ways.

Differential reinforcement affects students' behavior but only to a limited degree. Parents, teachers, and peers cannot decide for other individuals what they will think and how they will behave.

CONSTRUCTIVISM: COGNITIVE AWARENESS AND MODELING

Children voluntarily adopt some gender-stereotypical ways of behaving without having to be rewarded (11, 52–59). They become aware of and identify with their gender, and then copy behavior they believe is gender appropriate. In fact, as their conceptual abilities develop, they construct increasingly more elaborate schemes of gender-appropriate behavior and proceed to match their behavior to their constructs.

Maccoby and Jacklin described the process in the following way: "A child gradually develops concepts of 'masculinity' and 'femininity', and when he has understood what his own sex is, he attempts to match his behavior to his conceptions. His ideas may be drawn only very minimally from observing his own parents. The generalizations he constructs do not represent acts of imitation, but are organizations of information distilled from a wide variety of sources" (11, pp. 365–366).

There is ample evidence that adults, including parents, model gender-specific behavior and communicate gender-specific expectations to children and youth, which children tend to copy (16, 52–70). Considerable evidence also suggests that children as young as 2 and 3 years of age develop constructs of appropriate male and female behavior and tend to bring their behavior into line with these constructs (49, 52).

STRUCTURED REPRODUCTION

As noted in Chapter 3, reproduction theorists claim that schools purposely perpetuate the values, ideals, and attitudes European American middle- and upper-class males have set up throughout society to maintain their economic and social power and position. That is, such theorists believe that those who exercise control and power in U.S. society—middle- and upper-class European American males—

structure its institutions, including schools, to maintain their special positions by reproducing the inequality that serves their interests (71–77). According to these theorists, schools provide females and others with the kinds of educational experiences that maintain them as a source of cheap, though well-prepared, labor for their enterprises, whereas more affluent male students are trained to be the leaders of society. Also, at the same time, schools tend to teach females to accept the status quo—their economic and social inferiority.

RESISTANCE, PRODUCTION, AND TRANSFORMATION

Although students are exposed to gender and class biases in school and society at large, they are also exposed to ideas and experiences that contradict these biases (78–87). Nonsexist ideas have become more frequent in the media and in the materials students read in school. Many teachers and parents do not adhere to society's gender, ethnic, and socioeconomic-class stereotypic expectations for children and adolescents. Since they are given conflicting messages, students accept some and resist others.

Some students accept most of the stereotypic messages they receive. Many others do not; they understand that schools are structured to maintain gender inequality. And they know that even if they do well in school, a society stratified along gender lines will not afford them the same benefits that males, especially European American upper-class males, receive from succeeding in school. Therefore, instead of acquiescing to the educational system for payoffs they do not believe will be forthcoming, they strive to maintain their own sense of identity.

As noted in Chapter 3, some students accommodate more than they resist; others actively resist the biased education they receive and the inferior position it threatens to place them in. Some defy schools' gender and socioeconomic class biases in nonconstructive ways (79, 80, 84–87); others battle the same forces in constructive ways. They reject the biased ideas to which they are exposed. Instead, they gain a sense of self-identity and a better understanding of their gender and class, and begin to contribute to transforming society (75, 81–83).

CONCLUSIONS

Biology, differential reinforcement, modeling, cognitive awareness, and structured reproduction all interact in undetermined ways to lead a given individual to behave in a particular way in a specific situation. These factors can contribute to gender differences; however, they do not make male and female students behave differently. Physiological factors only predispose or incline the genders to act in dissimilar ways. Students can modify and channel their biological predispositions. Differential reinforcement, cognitive awareness and modeling, and educational structures reproduce gender stereotypes, but they can also produce students with new perspectives on gender issues.

THE SCHOOL'S ROLE

This section examines the school's role in the creation and maintenance of gender differences in students' achievement and participation in school and in their enrollment in special education.

Administrative Imbalance

Although females comprise the majority of classroom teachers, they are grossly underrepresented in administrative positions (88–91). In 1990, 83 percent of the nation's school principals and superintendents were male and the majority of these, 75 percent, were European American males (91). Thus, the current situation, especially in elementary schools, is no different than the situation described by Frazier and Sadker in 1973: "Elementary school is a woman's world, but a male captain heads the ship" (89, p. 96). What message does this situation communicate to students? Many authors believe that it teaches students that males, especially European American males, are and should be the authorities (88–91).

Curriculum Materials

Although curriculum materials such as textbooks, readers, and biographies that students currently use are not as sexist as the materials used in classes in the 1960s and 1970s, they continue to introduce society's gender biases into the school's structure (92–103). The disparity in the number of pictures in books of males and females has been reduced. The stereotypic portrayal of females as nurses and secretaries has been largely eliminated and working females are engaged in many more occupations. The preponderance of male characters in basal readers has been reduced by eliminating male characters from many stories and replacing them with nonhuman characters such as talking trees or animals without sex roles.

However, many problems still exist. For example, many authors and publishers still use male pronouns to describe individuals whose gender is unknown and use the word *man* to signify all people. The use of nonhuman characters in basal readers avoids the appearance of sexism but it does not increase the number of female characters or stories about females. In fact, stories about males still greatly outnumber stories about females in students' readers in the higher grades and in the biographies found in school libraries. In most of the material students read, fathers still work and mothers still stay home. At home, mothers do domestic chores such as taking care of children and cooking; fathers build and repair things. When parents work outside the home, they are still described as involved in gender-stereotypic jobs but to a lesser degree. Males are depicted as engaged in three times as many different occupations as females, and fathers are the executives, professionals, scientists, firefighters, and police officers. Males participate in a variety of different athletic activities; females are involved primarily in sports that have traditionally been considered "female" sports. Females are described as overemotional, dependent, concerned about their appearance, and watching others do things. Males are depicted as actively involved in solving problems and doing adventurous things. Females are still portrayed as receiving help and males as helping them.

In math books, boys learn to count by driving cars, flying planes, and engineering trains; girls learn to count by jumping rope, measuring cloth, and following cooking recipes. Males are still the scientists in science materials. Although the number of pictures of males and females is about equal in history textbooks, only 5 percent of the text deals with female experiences. When females' roles in history are included in the 5 percent devoted to female experiences, women whose contributions fulfill the more acceptable traditional female role are described almost to the exclusion of feminists or those who were involved in feminist issues.

Computer software is also biased against females. Woodill stated, "Much of computer software has been designed by males for males, as shown by the predominance of male figures in programs, computer ads, and on the software packaging" (103, p. 55). Thus, while changes have occurred, curriculum materials in general are still quite sexist.

Teacher Attention, Feedback, Evaluation, and Expectations

Teachers tend to create and maintain gender differences in school through the attention and feedback they give students, the ways they evaluate them, and the expectations they communicate to them. Chapter 3 described the adverse effects of teachers' biased expectations and evaluations. This section focuses on the harm done to students by gender bias in teacher attention and feedback.

Beginning in preschool, boys receive more attention from their teachers (11, 104–121). One reason for this is that teachers spend more time disciplining boys for misbehavior (115, 121, 136). Much of the difference, however, is due to the fact that teachers demonstrate a clear bias in favor of male participation in their classes. Teachers are more likely to call on males when students volunteer to recite and when they call on nonvolunteers. When students recite, teachers are also more likely to listen to and talk to males. They also use more of their ideas in classroom discussions and respond to them in more helpful ways (117).

The pattern of giving more attention to males is especially clear in science and mathematics classes. Beginning in preschool grades, teachers ask males more questions and give them more individual instruction, acknowledgment, praise, encouragement, corrective feedback, opportunities to answer questions correctly, and social interaction (104, 112–114, 120). In mathematics classes, teachers wait longer for males to answer questions before calling on someone else. They reward females for performing computational skills and males for higher-level cognitive skills, demonstrate more concern about giving males remedial help, and expect males to be more interested in math and better at solving math problems (149).

Gender differences do not favor males in all subjects, however. In reading, a course traditionally seen as in the so-called female domain, teachers tend to spend more time instructing and attending to girls (114, 119).

How do females interpret their teachers' apparent disinterest in them? No one knows for sure. However, Boudreau's conclusion about the probable interpretation students put on the message teachers give them may be correct. "The idea conveyed to girls is, although subtle, quite clear. What boys do matters more to teachers than what girls do" (106, p. 68).

Teachers also give males and females different kinds of attention. Again, the differential treatment favors males. Boys are given more praise and attention for high levels of achievement and correct responses (107–109, 111, 123). In fact, teachers give high-achieving girls the least amount of attention, praise, and supportive feedback, and the largest number of disparaging statements compared to low-achieving girls and all boys (98, 123). They praise girls more for neatness, following instructions exactly, and raising their hands. Even when they give the wrong answer, girls are often praised for raising their hands and volunteering (122, 126). Many teachers avoid criticizing girls' responses, even when they are wrong (126). This is unfortunate since girls learn better when they receive corrective feedback (124). There is some evidence that these biases are more characteristic of European American teachers than African Americans (127). This may be one more example of the fact that "blacks are less gender-typed and more egalitarian than whites" (125, p. 61).

What are teachers telling their female students by relating to them in these ways? Are they communicating that they do not expect their female students to be able to perform well in academic areas? Are they implying that they do not believe they can respond correctly? Are they saying that they feel females are too fragile to be criticized? Any and all of these explanations are possible in the absence of research data. How do female students interpret their teachers' behavior? A probable answer is that, with the exception of courses in the "female domain," they are still getting the message that teachers do not expect them to do as well as boys.

Research that needs updating suggests that teachers have different academic expectations for females and males (105, 128–134). Although educators generally do not expect males and females to have different achievement levels in school, they view high achievement as a masculine characteristic and low achievement as feminine. They believe that courses such as physics are more appropriate for students with masculine characteristics. In mathematics classes, they assign females to lower ability groups than their achievement would warrant. These differences can affect students' self-confidence about their academic ability and their motivation to succeed in school.

As noted in Chapter 3, the message African American females receive is even more destructive (135–138). Teachers, especially European American teachers, perceive and treat African American females in an even more biased manner than European American females (135, 137, 138). Their teachers seem to be telling them that all they are good for is the stereotypic roles such as housekeepers, maids, child-care providers, and so on that European Americans have historically assigned to African American females.

Gender and ethnic differences in teacher attention, feedback, expectations, and evaluations can have other negative effects on students (139–142). These disparities may help to explain why girls are more likely than boys to react poorly to failure or the threat of failure and to attribute their poor performance to lack of ability rather than lack of effort. They may also contribute to females' high anxiety during testing situations. Such differences may be one reason why European American females think such subjects as mathematics and science are less important to them and enroll in fewer math and science courses.

SELF-
QUIZ

TEACHER ATTENTION, FEEDBACK, AND EXPECTATIONS

Your answers to the questions in this and the following self-quizzes will help you determine if you treat male and female students the same or differently. Your replies will also help you evaluate the ways you deal with gender differences in your classroom. You may answer the questions by videotaping yourself during classes, but it would probably be more helpful to pair up with a colleague and observe one another in your classrooms.

- Do I provide the same amount and type of help to all students regardless of their gender?
- Do I coach males more than females by asking guiding or probing questions when their answers are not correct?
- Do I praise boys and girls equally for their intellectual/academic accomplishments?
- When male and female students raise their hands, do I call on them with equal frequency?
- Do I expect males to answer more questions correctly?
- Do I expect boys to do better than girls in math and science and girls to do better than boys in language arts, music, and art?
- Do I criticize girls' and boys' academic work with the same degree of objectivity and frankness?
- Am I more likely to ask girls easy questions and questions that require factual answers and to reserve the really difficult ones and those that involve critical thinking for boys?
- Do I attribute the cause of students' poor performance accurately or am I more likely to attribute boys' poor performance to lack of interest or effort and girls' poor performance to lack of ability?
- Am I more likely to stand nearer or touch students of my sex than students of the opposite sex or to engage them in conversations unrelated to school?
- Do I make eye contact more with males than females?

Courses and Activities

Many teachers believe that some courses belong in the "male domain" and others in the "female domain" (146). For example, teachers and counselors tend to reward boys more than girls for learning math. They encourage boys to enroll in math and science-related courses and discourage girls from taking advanced courses such as calculus and physics. Likewise, they discourage boys from enrolling in such "feminine" courses as languages and home economics. Many teachers and counselors believe that higher education and certain careers and occupations are more appropriate for one sex than the other, and vocational education teachers often harass female students enrolled in nontraditional vocational courses (143–145, 148).

Students receive sexist messages about participation in physical education activities. Schools tend to provide different sports experiences for males and females (147–149). Many schools, especially at the middle and high school level, continue to have separate physical education classes for boys and girls. The schedule for female teams' practice is often determined by when males are not using the facilities, and coaches of male teams are paid more than those coaching female teams. Girls are almost routinely excluded from contact sports such as football, rugby, and soccer, and boys are discouraged from participating in activities such as dancing, skipping rope, and using the balance beam. When students persist in pursuing activities reserved for the opposite sex, they are often labeled tomboys or sissies.

SELF-
QUIZ   **COURSES AND ACTIVITIES**

- Are you likely to encourage boys more than girls to go to college?
- Do you believe that women should be equally concerned, more concerned, or less concerned about marriage and childbearing than they are about academic and professional success?
- Do you think of some careers and vocational choices as more appropriate for one sex?

Gender Segregation/Separation

Studies done in the late 1970s and middle 1980s revealed that some teachers discouraged male-female interaction. Instead of encouraging mixed gender groups, some teachers assign different chores to boys and girls. For example, girls put things in order and boys move furniture. Teachers separate boys and girls when assigning seats or areas to hang up clothes and when forming study and work groups and committees (146, 150, 151). Lockheed and Harris reported a particularly pernicious management approach: "In classrooms, assignment to mixed-sex seating adjacencies or groups often is used as a punishment designed to reduce student interaction instead of as a learning technique designed to foster cooperative interaction" (151, p. 276). It is unclear how many teachers engaged in these practices in the past and whether teachers continue to do so now. Research is needed to determine if these practices continue today and if they are widespread.

GENDER SEGREGATION/SEPARATION

- Do you segregate boys and girls for some activities?
- Do you sometimes make a special effort to ensure that students do not sit, play, or work in same-sex groups even if they appear to prefer them?
- Do you think that some topics are better dealt with in single-sex groups?
- Do you sometimes assign students to single-sex groups in order to protect female students from being dominated or inhibited by male students or in order to allow boys to deal with certain topics in a male way?

Encouragement of Behavioral Differences

Although all teachers want their students to be well behaved, according to research that was conducted in the 1970s to middle 1980s, they appear to have different standards for males and females. Beginning in preschool, teachers tend to encourage gender-stereotypic behavior (106, 152–156). Teachers praise boys more than girls for creative behavior and girls more than boys for conforming behavior. Boys are rewarded for functioning independently, whereas girls are rewarded for being obedient and compliant. Boudreau stated that this form of discrimination harms females. "The pattern of reinforcement that young girls receive may lead them to stake their sense of self-worth more on conforming than personal competency" (106, p. 73). To the extent that these results are still current, teachers who encourage these gender differences can certainly cause problems for girls in situations that require creativity, assertiveness, or independence.

There is also evidence that teachers accept different kinds of inappropriate behavior from males and females without disciplining them for misbehaving. Huffine, Silvern, and Brooks found that kindergarten teachers discipline males and females for different kinds of misbehavior. They reported, "Aggression in boys is acceptable while in girls it is not. The reverse seems to be true of disruptive talking. Teachers expect and/or accept talking from girls, at least much more so than from boys. Thus, the stereotypic behaviors, aggressiveness and loquacity, may be acquired and/or maintained by the differential teacher responses to these behaviors" (154, p. 34).

ENCOURAGEMENT OF BEHAVIORAL DIFFERENCES

- Do you ever encourage girls to wear dresses?
- Do you ask boys to do the physical work such as move furniture and girls to decorate the room, organize the bulletin board, clean up, or other traditional female chores?
- Do you praise male students, but not female students, for being strong or athletic?
- Do you appreciate boys who are "all boy"?
- Do you believe that girls should act like ladies and boys like gentlemen?
- When males are dominating the group by monopolizing the conversation, making most of the suggestions and decisions, and so on, do you intervene on the females' behalf or encourage them to take a more active role in the group?
- Do you encourage females not to allow males to dominate them?
- Do you attempt to encourage female students who are passive or docile to be more assertive and competitive and to take more risks?
- Do you encourage boys to be less competitive and assertive and more cooperative?
- Are you annoyed by boys who do not express their feelings?

Intolerance of Male Behavior Patterns and Biased Classroom Management Techniques

As noted previously, educators, especially female educators, tend to be less tolerant of behaviors that are felt to be typical of males. African American males are especially likely to suffer the consequences of teachers' intolerance. Many African American males, and females as well, express their emotions much more intensely than most European Americans. When European American teachers observe African American males behaving aggressively and assertively, they tend to assume that the students are much angrier or upset than they actually are. Attributing a level of anger to African American students that would be correct for European American students who behaved in a similar way, teachers become uncomfortable, even anxious, and concerned about what they incorrectly anticipate will happen next. As a result, they intervene when no intervention is necessary. If teachers appreciated the cultural context of African American males' seemingly aggressive behavior toward others and understood that such behavior is unlikely to cause the physical fight or whatever else teachers expect to occur between African American students, teachers would be less likely to have to intervene to make themselves feel more at ease in the situation. This, in turn, would lessen the likelihood that African American males would get into trouble needlessly.

Teachers tend to reprimand males more often than females and in different ways (29–31, 106, 154). They tend to speak briefly, softly, and privately to girls but publicly and harshly to boys. With younger children, they tend to use physical methods like poking, slapping, grabbing, pushing, squeezing, and so on with boys and use negative comments or disapproving gestures and other forms of nonverbal communication with girls (154).

Teachers are more likely to use even harsher disciplinary techniques, such as corporal punishment and suspension, with poor, African American, and Hispanic American males than with middle-class European American males (26, 29, 154, 157–160). This is unfortunate because public and harsh reprimands and physical forms of discipline and severe punishments can cause students to react rebelliously to punishments that they feel are too harsh. This may help to explain why males get into trouble in school and are referred to special education programs for students with behavioral and emotional problems much more often than females. It may also explain why males from poor backgrounds and some non-European American backgrounds tend to get into more trouble than European American middle-class students (22–26).

SELF-
QUIZ

**APPROACHES TO CLASSROOM MANAGEMENT
AND BEHAVIOR PROBLEMS**

- Do you want students to behave in a conforming, quiet manner?
- Do you prefer students to relate cooperatively rather than competitively to their peers?
- Are you as concerned about the behavior of students who appear to be passive, inhibited, quiet, withdrawn, timid, or overdependent as you are about the behavior of active, assertive, aggressive students?
- Are you equally comfortable with students who are assertive and with students who are passive?
- Are you equally comfortable with students who are competitive and with those who are cooperative?
- Are you equally comfortable with students who prefer to work alone and with those who like to work in groups?
- If there is a conflict between students, do you feel as comfortable when they face it head-on as when they "sweep it under the carpet"?
- Are you equally comfortable with students who try to find a compromise solution to disagreements and with students who stand up for their rights as they see them?
- Do you monitor males more closely than females because you expect them to misbehave more often?
- Are you more likely to believe girls than boys because you think girls are more honest?
- Are you more likely to punish boys than girls for the same behavior?
- Do you use a sterner tone of voice with boys than girls?
- Do you believe that severe forms of punishment are more appropriate for males than females?

- Are you more likely to reprimand girls privately and calmly and to reprimand boys harshly and publicly?
- Do you use the same rewards for male and female students or attempt to select rewards that are gender appropriate?

Conclusions

The data presented clearly indicate that schools play an important role in the formation and maintenance of students' stereotypic views of gender roles. Meece stated, "Schools have been slow in adapting to recent changes in the social roles of men and women. As a result, schools may be exposing children to masculine and feminine images that are even more rigid and more polarized than those currently held in the wider society. Furthermore, the school setting does not seem to provide children with many opportunities to perform behaviors not associated with their gender. Therefore, schools seem to play an important role in reinforcing rigid gender distinctions" (125, p. 67).

SELF-QUIZ   **CRITICAL INCIDENTS**

It is not always easy to apply a set of principles to a real-life situation when some of the principles that apply to a specific situation appear to lead to contradictory solutions. Describe how you think teachers should handle each of the following critical incidents:

1. After raising her hand repeatedly to volunteer answers to her teacher's questions without being called on, a fifth-grade student complains that her teacher is unfair because the teacher always calls on the boys to answer the difficult questions. The teacher does not believe the student is correct.
2. An African American tenth-grade male in a predominantly poor neighborhood school tells his teacher in no uncertain terms to get off his case and stop telling him about the value of a high school diploma. He insists that a high school diploma does not help African Americans. The teacher tells the student he is wrong. The next day, the student brings in some articles that confirm that African American males who graduate high school do not earn significantly more than those who do not.
3. The immigrant mother of a developmentally disabled 15-year-old female refuses to give her daughter permission to attend school dances or go on coeducational school outings because she believes her daughter is both too young and too disabled to understand and deal with the physical desires of male teenagers. She explains that in her country even "normal" 15-year-old girls are expected to avoid such situations until they are much older.

SUMMARY

Many factors contribute to the gender differences observed in regular and special education. Males and females are biologically predisposed to function differently. Males are more vulnerable to the results of neurological damage. Males and females are reinforced for behaving differently and they learn different roles by observing adults behaving in gender-stereotypical ways. Further, they are exposed to gender-biased information. In addition, society is structured in ways that promote gender differences. For the present, it is unknown which combination of factors contribute to a particular gender difference, how these factors interact to produce the differences, and the relative amount of influence each factor exercises in the case of any particular difference. Nor are the reasons known why some individuals conform to these gender stereotypes and others do not. Much more research is needed before scientific answers can be provided to these important questions.

Schools play a significant role in creating and maintaining gender differences. Gender bias exists in the textbooks students use, the unequal amounts of attention and different kinds of feedback and encouragement they receive from their teachers, the gender segregation they experience, and so on. Although these factors tend to reproduce gender differences, substantial numbers of students resist their influences to varying degrees. Students belong to ethnic groups, socioeconomic classes, and gender groups. Bias against students in school occurs as a result of the interplay between the ways in which teachers relate to students in terms of these three characteristics. Bias against any group of students for any reason is undesirable and should be eliminated.

ACTIVITIES

1. Compare the way you relate to different groups of students by studying your behavior during a few 10-minute periods at convenient times during the day. You can study almost any aspect of your teaching. For example, count the number of times you call on students who volunteer, the number of times you assign students to particular chores, the number of times you praise students' work, and so on. Then compare the results for different groups of students such as males and females, European Americans and non-European Americans, and poor and middle-class students.

2. If you teach more than one subject, determine whether you relate to the genders differently during different subjects such as English or science.

3. Ask a colleague to evaluate some of your students' work that is difficult to judge objectively (e.g., essay questions or a writing sample rather than a math problem or a multiple-choice answer). Compare your colleague's evaluations with your own to see if your evaluations of particular groups of students are biased.

4. If you do not have teaching experience, study the way your master teacher or one or more of your professors relates to males and females and students from different ethnic backgrounds.

5. Interview males and females and students from different ethnic and socioeconomic backgrounds in the courses you are taking about some of the issues discussed in this chapter. What are their opinions about the origins of gender differences? Do students' opinions vary with their gender, ethnic, or socioeconomic-class backgrounds?

6. Review the textbooks and other materials your professors assign in the courses you are taking. Are they free from gender bias? Do they deal with the gender issues inherent in the topics they cover? Do they focus exclusively or primarily on European Americans to the exclusion of other ethnic groups?

7. Compare the amount of time your professors devote to the gender issues inherent in the courses they teach. Do you find that some professors are more sensitive to and interested in gender issues than others?

REFERENCES

References 1–21 present evidence that some gender differences in students' behavior in school and academic achievement may have a physiological base.

1. Frankenhaeuser, M., von Wright, M. R., Collins, A., von Wright, J., Sedvall, G., & Swahn, C. G. (1978). Sex differences in psychoneuroendocrine reactions to examination stress. *Psychosomatic Medicine, 40* (4), 334–343.
2. Grossman, H., & Grossman, S. (1994). *Gender Issues in Education.* Boston: Allyn and Bacon.
3. Halpern, D. F. (1986). *Sex Differences in Cognitive Abilities.* Hillsdale, NJ: Erlbaum.
4. Jacklin, C. N., Maccoby, E. E., & Doering, C. H. (1983). Neonatal sex-steroid hormones and timidity in 6- 18-month-old boys and girls. *Developmental Psychobiology, 16,* 163–168.
5. Jacklin, C. N., Maccoby, E. E., Doering, C. H., & King, D. R. (1984). Neonatal sex-steroid hormones and muscular strength in boys and girls in the first three years. *Developmental Psychobiology, 17,* 301–310.
6. Jacklin, C. N., Wilcox, K. T., & Maccoby, E. E. (1988). Neonatal sex-steroid hormones and intellect abilities of six year old boys and girls. *Developmental Psychobiology, 21,* 567–574.
7. Kimura, D. (1980). Sex differences in intrahemispheric organization of speech. *Behavior and Brain Sciences, 3,* 240–241.
8. Kimura, D. (1983). Sex differences in cerebral organization for speech and praxic functions. *Canadian Journal of Psychology, 37,* 19–35.
9. Kimura, D. (1985). Male brain, female brain: The hidden difference. *Psychology Today, 19,* 50–58.
10. Levy, J., & Gur, R. C. (1980). Individual differences in psychoneurological organization. In J. Herron (Ed.), *Neuropsychology of Left-Handedness.* New York: Academic Press.
11. Maccoby, E. E., & Jacklin, C. N. (1974). *The Psychology of Sex Differences.* Stanford, CA: Stanford University Press.
12. Maccoby, E. E., & Jacklin, C. N. (1980). Sex-differences in aggression: A rejoinder and reprise. *Child Development, 51,* 964–980.
13. Marcus, J., Maccoby, E. E., Jacklin, C. N., & Doering, C. H. (1985). Individual differences in mood: Their relation to gender and neonatal sex steroids. *Developmental Psychobiology, 18,* 327–340.
14. McGlone, J. (1980). Sex differences in human brain asymmetry: A critical survey. *Behavioral and Brain Sciences, 3,* 215–263.
15. McKeever, W. F. (1987). Cerebral organization and sex: Interesting but complex. In S. U. Philips, S. Steele, & C. Tanz (Eds.), *Language, Gender, and Sex in Comparative Perspective.* Cambridge, England: Cambridge University Press.
16. Parsons, J. E. (Ed.). (1980). *The Psychobiology of Sex Differences and Sex Roles.* Washington, DC: Hemisphere Publishing.

17. Ray, W. J., Newcombe, N., Semon, J., & Cole, P. M. (1981). Spatial abilities, sex differences and EEG functioning. *Neuropsychologia, 19*, 719–722.

18. Seward, J. P., & Seward, G. H. (1980). *Sex Differences: Mental and Temperamental*. Lexington, MA: Lexington Books.

19. Shucard, D. W., Shucard, J. L., & Thomas, D. G. (1987). Sex differences in the pattern of scalp-recorded electrophysiological activity in infancy: Possible implications for language development. In S. U. Philips, S. Steele, & C. Tanz (Eds.), *Language, Gender, and Sex in Comparative Perspective*. Cambridge, England: Cambridge University Press.

20. Springer, S. P., & Deutsch, G. (1981). *Left Brain, Right Brain*. New York: Freeman.

21. Susman, E. J., Inoff-Germain, G., Nottelmann, E. D., Loriaux, D. L., Cutler, G. B., & Chrousos, G. P. (1987). Hormones, emotional dispositions, and aggressive attributes in young adolescents. *Child Development, 58*, 1114–1134.

References 22–26 indicate that males exhibit more behavior problems and get into more trouble in school than females.

22. Center, D. B., & Wascom, A. M. (1987). Teacher perceptions of social behavior in behaviorally disordered and socially normal children and youth. *Behavior Disorders, 12* (3), 200–206.

23. Duke, D. L. (1978). Why don't girls misbehave more than boys in school? *Journal of Youth and Adolescence, 7* (2), 141–157.

24. Epstein, M. H., Cullinan, D., & Bursuck, W. D. (1985). Prevalence of behavior problems among learning disabled and nonhandicapped students. *Mental Retardation and Learning Disability Bulletin, 13*, 30–39.

25. Ludwig, G., & Cullinan, D. (1984). Behavior problems of gifted and nongifted elementary school girls and boys. *Gifted Child Quarterly, 28* (1), 37–39.

26. National Black Child Development Institute. (1990). *The Status of African American Children: Twentieth Anniversary Report*. Washington, DC: Author.

References 27–29 detail differences in teachers' tolerance for male and female behavior patterns.

27. Fagot, B. I. (1985). Beyond the reinforcement principle: Another step toward understanding sex roles. *Developmental Psychology, 21*, 1097–1104.

28. Marshall, J. (1983). Developing antisexist initiatives in education. *International Journal of Political Education, 6*, 113–137.

29. Wooldridge, P., & Richman, C. L. (1985). Teachers' choice of punishment as a function of a student's gender, age, race, and IQ level. *Journal of School Psychology, 23*, 19–29.

Teachers' use of different management techniques with the sexes is discussed in references 30–31.

30. Eccles, J. S., & Blumenfeld, P. (1985). Classroom experiences and student gender: Are there differences and do they matter? In L. C. Wilkinson & C. B. Marrett (Eds.), *Gender Influences in Classroom Interaction*. New York: Academic Press.

31. Fagot, B. I., & Hagan, R. (1985). Aggression in toddlers: Responses to the assertive acts of boys and girls. *Sex Roles, 12* (3), 341–351.

The role of male vulnerability to neurological damage in causing gender differences in special education enrollment is discussed in references 32–43.

32. Abramowicz, H. K., & Richardson, S. A. (1975). Epidemiology of severe mental retardation in children: Community studies. *American Journal of Mental Deficiency, 80*, 18–39.

33. Burgio, G. R., Fraccaro, M., Tiepolo, D. L., & Wolf, U. (1981). *Trisomy 21*. New York: Springer-Verlag.

34. Gualtierii, C. T., & Hicks, R. E. (1985). An immunoreactive theory of selective male affliction. *Behavioral and Brain Sciences, 8*, 427–441.

35. Lord, C., Schopler, E., & Revecki, D. (1982). Sex differences in autism. *Journal of Autism and Developmental Disabilities, 12*, 317–330.

36. McMilen, M. M. (1979). Differential mortality by sex in fetal and neonatal deaths. *Science, 204*, 89–91.

37. Nichols, P. L., & Chen, T. C. (1981). *Minimal Brain Dysfunction: A Prospective Study*. Hillsdale, NJ: Erlbaum.

38. Novitski, E. (1977). *Human Genetics*. New York: Macmillan.

39. Rossi, A. O. (1972). Genetics of learning disabilities. *Journal of Learning Disabilities, 5*, 489–496.

40. Taylor, D. C., & Ounsted, C. (1972). The nature of gender differences explored through ontogenetic analyses of sex ratios in disease. In C. Ounsted & D. C. Taylor (Eds.), *Gender Differences: Their Ontogeny and Significance*. New York: Churchill Livingstone.

41. Toivanen, P., & Hirvonen, T. (1970). Placental weight in human feotomaternal incompatibility. *Clinical and Experimental Immunology, 7,* 533–539.

42. Tsai, L. Y., & Beisler, J. M. (1983). The development of sex differences in infantile autism. *British Journal of Psychiatry, 142,* 373–378.

43. Wing, L. (1981). Sex ratios in early childhood autism and related conditions. *Psychiatry Research, 5,* 129–137.

References 44–47 document that parents reinforce children for behaving in gender-stereotypical ways.

44. Block, J. H. (1984). *Sex Role Identity and Ego Development.* San Francisco: Jossey-Bass.

45. Fagot, B. I. (1978). The influence of sex of child on parental reactions to toddler children. *Child Development, 49,* 459–465.

46. Lewis, M., & Weintraub, M. (1979). Origins of early sex-role development. *Sex Roles, 5* (2), 135–153.

47. O'Brien, M., & Huston, A. C. (1985). Development of sex-typed play behavior in toddlers. *Developmental Psychology, 21* (5), 866–871.

References 48–51 deal with the reinforcement of gender-appropriate behavior by toddlers and preschoolers.

48. Fagot, B. I. (1977). Consequences of moderate cross-gender behavior in preschool children. *Child Development, 48,* 902–907.

49. Fagot, B. I. (1985). Beyond the reinforcement principle: Another step toward understanding sex roles. *Developmental Psychology, 21,* 1097–1104.

50. Lamb, M. E., Easterbrook, A. M., & Holden, G. W. (1980). Reinforcement and punishment among preschoolers: Characteristics, effects, and correlates. *Child Development, 51,* 1230–1236.

51. Lamb, M. E., & Roopnarine, J. L. (1979). Peer influences on sex-role development in preschoolers. *Child Development, 50,* 1219–1222.

References 52–59 discuss the role of cognitive awareness and modeling in children's sex-role acquisition.

52. Andersen, E. S. (1978). *Learning to Speak with Style: A Study of the Socio-Linguistic Skills of Children.* Unpublished doctoral dissertation, Stanford University, Stanford, CA.

53. Bem, S. L. (1983). Gender schema theory and its implication for child development: Raising gender aschematic children in a gender schematic society. *Signs, 8,* 598–616.

54. Bem, S. L. (1985). Androgyny and gender schema theory: A conceptual and empirical integration. In T. B. Sonderegger (Ed.), *Nebraska Symposium on Motivation: Psychology of Gender.* Lincoln: University of Nebraska.

55. Busey, K., & Bandura, A. (1984). Influence of gender constancy and social power on sex-linked modeling. *Journal of Personality and Social Psychology, 47* (6), 1292–1302.

56. Eagly, A. H. (1987). *Sex Differences in Social Behavior: A Social-Role Interpretation.* Hillsdale, NJ: Erlbaum.

57. Fagot, B. I. (1985). Changes in thinking about early sex-role development. *Developmental Review, 5,* 83–98.

58. Hargreaves, D. J., & Colley, A. M. (1987). *The Psychology of Sex Roles.* New York: Hemisphere Publishing.

59. Weintraub, M., Clemens, L. P., Sockloff, A., Ethridge, T., Gracely, E., & Myers, B. (1984). The development of sex role stereotypes in the third year: Relationships to gender labeling, gender identity, sex-typed toy preference, and family characteristics. *Child Development, 55,* 1493–1503.

The role of parents' behaviors, expectations, and beliefs in fostering gender differences in students' confidence about their academic abilities and in their choice of academic courses is discussed in references 60–70.

60. Baker, D. P., & Entwisle, D. R. (1987). The influence of mothers on the academic expectations of young children: A longitudinal study of how gender differences arise. *Social Forces, 65,* 670–694.

61. Bempechat, J. (1990). *The Role of Parent Involvement in Children's Academic Achievement: A Review of the Literature Trends and Issues No. 14.* New York: ERIC Clearinghouse on Urban Education, Institute for Urban and Minority Education.

62. Eccles, J., Adler, T. F., & Kaczala, C. M. (1982). Socialization of achievement attitudes and beliefs: Parental influences. *Child Development, 53,* 310–321.

63. Eccles, J., & Jacobs, J. E. (1986). Social forces shape math attitudes and performance. *Signs, 11,* 367–389.

64. Eccles, J., Kaczala, C. M., & Meese, J. L. (1982). Socialization of achievement attitudes and beliefs: Classroom influences. *Child Development, 53,* 322–339.

65. Entwisle, D. R., & Baker, D. P. (1983). Gender and young children's expectations for performance in arithmetic. *Developmental Psychology, 19* (2), 200–209.

66. Entwisle, D. R., & Hayduk, L. A. (1982). *Early Schooling*. Baltimore: Johns Hopkins University Press.

67. Jacobs, J., & Eccles, J. (1985). Gender differences in math ability: The impact of media reports on parents. *Educational Researcher, 14* (3), 20–25.

68. Parsons, J. E., Adler, T. F., & Kaczala, C. M. (1982). Socialization of achievement attitudes and beliefs: Parental influences. *Child Development, 53,* 310–321.

69. Parsons, J. E., Kaczala, C. M., & Meese, J. L. (1982) Socialization of achievement attitudes and beliefs: Classroom influences. *Child Development, 53,* 322–339.

70. Yee, D. K., & Eccles, J. S. (1988). Parent perceptions and attributions for children's math achievement. *Sex Roles, 19* (5/6), 317–333.

References 71–77 discuss the role of schools in the reproduction of inequities in society.

71. Connell, R. W. (1989). Curriculum politics, hegemony, and strategies of social change. In H. A. Giroux & R. I. Simon (Eds.), *Popular Culture, Schooling and Everyday Life*. Granby, MA: Bergin & Garvey.

72. Grant, C. A., & Sleeter, C. E. (1988). Race, class, and gender and abandoned dreams. *Teachers College Record, 90* (1), 19–40.

73. Kelly, G., & Nihlen, A. (1982). Schooling and the reproduction of patriarchy: Unequal workloads, unequal rewards. In M. Apple (Ed.), *Culture and Economic Reproduction in Education*. Boston: Routledge Kegan Paul.

74. Valli, L. (1986). *Becoming Clerical Workers*. Boston: Routledge Kegan Paul.

75. Weiler, K. (1988). *Women Teaching for Change: Gender, Class & Power*. Granby, MA: Bergin & Garvey.

76. Witt, S. H. (1979). Native women in the world of work. In T. Constantino (Ed.), *Women of Color Forum: A Collection of Readings*. ERIC ED 191 975.

77. Wolpe, A. (1981). The official ideology of education for girls. In M. McDonald, R. Dale, G. Esland, & R. Fergusson (Eds.), *Politics, Patriarchy and Practice*. New York: Falmer Press.

References 78–87 deal with student resistance to gender bias in school.

78. Anyon, J. (1984). Intersections of gender and class: Accommodation and resistance by working class and affluent females to contradictory sex-role ideologies. *Journal of Education, 166* (1), 25–48.

79. Arnot, M. (1982). Male hegemony, social class and women's education. *Journal of Education, 164* (1), 64–89.

80. Connell, R. W., Dowsett, G. W., Kessler, S., & Aschenden, D. J. (1982). *Making the Difference*. Boston: Allen & Unwin.

81. Fuller, M. (1980). Black girls in a London comprehensive school. In R. Deem (Ed.), *Schooling for Women's Work*. Boston: Routledge and Kegan Paul.

82. Gaskell, J. (1985). Course enrollment in high school: The perspective of working class females. *Sociology of Education, 58* (1), 48–59.

83. Kessler, S., Ashenden, R., Connell, R., & Dowsett, G. (1985). Gender relations in secondary schooling. *Sociology of Education, 58* (1), 34–48.

84. Ogbu, J. U. (1987). Variability in minority school performance: A problem in search of an explanation. *Anthropology & Education Quarterly, 18* (4), 312–334.

85. Simon, R. (1983). But who will let you do it? Counter-hegemonic possibilities for work education. *Journal of Education, 165* (3), 235–256.

86. Thomas, C. (1980). *Girls and Counter-School Culture*. Melbourne Working Papers, Melbourne, Australia.

87. Willis, P. (1981). Cultural production is different from cultural reproduction is different from social reproduction is different from production. *Interchange, 12* (2–3), 48–68.

Administrative imbalance is the focus of references 88–91.

88. Fennema, E., & Ayer, M. J. (Eds.). (1984). *Women and Education: Equity or Equality?* Berkeley, CA: McCutchan.

89. Frazier, N., & Sadker, M. (1973). *Sexism in School and Society*. New York: Harper & Row.

90. Lockheed, M. E. (1984). Sex segregation and male preeminence in elementary classrooms. In E. Fennema & M. J. Ayer (Eds.), *Women and Education: Equity or Equality?* Berkeley, CA: McCutchan.

91. SUNY study finds school management still white male dominated. (1990). *Black Issues in Higher Education, 7* (5), 23.

References 92–103 provide evidence that gender bias in curriculum materials has been reduced but not eliminated.

92. Cooper, P. (1989). Children's literature: The extent of sexism. In C. Lont & S. Friedly (Eds.), *Beyond Boundaries: Sex and Gender Diversity in Education*. Fairfax, VA: George Mason University Press.

93. Cooper, P. (1987). Sex role stereotypes of stepparents in children's literature. In L. Stewart & S. Ting-Toomey (Eds.), *Communication, Gender and Sex Roles in Diverse Interaction Contexts*. Norwood, NJ: Ablex.

94. Dougherty, W., & Engel, R. (1987). An 80s look for sex equality in Caldecott winners and honors books. *Reading Teacher, 40*, 394–398.

95. Heinz, K. (1987). An examination of sex occupational role presentations of female characters in children's picture books. *Women's Studies in Communication, 11*, 67–78.

96. Hitchcock, M. E., & Tompkins, G. E. (1987). Basis readers: Are they still sexist? *Reading Teacher, 41* (3), 288–292.

97. Nilsen, A. P. (1987). Three decades of sexism in school science materials. *School Library Journal, 34* (1), 117–122.

98. Purcell, P., & Stewart, I. (1990). Dick and Jane 1989. *Sex Roles, 22* (3/4), 177–185.

99. Tetreault, M. K. T. (1985). Phases of thinking about women in history: A report card on the textbook. *Women's Studies Quarterly, 13* (3/4), 35–47.

100. Timm, J. (1988). *Cultural Bias in Children's Storybooks: Implications for Education*. Paper presented at the annual meeting of the American Educational Research Association, New Orleans.

101. Vaughn-Roberson, C., Thompkins, M., Hitchcock, M. E., & Oldham, M. (1989). Sexism in basal readers: An analysis of male main characters. *Journal of Research in Childhood Education, 4*, 62–68.

102. White, H. (1986). Damsels in distress: Dependency themes in fiction for children and adolescents. *Adolescence, 21*, 251–256.

103. Woodill, G. (1987). Critical issues in the use of microcomputers by young children. *International Journal of Early Childhood, 19* (1), 50–57.

References 104–121 deal with gender differences in teacher attention.

104. Becker, J. (1981). Differential treatment of males and females in mathematics classes. *Journal of Research in Mathematics Education, 12*, 40–53.

105. Benz, C. R., Pfeiffer, I., & Newman, I. (1981). Sex role expectations of classroom teacher, grade 1–12. *American Educational Research Journal, 18* (3), 289–302.

106. Boudreau, F. A. (1986). Education. In F. A. Boudreau, R. S. Sennott, & M. Wilson (Eds.), *Sex Roles and Social Patterns*. New York: Praeger.

107. Brophy, J. E. (1985). Interaction of male and female students with male and female teachers. In L. C. Wilkinson & C. B. Marrett (Eds.), *Gender Influences in Classroom Interaction*. New York: Academic Press.

108. Brophy, J. (1986). Teaching and learning mathematics: Where research should be going. *Journal for Research in Mathematics, 17*, 323–346.

109. Eccles, J. S., & Blumenfeld, P. (1985). Classroom experiences and student gender: Are there differences and do they matter? In L. C. Wilkinson & C. B. Marrett (Eds.), *Gender Influences in Classroom Interaction*. New York: Academic Press.

110. Fennema, E., & Peterson, P. L. (1985). Autonomous learning behavior: A possible explanation of gender-related differences in mathematics. In L. C. Wilkinson & C. B. Marret (Eds.), *Gender Influences in Classroom Interaction*. New York: Academic Press.

111. Fennema, E., & Peterson, P. L. (1986). Teacher student interactions and sex-related differences in learning mathematics. *Teaching and Teacher Education, 2* (1), 19–42.

112. Fennema, E., Reyes, L., Perl, T., Konsin, M., & Drakenberg, M.(1980). *Cognitive and Affective Influences on the Development of Sex-Related Difference in Mathematics*. Symposium presented at the annual meeting of the American Educational Research Association, Boston.

113. Gore, D. A., & Roumagoux, D. V. (1983). Wait-time as a variable in sex-related differences during fourth-grade mathematics instruction. *Journal of Educational Research, 76* (5), 273–275.

114. Leinhardt, G., Seewald, A. L., & Engel, M. (1979). Learning what's taught: Sex differences in instruction. *Journal of Educational Psychology, 71* (3), 432–439.

115. Lockheed, M. (1982). *Sex Equity in Classroom Interaction Research: An Analysis of Behavior Chains*. Paper presented at the annual meeting of the American Educational Research Association, New York City.

116. Minuchin, P. P., & Shapiro, E. K. (1983). The school as a context for social development. In P. Mussen & E. M. Hetherington (Eds.), *Handbook of Child Psychology* (Vol. 4, 4th ed.). New York: Wiley.

117. Morrison, T. L. (1979). Classroom structure, work involvement and social climate in elementary school classrooms. *Journal of Educational Psychology, 71,* 471–477.

118. Morse, L. W., & Handley, H. M. (1985). Listening to adolescents: Gender differences in science classroom interaction. In L. C. Wilkinson & C. B. Marrett (Eds.), *Gender Influences in Classroom Interaction.* New York: Academic Press.

119. Pflaum, S., Pascarella, E., Boswick, M., & Auer, C. (1980). The influence of pupil behaviors and pupil status factors on teacher behaviors during oral reading lessons. *Journal of Educational Research, 74,* 99–105.

120. Putnam, S., & Self, P. A. (1988). *Social Play in Toddlers: Teacher Intrusions.* ERIC ED 319 529.

121. Stake, J., & Katz, J. (1982). Teacher-pupil relationships in the elementary school classroom: Teacher gender and student gender difference. *American Educational Research Journal, 19,* 465–471.

References 122–127 deal with gender differences in teacher feedback.

122. Dweck, C. S., Davidson, W., Nelson, S., & Enna, B. (1978). Sex differences in learned helplessness: The contingencies of evaluation feedback in the classroom, an experimental analysis. *Developmental Psychology, 14* (3), 208–276.

123. Frey, K. S. (1979). *Differential Teaching Methods Used with Girls and Boys of Moderate and High Achievement Levels.* Paper presented at the annual meeting of the American Educational Research Association, Minneapolis.

124. Hodes, C. L. (1985). Relative effectiveness of corrective and noncorrective feedback in computer assisted instruction on learning and achievement. *Journal of Educational Technology Systems, 13* (4), 249–254.

125. Meece, J. L. (1987). The influence of school experiences on the development of gender schemata. *New Directions for Child Development, 38,* 57–73.

126. Parsons, J. E., Kaczala, C. M., & Meese, J. L. (1982). Socialization of achievement attitudes and beliefs: Classroom influences. *Child Development, 53,* 322–339.

127. Simpson, A. W., & Erickson, M. T. (1983). Teachers' verbal and nonverbal communication patterns as a function of teacher race, student gender, and student race. *American Educational Research Journal, 20,* 183–198.

Gender differences in academic expectations are discussed in references 128–134.

128. Bem, S. (1977). On the utility of alternative procedures for assessing psychological androgyny. *Journal of Consulting and Clinical Psychology, 45,* 196–205.

129. Bernard, M. (1979). Does sex role behavior influence the way teachers evaluate students? *Journal of Educational Psychology, 71,* 553–562.

130. Casserly, P. L. (1975). *An Assessment of Factors Affecting Female Participation in Advanced Placement Programs in Mathematics, Chemistry, and Physics.* Washington, DC: National Science Foundation.

131. Dusek, J. B., & Joseph, G. (1983). The bases of teacher expectancies: A meta-analysis. *Journal of Educational Psychology, 75,* 327–346.

132. Hallinan, M. T., & Sorensen, A. B. (1987). Ability grouping and sex differences in mathematics achievement. *Sociology of Education, 60* (2), 63–72.

133. Luchins, E. (1976). *Women Mathematicians: A Contemporary Appraisal.* Paper presented at the annual meeting of the American Association for the Advancement of Science, Boston.

134. Phillips, R. (1980). Teachers' reported expectations of children's sex-roles and evaluation of sexist teaching. *Dissertation Abstracts International, 41,* 995–996-A.

Ethnic differences in the ways teachers perceive and relate to students is the focus of references 135–138.

135. Grant, L. (1984). Black females' "place" in desegregated classrooms. *Sociology of Education, 57,* 98–110.

136. Grant, L. (1985). *Uneasy Alliances: Black Males, Teachers, and Peers in Desegregated Classrooms.* Paper presented at the annual meeting of the American Educational Research Association, Chicago.

137. Pollard, D. (1979). Patterns of coping in Black school children. In A. W. Boykin, A. Franklin, & F. Yates (Eds.), *Research Directions of Black Psychologists.* New York: Russell Sage.

138. Washington, V. (1982). Racial differences in teacher perception of first and fourth grade pupils on selected characteristics. *Journal of Negro Education, 51,* 60–72.

References 139–142 deal with the adverse results of gender differences in teacher attention, feedback, and expectations.

139. Brush, L. R. (1980). *Encouraging Girls in Mathematics: The Problems and the Solutions.* Boston: Abt Associates.

140. Eccles, J., Adler, T. F., Futterman, R., Goff, S. B., Kaczala, C. M., Meece, J., & Midgley, C. (1983). Expectations, values, and academic behavior. In J. T. Spence (Ed.), *Perspectives on Achievement and Achievement Motivation.* San Francisco: Freeman.

141. Fox, L., Brody, L. A., & Tobin, D. (Eds.). (1980). *Women and the Mathematical Mystique.* Baltimore: Johns Hopkins University Press.

142. Fennema, E., & Sherman, J. (1977). Sex-related differences in mathematics achievement, spatial visualization, and affective factors. *American Educational Research Journal, 14,* 51–71.

References 143–149 describe how teachers and other school personnel foster sex differences in the courses and activities students choose.

143. Farris, C. (1982). *Sex Fair Knowledge, Attitudes, and Behaviors of Vocational Educators: A Research Report.* Utica, NY: SUNY College of Technology.

144. Hopkins-Best, M. (1987). The effects of students' sex and disability on counselors' agreement with postsecondary career goals. *School Counselor, 35* (1), 28–33.

145. Parmley, J. D., Welton, R. F., & Bender, M. (1980). *Opinions of Agricultural Teachers, School Administrators, Students and Parents Concerning Females as Agriculture Students, Teachers and Workers in Agriculture.* ERIC ED 209 488.

146. Roberts, E. J. (Ed.). (1980). *Childhood Sexual Learning: The Unwritten Curriculum.* Cambridge, MA: Ballinger.

147. Schaffer, K. F. (1981). *Sex Roles and Human Behavior.* Cambridge, MA: Winthrop.

148. Stockard, J., Schmuck, P. A., Kemper, K., Williams, P., Edson, S. K., & Smith, M. A. (1980). *Sex Equity in Education.* New York: Academic Press.

149. Tavris, C., & Wade, C. (1984). *The Longest War: Sex Differences in Perspective* (2nd ed.). New York: Harcourt Brace Jovanovich.

Gender segregation and separation is the focus of references 150–151.

150. Guttenberg, M., & Gray, H. (1977). Teachers as mediators of sex-role standards. In A. Sargent (Ed.), *Beyond Sex Roles.* St. Paul, MN: West.

151. Lockheed, M. E., & Harris A. M. (1984). Cross-sex collaborative learning in elementary classrooms. *American Educational Research Journal, 21* (2), 275–294.

References 152–156 deal with the fact that teachers encourage different behaviors in male and female students.

152. Caplan, P. J. (1977). Sex, age, behavior, and school subject as determinants of report of learning problems. *Journal of Learning Disabilities, 10,* 60–62.

153. Fagot, B. I. (1977). Consequences of moderate cross-gender behavior in preschool children. *Child Development, 48,* 902–907.

154. Huffine, S., Silvern, S. B., & Brooks, D. M. (1979). Teacher responses to contextually specific sex type behaviors in kindergarten children. *Educational Research Quarterly, 4* (2), 29–35.

155. Lamb, M. E., Easterbrook, A. M., & Holden, G. W. (1980). Reinforcement and punishment among preschoolers: Characteristics, effects, and correlates. *Child Development, 51,* 1230–1236.

156. Schlosser, L., & Algozzine, B. (1980). Sex behavior and teacher expectancies. *Journal of Experimental Education, 48,* 231–236.

References 157–160 describe how teachers use different classroom management techniques with various ethnic and socioeconomic groups.

157. Glackman, T., Martin, R., Hyman, I., McDowell, E., Berv, V., & Spino, P. (1980). *Corporal Punishment in the Schools As It Relates to Race, Sex, Grade Level and Suspensions.* Philadelphia: Temple University, National Center for the Study of Corporal Punishment in the Schools.

158. Richardson, R. C., & Evans, E. T. (1991). *Empowering Teachers to Eliminate Corporal Punishment in the Schools.* Paper presented at the annual conference of the National Black Child Developmental Institute, Washington, DC.

159. Stevens, L. B. (1983). *Suspension and Corporal Punishment of Students in the Cleveland Public Schools, 1981–1982.* Cleveland, OH: Office of School Monitoring and Community Relations.

160. Woolridge, P., & Richman, C. (1985). Teachers' choice of punishment as a function of a student's gender, age, race and I.Q. level. *Journal of School Psychology, 23,* 19–29.

8

GENDER-APPROPRIATE SPECIAL EDUCATION

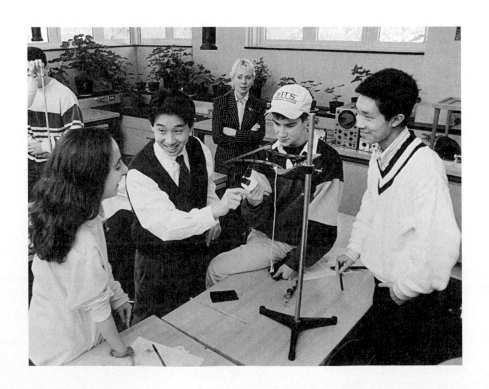

The goal of achieving equivalent outcomes in mathe-
matics education for males and females may require
that teachers actually should treat boys and girls
somewhat differently. (34, p. 155)

Chapters 1 and 3 explored a number of gender inequities such as misrepresentation in special education programs, gender disparities in educational outcomes, gender bias in the treatment of students, and gender differences in the roles for which schools prepare students. This chapter examines the advantages and disadvantages of four alternative ways of dealing with these inequities. Chapters 9 through 11 describe techniques special educators can use to implement these four approaches when they select assessment, instructional, and classroom management techniques. The chapter does not take a position about which of these four alternatives is the most appropriate in relation to any specific gender difference. Rather, it presents the arguments for and against each approach and includes exercises that will enhance your self-insight into your own views on gender issues. The chapter also describes the problems gay and lesbian students experience in and out of school, as well as what special educators can do to assist these students.

GENDER EQUITY IN SPECIAL EDUCATION: A CONTROVERSIAL ISSUE

What is gender equity and how can gender equity be achieved in school? Educators' opinions vary. Some educators equate equity with sameness. Their point of view is that gender equity is achieved when males and females participate in special education programs, courses of study, and extracurricular activities to the same degree; when their achievement is the same; when they are treated the same by their teachers; and when they are prepared for the same societal roles.

Other educators define equity in terms of fairness. Assuming that there are biologically or culturally based, educationally relevant differences between male and female students, they believe equity requires each gender to be treated in accordance with its biological makeups and cultural preferences. To them, educational equity is achieved when males and females are treated in accordance to their different needs in both regular and special education, when the genders have an opportunity to participate in whichever courses and activities they prefer and to achieve up to their different potentials, when they are placed in special educational in proportion to their different needs, and when they are prepared for different societal roles.

The way teachers define gender equity in school is extremely important because it influences how they perceive their students' behavior, the goals they set for them, and the way they relate to them. For example, some educators claim that there is gender misrepresentation in special education. They believe that many teachers focus their attention too exclusively on male-typical disruptive behavior and neglect students with problems that do not interfere with others. As a result, students who are anxious or depressed, who react poorly to challenging situations, who are overly dependent on others, and who have poor self-concepts do not receive the attention their problems require. These educators claim that since these are primarily female-typical behaviors, females are grossly underrepresented in special education programs for students with emotional and learning problems. Other educators believe that males require the special services provided by programs for students with developmental disabilities, behavior disorders, emotional disturbances, and learning disabilities more than females do because of innate physiological gender differences. These different beliefs have important implications for the ways in which special educators function on a day-to-day basis.

CONTROVERSIAL AND NONCONTROVERSIAL PRACTICES

Special educators may disagree about the broad issues involved in defining gender equity, but most would probably agree that certain current educational practices are unfair and should be corrected. For example, even though special educators have conflicts about the cause or causes of gender differences and different comfort levels with the status quo, most would probably agree that teachers should do the following:

- Decide whether to refer students to special education programs or accept students in special education programs without considering their gender.
- Select textbooks, readers, and biographies that include the contributions of both males and females.
- Pay equal attention to all students who volunteer answers or ask questions, regardless of their gender.
- Call on male and female students equally often.
- Provide the same kind and amount of help to all students.
- Praise female and male students equally for high achievement, creativity, and effort.
- Attribute the cause of students' academic problems accurately.
- Be equally attentive to the misbehavior of males and females.
- Avoid excessively harsh punishments with all students.
- Discourage dependent, helpless, and excessively conforming behavior in all students.

On the other hand, special educators probably disagree about whether teachers should do the following:

- Select textbooks and other reading materials that portray males and females fulfilling nontraditional roles.
- Permit males and females to choose to work and play in single-sex groups.
- Separate boys and girls for activities such as physical education and sex education.
- Assign students to single-sex groups during class to protect females from being dominated by males.
- Select male teachers for male students and female teachers for female students.
- Encourage students to conform to the same standards of behavior, regardless of their ethnic and socioeconomic backgrounds.
- Use similar classroom management procedures with males and females.
- Utilize the same instructional approaches and assessment procedures with all students, regardless of their ethnic and socioeconomic backgrounds.

POSITIONS ON GENDER DIFFERENCES

Excluding practices that most special educators would probably agree are unfair, the following are the four most common positions that have appeared in the literature regarding controversial gender issues such as the ones just listed.

1. *Educators should not treat males and females the same* (8, 9). Educators should prepare the genders to fulfill different societal roles because there are natural, physiological differences between the sexes. They should also accommodate their instructional practices to existing gender differences. The following quotation exemplifies the position that teachers should not treat males and females the same: "Boys who rise to the top in school often resemble girls in many important ways. . . . Scholastic honor and masculinity, in other words, too often seem incompatible. . . . The feminized school simply bores many boys: but it pulls some in one of two opposite directions. If the boy absorbs school values, he may become feminized himself. If he resists, he is pushed toward school failure and rebellion" (8, pp. 13, 33).

Do you agree that being a "real boy" is incompatible with being a good student? Do you agree that being a "real boy" in the sense that the term is usually used is a desirable personality characteristic? What is your opinion about the author's concern that schools feminize males?

2. *Educators should cease fostering gender-role differences that are unnatural, outdated, and harmful* (1–4, 6). Teachers should prepare students for the androgynous roles that are increasingly available to them in society. They should also encourage and prepare students to do what is necessary to transform the sexist society into a less sexist one. The following quote is an example of this position:

> In American society, men are supposed to be masculine, women are supposed to be feminine, and neither sex is supposed to be much like the other. If men are independent, tough, and assertive, women should be dependent, sweet, and retiring. A womanly woman may be tender and nurturant, but no manly man may be so. . . . I have come to believe that we need a new standard of psychological health for the sexes, one that removes the burden of stereotype and allows people to feel free to express the best traits of men and women. . . .
>
> Traditional sextyping necessarily restricts behavior. Because people learn, during their formative years, to suppress any behavior that might be considered undesirable or inappropriate for their sex, men are afraid to do "women's work" and women are afraid to enter a "man's world." Men are reluctant to be gentle, and women to be assertive. In contrast, androgynous people are not limited by labels. They are able to do whatever they want, both in their behavior and their feelings. (2, p. 32)

Do you agree that students should be encouraged to become androgynous? If you do, you probably favor discouraging students from accepting and acting out any gender-stereotypic roles, whatever they may be. "At the core of any radical pedagogy must be the aim of empowering people to recognize and work for a change in the social, political, and economic structure that constitutes the ultimate source of class-based power and domination" (4, p. 427). Do you agree that teachers should prepare students to change society in the ways suggested by the author of this statement?

3. *Educators should decide for themselves whether they want to prepare students to fulfill different gender roles or encourage students to fulfill similar roles* (5). The desirability or lack of desirability of gender roles is something for the individual professional or the group to decide.

> If we value the higher levels of aggressiveness in males, then schools should encourage aggression, competition, and assertion more in females. This might mean more emphasis on competitive athletics for girls, perhaps beginning in early elementary school, or perhaps even in the preschool years. In the academic classroom, it might mean encouraging reticent girls to speak up more forcefully in debates or to become more competitive about their success in mathematics courses. If, on the other hand, we value the low level of aggressiveness of females, we might seek to reduce the level of aggressiveness in boys, while simultaneously encouraging peaceful cooperation for them. . . . We might want to de-emphasize competitive sports in favor of cooperative sports or noncompetitive ones such as jogging. In the classroom, we would avoid competitively structured learning and work toward cooperatively structured learning. . . . Which of these alternatives is chosen, of course, is a matter of values. (5, pp. 64–65)

Do you agree that gender roles are inherently neither desirable nor undesirable, but depend on the values of different individuals and societies? If so, does that mean that societies have the right to establish different expectations for their male and female members? Does it also follow that different ethnic and socioeconomic groups have the right to expect the schools to respect their freedom to bring up their children to fulfill the gender roles they believe most appropriate? Or should the greater society determine the gender roles for all the subgroups living within its boundaries?

4. *Educators should empower students to decide for themselves whether to conform to any particular gender role or to be androgynous* (7). "To force everyone into the new mold may violate the individual as much as to force them into the older stereotypes. . . . Freedom to choose according to individual need would seem to be the preferred way of dealing with the complex problem of man/woman roles" (7, p. 202). Should teachers not involve themselves in shaping their students' attitudes about gender roles?

LEGAL REQUIREMENTS

Title IX of the Education Amendments Act was designed to correct the biased treatment received by males and females in school. Some of the provisions of Title IX that protect students from gender bias also restrict the rights of educators to decide for themselves how to respond to certain gender issues. The provisions of Title IX are less open to interpretation than those of Public Law (PL) 94-142.

Title IX requires schools to provide equal educational opportunities to all students, regardless of gender. As it did in the 1970s and 1980s, Title IX serves as the main legal basis for efforts to eliminate gender-discriminatory educational practices. Its requirements include the following:

- Students may not be denied admission to schools or subjected to discriminatory admissions practices on the basis of gender.
- Once admitted, students may not be excluded from participation in, be denied the benefits of, or subjected to discrimination while participating in any academic, extracurricular, research, occupational training, or other educational program or activity.
- All courses and activities, except human sexuality courses, must be open to all students, regardless of their gender. If offered, human sexuality courses must be available to all students, but they can be taught separately to males and females.
- Standards for student participation in physical education activities and ability groupings within these activities must be objective and applied equally to all students, regardless of gender. Separate athletic teams may be provided for males and females for contact sports or for other sports when the separation is justified by differences in skills. However, if a school has a contact sport for males only, a noncontact alternative team sport for females must be provided.
- Dress codes must be applied equally to males and females.

- Graduation requirements must be the same for both genders.
- Textbooks and other instructional materials are exempted from Title IX regulations due to potential conflicts with freedom of speech rights guaranteed by the First Amendment and other legislation.

CRITICAL INCIDENTS

This self-quiz is designed to provide you with some insight into the approaches you may use to resolve gender issues. First, describe how you think the teacher in the following examples should handle each of the incidents. Then, put yourself in the teacher's place. Disregard the description of the teacher's point of view. Instead, imagine what your viewpoint would be and how you would deal with the problem. If you prefer a number of different approaches to the incidents, try to determine the factors that led you to select the particular approaches you would use in each critical incident.

1. The father of a Hispanic American preschool student with learning disabilities comes to school irate because his son told him that the teacher encouraged him to play in the housekeeping/doll house area. He tells the teacher he does not want his son to play "girls' games" or with "girl things." The teacher believes that doll and housekeeping play are important for all children because they foster caring and nurturing qualities in children and androgynous gender roles.
2. A group of second-grade boys does not want some of the girls to join in their game on the schoolyard. The teacher believes students should learn to get along with both genders. The teacher also wants to encourage female students to participate in traditionally male activities and vice versa.
3. A fourth-grade student suggests that the class should have a spelling bee with the boys against the girls, like some other fifth-grade teachers do in their classes. The teacher, who feels that the students are already too competitive, wants them to learn to be more cooooperative. In addition, the teacher believes in bringing the genders together rather than indentifying them as competing groups.
4. One of a special educator's best students, an eighth-grade Hispanic American female in a program for gifted and talented youth, informs the teacher that she is not going to continue in the program in high school because she is not planning to go to college. When the teacher asks why, the student replies that in her family and culture, college is for boys. She says her plans are to finish high school, find a job for a while, get married, have four or five children, and stay home. The teacher believes that females should be encouraged to go on to college so they can have the career and other opportunities a college degree provides.

SELF-
QUIZ   **GENDER DIFFERENCES**

The following incident was reported by a school principal:

> Allen attended a parochial school where the playgrounds were segregated by gender. In one playground the girls skipped and jumped rope, in the other, the boys played football. Allen often stood on the sidelines and chatted with several other non-athletic boys. Allen's teacher was concerned and arranged privately with several of the male athletes to include Allen and his friends in the daily football game. The teacher warned that if they failed to do so, all of the boys in the class would be punished. (33, p. 208)

How do you feel about the gender separation that existed on the playgrounds? What is your opinion about the way the teacher responded to Allen and his friends' behavior? What might have been the teacher's reason for responding in that manner? How would you have responded?

SEXUAL ORIENTATION

Although adolescents have many problems around their emerging sexual drives and sexual orientation, people disagree about whether these topics are suitable for discussion in school. Many educators feel it is. However, in general, sexuality and especially sexual orientation is a forbidden subject in many schools, and many individuals and community groups demand that it remain so. For example, only 1 out of 28 school district boards in the New York City public school system voted to include the approved elementary school curriculum that deals with homosexual orientations in their schools (10).

Problems

Many heterosexual adolescents are concerned about their sexual orientation because of one or two homosexual experiences or fantasies. Although research indicates that there are no innate reasons why lesbian, gay, and bisexual students should have more problems than other students, many of them have a very difficult adolescence, primarily due to society's homophobic attitudes (11, 12, 14, 17, 19, 21, 24, 25, 28–30, 32). They experience a great deal of discrimination and prejudice, both in and out of school, and they also have a great deal of difficulty adjusting to their sexual orientation.

Because gay and lesbian students are brought up in a homophobic society and have little access to information that portrays lesbians and gays in a positive way, many of them suffer from homophobia and believe they are sick, evil, inferior, and disgusting. These ideas can lead to emotional problems such as depression, shame, and guilt, low self-esteem, and self-hatred, or at least ambivalence toward their sexual orientation. In turn, their emotional problems can cause them to drop out of school, abuse substances, and commit suicide. Some homosexual students attempt, usually unsuccessfully, to change their sexual orientation. Most students hide their homosexuality, thereby living in fear that they will be discovered. Kissen described their plight in the following manner:

> If, like most gay adolescents, they try to hide their identity, they live in constant fear that someone will discover they are gay. Even if they are successful at concealment, they must live every day as a lie, pretending to be someone they are not, and surrounded by homophobic jokes. . . . Anyone who spends time in a high school is surely aware that homophobia—fear and hatred of gay people—is the last "acceptable" form of bigotry among adolescents. Young people who would not dream of uttering (or would not dare to utter) a racial or religious epithet still unthinkingly toss around "queer" and "faggot"—probably the most often heard insults in any high school. (21, p. 2)

Sometimes the desire to be true to themselves, to feel good about themselves, and to stop hiding significant aspects of their selves from others in order to build a relationship based on honesty and trust leads gay, lesbian, and bisexual students to declare their sexual orientation to others (to "come out"). When they do, family conflicts and parental rejection can lead them to run away from home and to engage in prostitution. Loss of the friendship of and abuse by their heterosexual peers often follow. Ross-Reynolds offered this description of the problems of a gay and a lesbian student:

> Andy is a middle-class, White sixteen-year-old who ran away from his family home in Oregon after suffering years of abuse from his father after the man read his son's love letters from another boy. . . . Andy worked in a fast food restaurant in the evenings and attended high school during the day, resolving to complete high school and get his diploma, despite the obstacles caused by the relocation. Instead of a supportive environment at his new school, Andy found his peers hostile and harassing. Openly gay to his classmates and teachers, Andy was mocked during class time by other students, and received no support from teachers. After he was physically assaulted at the bus stop after school Andy felt pushed to the point of either quitting school or demanding action.
>
> Nina is a Black fifteen-year-old from Harlem. She had difficulty coping with the rejection she faced in her inner-city high school because she was up front about being a lesbian. . . . Name-calling, harassing notes, and verbal threats of violence, including rape, began to turn an upbeat, cheerful girl into a jumble of dysfunction and misery. As Nina faced the unpleasant task of steeling herself for two more years of such assaults, she found herself moving toward leaving school. (30, pp. 444–445)

Students who have difficulty accepting and adjusting to their gay or lesbian sexual orientation often develop emotional and behavior problems that can lead to their placement in special education programs. Anecdotal evidence also suggests that students with serious emotional problems often have difficulties around their sexual orientation (18). As a result, there is reason to believe that sexual orientation problems are more prevalent among teenagers in programs for students with emotional and behavioral problems than those in the general school population.

Causes

As already noted, students who are worried about their sexual orientation and gay, bisexual, and lesbian students need help and understanding, as do all students with serious problems. However, many educators believe that school is not the place to deal with or even discuss differences in sexual orientation. That may be why, in both regular and special education, sexual orientation problems and the presence of lesbian, bisexual, and gay students are denied or unnoticed at best. Dunham described the situation in the schools as follows: "While mental health professionals have worked to create positive and meaningful programs for the gay and lesbian population, educational systems have been considerably less eager to recognize and respond to the needs of this minority group. Public schools have continued to treat homosexuality as a forbidden subject" (15, p. 3).

Various causes of the current invisibility of gay and lesbian students in the schools have been identified. Some educators think it reflects society's justifiable desire to keep sexual orientation out of the school curriculum. Others, who are more critical of the schools, attribute the "problem" to homophobic attitudes among educators, their lack of the courage needed to advocate for the rights of gay and lesbian students, and the failure of school personnel to correct many educators' misinformation about the causes and "cures "of homosexuality.

A few school districts have developed projects, such as Project 10 in Los Angeles and the Harvey Milk School in New York City, that offer special services to homosexual and bisexual students (16, 30). Project 10 provides help to students who remain in their local schools. The Harvey Milk School offers an alternative school setting for those who wish to escape the difficulties inherent in being openly homosexual in a regular high school setting. Both types of programs have their share of critics who believe that homosexual students should be helped to convert to heterosexuals, but the Harvey Milk School has been criticized by supporters of gay and lesbian rights for capitulating to discrimination and homophobia, "ghettoizing" nonheterosexual students and removing them from the mainstream, and providing them with inferior educational opportunities. However, because these programs are rare, for the most part, lesbian, gay, and bisexual students have to rely on the assistance and understanding of individual teachers and counselors.

Solutions

Educators have offered the following suggestions for helping students who are concerned about their sexual orientation (13, 14, 22, 27, 30):

- Resist community pressure to avoid relating to the needs of students who are concerned about their sexual orientation.
- Refer students to community agencies and resources where they can obtain assistance.
- Protect students from harassment, criticize such incidents when they occur, and express disapproval of jokes about gays.
- Modify homophobic attitudes. Values are caught, not taught. Therefore, teach students to accept each other regardless of sexual orientation by modeling ac-

ceptance. Include issues and topics that affect gay and lesbian students in the curriculum (e.g., gay rights and contributions in social studies classes, gay life-styles in health and psychology courses, and gay and lesbian authors in English courses). Oppose censorship of texts and library material that demonstrate respect for lesbian and gay rights and life-styles. Dispel myths about people with nonheterosexual orientations. Have students experience the effects of discrimination and homophobic attitudes on students by role-playing. Advocate for students' rights.

- Include homosexual role models. "A healthy socialization process involves positive role models. Ideally, the socialization experiences for gay and lesbian adolescents will include learning from competent gay and lesbian adults. Observing how successful adults develop productive and ethical lifestyles, resolve problems of identity disclosure, obtain support, manage a career, and build relationships can be extremely valuable for teenagers" (17, p. 121).

It will not be easy for special educators to carry out these suggestions. Rofes pointed out the following:

> Because many educators believe that homosexuality is sick, sinful, or criminal, it is tremendously difficult for them to truly adopt an "objective" stance when addressing gay and lesbian issues in the classroom. . . . By allowing positive treatment of homosexuality in the classroom, teachers are vulnerable to witch-hunts by parents and school committees attempting to root out homosexual teachers. In certain parts of the nation, laws have been proposed and successfully passed that forbid positive discussion of homosexuality in public school classrooms. (31, p. 451)

In addition, since "gay and lesbian adolescents continue to be socialized to conceal their identities—educated to be invisible within the school community and the community at large" (15, p. 5)—they are often reluctant to disclosure their sexual orientation to others.

MYTHS ABOUT GAY AND LESBIAN STUDENTS

- *Effeminate boys and masculine females and those who like to cross-dress or play with toys that are thought of as in the domain of the opposite gender grow up to become gay and lesbian.* Research indicates that although some gay and lesbian students are more likely to exhibit cross-gender behaviors when they are children and adolescents, many do not. Also, many children who exhibit these behaviors do not grow up to be gay or lesbian.
- *One homosexual experience means that a person is and will be homosexual.* In reality, neither homosexual nor heterosexual experimentation is unusual. Human sexuality exists along a continuum from completely heterosexual to completely homosexual, with many people somewhere in between the extremes but close to the heterosexual end.
- *Discussing gay and lesbian issues encourages students to become homosexuals.* There is no evidence to support this notion.

- *Lesbian and gay teachers provide role models that encourage students to become lesbians and gays.* Homosexuality is not caught by observing lesbian and gay models.
- *Gay and lesbian adults sexually abuse children and recruit them to their life-styles.* Children and adolescents are much more likely to be abused by heterosexual adults.
- *Homosexuality is a sickness or a disorder.* The American Psychological Association and the American Psychiatric Association both state that homosexuality is not a disorder.
- *Homosexual behavior is rare in most animal species.* Research indicates that the opposite is true.
- *Because gays are incapable of establishing long-term relationships, they lead lonely, isolated lives.* Many gay and lesbian couples enjoy long-term relationships.
- *Homosexuality is a choice that one makes.* Research indicates that in our society, most homosexuals at first reject their homosexuality and resist thinking of themselves as homosexuals (20, 26, 31).

GAY AND LESBIAN SEXUAL ORIENTATIONS

SELF-QUIZ

1. "In a democratic country no citizen should be forced to live under the fear of homophobia. Fear is unhealthy for the individual and our democracy. . . . We need not endorse particular private sexual acts to protect the civil rights of all citizens" (23, p. 285). What do you think about this statement?
2. Should sexual orientation issues be included in the special education curriculum? Should special educators discuss their students' sexual orientation problems with students?
3. What should special educators do when community organizations and parents prefer or demand policies that conflict with their views of how to deal with sexual orientation issues and problems?

SUMMARY

Some of the ways some teachers treat the genders differently are clearly discriminatory or illegal, and some of the current differences in the schools outcomes for males and females are clearly undesirable. Except for these differences, educators disagree about their role vis-à-vis the current gender differences observed among many students. Educators' positions on gender issues include the following: teachers should stop fostering gender differences; they should treat each gender in accordance with their unique, natural, and desirable needs; each educator should decide how she or he wants to deal with gender differences; and they should empower students to make such decisions for themselves.

Although adolescents have many problems concerning their sexual orientation, it is a forbidden subject in many schools. Some educators believe that this is as it should be. Many others fault the schools for failing to help students with their problems. They suggest that educators should modify their own homophobic attitudes and those of their students; protect students from harassment; advocate for homosexual students' rights, include homosexual role models as well as issues and topics that affect gay and lesbian students in the curriculum; oppose censorship of texts and library material that demonstrate respect for lesbian and gay rights and life-styles; and dispel myths about people with nonheterosexual orientations. In today's environment, this will not be an easy things for regular educators or special educators to accomplish.

ACTIVITIES

1. Ask some of your colleagues or fellow students to respond to the critical incidents reported in this chapter. Do you notice any gender or ethnic differences in their responses?

2. How knowledgeable are your colleagues or fellow students about Title IX? Make up and administer a short quiz to them. Do you notice any gender differences in the extent of their knowledge?

3. Ask some gay or lesbian students if they have experienced any of the problems described in this chapter. Ask them if any of their teachers know about their sexual orientation, how they reacted to the information, and how they would have preferred them to react.

4. Administer a questionnaire based on the myths about homosexuality to some of your colleagues or fellow students. Do they believe the prevalant myths or do they know the facts? Do you notice any gender differences in their beliefs?

REFERENCES

References 1–9 discuss various positions on gender differences in school.

1. Becker, J. B. (1986). Influence again: An examination of reviews and studies of gender differences in social influence. In J. S. Hyde & M. C. Linn (Eds.), *The Psychology of Gender.* Baltimore: Johns Hopkins Press.

2. Bem, S. L. (1983). Traditional sex roles are too restrictive. In G. Leone & M. T. O'Neill (Eds.), *Male-Female Roles: Opposing Viewpoints.* St. Paul, MN: Greenhaven Press.

3. Block, J. H. (1984). *Sex Role Identity and Ego Development.* San Francisco: Jossey-Bass.

4. Giroux, H. A. (1981). Hegemony, resistance, and the paradox of educational reform. In H. A. Giroux, A. N. Penna, & W. F. Pinar (Eds.), *Curriculum & Instruction: Alternatives in Education.* Berkeley, CA: McCutchan.

5. Hyde, J. S. (1984). Gender differences in aggression. In J. S. Hyde & M. C. Linn (Eds.), *The Psychology of Gender: Advances through Meta-Analysis.* Baltimore: Johns Hopkins Press.

6. Jacklin, C. N. (1989). Female and male: Issues of gender. *American Psychologist, 44* (2), 127–133.

7. Schlafly, P. Personal communication.

8. Seward, J. P., & Seward, G. H. (1980). *Sex Differences: Mental and Temperamental.* Lexington, MA: Lexington Books.

9. Wardle, F. (1991). Are we shortchanging boys? *Child Care Information Exchange, 79,* 48–51.

Opposition to teaching about sexual orientations is documented in reference 10.

10. Columbia Broadcasting System. (1993, April 4). *Sixty Minutes: The Rainbow Curriculum.* New York: Author.

References 11–32 describe the problems of gay, lesbian, and bisexual students and their possible solutions.

11. Benvenuti, A. (1986). *Assessing and Addressing the Special Challenge of Gay and Lesbian Students for High School Counseling Programs.* ERIC ED 279 958.

12. Cates, J. A. (1987). Adolescent sexuality: Gay and lesbian issues. *Child Welfare, 66,* 353–364.

13. Chang, C. L. (1980). Adolescent homosexual behavior and the health educator. *Journal of School Health, 50* (9), 517–521.

14. Coleman, E., & Remafedi, G. (1989). Gay, lesbian, and bisexual adolescents: A critical challenge to counselors. *Journal of Counseling and Development, 68,* 36–40.

15. Dunham, K. L. (1989). *Educated to Be Invisible: The Gay and Lesbian Adolescent.* ERIC ED 336 676.

16. Friends of Project Inc. (1991). *Project 10 Handbook: Addressing Lesbian and Gay Issues in Our Schools. A Resource Directory for Teachers, Guidance Counselors, Parents and School-Based Adolescent Care Providers* (3rd ed.). ERIC ED 337 567.

17. Gonsiorek, J. C. (1988). Mental health issues of gay and lesbian adolescents. *Journal of Adolescent Health Care, 9,* 114–122.

18. Grossman, H. (1972). *Nine Rotten Lousy Kids.* New York: Holt, Rinehart and Winston.

19. Hetrick, E. S., & Martin, A. D. (1987). Developmental issues and their resolution for gay and lesbian adolescents. *Journal of Homosexuality, 14* (1/2), 25–42.

20. Hubbard, B. M. (1989). *Entering Adulthood: Living in Relationships.* Santa Cruz, CA: ETR Associates.

21. Kissen, R. M. (1991). *Listening to Gay and Lesbian Teenagers.* ERIC ED 344 220.

22. Krysiak, G. J. (1987). A very silent and gay minority. *School Counselor, 34* (4), 304–307.

23. Lenton, S. M. (1980). A student development response to the gay issue. In F. B. Newton & K. L. Ender (Eds.), *Student Development Practices.* Springfield, IL: Thomas

24. Martin, A. D. (1982). Learning to hide: The socialization of the gay adolescent. *Adolescent Psychiatry, 10,* 52–65.

25. Martin, A. D., & Hetrick, E. S. (1988). The stigmatization of the gay and lesbian adolescent. *Journal of Homosexuality, 15* (3), 163–183.

26. Public Broadcasting System. (1993) *Gay By Nature or Nurture.* New York: Author.

27. Powell, R. E. (1987). Homosexual behavior and the school counselor. *School Counselor, 34* (3), 202–208.

28. Remafedi, G. (1987). Adolescent homosexuality: Medical and psychological implications. *Pediatrics, 79* (3), 331–337.

29. Remafedi, G. (1987). Male homosexuality: The adolescent's perspective. *Pediatrics, 79* (3), 326–330.

30. Ross-Reynolds, G. (1982). Issues in counseling the "homosexual" adolescent. In J. Grimes (Ed.), *Psychological Approaches to Problems of Children and Adolescents.* Des Moines: Iowa State Department of Public Instruction, Division of Special Education.

31. Rofes, E. (1989). Opening up the classroom closet: Responding to the educational needs of gay and lesbian youth. *Harvard Educational Review, 59* (4), 444–453.

32. Schneider, M. S., & Tremble, G. (1985). Gay or straight: Working with the confused adolescent. *Journal of Social Work and Human Sexuality, 4,* 631–660.

The incident in the Self-Quiz entitled Gender Differences is taken from reference 33.

33. Hebert, T. P. (1991). Meeting the affective needs of bright boys through bibliography. *Roeper Review, 13* (4), 207–212.

The quotation at the beginning of the chapter is from reference 34.

34. Fennema, E., & Meyer, M. R. (1989). Gender, equity, and mathematics. In W. G. Secada (Ed.), *Equity in Education.* New York: Falmer Press.

9

ASSESSMENT
IN A DIVERSE SOCIETY

It should be borne in mind that an intelligence test administered in the English language to foreign-language-speaking children is not a fair test of the intelligence of such children. (1, p. 37)

This chapter describes how asessors' inattention to the cultural, linguistic, contextual, and gender differences among students can bias the results of assessments. It also examines various alternative solutions that may be employed by special educators and others when they assess students who may require special education services. Until recently, assessment procedures were not very effective when used with non-European American and poor students. The situation has improved somewhat in recent years; however, procedures still need improvement before educators can feel certain that the techniques in current use are unbiased and nondiscriminatory.

REFERRAL

Bias in the assessment process begins even before students are assessed for special education placement. Depending on the teachers involved, in comparison to females and European American middle-class students, teachers overrefer or underrefer poor, African American, Hispanic American, and Native American males to programs for students with learning disabilities, emotional/behavioral problems, speech and language disorders, and mild cognitive disabilities. Similarly, teachers underrefer poor, African American, Hispanic American, and Native American students to programs for gifted and talented students. (See Chapter 3.)

It is impossible to determine the actual percentage of students who are misplaced in or denied access to special education programs for which they are eligible. Figures would probably be greater for those categories where subjectivity can influence eligibility decisions than for programs for students with sensory impairment, physical disabilities, and severe cognitive disabilities for which eligibility criteria are much less subjective. Research indicates that programs for the gifted and talented enroll no more than 50 percent of the non-European American and poor students they would include if these students were represented proportionately (2–4). It has been estimated that approximately half of the students in classes for students with learning disabilities are actually students with other kinds of learning problems (6).

From the 1960s to the early 1980s, almost all of the students who were referred to programs for students with disabilities were assessed and most of them were deemed eligible and placed in a special education program (5, 8). In 1982, a national survey of directors of special education revealed that 92 percent of students referred to special education were evaluated, and 73 percent of those who were evaluated were found eligible (5). In 1992, some of the same researchers reported that in some cases, depending on the type of assessment procedures that are used, virtually all of the students referred are found to be eligible for special education (7). Results such as these support the following conclusion: "It is clear that the most important decision made in the entire assessment process is the decision by a regular classroom teacher to refer a student for assessment. Once a student is referred, there is a high probability that the student will be assessed and placed in special education" (8, p. 80).

Students without disabilities who are not referred for assessment cannot be misplaced in programs for students with disabilities; gifted and talented students who are not referred for assessment cannot be placed in the programs they deserve. Therefore, it is extremely important to reduce inappropriate and biased referrals to programs for students with disabilities and to increase the number of appropriate referrals to programs for gifted and talented students. This can be accomplished in part by increasing regular educators' knowledge of the contextual, cultural, gender, and socioeconomic factors that influence the way students behave and function in school and by making sure that appropriate prereferral procedures are followed before students who are thought to have disabilities are accepted for assessment. Chapters 5 and 6 discuss contextual and cultural factors. The information in Chapter 8 should help educators identify female students who may require special education intervention. The following section is designed to assist educators to identify potentially gifted and talented students.

African American, Hispanic American, Native American, limited-English-proficient, and poor students have always been underrepresented in programs for gifted and talented students. In the not too distant past, many educators did not expect them to be gifted and therefore they did not nominate them as potential candidates for such programs. Today, since theories of genetic inferiority and cultural deprivation are much less influential, educators tend to reject the notion that these students are unlikely to be gifted. Nevertheless, teachers tend to look for behaviors and personality characteristics to identify possibly gifted and talented students that do not always apply to African American, Hispanic American, Native American, and poor gifted and talented students.

Because cultures have different values, gifted and talented students demonstrate their superior abilities in different ways. For example, students brought up in competitive societies may demonstrate their abilities by excelling over others in certain endeavors, whereas gifted and talented students from cultures that value interpersonal relationships may demonstrate their abilities in their extraordinary leadership qualities and their skill at fostering good interpersonal relationships and cooperative behavior. Students from cultures that place high priority on academic achievement may excel on tests that measure such knowledge, but students who are brought up in cultures that value music, art, and the like may display their superior abilities in other ways. Rural gifted and talented students may receive low grades in academic areas but demonstrate their gifts and talents in nonacademic areas such as 4–H projects and auto and tractor repair because their environments foster their development in these areas.

Gifted and talented students from various cultural backgrounds may behave in different ways for other reasons as well. Some students may be reluctant to ask questions if they think to do so is a sign of disrespect for the teacher. Students who do not want to appear competitive with their peers may not demonstrate their advanced knowledge in class. Some gifted students who are bored with the work because they are not being challenged may hide their feelings, whereas others who are brought up to express their emotions and feelings may show their displeasure and get into trouble for behaving disrespectfully or disruptively. Poor and migrant gifted students may receive grades that do not reflect their abilities because they are seldom exposed to educational toys, books, and school-related materials at home and typically have parents who are undereducated. This is especially likely if these students do not have the time or opportunity to complete special projects or regular class assignments because they have to work or help out at home. For these reasons, teachers have to look for a variety of student characteristics that may indicate that their students are gifted and talented.

Limited-English-proficient gifted and talented students are especially difficult to identify. In English-submergence programs, limited English proficiency interferes with the students' ability to achieve at their potential and to demonstrate their superior skills. Therefore, it is essential to observe how these students function in situations in which their limited English proficiency does not impede their achievement.

The references at the end of the chapter describe behavior checklists and guidelines that are contextually, culturally, and linguistically appropriate for African American, Hispanic American, Native American, limited-English-proficient, and migrant students, depending on their type of acculturation to the European American life style, culture, and dialect. The references also include models that have proven to be effective for identifying gifted and talented students from non-European, rural, and/or low-income backgrounds.

Prereferral Process

Prereferral procedures attempt to eliminate inappropriate referrals in two ways—the preventive phase and the problem-solving phase. In the preventive phase, teachers determine whether the educational environment in which students function is one that fosters educational success for students in general; teachers then make any necessary modifications. This phase focuses on the needs that all students have in common and the characteristics that should be present in all learning environments. In the problem-solving phase, assistance designed to avoid referral for assessment is given to regular education teachers after they or other concerned persons identify students who have learning or behavior problems that may require special education services but before a formal referral to special education occurs. The following steps are usually included in such a process but not necessarily in the order indicated.

First, the teachers document the special efforts they have made to assist the students. This demonstrates that teachers actually require additional assistance to go beyond what they can do on their own. Teachers are then assisted by consultants or problem-solving teams, which often include special educators, to identify other possible reasons why students may not be succeeding. These reasons may include student-owned problems and needs, teacher-owned problems, or a a mismatch between teachers' instructional and classroom management styles and students' contextual, cultural, gender, and linguistic characteristics.

Next, the teachers and the consultants or problem-solving teams select contextually, culturally, linguistically, and gender-appropriate individualized instructional and classroom management techniques that regular classroom teachers can use to eliminate or ameliorate any problems that cannot be prevented by providing the best possible learning environments for students. In the case of Native American students, for example, these additional contextually, culturally, and linguistically appropriate interventions might include peer tutoring, cooperative learning, additional wait-time after calling on students, not singling out individual students by calling on them, eliminating competition among individuals in favor of competition between groups of students, replacing individual rewards with rewarding the whole group for the achievement of individual members, and providing students with additional time to complete assignments (13).

Chapters 5 through 8, 10, and 11 describe techniques educators can use to adapt their instruction and classroom management techniques to their students' needs before they refer students for possible placement. Descriptions of other prereferral intervention techniques and model prereferral programs are included in the references at the end of this chapter (9–25).

If these additional intervention approaches prove unsuccessful, the referral process proceeds. This makes good sense because if these classroom intervention techniques do not solve the problem, students are actually more likely to require special education services.

Prereferral intervention helps to avoid inappropriate student referrals to and placement in special education programs (11, 12, 21, 25). However, evidence that needs updating suggests that too often there is no prereferral intervention (16). Therefore, the following recommendation is as relevant today as it was in 1982: "It is the responsibility of teachers in the regular classroom to engage in multiple educational interventions and to note the effects of such interventions on a child experiencing academic failure before referring the child for special education assessment. It is the responsibility of school boards and administrators to ensure that needed alternative instructional resources are available" (18, p. 95).

LEGAL REQUIREMENTS

Students who have gone through the prereferral stage and a sessment must be assessed in an unbiased and nondiscrimina the 1970s, federal law, as embodied in Public Law (PL) 94-142, the U.S. Office of Civil Rights policy, and, with very few exceptions (31), various court cases have made it necessary for special education assessment procedures to be culturally and linguistically appropriate (26–32). Thus, PL 94-142 requires that states establish "procedures to assure that testing and evaluation materials and procedures utilized for the purpose of evaluation and placement of handicapped children will be selected and administered so as not to be racially or culturally discriminatory. Such materials or procedures shall be provided and administered in the child's native language or mode of communication unless it clearly is not feasible to do so."

The U.S. Office of Civil Rights Memorandum of May 25, 1975, requires that school districts must not assign minority-group students to classes for the mentally retarded on the basis of criteria that essentially measure or evaluate English language skills. *Diana* v. *the State Board of Education,* (1973) and *Jose P.* v. *Gordon M. Ambach et al.* (1979) require students to be assessed in the language or languages in which they can demonstrate what they know and can do. *Larry P.* v. *Wilson Riles,* Superintendent of Public Instruction for the State of California (1979), requires that assessment procedures be conducted in a culturally appropriate manner. *Guadalupe* v. *Tempe Elementary School District* (1971), *Lora* v. *Board of the City of New York* (465 F. Supp. 1211, 1977), and the U.S. Office of Civil Rights Memorandum state that school systems must avoid and correct any disproportionate representation of non-European and limited-English-proficient (LEP) students in special educational programs.

BIASED AND DISCRIMINATORY ASSESSMENT

Educators today are much more knowledgeable about the cultural and linguistic bias typically found in the assessment strategies and materials used with poor and non-European American students and the harmful effects of biased assessment on students. New, less biased procedures and materials have been developed. However, the sad fact is that many school districts do not use these approaches. Thus, many people feel that for a number of students not much has changed since the 1920s. As a result, today's critics of biased assessment are basically still repeating what has been written and said over and over again for more than 70 years (33, 34, 36, 37). For example, the following quote by Cummins is not very different from what concerned Hispanic American, African Americans, and European Americans wrote in the 1920s and 1930s:

Assessment is still oriented towards discovery of the *student's* problem. The societal context and the classroom context are taken for granted, thereby limiting possible explanations of academic difficulties to intrinsic characteristics or cultural background of students. . . . Location of the "problem" with the child is virtually inevitable when the conceptual base for the psychological assessment process is purely psycho-educational. If the psychologist's task is to discover the causes of a minority student's academic difficulties and the only tools at her disposal are psychological tests, then it is hardly surprising that the child's difficulties will be attributed to psychological dysfunction. . . . Psychologists who operate within this pattern of role definition ignore the possibility that the "learning disabilities" they have identified are pedagogically-induced. . . . Psychologists who operate within the traditional narrow-focus model of assessment unwittingly legitimize the educational disabling of many minority students. (35, pp.12–14)

STUDENT CHARACTERISTICS

Assessment procedures that are not suited to the characteristics of the students who are evaluated can provide misleading and biased information. This section describes some of the many differences among students that require adaptations in the assessment process to avoid bias. It also presents and evaluates suggestions for adapting the assessment process to these differences. As noted in the Preface, it is important to avoid overgeneralizations and stereotypical statements about students. The ethnic, socioeconomic-class, and gender differences discussed in this chapter are meant to sensitize assessors to differences that may possibly characterize students, not to encourage them to judge students by the contextual aspects of their lives, ethnic background, name, skin color, or gender.

Familiarity with the Assessment Process

Not all students are accustomed to being assessed, especially in a one-to-one situation. Students who are are unfamiliar with assessment procedures often become anxious when they are assessed (38–43). Research indicates that a small amount of anxiety can motivate students to do their best when they are assessed, but too much anxiety can interfere with their performance (41). "The way many standardized tests are composed and given do, in fact, elicit or at least allow strong debilitating motivational dynamics such as test anxiety to operate. Such motivational test bias will cause many children to perform well below their optimal level of functioning in the test situation, thereby invalidating their results if one is interested in what the children have learned, as opposed to whether they can demonstrate that learning under heavy testing pressure" (41, p. 4).

Immigrant and refugee students who have never been assessed, especially on a one-to-one basis, are likely to be anxious during the assessment process (39, 40,

42). There is also considerable evidence that many African American and poor students are more anxious in assessment procedures than European American and middle-class students (38, 41, 43). "Some Hispanics come from countries where students are seldom assessed individually as they are in the United States. The strangeness and unfamiliarity of this situation may make Hispanic students anxious to the point that their anxiety interferes with their ability to demonstrate their achievement and potential" (40, p. 175).

Students come to the assessment process with different test-taking skills. Their "test wiseness" and their capacity to utilize the characteristics and format of an assessment situation to solve the problems included in such a procedure affect their ability to perform up to their actual level. Students who have not acquired test-taking skills (such as when to ask the assessor for clarification or assistance, when to work fast, when to guess and to skip difficult items, how to rule out items in multiple-choice questions that are obviously meant to mislead or entrap students, how to mark an answer sheet, and so on) may be unable to demonstrate what they actually know and can do. "Many Native American Indian students fail to exhibit successful test-taking behaviors due to a multiplicity of underlying causes. Cultural beliefs in some tribes may bar competitive behaviors in an academic setting. The student may underestimate the seriousness of the test or fail to adopt a successful response strategy which may involve selective scanning for known items, techniques of using partial information to guess correct answers, or efficient time use" (47, p. 3).

Research has consistently indicated that improving students' test-taking skills—including those of African American, Hispanic American, Native American, and poor students as well as students with learning disabilities and behavior disorders—also improves their scores on assessment procedures (44, 46, 48, 50–55). From 5 to 14 hours of instruction time spread out over five to seven weeks appears to be the effective range of instructional time needed to improve students' "test wiseness." A number of researchers have recommended 10 hours. There is also some evidence that improving students' test-taking skills may also reduce their misplacement in special education (45).

Some educators disagree with this approach. They feel it is unethical and misleading to teach test-taking skills to students. Others argue that since students who lack test-taking skills are unable to demonstrate what they can do and what they know, improving their skills through training makes results of assessment more accurate and less biased. Haladyna and colleagues suggest that there are ethical and unethical ways to prepare students for standardized tests (49). Some of the approaches they consider unethical include modifying the curriculum to match the test, teaching students the actual items in the test, and practicing alternate forms of the test. Examples of approaches they believe to be ethical include teaching test-taking skills and motivating students to want to perform their best.

TEST-WISENESS

- Were you a test-wise student when you were younger?
- Which if any techniques did your teachers employ to improve your test-taking skills?
- Which techniques would you employ to improve your students' test-taking skills?
- Which techniques do you think are unethical?

Motivation

All students are not equally motivated to do their best when they are assessed. Some students may not realize that the assessment being conducted is designed to evaluate them. This is especially true of many Hispanic American, Native American, and Southeast Asian American students who come from cultures where they are not evaluated in the same way (40, 59). In fact, some Native American students who have not been exposed to a great deal of testing in reservation schools tend to view a test as a game. As a result, they do not try to do as well as they might if they understood the significance of the situation (59).

Many European American females, especially those from less affluent and working-class backgrounds, have mixed feelings about and are uncomfortable with success in courses or occupations traditionally thought to be in the so-called male domain. This applies to a lesser degree to African American females. (See Chapter 10.) There is also evidence that some African American students, especially males, are motivated to avoid success in school or at least are not motivated to try to succeed. (See Chapters 3 and 11.) Students who are not motivated to succeed in school may be equally unmotivated to perform their best on school-related assessments. Therefore, it may be necessary for assessors to motivate such students to try their best. If this fails, teachers should at least take students' lack of motivation into consideration when they interpret and report the results they obtain.

Students' motivational styles also affect their motivation to succeed. Assessors who are aware of students' motivational styles can utilize their knowledge to increase students' motivation to maximize their performance. For example, students who are brought up to view their family as their main reference point when evaluating themselves are more likely to respond positively to statements such as, "If you do your best during the assessment, your family will be proud of you and it will reflect positively on your family and community." This may be an especially effective approach with Hmong Americans who have extremely strong loyalty to their kinship group, as the following description indicates. The Hmong believe that "a person exists as a member of a specific kin group. . . . The fate of the group determines its individual members' status and identities. People think of themselves as a collective group with an identity and responsibility. Individuals' actions determine the status of the kin group by reflecting on its honor and on the public respect the group can command. Thus a person's achievements are important insofar as they reflect on her or his extended family, and, in turn, affect the well-being of its members" (60, pp. 6–7).

In comparison to European American students, Hispanic Americans are also brought up to have a greater loyalty to their families and communities. "Hispanics have a strong identification with and loyalty to their family and community. As a result, Hispanic students may be highly motivated to do things that have significance for their families, friends, and community" (40, p. 38).

When attempting to motivate students to do their best when they are assessed, it is also helpful to know whether individual recognition or anonymity is stressed in their culture. Some students try to do their best if they anticipate that their achievement will be recognized publicly; others try harder when they are assured that their anonymity will be preserved. Many non-European students and some European Americans, especially females, have difficulty with public recognition. An Hispanic American special educator reported, "When I was a student, I was tremendously embarrassed any time I was singled out. I would have preferred my recognition in private" (40, p. 87).

Are students brought up to behave cooperatively or to compete with others? Would students respond better to competitive or cooperative motivating techniques during the assessment process? Chamberlain and Medinos-Landurand pointed out that "in American society, students who do not value or are not skilled in competition are at a serious disadvantage in the testing process. These students do not understand or accept the concept of doing their 'best' and working to do better than others during a test" (57, p. 118).

As the following quotations show, Hispanic Americans, Hawaiian Americans, and Native Americans, among others, tend to prefer cooperative environments:

> Cooperative learning is very essential for Central Americans. Cooperation and collectivity are always regarded as very essential values, while in this country what is valued is individualism and competition. (Carlos Cordova, San Francisco University) (63, p. 19)

> Because of their belief that it is bad manners to try to excel over others, some Hispanic students may not volunteer answers or they may even pretend not to know the correct answer when called on. (61, p. 358)

> There is evidence that Hawaiians are seldom concerned with the pursuit of success for the purely personal satisfaction involved. . . . Hawaiians apparently derive little personal pleasure from competing successfully against others and, in fact, avoid individual competition. . . . As an illustration, many children in our school refused to accept material rewards (e.g., Cokes or candy) for high grades or successful competition unless the rewards could be shared with their friends. (64, pp. 55–56)

> Native American parents desire their children to be successful, just as any other parents, but in a manner that is consistent with the cooperative and non-competitive tribal, community, and family values and aspirations. (56, p. 46)

Would comparing students to their peers be an effective or ineffective motivational device? In some cases, especially with students who have been brought up in individualistic cultures, such comparisons can be highly motivating. However, students who have learned that such comparisons are bad may do whatever necessary to avoid appearing to be competitive with other individuals. After a friend has given the wrong answer, how will students who have been brought up to function cooperatively rather than competitively respond when they are called on to give the correct answer? Although it is difficult for many European American teachers to believe, many non-European American students, especially Hispanic Americans and Native Americans, pretend that they do not know the answer to a question or a problem if one of their peers has not given the right answer. "Calling upon a boy or girl to correct an answer or to supply information in response to a question missed by someone else, creates a problem situation for, in the Latino code of ethics, it is not considered proper for any individual to secure attention at the expense of another person (showing up his ignorance, for instance)" (58, p. 78). Also, "if a question is asked and one child cannot answer it, no one else [American Indian student] will because that means they would have placed themselves in a superior position over their peer" (62, p. 135).

Perception of Assessors

A number of questions exist in regard to students' perceptions of their assessors, such as the following:

- How are children brought up to relate to people who they do not know?
- Are children taught to give people the benefit of the doubt or to be wary of strangers until they prove to be trustworthy?
- What is the history of the relationship between the students' ethnic or socioeconomic group and the group the assessors represent?
- Have the students personally experienced prejudice, oppression, rejection, or abuse by members of the assessors' ethnic or socioeconomic group?
- Have the students been brought up to anticipate such treatment?
- How will students perceive and relate to assessors who are not members of their ethnic socioeconomic or regional group and who they do not know?
- Will students perform poorly during assessment sessions because they are suspicious of their assessors and not because of a lack of potential or achievement?
- Will students feel more relaxed and perform better if they are familiar with the assessor?

Students from low-income backgrounds tend to perform better on more difficult tasks when the assessor is a familiar person or acts in a warm, friendly manner (65, 66). Research that needs to be updated suggests that Hispanic American students perform better with Hispanic American examiners (68, 71).

As the following quotations reveal, in the 1970s and 1980s, many African American students were brought up to be suspicious of the motives and intentions of European Americans. There is little reason to believe that the situation has changed since then.

> A black child has to be aware that the mainstream white society often judges black people as less intelligent, less attractive, and less trustworthy. . . . To raise a black child without any notion that he is viewed differently because of his race would be disastrous. Eventually, he would explode in bitterness. He would be incensed when he discovers, as sooner or later he must, in his social life or at work, that he is seen not as a person. . . . but as "the black guy" or, worst of all, "that nigger." (75, p. 50)

> Black children are taught early to be suspicious of whites. . . . Thus Blacks grow up believing that whites cannot be trusted. Whether this is true or not is hardly the question, for we are dealing here with *perceptual* realities of Blacks. . . . The effect of such an attitude on any testing situation in which the instrument is administered by a white is obvious. . . . From an intercultural point of view the testing situation is even more complicated. The situation itself, in all probability is defined as being *cold* in the negative sense of that Black term. Black Americans looking at Euro-American interactional style often brand whites as cold and aloof. This feeling about whites will then be intensified if the situation is kept under the control of the tester. Not only does this environment ignore the means by which significant information is generally passed on among blacks. . . . but it eliminates the possibility of establishing the kind of relationship that makes anything but hostile responses seem appropriate to the testee. In this sense it is not the questions per se which cause Black children difficulty, it is the testing environment in general and especially the techniques that are used to ask the questions. (69, pp. 338–339)

Research about whether these attitudes actually affect the way African American students react to the ethnic background of assessors has yielded inconsistent results. Studies of African American students that do not consider student characteristics such as age, mistrust of European Americans, socioeconomic class background, or other situational factors (e.g., the level of difficulty of the assessment procedure and the role of the assessor) tend to find that assessors' ethnic background does not affect the results of assessment procedures. However, results that consider these factors have indicated the opposite. For example, preschool African American students perform better with African American assessors (72). African Americans students who mistrust European Americans also perform better with African American assessors, but ethnic background has no effect on those who do not mistrust European Americans (73). Although assessors' ethnic background does not affect the results of assessments of middle-class African American students, research that was done in the 1970s and early 1980s indicates that African Americans students from low-income backgrounds perform better with African American assessors. They score higher on standardized tests when given social reinforcement by African American assessors and provide longer and elaborate responses (67, 74).

The reasons for these age and socioeconomic-class effects have not been explored. Some researchers have suggested that because young children are likely to be unfamiliar with European Americans and have less interaction with them as individuals, they are less likely to trust them. They also propose that students from low-income backgrounds are better able to overcome their discomfort with an unfamiliar and/or threatening assessment procedure when their assessors are familiar. Although most assessors are unfamiliar to students, the administrative procedures for most standardized tests discourage assessor familiarity or friendliness. They also provide little or no opportunity for assessors to engage students in activities that will help them gain their trust.

There is also evidence that some students from some cultures may perform better with same-gender rather than different-gender assessors. In some cultures, students try harder with male assessors because in their culture they are more highly regarded and respected than females (70).

Communication Style

Students' communication styles can also influence the results of their assessments. As noted in Chapter 8, assessors who prefer direct expression may mistakenly think that African American and Hispanic American students who use a more poetic and analogous speech pattern are "beating around the bush," cannot think straight, or have communication problems (40, 61).

Also as noted previously, some students (e.g., Hispanic Americans and Japanese Americans) expect others to be sensitive enough to their feelings and problems that it is unnecessary for them to be open and direct about their needs. If they have to do so, they may experience a loss of self-respect and think that others have also lost respect for them as well (40, 76, 78). "Because Hispanics tend to feel that it reflects negatively on their self-worth to admit that they do not know something or cannot do something, Hispanic students who are less accustomed to asking questions and expressing doubts and confusions may not admit that they do not understand directions or items included in assessment procedures" (40, p. 176). Therefore, assessors should not assume that students who do not ask for help in understanding directions and so on are really ready to perform the required assessment task.

Children are brought up to be more or less loquacious with adults. For example, many Native American, Asian Pacific American, and Hispanic American students are expected to talk less and listen more when they converse with adults in comparison to European American students (40, 57, 77). Thus, these students may respond in as few words as possible during assessment procedures and be penalized for not saying enough or providing enough details.

Learning Style

Dependent versus Independent Learners

No children are brought up to be completely dependent on or independent of adults. However, some youngsters are trained to accomplish things on their own, and others are brought up to be more dependent on the aid, support, opinions, and feedback of their parents and other significant adults. Therefore, it is important to know whether students are prepared to be relatively self-reliant and independent during the assessment process or if they require a great deal of guidance and feedback to perform at their optimum level. Most standardized assessment procedures do not permit assessors to provide dependent learners with the supportive environment they require to demonstrate their accomplishments.

Students who are brought up to be less independent (e.g., Hispanic American students) may have acquired the skills that their parents expect them to acquire but not those that are typical of European middle-class youngsters. In most cultures, there are also gender differences in the independence training students receive. Chamberlain and Medinos-Landurand explained,

> In many traditional Colombian and Asian families, young boys are fed, dressed, and pampered; yet they may be allowed more independence than girls outside the home at an earlier age. Girls, on the other hand, care for younger siblings, clean, cook and are given a great deal of responsibility within the home; however, they are often restricted in their independence outside the house.
>
> In the assessment process, such gender differences can significantly affect a student's performance. . . . Often, behaviors that are not condoned within a student's culture generally will not be performed successfully by the student. Not only will the student lack experience in performing the task, but the emotional barrier to performing a task that the student views as inappropriate for his or her gender or culture will hamper performance. (57, p. 121)

Such students may score lower than expected on evaluations of their adaptive behavior if they are compared to norms developed on children who have been raised to be more independent. Assessors who are not aware of the cause of these students' lower performance may mistakenly believe that developmental problems are preventing them from functioning as independently as others.

Reflective/Analytical versus Spontaneous/Intuitive

No one is completely reflective/analytical or spontaneous/intuitive, but there are cultural differences among people along this continuum. Therefore, it is important to know whether children's cultures stress analyzing and reflecting on questions and problems and being sure to know the answer or solution before saying anything, or emphasize responding intuitively and spontaneously in terms of what occurs to them immediately. Shade described the difference as follows: "Some people are rather anxious to insure that they gather all the information possible before being asked to respond and they have a need to be accurate. These individuals are considered to be *reflective* while those individuals who respond immediately to what is presented without regard to the fact they may be erroneous are labeled as *impulsive* learners" (82, p. 17).

How long does it take for students to prepare their answers when called on in class or asked to respond to a question during the assessment process? African American students tend to respond promptly and spontaneously. On the other hand, Native American students tend to look at all sides of an issue, examine their possible implications, and make sure they know the answer before they are ready to express their opinion. Assessors who do not allow students sufficient time to prepare their answers before calling on someone else or moving on to the next item may mistakenly believe that students do not know something, are slow learners, and so on (83).

Risk Taking

How sure do students have to be that they know the answer, that they can complete a task, or that their opinion is correct before they will risk a response during assessment? How likely are they to choose an answer they are not completely sure of on a multiple-choice item that deducts for incorrect answers? One study reported, "A Japanese youth . . . should remain silent rather than exhibiting a faulty understanding or command of a skill. To put forth a mistaken answer or an unperfected skill is a personal disgrace and an insult to the teacher and the discipline" (76, p. 19). Another author stated, "A reluctance to try too soon and the accompanying fear of being 'shamed' if one does not succeed may account for the seemingly passive uninterested and unresponsive attitude of Indian students" (81, p. 28). Consider also Grossman's findings: "The Hispanic culture discourages guessing (*hablando sin saber*). Thus, Hispanic students may be penalized on assessment procedures which require students to respond when they are uncertain of the correct answer" (40, p. 177).

Global Perception versus Analysis of Details

Some students, such as African Americans and Hispanic Americans, tend to be global learners; others, including many middle-class European Americans, typically are more analytical. Global learners perceive things in a holistic manner. They perceive the whole of an event, idea, or image and the relationships between its parts simultaneously. They see everything as a part of the whole and use few discrete categories to notice differences among the parts. Analytic learners can easily divide the whole into subcategories based on differences. Therefore, students' performance on achievement and other types of assessment procedures may depend, in part, on whether the tasks they are required to perform fit their particular global or analytic learning style.

Stimulation and Variety

Students differ in terms of their tolerance for and willingness to continue to perform assessment tasks that are boring, monotonous, tedious, and repetitious. Research indicates that the performance of African American students who come from homes that are highly stimulating increases when the format of an assessment procedure includes more task variation, but the performance of African American and European American students from homes that are not highly stimulating does not improve with increased variability (80). Boykin explained this on the basis of the home environment to which many African Americans are accustomed.

> The home and immediate ecological environments of a preponderance of Black children afford levels of physical stimulation that are high in both intensity and variability. . . . One consequence of growing up in such environments may be a heightened responsiveness to stimulus change. . . . It would seem reasonable, moreover, that in a problem solving context, Black children would find tasks presented in a relatively monotonous fashion even more intolerable than their counterparts from more placid settings. Thus, it would seem that increased variation should have a greater positive effect on the task performance of Black children. (80, pp. 470–471)

Activity Level

Students' willingness to sit still for long periods of time is greatly influenced by their ethnic and socioeconomic-class backgrounds (79). Some students may have difficulty sitting quietly and completing sedentary assessment activities for long periods of time. Their performance may indicate their difficulty adjusting to the requirements of the assessment situation and not what they have achieved or learned or what they could accomplish if they were assessed in a more culturally appropriate manner.

Pace

People from different cultures work and play at different paces. Some students attempt to accomplish as much as possible within a given period of time; others prefer a relaxed steady pace. Slower-working students who correctly answer all the items that they have time to complete on standardized tests may receive a lower score than students who rush through the test and miss items that those working at a slower pace answer correctly. It is important, then, to determine whether students can demonstrate what they know and have achieved in school on timed evaluations or merely appear to have accomplished less than they have because they are unable to complete the evaluation procedure.

Some students who are accustomed to working at a slower pace (e.g., African Americans, Brazilian Americans, Filipino Americans, Hawaiian Americans, Samoan Americans, and others) may make more errors when required to work as fast as they can. Students accustomed to a faster pace (e.g., Japanese Americans and Chinese Americans) continue to perform as well when they are told to work as fast as they can (84–86). For all of these reasons, it is essential to use untimed procedures when assessing students who are not accustomed to rushing through things and to make sure that students are not recommended for placement in special education based on the results of evaluation procedures that are culturally inappropriate because they are timed.

Response Style

Cultures differ in the degree to which they encourage intense or subdued responses to life. For example, in comparison to European American students, African American students are more likely to respond intensely to things in general and to select extreme responses on scales that ask if they strongly agree or just agree or if they strongly disagree or just disagree (87, 88). Therefore, assessors should consider students' response style when they interpret their responses to items on assessment procedures.

ASSESSOR CHARACTERISTICS

Assessors' characteristics can also affect the results of the assessment process. Three factors are particularly important. As noted earlier, some groups of students may respond negatively to assessors because they have been brought up to mistrust the group to which the assessors belong. Some educators feel that since this may interfere with students' ability to perform at their best, if possible, assessors should have the same background as the students they assess. If this is not possible, it has been suggested that the mistrust factor should be taken into consideration when the results of an assessment are interpreted.

Many educators and psychologists evaluate non-European and poor students in a biased manner. (See Chapter 3.) The information and exercises in Chapters 3 through 6 are designed, in part, to help assessors avoid these problems. Assessors who are less knowledgeable about evaluating limited-English-proficient, non-European American students are more likely to attribute these students' difficulties to disabilities rather than to their incomplete mastery of English and more likely to believe that they require special education (89). Inexperienced assessors should consider this possibility when they make recommendations about students' placements.

ASSESSMENT MATERIALS AND PROCEDURES

The materials and procedures that assessors use are another significant source of bias. The primary sources of such bias are technical bias, content bias, format bias, linguistic bias, and gender bias.

Technical Bias

Assessment procedures must be reliable and valid. If they are not, then decisions based on the data they provide will be discriminatory. For an assessment procedure to be useful, the score or results that are obtained should be correct. For example, students who have emotional problems should appear that way to different observers and they should appear to have problems regardless of the particular time they are observed or evaluated or the particular situation in which they are evaluated. If this is not true, then judgments about students might depend on the persons who observe them, the time they are observed, or the situation in which they are observed. Procedures are reliable when they produce consistent results regardless of the observer, the time, or the situation.

Methods that are reliable for some students may be unreliable when used with other students. Since the reliability of most procedures is determined by studying their use with predominantly European American students, many procedures may be unreliable when used with non-European students. For example, observers who are biased against certain groups such as African American students or who do not know about the cultural determinants of their behavior may perceive their behavior differently than observers who are not prejudiced against them or knowledgeable about their culture.

Procedures that are valid measure what they claim to measure and accomplish what they are designed to achieve. For example, intelligence tests or tests of learning potential are supposed to measure students' ability to learn and to predict how much students will learn in certain situations when they are given certain kinds and amounts of assistance. If they do not measure a student's capacity to learn and predict accurately how he or she will function in specific learning situations, they are invalid, useless, and even harmful.

For instance, students' current knowledge about a particular item such as how far it is from one place to another or the height of the average American adult male, or their ability to perform a particular task such as forming a design from blocks, can indicate their learning potential or help assessors to predict how they will learn in the future, but only under certain conditions. The students must have been exposed to the information or task and have had sufficient practice to learn it. They must be motivated to demonstrate their knowledge or ability to assessors and they have to be permitted to do so in a way that fits their performance style. Non-European American, poor, and limited-English-proficient students are not always exposed to the same materials, tasks, environments, and so on as European American, middle-class and English-proficient students. They may not be as motivated to demonstrate their ability and knowledge to strangers during the assessment procedure and they will probably have different learning and communication styles. Therefore, procedures that are valid with European American middle-class students may be invalid when used with non-European American and poor students.

Content Bias

Content bias may occur because various teachers, schools, and school districts include different content in the courses they offer at each grade level and because students bring divergent experiences to the assessment situation for contextual and cultural reasons. Because of differences in the content of the curriculum to which students are exposed, students' scores on standardized achievement tests may depend on the match between what the procedure measures and what they have been taught (90, 93, 95). After determining that third- and fourth-grade students obtained different scores on each of four standardized reading achievement tests, Good and Salvia concluded that one cannot always determine whether "a student's reading score reflects deficient reading skills or the selection of a test with poor content validity for the pupils curriculum" (95, p. 56).

Inner city, rural, and suburban schools include very different skills in their curriculum. Migrant students who move from school to school may miss a considerable amount of course content. For these reasons, assessment procedures may mistakenly evaluate students on what they should have been taught, not on what they were actually taught (90).

Some educators believe curriculum-based assessment is an effective way to avoid content bias. Curriculum-based assessment is an approach that aims to assess students in terms of the curriculum they have actually been exposed to in class. This avoids the bias that results in assessing students on knowledge and skills that they have not studied or practiced and including items that depend on family and community values. The advantages and disadvantages of this approach are discussed later in this chapter.

Some teachers claim that the content of many assessment materials are biased against non-European American and poor students because the context of their lives and their cultural backgrounds expose them to very different experiences than those of middle-class American students. "A body of knowledge based on the experiences of a white middle class community cannot help but create a disadvantage for members of communities which differ from the mainstream" (93, p. 178). These educators suggest that questions such as how far is it from one place to another are only relevant if students are familiar with the places. Asking why it is better to pay bills by check rather than cash is not relevant to children whose parents cannot afford a checking account. Issues concerning whether it is better to build houses from bricks rather than wood depend on the geographic region in which students grow up.

Measuring independence or motor control by determining if a child can drink out of a cup, throw a ball overhand, or ride a tricycle can lead to incorrect conclusions if they still drink from a bottle, play soccer rather than baseball, or are too poor to own a tricycle or live in an area where the traffic makes it is too dangerous to ride a tricycle. Evaluating students' short-term memory by having them repeat a series of digits backward or forward can provide accurate information for students who have had an opportunity to practice remembering numbers in a series. However, some students come from places where they and their friends have telephone numbers and street addresses, whereas others come from rural areas where there is little reason to remember numbers.

Some items are biased because they involve family and community values. The answers to such items as what to do if a smaller child hits you, why is it better to give money to a charitable organization than to a street beggar, and what to do if you lose something that belongs to your friend depend on the values and experiences to which students have been exposed.

Other educators and psychologists question whether such items are really biased (92, 98). They claim that one cannot determine if an item or content is biased merely be examining it because that is too subjective. They maintain that one has to determine statistically whether an item is more difficult for one group than another. They also point out that some items that were judged to be biased have turned out to be no more difficult for the group that they are supposed to be biased against than any other group. Presently, there is very little research to support this point of view.

Educators who believe that there is a great deal of content bias in assessment procedures have suggested that one way to reduce such bias is to eliminate any items that are more difficult for some groups than for others (94, 98, 103). They complain that although test publishers eliminate items that are more difficult for one gender or the other in order to eliminate gender bias, they do not do the same thing for items that are more difficult for certain ethnic, socioeconomic-class, or regional groups. Other educators and psychologists feel that the differences in the scores that various groups receive on these items represent real differences in ability or achievement between groups (97). They advise test publishers to continue to include such items in their assessment materials.

In the 1970s and early 1980s, educators and psychologists developed a number of culture-specific assessment instruments, primarily for African Americans, that included content that was more relevant to their experiences, pictures of

African Americans in more culturally relevant situations, and so on. The majority of these instruments were designed to evaluate African Americans' personality characteristics, their priorities in life, the extent to which they are aware of and identify with their African heritage, their knowledge of the oppressive nature and effects of racism, their willingness to resist anti-African American pressures and threats, their attitudes toward African American issues, their mistrust of European Americans, and their identification with African American values, customs, and institutions (91, 96, 100, 101, 102, 104). Research indicates that persons assessed with these instruments provide more data and data that is more valid. They can be used to obtain information about certain aspects of students' personalities and their attitudes about European American teachers and European American values. However, they provide only a limited amount of the information needed to evaluate African American students who may have disabilities.

SAMPLE ITEMS FROM ASSESSMENT INSTRUMENTS DESIGNED FOR AFRICAN AMERICANS

Persons are asked to state whether they agree or disagree with items such as the following:

- Black people should have their own independent schools that consider their African heritage and values an important part of the curriculum.
- Whites are usually fair to all people regardless of race.
- I feel little sense of commitment to Black people who are not close friends or relatives.

They are asked to choose the response that best reflects their preferences regarding such questions as the following:

Where do you prefer to live?
a. All-Black community
b. A racially mixed community
c. Does not matter

Do you prefer to work for
a. All Blacks
b. Both Blacks and Whites
c. Only Whites
d. Does not matter

They are asked to complete a sentence that expresses their beliefs or feelings regarding such phrases as the following:

- Most Black people
- The NAACP

A number of culture-specific instruments have also been developed for use with Hispanic American students. Most of these instruments are designed to be administered in Spanish to limited-English-proficient students who have not adopted the mainstream European American culture. (See Linguistic Bias in this chapter.) Few of them are designed for use with English-proficient Hispanic American students. There are very few culture-specific assessment instruments available for other groups. This may indicate that it is not profitable to develop and market culture-specific procedures for small numbers of students. Thus, for the present, culture-specific instruments are not a viable option for assessors who wish to avoid content bias.

Format Bias

The format of an assessment procedure refers to the way tasks, questions, and so on are posed to students and the way in which students are required to respond to them. Format characteristics (e.g., whether students are asked to recognize the correct answer or solution to a problem or to produce it themselves; whether they respond orally, in writing, or perform a task; whether there are time limits; whether items get progressively more difficult, etc.), as well as the materials students work with, can affect students' performance. When there is a poor match between the ways students function and the format of an assessment procedure, students may not be able to show what they know and can do. Space permits a discussion of only a few examples of format problems.

Students who are immigrants or who have attended atypical schools on reservations may have difficulty adjusting to the unfamiliar format of many standardized tests. For example, some assessment procedures require students to fail 5, 6, or even 7 similar items before they can go on to the next group of items. This can be devastating to students who respond poorly to such experiences and to students who are not accustomed to taking tests in which they fail many items and still do well. Assessment materials that can be used with students who function at many different levels often contain both very easy and very difficult problems on the same page. This can be very frightening and demoralizing to students who see many problems or items that are too difficult for them and do not understand that the difficult ones are for students who are older or in a higher grade.

As noted earlier, some students (especially African Americans, Hispanic Americans, and Native Americans) cannot always show what they can do on timed procedures. Stringent time limits galvanize some students to work efficiently and perform at their optimal level, but those who are anxious or who work at a slower pace perform less adequately under time pressures (41). "Achievement tests with stringent time limits do not just measure what skills children have acquired or what they know but in addition whether or not they can demonstrate this knowledge quickly and under time pressure and testing stress" (41, p. 16). Providing these students with the time they need to complete an assessment at the pace at which they are accustomed to work provides more accurate information about what they know and can do (105).

Cultural factors may make it difficult for some students to engage in certain required activities during the assessment process. For example, on assessment of fine motor coordination, Hmong children would not demonstrate that they could use pincers to pick up an object because the raisins they were required to pick up resembled Hmong medicines that they were warned to avoid (106).

Whether students are required to respond orally or in writing, in a multiple-choice or short essay format, verbally or kinesthetically, and so on during the assessment process can determine if they are able to demonstrate their true capability and achievement. To deal with this problem, Gardner suggested, "Achievement tests should be designed so that students have some room for flexibility. For example a cluster of three or four items that examine a particular skill from different viewpoints and tests it in different ways could be set. . . . A pupil who can answer any one of them correctly will have demonstrated his/her mastery of that skill and should receive full credit for it—even if he/she had erred on some of the other items in that cluster" (85, p. 234).

Linguistic Bias

Assessments conducted in a language or dialect in which students are not proficient or in only one language when students require two languages to function adequately and explain themselves fully do not provide a true picture of what students know or can do. The biased results they provide can cause students to be misplaced in programs for students with disabilities or denied acceptance into programs for the gifted and talented.

Limited English Proficiency

Limited-English-proficient students are more likely to be found eligible for special education programs for students with learning disabilities and cognitive disabilities when they are assessed in English rather than in the language in which they are most proficient, regardless of whether they actually have disabilities (26, 109). At first glance, this suggests that limited-English-proficient students should be assessed in their native languages. However, the choice of which language or languages should be used to assess students is a much more complicated issue. Students who have no proficiency in English clearly need to be assessed in their native language. Those who are truly proficient in English can be assessed completely in English. However, many other students need to be assessed in two languages to demonstrate what they know and can do.

Many limited-English-proficient students have two vocabularies—a home vocabulary and a school vocabulary. Students in bilingual programs learn a great deal of curriculum content in their native language. Students in English as a second language programs or in regular English language classes learn much of the material in English. Thus, until students are completely proficient in English, those in bilingual programs may have to use their native language to demonstrate their mastery of school-related material, whereas those in English as a second language or English submergence programs will be unable to demonstrate their school-related achievement unless it is assessed in English.

Regardless of the program students are in, their English vocabulary is likely to be limited to what they are learning in school. As a result, students are likely to have to use their native languages to express most of what they have learned at home and in their community. These differences must be taken into account when decisions are made regarding the language or languages in which students should be assessed in general. Since students need to be assessed in the language in which they will function best on each particular task, skill, or knowledge area, individual differences in native language and English language proficiency must be considered when decisions are made about the language or languages in which each aspect of the assessment should be conducted. A general principle to follow is to make sure students are assessed in both English and their native language since research indicates that limited-English-proficient students usually score higher when assessed in both languages rather than in either their native language or English alone (105, 107).

The goal of providing students with linguistically appropriate assessment services in the more than 100 languages spoken by limited-English-proficient students in the United States has proved difficult to achieve for two reasons. Very few of the regular educators, special educators, and psychologists who are responsible for assessing students for possible placement in special education programs are bilingual. This is especially true for languages other than Spanish. Also, except for Spanish language materials, there is very little assessment material in the many languages spoken by the millions of limited-English-proficient students in the public schools. The two approaches that have been used to overcome these difficulties is to translate assessment materials into other languages and to use interpreters during the assessment process. Both of these approaches are problematic.

Translating materials into students' native languages can improve the performance of limited-English-proficient students (105, 108). However, there are a number of problems that must be avoided before these benefits can be achieved.

Poorly translated materials will not improve the validity of an assessment. Back translations can eliminate this problem. In a back translation, the material that has been translated from English is translated back into English in order to detect any distortion in meaning that resulted from original translation. If the meaning or the back translation and the original are equal, then the translation is probably correct. If they are different, there is good chance that the meaning was changed when the material was translated from English. It is also important to be sure that students speak the dialect of the translation to avoid linguistic bias. In addition, it is important to keep in mind that using material translated into students' native languages when their preferred language for the task or problem is English because they have learned it in English will not benefit students.

Translating material will not necessarily eliminate its content bias. Therefore, it is often necessary to adapt the content as well as the language of the material to

the cultural, contextual, and linguistic characteristics of the student
they are to be used. Actual examples of content change in translat
changing the question, How are a peach and a plum alike? to How ar   ˌrange
and a banana alike? or replacing a marble game with a card game, or modifying
How far is it from New York to Chicago? to How far is it from New York to
Puerto Rico?

Sometimes it is necessary to accept alternative correct answers to some items.
For example, what is absurd about a picture of a man carrying an umbrella upside
down to middle-class European American children is that the umbrella is in a position that it will not protect him from rain. However, to Puerto Rican children,
the absurdity is that a *man* is carrying an umbrella in any position since males do
not carry umbrellas. On a vocabulary test, a translated word may have more than
one meaning. For example, translating *courage* into *valor* becomes problematic because *valor* means value as well as bravery in Spanish. Translating material often
changes the level of difficulty of items. *Dog*, a very easy word to read or spell in
English, translates to *perro* in Spanish, a more difficult word because of double *rr*.
Translating *building* to *edificio* makes the item easier. Translating materials does
not make the norms of a standardized assessment procedure any more appropriate for students who are not well-represented in the norm sample. Nor does it
eliminate the format bias of procedures that provide students with only limited
amounts of time, require them to make many errors before they are allowed to go
on to the next group of problems, and so on.

UNANTICIPATED TRANSLATION PROBLEMS

It was discovered that some Vietnamese children, when asked to pick up the blue
block, would instead pick up the green block. The Vietnamese language classifies colors into four families: green, red, yellow, and purple. Blue is in the green family, so
that words for green and blue are similar (Xahn). To distinguish it is necessary to say
'Xahn lo' (blue like the sky) or Xahn la cay' (green like the leaves) to ensure that the
child correctly differentiates between green and blue. (106, p. 482)

Assessors who cannot evaluate limited-English-proficient students and interview students' parents in their native language require the assistance of interpreters. As the following quote indicates, when properly used interpreters can be
very helpful: "I strongly believe in the use of language and cultural mediators or
interpreters, as I have seen dramatic differences in the behaviors of both children
and adults. We find a significant difference in how quickly the family develops
trust and responds, how much information they volunteer, and how well they establish a relationship" (114, p. 9).

The use of untrained or poorly prepared interpreters, however, can create many problems (110). Untrained interpreters may identify with the students and want them to do well rather than demonstrate true abilities and disabilities. This may lead interpreters to prompt the right answer from students or to modify their answers so that students are closer to the acceptable response. Interpreters who are not equally fluent in both languages may translate incorrectly to the student or assessor. Interpreters who are fluent in students' languages but not knowledgeable about their cultural background may translate correctly but conduct the assessment in a culturally inappropriate manner or fail to notice content and format bias. If they are from a different socioeconomic class or religious, racial, or ethnic background than the students, they may be prejudiced against them.

To avoid or at least minimize these potential problems, interpreters should be trained in the principles of assessment, human development, special education, and so on. They should be equally competent in both languages, equally familiar with mainstream American culture and students' culture, and, if possible, familiar with the community in which students live and the subgroups to which they belong. The references at the end of the chapter contain much useful information on the training and use of interpreters in the assessment of culturally and linguistically different students (111–113).

Dialect
Although in the 1970s a few studies found that nonstandard dialect speakers are not penalized when they are assessed in Standard English (115–118), the vast majority of research at the time and virtually all that has been carried out since then indicates that nonstandard dialect-speaking students who are poor, African American, Native American, Hispanic American, or from Appalachian areas perform poorly when they are assessed in Standard English (119–122, 124, 125, 127–130, 132–136, 139–142). There is also considerable evidence that these biased results can lead educators to underestimate students' academic achievement and language ability and to incorrectly refer them to special education programs for nonexistent learning disabilities and communication disorders (123, 125, 128, 129).

The following are some causes of dialect bias during the assessment process:

- Educators and others discriminate against nonstandard English dialects. (See Chapter 6.)
- Questions on assessment procedures are often asked using vocabulary that is not familiar to students (e.g., "behind the sofa" rather than "in back of the couch," "beginning to climb" instead of "starting to climb") (142). As a result, students appear to lack information and skills that they actually possess and would be able to demonstrate if they understood the question or directions.
- Some dialect speakers may read material that is written in their own dialect better than material in Standard English (138).
- Students tend to be better at remembering material that is in their dialect (119, 128).

- Students are better able to discriminate between sounds that are present in their own dialect (122, 126, 136).
- Students may misunderstand items and directions because they are given in a different dialect. As an example, European American students who are asked to find which of four pictures shows "delight" may have little difficulty identifying the picture of a girl happily eating an ice cream cone. However, African American students who do not speak Standard English may hear "de (the) light" and select the picture of a boy reading who needs a light (131).
- What may appear to be articulation problems and other types of speech disorders can be omissions and substitutions that conform to speech patterns present in students' dialect (127, 140).

Suggestions for avoiding bias during the assessment of nonstandard English speakers include the following (125, 129, 132, 133, 137, 139, 140):

- Become knowledgeable about the characteristics of the dialects spoken by nonstandard English speakers. There are many descriptions of the major differences between Standard English and the various nonstandard English dialects that can help assessors avoid mistaking dialect differences for possible speech disorders (121, 143, 144).
- Examine personal attitudes about nonstandard dialects for possible bias.
- Avoid stereotyping all members of a group as nonstandard speakers. Determine whether each individual student is a standard or nonstandard dialect speaker. Keep in mind that working-class and younger students are more likely to use nonstandard dialects.
- Use assessment procedures only with students who use the dialect for whom the test has been standardized.
- Do not consider differences in oral reading due to dialect differences such as mispronunciations, adding or omitting endings that indicate plurals, tense, and the like as reading errors.
- Accept answers that conform to students' dialect as correct even though they may not be acceptable according to the manual.
- Make sure students understand the directions and the items included in any assessment procedure. Be prepared to use alternate instructions in both dialects and to express the content in both dialects.

Gender Bias

The content and language of an assessment procedure can also be biased against one gender or the other. Although the effect is not very large, each gender is more likely to answer correctly those test items that deal with objects and topics that interest them and those that use same-gender pronouns (i.e., male students do somewhat better when pronouns are *he, him,* and *his;* females tend to score higher when pronouns refer to *she, her,* and *hers).* Studies conducted in the 1970s and early 1980s indicate that test items tend to include more male pronouns and more material that fit stereotypical male interests. If this situation has not been corrected in recent years, female students may still be placed at a disadvantage when they are assessed with these materials (145–151).

FORMAL, STANDARDIZED, NORM-REFERENCED ASSESSMENT VERSUS INFORMAL, NONSTANDARDIZED, CRITERION-REFERENCED ASSESSMENT

Assessment procedures can be divided into two categories: formal, standardized, norm-referenced procedures and informal, nonstandardized, criterion-referenced procedures. Assessors use the terms somewhat differently and do not always agree about which are which. In general, formal assessment procedures are those that deviate from regular classroom practices. They are usually designed to determine how students are doing in relation to criteria that are more universal and less applicable or geared to the particular students' situations. In order to make such comparisons, formal procedures are administered and scored in a standardized way. The interpretation of the scores is typically accomplished by comparing an individual's score to norms obtained from a sample of students that are believed to represent the population of students with whom the procedure will be used. Standardized achievement tests are good examples of these procedures.

Informal procedures are those that can easily be incorporated into the classroom without interfering with daily activities. Informal procedures typically involve evaluating what students do, how they function, and what they have learned in relation to the curriculum they are exposed to or the goals and standards of their particular teacher or school. This can be done in an unstructured manner by observing how students function and evaluating their work or in a structured way by using observation checklists and scales as well as lists of specific evaluative criteria.

Unlike norm-referenced assessment approaches in which individual students are compared to a norm sample of students, criterion-referenced assessment is designed to compare an individual student to a set of criteria or performance standards such as the number of words spelled correctly or the skills needed to perform a specific task. Criterion-referenced assessment procedures describe students' achievement, knowledge, behavior, and so on, rather than compare students to each other (152, 153).

"In norm-referenced testing, learning a particular skill is important only to the extent that differential learning allows the examiner to rank individuals in order, from those who have learned many skills to those who have learned few. The emphasis is on the relative standing of children rather than on absolute mastery of content. On the other hand, criterion-referenced testing interprets achievement by describing in behavioral terms the child's performance regarding a particular instructional objective" (152, p. 222). Typically, criterion-referenced assessment materials are constructed by individual teachers, departments, or school districts to compare their students to some criteria that they have developed. However, criterion-referenced materials are also available from commercial publishers.

The results of a formal procedure might indicate that the student is functioning at the fourth-grade level in vocabulary (because her scores on the test were the same as the average of fourth-graders in the norm sample) or that she is in the top 10 percent of fourth-graders (because her scores on the vocabulary test were higher than 90 percent of the fourth-graders in the norm sample). The results of an informal nonstandardized procedure might indicate that a student has learned 85 percent of the vocabulary words that a teacher assigned the class.

Experts disagree about which of the two assessment approaches is most and least subject to bias. The advantages and disadvantages of using each approach with limited-English-proficient, non-European American, and poor students are discussed next.

Formal, Standardized, Norm-Referenced Assessment

Educators and other concerned persons have been criticizing the standardized tests used in regular and special education with poor and non-European American students since the early 1920s (33, 34, 36, 37). However, criticisms of standardized assessment approaches did not appear regularly nor receive a great deal of attention from special educators and psychologists until the Association of Black Psychologists, a subgroup of the American Psychological Association, called for a moratorium in 1968 on the standardized testing of African American students. The association criticized achievement, intelligence, aptitude, and performance tests because they were being used to

1. Label black people as uneducable
2. Place black children in special education
3. Perpetuate inferior education
4. Assign black children to lower educational tracks
5. Deny black children higher educational opportunities
6. Destroy positive intellectual growth and development of black people (157, pp. 17–18)

Williams, an officer and spokesperson for the Association claimed,

Classification systems based upon standardized tests have systematically labeled a disproportionately large number of minority group children as abnormal, intellectually subnormal and a disproportionately small number of minority group children as normal and gifted . . .

1. Children who are misclassified and labeled as "different" may be permanently stigmatized and may experience rejection by those in their immediate environment.
2. They may be assigned to inferior educational programs or deprived of their freedom through commitment to an institution.
3. They may be excluded from opportunities which are vital for the full development of their emotional and physical existences.
4. They may be committed to institutions, which define and confirm them as delinquent, retarded or emotionally disturbed. Thus, the child will manifest behaviors which are appropriate to his label. They become more inclined to crime, more disturbed than they would be under more normal growth conditions and less bright than they could be. (158, pp. 3–4, 8–9)

Other criticisms of standardized assessment include th following (154–156):

- Standardized assessment procedures do not accurately or validly describe how students function in the present nor do they predict how students will function in the future.
- They ask "Do you know what I know?" rather than "What is it that you know?" (155, p. 29)
- The data collected with standardized instruments are typically collected in nonclassroom situations under unusual circumstances by unfamiliar assessors and therefore do not reflect how students function in real-life classrooms with real-life teachers.
- Percentile ranking, grade-level placements, and other norms provided by standardized tests are not realistic because national norms are not necessarily true for a given school district, school, or class. The content of courses taught at the seventh-grade level in a predominantly middle-class suburban school may be very different than the course content in a school serving predominantly poor urban students. Thus, students who score at the seventh-grade level on a nationally normed reading test may actually be functioning much lower than the typical seventh-grade student in a middle-class neighborhood suburban school and much higher than the typical seventh-grade student in some other school districts.
- Standardized assessment procedures are not easily adapted to students' contextual, cultural, and linguistic characteristics.
- They measure different attributes with different groups of students. When used with limited-English-proficient, non-European American, and poor students, they measure what students have been exposed to, how fast they can work without making careless mistakes, how motivated they are to succeed and do their best, how well they can adapt to the particular format of the procedure, how they respond to pressure, and so on, not their achievement, learning potential, learning disabilities, or whatever else they may measure when used with European American middle-class students who are English proficient and speak Standard English.
- They require all students to fit a preconceived mold. "Despite the lip-service we pay to the myriad ways in which individuals differ, and claim to celebrate this variety, our practices speak otherwise. In fact it is performance on these tests—with their narrow and rigid definition both of when children should be able to perform particular skills and how they should be able to exhibit their knowledge—that determines whether we see children as 'okay' or not. In the process we damage all children—we devalue the variety of strength they bring with them to school. All differences become handicaps" (156, p. 47).

The Council of the American Psychological Association disagreed with the Black Psychological Association's call for a moratorium on standardized testing. The council stated,

Good psychological decisions require good evidence, and some of the most useful and reliable evidence comes from well-designed and properly interpreted standardized tests. . . . Yet for a variety of reasons, some valid and some not, testing has been the constant target of attack, joined in often by political figures or by the popular media. Testing continues to play an informative role in psychological decisions, for example in counseling practice and educational guidance, yet the science and profession of psychology are damaged by lopsided attacks, which often go without correction, comment or rebuttal.

Now, therefore, the Council of the American Psychological Association asserts the following:

1. Standardized testing, competently administered and evaluated, is a valuable tool in individual, educational, and personnel decision-making.
2. Abuses of testing, through unwarranted labeling or interpretation, are to be avoided as are abuses of any valuable tool. (160).

Arguments in support of the use of standardized assessment procedures include the following (159–163):

- Standardized assessment procedures provide reliable and valid data that describe what students know and can do and predict how much they will be able to learn and what they will be able to accomplish.
- Standardized assessment procedures are not biased. "A considerable body of literature fails to substantiate cultural bias against native-born American ethnic minorities with regard to the use of well-constructed, adequately standardized intelligence and aptitude tests. . . . Those concerned with special education cannot ethically fall prey to the socio-politico Zeitgeist of the times and infer bias where none exists" (162, pp. 255–256).
- Standardized tests predict how students will perform in biased and discriminatory schools. "Perhaps the inequities lie in the traditional education rather than merely in the tests. Intelligence tests are satisfactory predictors of success in traditional education. That the educational system fails to adjust to a culturally pluralistic society is not the fault of tests. Schools seem to prepare students to function in the mainstream, majority culture. If the nature of schools changed radically, mental tests might lose their high predictive validity and no longer be useful" (161, p. 78).
- The problem is not in the standardized tests themselves, but their misuse.
- The elimination of objective standardized approaches to assessment will lead to more subjective and less reliable and valid assessment procedures and to the very bias that objective standardized instruments are designed to avoid.
- Since students eventually are going to have to function in the mainstream, their performance should be assessed in terms of mainstream content, format, and norms.
- Objective and standardized measures are necessary to compare the achievement of different groups in order to identify inequities and problem areas that need to be corrected. "Test results provide a way for the public to moni-

tor educational standards over time. Test results also help teachers and school officials to indentify weaknesses in instruction and curriculum. Tests provide the data that enable parents and others to keep the pressure on communities, schools, and educators to 'close the gap' between the performance of black students and that of whites—pressure that is finally bringing results" (159, p. 624).

Pluralistic Norms

In the 1970s, a number of researchers attempted to improve the validity of norm-referenced tests by providing different norms for different groups of students. In theory, the use of pluralistic norms for different groups allowed assessors to compare students to others like them from a similar background, with the same motivation to do well, and the same exposure to the tasks and information. This approach was criticized on a number of grounds (92, 164–167), such as the following:

• Pluralistic norms do not compare students to others who are like them because students from similar ethnic or socioeconomic-class background are actually very different. For example, they are not all equally motivated to succeed either in school or when they are assessed, and their exposure at home to school-related information and the support they receive from their parents may be very different.

• The original national norms reflect the reality at the moment. Thus, if students are compared to a small select group using pluralistic norms, then the results cannot predict how they will function in mainstream America when they have to compete with many others who do not share the same socioeconomic-class, ethnic, or regional background. "If the question is how a particular Chinese-American fifth-grade boy compares in reading to other fifth-grade Chinese-American boys, then culturally appropriate norms would be used. On the other hand, if the question is how this same boy compares with other fifth-grade boys in general, then much broader norms naturally must be consulted" (166, p. 207).

• Lowering standards by using pluralistic norms will lead to the selection of students for programs such as gifted and talented who may not succeed. "If the goal of achieving a desegregated society is still seen as worth pursuing (a value judgment), then the minority child should be compared against a national reference group, for this is the group with which the minority child must compete. When one is looking for a physician to treat him, he does not add 10 points to the physician's competency score to offset limitations stemming from sociocultural background; instead, one looks for the most competent physician, regardless of racial or ethnic background" (92, p. 62).

• Pluralistic norms encourage educators, psychologists, and society in general to accept stereotypical ideas that all people in a group or subgroup are alike. Since pluralistic norms are usually lower for most non-European American groups, they encourage educators, psychologists, and others to believe these groups of students are less capable and to expect less from them. This can result in self-fulfilling prophesies.

Studies done in the late 1970s and early 1980s indicate that assessors' decisions based on pluralistic norms are no more valid than those based on traditional national norms when students' schools did not use multicultural approaches. Estimates of students' learning potential that were based on pluralistic norms yielded less valid predictions of their achievement in schools that were designed for the dominant European American middle-class culture than their original IQ scores (164, 167). Thus, it appears that pluralistic norms can identify students who should not be considered mildly developmentally disabled, but they do not predict how well students will do in school or whether they will learn more in regular education or special education programs.

SELF-
QUIZ   **CONTENT, FORMAT, AND NORMS**

- What is your opinion about modifying the content, format, and norms of assessment procedures?
- Do you think that adapting assessment procedures to students' culturally, contextually, and geographical backgrounds makes them less biased and more useful? Or do you believe that all students should be assessed on the same content, in the same way, and compared to norms based on a national sample? State the reasons for your opinion.

Informal, Nonstandardized, Criterion-Referenced Assessment

Educators have always used informal approaches to assess students. The typical weekly spelling, math, and social studies tests are examples of informal approaches to assessing students' academic progress. Determining if a student who is a refugee has emotional problems or is merely conforming to a cultural pattern by comparing his behavior to that of other students who have a similar contextual, ethnic, and socioeconomic-class background is an example of informal assessment of students behavior (167, 168). Asking parents to compare a student's adaptive behavior at home and in the community with those of her siblings, cousins, or other neighborhood children is an example of a culturally appropriate informal way of evaluating students' out-of-school achievement (169). The references at the end of the chapter include practical suggestions for special educators who wish to develop their own criterion-referenced procedures (153, 167, 168).

Informal, nonstandardized, criterion-referenced assessments can have many advantages over formal, standardized, norm-referenced assessments. Consider the following:

- The information they provide has a more direct relationship to the decisions teachers have to make about instructing and managing students (e.g., what their strengths and weaknesses are, what skills they have and have not acquired, and where to begin with particular students).
- The criteria students are measured against are those deemed important by the assessor rather than the standardized test developers.
- They evaluate students in terms of activities, skills, and subject matter that they have actually been taught and practiced.
- They can be used to determine if students have accomplished the goals set by the teacher, department, or school district.

However, some educators and psychologists have serious questions about informal, nonstandardized, criterion-referenced assessment approaches. The following are typical of their concerns:

- Because special educators are not as knowledgeable about principles of assessment as professional test developers, the criterion-referenced procedures they prepare may not be as reliable or valid.
- Many teachers have biased expectations for certain groups of students and evaluate them in a discriminatory manner. Standardized assessment can help avoid such discrimination; allowing biased teachers to develop their own assessment procedures would increase discriminatory assessment, not prevent it.
- Criterion-referenced assessment does not facilitate comparisons between schools and programs that employ different criteria to measure students' progress. Thus, it would be exceedingly difficult to determine if some programs and schools are succeeding more than others.
- Comparing students to a limited, particularistic set of criteria does not indicate how they are functioning in comparison to other students in general nor does it enable educators to predict how students will function in society where criteria may be very different.

In recent years, proponents of nonstandardized, informal assessment have developed a number of new well-developed and organized informal nonstandardized approaches that they believe to be superior to standardized assessment. Three approaches that are particularly popular are portfolio assessment, curriculum-based assessment, and test-teach-test.

Portfolio Assessment

Portfolio assessment—also called assessment in context, situational testing, and authentic assessment—is a particular form of criterion-referenced assessment that emphasizes assessing what students actually do or perform. Portfolio assessment has been defined as "a purposeful, chronological collection of student work, designed to reflect student development in one or more areas over time and student outcomes at one or more designated points in time" (170, p. 256).

Portfolios contain evidence of students' work that tells the story of their accomplishment and process of achieving it. The material in a portfolio can be constructed, created, or described by students; material may be audiotaped, written, videotaped, or photographed. Portfolios can contain only students' final, completed work or their work at different stages over time showing how their work improved. Portfolios may include a number of totally different tasks or the same task performed many times over the course of weeks, months, a semester, or a year.

"The portfolio collection should not be restricted simply to the student's best work. It should also include drafts, outlines, and early attempts; these are equally important to the task of demonstrating what the student has learned and the specific skills and concepts mastered" (174, pp. 12–13). Portfolios may also contain students' grades, test scores, honors, testimonies from others, teachers' observation and evaluation of students' performance, interview protocols, student self-reports, and so on.

Proponents of portfolio assessment believe it offers educators all of the advantages of criterion-referenced assessment noted earlier. In addition, they claim the following:

- Portfolio assessment evaluates students in terms of the real-life authentic tasks in the situations in which students are actually functioning.
- It provides much more detailed and comprehensive data than an answer on a multiple-choice item.
- It provides information about how students learn. Portfolio assessment "reaches well beyond the 'snapshot' examination that captures only the student's knowledge and capabilities at a specific moment" (174, p. 3).
- It enables students to use their preferred learning and communication styles and linguistic ability in English and their native language in order to demonstrate their accomplishments.
- It encourages students to take responsibility for their own learning.
- It assists teachers in establishing assessment targets standards (goals and priorities)—measurable objective standards against which students' progress is evaluated.

The concerns that have been expressed about criterion-referenced assessment in general also apply to portfolio assessment. Two concerns should be emphasized:

- It is important that assessors use objectives, standards, and goals against which students' performance can be measured in order to avoid subjectivity.
- Since teachers' evaluations of poor and non-European American students can be prejudiced, the use of subjective portfolio assessment may lead to even more bias than results from objective standardized procedures.

Research indicates that educators can be trained to evaluate portfolios in a reliable manner (171, 173). Anecdotal evidence suggests that portfolio assessment can produce useful assessment information about European American, non-European American, and limited-English-proficient students (172). However, there is little research evidence that decisions based on students' portfolios are more valid than those based on standardized norm-referenced assessment procedures. Therefore, French's conclusion about the validity of portfolio assessment with limited-English-proficient students probably applies equally well to all students. "There appears to be great potential in the use of portfolio with LEP students. However, the value is yet to be determined. Experimentation, perhaps as much as tens years of it, will be needed. Thankfully, that experiment is underway" (170, p. 271).

Curriculum-Based Assessment

Curriculum-based assessment is a relatively new and not very widely used approach that evaluates students in terms of the curriculum to which they have been and are being exposed (175–181). To use a curriculum-based evaluation approach, a school district or a similar entity establishes the content and objectives of a particular curriculum (such as fifth-grade math, third-grade spelling, American History 2, Spanish 3, etc.) and develops a series of probes—assessments that teachers and others can employ to determine how well students have achieved each of these objectives. Examples of typical probes include the number of words students read correctly in a reader or word list and the number of words spelled correctly from a spelling list in one or two minutes.

These probes can be used to compare students' achievement of the objectives of the curriculum to their peers' achievement on the same curriculum. This enables assessors to determine if students are far enough behind to warrant possible referral to or enrollment in special education. By evaluating students' achievement in many areas of the curriculum (i.e., reading, spelling, written language, and math computation), educators can obtain an estimate of students' overall ability. They can then compare this estimate to students' achievement in a particular subject area to determine whether it is significantly below their general potential to qualify them for programs for students with learning disabilities. Curriculum-based assessment can also be used to monitor students' progress in the curriculum, to determine whether students have achieved a particular goal, and whether they have progressed to the point that they no longer require special education services.

Curriculum-based assessment offers the following advantages over standardized tests:

- It avoids the problem of assessing students on tasks, skills, and knowledge that they have not been taught.
- It does not compare students to norms based on a national sample of students, many of whom attend schools that do not resemble theirs and live in other parts of the country.

- Since it can be administered informally as part of the regular classroom activities, it may make students less anxious and thereby provide a more accurate measure of their achievement.
- It can be used repeatedly with students, whereas standardized tests have to be administered sparingly because they usually do not come in many alternate forms.
- It is more sensitive to short-term improvement in student achievement and provides information that can be used to make day-to-day instructional decisions.

Curriculum-based assessment also has the following disadvantages and limitations:

- It requires a standardized schoolwide or districtwide curriculum.
- It focuses primarily on achievement of basic academic skills and objectives in reading, spelling, written language, and math computation.
- It can be very expensive to develop.
- Standardized test publishers almost always provide information about their reliability and validity, but school systems that develop curriculum-based assessment procedures have to do this for themselves. In the absence of such information, special educators and others cannot be confident that the assessment procedures accurately and reliably measure what they are supposed to measure.
- It does not provide information about the causes of students' lack of progress toward the attainment of curriculum objectives.
- The format is often too inflexible to be adapted to the needs of students from diverse socioeconomic-class, contextual, and cultural backgrounds.
- There appear to be few school districts that have used this approach to evaluate limited-English-proficient students.
- Although students are typically compared to other students in their districts, some groups may be so small (e.g., migrant students and non-European American students) that they may actually be compared to students very unlike themselves. This can be reduced by selecting class, schoolwide, or districtwide norms, if they are available, depending on which would be more representative of students' backgrounds.
- If students are functioning below their potential in most areas of the academic curriculum, estimations based on their average level of achievement may underestimate their potential.
- The use of local norms may encourage low expectations for students if able students' goals are based on the average or typical scores of their peers or if the local regular education or special education norms are below the national average.
- Although it has proven to be useful for making decisions on the elementary level about whether students are eligible for special education, there is little evidence of its usefulness on the secondary level.

Research indicates that curriculum-based assessment approaches can be used to differentiate low-achieving students from students with learning disabilities. Its use during the prereferral phase has reduced the number of students who are eventually assessed and the proportion of referred students found to require special education programs (178, 179).

Given these advantages and limitations, curriculum-based assessment approaches appear to be a promising method of obtaining information about students. However, for the present at least, because the information it provides is limited to academic achievement, especially in basic skills areas, and it does not necessarily provide information that is free from contextual, cultural, linguistic, and gender bias, its current usefulness with poor, non-European American, and limited-English-proficient students has not yet lived up to its promise.

Test-Teach-Test

The test-teach-test approach—also called assisted assessment, reciprocal teaching, and dynamic assessment—is an assessment method that is designed to evaluate students' learning potential by studying how they actually learn (182–185). As its name implies, the test-teach-test approach includes three steps. First, students' achievement or functioning is assessed. Then, assessors attempt to remediate or improve the students' functioning or achievement. Finally, students are reevaluated in order to determine the extent of improvement that can be expected as well as how much and what kinds of additional help are required for a given amount of improvement.

Traditional approaches are based on the assumption that students' learning potentials are reflected in what they have learned. They measure what students know and can do and they attribute more learning potential to students who know more of the information and can do more of the tasks included in the assessment procedure. The test-teach-test method, on the other hand, provides a direct measure of the extent to which students can learn if given additional help. It also reveals how much and what kinds of additional help students require to reach a specific goal or standard. It focuses on the trainability or educability of students' cognitive processes (learning ability).

Advantages claimed for the test-teach-test approach include the following (39, 182–185):

- It is a more valid measure of students' learning potential than traditional measures of IQ because it studies students' learning.
- Since it evaluates new learning rather than old learning, unlike traditional approaches, it does not require assumptions such as all students have been equally exposed to the information and have had equal opportunity to practice the tasks on which they are being assessed.
- It provides information about students' strengths and weaknesses and responds to their weaknesses by providing the feedback, practice, and support students may need to learn.

- It is a regular component of classroom activities rather than a test and therefore it is less threatening and anxiety provoking.
- It provides the initial guidance and modeling that students may require to learn.
- It teaches students the learning strategies they need for success and when and how to use them.

A number of concerns have been raised about the test-teach-test approach. Two that are especially important are the following:

- There is insufficient data to determine the validity and reliability of the data it produces.
- The method can produce biased data if assessors are not sufficiently knowledgeable about students to adapt the instructional techniques they use in the "teach" phase of the approach to students' cultural, contextual, gender, and linguistic characteristics. When assessors use inappropriate instructional techniques, they may incorrectly attribute the students' limited improvement to their supposedly limited learning potential rather than to the assessors' inappropriate teaching techniques.

SELF-QUIZ

FORMAL, STANDARDIZED, NORM-REFERENCED ASSESSMENT VERSUS INFORMAL, NONSTANDARDIZED, CRITERION-REFERENCED ASSESSMENT

- Do you have a preference between formal, standardized, norm-referenced, assessment and informal, nonstandardized, criterion-referenced assessment?
- State which type of assessment approach you would prefer to emphasize for each of the following tasks and explain the reasons for your preferences:

    To evaluate students' achievement

    To determine students' learning potentials

    To ascertain whether there is a significant discrepancy between students' learning potentials and their achievement

    To evaluate whether the goals of students' individualized educational plans have been reached

    To identify students' learning disabilities

    To determine whether students are eligible for programs for gifted and talented students

    To compare the effectiveness of different special education techniques and materials

---

INTERPRETATION OF DATA

Assessors' interpretation of the data they collect by means of formal, standardized, norm-referenced assessment; informal, nonstandardized, criterion-referenced assessment; and test-teach-test assessment can be problematic. Standardized procedures make it difficult for assessors to determine the reasons why students obtain their scores. Unless they examine students' answers carefully and/or interview them, they cannot tell from students' scores alone if students were familiar with the procedure, if they lacked sufficient time to complete the procedure, if they did not ask questions when they did not understand the directions, if they would not guess when guessing was to their advantage, if they were not motivated to perform their best, and so on.

Informal, nonstandardized, criterion-referenced assessment and test-teach-test assessment are also subject to assessor bias. As noted earlier, many assessors are biased against non-European American and poor students. Those who are not prejudiced may mistakenly interpret what they observe from their own cultural, contextual, and gender point of view. Hilliard stated many years ago, "A given style user will take the behavior of another style user and will not experience it as that behavior actually is, but will reinterpret that experience in terms of her own experiential views or her own experiential framework, thus frequently losing the essence of the experience of the person being observed. In some cases the assessor can comprehend the experiences of another style user only by actually 'changing' that person's experience" (155, p. 44).

To avoid such bias, assessment results should be reported along with a description of the context in which they were obtained and any limitations due to the assessors' lack of knowledge or experience (186). This should include such contextual factors as students' familiarity with the material and format of procedure, whether they were anxious or tense while they were being assessed, their motivation to perform well, whether they completed all parts and items of the procedure or were limited by time constraints, their reaction to the assessor, possible linguistic problems, and so on. Assessor limitations might include lack of fluency in the language spoken by students, inability to interpret the results obtained in terms of students' experiences, possible assessor bias, and so on.

GUIDELINES AND MODEL ASSESSMENT APPROACHES

A number of comprehensive guidelines have been published to assist individuals or schools during the assessment process to consider the various issues raised in this chapter and to avoid the many sources of bias. Many of them are listed in the references (153, 187–189). These guidelines can be quite helpful at avoiding bias in general. However, assessors also need specific assessment models and materials to supplement these guidelines, especially when they evaluate students who may have learning disabilities, mild cognitive disabilities, emotional and behavioral problems, and gifts and talents. Current approaches to avoiding bias when identifying students with learning disabilities, mild cognitive disabilities, and gifts and talents are briefly described next. The identification of students with emotional and behavioral problems is discussed in Chapter 11.

Learning Disabilities

There are a number of well-established comprehensive assessment models that are designed to assist educators to employ culturally and linguistically appropriate techniques to the evaluation of students who may require special education services for students with disabilities (190–193). The developers of the two models described here for assessing students who may have learning disabilities have prepared training materials to facilitate their adaptation by interested schools and individuals.

AIM for the BESt (Assessment and Intervention Model for the Bilingual Exceptional Student) is an approach to avoid misplacement of LEP students in special education (193). Major emphasis is placed on preventing inappropriate referrals by providing students with appropriate educational environments through "restructuring schools to open up communication with the school community . . . using participatory and cooperative teaching and learning approaches . . . and providing instructional content that is challenging and that is culturally and personally relevant" (193, p. v). Prereferral intervention consists of three phases: training regular classroom teachers and special educators in effective instructional strategies, training teachers to validate students' learning problems, and using campus student/teacher assistance teams to assist teachers in solving the problems of students who demonstrate problems despite these efforts. Those who are assessed after prereferral intervention are evaluated in a culturally and linguistically appropriate manner that stresses curriculum-based and other informal assessment procedures.

Exito is another comprehensive approach to eliminate the misplacement of LEP students in special education (190). The goals of the Exito model are: "1. to refine district policies and procedures concerning referrals of culturally and linguistically diverse students to special education, 2. to create an assessment environment that is student-need driven, and 3. to empower all members of regular education referral teams and special education assessment teams with the ability to formulate clinical judgements about the needs of culturally and linguistically different students" (190, p. 1). An eight-session training program is devoted to improving educators' competencies in the following areas: identifying how cultural factors impact on teachers' perceptions of students, understanding the effect of limited English proficiency on students' achievement, prereferral and referral processes, evaluating the match between the educational environment and students' needs, selecting and administering assessment instruments, informal assessment, and linguistically appropriate assessment.

Mild Cognitive Disabilities

Some progress has been made in reducing the overrepresentation of non-European American and poor students in programs for students with mild cognitive disabilities. This progress can be attributed to a number of factors, such as the following:

- Since court cases such as *Diana v. the State Board of Education* (1973) and *Larry P. v. Wilson Riles,* Superintendent of Public Instruction for the State of California (1979), and the passage of PL 94-142, the results of standardized intelligence tests are no longer the sole criteria for identifying students with limited cognitive potential. There has been a decrease in the inclusion of the results of primarily verbal standardized intelligence tests as one of the criteria for identifying such students. Although such intelligence tests are still used with non-European American and poor students in states where they are permitted, newer intelligence tests that in some studies appear to be less biased, such as the Kaufman Assessment Battery for Children, are being employed with increasing frequency. As noted earlier, other less biased means of evaluating students' cognitive ability, including the test-teach-test approach and portfolio assessment, are also being used.
- Limited-English-proficient students are somewhat less likely to be assessed by means of English language instruments.
- Decisions about students' cognitive development are no longer being made only on the basis of their functioning in school. Now it is necessary to evaluate the extent to which students meet societal expectations outside the classroom (adaptive behavior) in order to determine whether their so-called cognitive disabilities also affect their nonschool functioning. The inclusion of measures of students' adaptive behavior has reduced the number of students in programs for students with mild cognitive disabilities because students who have problems only in school do not have innate limitations and are not accepted into such programs.

Students' nonschool adaptive behavior can be evaluated formally or informally. The most widely used standardized instruments for measuring adaptive behavior are the Adaptive Behavior Inventory for Children, the American Association on Mental Deficiency Behavior Scale–Public School Version, and the Vineland Social Maturity Scale. Studies done in the late 1970s and early 1980s have shown that all of these instruments are culturally biased because they include behavioral expectations that may not be age appropriate for some cultural and socioeconomic-class groups and they compare students' performance with norms derived from a primarily European American middle-class group (194–198). They lack different norms for males and females, which appear to be necessary in some cases. They may not be equally applicable to students from different regions of the country. Also, they are not available in the various languages that are spoken by the many limited-English-proficient students' referred for evaluation. Thus, although their use tends to reduce the number of poor and non-European American students accepted in programs for students with mild cognitive disabilities, they cannot be used as the sole measure of students' adaptive behavior.

Assessors who use informal assessment procedures can avoid the ethnic, gender, regional, and socioeconomic-class bias associated with standardized instruments as long as they compare students' adaptive behavior to ethnic, gender, regional, and socioeconomic-class appropriate expectations. If assessors are not knowledgeable enough to accomplish this, the results of informal evaluations of students' adaptive behavior may be no more valid than those obtained from standardized instruments.

The Bilingual Home Inventory is an example of an instrument that is designed to provide assessors with some of this knowledge. It is a culture-specific instrument that assists assessors in involving the parents of limited-English-proficient students' who may have cognitive disabilities in the assessment and IEP process (169). It is published in four languages—Chinese, Portuguese, Spanish, and Vietnamese—with the non-English and English versions of the test on opposite sides of each page. It includes suggestions for conducting culturally appropriate interviews with parents and it enables bilingual assessors who speak these languages or teams of monolingual assessors and bilingual interpreters to obtain the culturally appropriate information required to assess students' adaptive behavior. Although the Bilingual Home Inventory has proven to be a reliable instrument, unfortunately there is no information about its validity.

An approach to nondiscriminatory assessment of students' learning potential that appears promising is assessing multiple intelligences. Proponents of the multiple intelligences approach propose that there are many different intelligences. One theory of multiple intelligences that has been extensively studied and widely disseminated proposes that there are seven different intelligences: linguistic (verbal), logical-mathematical, spatial, musical, body-kinsethetic, interpersonal (ability to understand others), and intrapersonal (ability to understand oneself) (199, 200).

Educators and others who prefer the multiple intelligences approach claim it has two important advantages over traditional means of assessing intelligence when used to identify students who may have mild cognitive disabilities. These advantages are the following:

- Almost all traditional approaches rely exclusively on measures of students' linguistic and logical-mathematical intelligences. Although such measures have some ability to predict how well students will perform in school, they are poor indicators of how students will do out of school in situations that require many other intelligences. Those few traditional tests that do measure other intelligences do so verbally. Because these other intelligences are measured verbally, students who are not strong in the linguistic area are often unable to demonstrate their other intelligences. For these reasons, traditional approaches are prone to overidentify students who are thought to be less capable in general and to misplace them in programs for students with cognitive disabilities. Multiple intelligences approaches avoid this problem.

- Traditional approaches that measure only students' linguistic and logical-mathematical intelligences do not provide assessors with information about students' strengths and weaknesses. Multiple intelligences approaches, on the other hand, provide the information educators require to select curriculum and teaching styles that match students' most developed, efficient, and powerful intelligences.

Gifted and Talented

As noted in this chapter and in Chapter 1, African American, Hispanic American, Native American, limited-English-proficient, and poor students continue to be underrepresented in programs for the gifted and talented. In part, this is due to an overreliance on biased teacher nominations and norm-referenced standardized IQ tests to identify and assess candidates for these programs (3).

Some progress has been made. Educators are becoming better prepared to use behavior checklists and the like to identify non-European, poor, and limited-English-proficient students who should be assessed because they behave in ways that indicate they may be gifted and talented (4, 201–203). Numerous alternative methods for assessing gifted and talented students have been developed. Instruments such as the Matrix Analogy Test and the Kaufman Assessment Battery for Children, which appear to avoid many of the problems of the original group of standardized IQ tests, are are being employed to identify non-European, poor, extremely bright students (204–206). Some assessors have adopted a multiple intelligences approach to identifying students' gifts and talents. A number of models for identifying gifted and talented students from non-European American, low-income, and rural backgrounds have also proved to be effective (155, 207–222).

CONCLUSIONS

A great deal of progress has been made in recent years toward the goal of non-biased assessment. Assessors are becoming more sensitive to the ways in which students' contextual, cultural, linguistic, and gender characteristics can affect the assessment process. New, promising approaches to assessment—such as curriculum-based assessment, portfolio assessment, and test-teach-test—appear to offer the possibility of less biased data. Guidelines for assessing students in a non-biased manner have been widely disseminated. Also, numerous models of non-biased assessment are available for adoption.

However, assessors still evaluate non-European American and poor students in a discriminatory manner. The validity of the new assessment approaches has not yet been established. In addition, the new models of identifying students with learning disabilities, mild cognitive disabilities, and gifts and talents have their limitations. Therefore, Sennett's conclusion that was made in the early 1980s about the assessment of limited-English-proficient students with disabilities applies equally well today to the assessment of English-proficient, non-European, rural, and poor students: "About the best that we can do is to move towards a system of 'least biases assessment' in which many safeguards are present to assure that cultural differences neither mask real deviance nor are mistaken for deviance" (223, p. 32).

SUMMARY

Assessment procedures have not been very effective when used with non-European American, limited-English-proficient, and poor students. The situation has improved somewhat in recent years, especially as a result of various federal laws and court cases. New approaches to identifying non-European American, limited-English-proficient, and poor students with learning disabilities, mild cognitive disabilities, and gifts and talents appear to be less biased than those they are replacing. However, there is still need for improvement. The major sources of bias in the assessment process continue to include failure to adapt procedures to the contextual, cultural, linguistic, and gender differences among students; assessors' discriminatory practices against and lack of information about non-European American and poor students; inadequacies in assessment materials and procedures; and mistakes in the interpretation of the information obtained.

ACTIVITIES

1. Describe yourself in terms of the student characteristics discussed in this chapter. Then ask a few of your peers whose backgrounds are unlike yours to do the same. Do you observe a great deal of similarity or difference among individuals from different backgrounds?

2. Most professors use one assessment approach with all students, regardless of their background. A few professors offer students a choice between oral and written exams or between multiple-choice and essay formats. Some provide students with as much time as they need to complete their exams; others typically require some of their students to rush through their exams or hand in incomplete work. Some professors are flexible about deadlines for completing work such as papers; others lower students' grades if their work is late or even refuse to accept it. A few professors use portfolio assessment, videotapes, and other innovative approaches to assess students. How have your professors evaluated you over the years? Which of them have used a multicultural approach to assess students? Which of them have employed the same approach with all students? Is there one particular format that you prefer? How often have your professors used it?

3. How would you like your achievement to be evaluated in the course in which you are using this text? Compare your preference to those of other students in the course. Are you basically in agreement or do many of you have different preferences?

4. Observe a class for gifted and talented students. Are there observable behavioral differences among students from different ethnic and socioeconomic-class backgrounds?

5. Compare the ethnic makeup of the students in a school district to their representation in programs for gifted and talented students and for students with learning disabilities and mild cognitive disabilities.

6. Compare the percentage of limited-English-proficient, immigrant, and migrant students in a school district to its percentage of students in programs for gifted and talented students.

7. Study the procedures that were followed by a school district in placing a few students in special education. Were adequate prereferral intervention techniques employed before students were evaluated for possible special education placement? In which languages were limited-English-proficient students assessed? Were the same assessment techniques or tests used with all students or were different procedures and materials selected for each student? Did the assessors describe and discuss the results of their assessment procedures in context or did they merely note the scores the students obtained?

REFERENCES

The quotation that begins this chapter is found in reference 1.

1. Mitchell, A. J. (1937, September). The effect of bilingualism in the measurement of intelligence. *Elementary School Journal*, pp. 29–37.

Lack of equity in the identification and enrollment of non-European American students in programs for the gifted and talented is discussed in references 2–4.

2. Cohen, L. (1990). *Meeting the Needs of Gifted and Talented Minority Language Students*. Reston VA: ERIC Clearinghouse on Handicapped and Gifted.

3. VanTassel-Baska, J., Patton, J., & Prillaman, D. (1989). Disadvantaged gifted learners at-risk for educational neglect. *Focus on Exceptional Children*, 22 (3), 1–16.

4. Yancey, E. (1990). *Increasing Minority Participation in Gifted Programs*. Washington, DC: Mid-Atlantic Equity Center.

References 5–8 discuss the high rate of student acceptance to and misplacement in special education.

5. Algozzine, B., Christenson, S., & Ysseldyke, J. (1982). Probabilities associated with the referral to placement process. *Teacher Education and Special Education*, 5 (3), 19–23.

6. Shepherd, L. (1987). The new push for excellence: Widening the schism between regular and special education. *Exceptional Children*, 53 (4), 327–329.

7. Ysseldyke, J. E., Algozzine, B. J., & Thurlow, M. L. (1992). *Critical Issues in Special Education*. Dallas, TX: Houghton Miflin.

8. Ysseldyke, J. E., Thurlow, M., Graden, J., Wesson, C., & Algozzine, B. (1983). Generalizations from five years of research on assessment and decision making: The University of Minnesota Institute. *Exceptional Education Quarterly, 4,* 75–93.

Prereferral intervention procedures and their effectiveness are the focus of references 9–25.

9. Avenida, L. (1988). *Preventing Inappropriate Referrals of Language Minority Students to Special Education.* San Francisco: Bilingual Education Department, San Francisco Unified School District.

10. Benavides, A. (1986). *Guidelines for the Implementation of the Initial Screening for Students from a Non-English Background.* ERIC ED 291 176.

11. Carter, J., & Sugai, G. (1989). Survey on prereferral practices: Responses from state departments of education. *Exceptional Children, 55* (4), 1–3.

12. Chalfant, J. C., & Van Dusen Pysh, M. (1989). Teacher assistance teams: Five descriptive studies on 96 teams. *Remedial and Special Education, 10* (6), 49–58.

13. Dodd, J. M. (1992). *Preventing American Indian Children from Overidentification with Learning Disabilities: Cultural Considerations during the Prereferral Process.* Paper presented at the Council for Exceptional Children Topical Conference on Culturally and Linguistically Diverse Exceptional Children, Minneapolis.

14. Fuchs, D., Fuchs, L. S., Bauhr, M. W., Fernstrom, P., & Stecker, P. M. (1990). Prereferral intervention: A prescriptive approach. *Exceptional Children, 56* (6), 493–513.

15. Garcia, S. B., & Ortiz, A. A. (1988). *Preventing Inappropriate Referrals of Language Minority Students to Special Education. Occasional Papers in Bilingual Education.* ERIC ED 309 591.

16. Gartner, A. (1986). Disabling help: Special education at the crossroads. *Exceptional Children, 53* (1), 72–76.

17. Graden, J. (1989). Redefining "prereferral" intervention as intervention assistance: Collaboration between general and special education. *Exceptional Children, 56* (3), 227–231.

18. Heller, K. A., & Holtzman, W. H. (1982). *Placing Children in Special Education: A Strategy for Equity.* Washington, DC: National Academy Press.

19. Michigan State Board of Education. (1987). *Program Suggestions for the Provision of Special Education Services to Limited English Proficient Students in Michigan Schools.* ERIC ED 303 953.

20. Moscoso, R. W. (1989). *The Praise Intervention Checklist for Teachers: Prereferral Accommodations and Interventions for Students in ESL.* Unpublished manuscript, Washington, DC, McFarland Special Education Center, District of Columbia Public Schools.

21. Ortiz, A. A. (1992). Assessing appropriate and inappropriate referral systems for LEP special education students. In *Proceedings of the Second National Research Symposium on Limited English Proficient Student Issues: Focus on Evaluation and Measurement, Vol I.* Washington, DC: U.S. Department of Education, Office of Bilingual Education and Minority Languages Affairs.

22. Ortiz, A. A., & Maldonado-Colon, E. (1986). Recognizing learning disabilities in bilingual children: How to lessen inappropriate referrals of language minority students to special education. *Journal of Reading, Writing, and Learning Disabilities International, 1* (1), 47–56.

23. Phillips, V., & McCullough, L. (1990). Consultation-based programming: Instituting the collaborative ethic in schools. *Exceptional Children, 56* (4), 291–304.

24. Ramage, J. C. (1988). *Policy and Alternative Assessment Guideline Recommendations: A Report of the Larry P. Task Force.* Sacramento: California State Department of Education.

25. Reschly, D. J. (1988). Minority MMR overrepresentation and special education reform. *Exceptional Children, 54* (4), 316–323.

Court cases and federal laws that pertain to nondiscriminatory assessment are discussed in references 26–32.

26. *Diana* v. *The State Board of Education* (1973). Education for Handicapped Children Act of 1974 (Public Law 94-142).

27. *Guadalupe* v. *Tempe Elementary School District* (1971).

28. *Jose P.* v. *Gordon M. Ambach et al.* (1979).

29. *Larry P.* v. *Wilson Riles,* Superintendent of Public Instruction for the State of California (1979).

30. *Lora* v. *Board of the City of New York* (465 F. Supp. 1211) (1977).

31. *PASE (Parents in Action on Special Education) et al. v. Hannon et al.* (1980).
32. U.S. Office of Civil Rights Memorandum of May 25, 1975.

References 33–37 discuss current and historical criticisms of discriminatory assessment.

33. Bond, H. M. (1924). What the army "intelligence" tests measured. *Opportunity, 2,* 197–202.
34. Colvin, S. S., & Allen, R. D. (1923). Mental tests and linguistic ability. *Journal of Educational Psychology, 14* (1), 1–20.
35. Cummins, J. (1986). Psychological assessment of minority students: Out of context, out of focus, out of control. *Journal of Reading, Writing, and Learning Disabilities International, 2* (1), 9–19.
36. Frazier, E. F. (1928). The mind of the American Negro. *Opportunity, 6,* 263–266.
37. Thompson, C. H. (1928). The educational achievement of Negro children. *Annals of the American Academy of Political and Social Sciences, 140,* 193–205.

Test anxiety is the focus of references 38–43.

38. Clawson, T. W., Firment, C. K., & Trower, T. L. (1981). Test anxiety: Another origin for racial bias in standardized testing. *Measurement and Evaluation in Guidance, 13* (4), 210–215.
39. Dao, M. (1991). Designing assessment procedures for educationally at-risk Southeast Asian-American students. *Journal of Learning Disabilities, 24* (10), 594–601.
40. Grossman, H. (1984). *Educating Hispanic Students: Cultural Implications for Instruction, Classroom Management, Counseling, and Assessment.* Springfield, IL: Thomas.
41. Hill, K. T. (1980). *Eliminating Motivational Causes of Test Bias. Final Report, October 1, 1976 through March 31, 1980.* ERIC ED 196 936.
42. Nguyen, K. T. (1984). *Assessing and Counseling Vietnamese Exceptional Students: Some Cultural Factors to Be Considered.* Santa Clara, CA: Santa Clara County Office of Education.
43. Payne, B. D. (1984). The relationship of test anxiety and answer-changing behavior: An analysis by race and sex. *Measurement and Evaluation in Guidance, 16* (4), 205–211.

References 44–55 discuss students' familiarity with assessment procedures and the effects of training in "test-wiseness" on students' subsequent performance and enrollment in special education.

44. Bangert-Drowns, R. L., Kulik, R. L., & Kulik, C. C. (1983). Effects of coaching programs on achievement test scores. *Review of Educational Research, 53,* 571–585.
45. Bell-Mick, L. (1983). *Assessment Procedures and Enrollment Patterns of Cuban-American, Mexican-Americans, and Puerto Ricans in Special Education Programs.* Paper presented at the annual meeting of the American Educational Research Association, Montreal.
46. Benson, J., Urman, H., & Hocevar, D. (1986). Effects of test-wiseness training and ethnicity on achievement of third-and fifth-grade students. *Measurement and Evaluation in Counseling and Development, 18* (4), 154–162.
47. Brescia, W., & Fortune, J. C. (1988). *Standardized Testing of American Indian Students.* Las Cruces, NM: ERIC/CRESS.
48. Bridgeman, B., & Buttram, J. (1975). Race differences on nonverbal analogy test performance as a function of verbal strategy training. *Journal of Educational Psychology, 67* (4), 586–590.
49. Haladyna, T. M., Nolen, S. B., & Hass, N. S. (1991). Raising standard achievement scores and the origins of test score pollution. *Educational Researcher, 20* (5), 2–7.
50. Kalechstein, P., Kalechstein, M., & Doctre, R. (1981). The effects of instruction on test-taking skills in second-grade black children. *Measurement and Evaluation in Guidance, 13* (4), 198–202.
51. McPhail, I. P. (1985). Instructional strategies for teaching test-wiseness. In C. Brooks (Ed.), *Tapping Potential: English Language Arts for the Black Learner.* Urbana IL: National Council of Teachers of English.
52. Samson, G. E. (1985). Effects of training in test-taking skills on achievement test performance: A quantitative synthesis. *Journal of Educational Research, 78* (5), 266.
53. Sarnacki, R. E. (1979). An examination of test-wiseness in the cognitive test domain. *Review of Educational Research, 49,* 252–279.
54. Schubert, J., & Cropley, A. (1972). Verbal regulation of behavior and IQ in Canadian Indian and white children. *Developmental Psychology, 7,* 295–301.

55. Scruggs, T. E. (1984). *The Administration and Interpretation of Standardized Achievement Tests with Learning Disabled and Behaviorally Disordered Elementary School Children.* Unpublished paper, Salt Lake City, Utah University.

The relationship between students' motivation and their functioning during assessment procedures is discussed in references 56–64.

56. Burgess, B. J. (1978). Native American learning styles. In L. Morris, G. Sather, & S. Scull (Eds.), *Extracting Learning Styles from Social/Cultural Diversity: A Study of Five American Minorities.* Norman, OK: Southwest Teacher Corps Network.

57. Chamberlain, K. P., & Medinos-Landurand, P. (1991). Practical considerations for the assessment of LEP students with special needs. In E. V. Hamayan & J. S. Damico (Eds.), *Limiting Bias in the Assessment of Bilingual Students.* Austin, TX: PRO-ED.

58. Condon, E. C., Peters, J. Y., & Sueiro-Ross, C. (1979). *Special Education and the Hispanic Child: Cultural Perspectives.* Philadelphia: Temple University, Teacher Corps Mid-Atlantic Network.

59. Deyhle, D. (1987). Learning failure: Tests as gatekeepers and the culturally different child. In H. E. Trueba (Ed.), *Success or Failure?* Rawley, MA: Newbury House.

60. Goldstein, B. L. (1988). In search of survival: The education and integration of Hmong refugee girls. *Journal of Ethnic Studies, 16* (2), 1–27.

61. Grossman, H. (1990). *Trouble Free Teaching: Solutions to Behavior Problems in the Classroom.* Mountain View, CA: Mayfield.

62. Lyons, G. (1979). A high school on an Indian reservation: A question of survival, developing goals, and giving leadership. *British Educational Administration Society, 7,* 130–138.

63. National Coalition of Advocates for Students. (1988). *New Voices: Immigrant Students in U.S. Public Schools.* Boston: Author.

64. Slogett, B. B. (1971). Use of group activities and team rewards to increase individual classroom productivity. *Teaching Exceptional Children, 3* (2), 54–66.

The effects of assessor characteristics on the outcome of assessment procedures is discussed in references 65–75.

65. Fuchs, L. S., & Fuchs, D. (1984). Examiner accuracy during protocol completion. *Journal of Psychoeducational Assessment, 2,* 101–108.

66. Fuchs, D., & Fuchs, L. S. (1986). Test procedure bias: A meta-analysis of examiner familiarity effects. *Review of Educational Research, 56* (2), 243–262.

67. Gantt, W. N., Wilson, R. M., & Dayton, C. M. (1974–1975). An initial investigation of the relationship between syntactical divergency and the listening comprehension of black children. *Reading Research Quarterly, 10* (2), 193–211.

68. Garcia, A. B., & Zimmerman, B. J. (1972). The effect of examiner ethnicity and language on the performance of bilingual Mexican-American first graders. *Journal of Social Psychology, 87,* 3–11.

69. Gay, G., & Abrahams, R. D. (1973). Does the pot melt, boil, or brew? Black children and white assessment procedures. *Journal of School Psychology, 11* (4), 330–340.

70. Gollnick, D., & Chinn, P. (1988) *Multicultural Education in a Pluralistic Society.* St Louis: Mosby.

71. Mishra, S. P. (1980). The influence of examiners' ethnic attributes on intelligence test scores. *Psychology in the Schools, 17* (1), 117–121.

72. Ratusnik, D. L., & Koenigsknecht, R. A. (1977). Biracial testing: The question of clinicians' influence on children's test performance. *Language, Speech, and Hearing Services in Schools, 8* (3–4), 5–14.

73. Terrell, F., & Terrell, S. L. (1983). The relationship between race of examiner, cultural mistrust, and the intelligence test performance of black children. *Psychology in the Schools, 20,* 367–369.

74. Terrell, F., Terrell, J. L., & Taylor, J. (1981). Effects of type of reinforcement on the intelligence test performance of retarded black children. *Psychology in the Schools, 18,* 225–227.

75. Williams, J. (1988). The color of their skin. *Parenting, 2* (2), 48–53.

References 76–78 deal with the relationship between communication style and assessment results.

76. California State Department of Education. (1987). *Handbook for Teaching Japanese-Speaking Students.* Sacramento, CA: Author.

77. Crago, M. (1988). *Cultural Context in Communicative Interaction of Inuit Children.* Unpublished doctoral dissertation, Montreal, McGill University.

78. National Council of La Raza. (1986). *Beyond Ellis Island: Hispanics—Immigrants and Americans.* Washington, DC: Author.

The influence of students' learning style on their functioning during the assessment process is the focus of references 79–83.

79. Almanza, H. P., & Mosley, W. J. (1980). Cultural adaptations and modifications for culturally diverse handicapped children. *Exceptional Children, 46* (8), 608–614.

80. Boykin, A. W. (1982). Task variability and the performance of black and white school children. *Journal of Black Studies, 12* (4), 469–485.

81. Longstreet, E. (1978). *Aspects of Ethnicity.* New York: Teachers College Press.

82. Shade, B. J. (1979). *Racial Preference in Psychological Differentiation: An Alternative Explanation for Group Differences.* ERIC ED 179 672.

83. Tharp, G. (1989). Psychocultural variables and constants: Effects on teaching and learning in schools. *American Psychologist, 44* (2), 349–359.

References 84–86 focus on how the pace at which students work and play can affect the results of assessments.

84. Ayabe, H. I. (1978). Ethnic-culture, reflection impulsivity and locus of control. *Educational Perspectives, 17* (4), 10–12.

85. Gardner, W. E. (1977). A model for creating a more hospitable achievement test environment for black elementary students. *Negro Educational Review, 28* (3/4), 229–236.

86. Levine, R. V., West, L. J., & Reis, H. T. (1980). Perceptions of time and punctuality in the United States and Brazil. *Journal of Personality and Social Psychology, 38* (4), 541–550.

The tendency of African American students to select extreme responses on Likert Scales is documented in references 87–88.

87. Bachman, J. G., & O'Malley, P. M. (1984). Yea-saying, nay-saying and going to extremes: Are black-white differences in survey results due to response styles? *Public Opinion Quarterly, 48,* 409–427.

88. Bachman, J. G., & O'Malley, P. M. (1984). Black-white differences in self-esteem: Are they affected by response styles? *American Journal of Sociology, 90* (3), 624–639.

Reference 89 describes the relationship between assessors' inexperience and the likelihood that students will be referred to special education.

89. Carpenter, L. J. (1992). The influence of examiner knowledge based on diagnostic decision making with language minority children. *Journal of Educational Issues of Language Minority Students, 2,* 139–161.

References 90–104 deal with content bias in assessment procedures.

90. Bagby, S. A. (1981). *Educational Testing for Migrant Students.* Las Cruces, NM: ERIC Clearinghouse on Rural Education and Small Schools.

91. Baldwin, J. A., & Bell, Y. R. (1985). The African Self-Consciousness Scale: An Africentric personality questionnaire. *Western Journal of Black Studies, 9* (2), 61–68.

92. Clarizio, H. F. (1982). Intellectual assessment of Hispanic children. *Psychology in the Schools, 19* (6), 61–71.

93. Conroy, A. A. (1992). The testing of minority language students. *Journal of Educational Issues of Language Minority Students, 2,* 175–186.

94. Fagen, J. (1987). Golden Rule revisited: Introduction. *Educational Measurement: Issues and Practice, 6* (2), 5–8.

95. Good, R. H. III, & Salvia, J. (1988). Curriculum bias in published norm-referenced reading tests: Demonstrable effects. *School Psychology Review, 17* (1), 51–60.

96. Hawley, L., & Williams, R. L. (1981). Feeling-tone and card preference of black college students for the TCB and TAT. *Journal of Non-White Concerns, 10* (1), 45–48.

97. Jaeger, M. M. (1987). NCME opposition to proposed Golden Rule legislation. *Educational Measurement: Issues and Practice, 6* (2), 21–22.

98. Rooney, J. P. (1987). Golden Rule on "Golden Rule." *Educational Measurement: Issues and Practice, 6* (2), 9–12.

99. Sandoval, J., & Mille, M. (1980). Accuracy of judgments of WISC-R item difficulty for minority groups. *Journal of Consulting and Clinical Psychology, 48,* 249–253.

100. Terrell, F., & Taylor, J. (1978). The development of an inventory to measure certain aspects of black nationalist ideology. *Psychology: A Quarterly Journal of Human Behavior, 15,* 31–33.

101. Terrell, F., & Terrell, S. (1981). An inventory to measure cultural mistrust among blacks. *Western Journal of Black Studies, 5* (3), 180–185.

102. Weaver, V. (1981). Racial attribution, story length, and feeling-tone of young black males to TCB and TAT. *Journal of Non-White Concerns, 10* (1), 31–43.

103. Weiss, J. (1987). The Golden Rule bias reduction principle: A practical reform. *Educational Measurement: Issues and Practice, 6* (2), 23–25.

104. Williams, R. L., & Johnson, R. C. (1981). Progress in developing Afrocentric measuring instruments. *Journal of Non-White Concerns, 10* (1), 3–18.

Format bias is the focus of references 105–106.

105. Llabre, M. M. (1988). *Test-Related Factors Affecting Test Performance of Hispanics.* Paper presented at the Annual Conference of the American Education Research Association, New Orleans.

106. Miller, V., Onotera, R. T., & Deinard, A. S. (1984). Denver Developmental Screening Test: Cultural variations in Southeast Asian children. *Journal of Pediatrics, 104* (3), 481–482.

The effects of linguistic bias is the focus of references 107–109.

107. Bergan, J. R., & Marra, E. B. (1979). Variations in IQ testing and instruction and the letter learning and achievement of Anglo and bilingual Mexican-American children. *Journal of Educational Psychology, 71* (6), 819–826.

108. Levandowski, B. (1975). The difference in intelligence test scores of bilingual students on an English version of the intelligence test as compared to a Spanish version of the test. *Illinois School Research, 11* (3), 47–51.

109. Wilkinson, C. Y., & Holtzman, W. H. (1988). *Relationship among Language Proficiency, Language of Test Administration and Special Education Eligibility for Bilingual Hispanic Students with Suspected Learning Disabilities.* ERIC ED 301 604.

References 110–114 deal with effective use of interpreters during the assessment process.

110. Del Green Associates. (1983). *A Review of Research Affecting Educational Programming for Bilingual Handicapped Students. Final Report.* ERIC ED 267 555.

111. Figueroa, R. A. (1989). Using interpreters in assessments. *Communique, 17,* 7, 19.

112. *Meet the Needs of Handicapped Language Minority Students and Their Families.* Washington, DC: National Clearinghouse for Bilingual Education.

113. Langdon, H. W. (1988). *Interpreters/Translators in the School Setting Module.* Sacramento: California State Department of Education.

114. Metz, I. B. (1991) Comments. In M. Anderson & P. F. Goldberg (Eds.), *Cultural Competence in Screening and Assessment: Implications for Services to Young Children with Special Needs Ages Birth through Five.* Minneapolis: PACER Center.

Authors of references 115–118 have not found bias when nonstandard dialect speakers are assessed in Standard English.

115. Desberg, P., Marsh, G., Schneider, L. A., & Duncan-Rose, C. (1979). The effects of social dialect on auditory sound blending and word recognition. *Contemporary Educational Psychology, 4,* 14–144.

116. Frentz, T. S. (1971). Children's comprehension of standard and Negro nonstandard English sentences. *Speech Monographs, 38,* 10–16.

117. Hockman, C. H. (1973). Black dialect reading tests in the urban schools. *Reading Teacher, 26,* 581–583.

118. Nolen, P. (1972). Reading of non-standard dialect materials, a study at grades two and four. *Child Development, 43,* 1092–1097.

References 119–142 describe bias resulting from assessing nonstandard dialect speakers with Standard English procedures and how to avoid it.

119. Baratz, J. (1969). *Language and Cognitive Assessment of Negro Children: Assumptions and Research Needs.* Paper presented at the annual meeting of the American Speech and Hearing Association, Washington, DC.

120. Benmaman, V., & Schenck, S. J. (1986). *Language Variability: An Analysis of Language Variability and Its Influence upon Special Education Assessment.* ERIC ED 296 532.

121. Bliss, L. S., & Allen, D. V. (1981). Black English responses on selected language tests. *Journal of Communication Disorders, 14,* 225–233.

122. Bryen, D. N. (1976). Speech-sound discrimination ability on linguistically unbiased tests. *Exceptional Children, 42* (4), 195–201.

123. Burke, S. M., Pflaum, S. W., & Knafle, J. D. (1982). The influence of Black English on diagnosis of reading in learning disabled and normal readers. *Journal of Learning Disabilities, 15* (1), 19–22.

124. Byrd, M. L. , & Williams, H. S. (1981). *Language Attitudes and Black Dialect: An Assessment. (1) Language Attitudes in the Classroom. (2) A Reliable Measure of Language Attitude.* ERIC ED 213 062.

125. Cartledge, G., Stupay, D., & Kaczala, C. (1984). *Formal Language Assessment of Handicapped and Nonhandicapped Black Children.* ERIC ED 250 348.

126. Evans, J. S. (1972). Word-pair discrimination and imitation abilities of preschool Spanish-speaking children. *Journal of Learning Disabilities, 7* (9), 49–56.

127. Fisher, D., & Jablon, A. (1984). An observation of the phonology of black English speaking children. In Queens College Department of Communication Arts and Sciences. *Working Papers in Speech-Language Pathology and Audiology.* Flushing: City University of New York.

128. Harber, J. R. (1980). Issues in the assessment of language and reading disorders in learning disabled children. *Learning Disability Quarterly, 3* (4), 20–28.

129. Hemingway, B. L., Montague J. C. Jr., & Bradley, R. H. (1981). Preliminary data on revision of a sentence repetition test for language screening with black first grade children. *Language, Speech, and Hearing Services in Schools, 12,* 145–152.

130. Jensen, L. J. (1976). Dialect. In P. A. Allen (Ed.), *Findings of Research in Miscue Analyses: Classroom Implications.* Urbana, IL: National Council of Teachers of English.

131. Mackler, B., & Holman, D. (1976). Assessing, packaging, and delivery: Tests, testing, and race. *Young Children, 31* (5), 351–364.

132. Musselwhite, C. R. (1983). Pluralistic assessment in speech-language pathology: Use of dual norms in the placement process. *Language, Speech, and Hearing Services in Schools, 14,* 29–37.

133. Norris, M. K., Juarez, M. J. & Perkins, M. N. (1989). Adaptation of a screening test for bilingual and bidialectal populations. *Language, Speech, and Hearing Services in Schools, 20* (4), 381–390.

134. Ramstad, V. V., & Potter, R. E. (1974). Differences in vocabulary and syntax usage between Nez Perce Indian and white kindergarten children. *Journal of Learning Disabilities, 7* (8), 35–41.

135. Rivers, L. W. (1978). The influence of auditory-, visual-, and language-discrimination skills on the standardized test performance of Black children. *Journal of NonWhite Concerns, 6* (3), 134–140.

136. Ross, H. W. (1979). Wepman Test of Auditory Discrimination: What does it discriminate? *Journal of School Psychology, 17* (1), 47–54.

137. Seymour, H. N., & Seymour, C. M. (1977). A therapeutic model for communicative disorders among children who speak Black English vernacular. *Journal of Speech and Hearing Disorders, 42,* 238–246.

138. Thurmond, V. B. (1977). The effect of Black English on the reading test performance of high school students. *Journal of Educational Research, 70* (3), 160–163.

139. Vaughn-Cooke, F. B. (1980). Evaluation the language of black English speakers: Implications of the Ann Arbor decision. In M. F. Whileman (Ed.), *Reactions to Ann Arbor: Vernacular Black English and Education.* Arlington VA: Center for Applied Linguistics.

140. Wartella, A. B., & Williams, D. (1982). *Speech and Language Assessment of Black and Bilingual Children.* ERIC ED 218 914.

141. Weiner, F. D., Lewnay, L., & Erway, E. (1983). Measuring language competence of Black American English. *Journal of Speech and Hearing Disorders, 48,* 76–84.

142. Williams, R. L., & Rivers, L. W. (1972). *The Use of Standard Versus Non-Standard English in the Administration of Group Tests to Black Children.* Paper presented at the annual meeting of the American Psychological Association, Honolulu.

References 143–144 provide descriptions of expected differences that may occur in responses on some standardized tests given to speakers of nonstandard dialects.

143. Deyhle, D. (1985). Testing among Navajo and Anglo students: Another consideration of cultural bias. *Journal of Educational Equity and Leadership, 5,* 119–131.

144. Hunt, B. C. (1974–1975). Black dialect and third and fourth graders' performance on the Gray Oral Reading Test. *Reading Research Quarterly, 10,* 103–123.

References 145–151 discuss gender bias in test items.

145. Brown, F. G. (1980). Sex bias in achievement test items: Do they have any effect on performance? *Teaching of Psychology, 7* (1), 24–26.

146. . Doolittle, A. E. (1986). *Gender-Based Differential Item Performance in Mathematics Achievement Items.* ERIC ED 270 464.

147. Dwyer, C. A. (1979). The role of tests in producing sex-related differences. In M. A. Witting & A. C. Peterson (Eds.), *Sex-Related Differences in Cognitive Functioning: Developmental Issues.* New York: Academic Press.

148. Ekstrom, R. B., Lockheed, M. E., & Donlon, T. F. (1979). Sex differences and sex bias in test content. *Educational Horizons, 58* (1), 47–52.

149. Faggen-Steckler, J., McCarthy, K. A., & Tittle, C. K. (1974). A quantitative method for measuring sex "bias" in standardized tests. *Journal of Educational Measurement, 11,* 151–161.

150. Plake, B. S., Hoover, H. D., & Loyd, B. H. (1980). An investigation of the Iowa Test of Basic Skills for sex bias: A developmental look. *Psychology in the Schools, 17* (1), 47–52.

151. Tittle, C. K. (1974). Sex bias in educational measurement: Fact or fiction? *Measurement and Evaluation in Guidance, 6,* 219–226.

The differences between formal, standardized, norm-referenced assessment and informal, nonstandardized, criterion-referenced assessment are discussed in references 152–153.

152. Olion, L., & Gillis-Olion, M. (1984). Assessing culturally diverse exceptional children. *Early Childhood Development and Care, 15,* 203–232.

153. Plata, M. (1982). *Assessment, Placement, and Programming of Bilingual Exceptional Pupils: A Practical Approach.* Reston, VA: ERIC Clearinghouse on Handicapped and Gifted Children.

The disadvantages and limitations of standardized assessment procedures are discussed in references 154–158.

154. Executive Committee of the Council for Children with Behavior Disorders. (1989). Best assessment practices for students with behavioral disorders: Accommodation to cultural diversity and individual differences. *Behavior Disorders, 14* (4), 263–278.

155. Hilliard, A. G. III. (1976). *Alternatives to IQ Testing: An Approach to the Identification of Gifted "Minority" Children.* ERIC ED 148 038.

156. Howe, H., & Edelman, M. (1985). *Barriers to Excellence: Our Children At Risk.* Boston: National Coalition of Advocates for Students.

157. Williams, R. L. (1974). A history of the Association of Black Psychologists: Early formation and development. *Journal of Black Psychology, 1* (1), 9–24.

158. Williams, R. L. (Guest Editor). (1975). Testing of the Afro-American. *Journal of Afro-American Issues, 3.* As quoted in R. L. Williams & H. Mitchell (Eds.), *Whatever Happened to ABPSI's Moratorium on Testing: A 1968–1977 Reminder.* St. Louis: Washington University.

References 159–163 present the point of view of authors and groups who favor the continued use of standardized assessment procedures.

159. Anrig, G. R. (1985). Educational standards, testing, and equity. *Phi Delta Kappan, 66* (9), 623–625.

160. Council of the American Psychological Association. (1976). *Resolution on Standardized Testing.* Washington, DC. Quoted in R. L. Williams & H. Mitchell, *Whatever Happened to ABPSI's Moratorium on Testing: A 1968–1977 Reminder.* St. Louis: Washington University.

161. Muir, S. P. (1984). IQ tests: Should they be used? *Social Education, 84,* 72–78.

162. Reynolds, C. R. (1983). Test bias: In God we trust; all others must have data. *Journal of Special Education, 17* (3), 241–260.

163. Reschly, D. J. (1981). Psychological testing and educational classification and placement. *American Psychologist, 36* (10), 1094–1102.

References 164–167 discuss the validity of pluralistic norms.

164. Oakland, T. (1983). Concurrent and predictive validity estimates for the WISC-R IQs and ELPs by racial-ethnic and SES groups. *School Psychology Review, 12* (1), 57–61.

165. Richardson, J. C. (1989). Pro IQ testing: We're not the bad guys. *Diagnostique, 14* (2), 136–146.

166. Tolor, A. (1978). Assessment myths and current fads: A rejoinder to a position paper on nonbiased assessment. *Psychology in the Schools, 15* (2), 205–209.

167. Wilen, D. K., & Sweeting, C. M. (1986). Assessment of limited English proficient Hispanic students. *School Psychology Review, 15* (1), 59–75.

References 168–169 describe informal assessment approaches.

168. Alessi, G. J., & Kaye, J. H. (1983). *Behavior Assessment for School Psychologists.* Kent, OH: National Association of School Psychologists.

169. Pelligrini, S., & Grossman, H. (1985) *Bilingual Home Inventory.* Sacramento: California State Department of Education, Office of Special Education.

Portfolio assessment is the focus of references 170–174.

170. French, R. L. (1992). Portfolio assessment and LEP students. In *Proceedings of the Second National Research Symposium on Limited English Proficient Student Issues: Focus on Evaluation and Measurement. Vol I.* Washington, DC: U.S. Department of Education, Office of Bilingual Education and Minority Languages Affairs.

171. Goldstein, H., & Wolf, A. (1991). Recent trends in assessment: England and Wales. In L. C. Wing & B. R. Gifford (Eds.), *Trends in Educational Testing and Assessment.* Boston: Kluwer.

172. Heath, D. (1993). Using portfolio assessment with secondary LEP students yields cross-cultural advantages for all. *BEOutreach, 4* (1), 27.

173. Resnick, L. B., & Resnick, D. P. (1989). *Assessing the Thinking Curriculum: New Tools for Educational Reform.* Unpublished manuscript, Pittsburgh, Learning Research and Development Center, University of Pittsburgh and Carnegie-Melon University.

174. Walters, J. (1992). Application of multiple intelligence research in alternative assessment. In *Proceedings of the Second National Research Symposium on Limited English Proficient Student Issues: Focus on Evaluation and Measurement. Vol I.* Washington, DC: U.S. Department of Education, Office of Bilingual Education and Minority Languages Affairs.

References 175–181 deal with curriculum-based assessment.

175. Howell, K. W., Fox, S. L., & Morehead, M. K. (1993). *Curriculum-Based Evaluation: Teaching and Decision Making* (2nd ed.). Pacific Grove, CA: Brooks/Cole.

176. Marston, D. (1988). Measuring academic progress on IEP's: A comparison of graphic approaches. *Exceptional Children, 55* (1), 38–44.

177. Marston, D., & Magnusson, D. (1988). Curriculum-based measurement: District level implementation. In J. Graden, J. Zins, & M. Curtis (Eds.), *Alternative Educational Delivery Systems: Enhancing Instructional Options for All Students.* Washington, DC: National Association of School Psychologists.

178. Ponti, C. R., Zins, J. E., & Graden, J. L. (1988). Implementing a consultation-based service delivery system to decrease referrals for special education: A case study of organizational considerations. *School Psychology Review, 17* (1), 89–100.

179. Shinn, M. R. (1988). Development of curriculum-based local norms for use in special education decision-making. *School Psychology Review, 17* (1), 61–80.

180. Shinn, M. R., & Hubbard, D. D. (1992). Curriculum-based measurement and problem-solving assessment: Basic procedures and outcomes. *Focus on Exceptional Children, 24* (5), 1–20.

181. Tindal, G. A., & Marston, D. B. (1990). *Classroom-Based Assessment.* Columbus, OH: Merrill.

The test-teach-test approach is the topic of references 182–185.

182. Brown, A. L., Campione, J. C., Webber, L. S., & McGilly, K. (1992). Interactive learning environments: A new look at assessment and instruction. In B. R. Gifford & M. C. O'Connor (Eds.), *Changing Assessments: Alternative Views of Aptitude, Achievement, and Instruction.* Boston: Kluwer.

183. Brown, A. L., & Campione, J. C. (1987). Linking dynamic assessment with school achievement. In C. S. Lidz (Ed.), *Dynamic Assessment.* New York: Guilford.

184. Campione, J. C. (1989). Assisted assessment: A taxonomy of approaches and an outline of strengths and weaknesses. *Journal of Learning Disabilities, 22,* 151–165.

185. Feurerstein, R. (1979). *The Dynamic Assessment of Retarded Performers: The Learning Potential Assessment Device, Theory, Instruments, and Techniques.* Baltimore: University Park Press.

Reference 186 discusses interpretation bias.

186. Davis, J. D. (1986). *Proposals for Improving the NAEP Mathematics Assessment of Black Youth.* ERIC ED 279 674.

References 187–189 include guidelines for providing the least biased assessment.

187. Holtzman, W. H. Jr., & Mendoza, P. (1984). *Decision Models to Assist in Assessment Procedures for Bilingual Exceptional Children.* ERIC ED 252 986.
Northeast Regional Resource Center. (1979). *Nondiscriminatory Speech and Language Testing of Minority Children: Linguistic Differences.* Atlanta, GA: American Speech and Hearing Association.

188. Reichman, S., & Zyskowski, G. (1988). *Testing Approaches and Uses with Bilingual, Special Education Students.* ERIC ED 300 944.

189. Rydell, L. (1990). *The Least Biased Assessment: Implications for Special Educators.* Sacramento, CA: Resources in Special Education.

Models for assessing students with possible learning disabilities are described in references 190–193.

190. Baca, L., & Clark, C. (1992). *Exito: A Dynamic Team Assessment Process.* Boulder: BUENO Center, University of Colorado.

191. Gonzalez, V. (1992). *A Model of Psychoeducational Strategies that Integrates Diagnosis of Normal versus Genuine Handicapping Conditions with Successful Instructional Practices for Language Minority Children.* Paper presented at the Topical Conference on Culturally and Linguistically Diverse Exceptional Children, Minneapolis.

192. Minnesota Department of Education. (1987). *A Resource Handbook for the Assessment and Identification of LEP Students with Special Needs.* Minneapolis: Author.

193. Ortiz, A. A., Wilkinson, C. Y., Doutrney-Robertson, P., & Kushner, M. I. (1991). *AIM for the BESt: Assessment and Intervention Model for the Bilingual Exceptional Student.* Austin: University of Texas, Department of Special Education.

The validity of standardized adaptive behavior inventories with non-European American and poor students and their gender bias is the focus of references 194–198.

194. Baca, L., & Cervantes, H. (1978). The assessment of minority students: Are adaptive behavior scales the answer? *Psychology in the Schools, 15* (3), 366–370.

195. Fisher, A. T. (1977). *Adaptive Behavior in Non-Biased Assessment: Effects on Special Education.* ERIC ED 150 514.

196. Kazimour, K. K., & Reschly, D. J. (1981). Investigation of the norms and concurrent validity for the Adaptive Behavior Inventory for Children (ABIC). *American Journal of Mental Deficiency, 85* (5), 512–520.

197. Lambert, N. M. (1979). Contributions of school classification, sex, and ethnic status to adaptive behavior assessment. *Journal of School Psychology, 17* (1), 3–16.

198. Slate, N. M. (1983). Nonbiased assessment of adaptive behavior: Comparison of three instruments. *Exceptional Children, 50* (1), 67–70.

References 199–200 discuss the assessment of multiple intelligences.

199. Gardner, H. (1983). *Frames of Mind: The Theory of Multiple Intelligences.* New York: Basic Books.

200. Gardner, H. (1993). *Multiple Intelligences: The Theory in Practice.* New York: Basic Books.

General guidelines and models for identifying non-European American, poor, and limited-English-proficient students who are gifted and talented are included in references 201–203.

201. Cummings, W. B. (1980). *Cummings Checklist of Characteristics of Gifted and Talented Children.* ERIC ED 187 065.

202. Gregory, D. A., Starnes, W. T., & Blaylock, A. W. (1986). *Finding and Nurturing Potential Giftedness among Black and Hispanic Students.* ERIC ED 298 707.

203. Sisk, D. A. (1987). Children at risk: The identification of the gifted among the minority. *Gifted International, 4* (2), 33–41.

Less biased instruments for identifying gifted and talented students are described in references 204–206.

204. Kaufman, A. S., & Kaufman, N. L. (1983). *Kaufman Assessment Battery for Children (K-ABC).* Circle Pines, MN: American Guidance Company.

205. Naglieri, J. A. (1985). *Matrix Analogy Test-Short Form.* New York: Psychological Corporation.

206. Naglieri, J. A. (1985). *Matrix Analogy Test-Expanded Form.* New York: Psychological Corporation.

References 207–209 are concerned with identifying gifted and talented, limited-English-proficient, immigrant, refugee students.

207. Berney, T. D., & Moghadam, V. (1989). *Scholarly Transition and Resource Systems (Project STARS), 1987–1988 OREA Evaluation Report.* ERIC ED 311 725.

208. Harris, C. R. (1990). *Identifying and Serving the Gifted New Immigrant/Refugee: Problems, Strategies, Implications.* ERIC ED 319 209.

209. Hartford Public Schools. (1986). *Encendiendo una Llame. Bilingual Gifted and Talented Program: Overview, Identification of Students, and instructional Approaches.* ERIC ED 287–274.

The identification of gifted and talented students in rural areas is the focus of references 210–211.

210. Spicker, H. H. (1992). Identifying and enriching rural gifted children. *Educational Horizons, 70* (2), 60–65.

211. Spicker, H. H. (1992). *Project Spring.* Paper presented at the Topical Conference on Culturally and Linguistically Diverse Exceptional Children, Minneapolis.

References 212–215 describe procedures for identifying African American students who are gifted and talented.

212. Frasier, M. M. (1987). The identification of gifted black students: Developing new perspectives. *Journal for the Education of the Gifted, 10* (3), 15–18.

213. Johnson, S. T., Starnes, W. T., Gregory, D., & Blaylock, A. (1985). Program of Assessment, Diagnosis, and Instruction (PADI): Potentially gifted and talented minority students. *Journal of Negro Education, 54* (3), 416–430.

214. Patton, J. M. (1992). Assessment and identification of African-American learners with gifts and talents. *Exceptional Children, 59* (2), 150–159.

215. Patton, J. M., & Baytops, J. L. (1992). *Families and Schools Connecting: Lessons Learned from Project Mandala.* Paper presented at the Topical Conference on Culturally and Linguistically Diverse Exceptional Children, Minneapolis.

Reference 216 describes procedures and models for identifying Hispanic American gifted and talented students.

216. Melssky, T. J. (1987). Identifying and providing for the Hispanic gifted child. *NABE Journal, 9* (3), 43–56.

Guidelines for identifying Native American gifted and talented students are discussed in references 217–222.

217. Daniels, R. R. (1988). Gifted, talented, creative, or forgotten? *Roeper Review, 10* (4), 241–244.

218. Florey, J. E., Nottle, D., & Dorf, J. H. (1986). *Identification of Gifted Children among the American Indian Population.* ERIC ED 273 399.

219. George, K. R. (1987). *A Guide to Understanding Gifted American Indian Students.* Las Cruces: New Mexico State University, ERIC CRESS.

220. Kirschenbaum, R. (1988). Methods for identifying the gifted and talented American Indian student. *Journal for the Education of the Gifted, 11* (3), 53–63.

221. Montgomery, D., Bull, K. S., & Salyer, K. (1990). *Screening for Giftedness among American Indian Students*. ERIC ED 321 918.

222. Tonemah, S. (1987). Assessing American Indian gifted and talented students' abilities. *Journal for the Education of the Gifted, 10* (3), 181–194.

Reference 223 includes the quote in the Conclusions section.

223. Sennett, K. H. (1981). *Special Needs Assessment for Linguistically, Minority Students in the Brockport Public School System*. Paper presented at the Council for Exceptional Children Conference on the Exceptional Bilingual Child, New Orleans.

10

INSTRUCTION
IN A DIVERSE SOCIETY

Special education classes are likewise not set up to meet the needs of culturally different students. For example, special education classes rely on individual performance and don't allow for group rehearsal the same as in regular education classes; whereas it has been shown that Black students benefit from group rehearsal and resist individual performance in a learning environment. Thus when the student is moved from the regular classroom to a special education classroom he/she is moved from one type of "white classroom" to another, slower paced "white classroom." (1, p. 22)

Students' contextual, ethnic, linguistic, and gender characteristics influence how they learn. As noted in Chapter 4, students learn more when educators adapt their instructional approaches to students' characteristics. When educators do not take their students' characteristics into account, students who do not have disabilities are often referred to special education because of supposed learning and cognitive problems, and students who are correctly placed in special education programs learn less efficiently.

Previous chapters described how special educators can adapt their instructional approaches to students' contextual and linguistic characteristics. The goal of this chapter is to improve special educators' ability to adapt their instructional methods to the ethnic and gender diversity among students with disabilities. The chapter describes the ways in which students' relationship style, cognitive style, and motivational style, as well as time orientations, degree of self-confidence, interests, and comfort level with certain educational activities differ. It also suggests how special educators can accommodate their instructional techniques to these differences.

RELATIONSHIP STYLE

The ways students have learned to relate to adults and peers affect the way they learn in school. The ways students have learned to relate to their parents, other adults, and peers affect the ways in which they are comfortable relating to others in school. Their learning is enhanced when others compliment their preferred relationship styles; it is impeded when they cannot relate in ways that make them comfortable.

Participatory versus Passive Learning

Some children are brought up to be active participants in the learning process. They are expected to ask questions of adults, discuss ideas, and so on. These students perceive educators as guides who lead and stimulate students' active learning. Other children are expected to be less active and more passive recipients of instruction and information. They tend to perceive teachers as fountains of information and themselves as passive learners. Active participatory learning has proven to be more effective than passive learning with most students. However, all students are not equally prepared to function in such an environment. African American students prefer and learn more effectively in an interactive, participatory learning environment (2). On the other hand, many Hispanic Americans and Asian Pacific American students are expected to be passive learners. The following quotations describe the passive learning styles of Hispanic Americans and Southeast Asian Americans:

> The Hispanic culture requires good students to be passive learners—to sit quietly at their desks, pay attention, learn what they are taught and speak only when they are called upon. Anglo educational methods often require students to be active students— to show initiative and leadership, to volunteer questions and answers, and to question the opinion of others. (3, p. 188)

> Since they have been taught to learn by listening, watching (observing), and imitating, these students may have a difficult time adjusting to learning by active doing and discovering. . . . There is a lesser emphasis, as compared to the American school system, on critical thinking and judgmental questions. If a teacher were to ask a question on the relationship between two concepts, one might see Indochinese students searching through their notes or books for the answers, or they may display reluctance or discomfort. (4, p. 42)

In recent years, special educators have begun stressing the value of active participatory learning. However, students who are not comfortable with this approach may require a great deal of direct instruction and supervision during self-directed activities until they become comfortable in their more active role. Meanwhile, some students may not fulfill their academic potential and their behavior may be incorrectly attributed to insecurity, shyness, or excessive passivity. The following quote describes how this applies to some Asian Pacific American students: "The child does not volunteer to answer. He just sits and waits for his teacher to call upon him. So in the eyes of the American teacher, Asian children, as compared to American students, are dull, passive, unresponsive, and lack initiative. Most of the time, Asian children are ignored because of their absolute silence in class" (5, p. 11).

Aloof, Distant versus Involved Personal Relations

Cultures differ in terms of the degree of personal involvement teachers are supposed to have with their students. In some cultures, educators' interest in and involvement with students are expected to be restricted to their functioning in school. In other cultures, they are expected to be interested and involved with them as persons who are also students. In comparison to males, females prefer closer personal relationships with their teachers. Hispanic American and Native American students, among others, may learn more when their teachers show more interest in their out of school life. One author stated, "While I was in school in Mexico I felt as if my teachers, the nuns, were my friends as well as my teachers. They asked about my family and my personal life. When I came here the teachers seemed very cold and aloof. It was very hard for me to adjust to the differences" (3, p. 46). Another wrote, "Village students tend to expect highly personalized, emotionally intense relationships . . . with their teachers. . . . Village students consider it legitimate to expect a teacher to 'care about' them as total persons, not as learners of a particular subject matter" (6, p. 312). Because special educators typically work with fewer students than regular educators, they are in a better position to satisfy the preferences of students who prefer to have more personal and involved relationships with them.

Teacher versus Self-Directed

There are significant ethnic and gender differences in the extent to which students are trained to accomplish things on their own and to arrive at their own independent opinions and decisions or are brought up to be dependent on the aid, support, opinions, and feedback of their parents and other adults. Compared to European American students, many, but not all, non-European American students (especially Hispanic Americans, Native Americans, Filipino Americans, and Southeast Asian Americans) tend to be more interested in obtaining their teachers' direction and feedback (3, 9, 12, 16). "Filipino Children may be passive and may not show initiative, creativity, or independence. They may be reluctant, afraid, or slow to make decisions in the classroom. . . . To Filipino children, family approval is very important, and they usually rely on their parents to make decisions for them" (9, p. 34).

In most cultures, females, especially young ones, are more adult oriented than males. Females achieve more when adults are present than when they are absent (10). There is suggestive evidence that when they are young, females' self-esteem is more dependent on feedback from others; males' self-esteem, however, may be more dependent on their ability to master their environment (8). European American females are also more likely to use learned helplessness when they are older as a way of influencing others (14). This is not true of African American females.

The genders are not equally susceptible to the influence of other people (7, 11, 13, 15, 17). Although some research indicates the contrary (15), girls are more likely than boys to modify their opinions and attitudes to conform to others and to copy what others model; boys tend to maintain their ideas and opinions despite what others may think or feel.

The reason why many females seek their teachers' feedback, learn more in their presence, and are more willing to modify their opinions to conform to those of others while males function independently is unclear. Some educators argue that females learn better in interpersonal situations and males learn better in impersonal ones. They believe females' learning is enhanced when they and their teachers are equally involved in the process of examining their experiences together. Also, teachers tend to evaluate the female style more favorably than the male style. Other educators attribute the difference to what they believe is female students' inability to function independently and feel that females need to develop independent learning skills.

Both learning styles have advantages and disadvantages. Some situations call for the ability to work independently and to maintain one's own opinions and attitudes in the face of opposition. Other situations require students to be able to work well with others and to modify their ideas and opinions when others have more experience, knowledge, and training. Students who cannot distinguish between these two situations and those who are too inflexible to adjust to others' opinions as the situation demands are at a distinct disadvantage. Thus, the most helpful approach special educators can use may be to help all students learn to function in a bicultural manner.

Peer versus Adult Oriented

In some cultures, children look primarily to adults for guidance, support, and direction; children in other cultures (e.g., Hawaiian Americans) tend to learn from and are guided by other children and youth. Thus, research suggests that Hawaiian American students prefer to work with their peers in study groups rather than have teachers lecture to them, and they learn more effectively in peer groups (18, 19). In addition, females are more adult oriented; they seek the help, support, and feedback of their teachers. Males are more responsive to feedback from their peers (20–23, 25). However, males who lack self-confidence in their abilities also require teacher feedback to perform well (24). Special educators would do well to consider these differences when they select students for instructional activities such as peer tutoring and to decide how much teacher supervision to provide.

Individualistic versus Group Oriented

No culture expects children to be completely individualistic or group oriented, but there are important cultural differences in the degree to which these relationship styles are emphasized. In some cultures, children are brought up to be relatively individualistic. Such children prefer to work alone. When they are assigned to groups, in comparison to more group-oriented students, they are likely to continue to work independently, neither soliciting nor offering assistance. Native American children are an example of such children (18, 26). Although they may not be competitive with their peers, students who prefer to work alone may require considerable assistance before they can function well in cooperative learning environments.

COGNITIVE STYLE

All students do not perceive things the same way or use the same problem-solving techniques. Some of the most important cognitive style differences among students are discussed next. Again, these differences should be considered as different points on a continuum, not mutually exclusive styles.

Reflective/Analytical versus Impulsive/Spontaneous/Intuitive

Students differ in terms of how long they think about things before arriving at conclusions. Some children are brought up to analyze and reflect on questions and problems and to be sure they know the answer or solution before saying anything. Others respond more intuitively and spontaneously to problems in terms of what occurs to them immediately. "Some people are rather anxious to insure that they gather all the information possible before being asked to respond and they have a need to be accurate. These individuals are considered to be *reflective* while those individuals who respond immediately to what is presented without regard to the fact they may be erroneous are labeled as *impulsive* learners" (30, p. 17).

Temperamental, ethnic, and gender factors help to determine which of these cognitive styles students use (29). Native Americans are an example of students who tend to look at all sides of an issue, examine every possible implication, and make sure they know the answer before they are ready to express their opinion (18).

Research conducted in the 1970s indicated that in comparison to males, females are better able to delay judgment until they have the information they need to begin a task. They are also able to wait for a more desirable reward or outcome rather than to settle immediately for something less desirable (27, 28). More research is needed to determine whether this is still the case.

In schools, students who are more reflective usually have an advantage over their more spontaneous peers. Believing that all students should be reflective/analytical learners, some special educators use techniques that have been recommended to modify the learning style of students who have attention deficit disorders with students who have culturally determined impulsive, spontaneous, intuitive learning characteristics. This practice remains controversial among educators who appreciate straightforwardness and directness. In addition, some special educators do not allow reflective students sufficient time to prepare their answer (wait time) before calling on someone else. This impedes students' learning and may lead teachers to conclude that these students are unprepared or slow learners.

Global Perception versus Analysis of Details

As noted in the previous chapter, global learners perceive things in a holistic manner. They perceive the whole of an event, idea, or image and the relationships between its parts simultaneously. They see everything as a part of the whole and use few discrete categories to notice differences among the parts. Analytic learners can easily divide the whole into subcategories based on differences. Global learners tend to do better in whole-language approaches and sight vocabulary. Because analytic learners process individual parts sequentially and gradually build up to an understanding of the whole, a phonetic approach in which the parts of words are analyzed to obtain the meaning of the whole word is more to their liking. In comparison to European American students, African American, Asian Pacific American, Hispanic American, and Native American students have a more global perceptual style (31–35).

> The Native American sees little or no differentiation between religion and daily life, has little trouble with the anthropomorphism of inanimate objects, [and] practices holistic medicine. . . . The Anglo, on the other hand, sees medicine as separate from nutrition and reading as separate from science or social studies or math. . . . The Anglo compartmentalizes by subject rather than seeing them all as a part of the relation to the person. (35, p. 24)

> Afro-American people tend to prefer to respond to and with "gestalts" rather than to or with atomistic things. Enough particulars are tolerated to get a general sense of things. There is an impatience with unnecessary specifics. Sometimes it seems that the predominant pattern for mainstream America is the preoccupation with particulars along with a concomitant loss of a sense of the whole. (32, p. 38)

Unfortunately for global learners, the teaching style of many European American educators does not match their learning style.

> Many a new topic in school is approached in an analytic, sequential manner. The topic is introduced a little bit at a time, in a carefully sequenced manner. Often the overall picture (global view) of a topic is not presented until the end of a teaching sequence. For many Native Indian children (ands others) this approach would be much more effective if the overall purpose and the overall structure were described before the analytic sequence was begun. The term "advance organizers" has been used by some educators to describe this approach. (33, p. 26)

> There is the belief that anything can be divided and subdivided into minute pieces and that these pieces add up to a whole. Therefore dancing and music can be taught by the numbers. Even art is sometimes taught this way. This is why some people never learn to dance. They are too busy counting and analyzing. (32, p. 38)

Aural, Visual, and Verbal Learners

Although all children without visual or auditory impairments learn both visually and aurally, there are significant culturally influenced differences among students. It is important to know whether students' cultures prepare people to be primarily aural or visual learners, or both, since this would influence whether particular students would learn more efficiently if material were presented orally or visually.

Do people learn visually by observing what transpires in their worlds or by reading about things? Are students better at remembering what they have seen or what they have read? Because of their life-styles, Native American students tend to be visual learners (33, 37, 39).

> They scrutinize the face of adults; they recognize at great distances their family's livestock. They are alert to danger signs of changing weather or the approach of predatory animals. (37, p. 333)

> Native Indian students frequently and effectively use coding with imagery to remember and understand words and concepts. That is, they use mental images to remember or understand, rather than using word association. This suggests that use of metaphors, images or symbols is more effective than dictionary-style definitions or synonyms in helping many Native Indian students learn difficult concepts. (33, p. 26)

On the other hand, many other students—including African American, Hispanic American, Haitian American, and Hmong American—tend to be aural learners (3, 29, 36, 38). "Haitians usually have a highly developed auditory ability as evidenced by the oral traditions and rote learning methods. When presented with flow charts and diagrams they may require additional assistance in attaching meaning to the visual presentation" (36, p. 33).

The Hmong do not have a written language; therefore they have highly developed aural skills. "The Hmong are used to hearing long songs one or two times and then repeating them. Use of repetitive patterns and rhymes assists memorization" (38, p. 33).

Thus, it is extremely important to adapt special educational instructional techniques to students' preferences for aural, visual, kinesethetic, or verbal cognitive styles. At the very least, special educators should employ a multisensory approach when they instruct a group of diverse learners.

Kinesthetic, Active, Energetic Learning versus Calm, Inactive, Verbal Learning

Students' ability to sit still for long periods of time is greatly influenced by their cultural background. Knowledge of whether youngsters are expected to sit in a quiet and controlled manner in most situations or are allowed to be active and noisy enables special educators to use instructional techniques that permit students a level of activity that approximates what they are accustomed to and to provide them with ways to discharge their energy. Such knowledge also helps special educators distinguish between students who are truly hyperactive and those whose highly active behavior patterns are culturally determined.

In general, in comparison to European Americans, African American students are more active and less able to adjust to the sedentary learning environments of U.S. schools. "In many American schools and especially in inner city schools, children are expected to talk or to move about only when directed to do so by teachers. . . . Those children who talk and move about with or without teacher directions do not meet normative standards and expectations. . . . Euro-American children possess the movement repertoire that will satisfy the normative standards and expectations governing child behavior in elementary classrooms while the richer movement repertoire of Black children does not satisfy those normative standards" (40, p. 610).

In comparison to females, males prefer learning that involves active manipulation to more sedentary learning environments (42). Because of these ethnic and gender differences, special educators should know which of their students learn best by doing, manipulating, touching, and experiencing, and which prefer more sedentary approaches such as lectures, reading, written and oral explanations, and discussions of ideas.

Students also differ in terms of whether they function better in highly stimulating or more calm learning environments. African American and Hispanic American students are used to more stimulation than most students typically experience in school. That may be why African American and Hispanic American students perform better and achieve more when the curriculum includes many different materials, makes frequent use of nonverbal instructional forms such as visual media or manipulative games, and allows student autonomy. This type of classroom would be more conducive to learning than a classroom that is teacher controlled, uses a great deal of verbal learning, and involves limited use of different materials (44).

Numerous authors have suggested adapting the instruction techniques to African American and Hispanic American students' interest in music, singing, movement, and variety (41, 43). The following quote is an example of such suggestions:

> Many African American children are exposed to high-energy, fast-paced home environments, where there is simultaneous variable stimulation (e.g., televisions and music playing simultaneously and people talking and moving in and about the home freely). Hence, low-energy, monolithic environments (as seen in many traditional school environments) are less stimulating. . . . Variety in instruction provides the spirit and enthusiasm for learning. When instructional strategies facilitate stimulus variety, using combinations of oral, print, and visual media, African-American students perform better. Instructional activities should include music, singing, and movement. (43, pp. 118–119)

Nonverbal Cues

Students' sensitivity to nonverbal clues is influenced by their ethnic background and gender. As noted previously, African Americans, Asian Pacific Americans, and Hispanic Americans tend to be more aware of and tuned in to subtle nonverbal cues than European Americans. Females are also more sensitive than males to nonverbal cues (45, 46). Since people sometimes say things they do not mean and mean things they do not say, students who are sensitive to special educators' nonverbal communication as well as their verbal communication may learn and understand more because they perceive more.

Trial and Error versus "Watch Then Do"

In some cultures, people, especially children, tend to learn by trial and error. They observe, read about, or are told how something is done. Then they practice it under the supervision of a more knowledgeable and skilled individual. Learners are expected to make mistakes and to learn from those mistakes. In other cultures, individuals are expected to continue to watch how something is done as many times and for as long as necessary until they feel they can do it. Only when they are sure they can succeed do they demonstrate their ability to others.

Students who grow up in trial-and-error cultures can usually take in stride the mistakes they make in public when they volunteer answers or are called on. Those who are accustomed to a "watch then do" approach have greater difficulty exposing themselves in public while they are learning from their mistakes. This is especially true of Native American students (35, 47, 48).

> Native Americans spend much more time watching and listening and less time talking than do Anglos. If they are interested in something they watch how it is done, they inspect the product, they watch the process, they may ask a quiet question or two. Then they may try it for themselves, often out of the public eye. They are their own evaluator to determine whether their effort was successful or needs improvement. When they feel comfortable, they will show what they have done to someone else, usually someone they trust. (35, p. 26)

> A reluctance to try too soon and the accompanying fear of being "shamed" if one does not succeed may account for the seemingly passive uninterested and unresponsive attitude of Indian students. (47, p. 28)

Students who are uncomfortable with trial-and-error learning and exposing their errors to others may need special educators to supervise them less and not pressure them to try things before they are ready to do so. This may be a difficult adjustment for special educators who realize that most students with learning and cognitive disabilities, sensory impairments, or emotional problems need someone to look over their shoulders and encourage them to try to do things when they are unsure of themselves.

Argumentative/Forensic Instruction versus Direct Instruction

All cultures use many different teaching techniques with children, but only in some cultures do adults teach children by raising leading questions about their beliefs in order to guide them to a more correct or accurate understanding of things. In other cultures, children are accustomed to being told what is correct and unaccustomed to having their beliefs questioned critically. "Anglo education emphasizes verbal inquisitiveness, an argumentative discourse that is termed 'forensics.' In the Anglo-dominated school system, the child is encouraged, even pressured, both to ask and analyze questions. . . . There is consequently a built-in clash between the ethnic (Raza) home tradition and the Anglo school tradition of constant and formal questioning. The WASP 'inquisition' would be highly hostile to the Mexican-American attitude of tolerance" (49, p. 64). As a result, special educators may have to consider students' cognitive styles when deciding whether and how often to use instructional approaches that involve class discussions, debates, analysis of controversial topics, and the examination of students' opinions and beliefs.

Learning from Examples, Stories, and Morals versus Direct Instruction

In some cultures—for example, Native American cultures—in addition to being told things directly, children are led to an understanding of life through the legends they learn, the morals of the stories they are told, and the examples they are shown. For them, direct instruction can be effectively supplemented by these more seemingly time-consuming instructional strategies.

MOTIVATIONAL STYLE

In some respects, all students are similarly motivated. They would rather succeed than fail and learn to read than remain illiterate. However, because their cultural backgrounds help shape their perceptions about the value and role of education, students also have different motives.

Motivation to Succeed in School

Although students' desires to succeed in school are often influenced by a number of interrelated motivations, typically one or two reasons are paramount. Some students may desire to succeed academically, to go to college, to earn a lot of money, and to be successful materialistically. Others strive to succeed in order to receive honor and prestige. Still others may believe it is important to learn for the sake of learning.

Students' motivation to succeed in school is affected by ethnic, socioeconomic-class, and gender factors. As noted in Chapter 3, some older African American and Hispanic American students, especially poor males, are motivated to avoid success in school or have lost their motivation to try to succeed (50–55). Many non-European American and poor students are alienated, distrustful, angry, and disillusioned about the schools they attend and the teachers who instruct them because of the prejudice and discrimination they encounter. They believe that even if they do well in school, they will not obtain the same benefits that European American upper-class males receive from succeeding in school, especially in the vocational area. Also, some of them are pressured by their peers not to conform or to do well in school because to do so is to "act White."

For these reasons, numerous African American and Hispanic American students, especially males, purposefully avoid academic success by cutting school and not studying. Many students who do achieve up to their potential hide their true motives by becoming disciplinary problems, being the class clown, or keeping their efforts and accomplishments from their peers.

Although the evidence is somewhat inconsistent, it appears that many European American and Hispanic American females, especially those from less affluent and poor backgrounds, have mixed feelings about and are uncomfortable with success in courses or occupations traditionally thought of as being in the so-called male domain (57–61, 63). This applies to a lesser degree to African American females. Research indicates that there are at least three reasons for this (63, 56, 57, 61). Some females are concerned that they may seem less feminine and be less popular with males if they outperform them in these areas. A second reason why some females are uncomfortable with success is that success provokes a conflict between their desires to achieve and their more traditional perception of the ideal female as less oriented to achievement and individualism than to collaboration and egalitarianism. In this vein, Tanner explained, "Appearing better than others is a violation of the girls' egalitarian ethic: People are supposed to stress their connection and similarity. . . . It is no wonder that girls fear rejection by their peers if they appear too successful and boys don't. Boys from the earliest age, learn that they can get what they want—higher status—by displaying superiority. Girls learn that displaying superiority will not get them what they want—affiliation with their peers. For this they have to appear the same as, not better than their friends" (63, pp. 217–218).

A third reason is the belief held by many non-European Americans, including Hispanic Americans and Asian Pacific Americans, that a female's place is in the home (3, 38). For example, Lewis and colleagues explained, "There is also a suspicion among the Hmong regarding girls who are educated beyond the three or four years required for basic literacy and math skills. . . . The fear is that they will become like western women" (38, p. 32). There is also suggestive evidence that some males may be uncomfortable with success if they perceive success in school as a feminine characteristic (62).

Because of these gender, socioeconomic-class, and ethnic differences, special educators should not assume that all of their students are equally motivated to succeed in school. They should be knowledgeable about each student's motivation and then decide how to handle each individual case. This may be a difficult task for regular education teachers who have many students in their classes, but the lower student-teacher ratios that prevail in special education make this goal quite feasible.

Learning on Demand versus Learning What Is Relevant or Interesting

Are students prepared to spend equal time and energy learning whatever material is presented to them by teachers, regardless of what the students think and feel about the material? Or will their reactions to material depend on whether or not it interests them? All cultures require all children to learn many things, whether they want to or not. Some students, however, have been brought up in cultures in which they have considerable leeway to learn what is useful and interesting to them rather than what some others have decided they should learn. Other students are better prepared to study whatever teachers present to them. For example, Cortes stated that Hispanic American students whose parents are not well-educated are less willing to learn things that do not interest them. "Relevance is particularly important for students who do not come from families with high educational attainment. For students from families with examples of significant school achievement, education has built in relevance. They have role models. . . . They are raised with the concept of a career. . . . Such a student is more likely to accept and play the educational game" (64, pp. 34–35).

Other authors agree that Hispanic American students are less able to learn on demand. "Anecdotal evidence suggests that efficiency, automation and technology tend to be highly prized among Anglos, whereas humanistic concerns and open acceptance of affective temperament take precedence among Chicanos. Given such variations in cultural concerns, it is not surprising that the tendency to learn liked materials more readily than disliked materials is more intensified among Chicanos than Anglos" (65, pp. 114–115). Also, consider the following: "To the extent that response to demand could be called a learning style, the Hispanic population tends to demonstrate that tendency much less frequently than a middle-class, white group that is socialized almost from early childhood to produce on demand as is expected in school" (67, p. 19).

Native American students have been described in the following way: "They prefer to learn information that is personally interesting to them; therefore, interest is a key factor in their learning. When these students are not interested in a subject, they do not control their attention and orient themselves to learning an uninteresting task. Rather, they allocate their attention to other ideas that are more personally interesting, thus appearing detached from the learning situation" (68, p. 69).

Some educators believe that students should attend to whatever their teachers present to them since their teachers know best. Other educators think that students should not be so compliant if what they are expected to learn is busywork that has no apparent relationship to their interests and goals or is not at their level. These educators tend to believe that special educators should not be quick to capitalize on students' willingness to learn whatever they are given. Instead, they should use the feedback from their students to improve their instructional practices.

Students who are not ready to learn on demand may be willing to attend to material that does not interest them if teachers personally appeal to them to do so. For example, Kleinfeld reported that Native American students may be motivated to learn in order to please others and to avoid offending or hurting them. "Appealing to interpersonal values rather than purely academic values in a learning situation often motivates village students" (66, pp. 18–19).

Kleinfeld also pointed out that although Native American educators are comfortable appealing to such motives, European American teachers who believe that students should be motivated to learn for intrinsic reasons may be reluctant to make the kinds of personal appeals that are necessary to motivate students. A Native American teacher's response to Native American students follows: "He just wouldn't attend speech class. Then I told him he was hurting the teacher's feelings because she thought he didn't like her. At that point he said he would go" (66, pp. 18–19). On the other hand, a European American teacher reported, "He said he would study if I wanted him to. But I felt I should tell him that he should study it for himself not me" (66, pp. 18–19). Asian Pacific American students may also respond to personal appeals. "Asian children are often found to be motivated extrinsically by their parents and relatives. They study hard because they want to please their parents and impress their relatives" (69, p. 84).

It is important to enhance the intrinsic motivation of students with disabilities, especially if they have become discouraged because of the frustrations many of them experience in school. However, with some students, it may be effective to use personal appeals temporarily to encourage students to engage in schoolwork that will provide them with the successful experiences necessary to increase their intrinsic motivation.

Object-Oriented versus People-Oriented Learners

All children in all cultures must learn many abstract concepts. However, some cultures deemphasize abstract learning and are more people oriented. As a result, some students are more interested in solving math problems about people than those that involve only numerical computations, and human geography (how people live) rather than physical geography (rivers, topography, etc.), whereas other students may prefer more abstract, object-oriented curricular contents. In comparison to European Americans in general, Hispanic Americans, African Americans, and Native American are more people oriented (3, 70, 71).

> In comparison to the Anglo culture, the Hispanic culture emphasizes people over ideas. . . . As a result some Hispanic students may relate better to a person-centered rather than thing-or idea-centered curriculum. (3, pp. 42–43)

Research has suggested that white children are very object-oriented. That is, they have numerous opportunities to manipulate objects and discover properties and relationships. Consequently, this society's educational system is very object oriented. Classrooms are filled with educational hardware and technology. . . . Research with black children, in contrast, has found them to be very people-oriented. Most black children grow up in large families where they have a great deal of human interaction. . . . When this cultural trait is acknowledged, the result will be more human interaction in the learning process. (71, pp. 19–20)

Cooperative, Competitive, and Individualistic Learners

Cultures differ in the degree to which they stress cooperation, competition, and individualism. Therefore, it is important to know whether particular students respond better to competitive, individualistic, or cooperative motivating techniques and learning environments. Special educators are encouraged to use cooperative learning and peer tutoring with students with disabilities, but some students are less receptive than others to these approaches.

There are many significant ethnic, socioeconomic-class, and gender differences in students' preferences for competitive or cooperative learning environments. As noted in the previous chapter, some students—including African Americans, Asian Pacific Americans, Filipino Americans, Hawaiian Americans, and Hispanic Americans—tend to be brought up to be cooperative, whereas other cultures typically encourage students to be more competitive and/or individualistic.

European American gifted, average, and low-ability females, especially those from poor backgrounds, usually prefer cooperative learning environments and may learn better in certain kinds of cooperative situations. In group settings, they are more oriented toward group rather than individualistic goals. European American males tend to respond better to competitive and individualistic situations, whether they are high or low achievers (21, 72–77, 79, 81, 82, 84, 85, 88, 89). These gender stereotypes do not apply to the same degree to Native American and Hispanic American males who grow up in much less competitive environments (80, 83, 86, 87).

Ethnic groups also have different approaches to cooperation. For example, in the European American culture, when people are working cooperatively, everyone is supposed to do her or his share. To carry one's load is a guiding principle. Because this is not true of all cultures, the difference can create problems for teachers. Jaramillo pointed out that an European American teacher "is likely to be personally irked if he finds that some child isn't doing his share when engaged in a group task. Latin cultures typically do not put such requirements on individuals when they are working as part of a group. A group member who does not happen to be working will not be offensive. Those members of the group who best qualify or are most interested in performing the task will probably take it upon themselves to do the bulk of the labor. It is generally understood that each individual has special talents, and he will contribute when these talents are called for" (78, p. 9).

Some students are taught to be self-reliant—to be individualistic and to rely only on themselves to accomplish their goals and deal with the challenges, difficulties, and problems they face. Other students are brought up to expect and count on the help and the cooperation of others and to reciprocate in kind. Individualistic students who prefer to work on their own may have difficulty adjusting to working in groups or committees even though they are noncompetitive.

These ethnic and gender differences have important educational implications. Since some students learn more efficiently in cooperative learning environments, whereas others learn more in competitive or individualistic settings, their achievement depends in part on whether their teachers' instructional style matches their cooperative, competitive, or individualistic learning style. Special educators should consider these ethnic differences when they select learning environments and reward systems for students. In regular education, students who learn better in competitive or individualistic situations may have an advantage since these environments predominate (90). This is less likely to be true in special education programs where cooperation rather than competition is stressed.

The positive results of cooperative learning on many students' achievement, attitudes, and interpersonal relationships has been demonstrated repeatedly (91–101). Typically, interethnic relationships improve and students learn more, get along better with their peers, and feel better about themselves, their peers, and school when they learn in cooperative environments.

Research also indicates, however, that these results characterize only some, not all, students. In general, females, African Americans, Hispanic Americans, and students who have a cooperative learning style, regardless of gender or ethnicity, tend to experience the greatest academic gains from cooperative learning (21, 102, 103). Students who prefer competitive learning environments do better under competitive situations (104).

Female students tend to achieve more in single-sex cooperative learning situations than in mixed-sex cooperative groups (105, 106). There are many possible reasons for this. Moody and Gifford stated that one of the reasons for this is that females participate and lead less in mixed-gender groups. They suggested, "Females are forced to take leadership and responsibility in laboratory groups when working with only other females. . . . If increased female leadership and participation is desired, then grouping by gender can accomplish this objective" (106, pp. 16, 17).

Another reason why females are often the losers in mixed-sex groups is because although they tend be the providers of assistance, they are rejected by males when they ask for assistance. In addition, as noted earlier, in mixed-sex cooperative groups, females often revert to a pattern of not interacting with male students, allowing males to dominate them, and viewing themselves as less helpful, less important, and less visible (107, 109, 112, 113, 114, 116, 118). There is some evidence that they may behave more competitively than they otherwise do (115). Males may actually learn more and perform better than females in cooperative mixed-sex groups because they often ignore females, contribute most of the ideas, do most of the talking, and typically function as the group leaders (108, 109, 110, 117).

Peterson and Fennema pointed out other problems that can result in mixed-sex cooperative groups (111). They suggested that although girls' achievement may improve in cooperative learning groups, such groups may make girls even less independent and that could further impair their already inadequate high-level thinking skills in courses such as mathematics. The authors are also concerned that cooperative activities may impede the higher-level mathematics achievement of independent, competitive boys. In mixed groups, girls tend to be equally responsive to requests from and reinforcement by either sex. However, boys are responsive primarily to other males (119–122). Females are also less likely than males to participate in group discussions and to assume leadership positions (123–126).

Females can benefit from mixed-gender cooperative groups. They are more likely to do so when they have been given advanced training so they can function as expert/leaders of the group, when they have had prior experience with the group task so they are familiar with what is to be learned, and when educators prepare students to function in a more egalitarian manner.

The experiences of some African American students in mixed-ethnic cooperative groups may be similar to the negative experiences of many females (112, 127). Piel and Conwell stated, "White children and black children may not be getting the same experience from a cooperative learning experience. . . . If white children assume leadership roles and black children assume more subservient roles then the purpose for cooperative groups seems to be somewhat diminished" (112, p. 14). There is also some evidence that some African American students perform best when they cooperate with other African Americans and compete with European Americans (128). Finally, there is suggestive evidence that whether students benefit from cooperative learning depends in part on their self-concepts (129). When students with high and low self-concepts work together, those with high self-concepts are less likely to function cooperatively, thereby thwarting the goals of the cooperative learning experiences.

Thus, special educators should not assume that cooperative learning experiences will automatically benefit all students. Students, especially those who are likely to dominate others and those who tend to allow others to assume dominant positions, must be prepared for cooperative learning in order for all of the members of the group to reap the benefits associated with this approach.

Cooperative learning has proven to be an effective approach with some students with disabilities. However, all students are not equally prepared to engage in cooperative learning activities. For example, students with developmental disabilities may have difficulty cooperating with others because their cognitive delays may make it difficult for them to learn cooperative skills. Students with conduct disorders may be unwilling to work cooperatively with others unless they are forced to do so or perceive that it is to their advantage to do so. Students with serious emotional problems may be too frightened, angry, rebellious, or withdrawn to participate effectively in cooperative learning activities without a great deal of support and assistance from their teachers and peers. Students with attention deficit disorders may have difficulty conforming to the pace, schedules, and routines of the other members of their group. Also, regular education students may have to be sensitized to the special needs of the students with disabilities who are mainstreamed into their classes before they can work cooperatively with them. For the many reasons discussed in this section, special educators should not assume that cooperative learning benefits all students with disabilities or that all students are equally able and motivated to work cooperatively. Effective utilization of cooperative learning with students with disabilities requires a great deal of thoughtful planning and preparation.

Experts suggest that certain components are required for an effective cooperative learning experience. The following steps should be considered as a list of characteristics of effective cooperative learning approaches rather than as steps to follow exactly as listed:

- Become familiar with the variety of cooperative learning techniques available to teachers. The references in the bibliography are a good source of information.
- Inform students of the cooperative procedures they should follow and teach them how to follow them.
- Prepare all students, especially those who are accustomed to accepting subservient positions, to assume the expert/leadership role.
- Sensitize all students, especially male students and others who are prone to use group situations to dominate others, to the importance of allowing all students to take on all the roles available to group members.
- Determine the learning styles of the students. Those who have a cooperative learning style may be ready to profit from such experiences. However, those who tend to do better in competitive or independent learning situations may need to be taught to function better in more cooperative settings before they can profit from them.
- Monitor the groups closely to discourage the kinds of problems that have been discussed here and intervene as quickly as possible when problems arise.

SELF-QUIZ

SELECTING STUDENTS FOR COOPERATIVE LEARNING EXPERIENCES

- With which students do you think cooperative learning should be used?
- Do you think that cooperative learning should be used primarily with those who appear to favor this type of learning or with all students?
- Would you assign students to cooperative learning groups? If so, what criteria would you use to determine which students to assign to such groups?
- Would you allow students to choose their own learning environments?

Risking Failure and Rejection

Will students choose tasks that are challenging and novel if they also involve risk of failure or rejection or will they stick to those that are familiar? Will they be adventurous or play it safe? How sure do students have to be that they know the answer or that their opinion is correct before they will risk responding to their teacher's question?

With many exceptions, girls tend to react less positively than boys to situations that they believe are difficult and challenging. They often are less persistent when faced with difficult tasks in school and are less likely to take risks (130–132). In addition, girls tend to expect to do less well and perform less adequately than boys following failure or the threat of failure (133, 134). European American students appear more willing to take these kinds of risks than Asian Pacific American students (135, 136).

These cultural inhibitions may make it difficult for some Asian Pacific American students and other groups of non-European American students with similar inhibitions and females who have developmental and learning disabilities, sensory impairments, and serious emotional problems to take risks or bounce back from failure. These cultural inhibitions may also make it difficult for some gifted and talented students from these backgrounds to capitalize on their gifts and talents in creative ways.

The section in this chapter entitled Self-Confidence Enhancement describes a number of techniques that may be used to help students with disabilities overcome their reluctance to take risks and improve the way they deal with failure. Suggestions for helping gifted and talented students include the following:

- Provide a nonevaluative atmosphere because external teacher and peer evaluations may produce shame and loss of face and thereby reduce risk taking and creativity.
- Provide assignments that encourage creativity, such as "Think of all the ways this story could possibly end," "Draw something that no one else could possibly think of," and "Make as many designs as you can from these lines." Use a program designed to encourage creative thinking such as attribute listing, creative problem solving, and guided fantasy (136).

TIME ORIENTATION

Because time is a primary concern in the United States, it is easy to assume that all cultures have similar attitudes about time. This, however, is not the case.

Present versus Future Orientation

There are significant differences in the extent to which people sacrifice present satisfactions for future goals. Although all ethnic groups are concerned about and prepare for the future, some are more present oriented than future oriented.

The time many Mexican Americans value most is the present. Finishing a conversation with an old friend may be more important than keeping an appointment with a doctor. Making plans for the future may be less important than living to the fullest in the moment at hand. Many Mexican Americans perceive the time-serving ways of the Anglo as a misappropriation of the present. . . . The entire system of American education revolves about a ritualistic adherence to the ticking of the clock. What is the Mexican American child's reaction to the rigid schedules and the incessant pressures to plan for the future? How does he view a reward system that is programmed to respond to him at six week intervals? (142, p. 641)

Pacific peoples have learned to focus on meeting present needs and expecting little change. Americans value change, are future oriented, and expect that objectives will be achieved as a result of hard work. (139, p. 264)

Other ethnic groups such as European Americans and some Asian Americans are more future oriented. Because individuals differ in these respects, it is important to know whether students can work toward the accomplishment of long-term goals and rewards or are more responsive to short-term goals, immediate satisfaction, and immediate reinforcement. It is also important to ask whether students who have a tedious, boring, or irksome job to do will start it immediately, postpone it to a more convenient time, or wait until it is almost too late to complete it.

Punctuality

Do people keep to rigid schedules or do they have flexible beginning and ending times? Is time measured exactly or approximately? When students arrive late to class or a meeting, are they unmotivated or merely operating in a different time frame? How do people perceive lateness? In some cultures, when a person is late it reflects primarily on the late person who is seen as irresponsible. In others, lateness is perceived as a statement about the late person's disrespectful attitude toward those who have been kept waiting.

Are students accustomed to starting tasks when they are supposed to and completing them within a specified time period? If they are not, they will have problems functioning in U.S. schools. African Americans, Hispanic Americans, and Native Americans, among others, have a much more flexible attitude about time and punctuality (141, 144).

On the whole, Anglo Americans perceive time as a precious commodity to be conserved and budgeted carefully. . . . Hispanic societies, on the other hand, tend to treat time in a casual manner, accommodating its passage to their needs, rather than letting themselves be controlled by it. . . . In school, all activities are segmented into a strict time schedule which orchestrates the entire class to perform the same tasks in exact unison. For the Hispanic student, this imposition of a rigid chronological regimentation brings unfamiliar confusion and confinement for, at home, he has always been master of his "time" and been allowed to exercise his individuality within the casual rhythm of family life. (140, p. 67)

Three Eskimo high school seniors given scholarships to a Washington university flunked out after their first semester. High school counselors who came to investigate the failure of such promising students found them cowering in their dormitory rooms and discovered they had been terrified by the ringing of bells and classes ending in such a flurry of activity and of the rush of students to other classes to be on time. No one in their village had owned a watch or clock; thus they were unprepared for the university situation. (137, p. 5)

Pace

As noted in the previous chapter, students who are accustomed to working at a slower pace make more errors when instructed to work as fast as they can. Students accustomed to a faster pace continue to perform as well when they are told to work as fast as they can (138, 143). Condon and colleagues pointed out that Hispanic American students often have difficulty keeping to the fast pace set by many European American teachers. "The entire curriculum of the school is crowded into a tight schedule which features endless sequences of fast-moving and closely-timed activities, such as quizzes, tests and spelling bees. The emphasis placed on a 'clock-watch' performance of assigned tasks becomes a haunting nightmare for any learner functioning at a slower tempo, as is the case for Hispanic children who have been brought up in a relaxed home atmosphere where minutes (sometimes hours or days) are not seen as critical factors" (140, p. 68).

Special educators who reward students for the amount of work they accomplish—how many problems or pages they have done, rather than the quality of their work—may unwittingly cause some of them to make mistakes. They may also give students the message that it is more important to complete something fast than to do it correctly. This can be especially harmful for the many students with disabilities who lack confidence in their academic ability.

SELF-CONFIDENCE

Students' self-confidence about school success depends on their beliefs in their ability to learn and their ability to control their own lives (their locus of control). Males and females tend to differ in both of these respects. Ethnic and socioeconomic-class differences appear to be primarily in the area of students' beliefs about their abilities to control their lives.

Ability to Learn

Gender differences in students' self-confidence about school has been the subject of considerable research. Although it is not true of African Americans, in most ethnic groups, females tend to be less self-confident than males about school, especially in situations that are in the so-called male domain such as mathematics and science courses, in competitive situations, and when they lack objective information about how well they have done or can do in situations that involve mastery of tasks in the male domain (146–152). Females are not less self-confident than males in courses that are not perceived to be in the male domain such as reading and in situations that involve their perceived ability to develop friendly relationships with others, to be popular, to resolve conflicts with others, to break bad habits, to gain self-insight, and so on. There is little evidence that there also are gender differences in students' overall self-concepts and self-esteem (21).

As noted in Chapter 3, students from different ethnic and socioeconomic-class backgrounds start school equally confident about their ability to learn. Unfortunately, after spending a number of years in school, many, but far from all, poor, African American, Hispanic American, and Native American students lose much of their self-confidence about school.

Locus of Control

Students differ in terms of the extent to which they believe they are in control of and responsible for what happens to them in their lives in general and in school in particular. There is no consistent evidence that males and females differ in the extent to which they believe they are in control of and responsible for what happens to them outside of school. The results of studies that have examined how students explain their school-related experiences rather than in their lives in general paint a different picture. Although a few researchers have found no gender differences, most studies indicate that males and females attribute their academic successes and failures to different factors. Researchers who have compared males' and females' beliefs about whether they or external factors have greater influence over their general school performance have found that in comparison to males, females, especially those from a poor background, are more likely to attribute their general academic performance to internal factors (153, 157, 165). In courses such as math and science that are thought to be in the so-called male domain, females tend to attribute their poor performance to internal factors such as lack of ability and their success to external factors such as luck rather than effort or ability (154–156, 158, 160, 162, 163, 166). Males' attributions are different. They are more likely to attribute their failures to external factors and their success to internal factors across courses and subjects (159, 161–164).

There are significant ethnic differences in students' locus of control (140, 167–170). European American students are most likely to believe that they, rather than external factors, control what happens to them. Japanese Americans and Chinese Americans follow close behind. Hispanic American students tend to have a more external locus of control (168). The optimistic European American view embodied in the expression "If at first you don't succeed, try, try again," is compared to the fatalism of Hispanic Americans who are more likely to believe that forces beyond their control exert considerable influence over their lives. "This optimistic outlook on life is not shared by most Spanish speakers who have learned that one should not expect too much of life, and that it is best to dismiss the future with a fatalistic shrug of the shoulders—que sera, sera (what will be will be)" (140, p. 63).

As noted in Chapter 3, some African Americans and Native Americans do not assume that they can control many aspects of their lives because they are aware of their lack of power in an environment characterized by pervasive prejudice against them. Because of this they are less optimistic that they can assure themselves a good life by their own efforts (167, 169). "White folks think that because they have a good day today every day has to be good. They can't take bad times. Black folks know better. They're happy for any good days that come their way because they know they can't have them all the time" (167).

In general, research conducted primarily in the 1960s indicates that students with an internal locus of control tend to achieve more in school than those whose locus of control is external, because they try harder to succeed and to improve when they do poorly (171–174). However, whether this principle applies to poor, African American, Native American, and Hispanic American students has been a matter of controversy. Some educators argue that since many of these students grow up in a racist and prejudiced environment, it may be self-destructive for them to believe that they are completely in control of their lives in spite of the racism and prejudice that surrounds them. Students who correctly understand when external factors beyond their control are to blame for their failures may strive to change them. But students who incorrectly blame themselves or hold themselves responsible for failure caused by unfairness, prejudice, and economic injustice may give up.

Sometimes students who are often the victims of prejudice and discrimination incorrectly blame these factors for problems that they cause themselves. This can shield them from the self-criticism that is necessary for self-improvement. Thus, although it is important for students not to blame themselves for the problems others cause them, it is also important for them not to blame others for problems that they cause themselves. To date, there is insufficient research to determine the relationship between locus of control and school achievement for students who belong to groups that experience prejudice and discrimination.

Students with disabilities typically lack confidence in their ability to learn and they have an external locus of control. If they happen to be non-European, poor, or female, they are doubly at risk for having insufficient confidence in themselves. Students with disabilities who are self-confident are more likely to succeed than those who do not believe they have what it takes to succeed. Likewise, students who can attempt to accomplish things that involve the possibility of failure and can bounce back from the unavoidable failures that all students experience from time to time will do better over time than those who avoid possible failure and who are too discouraged by failure to try again. Students who avoid difficult and challenging situations deny themselves growth opportunities. Also, students who incorrectly attribute their poor performance to their learning, cognitive, sensory, or motor disabilities are less likely to attempt to succeed the next time they face a similar challenge.

Self-Confidence Enhancement

Research indicates that dedicated teachers can improve their students' self-concepts and self-esteem when they make the effort to do so (175–181). The first step is to identify students who lack self-confidence. This can be done informally by observing students at work, at play, and during their interactions with others. Teachers can also talk with students about what the students think of themselves. Several validated formal assessment instruments are available for this purpose. The Piers-Harris Children's Self-Concept Scale (186) and the Self-Observation Scales (184) provide information about students' overall perceptions of themselves. Other instruments such as the Perceived Competency Scale for Children (183), the Nowicki Strickland Locus of Control Scale for Children (185), and the Coopersmith Self-Esteem Inventory (182) have a more narrow focus. Some of these instruments may be dated since they were developed in the late 1960s and early 1970s. In addition, they may not be culturally appropriate for some students. A culture-specific instrument might be more valid for some purposes, especially when working with African American students

Many suggestions have been offered to enhance students' self-confidence in their ability to learn and control their lives. The following techniques can be used to improve students' confidence in their ability to learn (21, 175–181):

- Good instructional techniques individualized to students' strengths and weaknesses are probably the most effective way to enhance students' self-confidence. Selecting work at their ability levels, organizing their assignments to ensure success, and providing support and information when they need it can help many students with poor self-concepts succeed, despite their beliefs that they cannot.
- Students' pessimistic self-perceptions may be counteracted by helping them see the strengths and skills they bring to each task, by expressing a personal belief that they can succeed, and by explaining how their past experiences can be poor predictors of the present if they practice, study, and concentrate more and learn from their mistakes. Students can learn vicariously by reading books and seeing films about others who have had experiences like theirs. Exposing students who do not believe that they can succeed to stories of real people who have actually done so can be inspirational.
- If students see their accomplishments as inadequate because they judge themselves by culturally inappropriate standards, help them be more accepting of themselves and their cultural styles.
- Provide students with opportunities to succeed in areas where they feel adequate so their positive feelings in one area will generalize to other areas.
- Encourage students to make positive rather than negative statements about themselves and reinforce them when they do so.

The following approaches can help students believe that they have the power to achieve what they set out to accomplish:

- Demonstrate trust and faith that the students can be self-managing and self-motivating enough to attain the goals they determine themselves with a minimum of external guidance.
- In keeping with their maturity level, allow students to choose among alternative learning activities, centers, manipulatives, and instructional materials and permit them to generate or develop some of the alternatives themselves within set limits. This will enhance their perceptions that they, not others, are responsible for what they do in class. This also gives them another opportunity to experience the teacher's faith in them.
- Provide dependent students with assistance only when they request it, and gradually wean them from needing assistance.
- Ask students what they think about their own work rather than expressing a personal opinion. This demonstrates the teacher's faith in them that they can evaluate themselves.
- Teach students who seek extrinsic rewards to reward themselves.

As noted throughout this book, students from certain ethnic groups are more likely to suffer experiences that attack their self-confidence. Thus, many, but certainly not all, of the students in these ethnic groups can profit from instructional techniques that are designed to counteract these harmful experiences. Pepper listed the following aspects that should be included in a self-concept enhancement program for Native American students with disabilities: "Teach the true history of the American Indian and the value of Indian culture to all children. . . . Value and accept the Indian child as he is. . . . Use words that build the Indian child's self-esteem and feelings of adequacy. . . . Show faith in the Indian child so he can believe in himself. . . . Plan for experiences that are guaranteed to give success" (192, pp. 143–144).

The following seven-step process has been shown to be effective with African American students (188):

- Students discuss people's dreams and aspirations and what might become of them.
- Students analyze their ability to make decisions and their power at home in their community and at school.
- Students identify their personal desires and dreams and the kind of person they would like to become.
- Students set a short-term goal.
- Students prepare a plan of action to obtain the goal and identify the individuals and material resources available to them.
- Students' progress toward the achievement of the goal is monitored periodically.
- At the end of the period, students analyze their actions to understand why their goals were or were not met.

The many multicultural activities described in Chapter 4 can improve students' faith in their ability to learn and control their lives. As Wood pointed out, studying the history and contributions of non-European Americans increases students' self-confidence.

> When students become aware of the worth of their own histories, they can come to value their own perceptions and insights. They will not have to rely upon the history of the dominant culture to validate their experiences and truths. Rather they can look to themselves as useful members of a cultural tradition that empowers them to speak with their own voices. This has indeed been the experience of minorities in this country as they have strived to recover a sense of their own worth within an understanding of their value to the culture at large. Teachers need to incorporate such a historical perspective within the curriculum for all children, so that this sense of self-worth will permeate their social actions. (193, p. 235)

INTERESTS

As noted previously, some educators believe that schools cater to the interests of European Americans and offer non-European American students an irrelevant curriculum that contributes to their school-related problems. African American educators are particularly critical of the "Eurocentric" curriculum of most schools in the United States. To correct this, they suggest that teachers should include ethnocentric materials and content in the daily curriculum that deal with topics and themes that are relevant to other ethnic groups. "Most African-American children sit in classrooms, yet are outside the information being discussed. The white child sits in the middle of the information, whether it is literature, history, politics or art. The task of the Afrocentric curriculum is finding patterns in African-American history and culture that help the teacher place the child in the middle of the intellectual experience. This is not an idea to replace all things European, but to expand the dialogue to include African-American information" (194, p. 46).

Other educators disagree. For example, William Bennet, former Secretary of Education, stated, "I think it will further alienate the poor who are already tenuously connected to American culture. . . . It's a mistake to think that these kids are going to get any more interested in schools by studying more about Africa" (195, p. 45). Research is not very supportive of this latter position. Although children and youth share many interests in common, ethnic and gender groups do have somewhat different interests. For example, a study of the reading interests of sixth-grade African American and European American students found that the two books most preferred by African American students were the books least preferred by European American students (200). Chapter 4 and the references at the end of this chapter include many suggestions for making the curriculum more relevant to all students, not just European American males (194–201).

ACCEPTABLE AND UNACCEPTABLE LEARNING ACTIVITIES

Students differ not only in how they prefer to learn but also in what they prefer to learn. For example, because of their religious or moral upbringing, some students are unable to participate in various school activities. Jehovah's Witnesses do not allow their children to participate in holiday celebrations. Some Christian groups do not want their children to participate in discussions of morality. Hispanic American females may be uncomfortable about participating in physical education activities that require them to wear shorts. Also, "Indian students may not feel comfortable participating in some activities required in biology and other science classes. Destruction of life for the sole purpose of examining an organism may not be tolerable" (202, p. 44).

FIELD-SENSITIVE AND FIELD-INDEPENDENT LEARNING AND BEHAVIORAL CHARACTERISTICS

There is considerable evidence that some learning characteristics are interrelated. Researchers have identified two groups of learning characteristics that have been labeled *field sensitive* and *field independent*. Research conducted in the 1970s indicates that some ethnic groups tend to be primarily field sensitive (e.g., African Americans and Hispanic Americans) and others are predominantly field independent (e.g., European Americans). Within most ethnic groups, females tend to be more field sensitive than males.

No group or individual is completely field independent or field sensitive. An individual or an ethnic group may function in a predominantly field-sensitive or field-independent way, but aspects of the opposite styles also exist in their personalities. The following are examples of characteristics that tend to belong to either the field-sensitive or field-independent personality type (29):

- People rely more on internal clues—such as their own feelings, ideas, values, and experiences—to understand the world around them (field independent) or on information from their surroundings (field dependent/sensitive).
- People prefer solitary activities, personal time, and more distant, aloof relationships (field independent) or are sociable, gregarious, and interested in helping people (field dependent/sensitive).
- People work better individually (field independent) or in groups (field dependent/sensitive).
- People are relatively indifferent to the feelings, ideas, opinions, attitudes, and so on of others when they decide what to do or how to do it (field independent) or are sensitive to and responsive to what others feel and think and consider how their actions may affect others (field dependent/sensitive).
- People prefer to maintain considerable physical distance when they talk with others (field independent) or to be in close proximity to them (field dependent/sensitive).

- People are indifferent to praise and criticism from others (field independent) or react intensely to being praised and criticized (field dependent/sensitive).
- People function better in competitive situations (field independent) or under cooperative conditions (field dependent/sensitive).
- People prefer to work independently (field independent) or seek feedback, guidance, and approval from others (field dependent/sensitive).
- People prefer abstract, theoretical tasks such as math computational problems (field independent) or tasks that involve human issues and concerns such as math word problems (field dependent/sensitive).
- People respond better to impersonal rewards such as money, toys, candy, time off, and so on (field independent) or personal rewards such as praise, smiles, pats on the back, and the like (field dependent/sensitive)

AVOIDING MISLEADING STEREOTYPES

As noted in the Preface and throughout this text, the learning characteristics discussed in this chapter do not apply to all members of a given ethnic or gender group. Whether people conform to a particular ethnic or gender stereotype depends on many different factors. Two of these factors, their socioeconomic-class background and their type of acculturation, are discussed next.

Socioeconomic-Class Effects

In the United States, middle-class students are less likely to conform to traditional gender stereotypes. Research that was conducted primarily in the 1970s shows that ethnic stereotypes do not apply equally to all socioeconomic classes (203–211). In the United States, ethnic differences between African Americans or Hispanic Americans and European Americans are greatest among poor individuals and smallest among middle- and upper-class individuals. This may be because members of these groups may have to reject their ethnic background and accept the European American middle-class culture in order to succeed in a European American, middle-class dominated society. There is also suggestive evidence that socioeconomic class does not play as important a role among some other ethnic groups—for instance, Jewish Americans, Chinese Americans, and Japanese Americans. The cause of this may be that it is less necessary for them to deny their cultural heritages in order to enter the middle class.

It is often difficult to determine whether ethnicity or socioeconomic class is more influential in a particular situation. Thus, Havighurst asked, "A given person is a middle-class black, or a working-class black. Is he more accurately described by his social class or by his ethnicity? Another person is an upper-working-class Pole or an upper-middle-class Pole. Which takes precedence for him, his ethnicity or his social class?" (206, pp. 56–57).

Because ethnicity and socioeconomic-class factors interact to influence ethnic and gender traits, numerous educators attribute some of the learning characteristics of many non-European American students described in this text to socioeconomic class, not ethnic factors. They claim that in the United States the poor and the middle and upper classes have vastly different degrees of access to the many advantages offered to U.S. citizens, enjoy different standards of living, employ different child-rearing practices and learning and behavior styles, and have very different experiences. They believe that because African American, Native American, and Hispanic American students are more likely than European American students to come from poor backgrounds, many of the differences some people attribute to ethnicity are actually the result of contextual factors associated with socioeconomic class. (See Cultural versus Contextual Factors in Chapter 5.)

Unfortunately, few researchers have studied socioeconomic-class differences within the many ethnic groups in the Unites States. Given the lack of research in this area, it is presently impossible to state with any degree of accuracy which, if any, of the learning characteristics attributed in this chapter to an ethnic group in general or to a particular gender within that ethnic group are actually restricted to a particular socioeconomic class within that group. Perhaps the most reasonable conclusion at this time is that educators should not assume that any particular learning trait is equally characteristic of all socioeconomic classes within a particular ethnic group.

Acculturation Effects

Poor and non-European American students have at least four options for resolving the cultural conflicts they experience when their learning and behavioral characteristics do not meet the expectations of the middle-class, European American-oriented schools (212, 213). These students can (1) maintain the values, beliefs, and practices of their cultural heritage and reject the mainstream culture (traditional/cultural resistance); (2) reject their heritage culture and adopt the mainstream culture (assimilated/nontraditional/cultural shift); (3) identify with and accept both cultural systems and select which one is most appropriate for a given situation (bicultural/cultural incorporation); and (4) combine and alter both their original cultural norms and the alternate ones to create a new unique set of norms (cultural transmutation).

Many non-European American students have maintained most aspects of their culture, including learning and behavioral characteristics that are different than those expected by school personnel. The learning and behavioral characteristics of others who have lost or given up a great deal of their traditional culture parallel those of European American middle-class students. Some are bicultural and have neither lost nor given up much of their culture, and some are functioning in a way that represents, at least to some degree, cultural transmutation.

The pace at which individuals acculturate to a different culture, the type of acculturation they choose, and the areas in which they manifest these different types of acculturation depend on many factors. Some of these factors are the following:

- Age at immigration
- Gender
- Level of education
- Whether they are immigrants or refugees
- Number of generations the family has been living in the other culture
- Previous intercultural experience
- Length of time they have been exposed to the other culture
- Degree to which they interact with members of the other culture
- Ability to speak the language of the other culture
- Amount of compatibility between the two cultures
- Attitudes about the other culture
- Relationship between members of the original and the other cultures
- Amount of support they have within their original cultural group
- Ethnic makeup of the neighborhood
- Types and degree of pressure and encouragement they experience to maintain their original culture or to assimilate (213, 215, 217–220, 224, 227, 229, 231).

ASSESSING LEARNING CHARACTERISTICS AND ACCULTURATION

For the many reasons just cited, one cannot understand students' learning characteristics on the basis of their names, ethnic backgrounds, or skin shade. It is necessary to understand each student as a unique individual rather than stereotypically. To do so, educators can assess the learning styles of all students, regardless of their gender, ethnic background, and degree and type of acculturation of non-European and poor students.

Learning Characteristics

Students' learning characteristics can be evaluated informally. The various characteristics discussed in this chapter can serve as checklists or guides for observing how students learn. Special educators can also choose from a wide selection of formal assessment procedures for evaluating students' learning characteristics (233–237). Some are designed for students in general, such as the Learning Style Inventory (234, 237); others are aimed at non-European American students in particular, such as the Ramirez and Castaneda Behavior Rating Scales (212).

The regular and primary versions of the Learning Style Inventory involve students in the assessment process by having them state whether or not various statements apply to them. The following are some sample items from the instrument:

- The things I remember best are the things I hear.
- Noise usually keeps me from concentrating.
- I like to be given choices of how I can do things.
- I like to be told exactly what to do.

TABLE 10–1   The Ramirez and Castenada Behavior Rating Scale

Field-Sensitive Student	Field-Independent Student
• Likes to work with others to achieve a common goal	• Prefers to work independently
• Seeks guidance and demonstration from teacher	• Likes to try new tasks without teacher's help
• Is sensitive to feelings and opinions of others	• Is task oriented; is inattentive to social environments when working

Field-Sensitive Teacher	Field-Independent Teacher
• Encourages cooperation and development of group feeling; encourages class to think and work as a unit	• Encourages competition between individual students
• Humanizes curriculum; attributes human characteristics to concepts and principles	• Relies on graphs, charts, and formulas
• Is sensitive to children who are having difficulty and who need help	• Encourages independent student achievement; emphasizes individual effort

The Ramirez and Castenada Behavior Rating Scale is designed to evaluate whether students are field-sensitive or field-independent learners. Although the instrument was designed for use with Hispanic American students, it is useful in evaluating students from other ethnic groups. It is also a helpful tool in examining some gender stereotypes since many, but certainly not all, females prefer a field-sensitive learning style and males tend to be more field independent.

The scale also has items to evaluate whether teachers employ field-sensitive or field-independent instructional styles. By using both the teaching style and learning characteristics sections of this instrument, teachers can determine whether their teaching style matches a particular student's learning characteristics and thus accommodate their teaching to her or his needs. Table 10–1 shows examples of items in the students' and teachers' versions of the Ramirez and Castenada Behavior Rating Scale.

Acculturation

As noted in the previous chapter, it takes immigrant students who have spent the first four or more years of their lives somewhere else a number of years to adjust to a significant degree to the way things are done in the United States, even if they and their parents want to learn the new ways as quickly as possible. Thus, if immigrant students have not been in the United States at least for a few years, their classroom functioning will be affected by many of the cultural factors they or their parents brought with them. The same principle would apply to many other students who have to adjust to unfamiliar school environments, including Native American students, rural students in urban schools, and students who attend schools that serve children and youth from a different socioeconomic class.

Students' cumulative folders should include the information needed to determine how long they have been in the United States, whether they attended school prior to coming here, and, if so, the kind of school experiences they had. Some information about Native American or rural students can also be obtained from their cumulative folder. However, one may have to rely on the students themselves and their parents and sometimes agencies that are working with the students for most of the information that is needed. Additional information can be obtained in the following ways:

- *Observe the students' behavior.* Answer the following questions about students' behavior:

1. Do students socialize only with students from their same ethnic or social backgrounds, only with European American students, or with all types of students?
2. What language do bilingual students prefer to use when they are not in class (at lunch, recess, after school): English only, their native language, or a mixture of both?
3. Do students dress like typical European American students or in ways that identify them as members of a different group?
4. What do the statements students make about the European American culture and the culture of their homes reflect about their cultural identity? Do they express pride in their ethnic or racial background or reject it? Do they comment positively or negatively about the European American culture?
5. Do students' reactions to national and ethnic holidays indicate a bicultural identity or a preference for one type of holiday over the other?

- *Consult with colleagues.* Ask colleagues (other teachers, paraprofessionals, and so on) who are knowledgeable about students' cultures to observe students and determine if their actions indicate they are traditional, assimilated, or bicultural.

- *Interview the student.* Ask students if any of the classroom procedures, routines, rules, or social patterns are difficult for them to follow or conflict with how they are used to doing things at home. Inquire about whether they ever feel pressured in school to behave in ways that make them uncomfortable because they behave differently at home or in their neighborhoods. Determine whether students listen to and watch music, radio, movies, and television programs in their native language, English, or both languages. Listen to how students describe themselves. Do they say that they are Mexican, Vietnamese, Russian, and so on; Mexican American, Vietnamese American, Russian American, and so on; or just American?

INFORMAL ASSESSMENT

- Compare the following three Korean American teenagers in terms of their type of acculturation to the United States along the traditional, bicultural, assimilated continuum.
- Would you use different instructional strategies with each student because of their different types of acculturation? If so, how would you teach them differently?

Jae came to the United States when he was almost 10 years old. He has been here for 5 years. He speaks both Korean and English with friends and also at home. He reads English and Korean newspapers and magazines, watches Korean and English TV, eats European American and Korean food, and admires both Americans and Koreans. He belongs to some American groups but goes to a Korean church. His friends speak many languages but most of them are English speaking. His closest friend is a Vietnamese American immigrant.

Jae does not want to lose his ability to speak Korean. He deplores the fact that there are no Korean language books for his age group to read. Responding to a question about how he identifies himself, he stated,

> I'm Korean . . . because I'm from Korea. . . . My brains, you know, are washed up by Korean culture. Then I speak Korean. Even though I work with American Kids, I still don't forget I'm Korean and I look forward to getting along more with Korean people. And when I get a job, I'll look Korean even though I'll have citizenship because I don't have white skin. They'll still be prejudiced a little bit that I'm Oriental. They're not going to look at me as American. . . . So I'm Korean. (232, p. 13)

Mi Cha has been in the United States for 7 years, since she was 9 years old. She considers herself Korean American. Her friends speak English and Korean, but she spends most of her time with a group of Korean American teenagers who belong to a Korean church. She describes herself in the following way:

> I can't really speak good English. I can speak fluently in Korean but I don't know about deep words, you know. So I'm in the middle. Half English and half Korean. I know I'm Korean. I'm more into Korea than America. That's why I hang around a lot with Korean people who are older than me. They teach me a lot in Korean and I really learn a lot of Korean there. I will probably live my whole life here, probably learn American as I grow. But if you don't join Korean people you don't learn.
>
>   I would marry a Korean guy. . . . I think we could get along better. . . . American people think differently than Korean people. . . . I'm not going to be over men. It's better if they're over me. But they'll not rule me where I have to do every little thing like that. . . . I want an equal chance but I could serve him. It will be easier for me. (232, p. 13)

Danny has been in the United States for 11 or 12 years, since he was 5 or 6 years old. He does not remember anything about Korea. He does not know much about Korea and would like to learn more. However, Danny does not appear to be too interested in visiting his native land. He speaks both languages fluently, but he prefers to speak English because he is embarrassed by the mistakes he makes in Korean. He cannot read Korean. He would like to learn but does not have the time. Although he identifies himself as Korean-American, Danny feels more American than Korean.

He dates both Korean American and European American girls. His best friend is European American. He only knows a few Korean American friends and they all speak English. He says that the new Korean kids in school have their own friends. He would like to help them but he is too busy with football practice and other things.

Danny's mother cooks Korean food at home. Although he claims to like Korean foods, he does not eat much spicy Korean food any more.

Source: From "The Acculturation of Three Korean American Students" by J. G. Golden, 1990, *Teaching and Learning, 5,* pages 9–20. Copyright 1990 by *Teaching and Learning: The Journal of Natural Inquiry.* Adapted by permission.

There are numerous formal assessment instruments for evaluating students' acculturation (214, 216, 217, 222–226, 228, 230). These instruments study the extent to which students are involved in their original and the European American cultures by requiring them to respond to a series of questions about their friendships both in and out of school, the activities they engage in, their recreational habits, the language or languages they speak, their attitudes and values, the way they identify themselves, and so on. Typical items include the following: What is the ethnic origin of your friends—exclusively Hispanic, Vietnamese, Chinese, Americans; mostly Hispanic, Vietnamese, Chinese Americans; both Hispanic, Vietnamese, Chinese, Americans and European Americans; mostly European Americans; or exclusively European American? How do you call yourself—Hispanic, Vietnamese, Chinese; Hispanic Vietnamese Chinese American; or American? What kind of music do you prefer to listen to—Hispanic, Vietnamese, Chinese, or American?

Some instruments also include questions about students' parents—such as their citizenship, the languages they speak, the kind of jobs they work at, the amount of education they have completed, and the number of children they have had—because assimilated and nonassimilated families tend to differ along these lines. One instrument is based on a series of questions designed to determine whether the persons being assessed consider themselves to be "insiders" or "outsiders" in relation to the dominant culture (222). The students' answers are then compared to a sample group of students from similar backgrounds. The results enable educators to determine the extent to which students have remained traditional, have assimilated, or become bicultural, whether they identify with one or both cultures, and whether they are growing up in a nontraditional/assimilated or traditional home.

Until recently, most experts viewed acculturation as a process of change along a continuum from unassimilated to highly assimilated (215–217, 221, 223, 225, 227, 228, 230). Therefore, most instruments indicate students' acculturation along this continuum—the extent to which they are traditional, assimilated, or bicultural. Because these instruments yield a score that indicates students' general level of acculturation, they can easily be misinterpreted. Today, experts realize that students and others do not assimilate at the same pace in all areas of their lives. Thus, an overall score can underestimate the extent of students' assimilation in one area and overestimate their adaptation in another. Mendoza and Martinez stated, "Some cultural traits tend to be assimilated more rapidly than others. Language usage, dress customs, and technological necessities, for instance, are generally incorporated much faster than abstract or less tangible qualities that involve values, sentiments, esthetic preferences, or attitudes on various socialization practices" (224, p. 73).

Despite the limitation of the instruments currently available, the information they provide can serve as a starting point for continued examination of the ways in which students deal with cultural incompatibilities. Most of the instruments currently available assess Hispanic Americans. However, they can be adapted and translated if necessary for use with other ethnic and language groups.

These formal and informal procedures will furnish the teacher with a place to begin. They will provide a general understanding of the degree to which students are assimilated and they will help alert the teacher to the possible existence of cultural differences. However, these procedures do not provide the information needed to determine whether students are characterized by a particular cultural trait—information that is necessary to enable the teacher to consider individual students' cultural characteristics when choosing educational approaches to use with them. To do this requires more detailed information about the way individual students function in school.

SUMMARY

There are significant gender and ethnic differences in students' relationship, cognitive, and motivational styles; time orientations; interests; degree of self-confidence; and comfort level with certain educational activities. When special educators adapt their instructional approaches to to these learning characteristics, students learn more efficiently.

These learning characteristics do not apply to all members of a given ethnic or gender group. Students' socioeconomic-class background and type of acculturation help to determine whether particular students will conform to a particular ethnic or gender stereotype. In order to understand each student with disabilities as a unique individual, special educators can assess their learning characteristics and the degree and type of their acculturation to European American middle-class-oriented schools.

ACTIVITIES

1. If you are a teacher, observe your students' learning styles. Do students work at different paces, volunteer to answer question equally often, and so on? Do you notice any of the cultural differences reported in this chapter? If you

are a preservice teacher, ask some students from different cultural backgrounds in the courses you are taking or some friends to describe their learning style preferences. You can interview them informally or prepare an informal questionnaire. Do you notice any of the cultural differences reported in this chapter?

2. Using the list of learning characteristics included in this chapter as a guide, prepare descriptions of the traits that you believe are characteristic of male and female students. Then ask a few of your colleagues, peers, or students to review your list and tell you which traits they do and do not accept as being characteristic of their group.

3. Interview some individuals from an ethnic group that interests you and prepare a description of the educationally relevant cultural characteristics of the group as they perceive them.

4. Ask a colleague to evaluate your teaching style with the Ramirez and Castaneda Behavior Rating Scale and compare your teaching style to the learning styles of your students.

5. Use the Ramirez and Castaneda Behavior Rating Scale to compare the learning characteristics of some of your male and female students or peers. Do you observe any of the gender differences reported in the literature?

6. Ask your colleagues to use the Ramirez and Castaneda Behavior Rating Scale to evaluate their instructional style. Do you observe any gender differences?

REFERENCES

The initial quote is found in reference 1.

1. Serwatka, T., Dove, T., & Hodge, W. (1986). Black students in special education: Issues and implications for community involvement. *Negro Educational Review, 37* (1), 17–26.

References 2–5 discuss participatory and passive learning.

2. Gersten, R., & Keating, T. (1987). Long-term benefits from direct instruction. *Educational Leadership, 44,* 28–31.

3. Grossman, H. (1984). *Educating Hispanic Students: Cultural Implications for Instruction, Classroom Management, Counseling, and Assessment.* Springfield, IL: Thomas.

4. Kang-Ning, C. (1981). Education for Chinese and Indochinese. *Theory into Practice, 20* (1), 35–44.

5. Wong, M. K. (1978). Traditional Chinese culture and behavior patterns of Chinese students in American classrooms. In *Second Annual Forum on Transcultural Adaptation (Proceedings): Asian Students in American Classrooms.* Chicago: Illinois Office of Education.

Ethnic differences in whether students prefer aloof and distant or involved and personal relations with teachers is included in reference 6.

6. Kleinfeld J. (1975). Effective teachers of Indian and Eskimo high school students. *School Review, 83* (2), 301–344.

Ethnic and gender variability in students' preferences for dependent or independent learning is the focus of references 7–17.

7. Becker, B. J. (1986). Influence again: An examination of reviews and studies of gender differences in social influence. In J. S. Hyde & M. C. Linn (Eds.), *The Psychology of Gender.* Baltimore: Johns Hopkins University Press.

8. Brutsaert, H. (1990). Changing sources of self-esteem among girls and boys in secondary school. *Urban Education, 24* (40), 432–439.

9. California State Department of Education. (1986). *Handbook for Teaching Pilipino-Speaking Students.* Sacramento, CA: Author.

10. Caplan, P. (1979). Beyond the box score: A boundary condition for sex differences in aggression and achievement striving. In B. Maher (Ed.), *Progress in Experimental Personality Research* (Vol. 9). New York: Academic Press.

11. Cooper, H. M. (1979). Statistically combining independent studies: A meta-analysis of sex differences in conformity research. *Journal of Personality and Social Psychology, 37,* 131–146.

12. Dao, M. (1987) *From Vietnamese to Vietnamese American.* San Jose, CA: San Jose State University.

13. Eagly, A. H., & Carli, L. L. (1981). Sex of researchers and sex-typed communications as determinants of sex differences in influenceability: A meta-analysis of social influence studies. *Psychological Bulletin, 90,* 1–20.

14. Parsons, J. E. (1982). Sex differences in attributions and learned helplessness. *Sex Roles, 8* (4), 421–432.

15. Van Hecke, M., Tracy, R. J., Cotter, S., & Ribordy, S. C. (1984). Approval versus achievement motives in seventh-grade girls. *Sex Roles, 11* (1), 33–41.

16. Wauters, J. L., Bruce. K. M., Black, D. R., & Hocker, P. N. (1989, August). Learning styles: A study of Alaskan Native and non-Native students. *Journal of American Indian Education,* Special Issue, pp. 53–62.

17. Wulatin, M. L., & Tracy, R. J. (1977). *Sex Differences in Children's Responses to Achievement and Approval.* Paper presented at the meeting of the Midwestern Psychological Association, Chicago.

References 18–19 discuss factors that influence whether students are peer oriented or adult oriented.

18. Tharp, R. G. (1989). Psychocultural variables and constants: Effects on teaching and learning in schools. *American Psychologist, 44* (2), 349–359.

19. Tharp, R. G., & Gallimore, R. (1988). *Rousing Minds to Life: Teaching, Learning and Schooling in Social Context.* Cambridge, England: Cambridge University Press.

Gender differences in seeking teacher help, support, and feedback are the focus of references 20–25.

20. Eiszler, C. F. (1982). *Perceptual Preference as an Aspect of Adolescent Learning Styles.* ERIC ED 224 769.

21. Grossman, H., & Grossman, S. (1994). *Gender Issues in Education.* Boston: Allyn and Bacon.

22. Henry, S. E., Medway, F. J., & Scarbro, H. A. (1979). Sex and locus of control as determinants of children's responses to peer versus adult praise. *Journal of Educational Psychology, 71* (5), 604–612.

23. Nelson-LeGall, S., & Glor-Scheib, S. (1983). *Help-Seeking in Elementary Classrooms: An Observational Study.* ERIC ED 230 286.

24. Stewart, M. J., & Corbin, C. B. (1988). Feedback dependence among low confidence preadolescent boys and girls. *Research Quarterly for Exercise and Sport, 59* (2), 160–164.

25. Sullivan, H. J. (1986). Factors that influence continuing motivation. *Journal of Educational Research, 80* (2), 86–92.

Reference 26 explores student differences in individualistic or group orientation.

26. Barnhardt, C. (1982). Tuning-in: Athabaskan teachers and Athabaskan students. In R. Barnhardt (Ed.), *Cross-Cultural Issues in Alaskan Education* (Vol 2). ERIC ED 232 814.

Factors that contribute to differences among students in terms of reflective/analytical versus impulsive/spontaneous/intuitive cognitive styles are discussed in references 27–30.

27. Farkas, G., Grobe, R. P., Sheenan, D., & Shuan, Y. (1990). Cultural resources and school success: Gender, ethnicity, and poverty groups within an urban school district. *American Sociological Review, 55,* 127–142.

28. Forslund, M. A., & Hull, R. E. (1974). Teacher sex and achievement among elementary school pupils. *Education, 95,* 87–89.

29. Grossman, H. (1990). *Trouble Free Teaching: Solutions to Behavior Problems in the Classroom.* Mountain View, CA: Mayfield.

30. Shade, B. J. (1979). *Racial Preference in Psychological Differentiation: An Alternative Explanation for Group Differences.* ERIC ED 179 672.

Ethnic contributions to students' preferences for global perception or analysis of details is the subject of references 31–35.

31. Chan, D. M. (1986). Curriculum development for limited English proficient exceptional Chinese children. *Rural Special Education Quarterly, 8* (1), 26–31.

32. Hilliard, A. (1976). *Alternatives to I.Q. Testing: An Approach to the Identification of Gifted Minority Children.* Sacramento, CA: Final Report to the California State Department of Education.

33. More, A. J. (1987). Native Indian learning styles: A review for researchers and teachers. *Journal of American Indian Education, 27* (1), 17–29.

34. More, A. J. (1989, August). Native Indian learning styles: A review for researchers and teachers. *Journal of American Indian Education,* Special Issue, pp. 15–28.

35. Rhodes, R. W. (1988). Holistic/teaching learning for Native American students. *Journal of American Indian Education, 27* (2), 21–29.

References 36–39 discuss the effects of ethnic background on students' preferences for aural, visual, or verbal learning situations.

36. Hallman, C. L., Etienne, M. R., & Fradd, S. (1982). *Haitian Value Orientations. Monograph Number 2.* ERIC ED 269 532.

37. John, B. (1972). Styles of learning—Styles of teaching: Reflections of the education of Navajo children. In D. Cazden, V. John, & D. Hymes (Eds.), *Functions of Language in the Classroom.* New York: Teachers College Press.

38. Lewis, J., Vang, L., & Cheng, L. L. (1989). Identifying the language-learning difficulties of Hmong students: Implications of context and culture. *Topics in Language Disorders, 9* (3), 21–37.

39. Swisher, K., & Deyhle, D. (1989, August). The styles of learning are different, but the teaching is just the same: Suggestions for teachers of American Indian youth. *Journal of American Indian Education,* Special Issue, pp. 1–14.

References 40–44 contrast kinesthetic/active/energetic stimulating learning environments and calm/inactive/verbal learning environments.

40. Almanza, H. P., & Mosley, W. J. (1980). Cultural adaptations and modifications for culturally diverse handicapped children. *Exceptional Children, 46* (8), 608–614.

41. Boykin, A. W. (1984). Reading achievement and the social-cultural frame of reference of Afro-American children. *Journal of Negro Education, 53* (4), 464–473.

42. Eiszler, C. F. (1982). *Perceptual Preference as an Aspect of Adolescent Learning Styles.* ERIC ED 224 769.

43. Franklin, M. E. (1992). Culturally sensitive instructional practices for African-American learners with disabilities. *Exceptional Children, 59* (2), 115–122.

44. Simpson, C. (1981). Classroom organization and the gap between minority and non-minority student performance levels. *Educational Research Quarterly, 6* (3), 43–53.

References 45–46 indicate that females are more sensitive to nonverbal cues.

45. Hall, J. C. (1978). Gender effects in decoding nonverbal cues. *Psychological Bulletin, 85,* 845–857.

46. Rosenthal, R., Hall, J. A., DiMatteo, M. R., Rogers, P. L., & Archer, D. C. (1979). *Sensitivity to Non-Verbal Communication.* Baltimore: Johns Hopkins University Press.

References 47–48 focus on trial and error versus "watch then do."

47. Longstreet, E. (1978). *Aspects of Ethnicity.* New York: Teachers College Press.

48. Rhodes, R. W. (1990). Measurement of Navajo and Hopi brain dominance and learning styles. *Journal of American Indian Education, 29* (2), 29–40.

Argumentative/forensic instruction versus direct instruction are discussed in reference 49.

49. Burger, H. G. (1972). Ethno-lematics: Evoking "shy" Spanish-American pupils by cross-cultural mediation. *Adolescence, 6* (25), 61–76.

Ethnic and gender variations in students' motivation to succeed in school are the focus of references 50–55.

50. Comer, J. P. (1990). What makes the new generation tick? *Ebony, 45* (10), 34, 37, 38.

51. Ford, D. Y. (1991). *Self-perceptions of Social, Psychological, and Cultural Determinants of Achievement among Gifted Black Students: A Paradox of Underachievement.* Unpublished doctoral disser-

tation, Cleveland State University, Cleveland, OH.

52. Ford, D. Y. (1992). The American achievement ideology and achievement differentials among preadolescent gifted and nongifted African American males and females. *Journal of Negro Education, 61* (1), 45–64.

53. Fordham, S. (1988). Racelessness as a strategy in Black students' school success: Coping with the burden of "acting White." *Urban Review, 18,* 176–207.

54. MacLeod, J. (1987). *Ain't No Makin' It: Leveled Aspirations in a Low-Income Neighborhood.* Boulder, CO: Westview.

55. Ogbu, J. U. (1990). Minority education in comparative perspective. *Journal of Negro Education, 59,* 45–57.

References 56–63 deal with gender differences in motivation to avoid success.

56. Crovitz, E. (1980). A decade later: Black-white attitudes toward women's familial roles. *Psychology of Women Quarterly, 5* (2), 170–176.

57. Fleming, J. (1978). Fear of success, achievement related motives and behavior in Black college women. *Journal of Personality, 46,* 694–716.

58. George, V. D. (1981). *Occupational Aspirations of Talented Black Adolescent Females.* ERIC ED 206 976.

59. George, V. D. (1986). Talented adolescent women and the motivation to avoid success. *Journal of Multicultural Counseling and Development, 14* (3), 132–139.

60. McCorquodale, P. (1983). *Social Influences on the Participation of Mexican American Women in Science* (N.I.E. Final Report 6-79-011). Tucson: University of Arizona.

61. Roberts, L. R. (1986). *Gender Differences in Patterns of Achievement and Adjustment during Early Adolescence.* ERIC ED 288 134.

62. Stockard, J., Schmuck, P. A., Kemper, K., Williams, P., Edson, S. K., & Smith, M. A. (1980). *Sex Equity in Education.* New York: Academic Press.

63. Tanner, D. (1990). *You Just Don't Understand.* New York: William Morrow.

References 64–69 focus on learning on demand versus learning what is relevant or interesting.

64. Cortes, C. E. (1978). Chicano culture, experience and learning. In L. Morris, G. Sather, & S. Scull (Eds.), *Extracting Learning Styles from So-cial/Cultural Diversity: A Study of Five American Minorities.* Norman, OK: Southwest Teacher Corps Network.

65. Garza, R. T. (1978). Affective and associative qualities in the learning styles of Chicanos and Anglos. *Psychology in the Schools, 15* (1), 111–115.

66. Kleinfeld, J. (1975). *Effective Teachers of Indian and Eskimo Students.* Fairbanks: Institute of Social, Economic, and Government Research, University of Alaska, Fairbanks.

67. Rabiannski-Carriuolo, N. (1989). Learning styles: An interview with Edmund W. Gordon. *Journal of Developmental Education, 13* (1), 18–20, 22.

68. Walker, B. J., Dodd, J. , & Bigelow, R. (1989, August). Learning preferences of capable American Indians of two tribes. *Journal of American Indian Education,* Special Issue, pp. 63–71.

69. Yao, E. L. (1987). Asian-immigrants students—Unique problems that hamper learning. *NASSP Bulletin, 71* (503), 82–88.

References 70–71 argue that Native American and African American students are less object-oriented and more people-oriented learners.

70. Burgess, B. J. (1978). Native American learning styles. In L. Morris, G. Sather, & S. Scull (Eds.), *Extracting Learning Styles from Social/Cultural Diversity: A Study of Five American Minorities.* Norman, OK: Southwest Teacher Corps Network.

71. Hale, J. (1978). Cultural influences on learning styles of Afro-American children. In L. Morris, G. Sather, & S. Scull (Eds.), *Extracting Learning Styles from Social/Cultural Diversity: A Study of Five American Minorities.* Norman, OK: Southwest Teacher Corps Network.

References 72–89 focus on ethnic and gender differences in preferences for competitive, cooperative, and individualistic learning environments.

72. Allen, J. L., O'Mara, J., & Long, K. M. (1987). *The Effects of Communication Avoidance, Learning Styles and Gender upon Classroom Achievement.* ERIC ED 291 111.

73. Alvino, J. (1991). An investigation into the needs of gifted boys. *Roeper Review, 13* (4), 174–180.

74. Dalton, D. W., Hannafin, M. J., & Hooper, S. (1989) Effects of individual and cooperative computer assisted instruction on student performance and attitudes. *Educational Technology Research and Development, 37* (2), 15–34.

75. Englehard, G., Jr., & Monsas, J. A. (1989). Performance, gender and the cooperative attitudes of third, fifth, and seventh graders. *Journal of Research and Development in Education, 22* (2), 13–17.

76. Fennema, E. H., & Peterson, P. L. (1985). Autonomous learning behavior: A possible explanation of gender-related differences in mathematics. In L. C. Wilkinson & C. B. Marrett (Eds.), *Gender Influences in Classroom Interaction*. New York: Academic Press.

77. Harpole, S. H. (1987). *The Relationship of Gender and Learning Styles to Achievement and Laboratory Skills in Secondary School Chemistry Students*. ERIC ED 288 728.

78. Jaramillo, M. L. (1973). *Cautions When Working with the Culturally Different Child*. ERIC ED 115 622.

79. Kagan, S., & Madsen, M. C. (1972). Rivalry in Anglo-American and Mexican children of two ages. *Journal of Personality and Social Psychology, 24*, 214–220.

80. Kagan, S., Zahn, G. L., & Gealy, J. (1977). Competition and school achievement among Anglo-American and Mexican-American children. *Journal of Educational Psychology, 69* (4), 432–441.

81. Lewis, M. A., & Cooney, J. B. (1986). *Attributional and Performance Effects of Competitive and Individualistic Feedback in Computer Assisted Mathematics Instruction*. ERIC ED 271 287.

82. Lockheed, M. E., Harris, A. M., & Nemceff, W. P. (1983). Sex and social influence: Does sex function as a status characteristic in mixed-sex groups of children? *Journal of Educational Psychology, 75*, 877–888.

83. McClintock, C. (1974). Development of social motives in Anglo-American and Mexican children. *Journal of Personality and Social Psychology, 29*, 348–354.

84. Moely, B. E., Skarin, K., & Weil, S. (1979). Sex differences in competition-cooperation behavior of children at two age levels. *Sex Roles, 5* (31), 329–342.

85. Peterson, P., & Fennema, E. (1985). Effective teaching, student engagement in classroom activities, and sex-related differences in learning mathematics. *American Educational Research Journal, 22* (3), 309–334.

86. Strube, M. J. (1981). Meta-analysis and cross-cultural comparison: Sex differences in child competitiveness. *Journal of Cross-Cultural Psychology, 12* (1), 3–20.

87. Swisher, K. (1990). Cooperative learning and the education of American Indian/Alaskan Native students: A review of the literature and suggestions for implementation. *Journal of American Indian Education, 29* (2), 36–43.

88. Webb, N. M., & Kenderski, C. M. (1985). Gender differences in small-group interaction and achievement in high- and low-achieving classes. In L. C. Wilkinson & C. B. Marrett (Eds.), *Gender Influences in Classroom Interaction*. New York: Academic Press.

89. Wilkinson, L. C., Lindow, J., & Chiang, C. P. (1985). Sex differences and sex segregation in students' small-group communication. In L. C. Wilkinson & C. B. Marrett (Eds.), *Gender Influences in Classroom Interaction*. New York: Academic Press.

Reference 90 documents the fact that competitive learning environments predominate in U.S. schools.

90. Johnson, D. W., & Johnson, R. T. (1987). *Learning Together and Alone: Cooperation, Competition and Individualization* (2nd ed.). Englewood Cliffs, NJ: Prentice Hall.

References 91–101 document the positive effects of cooperative learning.

91. Aronson, E., Blaney, N., Sikes, J., & Snapp, M. (1978). *The Jigsaw Classroom*. Beverly Hills, CA: Sage.

92. Asher, C. (1986). Cooperative learning in the urban classroom. *ERIC Digest, 30*.

93. DeVries, D. K., Edwards, K. J., & Slavin, R. (1978). Biracial learning teams and race relations in the classroom: Four field experiences using Teams-Games-Tournament. *Journal of Educational Psychology, 70*, 356–362.

94. DeVries, D., & Slavin, R. E. (1978). Teams-Games-Tournaments: A research review. *Journal of Research and Development in Education, 12*, 28–38.

95. Humphreys, B., Johson, R. T., & Johnson, D. W. (1982). Effects of cooperative, competitive and individualistic learning on students' achievement in science class. *Journal of Research in Science Teaching, 19* (5), 351–356.

96. Johnson, R. T., & Johnson, D. W. (1981). Effects of cooperative and individualistic learning experiences on interethnic interaction. *Journal of Educational Psychology, 73*, 444–449.

97. Johnson, D. W., Johnson, R. T., Holubec, E. J., & Roy, P. (1984). *Circles of Learning*. Alexandria, VA: Association for Supervision and Curriculum Development.

98. Johnson, R. T., Johnson, D. W., Scott, L. E., & Ramolae, B. A. (1985). Effects of single-sex and mixed-sex cooperative interaction on science achievement and attitudes and cross-handicap and cross-sex relationships. *Journal of Research in Science Teaching, 22* (3), 207–220.

99. Johnson, D. W., Maruyama, G., Johnson, R., Nelson, D., & Skon, L. (1981). Effects of cooperative, competitive, and individualistic goal structures on achievement: A meta analysis. *Psychological Bulletin, 89,* 47–62.

100. Schofield, J. W. (1982). *Black and White in School: Trust, Tension, and Tolerance.* New York: Praeger.

101. Slavin, R. E., & Oickle, E. (1981). Effects of cooperative learning teams on student achievement and race relations: Treatment by race interactions. *Sociology of Education, 54,* 174–180.

The selective benefits of cooperative learning are described in references 102–104.

102. Calderon, M. E., Tinajero, J. V., & Hertz-Lazarowitz, R. (1992). Adapting cooperative integrated reading and composition to meet the needs of bilingual students. *Journal of Educational Issues of Language Minority Student,* Special Issue, pp. 79–106.

103. Glassman, P. (1988). *A Study of Cooperative Learning in Mathematics, Writing and Reading as Implemented in Third, Fourth and Fifth Grade Classes: A Focus upon Achievement, Attitudes and Self-Esteem for Males, Females, Blacks, Hispanics and Anglos.* ERIC ED 292 926.

104. Knight, G. P., Nelson, W., Kagan, S., & Gumbiner, J. (1982). Cooperative-competitive social orientation and school achievement among Anglo-American and Mexican-American children. *Contemporary Educational Psychology, 7,* 97–106.

The positive effects of single-sex cooperative groups on females are discussed in references 105–106.

105. Kahle, J. B., & Lakes, M. K. (1983). The myth of equality in science classrooms. *Journal of Research in Science Teaching, 20,* 131–140.

106. Moody, J. D., & Gifford, V. D. (1990). *The Effect of Grouping by Formal Reasoning Ability, Formal Reasoning Ability Levels, Group Size, and Gender on Achievement in Laboratory Chemistry.* ERIC ED 326 443.

Documentation of the effects of mixed-sex groups on students is found in references 107–118.

107. Chalesworth, W. R., & LaFrenier, P. (1983). Dominance, friendship utilization and resource utilization in preschool children's groups. *Ethology and Sociobiology, 4,* 175–186.

108. DeVries, D. K., & Edwards, K. J. (1974). Student teams and learning games: Their effects on cross-race and cross-sex interaction. *Journal of Educational Psychology, 66* (5), 741–749.

109. Lockheed, M. E., & Harris, A. M. (1984). Cross-sex collaborative learning in elementary classrooms. *American Educational Research Journal, 21* (2), 275–294.

110. Lockheed, M. E., Harris, A. M., & Nemceff, W. P. (1983). Sex and social influence: Does sex function as a status characteristic in mixed-sex groups of children? *Journal of Educational Psychology, 75,* 877–888.

111. Peterson, P., & Fennema, E. (1985). Effective teaching, student engagement in classroom activities, and sex-related differences in learning mathematics. *American Educational Research Journal, 22* (3), 309–334.

112. Piel, J. A., & Conwell, C. R. (1989). *Differences in Perceptions between Afro-American and Anglo-American Males and Females in Cooperative Learning Groups.* ERIC ED 307 348.

113. Powlishta, K. (1987). *The Social Context of Cross-Sex Interactions.* Paper presented at the biennial meetings of the Society for Research in Child Development, Baltimore.

114. Siann, G., & Macleod, H. (1986). Computers and children of primary school age: Issues and questions. *British Journal of Educational Technology, 17,* 133–144.

115. Skarin, K., & Moely, B. E. (1974). *Sex Differences in Competition-Cooperation Behavior af Eight-Year Old Children.* ERIC ED 096 015.

116. Underwood, G., McCaffrey, M., & Underwood, J. (1990). Gender differences in a cooperative computer-based language task. *Educational Research, 32* (1), 44–49.

117. Webb, N. (1984). Microcomputer learning in small groups: Cognitive requirements and group processes. *Journal of Educational Psychology, 76* (6). 1076–1088.

118. Wilkinson, L. C., Lindow, J., & Chiang, C. P. (1985). Sex differences and sex segregation in students' small-group communication. In L. C. Wilkinson & C. B. Marrett (Eds.), *Gender Influences in Classroom Interaction.* New York: Academic Press.

Gender differences in responsiveness to peers' requests and reinforcement are discussed in references 119–122.

119. Fagot, B. I. (1985). Beyond the reinforcement principle: Another step toward understanding sex roles. *Developmental Psychology, 21,* 1097–1104.

120. Lamb, M. E., Easterbrook, A. M., & Holden, G. W. (1980). Reinforcement and punishment among preschoolers: Characteristics, effects, and correlates. *Child Development, 51,* 1230–1236.

121. Serbin, L. A., Sprafkin, C., Elman, M., & Doyle, A. B. (1984). The early development of sex differentiated patterns of social influence. *Canadian Journal of Social Science, 14* (4), 350–363.

122. Wilkinson, L. C., & Marrett, C. B. (Eds.). (1985). *Gender Influence in Classroom Interaction.* New York: Academic Press.

Gender differences in leadership assumption and participation in mixed-sex groups are treated in references 123–126.

123. Lockheed, M. E. (1977). Cognitive style effects on sex status in student work groups. *Journal of Educational Psychology, 69,* 158–165.

124. Lockheed, M. E. (1985). Sex and social influence: A meta-analysis guided by theory. In J. Berger & M. Zeldich (Eds.), *Status, Attributions, and Rewards.* San Francisco: Jossey-Bass.

125. Lockheed, M. E., & Hall, K. P.(1976). Conceptualizing sex as a status characteristic: Application to leadership training strategies. *Journal of Social Issues, 32* (3), 111–124.

126. Webb, N. M., & Kinderski, C. M. (1985). Gender differences in small group interaction and achievement in high- and low-achieving classes. In C. Wilkinson & C. B. Marrett (Eds.), *Gender Influence in Classroom Interaction.* New York: Academic Press.

References 127–128 discuss the experiences of different ethnic groups in cooperative learning groups.

127. Conwell, C. R., Piel, J. A., & Cobb, K. B. (1988). *Students' Perceptions When Working in Cooperative Problem Solving Groups.* ERIC ED 313 455.

128. Fry, P. S., & Coe, K. J. (1980). Achievement performance of internally and externally oriented black and white high school students under conditions of competition and cooperation expectancies. *British Journal of Educational Psychology, 50,* 162–167.

Reference 129 discusses the relationship between students' self-concepts and the outcome of cooperative learning activities.

129. DeVoe, M. W. (1977). Cooperation as a function of self-concept, sex and race. *Educational Research Quarterly, 2* (2), 3–8.

The focus of references 130–134 is gender differences in risk taking and reactions to challenges and failure.

130. Ginsburg, H. J., & Miller, S. M. (1982). Sex differences in children's risk-taking behavior. *Child Development, 53* (2), 426–428.

131. Licht, B. G., Kistner, J. A., Ozkaragoz, T., Shapiro, S., & Clausen, L. (1985). Causal attributions of learning disabled children: Individual differences and their implications for persistence. *Journal of Educational Psychology, 77* (2), 208–216.

132. Licht, B. G., Linden, T. A., Brown, D. A., & Sexton, M. (1984). *Sex Differences in Achievement Orientation: An "A" Student Phenomenon.* ERIC ED 252 783.

133. Miller, A. (1986). Performance impairment after failure: Mechanisms and sex differences. *Journal of Educational Psychology, 78* (6), 486–491.

134. Reyes, L. H. (1984). Affective variables and mathematics education. *Elementary School Journal, 84* (5), 558–581.

References 135–136 discuss ethnic difference in risk taking.

135. Kishi, G., & Hanohano, M. (1992). *Hawaiian-American vs. Caucasian-American Values.* Paper presented at the Council for Exceptional Children Topical Conference on Culturally and Linguistically Different Exception Children, Minneapolis.

136. Kitano, M. K. (1986). Gifted and talented Asian children. *Rural Special Education Quarterly, 8* (1), 9–13.

References 137–144 deal with different ethnic concepts of time.

137. Allameh, J. (1986). *Learning among Culturally Different Populations.* ERIC ED 273 137.

138. Ayabe, H. I. (1978). Ethnic-culture, reflection impulsivity and locus of control. *Educational Perspectives, 17* (4), 10–12.

139. Brady, M. P., & Anderson, D. D. (1983). Some issues in the implementation of P.L. 94-142 in the Pacific Basin Territories. *Education, 103* (3), 259–269.

140. Condon, E. C., Peters, J. Y., & Sueiro-Ross, C. (1979). *Special Education and the Hispanic Child: Cultural Perspectives.* Philadelphia: Temple University, Teacher Corps Mid-Atlantic Network.

141. Dodd, J. M. (1992). *Preventing American Indian Children from Overidentification with Learning Disabilities: Cultural Considerations during the Prereferral Process.* Paper presented at the Council for Exceptional Children Topic Conference on Culturally and Linguistically Diverse Exceptional Children, Minneapolis.

142. Felder, D. (1970). The education of Mexican Americans: Fallacies of the monocultural approach. *Social Education, 34* (6), 639–642.

143. Levine, R. V., West, L. J., & Reis, H. T. (1980). Perceptions of time and punctuality in the United States and Brazil. *Journal of Personality and Social Psychology, 38* (4), 541–550.

144. Morgan, C. O., Guy, E., Lee, B., & Celini, H. (1986). Rehabilitation services for American Indians: The Navajo Experience. *Journal of Rehabilitation, 52* (2), 25–31.

Gender differences in students' confidence in their ability to succeed in school are the focus of references 145–152.

145. Eccles, J., Adler, T. F., & Meece, J. L. (1984). Sex differences in achievement: A test of alternate theories. *Journal of Personality and Social Psychology, 68,* 119–128.

146. Hyde, J., & Fennema, E. (1990). *Gender Differences in Mathematics Performance and Affect: Results of Two Meta-Analyses.* Paper presented at the annual meeting of the American Educational Research Association, Boston.

147. Levine, G. (1990). *Arithmetic Development: Where are the Gender Differences?* Paper presented at the annual meeting of the American Educational Research Association, Boston.

148. Matyas, M. L. (1984). *Science Career Interests, Attitudes, Abilities, and Anxiety among Secondary School Students: The Effects of Gender, Race/Ethnicity, and School Type/Location.* ERIC ED 251 309.

149. Meece, J. L., Parsons, J. E., Kaczala, C. M., Goff, B., & Futterman, R. (1982). Sex differences in math achievement: Toward a model of academic choice. *Psychological Bulletin, 91,* 324–348.

150. Richman, C. L., Clark, M. L., & Brown, K. P. (1984). General and specific self-esteem in late adolescent students: Race × gender × SES effects. *Adolescence, 20* (79), 555–566.

151. Stevenson, H. W., & Newman, R. S. (1986). Long-term prediction of achievement and attitudes in mathematics and reading. *Child Development, 57,* 646–659.

152. Travis, C. B., McKenzie, B. J., & Wiley, D. L. (1984). *Sex and Achievement Domain: Cognitive Patterns of Success and Failure.* ERIC ED 250 601.

References 153–166 deal with gender differences in students' perceptions of their ability to exert control over their lives and their attribution of the cause of their successes and failures in school.

153. Dyal, J. A. (1984). Cross-cultural research with the locus of control construct. In H. M. Lefcourt (Ed.), *Research with the Locus of Control Construct. Vol. 3: Extensions and Limitations.* New York: Academic Press.

154. Evans, E. D., & Engleberg, R. A. (1988). Student perceptions of school grading. *Journal of Research and Development in Education, 21* (2), 45–54.

155. Frey, K. S., & Ruble, D. N. (1987). What children say about classroom performance: Sex and grade differences in perceived competence. *Child Development, 58,* 1066–1078.

156. Lewis, M. A. (1989). *Consistency of Children's Causal Attributions across Content Domains.* ERIC ED 306 488.

157. Lopez, C. L., & Harper, M. (1989). The relationship between learner control of CAI and locus of control among Hispanic students. *Educational Technology Research and Development, 37* (4), 19–28.

158. McMahan, I. D. (1982). Expectancy of success on sex-linked tasks. *Sex Roles, 8,* 949–958.

159. Powers, S., & Wagner, M. J. (1983). *Achievement Locus of Control of Hispanic and Anglo High School Students.* ERIC ED 230 355.

160. Reyes, L. H., & Padilla, M. J. (1985). Science math and gender. *Science Teacher, 52* (6), 46–48.

161. Ryckman, D. B., & Peckman, P. D. (1986). Gender differences in attribution patterns in academic areas for learning disabled students. *Learning Disabilities Research,1* (2), 83–89.

162. Ryckman, D. B., & Peckman, P. D. (1987). Gender differences in attribution for success and failure. *Journal of Early Adolescence, 7,* 47–63.

163. Ryckman, D. B., & Peckman, P. D. (1987). Gender differences in attribution for success and failure across subject areas. *Journal of Educational Research, 81,* 120–125.

164. Stipek, D. J. (1984). Sex differences in children's attributions for success and failure on math and spelling tasks. *Sex Roles, 11* (11–12), 969–981.

165. Turner, R. R. (1978). Locus of control, academic achievement, and follow through in Appalachia. *Contemporary Educational Psychology, 3,* 367–375.

166. Willig, A. C., Harnisch, D. L., Hill, K. T., & Maehr, M. L. (1983). Sociocultural and educational correlates of success-failure attributions and evaluation anxiety in the school setting for Black, Hispanic and Anglo children. *American Educational Research Journal, 20* (3), 385–410.

References 167–170 focus on ethnic differences in students' perceptions of their ability to exert control over their lives.

167. Ashe, R. (n.d.). Personal comment.

168. Ayabe, H. I. (1977). *Measuring Locus of Control at the College Level.* Paper presented at the annual conference of the Hawaiian Psychological Association, Honolulu.

169. Shade, B. J. (1979). *Racial Preference in Psychological Differentiation: An Alternative Explanation for Group Differences.* ERIC ED 179 672.

170. Tashakkori, A., & Thompson, V. D. (1990). *Race Differences in Self-Perception and Locus of Control During Adolescence and Early Adulthood.* ERIC ED 327 806.

The relationship between locus of control and school achievement is discussed in references 171–174.

171. Coleman, J. S., Campbell, E. Q., Hobson, C. J., McPartland, J., Mood, A. M., Weinfeld, F. D., & York, R. L. (1966). *Equality of Educational Opportunity.* Washington, DC: U.S. Government Printing Office.

172. Crandall, V., Katkovsky, W., & Crandall, V. (1965). Children's beliefs in their own control of reinforcement in intellectual and academic achievement situations. *Child Development, 36,* 91–109.

173. Epps, E. G. (1969) Negro academic motivation and performance: An overview. *Journal of Social Issues, 25* (3), 5–11.

174. Wilson, K. R., & Allen, W. R. (1987). Explaining the educational attainment of young black adults: Critical familial and extra-familial influences. *Journal of Negro Education, 56* (1), 64–76.

References 175–181 discuss the efficacy of efforts to improve students' self-confidence.

175. Canfield, J., & Wells, H. C. (1976). *100 Ways to Enhance Self-Concept in the Classroom.* Englewood Cliffs, NJ: Prentice Hall.

176. De Charms, R. (1976). *Enhancing Motivation.* New York: Irvington.

177. Hauserman, N., Mitler, J. S., & Bond, F. T. (1976). A behavioral approach to changing self-concept in elementary school children. *Psychological Record, 26,* 111–116.

178. Lane, J., & Muller, D. (1977). The effect of altering self-descriptive behavior on self-concept and classroom behavior. *Journal of Psychology, 97,* 115–125.

179. Olszewski, P., Kulieke, M. J., & Willis, G. B. (1987). Changes in the self-perceptions of gifted students who participate in rigorous academic programs. *Journal for the Education of the Gifted, 10* (4), 287–303.

180. Scheier, M. A., & Kraut R. E. (1979). Increasing educational achievement via self-concept change. *Review of Educational Research, 49,* 131–149.

181. Schulman, J. L., Ford, R. C., & Busk, P. (1973). A classroom program to improve self-concept. *Psychology in the Schools, 10,* 481–487.

Instruments for assessing students' self-confidence are described in references 182–186.

182. Coopersmith, S., & Feldman, R. (1974). Fostering a positive self-concept and high self-esteem in the classroom. In R. H. Coop & K. White (Eds.), *Psychological Concepts in the Classroom.* New York: Harper & Row.

183. Harter, S. (1982). The perceived competency scale for children. *Child Development, 53,* 87–97.

184. Katzenmer, W. G., & Stenner, A. J. (1970). *Self-Observation Scale.* Durham, NC: NTS Research Corporation.

185. Norwicki, S., & Strickland, B. (1973). A locus of control scale for children. *Journal of Consulting Psychology, 40,* 148–154.

186. Piers, E. V., & Harris, D. B. (1969). *Children's Self-Concept Scale (The Way I Feel About Myself).* Nashville: Counselor Recordings and Tests.

Suggestions for enhancing the self-confidence of poor and non-European American students are included in references 187–193.

187. Draper, I. L., Kimbrough, A. H., Jones, J. W., & Pierce, B. (1992). *Using "Self-Esteem through Culture Leads to Academic Excellence (SETCLAE)" Transmission of Culture.* Paper presented at the Council for Exceptional children Topical Conference on Diverse Exceptional Children, Minneapolis.

188. Frasier, M. M. (1979). Rethinking the issues regarding the culturally disadvantaged gifted. *Exceptional Children, 45* (7), 538–542.

189. Hale-Benson, J. E. (1986). *Black Children: Their Roots, Culture, and Learning Styles.* (rev. ed.). Baltimore: Johns Hopkins University Press.

190. Hankerson, H. E. (1980). Understanding the young black exceptional child: An overview. In E. Jackson (Ed.), *The Young Black Exceptional Child: Providing Programs and Services.* ERIC ED 204 919.

191. Mack, F. R-P. (1987). Understanding and enhancing self-concept in black children. *Momentum, 18* (1), 22–25.

192. Pepper, F. C. (1976). Teaching the American Indian child in mainstream settings. In R. L. Jones (Ed.), *Mainstreaming and the Minority Child.* Reston, VA: Council for Exceptional Children.

193. Wood, G. H. (1984). Schooling in a democracy: Transformation or reproduction: *Educational Theory, 34* (3), 219–239.

References 194–201 offer guidelines and suggestions for how to make course content more relevant and interesting to non-European American students.

194. Asante, M. K. (1991). Putting Africa at the center. *Newsweek, 118* (13), 46.

195. Kantrowitz, B. (1991). A is for ashanti, b is for black. *Newsweek, 118* (13), 45–48.

196. Cheng, L. (1989). Intervention strategies: A multicultural approach. *Topics in Language Disorders, 9* (3), 84–91.

197. Flores, J. M. (1989). Barrio folklore as a basis for English composition. *Equity & Excellence, 24* (2), 72.

198. Gay, G. (1988). Designing relevant curricula for diverse learners. *Education and Urban Society, 20* (4), 327–340.

199. Martinez, D. I., & Ortiz de Montellano, B. R. (1988). *Improving the Science and Mathematic Achievement of Mexican American Students through Culturally Relevant Science.* Las Cruces, NM: ERIC/CRESS, New Mexico State University.

200. Palmer, P. A., & Palmer, B. C. (1983). Reading interests of middle school black and white students. *Reading Improvement, 20* (2), 151–155.

201. Pugh, S. L. (1989). Literature, culture, and ESL: A natural convergence. *Journal of Reading, 34* (4), 320–329.

Reference 202 provides examples of acceptable and unacceptable learning experiences.

202. Nazzaro, J. N. (1981). Special problems of exceptional minority children. In J. N. Nazzaro (Ed.), *Culturally Diverse Exceptional Children in School.* ERIC ED 199 993.

References 203–211 discuss the interrelationship between socioeconomic class and ethnicity.

203. Chan, K., & Rueda, R. (1979). Poverty and culture in education: Separate but equal. *Exceptional Children, 45,* 422–427.

204. Cooper, J. G. (1977) *The Effects of Ethnicity upon School Achievement.* ERIC ED 157 675.

205. Dillard, J. M., & Perrin, D. W. (1980). Puerto Rican, Black, and Anglo adolescents' career aspirations, expectations, and maturity. *Vocational Guidance Quarterly, 28,* 313–321.

206. Havighurst, R. J. (1976). The relative importance of social class and ethnicity in human development. *Human Development, 19,* 56–64.

207. Johnson, N. J., & Sanaday, P. R. (1971). Subcultural variations in one urban poor population. *American Anthropologist, 73,* 128–143.

208. Kagan, S., & Ender, P. B. (1975). Maternal responses to success and failure of Anglo-American, Mexican American, and Mexican children. *Child Development, 46,* 452–458.

209. Laosa, L. M. (1977). Socialization, education and continuity: The importance of the sociocultural context. *Young Children, 32* (5), 21–27.

210. Sarason, S. B. (1973). Jewishness, blackness, and the nature-nurture controversy. *American Psychologist, 28,* 962–971.

211. Wilson, W. J. (1978). *The Declining Significance of Race.* Chicago: University of Chicago Press.

References 212–232 discuss students' acculturation and how to evaluate it.

212. Ramirez, M., & Castaneda, A. (1974). *Bicultural Democracy, Bicognitive Development and Education.* New York: Academic Press.

213. Berry, J. W., Kim, U., Minde, T., & Mok. (1987). Comparative studies of acculturative stress. *International Migration Review, 21* (30), 491–511.

214. Cloud, N. (1990). *Measuring Level of Acculturation in Bilingual, Bicultural Children.* Paper presented at the annual meeting of the American Educational Research Association, Boston.

215. Cloud, N. (1991). Acculturation of ethnic minorities. In A. M. Ambert (Ed.), *Bilingual Education and English as a Second Language: A Research Handbook 1988–1990.* New York: Garland.

216. Cuellar, I., Harris, L. C., & Jasso, R. (1980). An acculturation scale for Mexican American normal and clinical populations. *Hispanic Journal of Behavioral Sciences, 2* (3), 199–217.

217. Franco, J. N. (1983). An acculturation scale for Mexican-American children. *Journal of General Psychology, 108,* 175–181.

218. Koh, T., & Koh, S. D. (1982). A note on the psychological evaluation of Korean school children. *P/AAMHRC Research Review, 1* (3), 1–2.

219. Lee, E. (1988). Cultural factors in working with Southeast Asian refugee adolescents. *Journal of Adolescence, 11,* 167–179.

220. Leung, E. K. (1988). Cultural and acculturational commonalities and diversities among Asian Americans: Identification and programming considerations. In A. A. Ortiz & B. A. Ramirez (Eds.), *Schools and Culturally Diverse Exceptional Students: Promising Practices and Future Directions.* Reston, VA: ERIC Clearinghouse on Handicapped and Gifted Children, Council for Exceptional Children.

221. Lin, K., & Masuda M. (1983). Impact of refugee experience: Mental health issues of Southeast Asian refugees. In R. F. Morales (Ed.), *Bridging Cultures.* Los Angeles: Asian American Health Center.

222. Mainous, A. G., III. (1989). Self concept as an indicator of acculturation in Mexican Americans. *Hispanic Journal of Behavioral Sciences, 11* (2), 178–189.

223. Martinez, R., Norman, R. D., & Delaney, H. D. (1984). A Children's Hispanic Background Scale. *Hispanic Journal of Behavioral Sciences, 6* (2), 103–112.

224. Mendoza, R. H., & Martinez, J. L. (1981). The measurement of acculturation. In A. Baron, Jr. (Ed.), *Explorations in Chicano Psychology.* New York: Holt.

225. Olmedo, E. L. (1980). Quantitative models of acculturation: An overview. In A. M. Padilla (Ed.), *Acculturation: Theory, Models and Some New Findings.* Boulder, CO: Westview Press.

226. Olmedo, E. L., & Padilla, A. M. (1978). Empirical and construct validity of a measure of acculturation for Mexican Americans. *Journal of Social Psychology, 105,* 179–187.

227. Padilla, A. M. (1980). The role of cultural awareness and ethnic loyalty in acculturation. In A. M. Padilla (Ed.), *Acculturation: Theory, Models, and Some New Findings.* Boulder, CO: Westview Press.

228. Suinn, R. M., Rickard-Figueroa, K., Lew, S., & Vigil, P. (1987). Asian Self-Identity Acculturation Scale: An initial report. *Educational and Psychological Measurement, 47,* 401–407.

229. Szapocznik, J., & Kurtines, W. (1980). Acculturation, biculturalism and adjustment among Cuban Americans. In A. M. Padilla (Ed.), *Acculturation: Theory, Models, and Some New Findings.* Boulder, CO: Westview Press.

230. Szapocznik, J., Kurtines, W. M., & Fernandez, T. (1979). *Bicultural Involvement and Adjustment in Hispanic American Youth.* ERIC ED 193 374.

231. Wong-Rieger, D., & Quintana, D. (1987). Comparative acculturation of Southeast Asian and Hispanic immigrants and sojourners. *Journal of Cross-cultural Psychology, 18* (3), 345–362.

232. Golden, J. G. (1990). The acculturation of three Korean American students. *Teaching and Learning, 5* (1), 9–20.

Instruments for evaluating students' learning styles are listed and discussed in references 233–237.

233. Dunn, R., & Dunn, K. (1978). *Teaching Students Through Their Individual Learning Styles: A Practical Approach.* Reston, VA: Reston Publishing.

234. Keefe, J. (1979). Learning style: An overview. In *Student Learning Styles: Diagnosing and Prescribing Programs.* Reston, VA: National Association of Secondary School Principals.

235. McCarthy, B. (1980). *The 4 Mat System: Teaching to Learning Styles with Right/Left Mode Techniques.* Oak Brook, IL: Excel.

236. Perrin, J. (1982). *Learning Style Inventory: Primary Version.* Jamaica, NY: St. John's University.

237. Renzulli, J., & Smith, L. (1978). *The Learning Style Inventory: A Measure of Student Preference for Instructional Techniques.* Mansfield Center, CT: Creative Learning Press.

11

CLASSROOM/BEHAVIOR MANAGEMENT IN A DIVERSE SOCIETY

"Do unto others as you would have others do unto you" only works to the extent that both parties prefer to be treated the same way.

This chapter provides special educators with the information they require to consider their students' unique characteristics when they select classroom/behavior management techniques. It begins by noting that many special educators contribute to students' behavior problems by relating to them in a discriminatory manner. Then it describes the typical ways special educators can misperceive and misunderstand students' behaviors and use inappropriate responses to deal with them when they interpret students' behavior from their own perspective. Next is a discussion of some student characteristics that special educators should be aware of in order to understand why students are behaving in a particular way and what techniques might help them to behave differently. The final section discusses the importance of using classroom/behavior management techniques that empower rather than disempower students.

DISCRIMINATORY CLASSROOM/BEHAVIOR MANAGEMENT APPROACHES

There is still considerable ethnic, socioeconomic-class, and gender bias in U.S. schools. As noted in Chapters 3 and 7, many regular educators and special educators have lower expectations for poor, African American, Hispanic American, and Native American students. They tend to evaluate them lower than objective evidence warrants, praise and call on them less often, criticize them more often, and use harsher and more punitive disciplinary techniques with them. Teachers' gender biases are demonstrated in the different expectations, attention, and feedback they typically have for male and female students, their encouragement of different behaviors in male and female students, their intolerance of male behavior patterns, and their use of more severe classroom management techniques with males. No one knows the exact degree to which behavior problems in school are caused by prejudice. However, when the evidence is considered as a whole, it is inconceivable that the discriminatory manner in which many students are treated by their teachers does not affect their attitudes and behavior. Therefore, elimination of teacher prejudice is one of the most important steps special educators can take to eliminate disciplinary problems.

Chapters 3 and 4 include a number of self-quizzes and activities designed to assist teachers in identifing and correcting their biases. This chapter will also provide some of the additional knowledge teachers require to provide students with nondiscriminatory classroom/behavior management.

MISPERCEPTIONS

Educators do not have to be prejudiced to use biased management techniques with students. Even well-meaning teachers can misperceive and misunderstand students' behaviors when they interpret them from their own perspective. They can perceive behavior problems that do not exist, not notice problems that do exist, misunderstand the causes of students' behaviors, and use inappropriate techniques to deal with students' behavior problems.

Nonexistent Problems

Students who come from different ethnic or socioeconomic backgrounds than their teachers and school administrators may have values, goals, and interests that are acceptable to their families and communities but not to the school system. As a result, educators may not be able to accept behavior that the students and their parents find completely appropriate. For example, teachers may incorrectly think that students brought up not to be assertive or to volunteer their opinions unless encouraged by adults are shy, insecure or passive. They may also believe that students who are encouraged at home to work independently rather than with others and to judge their accomplishments for themselves rather than rely on the opinions of others do not care about others. Some specific examples of how educators may perceive nonexistent problems in the case of African American, Asian Pacific Americans, and Hispanic American students follow.

African American students are especially prone to have difficulty in school because of incompatibilities between the way many of them are encouraged to behave in their communities and the expectations of their teachers (1, 3, 4, 6, 8, 11). Many African American males, as well as females, express their emotions much more intensely than most European Americans. When European American teachers observe African American males behaving aggressively and assertively, too many of them assume that the students are much angrier or upset than they actually are. Attributing a level of anger to African American students that would be correct for European American students who behaved in a similar way, the teachers can become uncomfortable, even anxious, and concerned about what they incorrectly anticipate will happen next. As a result, they often intervene when no intervention is necessary. If teachers appreciated the cultural context of African American males' seemingly aggressive behavior toward others and understood that such behavior is unlikely to cause the physical fight or whatever else they expect to occur between African American students who appear to be acting aggressively toward each other, they would be less likely to intervene in order to make themselves feel more at ease in the situation. This would lessen the likelihood that African American males would get into trouble needlessly. Two African American professionals stated,

> Urban schooling patterns, for the most part, promote quietness and docility. Such classrooms are therefore designed to suit the learning norms of children from white families and opposed to the characteristics of Black children, making it difficult for them to comply with the demands made upon them by that system. . . . A troubled teacher-pupil relationship is the outcome. The resentful teacher and the balking student's interactions erode with daily incidents. School policy leads to a compilation of a dossier on these students so as to build up a string of minor offenses, which, when presented all at once, appear to be a massive campaign of misdeeds. (11, pp. 51–52)

> Most teachers are unprepared to accept the active, aggressive behavior of Black boys. The aggressive behavior of a Black child is immediately interpreted as hostile. The teacher's expectation is that the student should be compliant, docile, and responsive to authority. The student is expected to conform to a standard of behavior that the teacher is familiar with, the compliant child standard that was indicative of the teacher's upbringing. It is as though the teacher makes an unwritten contract with the student, "If you don't behave, I won't (or can't) teach you."
>
> The next step in the process is that the teacher will make futile attempts to control the aggressive, active behavior, but abandon those efforts very quickly and conclude that the child is unmanageable. The child resists the teacher's efforts to control the behavior. More often than not, the behavior becomes more unmanageable. As the disruptive behavior increases, the amount of time and effort available to devote to attending to the instructions and acquiring academic skills decreases. In all likelihood the student prefers to avoid the academic work. Within a short period of time it becomes apparent that this unmanageable student is not functioning at grade level. This then can be interpreted, depending on the tolerance level of the teachers, as a learning problem and a justification for referral for special placement. The longer the time span involved, the greater the learning problem. (1, pp. 78–79)

An African American educator describes how other behavior patterns that are acceptable in the African community can cause problems for students in school:

> Blacks are accustomed to integrating mental, emotional, and physical activities. Schools tend to encourage compartmentalizing these areas. The Black child's involvement in cognitive classroom activities is likely to be signaled by vocal responses, exuberance, and physical movement. Teachers consider this behavior disruptive because they expect that one can be highly stimulated to intellectual activities without involving affective or psychomotor dimensions.
>
> What teachers view as total chaos and noise may be structured activity to Blacks. What teachers consider planned activities may be perceived by Black students as prohibiting constraints. The problem of perception stems from different sets of expectations and cultural sensibilities. (3, pp. 32–33)

Elaborating on the way African Americans respond to others when they are reciting, performing, and so on, Gay stated the following:

> There is more total interaction involved; all those in the social environment must play some active response role if it is only through such responses as "right on brother." . . .

The Black child in performing looks for verbal and kinesthetic support from his peers. The teacher hears noise and is threatened. The child's success is measured by his peers by the extent to which he stimulates the others to provide responses. When this behavior is manifested, teachers see an undisciplined and discourteous group of Blacks.

This situation arises because contrarily in white, middle-class culture the relationship between a performer and his audience demands a show of passivity on the part of the latter. . . . When Black children's classroom behavior is assessed using this frame of reference, the conclusions are foreordained. The culturally determined Black ways of demonstrating interest and involvement are interpreted as restlessness, inattentiveness, and sometimes hostility. (4, p. 338)

A final example of these many incompatibilities between acceptable African American students' behavior at home and the expectations of the schools is the verbal dueling games such as "playing the dozens," "ribbin' and jivin'," and so on that African American students play. Although they know that these are merely part of a competitive game, European American and other non-African American teachers often perceive them as a prelude to a fight. (8)

Commenting on the way European American teachers may misperceive the origin and meaning of the field-sensitive/dependent relationship style of Hispanic American students, Jaramillo stated, "An Anglo teacher is likely to consider many of the Spanish speaking children in his class dependent in a negative sense, or perhaps he will say they are immature, or that they are retarded in their social development. In reality, these differences are purely cultural, and viewed from another perspective, these children are perfectly normal and mature for their age" (7, p. 13).

The following quotation provides insight into the kinds of cultural misperceptions educators can make with Chinese American students: "The child does not volunteer to answer. He just sits and waits for his teacher to call upon him. So in the eyes of the American teacher, Asian children, as compared to the American students, are dull, passive, unresponsive, and lack initiative. Most of the time, Chinese (Asian) students are ignored because of their absolute silence in class" (14, p. 11).

Examples of the kinds of cultural misperceptions educators can make with Southeast Asian students are illustrated in the quotations that follow.

American straightforwardness is considered at best impolite, if not brutal. In Indochina, one does not come directly to the point. To do so is, for an American, is a mark of honesty and forthrightness while a person from Indochina sees it as a lack of intelligence or courtesy. Falsehood carries no moral structure for a Cambodian, Laotian, or Vietnamese. The essential question is not whether a statement is true or false, but what the intention of the statement is. Does it facilitate interpersonal harmony? Does it indicate a wish to change the subject? Hence, one must learn the "heart" of the speaker through his/her words. In Indochina, one thinks very carefully before speaking. The American style of "speaking one's mind" is thus misunderstood. . . .

The Vietnamese literal equivalent of the English word "Yes" is "Da" (pronounced "Ya" in the Southern Vietnamese dialect). However, whereas the English "Yes" means unequivocally "Yes," the Vietnamese "Da" means a variety of things. In the final analysis, it can mean "Yes," but in general usage it merely means "I am politely listening to you," and it does not at all mean that "I agree with you." The listener may disagree with what he hears, but due to his politeness, cannot say no. His English "Yes" for him conveys the polite and noncommittal Vietnamese "Da," but to the American it can carry only its English meaning. Thus, the Vietnamese may appear insincere, or even stupid, to the American. (12, pp. 6, 7, 19)

It is easy to understand how educators who do not know these facts could misinterpret their students' responses. For example, they may think their students have just agreed to do what they have been asked to do and so become angry and frustrated when the students do not follow through after saying "yes."

Unnoticed Problems

Educators who are attuned to the ways students from other cultures communicate can miss a request for help or assistance. They may not even realize that their students have problems. As noted previously, Hispanic American and Asian Pacific American students are usually brought up not to ask teachers for help. Hispanic Americans typically are expected to be sensitive to the needs, feelings, and desires of others so that it is unnecessary for others to be embarrassed by asking for help, and many Asian Pacific American students believe to do so would insult their teachers.

Incorrect Causes

Educators may mistakenly attribute behavior problems that are culturally determined to other causes. For example, teachers who are unaware of their students' identity conflicts may attribute their behavior to lack of interest and motivation to succeed in school, lack of respect for the teacher, poor parenting, and other reasons. Then, instead of responding with understanding to their students' identity conflicts or helping them resolve these conflicts, the educators are likely to use inappropriate techniques to squash the objectionable behavior. Some of the ways non-African American teachers can misunderstand the causes of African American students' behavior are revealed in the following description of the faculty of a desegregated school:

> The Black children displayed unfamiliar behavior that teachers found difficult to adjust to and cope with. At one time or another teachers commented:
>
>> "There's so much pent-up anger in them."
>> "They talk so loud."
>> "When he came here he was totally nonverbal."
>> "Did you ever see such antsyness?"
>
> Teachers called attention to kids who used "foul" language ("I'll never get used to that"), to children who spoke out in class, to antisocial behavior (fighting, spitting at other children, stealing), to short attention spans, to immaturity (e.g., thumb sucking). Each of these behaviors made the job of teaching much more difficult than it had been prior to desegregation. . . . The first and most basic teacher response to the number of

problems presented by the Black children was to devise some personal explanation for the unfamiliar behavior. While these explanations varied somewhat from teacher to teacher, a common theme emerged. On several occasions unfamiliar and disturbing behavior (whether antisocial actions or difficulty mastering classroom work) was attributed to problems in a child's environment. Comments such as "I think Ben is brutalized at home" were offered as explanations for children's actions or attitudes. To a lesser extent I heard references made to children's previous schools not having demanded enough of them. Whether these explanations accurately represented fact or not, they made the problems understandable and to some extent served to legitimate the approach taken by the teachers to ameliorate the problems. (10, p. 21)

The next two quotations describe some of the possible causes of behavior problems that teachers should consider when they interpret the behavior of Asian Pacific American students.

When a Southeast Asian student misbehaves this misbehavior may be the result of one or more of the following sources of tension: frustration due to language problems and misunderstanding, imitation out of a desire for rapid adaptation, behavior learned in refugee camps where survival was paramount and included stealing and violent self defense, intragroup historical animosity among various Southeast Asian groups, adjustment difficulties because school rules here are less strict and well-defined, culture-gap in the family resulting from different rates of assimilation. (2, p. 58)

One teacher was puzzled by an Asian child, because he responded with a smile when scolded. Asian children tend to "camouflage" their embarrassment by smiling. (9, p. 1)

The final quotation reminds special educators not to overlook the possibility that some of the behavior problems of limited-English-proficient students can be caused by their language difficulty.

Problem behaviors such as difficulty following directions, poor eye contact, inattention, and daydreaming could be associated with a handicapping condition, but they could also reflect a lack of English proficiency. (13, p. 52)

Inappropriate Techniques

Even when educators recognize when students' behavior problems are culturally determined, they may still respond with techniques that are inappropriate if they do not have the knowledge needed to adapt their approaches to the cultural realities of their students. An educator who wishes to communicate effectively with Hispanic American students benefits from understanding the differences between the cultures and how these impact the classroom.

Hispanic parents tend to speak more politely and indirectly when they criticize or discipline their children. In the United States educators are much more gruff and direct with students. . . . Some Hispanic students, especially males, may interpret the gruff or more direct manner of Anglos as an indication that educators do not consider them worthy or deserving of a proper relationship. When educators speak to them in a matter-of-fact or authoritarian manner, they may feel insulted, angry, or resentful and lose respect for these educators and the desire to cooperate or conform. (5, p. 102)

At times, the techniques teachers choose to motivate individual students backfire because of different cultural values. For example, as described in Chapter 9, rewarding individual Hawaiian American students for appropriate behavior can cause them to behave in less desirable ways in order to avoid being singled out for praise and recognition. On the other hand, rewarding the whole group for the improvement of one or more members of the group can cause those individuals who are not behaving appropriately to behave in a more desirable manner.

STUDENT CHARACTERISTICS

There are numerous ways students' behavioral characteristics differ. Knowledge of how ethnic, socioeconomic-class, and gender factors influence these characteristics may help in understanding how students actually behave, why they behave as they do, and which management techniques might help them to behave differently.

Which of the four approaches described in Chapter 6 the teacher decides to use (assimilation, accommodation, biculturalism, or empowerment) when he or she discovers that students' behavior is the result of ethnic, socioeconomic-class, or gender factors is a personal matter. However, the awareness that one or more of these factors is contributing to students' behavior problems should help the teacher avoid misperceiving and misunderstanding the behavior. It will also enable the teacher to to use effective management techniques.

Previous chapters discussed students' communication, motivational, and cognitive styles; time orientation; interests; and attitudes about acceptable and unacceptable learning activities. This chapter focuses on other student characteristics.

Perception of Authority Figures

Are students expected not to speak unless spoken to, not to ask questions, and to obey their elders just because they are authorities? Or can they disagree with adults and ask their elders to justify why they are requiring them to do certain things or punishing them? Can teachers expect students to accept their opinions, rules, and consequences simply because they are in charge, or are they expected to justify themselves to their students?

Although many experts advise teachers to be authoritative rather than authoritarian, students from other cultures may require help in adjusting to an adult who is authoritative and not authoritarian. These students may also have difficulty participating in democratic classrooms in which the students are actively involved in establishing rules, procedures, and consequences. For example, a Filipino American teacher stated, "Especially to a small child from grade one to grade six, the democratic atmosphere that is being provided here is an entirely new aspect. Perhaps, during the first months the Filipino student is somewhat lost. He doesn't know what to do. The Filipino child may feel insecure. In the Philippines, the teacher usually says, 'do this, make this'" (19, p. 21).

Is the relationship between adolescents and adult authority figures more like that between children and adults or between adults and adults? What special rights and privileges do adolescents enjoy that are denied to children? What special instructional and classroom management techniques should teachers use with adolescents? Which techniques that are appropriate with younger students are inappropriate with adolescents?

Are the authority roles of male and female adults the same? Is one gender the authority figure and the other the nurturer? Does each gender express and enforce its authority in the same or different ways? Are students ready to accept teachers of either gender as authority figures? Are students prepared to accept the same disciplinary techniques from teachers regardless of their teachers' gender? An Hispanic American educator offered the following comment about Hispanic American males' perceptions of their female teachers: "One should be conscious of a male Chicanos' lack of understanding in trying to take orders from a female teacher. He will really look up to or listen with better interest if an adult male is talking to him" (5, p. 104). Because some Hispanic American males may have difficulty accepting the authority of female teachers, some educators suggest that females should stress nonauthoritarian methods, such as requesting rather than ordering and asking a male administrator to intervene if it becomes necessary to deal in a stern way with male students (5).

How do students express their respect for authority? As noted in Chapter 6, in some cultures, looking an adult in the eye is a sign of respect and submission. In other cultures, avoiding eye contact communicates the same message. As a result, teachers may misinterpret the nonverbal messages communicated by students from other cultural backgrounds. The ways African American, Asian Pacific American, Hispanic American, and other non-European American students are taught to show respect is typically different from the ways European American students are expected to behave.

Relationships with Others

Individual versus Group Rights

Are the rights of individuals or the obligations of individuals to the group emphasized? Are youngsters encouraged to establish their own goals and strive for individual excellence or are they expected to be sensitive and responsive to the needs and desires of the group? Are students likely to sacrifice their desires for the benefit of their classmates?

Which group rights are respected? Some cultures expect individuals to consider the effect of their actions on other people's sensibilities. Cultures that stress people's individuality—their right to determine for themselves the way they satisfy their desires—require their members to learn to tolerate the inconvenience created by the rights of others. Thus, some children are taught to be considerate by keeping the volume on the TV or stereo low so as to avoid disturbing others. Other children are taught to be considerate of others by learning how to do what they have to do even when the volume is high. Teachers who are unaware of this difference may mistakenly believe that some students are inconsiderate and self-centered rather than merely behaving in a culturally approved manner. The following is a description of the different approaches of many African Americans and European Americans in this respect:

> Whites have been taught that to act on behalf of their own feelings is unjustified if someone else's sensibilities might become offended as a result. So strongly ingrained is this rule that it has the force of a moral injunction. Rather than violate it and feel guilty . . . whites will hold back what they truly feel even if this will result in an injustice to their feelings or create for themselves an unwanted social situation.
>
> From a black standpoint, individuals asserting themselves in accordance with their feelings are seen not as violating the sacred rights of others but, rather, as preserving the sacred rights of self. (22, pp. 121, 123)

How should special educators deal with this issue? Should they teach students to be tolerant of each other's styles or to be sensitive to the needs and sensibilities of others? Some students with serious emotional problems have great difficulty accepting and coping when others express strong feelings. Other students may have strong needs to express themselves. How should special educators reconcile the conflicting needs of students in such situations?

Giving and Sharing

Some cultures train children to be generous with their possessions because it is better to give than to receive. Other cultures stress private ownership and property rights. Some students have more practice in sharing because their cultures do not provide many experiences in private ownership and personal space. Instead of having their own room, area, chair, and so on, they have to share space, belongings, and the like. Their different experiences at home can affect how they prefer to function in school.

To what extent are children and youth expected to share their things with others? How prepared are students to share their belongings with others? Will they also expect their peers to reciprocate? How will students react if their peers do not share their things with them? Condon, Peters, and Sueiro-Ross stated, "Humanism in Hispanic children is also expressed in their unusual generosity with toys and other personal belongings, an openness of attitude which they frequently discover is not reciprocated by their Anglo-Saxon peers" (18, p. 75). Grossman added, "When educators attempt to resolve sharing difficulties among students by explaining the rights of owners—emphazing private property or what's mine is mine and what's yours is yours, Hispanic students may feel bewildered, confused or even rejected and insulted" (5, p. 89).

Students' motives for doing favors for and giving presents to teachers and peers differ. In some cultures, when students do favors for and give gifts to their peers and teachers, they do so in order to curry favor with them. In other cultures, they do so in order to place others in their debt. In still others, the purpose is to express friendship. Therefore, special educators should not assume they understand why students do favors for others or give them gifts if they are not knowledgeable about students' cultural backgrounds.

Do students regard helping a friend during a test as cheating and think of it as a bad or dishonest way of demonstrating their helpfulness, friendliness, and brotherhood? Some Hawaiian American and Hispanic American students may feel that helping friends during a test or when they are called on to recite is necessary, despite their teachers' view that it is cheating (5, 17). How should special educators react to students whose ethnic backgrounds lead them to have different attitudes about sharing their belongings and helping their peers when they are called on to recite or taking a test? Should they treat all students the same regardless of the students' beliefs or take their beliefs into consideration when they establish rules, procedures, and expectations?

Relationships with the Opposite Gender

How do children and youth relate to the opposite sex at different ages? The brother-sister and male-female relationships in the Hispanic American community have been described as follows:

> Older boys, for instance, tend to assume a protective and responsible attitude toward their sisters—escorting them to and from school, dispensing lunch money to them, and defending them against intruders; as a result of their protective upbringing, girls tend to be shy and submissive toward their brothers and other boys. Neither of these typical male and female Hispanic behaviors meets the wholehearted approval of the egalitarian Anglo-American educator who tends to translate them as overaggressiveness on the one hand, and excessive dependence on the other. (18, p. 61)

At what age are students comfortable relating to peers of the opposite sex? Should they be allowed to choose to work in same-sex groups or required to participate in groups with the opposite sex? Does the students' age or the nature of the activity play a role in their ability to participate comfortably in mixed-gender groups? In recent years, an increased emphasis on nonsexist coeducational activities in the schools has been required by Title IX and supported by the courts. (See Chapter 9.) Yet, students from some cultural backgrounds may both overtly and covertly resist being required to engage in activities that are reserved for the opposite sex in their cultures. They may also balk at being made to engage in coeducational activities that are usually carried out in sexually segregated groups in their home culture. The problems that many Native American and East Indian American students experience in mixed gender groups is described as follows:.

> At a school dance in which Anglo teachers were instructing Navajo students in the expected social behavior of adolescents in the dominant society, these harbingers of "culture" randomly selected young males and females and forced them to dance together. As some of these students were from the same clan, this physical contact was akin to a sexual encounter. In their minds, incestuous relations were forced upon these students. (24, p. 23)

> East Indian American students expressed great discomfort about working with someone of the opposite sex on a class assignment about how to run a household as a married couple. The Indian culture segregates males and females in all environments especially until they are married. Thus coming from a culture that believes it would be wrong to work in close contact with each other it is uncomfortable for most students to do so. All of the European American students felt totally comfortable with the project and stated that it would be a great learning experience. (28, p. 3)

How should special educators deal with the requirements of Title IX? Should they respect students' ethnic preferences, encourage students to comply with them, or require them to do so?

How do males and females express interest in one another? What one group may consider an insulting form of attention or show of interest may be deemed acceptable by another group. This is especially true of African Americans and Hispanic Americans. Thus, *piropos*—compliments said to females who one does not know about how great they look or how sexy they are—are acceptable in many Hispanic American and African American communities, but insulting to many European Americans (22, 23). How should special educators deal with the problems that occur when males relate to females from different ethnic backgrounds in ways that they think are acceptable but in which the females feel insulted or harassed?

Social Space

People from different cultural backgrounds prefer different amounts of personal space between them and the individuals with whom they are interacting. Thus, European American special educators may find that some Hispanic American students make them uncomfortable by standing to close to them, while the students feel rejected every time the teachers back away in order to feel more comfortable. These same teachers may have the exact opposite experience with some Asian Pacific American students who require even more personal space than they do.

> The concept of social space is interpreted in widely different manners in Hispanic and American societies, with the former opting generally for a narrower interaction distance than that preferred by the latter. . . . Many an Anglo American has reacted negatively without realizing it to the "crowding" behavior of Latino children, and his instinctive withdrawal has been interpreted by them as a sign of exclusion from the inner circle of favorite students. (18, p. 65)

> In the classroom situation, Oriental American students, particularly those newly arrived, have often demonstrated uneasiness when teachers sit too close to them. This is because they are not used to proximity between an adult and a youngster. In Asia, teachers are respected by both students and their parents, and the size of the spatial bubble is rather extensive. Oriental teachers seldom mingle with students to help them with schoolwork. (32, pp. 68–69)

DISCIPLINARY STYLE

People from various cultures attribute disciplinary problems to different causes and use assorted techniques to motivate children and youth to behave in acceptable ways. Some ethnic groups rely heavily on the use of consequences to modify children's behavior; others do not. Some are quick to resort to punishments; others emphasize rewards. Some stress materialistic rewards; others train children and youth to respond to more personal rewards. Therefore, it is helpful to know the kinds of disciplinary techniques that students are accustomed to in their homes and communities. The following quotations describe how this principle applies to African American students:

> Many districts offer a single program for improving the behavior of all students based on the assumption that the students' population is homogeneous. But . . . it is likely that those activities necessary to improve the behavior of African-American students will involve efforts that address those behavioral differences. Identifying alternative disciplinary actions is perhaps the most difficult of the tasks included in this approach because it involves trying to determine what actions may be more effective.
>
> The difficulty of the task partially reflects the reluctance of schools to develop and use strategies that specifically address the needs and problems of African-American students because they fear that they will be charged with having dual standards of discipline. (31, p. 34)

> In many instances white teachers are unable to discipline Black children because they do not "connect" culturally; the teachers do not behave as Black children expect authority figures to behave. . . . It seems that when white teachers practice the disciplinary techniques they are taught in college, Black children "run over them." (20, p. 172)

> It is much easier to dish out punishment to the child of a Black maid than to the child of a white school board president. (27, p. 16)

Permissive versus Strict Management

Although special educators are being advised to be more accepting and understanding of their students' behavior problems, some educators believe that a lenient, permissive approach to classroom management can backfire with students who are used to a more authoritarian approach (2, 20, 30). For example, speaking of African American students, Bacon advised that "those who are accustomed to a more authoritarian approach to behavior management are particularly difficult to control in an atmosphere of permissiveness, of being given freedom to choose prematurely and without training" (15, p. 7).

In a somewhat similar vein, Tharp advised that teachers of Hawaiian Americans need to be tough: "To be tough, the teachers must be firm, clear, and consistent in insisting that the children comply with their directions and requests. They must dispense contingently the resources they control, such as recess, access to peers, and praise" (30, p. 354). However, Tharp reported that the opposite is true for Navajo students: "For Navajos, neither extreme of 'tough' or 'nice' is appropriate, and the reinforcing and punishing value of identical teacher behaviors is often reversed. Navajo adults are more reserved in their affectionate displays but are highly respectful of children's individuality and of children's sovereignty over their own persons. Punishment, contingent reward, or any openly manipulative effort to control the behavior of others—including children—is a violation of cultural values" (30, p. 354).

Positive Consequences

How much praise and reward do students receive from adults? Will students expect to be rewarded and praised more often, less often, or about as often as teachers habitually praise and reward them? Providing students with less than their customary amount of praise and rewards may cause them to think that their teachers do not value them or their work. On the other hand, rewarding and praising students excessively can cause learned helplessness. Special educators understand the importance of using praise to motivate students with disabilities. Their problem lies in the fact that what is an unnecessary or excessive amount of praise for some students may be just the amount or less than what others are accustomed to receiving.

For example, as the following quote indicates, Southeast Asian American children usually are not rewarded and praised as often as children from many other cultures: "The child should not receive rewards for the behaviors he is expected to demonstrate. Accomplishments are usually acknowledged in the form of parent encouragement to do even better and strive for higher levels of achievement. This attitude is also reflected in the family discouragement of praising oneself or family members in the presence of non-family members. When a child (or adult) is given a compliment, it is often dismissed or negated by immediate discussion of one's faults through self-deprecating remarks" (26, p. 4). Students' ethnic backgrounds also affect which consequences they experience as rewarding.

There are many other questions that special educators should consider when they make decisions about whether and how to reward students. Are students brought up to strive for individual recognition or is anonymity stressed? Will students respond better to individual rewards or when the group is praised and rewarded? Should teachers recognize students' accomplishments or those of the group as a whole? When recognizing students' accomplishments, should teachers do so publicly by placing their work on the walls, referring to their achievement, and using them as peer models or privately? Many non-European students—especially Asian Pacific Americans, Hawaiian Americans, Hispanic Americans, Native Americans, and European American females—have such difficulty in classrooms that stress individual goals and individual recognition that it is often better to recognize their achievement in a less public manner (5, 29).

Are students accustomed to receiving personal or impersonal rewards at home? Will they respond better to personal, positive reinforcements—such as statements of approval, smiles, pats on the back, and so on—or impersonal ones— such as treats, toys, gold stars, sweets, and the like? Is it possible that students are not changing their behavior because they are relatively indifferent to praise and criticism from others?

Negative Consequences

Special educators should also be aware of their students' characteristics when they decide to use negative consequences with them. Various issues should be considered. What kinds of negative consequences do adults use to discipline youngsters—physical punishments (spanking and slapping); loss of affection, attention, or social interaction (statements of disappointment and anger, removal from the presence of others); loss of privileges (being grounded, no TV); or loss of material things (desserts, allowances)? What kinds of negative consequences will be unacceptable to them or their parents? The following are a few examples of cultural differences among Hispanic Americans, Native Americans, Hawaiian Americans, and Southeast Asian Americans:

> Hispanics tend to use corporal punishment more and deprivation of love and affection less when disciplining their children. (5, p. 161)

> Native American children are seldom, if ever, struck by an adult: no parents, uncles, aunts, no adults. (16, p. 45)

> 'Time out' from the social interaction of recess or in-class activities is a sharp punishment for Hawaiian children. In Navajo classrooms, children are quite content to be alone. (30, pp. 354–355)

> Such forms of punishment as locking the child outside the house, isolating the child from the family social life, shaming the child, scolding or guilt induction that results in a "loss of face" are commonplace in Southeast Asia. (25, p. 145)

What are the acceptable and unacceptable ways of criticizing or punishing children and teenagers? Are they given feedback about their behavior in public or only in private? Can students accept direct criticism or only indirect and subtle feedback? Can they tolerate being criticized in public or will they respond positively only to private criticism? Should special educators write students' names on the blackboard when they misbehave and comment about their inappropriate behavior in front of others or should they correct students only in private to make sure they do not "lose face"?

Many non-European American students may react extremely negatively to public criticism. The following describes the likely response of Filipino American students to criticism: "Correction of students' mistakes must be done tactfully. Pilipino students often have difficulty detaching themselves from their work and may view adverse comments as direct criticisms of themselves. . . . Pilipino children are particularly sensitive to criticism. When embarrassed the child may withdraw and become uncooperative. The teacher may be frustrated in all attempts to discover what is wrong" (21, p. 19).

What tone of voice do adults use when they discipline and criticize children and teenagers? Are they gruff, emotional, and direct or are they gentle and indirect? European Americans tend to be more emotional and direct than many other groups. For example, among Native Americans, "talking loud, especially while correcting children, is highly disapproved" (16, p. 45).

Group Consequences

To what extent are students motivated by the attitude of their peer group? Can teachers motivate students to change their behavior by referring to its effect on the students' peer group? As noted earlier, in comparison to European Americans, many non-European Americans are more sensitive to the effects their behavior has on their peers.

> What motivates Hispanics to be punctual are not impersonal reasons such as it's efficient for everyone to arrive at the same time and begin at the same time. Hispanics may feel that the meeting or work could have started without them if necessary. . . . On the other hand, personal relationships do concern them. For example they may be very concerned that their lack of punctuality not be interpreted as a sign of disrespect or a lack of courtesy toward others and arrive on time to make sure they do not seem disrespectful. . . . Statements such as "if you respect your classmates you will get here when we need you" may have more effect than statements such as "we could not finish on time" or "we wasted fifteen minutes because we had to wait for you." (5, p. 95)

Shame and Guilt

Do parents emphasize guilt (feeling bad about one's self for misbehaving), shame (feeling bad because others know one has misbehaved), or neither when they discipline children? When motivating students to behave well, should educators focus on what the students themselves should think about their behavior (guilt), how others will think of them (shame), or neither? Special educators are typically advised not to make students feel guilty or to shame them, even in private. In fact, many readers may feel that this discussion of the possibility of using guilt or shame to motivate students is inappropriate. However, shame and its avoidance can be a very effective and acceptable motivator with some Hispanic American, Native American and Southeast Asian American students (7, 16, 18, 25, 26).

> For Native Americans, warnings about the consequences of bad behavior are couched in community terms like, "What will people say—they will laugh at you." . . . Shame, otherwise known as embarrassment, is a common disciplinary tool with Native Americans. (16, p. 48)

> Shame is, indeed, a powerful instrument for discipline in Hispanic culture. . . . Where the threat of a failing grade or detention may not succeed in producing the desired change of behavior with the student, a private and strong reminder of his family obligations may do wonders. (18, pp. 72–73)

SELF-
QUIZ **ACCOMMODATING MANAGEMENT TECHNIQUES
TO STUDENT CHARACTERISTICS**

- How should special educators handle problems between male and female students from different ethnic or socioeconomic-class backgrounds that result from their different perceptions of what are and are not acceptable ways for students to relate to the opposite gender?
- Do you agree that female educators should use less direct management techniques with those Hispanic American males who are not accustomed to direct disciplinary approaches from females?

- With which of the following ways of accommodating management techniques to students' behavioral characteristics would you feel comfortable?
  1. Being authoritarian with some students and authoritative with others
  2. Being tough with some students and the opposite with others
  3. Using time out as a negative consequence with some students but not with others
  4. Recognizing some students' achievements, progress, and improvements publicly and those of others privately
  5. Using corporal punishment, scolding, or peer pressure with students who are accustomed to such forms of discipline at home and in their communities

EMPOWERING APPROACHES

Students who are empowered by their teachers are helped to believe they can achieve their goals, control their behavior, and meet the challenges that confront them. This occurs because they themselves have the power to shape their destinies and futures. Those who are disempowered come to believe they lack the ability or potential to do so. Behavior management techniques that can disempower students will be discussed next. (See Locus of Control in Chapter 10.)

Deprecating students' backgrounds and treating them prejudicially has a harmful effect on their self-concepts and sense of power. Routinely and unnecessarily rewarding students may teach them to strive to please others rather than to accomplish their own internal motives and contribute to their "learned helplessness" (33). Praising poor or non-European American students for trying, even though they do not succeed, or for achieving less than what is expected of others with the same ability can cause them to doubt whether they can succeed or accomplish what others can. Also, emphasizing teacher-management techniques over self-management techniques can lead students to believe that they are unable to manage themselves (33).

The following quotation exemplifies the view of many African American educators that using extrinsic consequences to modify the behavior of African American students with disabilities does them more harm than good:

> Perhaps one of the most overriding criticisms of externally oriented management techniques is the tendency of teachers to use these approaches as control tactics rather than teaching students to become self-directing individuals. . . . Many otherwise promising teachers resort to interpreting and utilizing traditional management approaches as control tactics, which then results in making students behaviorally stifled, docile, overcompliant, and further doubt their abilities. Additionally, the use of these approaches in this vein has the tendency to foster impulsive conformity in students and often turns them off to school and learning. . . . Many behaviorally disordered Black children have histories of failure and have developed predispositions to expect failure and, thus, are often unwilling to take chances in learning situations. . . . Given this re-

ality, management approaches which result in these students doubting their abilities further exacerbate an already regressive situation for the life progression of exceptional Black children. (34, pp. 1–4)

To empower students, special education teachers should demonstrate their conviction that students can and will control their own behavior. In addition, teachers should assist students to do so without making them dependent on excessive or unnecessary teacher praise, assistance, or supervision. "Our society thinks that 'more discipline' will make a better world and certainly better schools. But doesn't the cry for discipline really translate to, 'let's try to help people act in a responsible manner'? This society desperately needs people who accept responsibility, not simply accept discipline" (35, p. 188).

SELF-
QUIZ   **EMPOWERMENT**

- If you have been an in-service teacher or have completed a teaching practicum, list the various classroom/behavior management techniques that you tend to use with students. Categorize them into empowering and disempowering approaches and determine which approach you employ most often.

SUMMARY

There are many ways special educators can improve their classroom/behavior management approaches. Since many special educators contribute to students' behavior problems by relating to them in a discriminatory manner, they can correct their ethnic, socioeconomic-class, and gender biases. Rather than interpreting students' behavior from their own perspective, special educators can avoid misperceiving and misunderstanding students' behaviors by taking students' behavioral styles into consideration. Finally, teachers can use classroom/behavior management techniques that empower rather than disempower students.

ACTIVITIES

1. If you are a teacher, interview some of your students about their behavior styles. Do you notice any of the differences reported in this chapter? If you are a preservice teacher, ask some students from different backgrounds in the courses you are taking or some friends to describe their behavior style preferences. Do you notice any of the differences reported in this chapter?

2. Using the list of characteristics included in this chapter as a guide, prepare descriptions of the traits that you believe are characteristic of male and female students. Then ask a few of your colleagues, peers, or students to review your list and tell you which traits they do and do not accept as being characteristic of their group.

3. Interview some individuals from an ethnic group that interests you and prepare a description of the characteristics of their group that they think special educators should consider when they select management techniques.

4. Ask your colleagues or fellow students to answer the self-quiz on accommodating management techniques to student characteristics. Do you observe any differences between persons of different genders or persons of different ethnic backgrounds? How do your answers compare to theirs?

5. List the various classroom/behavior management techniques that your professors tend to use with students. Categorize them into empowering and disempowering approaches and determine which approach each professor employs most often. Are there any differences between male and female professors?

REFERENCES

Misperceptions and misunderstandings that can affect special educators' choices of management approaches are discussed in references 1–14.

1. Dent, J. L. (1976). Assessing black children for mainstream placement. In R. L. Jones (Ed.), *Mainstreaming and the Minority Child*. Reston, VA: Council for Exceptional Children.

2. ERIC Clearinghouse on Urban Education. (1985). The social and psychological adjustment of Southeast Asian Refugees. *Equity and Choice, 1* (3), 55–59.

3. Gay, G. (1975, October). Cultural differences important in the education of Black children. *Momentum*, pp. 30–33.

4. Gay, G., & Abrahams, R. D. (1973). Does the pot melt, boil, or brew? Black children and white assessment procedures. *Journal of School Psychology, 11* (4), 330–340.

5. Grossman, H. (1984). *Educating Hispanic Students: Cultural Implications for Instruction, Classroom Management, Counseling, and Assessment*. Springfield, IL: Thomas.

6. Irvine, J. J. (1991). *Black Students and School Failure: Policies, Practices, and Prescriptions*. New York: Praeger.

7. Jaramillo, M. L. (1973). *Cautions When Working with the Culturally Different Child*. ERIC ED 115 622.

8. Johnson, S. O. (1980). Minorities and discipline games. *High School Journal, 63* (5), 207–208.

9. Koh, T., & Koh, S. D. (1982). A note on the psychological evaluation of Korean school children. *P/AAMHRC Research Review, 1* (3), 1–2.

10. Kritek, W. J. (1979). Teachers' concerns in a desegregated school in Milwaukee. *Integrated Education, 17*, 19–24.

11. Morgan, H. (1980). How schools fail black children. *Social Policy, 10* (4), 49–54.

12. Nguyen, L. D. (1986). Indochinese cross-cultural adjustment and communication. In M. Dao & H. Grossman (Eds.), *Identifying, Instructing and Rehabilitating Southeast Asian Students with Special Needs and Counseling Their Parents*. ERIC ED 273 068.

13. Ortiz, A. A., & Yates, J. R. (1988). *Characteristics of Learning Disabled, Mentally Retarded, and Speech-Language Handicapped Hispanic Students at Initial Evaluation and Reevaluation*. ERIC ED 298 705.

14. Wong, M. K. (1978). Traditional Chinese culture and the behavior patterns of Chinese students in American classrooms. In *Second Annual Forum on Transcultural Adaptation (Proceedings): Asian Students in American Classrooms.* Chicago: Illinois Office of Education.

References 15–32 discuss student characteristics that special educators should consider when selecting classroom/behavior management approaches.

15. Bacon, M. M. (n.d.). *Coping Creatively with Adolescence: Culturally Relevant Behavior Management Strategies for the Twenty-First Century.* Unpublished manuscript, Palo Alto Unified School District, Palo Alto, CA.

16. Burgess, B. J. (1978). Native American learning styles. In L. Morris, G. Sather, & S. Scull (Eds.), *Extracting Learning Styles from Social/Cultural Diversity: A Study of Five American Minorities.* Norman, OK: Southwest Teacher Corps Network.

17. Chan, K., & Rueda, R. (1979). Poverty and culture in education: Separate but equal. *Exceptional Children, 45,* 422–427.

18. Condon, E. C., Peters, J. Y., & Sueiro-Ross, C. (1979). *Special Education and the Hispanic Child: Cultural Perspectives.* Philadelphia: Temple University, Teacher Corps Mid-Atlantic Network.

19. Geschwind, N. (1974). *Cross-Cultural Contrastive Analysis: An Exploratory Study.* Unpublished master's thesis, University of Hawaii, Honolulu.

20. Hale-Benson, J. E. (1986). *Black Children: Their Roots, Culture, and Learning Styles* (rev. ed.). Baltimore: Johns Hopkins University Press.

21. Howells, G. N., & Sarabia, I. B. (1978). Education and the Pilipino Child. *Integrated Education, 16* (2), 17–20.

22. Kochman, T. (1981). *Black and White Styles in Conflict.* Chicago: University of Chicago Press.

23. Leggio, P. (n.d.). *Contrastive Patterns in Nonverbal Communication among Different Cultures.* Trenton, NJ: Office of Equal Opportunity, New Jersey State Department of Education.

24. Medicine, B. (1985). Child socialization among Native Americans: The Lakota (Sioux) in cultural context. In *Indian Studies.* Cheney, WA: Eastern Washington University.

25. Morrow, R. D. (1987). Cultural differences—Be aware. *Academic Therapy, 23* (2), 143–149.

26. Morrow, R. D., & McBride H. J. (1988). *Considerations for Educators in Working with Southeast Asian Children and Their Families.* ERIC ED 299 730.

27. Robinson, S. (198⁰). Quoted in Wiley, E., III. (1989). Educators call for fairer, more effective means of discipline in schools: Black males most likely to be punished. *Black Issues in Higher Education, 5* (21), 3, 16.

28. Sra, D. (1992) *A Comparison of East Indian American and European American Students.* Unpublished manuscript, San Jose State University, Division of Special Education, San Jose, CA.

29. Swisher, K. (1990). Cooperative learning and the education of American Indian/Alaskan Native students: A review of the literature and suggestions for implementation. *Journal of American Indian Education, 29* (2), 36–43.

30. Tharp, G. (1989). Psychocultural variables and constants: Effects on teaching and learning in schools. *American Psychologist, 44* (2), 349–359.

31. Williams, J. (1989). Reducing the disproportionately high frequency of disciplinary actions against minority students: An assessment-based policy approach. *Equity and Excellence, 24* (2), 31–37.

32. Yao, E. L. (1979) Implications of biculturalism for the learning process of middle-class Asian children in the United States. *Journal of Education, 16* (4), 61–72.

The importance of empowering students is discussed in references 33–35.

33. Grossman, H. (1990). *Trouble Free Teaching: Solutions to Behavior Problems in the Classroom.* Mountain View, CA: Mayfield.

34. Patton, J. M. (1981). *A Critique of Externally Oriented Behavior Management Approaches as Applied to Exceptional Black Children.* ERIC ED 204 902.

35. Sleeter C. E., & Grant, C. A. (1988). *Making Choices for Multicultural Education: Five Approaches to Race, Class, and Gender.* Columbus, OH: Merrill.

INDEX